The City

The City

Los Angeles and Urban Theory at the End of the Twentieth Century

EDITED BY

Allen J. Scott
Edward W. Soja

UNIVERSITY OF CALIFORNIA PRESS

Berkeley   Los Angeles   London

University of California Press
Berkeley and Los Angeles, California
University of California Press
London, England

Copyright © 1996 by The Regents of the University of California

Library of Congress Cataloging-in-Publication Data
Printed in the United States of America

Library of Congress Cataloging-in-Publication Data

The city : Los Angeles and urban theory at the end of the twentieth
century / edited by Allen J. Scott, Edward W. Soja.
    p.   cm.
   Includes bibliographical references and index.
   ISBN 0–520–20424–7 (alk. paper)
      0–520–21313–0 (pbk : alk. paper)
   1. Los Angeles (Calif.)   2. Los Angeles (Calif.)—Social
conditions.   3. City planning—California—Los Angeles.
4. Sociology, Urban—California—Los Angeles.   I. Scott, Allen
John.   II. Soja, Edward W.
HN80.L7C57   1996
307.76'09794'94—dc20   96-5512
                                               CIP

1 2 3 4 5 6 7 8 9

CONTENTS

PREFACE

Over the last decade or so, urban theorists, cultural critics, and social commentators have devoted a tremendous amount of attention to the study of Los Angeles. This attention derives not just from the fact that Los Angeles is one of the world's largest metropolitan regions with an exuberant, if brief, history and an extraordinarily diverse population and human geography or from its unenviable and notorious urban problems ranging from chronic atmospheric pollution to widespread social violence. Interest in Los Angeles is in part a function of these circumstances, but it is related most of all to its emergence as one of the most dramatic and concentrated expressions of the perplexing theoretical and practical urban issues that have arisen at the end of the twentieth century.

Los Angeles today is a vigorous complex of economic and industrial activities, the largest industrial metropolis in America. Its urban industrial development, however, has diverged considerably from the paradigmatic American industrial metropolises such as Chicago, Detroit, and Pittsburgh that came to the fore in the earlier part of the twentieth century. Its economy is not, like theirs, based on huge growth poles focused on Fordist mass production industries churning out products like automobiles, steel, machinery, and domestic appliances. Rather, it is a compound of enormously diverse, flexible production sectors, including financial and business services, high-technology industry, and various craft, fashion, and cultural products industries ranging from clothing and jewelry to motion pictures and music recording.

At the same time, and in contrast to the classical cases of Chicago or Detroit in the interwar years, the social structure of Los Angeles is no longer characterizable in terms of a (numerically) dominant and relatively affluent blue-collar working class but is deeply divided into two distinctive segments, as represented on the one side by an upper tier of highly paid managers, professionals, and technicians and on the other side by a lower tier composed of low-skill, low-wage workers, the vast majority of whom are immigrants, many of them undocumented. Moreover, the immigrants who occupy such a conspicuous position in this lower tier are predominantly from Latin America and Asia, part of an extraordinary global migration stream that has made Los Angeles one of the most culturally heterogeneous metropolises the world has ever seen. These circumstances have had profound implications for the shape and form of metropolitan development in Southern California and for the social and political dynamics that drive this development forward.

The contributors to this volume seek to deal with these complicated issues in part by explicit theoretical analysis, but more often by means of case studies, empirical vignettes, historical-geographic illustration, and policy-oriented critiques. Although there is much that is shared among the authors, each has been encouraged to express her or his distinctive approach to understanding Los Angeles, even if this results in conflicting views of the same subject. No grouping of the chapters has been made, but there is nevertheless an orderliness in the sequence that results both from overlapping themes and from substantial differences and contrasts in perspective. The overall aim is to present an interlocking mosaic of descriptions of different aspects of Los Angeles and in this way to move tentatively toward a new kind of urban analysis, one that is open to a diversity of interpretive positions yet is committed to a collective project that is theoretical and practical at the same time. It is our hope to set in motion future and more ambitious investigations that will chart in forceful ways the emergence and dynamics of what we shall refer to here (for want of a less ambiguous and problematical vocabulary) as the post-Fordist/postmodern metropolis.

The book as a whole is a project of the Lewis Center for Regional Policy Studies at the University of California, Los Angeles (UCLA). The editors and authors wish to extend their thanks to Ralph and Goldy Lewis for their support of the Center and, above all, for their generous endowment gift that gave birth to the Center and that has subsequently supported its active programs of research, publication, and outreach to the wider social and policy community of Southern California. We also wish to thank the Ford Foundation for its financial support of this project, making it possible for the editors and authors to come together as a team in the development of the book. Richard Weinstein, former dean of the Graduate School of Architecture and Urban Planning at UCLA, was instrumental in negotiating this support and in helping to plan the initial outline of this book. We are also grateful to Vanessa Dingley, assistant director of the Lewis Center, for her indefatigable and always enthusiastic efforts in organizing the various stages in the preparations for this book.

The City: Los Angeles and Urban Theory at the End of the Twentieth Century is not intended to be a final substantive statement about Los Angeles. Instead, our aim is to whet the appetite and stimulate the quest for a more systematic and insightful understanding of the issues and problems raised, in Los Angeles and in other major world cities.

Allen J. Scott and Edward W. Soja

CONTRIBUTORS

Susan Anderson is external affairs director for the Local Initiatives Support Corporation (LISC) of Los Angeles.

Evelyn Blumenberg is a doctoral student in urban planning at UCLA.

Mike Davis teaches urban history, theory, and criticism at the Southern California Institute of Architecture.

Michael Dear is professor of geography at the University of Southern California in Los Angeles.

Margaret FitzSimmons, formerly associate professor in urban planning at UCLA, is now on the faculty of the Environmental Studies Board at the University of California, Santa Cruz.

Robert Gottlieb is a lecturer in urban planning at UCLA.

Charles Jencks is adjunct professor of architecture and urban design at the School of Arts and Architecture, UCLA.

Harvey Molotch is professor of sociology at the University of California, Santa Barbara.

Paul Ong is professor of urban planning and chair of the department at UCLA.

Raymond A. Rocco is professor of political science at UCLA.

Allen J. Scott is associate dean of the School of Public Policy and Social Research, director of the Lewis Center for Regional Policy Studies, and professor of geography at UCLA.

Edward W. Soja is professor of urban planning and chair of the department at UCLA.

Martin Wachs is professor of urban planning and director of the Institute for Transportation Studies at UCLA.

Richard S. Weinstein is associate dean of the School of Arts and Architecture and professor of architecture and urban design at UCLA.

Jennifer Wolch is professor of geography at the University of Southern California in Los Angeles.

ONE

Introduction to Los Angeles

City and Region

Edward W. Soja and Allen J. Scott

SETTING THE SCENE

For close to a century now, Southern California has been the magnet for enormous population movements both from other parts of the United States and from other parts of the world. In an ever-widening orbit of attraction, a series of migratory waves have given rise to a net population growth averaging close to two million per decade, or over five hundred every day for almost one hundred years.[1] Anchoring this phenomenal growth has been a process of urban and regional development that has engendered one of the world's largest metropolitan agglomerations. The regional metropolis of Los Angeles, centered around the original settlement of El Pueblo de Nuestra Señora la Reina de los Angeles de Porciúncula but now stretching outward for sixty miles in almost every direction, encompasses more than 160 separate municipalities in five counties, with a current population of fifteen million. It is the sixth or seventh largest of the world's "megacities."[2]

The emergence of Los Angeles out of a scattered collection of towns and villages as one of the major metropolitan regions of the contemporary world gives it a special place in the history and geography of city building. Just what this "place" represents, however, has always been a controversial issue, perhaps never more so than today. It is still an open question, for example, whether to view Los Angeles as an exceptional case, a persistently peculiar and unreproducible type of city, or as an exemplary, if not paradigmatic, illustration of the essential and generalizable features of late-twentieth-century urbanization. Similarly, the historical geography of Los Angeles invites continuing debate between those who see in it the achievement of a sort of urban utopia and the American Dream and those who see little more than the dystopian nightmares of a "Hell Town"[3] grown to gargantuan proportions.

In the essays contained in this volume, a diversity of views on these—and other—issues is represented. By maintaining this multiplicity of positions, we hope to dissolve the either/or logic that has commonly characterized debates about the region and to foster, as a means of understanding and interpreting late-twentieth-century Los Angeles, a more encompassing purview capable of holding several different standpoints simultaneously in perspective. In every urban space one can find liberating and oppressive forces, the unique and the general, the utopian and dystopian, mixed together in complex ways. Recognition of the stubborn coexistence of these conflicting circumstances and their often revealing interdependence and inseparability is the starting point for making sense of the urbanization of Los Angeles—or, for that matter, any other contemporary metropolis.

This multisided approach to understanding Los Angeles does not mean that there is no common ground to the chapters that follow, other than one of simple context. All of the chapters are imbued with a strong geographic or spatial perspective, a point of view that focuses our attention on the regional development and built environment of Los Angeles, that is, on what can be described as the social and spatial construction of the metropolis. This emphasis is complemented by a shared concern for policy issues and the political challenges posed in Los Angeles by the tasks of creating more progressive forms of urban and regional planning, architecture and urban design, community development, and environmental regulation. In one way or another, every contributor to this book has been or is actively involved in public policy debates in Southern California, giving the collection a unifying sense of immediacy and of commitment to social justice and the improvement of urban life.

The essays focus primarily on the dramatic changes that have been occurring in Los Angeles over the past thirty years. Making practical sense of this broadly defined urban *restructuring* as it has unfolded in the period marked by the two most disruptive urban insurrections in twentieth-century America, in 1965 and then again in 1992, is an insistently recurrent theme. It influences how far back into the past each contributor delves and how far into broader theoretical debates and discourses each essay extends. In this attempt to make practical sense of the restructuring of Los Angeles, some but not all authors link their essays to wider debates on contemporary social change, particularly on issues of modernity and postmodernity. What is being suggested by this linkage is that the restructuring of Los Angeles is part of a more global restructuring process affecting everyone, everywhere in the world, albeit unevenly, during the closing decades of the twentieth century. Moreover, there is an additional inflexion to this argument, an implied presentation of Los Angeles as a particularly revealing place from which to understand and interpret global phenomena of urbanization and regional development in relation to broadly based transformations of contemporary capitalist society.

THE GROWTH AND DEVELOPMENT OF LOS ANGELES:
A BRIEF HISTORICAL GEOGRAPHY

Every city has had its boom, but the history of Los Angeles is the history of booms. Actually, the growth of Southern California since 1870 should be regarded as one continuous boom punctuated at intervals with major explosions.
CAREY McWILLIAMS, *SOUTHERN CALIFORNIA: AN ISLAND ON THE LAND*

Taking our cue from Carey McWilliams, one of the finest critical historians of Southern California, a panoramic picture of the historical and geographic growth of the regional metropolis of Los Angeles can be described in terms of a virtually continuous boom periodically slowed by national and global economic recession and punctuated by some of the most violent urban social upheavals in American history. This rhythm can be broadly seen in the array of decennial census figures presented in table 1.1. Starting in 1870, five surges of urban expansion can be identified, peaking first in the 1880s and then in the 1900s during the Progressive Era, the Roaring Twenties, the two decades following the end of the Second World War, and finally

TABLE 1.1   Population Growth in the Five-County Region of Los Angeles (000s)

Census Year	Los Angeles (*)		Orange	San Bernardino	Riverside	Ventura	Five-County Region
1870	15	(79)	—	4	—	—	19
1880	33	(72)	—	8	—	5	46
1890	101	(67)	14	25	—	10	151
1900	170	(68)	20	28	18	14	250
1910	504	(78)	34	57	35	18	648
1920	936	(81)	61	73	50	28	1,150
1930	2,209	(85)	119	134	81	55	2,597
1940	2,786	(86)	131	161	106	70	3,253
1950	4,152	(84)	216	282	170	115	4,934
1960	6,011	(78)	709	501	303	199	7,724
1970	7,042	(71)	1,421	682	457	378	9,981
1980	7,478	(65)	1,932	893	664	530	11,496
1990	8,863	(61)	2,411	1,418	1,170	669	14,531

(*) = Los Angeles County as percentage of total regional population.

the contemporary period of restructuring, which seems clearly to have reached its crest some time in the late 1980s.

Surge 1, 1870–1900

The inaugural punctuation point in the urbanization of Los Angeles was the Chinese Massacre of 1871, perhaps the first time the Americanized pueblo made headline news all around the world. The event took place in and around the Calle de los Negros (called "Nigger Alley" at the time), for several decades the multiethnic main street of violent Hell Town, located not far from present-day Union Station. It resulted in the murders of about twenty Chinese (out of a total Chinese population of 200) by an angry mob of Anglo vigilantes, police officers (apparently led by the chief of police), and a few Mexicans seeking revenge for the accidental killing of a white man. The shocked citizenry responded with something very much like the Rebuild LA Committee that was set up in the immediate aftermath of the riots of 1992, representing (in both cases) an effort to reestablish social order and to improve the severely tarnished external image of the city. This first burst of boosterism in the late 1800s contributed significantly to an urban boom that would last from the 1880s to the national depression years of the mid-1890s.

Despite continued anti-Asian hysteria along the entire Pacific Coast, the Chinese were to play a significant role, as merchants, laborers, fishermen, and vegetable farmers, in the 1880s surge of urban expansion. Thriving Chinatowns grew up in almost every urban center in Southern California. By the end of the century, however, racial discrimination, exacerbated by an influx of Mexican labor and Japanese farmers, effectively squeezed the Chinese population into the small Chinatown that still exists adjoining the old pueblo. A pattern was set by the Chinese Massacre and the subsequent social disciplining of the "troublesome" minority. The massacre exposed an undercurrent of racism and xenophobia that would periodically burst to the surface, briefly interrupting as well as redirecting the urbanization process. In the aftermath of riot and social upheaval, private interests would gather in force to plan and promote their visions of an idealized urban future, often in the absence of effective public leadership and at the expense of a perceived "problem minority."

The first surge of urban growth saw the addition of over 230,000 people to the tiny regional population of about 20,000 in 1870. The long-resident Mexican "Californio" population, the primary target for Protestant racial purification after the American conquest of the Mexican Southwest, dwindled in relative size and absolute importance over this period, as the region was flooded with WASP migrants mainly from small-town mid-America who were attracted to the sunny subtropical vineyards, orange groves, and southern comforts of such new towns as Pasadena, Santa Monica, Anaheim, Santa Ana, Pomona, Riverside, and Redlands. Key rail connections broke the region's isolation from the national economy, and local boosters effectively began to promote the image of healthy and bountiful Southern California, the imminent home place for the first truly American city.

Twenty new municipalities were created in this period, adding to the three established cities of Los Angeles (incorporated in 1850), San Buenaventura (1866), and San Bernardino (1869). The region was on its way to becoming the richest agricultural area in the country, a position it would maintain well into the twentieth century. So intense was its self-advertisement and dependency on land development and speculation that as early as 1886 local observers were claiming that there were more real estate agents per acre than in any other city in the world. The economic development and urbanization of Southern California had begun.

Surge 2, 1900–1920

The first surge sold an idyllic Los Angeles to Protestant America and created a regional economy based in agriculture, land speculation, real estate boosterism, and the provision of specialized health and leisure services, particularly to wealthy white retirees.[4] The depression of the mid-1890s, however, demonstrated the weaknesses of this economic base for further urban growth. In the next surge, the public and private promoters of Los Angeles turned increasingly to industrial development and succeeded in plugging the city into the dynamo of the American Manufacturing Belt in the northeastern states. In 1920, Los Angeles was still behind most other major American cities in manufacturing employment but had clearly begun the trajectory that would make it the country's leading industrial metropolis seventy years later.

Rapid economic development between 1900 and 1920 helped to quadruple the regional population to well over one million. There were many key developments in this expansion. By 1920, Los Angeles had become one of the major petroleum-producing regions in the world and its leadership in motion picture production was firmly established. A budding aircraft industry was born from the talents of local entrepreneurs like Donald Douglas and the Loughead (Lockheed) brothers. An expanded port complex in San Pedro (annexed to the City of Los Angeles in 1906) and in Long Beach (by this time well established as the region's "second city") had already surpassed nearly all its Pacific Coast competitors, and the completion of the California Aqueduct in 1913 (which triggered many other annexations to the city, including Hollywood in 1910) assured a sufficient water supply for large-scale urban growth.

Significant migration streams from southern and central Europe, Japan, and especially Mexico created a highly diverse industrial labor force. In 1920, Mexicans had become the largest immigrant group in Los Angeles and were for the first time since the late nineteenth century more numerous than African-Americans. These trends reinforced the character of Los Angeles as the most racially diverse—and racially segregated—of Pacific Coast cities.[5] Finally, the booming regional complex was effectively forged into a single functional unit by the automobile (in 1920, Los Angeles was already ahead of all other major American cities in automobile registration and use) and by what was probably the most extensive network of metropolitan mass transit in the world, dominated by the Red Cars of the Pacific Electric Railway Company.

Over forty new cities were incorporated in this period in the five-county region, reinforcing the sprawling, polycentric character of the urban built environment. Many were "black gold suburbs" built on the scattered pools of petroleum underlying the region, while others grew at new industrial sites, as the interplay of urbanization and industrialization began its forceful impact on the regional landscape. A very different kind of American metropolis was now taking shape, one in which the oil derrick, the automobile, the airfield, the movie studio, the beach and mountain community, the immigrant labor camp and factory town, and the all-purpose tourist resort both stretched the urban fabric and pinned it down in an extensive multiplicity of urban places and experiences.

At the same time, the City of Los Angeles was taking on its peculiar shape, spreading into the San Fernando Valley to the north, extending an annexed ribbon of land south to the port at San Pedro, and gobbling up most of the communities in its western march to the Pacific (leaving a series of "holes" as represented by the independent municipalities of Beverly Hills and Culver City, where local movie moguls and real estate developers were powerful enough to resist annexation and incorporate on their own). Anchoring this expansion was the new central city of Los Angeles, just south of the old pueblo, a bustling downtown clogged with automobiles and the worst traffic jams of any major American city. The Progressive movement was particularly successful in Los Angeles, introducing such populist local government reforms as the initiative, the referendum, and the recall; and by the end of the century's first decade, Los Angeles had become a vital center of the American labor movement and seemed ready to elect a socialist mayor.

The punctuating explosion of this growth surge was the bombing of the *Los Angeles Times* building in late 1910, in retrospect a key turning point in the Progressive Era, the labor movement, and the development of socialism in America. Over the next few years, not only were the alleged "radical anarchist" perpetrators thrown in jail and the socialist candidate for mayor defeated (he retreated to the desert to found the short-lived socialist com-

munity of Llano del Rio) but the local labor movement was decimated, the
"open shop" was given new life (it would last for another three decades),
and the industrialization of Los Angeles was placed even more firmly in
the hands of business interests linked to the triumphant *Los Angeles Times*
and the powerful Merchants and Manufacturers Association. After this
brief but volatile interruption, the regional metropolis was prepared to
boom again.

Surge 3, 1920–1940

The 1920s may have roared more loudly in Los Angeles than anywhere else
in America. The regional population more than doubled over the decade
to 2.6 million. Although population growth would slow down dramatically
following the stock market crash in 1929, the persistence of the "continuous
boom" softened the impact of the Great Depression, at least in relation to
other American metropolitan areas. The most powerful engines of the regional economy recovered rapidly in the 1930s, and, as occurred after key
turning point explosions in the past, Los Angeles seemed on the edge of
yet another growth surge as the era ended in the global explosions of the
Second World War.

In addition to a renewed land boom, petroleum production and refining
experienced a resurgence, especially in southern Los Angeles County,
stimulating the growth of the ports of Los Angeles-Long Beach and the
emergence of a vast urban industrial zone stretching northward from the
ports to downtown. The motion picture industry grew more rapidly than
ever as it moved beyond the silent era. It was the leading industry throughout this period and employed between thirty and forty thousand workers.
Still centered in Hollywood, "the industry," as it came to be called, developed in a band stretching from North Hollywood through the central axis
of Hollywood to Culver City. The Los Angeles aircraft industry also boomed
in the interwar years, although it required the impetus of the Second World
War before it assumed unquestioned national leadership, and it became the
conduit through which the main high-technology industrial base of the regional metropolis would be established in later years.

The 1920s and 1930s marked the peak period of growth of Los Angeles
County. A map of the built-up area in 1940 would show an almost complete
filling in of the county's southwest quadrant, that is, virtually all of the City
of Los Angeles and the array of working-class suburbs attached to the industrial zone stretching from downtown to Long Beach. The population of
Los Angeles County in 1940 was 86 percent of the total for the five-county
region, the highest percentage it would ever reach. Municipal incorpora-
tions between 1920 and 1940 slowed significantly to only nineteen, but the
majority were in Los Angeles County in and around the industrial zone:

Torrance, Signal Hill, South Gate, Maywood, Lynwood, Bell, Hawthorne, Gardena, Montebello, West Covina. Only Detroit compared with Los Angeles in the net increase of manufacturing workers over this period, and Los Angeles would continue to lead all other metropolitan areas decade by decade for the next fifty years as well. By 1935, Los Angeles was the fifth-largest industrial county in the United States; it led the country in motion picture production, oil refining, aircraft manufacturing, and secondary automobile assembly; it was second in tires and fourth in furniture and apparel.

Despite this industrial growth, there has been little appreciation until recently that Los Angeles has for a long time been a major manufacturing center. In part, this was due to the triumphant character of industrial development in the Northeast during the Fordist era, with its enormous corporate power and giant manufacturing plants. Perhaps even more important, however, was the enveloping imagery that had developed which proclaimed the "exceptionalism" of Los Angeles, its representation as Hollywood, a bizarre Babylon by the sea, a unique and inimitable city of dreams. But beneath this thickly layered imagery there was a fulsome industrial job machine that had begun rolling in the 1920s. What has turned out to be the largest internal migration in U.S. history focused geographically on Los Angeles County starting in the 1920s, increasing with the dust bowl migration of poor white farmers in the 1930s and climaxing with the great black migrations during the three decades following the Second World War.

Surge 4, 1940–1970

As in the Roaring Twenties, the long postwar economic boom in America was nowhere more intense than in the Los Angeles metropolis. Between 1940 and 1970, the regional population tripled in size to nearly 10 million, a net addition of almost 7 million new residents. Los Angeles County grew from a population of 2.8 million to over 7 million, and the rate of population growth in the peripheral counties was even greater. Starting the surge at under half a million, the four outer counties' population reached nearly 3 million in 1970. The largest growth took place in Orange County, which increased more than tenfold to 1.4 million, about equal to the other three peripheral counties combined. What was occurring in the regional metropolis of Los Angeles was mass suburbanization on a scale never before encountered.

An unprecedented housing boom resulted in a proliferation of suburban tracts that quickly grew into independent municipalities. Nearly sixty cities were incorporated between 1940 and 1960 as the built-up area of the metropolis expanded ever more insistently outward. Lakewood (incorporated in 1954) was the exemplary model—Los Angeles's Levittown—of the new, primarily white and largely working-class suburban municipality. A "city by contract," it purchased its basic services from the county in a scheme that would stimulate an "incorporation game" of unusual intensity and creativity. New municipalities sprouted to serve highly specialized local constituencies: the City of Industry (incorporated in 1957), the City of Commerce (1960), a city zoned for the horsey set (Bradbury, 1957), and others gated, walled, and protected by armed guards (Rolling Hills and Rolling Hills Estates, 1957). There was an incorporated place for everyone, it seemed, except for those in the black ghetto inside the City of Los Angeles and the major Mexican barrio, concentrated on county land in what is still unincorporated East Los Angeles. Here, housing problems were compounded until they became stubborn community crises beyond the pale of private development solutions.

Sustaining this surge of growth was the series of Pacific wars—the Second World War, the Korean War, Vietnam—that propelled the Los Angeles region into a primary position within what President Dwight D. Eisenhower would call, warning the people of its power, the American "military-industrial complex." While all the other engines of the regional economy continued to expand through this period, the aerospace industry emerged as by far the leading local sector, accompanied by an extensive network of components manufacturers, service providers, research centers, and a growing electronics industry. After a brief lull following the Second World War, the outbreak of fighting in Korea gave renewed vigor to the aerospace-defense-electronics industry and initiated the unfolding over the following decades of a series of generations of technopoles, or high-technology industrial districts. Each new generation shifted farther outward from the central industrial core of Los Angeles, the most pronounced expansion in this period occurring in the northern half of Orange County.[6]

The Second World War and the Korean War were periods of intensified social tensions that brought back to the surface the long history of white American racism and xenophobia in Los Angeles. In the war years of the 1940s, the long-standing anti-Mexican tradition exploded again after the so-called Zoot Suit riots of 1943, while the equally long-standing anti-Asian tradition reached another low point in the confinement of more than thirty thousand Japanese-Americans from Los Angeles in concentration camps following Executive Order 9066 of 1942. In the early 1950s, after forty years of relative quiescence, socialism and militant unionism again entered the local political agenda, especially in two important areas of the booming regional economy: housing and Hollywood.

In the years following the Second World War, the City of Los Angeles was poised to become a national center for the provision of public housing. In a counteroffensive reminiscent of the events of 1910–1911, the *Los Angeles Times* and a cohort of probusiness organizations crushed these initiatives under the guise of American resistance to a socialist plot. No significant public housing for the poor has been built since the early 1950s. Hollywood provided another target. By the late 1940s, unions and guilds associated with the motion picture industry had become perhaps the most militant in the region. Large numbers of European intellectuals and others fleeing Fascism had moved to Los Angeles, and their growing influence intensified fear of a Socialist/Communist takeover of the movie industry, which had a powerful capacity for the mass propagation of social and political ideas and imagery. Aside from federal government officials and members of Congress, the Joseph McCarthy-led House Un-American Activities Committee inquisitions of the time focused primarily on Los Angeles, in a fierce and locally supported eradication of the Left that was also, as in the Progressive Era, accompanied by a reinforcement of private business control over the economic development of Los Angeles.

Hollywood and the housing market, however, were only two of the key sectors leading the postwar boom. A major new ingredient in this surge of economic expansion was the net addition of about 600,000 African-Americans to the Los Angeles growth machine. Attracted in part by federal legislation that reduced racial discrimination in the aerospace-defense industries and some local changes in discriminatory building codes and contracts, African-Americans succeeded in creating the country's first large suburban ghetto in what has come to be called South Central Los Angeles and began to play an increasingly important role in the regional economy and in urban politics. This expansion of black Los Angeles intensified white flight, sprawling suburbanization, and new forms of racial discrimination in industrial employment and housing.

The increasingly peripheralized technopoles in western Los Angeles County, in Orange County, and in the San Fernando Valley employed almost entirely white workers, often pooled into large, new, white-flight suburbs such as Simi Valley, incorporated in 1969 in Ventura County just over the Los Angeles County border. African-American blue-collar workers were relatively few in number even in the older industrial zones, which coincided throughout this period with overwhelmingly white working-class communities. To previous clusters populated by dust bowl Arkies and Okies, new incorporated municipalities were added, filling in southeastern Los Angeles County (Artesia, Baldwin Park, Bellflower, Bell Gardens, Cerritos, Cudahy, Downey, Hawaiian Gardens, La Mirada, Lakewood, Norwalk, Paramount, Pico Rivera, Santa Fe Springs) and pushing the continuously built-up area into the northern half of Orange County (Buena Park, Costa Mesa, Cypress, Fountain Valley, Garden Grove, La Palma, Los Alamitos, Stanton, Westminster, Yorba Linda). By 1970, sociological studies were beginning to show that Los Angeles now rivaled Chicago as the most racially segregated of all American cities.

The primary punctuating explosion of this period was the Watts rebellion in 1965, the most violent urban upheaval in American history up to that time. The continuous boom was interrupted again by racial and economic tensions, but this time the interruption was much less localized in its causes and consequences and the regional metropolis took a much longer time to recover. In the next surge, the rates of growth in population and industry would be lower than in previous periods, but in the Great U-Turn experienced by the national and world economies over the 1970s, the regional metropolis of Los Angeles would continue (relative to most other U.S. metropolitan areas) its century of boom.

Surge 5, 1970–1990

Although rates of population growth in the contemporary period are much lower than in earlier surges, the absolute growth of the regional metropolis has been greater than that of any other metropolitan area in the country. For the first time, the outer four counties surpassed Los Angeles County in total population growth, adding 2.7 million compared to Los Angeles's still very substantial increase of 1.8 million. Postsuburban Orange County[7] continued to grow into a protometropolis in its own right, by far the largest metropolitan area in the country with no central city of more than 350,000 residents, and San Bernardino and Riverside were at the top of the list of America's fastest-growing counties. More than thirty new municipalities were incorporated, mainly in the regional periphery. Among them were the fastest-growing small cities in the United States: Irvine, Mission Viejo, Lancaster, Moreno Valley, Santa Clarita.

With the growth of the outer cities of the greater Los Angeles region, the metropolis as a whole moved from a period of mass suburbanization to one of, for want of a better term, mass regional urbanization. This shift was accompanied by a growing sense that the late-twentieth-century urbanization process was being redirected into new forms and expressions. The notion of postsuburbanization was assimilated into discussions of the emergence in Los Angeles of a postmodern political culture and a post-Fordist political economy, each maintaining some continuity with the past but nevertheless raising new issues and new challenges to contemporary urban and regional studies. Reinforcing these views has been a series of profound changes in the economy and demography of the regional metropolis.

By 1990, Los Angeles had developed an extremely varied economy based on a diversity of high- and low-technology industries, as well as a thriving business and financial services sector. The growth of the latter dates mainly from the late 1970s and is expressed in a large downtown business complex with a major appendage extending westward along the Wilshire Boulevard corridor to Century City (built on part of the old Twentieth Century-Fox movie lot) and a series of outlying satellite complexes, the largest being in Orange County. Much of this growth has been the result of the increasing internationalization of the Los Angeles regional economy and its insertion into the expanding development of the Pacific Rim. These global ties have confirmed the emergence of Los Angeles as a World City, a major nodal point in the ebb and flow of the new global economy.

Over this period of economic restructuring, and running parallel to deeply rooted processes of deindustrialization in America at large, the relatively small Fordist manufacturing sectors in Los Angeles (automobile assembly, tires, glass, steel, consumer durables) have virtually disappeared, whereas those based either on labor-intensive forms of craft production (including motion pictures, clothing, furniture, jewelry, leather-working) or on flexible high-technology production systems (led by electronics and aerospace) continued to expand, at least until the late 1980s. Today, the contemporary industrial landscape consists of a set of specialized craft industrial districts or agglomerations, mainly concentrated in the center of the region, a group of technopoles located outside the old industrial core, and a spatially extended complex of small metallurgical and machinery industries, mostly in and around the older central industrial zones (see fig. 1.1). While metropolitan areas in the northeastern states were losing manufacturing industries and employment at a rapid rate, Los Angeles continued to grow.

The economic vitality of the Los Angeles region after the turbulent late 1960s and early 1970s was accompanied by an intensified bifurcation of regional labor markets. On the one hand, there has been a growing high-wage, high-skill group of workers (managers, business executives, scientists, engineers, designers, and celebrities and many others in the entertainment industry); on the other hand, there has been an even more rapidly expanding mass of marginalized, low-wage, low-skill workers, the majority of whom are women and often undocumented Latino and Asian immigrants, who find employment throughout the service sector and in a widening pool of manufacturing sweatshops, from the garment industry to electronics assembly. Between these two strata is the traditional skilled and semiskilled blue-collar working class, which has been shrinking with such rapidity that it is now commonly referred to as the disappearing middle stratum of Southern California society. Many industrial sectors have based their main competitive strategies over this period on labor cost reductions rather than on reskilling workers or on product and process quality improvements, thus capturing much of the labor force in a vicious circle of cost squeezing. This has been made easier by the dramatic decline of industrial unionization throughout the region. As a result, the wages of production workers have declined in real terms since the 1970s, even as the overall economy boomed.

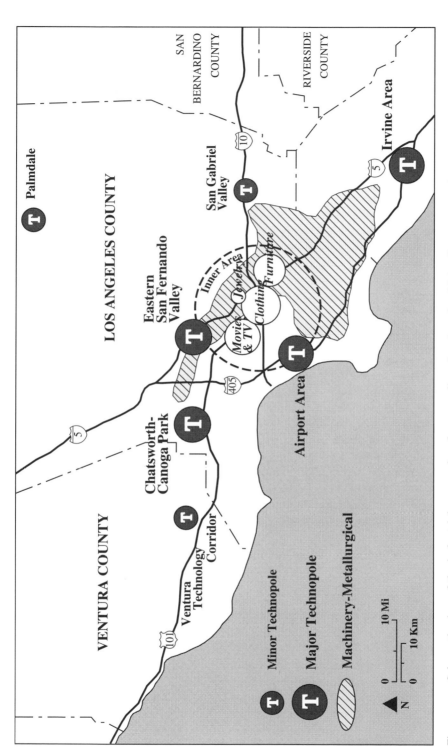

Figure 1.1. Schematic view of the industrial geography of metropolitan Los Angeles. Major freeways are shown.

In the 1980s, manufacturing employment began to decline in Los Angeles County, ending its century of virtually continuous expansion, and by the end of the decade, it had started to drop in the four outer counties as well. The end of the cold war and the major cuts in Department of Defense prime contracts sparked a new economic crisis in the region as it entered the 1990s. Employment in Los Angeles County aerospace-defense industries fell from 312,500 in 1987 to 259,600 in 1990 (a result of a more than 20% cut in real terms in prime contracts over the same years) and declined again to 234,800 in 1991. As it is assumed that one job in the defense sector generates through multiplier effects 1.5 to 2.5 jobs in other local sectors, the impact of these declines is far-reaching indeed. Waves of decline have also spread in the early 1990s to the FIRE (finance, insurance, real estate) sector, the construction industry, and much of the region's low-technology, low-wage, craft industries, which are now feeling the pinch of cheap foreign competition more than ever before.

The restructuring of the regional economy of Los Angeles was associated with a dramatically changing demographic pattern. As in earlier surges of urban development, waves of new immigration provided abundant cheap labor to fuel economic expansion and control labor costs, typically at the expense of established working-class communities. After the late 1960s, however, the migration waves reached unprecedented heights, transforming Los Angeles into the country's major port of entry for immigrants and making it probably the world's most ethnically and racially diverse metropolis. This demographic and cultural transformation and diversification has been most pronounced in Los Angeles County. The county's population shifted from 70 percent Anglo to 60 percent non-Anglo between 1970 and 1990, as what was once the most white and Protestant of American cities changed into what some commentators now call America's leading Third World city. The geographic distribution of the region's major ethnic groupings is shown in figure 1.2.

African-Americans numbered close to one million in 1990, an increase of about 230,000 over the two decades, but their rate of growth and their proportion of the total county population has been declining, and there are signs of an actual decrease in total numbers of African-Americans in the 1990s. Between 1970 and 1990, the old core of African-American Los Angeles was reduced in density and shifted to the west, with its once-rigid eastern black–white boundary dissolved by new Latino migrations.

The census category of Asian and Pacific Islander has experienced the highest rate of growth, as large numbers of Koreans, Chinese, Vietnamese, Thais, Filipinos, and Cambodians moved into the metropolitan region and raised the representation of these groups within Los Angeles County's population to more than 10 percent, almost equal to the percentage of African-Americans. Several new Asian neighborhoods have emerged since

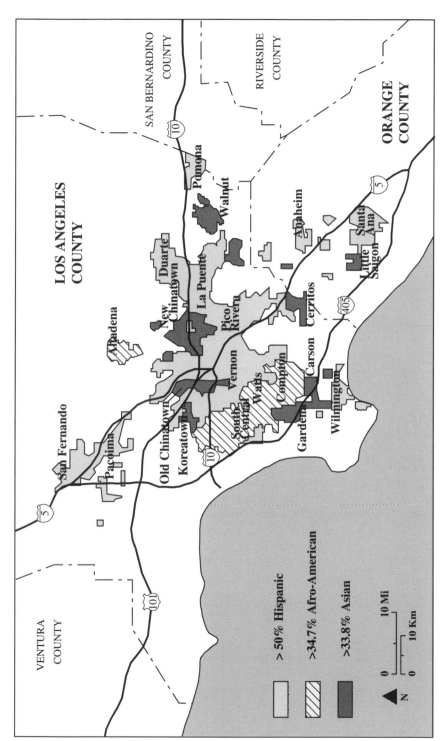

Figure 1.2. Afro-American, Hispanic, and Asian neighborhoods in Los Angeles and Orange counties. Major freeways are shown.

1970, including the large and expanding Koreatown west of the central city, the new "suburban Chinatown" centered in Monterey Park to the east, and a band of Vietnamese and Cambodian settlements to the south stretching from the older, predominantly Japanese community of Gardena to Long Beach and into Orange County, where a "Little Saigon" developed after the mid-1970s and now represents the largest concentration of Vietnamese people in the United States.

The greatest inward flow of population has led steadily to the re-Latinization of Los Angeles, more specifically, its re-Mexicanization. New migrants from Mexico, perhaps as many as two million, account for the vast majority of the increase in the Hispanic census category, with perhaps another half million coming from Guatemala, El Salvador, and other Central American countries. Probably undercounted in the 1990 census, the entire Latino population of Los Angeles County (including migrants from all countries south of the U.S. border as well as a resident Chicano population) is today approaching majority status. Population growth has been especially marked in the old Mexican barrio of East Los Angeles, and a new and largely Central American barrio has developed just west of downtown. In addition, a surge of growth has transformed some communities in southeastern Los Angeles County from more than 75 percent Anglo to over 90 percent Latino. While these areas of exceptional concentration have expanded, the Latino population has also spread broadly throughout the entire metropolitan region and into almost every economic sector.

This massive new wave of migration has been absorbed primarily into low-wage, low-skill service jobs in hotels, hospitals, restaurants, domestic service, and retail stores, as well as into the sweatshops that are now such an important part of the entire manufacturing system of Los Angeles. This has increasingly segmented local labor markets along ethnic lines. Latinos, for example, dominate in the furniture and clothing industries, and Asians are overrepresented in electronics assembly operations. At the same time, like immigrants throughout the history of the United States, many of the new arrivals to Los Angeles have moved out from these initial bases to become small entrepreneurs in their own right—ethnic restaurant owners, Korean clothing industry contractors, Mexican jewelry manufacturers—adding significantly to the continued entrepreneurial energies of the region and providing, for many contemporary observers, a key source for recovery from the current economic crisis.

The new urban landscape that has emerged since the early 1970s in many ways reflects earlier historical trends and trajectories. At the same time, it is filled with expressions of very different urbanization processes, much less susceptible to traditional forms of analysis and interpretation. This increasingly complex and volatile mix of the old and the new, the unique and the paradigmatic, has rekindled interest in Los Angeles as an object of urban inquiry and has produced a great expansion of both academic and journalistic writing filled with new ways of looking at and making sense, through Los Angeles, of the urban experience at large. It has also produced more troublesome problems and challenges for local policy makers and planners than ever before, especially after the most recent of the many explosions that have punctuated the continuous boom of the last one hundred twenty years. We are referring here to the massive urban uprising of the poor and the dispossessed that occurred throughout Los Angeles—but above all in South Central Los Angeles—in the last days of April 1992.

POLITICS AND PLANNING IN CONTEMPORARY LOS ANGELES

Once again Los Angeles is facing the task of recovering from explosive social unrest and reigniting its flagging economy. Again it seems to be turning primarily to an alliance of private business interests to lead the way, a turn that has been reinforced by the recent election of a Republican mayor on the heels of Tom Bradley, a Democrat and an African-American who held the post for well over two decades. Whether there will be an opportunity in this new configuration of urban political forces for a significant role to be played by community leaders, labor activists, and representatives of the new ethnic minorities and the poor has important implications for the future trajectory of development of Los Angeles at the end of the second millennium. It seems evident at this point that the economy is going through a further major round of restructuring involving a significant shift away from aerospace-defense work and toward more flexible forms of industrial development in sectors such as financial services, civilian high-technology production (such as medical instruments, computers, and biotechnology), and a great expansion of the region's craft, fashion, and cultural products industries. The major political question is, will this restructuring be the centerpiece of a new right-wing version of the post-Fordist/postmodern metropolis? Or will it be a foundation for the growth of new kinds of local social democracy, a new vision of citizenship (literally, the quality of being a denizen of a city) and the responsibilities it entails, and a concern for the quality of life rather than for a narrowly defined notion of the business climate? To conclude this introductory chapter, we will identify some of the key issues likely to affect the future of Los Angeles and the political, public policy, and planning arenas in which they are most likely to be addressed.

First on the agenda is the need to mobilize the new urban majority of Latino, Asian, and African-American communities. Within the existing system of local government, this will mean in part increased representation at the municipal (city council) and county (board of supervisors) levels, a process that has recently begun to be apparent in the case of Latino and Asian politicians. Changes in local election procedures will also be necessary to allow citizens without U.S. nationality to vote on issues that significantly affect their lives (e.g., school boards and local transportation), and new ways will have to be developed to promote neighborhood development and community planning, especially in building coalitions of community groups across ethnic and local government boundaries. These forms of political mobilization and empowerment will involve a major rethinking of state and local (and perhaps even federal) government institutions and procedures.

The provision of affordable housing must also be given high priority. The restructuring of the regional metropolis has directly and indirectly created one of the worst housing crises in urban America. Homelessness and overcrowding have risen to record levels, and an unresponsive private housing market and the federal government's almost complete withdrawal from providing new public housing have deepened the problems still further. Short of a revivified public housing program, the future here is likely to revolve around public intervention via partnerships with community groups and private developers and the establishment of a system of community housing banks, fostering such innovations as limited equity affordable housing cooperatives.

The issues of housing and community development must be broadened into a regional and multisectoral planning process that deals systematically with employment, mass transit, land use, and environmental issues. Urban restructuring has had a turbulent effect on the jobs–housing balance, lengthening journeys to work in many outlying areas, clogging the freeways everywhere, and increasing pollution. Some way must be found to coordinate the many different sectoral agencies that deal with these issues to promote an integrated, yet flexible, approach to policy formulation and implementation in the larger metropolitan area, one that is responsive to local community needs. Transportation planning is likely to be a key to the success of such efforts, for a major investment of federal and local funds (up to $180 billion) in mass transit development in Los Angeles is planned over the next thirty years—the largest direct public financial stimulus ever given to any metropolitan region. Ways to make this enormous investment benefit the entire region and to use it to stimulate local economic development, in particular by creating new kinds of advanced ground transportation equipment industries in the region, are now being considered.[8]

Important to this multisectoral planning process is the development of regional industrial and employment planning, first and foremost to guide the critical process of defense conversion. This will not only involve assistance to management in promoting technology sharing, the development of new products (such as nonpolluting automobiles, buses, and other mass transit vehicles), and the creation of networks for industrial innovation but should also serve labor through job retraining, skills maintenance, a reinvigorated labor movement, and the encouragement of greater labor participation in decision making at all levels. Several complementary programs need to be developed to (1) bring industrial and environmental planning closer together so as to streamline environmental regulation procedures while at the same time generating more effective programs for smog control, water quality, and the disposal of hazardous waste; (2) build on the continuing strengths of the regional economy, especially in the craft, fashion, and cultural products industry (which includes the entertainment industry), and in all associated facets of design, from architecture to automobiles;[9] (3) focus new industrial development on job generation, especially for the core poverty areas; and (4) promote and sustain new institution building at the local level, from regional manufacturing networks to neighborhood self-help organizations.

Behind all these efforts looms the need to rethink and reorganize regional government and planning. None of the programs identified above is likely to be successful if the present highly fragmented governance structure of the region remains intact. For if there is any lesson to be learned from a study of the causes and consequences of urban restructuring in Los Angeles, it is that the new metropolis that has emerged over the past thirty years is regional in scale, scope, functioning, and patterns of daily life, much more than it ever was before. In particular, in view of the intricate interdependencies that run throughout the many different clusters of industrial activity within the local economy, some organizational structure for coordinating local economic development strategies and for seeking to build agreements between important and relevant local constituencies (e.g., industrial associations, banks, labor organizations, local government agencies) about ways of moving forward is highly desirable. Many regions in different parts of the world have now put into place systems of local economic coordination, such as regional economic councils or development consortia, and there is much that such a system might accomplish for the economy of Los Angeles. Indeed, the Southern California Association of Governments has recently proposed the formation of a regional economic strategies consortium to promote local economic development.[10]

In its most recent incarnation, Los Angeles is a major node within a worldwide network of urban and regional economies. It is at once an important actor within the new global economy and a dependent organism, subject to intense buffeting by currents that lie far beyond its control. The entire pattern of postwar economic growth and development in the region has been seriously disturbed of late, and its social life—which has never in any case attained anything remotely approaching equilibrium—is now threatened by new rounds of intense turmoil and turbulence. The region seems to lie at a critical turning point in its history, as it did especially in the early years of the present century and immediately after the Second World War. The policy problems that it currently faces and the solutions that are brought to bear on them will provide crucial lessons and reference points for other localities in the United States as they, too, tackle the stresses and strains of the turn to post-Fordist/postmodern forms of urban development at the end of the twentieth century.

NOTES

1. What we will describe as the greater Los Angeles region is defined by the five counties of Los Angeles, Orange, Riverside, San Bernardino, and Ventura. In addition, the wider area of Southern California is defined as including San Diego and Imperial counties to the south and San Luis Obispo, Santa Barbara, and Kern counties to the north. In 1993, Southern California had a total population of close to 20 million.

2. A recent ranking of the largest metropolitan regions by Rand-McNally puts Los Angeles in sixth place, behind Tokyo-Yokohama, New York, Osaka-Kobe-Kyoto, São Paulo, and Seoul. Just behind Los Angeles is Mexico City.

3. Hell Town was the name given to Los Angeles in the period after the end of the Mexican-American War and the beginning of the great California gold rush. Reminiscent of the bloodiest Hollywood westerns, in the early 1850s there was an average of one murder every day in the newly established Los Angeles County (which had a total population of about 3,600) and even more frequent displays of racial hatred, violence, and Yankee vigilantism, a tradition that continues even to the present day.

4. Already in 1900, Los Angeles contained a higher proportion of elderly people than most comparable American cities.

5. For a detailed description of multiethnic Los Angeles in the 1920s, see Robert M. Fogelson, *The Fragmented Metropolis: Los Angeles, 1850–1930* (Cambridge: Harvard University Press, 1967; reissued in 1993, Berkeley, Los Angeles, and Oxford: University of California Press).

6. See Allen J. Scott, *Technopolis: High Technology Industry and Regional Development in Southern California* (Berkeley, Los Angeles, and Oxford: University of California Press, 1993).

7. See R. Kling, S. Olin, and M. Poster, eds., *Postsuburban California: The Transformation of Orange County since World War II* (Berkeley, Los Angeles, and Oxford: University of California Press, 1991).

8. Allen J. Scott and David Bergman, *Advanced Ground Transportation Equipment Manufacturing and Local Economic Development: Lessons for Southern California,* University of California, Los Angeles, Lewis Center for Regional Policy Studies, Working Paper no. 8, 1993.

9. Southern California is now one of the world's major centers of automobile design, with about twenty-five principal design studios belonging to car manufacturers from North America, Japan, and Europe.

10. *SCAG Regional Comprehensive Plan* (Los Angeles: Southern California Association of Governments, 1994).

TWO

The First American City

Richard S. Weinstein

Los Angeles is the first consequential American city to separate itself deci-
sively from European models and to reveal the impulse to privatization embedded in the origins of the American Revolution. Some have emphasized
the operation of economic factors in the development of Los Angeles, but
these need to be understood in relation to cultural and ideological forces
of singular power and resilience. While these forces influenced the economic marketplace, they cannot be explained as arising exclusively from its
operation.

To understand Los Angeles and the many places like it, certain recurring
themes in American culture need to be examined, themes that arise from
attitudes toward nature and society and the city as they were affected by
the experience of settling a new continent, by the transformation of that
experience by science and industrial change, and by the optimistic linkage
of both to our national destiny, to the conquest of western space, and to
the destruction of native populations. These experiences and their representation in art, literature, and thought provide the context of values that
guide our choices as a people. The operation of the marketplace is an in-
dicator of these deeper inclinations as they interact with the uncertainties
of the modern condition but is itself formative of their ultimately American
expressions in the political and institutional arrangements we have made,
in new sensibilities that alter our perceptions, and in the environment we
have built—which is their reflection and which reaches a culmination in
the urban pattern of Los Angeles.

ORIGINS AND SOURCES

. . . No occupation; all men idle, all;
And Women too,—but innocent and pure;
No sovereignty,— . . .
All things in common nature should produce
Without sweat or endeavor: treason, felony,
Sword, pick, knife, gun, or need of any engine,
Would I not have, but nature should bring forth,
Of its own kind, all foison, all abundance,
To feed my innocent people.

GONZALO, IN *THE TEMPEST*, ACT 2, SCENE 1

Those who made the American Revolution had already inherited a continent that haunted the European imagination by the plentitude and purity of its natural abundance, its immense reaches of space, and the potential these represented for beginning the work of civilization without the compromise of historical residue.

Individuals of intelligence, for example, Benjamin Franklin, also understood the immense power that would ultimately accrue to a people for whose growth and resources no limit was imaginable. This was the principal argument Franklin used in trying to persuade his countrymen in England that, in the long run, compromise was worth the prize of confirmed union with the colonies. When he finally failed in these loyal efforts at conciliation, he set to work with equal vigor in establishing the independence of the new settlements. Thomas Jefferson, far younger in years, was less attached to England and the ideals of urbanity than was Franklin. His Declaration not only asserts the rights of each individual to the pursuit of happiness but also rejects the system of controls employed by the British to govern from a distance. The Jeffersonian mind also rejects the urban civilization linked to this failure of governance. Instead he proposes a "dominant image of an undefiled green republic, a quiet land of forests, villages, and farms dedicated to the pursuit of happiness."[1] Jefferson grounded this happy, classless state in the farmers' actual possession of land; in such a society all would adopt an aloof patrician attitude toward acquisitive behavior. These sentiments will forcefully reemerge in Frank Lloyd Wright's vision of Broadacre City, which expressed an enhanced contempt for commerce and its consequences.

But the seeds of empirical science, practical invention, and manufacturing were already active in the American imagination and embodied in the person of Franklin, who was widely regarded in Europe as one of the world's great scientists because of his work with electricity. The kiss that Voltaire

and Franklin bestowed on each other at the culmination of a public ceremony symbolized the bond of genius between the new world and the old,
and of empirical science with philosophy.

The hope that the new world inspired in the European mind was premised in part in the dream of Arcadia, but from the beginning the idea of
the United States was also bound up with the idea of economic self-suf-
ficiency, improvisation, tinkering, ingenuity, and the empirical and the
practical, within the abundant context of a natural bounty. Thus began the
American drama opposing the hope for material progress to the dangerous
mystery of nature.

In Los Angeles, however debased, however partial in its expression, however compromised has been the sublime principle of desert, mountain, and
sea, these great cultural themes have found their most complete expression.

> The houses and the automobiles are equal figments of a great dream, the
> dream of the urban homestead, the dream of a good life outside the squalors
> of the European type of city, and thus a dream that runs back not only into
> the Victorian railway suburbs of earlier cities, but also to the country-house
> culture of the fathers of the US Constitution, or the whig squirearchs whose
> spiritual heirs they sometimes were, and beyond them to the "villegiatura" of
> Palladio's patrons, of the Medicis' "Poggio a Caiano." Los Angeles cradles
> and embodies the most potent current version of the great bourgeois vision
> of the good life in a tamed countryside.[2]

NATURAL CRIMES

The early citizens of the United States occupied a neutral, middle ground
between a remove from European influence and the sense of a violent frontier to the west where Native Americans resisted the encroachment of a
more powerful civilization. The protection of private rights afforded by the
Constitution was enhanced in the agricultural countryside bordering the
frontier by the reality and dangers of spatial isolation. Whatever was other,
became a threat. The destruction of native populations was rationalized on
the basis of survival, on the basis of conversion to the faith, and on the
basis of the "superior" message of Western civilization. The dismal record
of broken treaties nevertheless recognized certain entitlements that the native populations had and were perhaps influenced by ideas about the noble
savage, closeness to nature, and even the evidence of native genius. What
is relevant is the strategy of sequestering the other within defined spatial
borders (the reservations) and the use of violent action to achieve these
ends. In the process, violence became a justified instrument of segregation
and conquest, and racial difference became an acceptable cause for such
action when it served the collective interest of the pioneers. As a result,

fundamental contradictions, if not crimes, were built into the formative experience of the nation that proclaimed the equality of all men and their right to the pursuit of happiness. These means corrupted the moral underpinning of democratic institutions that sought a system of governance that would resolve disputes before violent means became necessary. These violent means applied to native populations were also applied to nature, which was savaged and consumed in the movement west.[3]

Racism and violence in American culture, and its expression in spatial terms, was both rationalized by dangerous encounters on the frontier and supported by the attitudes and practices of slavery in the South. It was reinforced by private entitlement that gave emphasis to the idea of the other and haunted by the influence of nature as simultaneously a source of redemptive knowledge and the carrier of savage threats to survival.

CULTURE AS EMPIRICISM AND MACHINE

The distrust of urban civilization, joined with the sense of boundless space, movement, and opportunity, was strengthened as industry changed the character of the great urban centers. Pollution, crime, immigration, noise, traffic, and poverty were increasingly seen as a threat to the good life and in fundamental opposition to the Jeffersonian strain in the American character. These sentiments are given new form by Henry David Thoreau and Ralph Waldo Emerson, though with a transcendental, romantic coloring. Accelerated by the railroads, the suburbs "express a complex and compelling vision of the modern family freed from the corruption of the city, restored to harmony with nature, endowed with wealth and independence, yet protected by a close-knit, stable community.[4] As Lewis Mumford said in *The Culture of Cities,* "The suburbs are a collective effort to live a private life."

By the mid-1850s, urban areas were feeling the impact of industrialization, and Emerson had begun to state his case against scientific rationality and its industrial consequences. In an article in *Nature,* published in 1836, he argues that experimental science is necessarily preoccupied with function and process and that "a dream may let us deeper into the secrets of nature than a hundred concerted experiments." Emerson sensed a turning point in American values when he further criticized practical intelligence as being morally neutral and potentially dangerous. He thus prescribed immersion in the natural landscape as spiritual therapy. To paraphrase George Orwell's observation, as long as a machine is *there,* one is under an obligation to use it. Siegfried Gideon believed that if progress were possible, then it was necessary, and William Mulholland said, "There it is, take it."[5]

This American ideology of industrialization was thus premised and rationalized on the notion of nature as a divine machine and identified with the notion of progress itself. The invention of machines to do the labor of humans became associated with the American myth of unlimited progress and hope.

The image of suburban America in the early part of the twentieth century domesticates some of these themes. It was Frederick Law Olmsted, designer of Central Park, who advocated the continuity of suburban front lawns as a means of expressing amplitude and democratic communal solidarity. The American obsession with front lawns reveals a deeper ideological inclination.[6] The lawn also represents a subjugation of nature to the rule of civilization. It is an abstraction of the presence of nature, like the whiteness of Moby Dick; it is nature known and therefore tamed. The democracy of the suburban lawn is simultaneously benign, excessive, and obsessive in the sense that it imposes a sameness irrespective of geographic difference and the particularity of ecological place. At the same time the lawn is pleasing, ordinary, and democratic and allows each citizen a symbolic share in a domesticated ritual of subjugation and aggrandizement. The lawn is a middle-class embodiment of the American conflict between the value of nature as a principle and its management as a means toward material progress. Walt Whitman's poetry earlier expressed these contradictions, with more explicit expansionist overtones. His was a kind of romantic poetry of the democratic collective that was self-justifying and gave a moral gloss to those who in celebrating themselves, were also identifying with the spirit of patriotic conquest and manifest destiny.

Los Angeles emerges as the dominant expression of these contradictory impulses and values that need to be understood as they interact with other powerful forces: the natural landscape and climate, economic growth, the character of migration, the national impulse toward suburbanization, the railroad, and later the automobile.

CULTURE AS INDIVIDUAL FULFILLMENT

I celebrate myself and sing myself.
        WALT WHITMAN, "SONG OF MYSELF"

To American attitudes toward nature and industrialization, the linkage between the nuclear family and the suburban impulse, and the practical optimism associated with an expanding frontier must be added a changing view of individual fulfillment. Once again it is Emerson who gives concentrated expression to the more general sentiment when he declared that wealth is less a measure of achievement than a means to "the legitimate comforts of [a well-rounded] life." The significance of this attitude lies in what it tells us about the waning of the agrarian myth and the Protestant ethic.

Work is no longer conceived as possessing inherent, if not religiously justified value; rather, it is perceived as standing in relation to a holistic notion
of the good life, centered on individual rather than collective experience,
emphasizing the transcendental and later the romantic impulse rather than
traditional Protestant virtue: "To believe your own thought, to believe that
what is true for you in your private heart is true for all men, that is genius.
Speak your latent conviction, and it shall be the universal sense."[7]

The rise of evangelical Christianity in various forms, including Mormon-
ism, may be seen as a counterrevolutionary and conservative move to protect religious values threatened both by the industrial revolution and by the
privatization of religious experience proposed by Emerson, Thoreau, and
Whitman.

> I make my circumstance. Let any thought or motive of mine be different from
> what they are, and the difference will transform my condition and economy.
> I—this thought which is called I—is the mold into which the word is poured
> like melted wax. . . . You call it the power of circumstance, but it is the power
> of me.[8]

In the last half of the nineteenth century, there were significant changes in
the American idea of success. The shift was away from the work ethic toward mental self-determination.

> The success myth's popularity was, in large measure, due to the moral cer-
> tainty it offered in a period of profound dislocation and confusion. The in-
> equities produced by industrialization did not merely outrage the sense of
> justice; they threatened to shatter an habitual way of viewing the world and
> interpreting experience. Purveyors of the protestant ethic sensed this threat
> and responded with assertions of traditional morality. Social, economic, and
> intellectual changes, however, challenged more than ideal conceptions of be-
> havior; these changes fostered a deterministic view of man which ran counter
> to the world view implicit in success mythology. The cult of mind and mind-
> power was a response to this deeper challenge. Proponents of the mentalist
> success cult were self-conscious defenders of an idealistic view of man and
> the cosmos. Their idealism struck a responsive chord because it made possi-
> ble the continued belief in the individual's power to mold his own life in a
> society where men seemed increasingly subject to forces beyond their control.
> The idea which links the two success mythologies in their common definition
> of the successful life is one which is self-willed, self-directed, and self-con-
> trolled. Preserving this belief in the power of self-determination as a possi-
> bility for all men was the chief factor operating in the change from the old
> to the new success tradition.[9]

In the early 1900s, William James emphasized the essential unity of
physical and mental action and pointed to the efficacy of the brain in helping to overcome the actual, physical difficulties of life. In this he shows

himself to be in the tradition of Emerson and related to the "new thought" that included the contemporary mentalist religion Christian Science. James argues that belief can condition reality, that "faith in a fact can help create the fact."[10] Such optimistic proclamations contain the seeds of the power of positive thinking later advocated by Norman Vincent Peale. They can be found pervasively in the popular literature of the time, which emphasizes fulfillment and self-realization, time for leisure, the avoidance of conflict, and the generally positive view of life that has come to be identified with Southern California.

Those who found comfort and motivation in these ideas, which James likened to a pervasive religious awakening, were drawn to Southern California, where, they were persuaded, climate and lifestyle would support their inclination. Here they could, like Emerson, ignore "experience whenever it was in harsh or ugly conflict with [their] optimism."[11] George Santayana, then at Harvard University with James and Josiah Royce, remarked that these future citizens of Southern California were the "sentimentalists, mystics, spiritualists, wizards, cranks, quacks, and impostors, . . . those groping, nervous, half-educated, spiritually disinherited, passionately hungry, individuals of which America is full."[12] They were not only produced by the place, or by the character of economic forces, they also constructed the place in the image of their inclinations.

By the turn of the century, these attitudinal changes had ripened in the affluent small-town Middle West. As Robert M. Fogelson notes, "Holding traditional sentiments about the moral superiority of the countryside they were increasingly reluctant to be bound to rural drudgery."[13] And it was to this population that the boosters of Southern California turned their avid attention with great success in the early years of the century. The village was the settlement pattern that most appealed to those who considered moving to Southern California: it was promoted as the return to village ideals and the simple life, an antidote to the blight of demoralizing metropolitanism. These provincial ideals also placed a value on social harmony and the absence of conflict, and hence this exclusion of nonconforming racial groups, to allay the anxieties associated with the move west. The promoters of Southern California real estate promised at the same time the recovery of an idealized life of the village in a rural setting and the opportunity for personal fulfillment.

The Red Cars of Huntington provided a decentralized mass transit network of trolleys that facilitated the pattern of linked suburban village settlements dispersed over the landscape which irreversibly established the fundamental pattern of Los Angeles' regional growth. This pattern, reinforced by land values and accessibility, responded to the persistent yearning in the American character for a redemptive contact with nature represented by the West, an escape from the failures of the industrial metropolis, and changes in the notion of the good life, family, and personal destiny.

That this paradigmatic postmodern urban form should have found its first and still most comprehensive expression in Los Angeles is in part the result of the dispersed spatial infrastructure of the first significant immigrations that permitted, enabled, and even encouraged the transformations that have occurred since the 1960s.

THE EXTENDED CITY

The prevailing extended city is now characterized by a medium-density housing tissue of subdivisions laced with commercial strips, including small industrial spaces, and periodically marked by centers of varying size that consist of a shopping mall with a cineplex, a cluster of commercial buildings, and a health care facility. At intervals, zones of industrial space form the hinterland behind the commercial arteries. This pattern occurs with variations at more or less regular intervals governed by the appetites of the marketplace in which each commercial or retail use depends for its success on access to a certain residential population. Because much of the U.S. population now lives in the extended city, it is possible to describe its characteristics as a particular kind of market in which predictable topologies regularly occur in response to subsets of population.

Three characteristics may serve to describe this built environment. The *matrix* is the prevailing latticework of intersecting grids in which a variety of uses are distributed. This matrix is laced by *linear developments* of greater commercial density from boulevards down to strips. Density is also clustered at *nodes,* or activity centers. These repetitive patterns are also reflected in the fragmented institutional and political structure of the region that is composed of multiple municipalities, county governments, and a variety of powerful, autonomous, single-purpose air quality, transportation, water, waste management, and redevelopment agencies. Many citizens are most directly affected by home owners' associations, and voting rights are proportionate to the value of the owner's property. At the periphery of the extended city, development may occur in unincorporated territory without adequate political representation. In addition, the rapid growth of the extended city corresponds with the accelerated entry of women into the workforce in the 1970s and the consequent proliferation of automobile ownership.[14]

Among the causes of this social transformation were economic pressures and the destabilizing uncertainties associated with rapid change, but also the burdens associated with individual choice, unsupported by a prevailing system of public values. "The enchantment of our souls by myth, philosophy, and revelation, has been replaced by more immediate meaning—the building of free and equal men by the overcoming of chance."[15] Disneyland may be a response to this challenge. As Karal Ann Marling describes it, "History has no dominion over such a world. Instead time was contingent and malleable. Without a past firmly situated in relation to a future, there were no beginnings or endings, no death."[16]

The interchangeability, predictability, and ordinariness of this urban landscape also offers comfort and security to a mobile population, anxiety ridden in the pursuit of profit, pleasure, individual self-definition, and the control of chance. Yet the ordinary, common, and conforming still contribute to this anxiety by a tense relation to the singular, individual, and privatized.

The complexity and fragmentation of governance arrangements and the multiple regulatory maze that is precipitated by their operation make political accountability almost impossible. The physical and spatial structure of the region is therefore inseparably related to the institutional and political arrangements that constitute its governance. The primary image of the city is an extended repetitive fabric, bounded by the sea or mountain edge overlaid with a discontinuous, contrapuntal net of freeways, with periodic concentrations of high-rise developments that are conceptually mapped during high-speed travel. The physical characteristics of the place are the objective correlative for its privatized, insular, fragmented, institutional structure, bound to some rule of reason, as by the freeways, through the establishment of imperial bureaucracies. The absence of integrated hierarchical order in either the built or the institutional environment is in some sense the complete expression of the kind of democracy that accompanies an apotheosis of privatization in which the multiplicity of competing parts leads to a uniform texture of political activity. John Cage, who lived in Los Angeles, developed a musical metaphor that embodies the same characteristics. He described his compositions as "setting a process going which has no necessary beginning, no middle, no end, and no sections."[17]

These fragmenting discontinuities operated on both the new development and the infill between existing (but already dispersed) communities that preceded the automobile, becoming the nonhierarchical, flexible, extended matrix that characterizes Los Angeles. The spatial porosity of the system, its void/positive character, together with the blockages represented by parking structures and the emptiness of parking lots, effectively preclude the hierarchical, linear, narrative ordering of traditional urban space with its organized public realms that depend on either consensual or authoritarian politics and the traditionally clear separation of public and private space.

In the European city, the public realm is usually apprehended as an open space within a communal solid; our impression of such cities is that they are mass-positive residuals of the feudal city, out of which were carved the piazzas and boulevards. Were it possible to oppose the deep impulse toward democratic privatization, the urban design strategies to create a similar postmodern public realm are not obvious. In Los Angeles, such realms are natural: the beach, the mountains, the desert. But these are not civic realms; they are essentially private experiences of nature.

To them must be added the theme park, which appeals to our lost sense of community. "In a pluralistic society, where experiences of church, school, and ethnicity were not universally shared, Disney motifs constituted a common culture, a kind of civil religion of happy endings, worry-free consumption, technological optimism, and nostalgia for the good old days."[18] Disneyland "is keyed to the kind of participation without embarrassment . . . we crave."[19] Themed developments are increasingly a part of Southern California life and real estate strategies.

Repetitive patterns and typologies, however they respond to valid psychic needs that underlie and motivate the behavior of the market, also address issues of efficient mass production and convenience for the majority population. "The strip is trying to tell us something about ourselves: namely that most Americans prefer convenience, are determined to simplify as much of the mechanical service and distribution sides of life as possible, and are willing to subsidize any informal geographic setting that helps."[20] These strategies combine to undermine the authenticity of unique places, in favor of uniformity of treatment; in fact, "the absence of place permits the attainment of greater levels of spatial [economic] efficiency."[21] The strip and its perfection, the shopping mall, are a logical solution to the problem of optimizing the acquisition of goods and services. The persistence of the form everywhere offers familiar access to the newcomer and minimizes adjustment (and presumed discomfort) to a new setting.

Much has been made of the homogeneity of subdivision design; despite the stylistic surface distinctions between New England or Spanish themes, houses and their internal arrangement are essentially the same from place to place. This has been attributed to the national mobility of the buyers, who move on an average of every six years to pursue new job opportunities and may move perhaps four or five times in their working lives. Homes are treated as investments, and by avoiding eccentricities, a more uniform market is created which appeals to a broader spectrum of buyers. The anxiety associated with job mobility and the uprooting of the family from place to place may also account in part for the value attached to the predictability (interchangeability) of environments and their signal features such as gated entrances.

LOS ANGELES AS BROADACRE CITY

Broadacre is everywhere or nowhere.
FRANK LLOYD WRIGHT, *The Living City*

Of all the architectural creators and thinkers of the last century, Frank Lloyd Wright now seems closest to the American urban ideal and its expression in contemporary Los Angeles. He is central to the cultural themes we have been examining, which have contributed to the evolving shape of American urbanism. Wright's vision of a decentralized extended and repetitive pattern based on the automobile and preserving contact with the earth can be discerned underneath the messy and inchoate surface of the extended city. In proposing a decentralized urban form, Wright recalls Jefferson's idea of unbounded checkerboard development wherein squares of agrarian land alternate with urbanized land. These extended grids also recall Marxist proposals calling for the gradual abolition of the distinction between town and country. In their contempt for the industrial city as "a wholly degenerate effusion of capitalism,"[22] the first generation of Soviet architects and planners came close to Wright's own sentiments about consumerism and the democratic "mobocracy." Wright, however, sought an alternative in a conservative reestablishment of the nuclear family in relation to the land and nature, a reinterpretation of the basic building blocks of Jeffersonian democracy.

Wright also sought to reestablish a meaningful connection between work and the products of labor, through the periodic introduction of regional markets. "Great spacious roadside pleasure places; like some flexible form of pavilion; a place of cooperative exchange: not only of commodities but cultural facilities."[23] These pavilions, as they emerge in Wright's sketches, feature airy glass roofs reminiscent of the Crystal Palace and Parisian arcades. The glass-covered market also formed the centerpiece of Ebenezer Howard's Garden City and was similarly proposed as a center for exchange and culture.

The identification of the glass pavilion and its promise of a controlled environment with an antiurban tradition goes back, as Marshall Berman has shown, through Ebenezer Howard to Nikolay Chernyshevsky. In *What Is To Be Done?* Chernyshevsky proposes huge air-conditioned, glass megastructures scattered without limit through the countryside, each of which contains harmonious self-contained communities of several thousand people.

In speaking of Dostoyevsky, Berman observes that "if the Crystal Palace is a denial of 'suffering, doubt and negation,' the streets and squares and bridges and embankments of Petersburg are precisely where these experiences and impulses [the acting- and working-out of personal and social conflict] . . . find themselves most at home."[24] Here the central opposition is defined as that between the urban street and its potential for productive humane conflict and Chernyshevsky's cleansing prophylactic exurban dreams of Paradise.

The aesthetic potential of glass and steel construction first completely realized in the Crystal Palace can be employed as an expression of the urban vitality and adventure that Dostoyevsky prized on the Nevsky Prospect (see also the Galleria Vittorio Emmanuel in Milan and the market building by Eiffel in Budapest), or as the expression of corporate American power and bureaucratic routine, for example, the Seagram building and its imitations in New York. Elias Canetti speaks of "smoothness and order, . . . [which] have entered into the very nature of power. They are inseparable from it and, in every manifestation of power, they are the first things to be established."[25] These dangerous, deadening, and Fascist expressions of routine are antiurban and as threatening to the public realm in the city, where they destroy the life of the street, as they are when they support the fragmentation of the extended city, where the street doesn't matter at all.

There is an additional aspect of the modern sensibility as it may be associated with the Crystal Palace that deserves attention because it contributes to the complex variations underlying American cultural themes of the extended city. Once again Berman has identified a crucial issue. Here is a contemporary description of the Crystal Palace:

> If we let our gaze travel downward it encounters the blue-painted lattice girders. At first these occur only at wide intervals; then they range closer and closer together until they are interrupted by a dazzling band of light—the transept—which dissolves into a distant background where all materiality is blended into the atmosphere.[26]

Berman links these impressions directly to a primary passage in Marx that illuminates the transformation of the modern sensibility:

> Constant revolutionizing of production, uninterrupted disturbance of all social relations, everlasting uncertainty and agitation, distinguish the bourgeois spark from all earlier times. All fixed, fact-frozen relationships, with their train of venerable ideas and opinions, are swept away, all new-formed ones become obsolete before they can ossify. All that's solid melts into air, all that is holy is profound, and men at last are forced to face with sober sense the real condition of their lives and their relations with their fellow men.[27]

The irreversible erosion of materiality "blended into the atmosphere," the melting of "all that is solid" into air, joins the deepest structuring of the modernist sensibility with its expression in architectural form. This was the beginning of a process in architecture, most completely realized by Wright, of the erosion of the solid materiality of buildings by active space, until a balance of boundary and void was achieved, producing a fluid interaction between solids and voids within the envelope of a building and its surrounding environment. A supreme example of this interaction can be found in Wright's house over a waterfall, Fallingwater.

Wright used such an extended grid that the coherence of concentrated urban settlement was lost in favor of the articulation of the natural landscape. In this effort we sense a deeply conservative yearning to recover what is holy and venerable in the agrarian tradition. At the same time, Wright, while consistent with this larger conservative vision, addresses in his architectural compositions the ambiguous condition of the modern sensibiliity, noted by Marx, with unequaled artistic depth.

The yearning for the fulfillment of this ideal can be sensed underneath the distraught conditions of contemporary Los Angeles, in the arrangements of its built form in relation to nature, in the managed innocence of its themed cultural productions. However, the sense of tragic limit, arising from the sediment of history out of which the structure of older cities is made, is crucially absent here, where the individual pursuit of paradise, the will "to triumph by earthly happiness," has become the shaping influence.

THE EXPERIENCE OF THE EXTENDED CITY

In the United States there is more space where nobody is than where anybody is. That is what makes America what it is.
GERTRUDE STEIN, *THE GEOGRAPHICAL HISTORY OF AMERICA*

In an extended city like Los Angeles, we come closer to the spatial compositions of Wright's architecture and even closer to the condition of modernity described by Marx. The shape and patterns of Los Angeles and other extended cities, in contrast to Broadacre, are derived from the behavior of markets, from industrial clusters, and from the preferences of consumers as they are influenced by advertising media. But these media strategies are based on assumptions of preference linked to the cultural tendencies discussed here as well as to cynical manipulation and the artificial promotion of appetite. It would be a mistake, however, to understand the built form of the extended city only as the result of consumerist conspiracies. Much more is at work which has little to do with economic determinism.

The uncertainty, the dissolving and chance conditions of contemporary life are reflected in the ad hoc texture of the Los Angeles urban landscape; it is the lack of hierarchical organization at the scale of neighborhoods that permits this impression to flourish. Vacant lots, parking lots, irrational leftover spaces that are the residual of freeway construction, impermeable parking structures, and the repetitive patterns that destroy the possibility of an ascending order promote the sense of porosity, flux, and impermanence. Further, the temporary and flimsy character of much construction contributes to the sense of instability and impermanence, which, in the early state of decay, forms a kind of inexpensive mulch in which the small industrial entrepreneurs who form the base of the region's manufacturing economy appear to flourish.

The city is experienced as a passage through space, with constraints established by speed and motion, rather than the static condition of solids, of buildings that define the pedestrian experience of traditional cities. The resulting detachment further privatizes experience, devalues the public realm, and, by force of the time spent in travel, contributes to isolation. Increasingly, social interaction is structured not by shared experience but by the comparison of solitary encounters with televised events—even when the event is riot or war. Our experience of the physical structure of Los Angeles, its nonhierarchical, unordered presence, and our compartmentalized, multileveled, multiscaled, and fragmented impression of it seems to be the world Marx described as melting into air.

Yet there is a subtext of concern for the development and discovery of the self as a moral exercise which touches on the idea of a moral commonwealth, a concern for the natural environment, an immediate pleasure in nature that has contributed to an open, informal, and inclusive lifestyle, and the development of a regional architecture inspired by the work of Frank Gehry that suggests the existence of deeper forces at work. Edmund Wilson could have been describing Gehry's architecture when in commenting on Southern California literature, he noted that it was "easy going, good natured, too lacking in organization, always dissolving into an even sunshine, always circumventing by ample detour what one expects to be sharp and direct."[28] What may have troubled Wilson was the working out in artistic style of the American suspicion of privilege and rules of inherited rank, the impulse to even out (dissolve into sunshine, melt into air?) precisely the inclusive, the informal—the against formality—raised to a principle of art and life. Much that is positive in such attitudes has so far been confounded by acquisitiveness and disturbed by the creation of new class distinctions based on wealth and ethnicity. Yet these attitudes may evolve and someday give more substance to the idea of Jefferson's moral commonwealth that continues to haunt contemporary confusions and despairs.

In assessing what is deficient and dangerous in the extended city, it is also important to point out opportunities for change that also inhere in the way its physical frame is constructed. First, the extended city lends itself to change because so much of it is open space. Second, because the quality of much construction is ersatz, in part due to the permissiveness of climate, it is relatively easy to renew and change. Third, because density is dispersed, it is possible to provide for growth in almost unnoticeable increments if it were to be uniformly distributed. The capacity to absorb growth also implies the flexibility to allow for selective concentrations of denser mixed-use development. Fourth, the cultural preferences that underlie the organization of the Southern California region, particularly the sanctity of privatized space, may be more adaptable to constraints than previously imagined. Environmental, traffic, and even social constraints may be accepted if they are seen as a way of preserving the essential freedoms of a middle-class lifestyle. Fifth, the underlying strengths of a diversified, flexible, regional economy, deriving in part from the dispersed pattern of regional settlement and its inherent spatial flexibility, could, if properly managed, provide increased social and economic mobility for the poor.

The relation between extreme poverty in the vestigial core and the middle-class character of the extended city has been insufficiently examined. We need a much more comprehensive understanding of its sociology, to see whether inclusionary (and even empowering) opportunities exist in the boundary conditions and voids between self-regulation parts. Pockets of ethnic poverty, for example, have now appeared throughout the region. We know much more about the dynamics of poverty, its statistical realities and geography, than we do of the porous middle-class matrix. A far more sophisticated, balanced, and even fair-minded understanding of the nature of this realm is required if the community advocates of the disenfranchised are to realize lasting advantages for their constituency in the only place it is reasonable to look for advantage, the sprawling, complicated, essentially middle-class matrix that still thrives in the extended city.

A NEW BASIS FOR THE PUBLIC REALM

Each person, withdrawn into himself, behaves as though he is a stranger to the destiny of others. His children and his good friends constitute for him the whole of the human species. As for his transactions with his fellow citizens, he may be among them, but he sees them not; he touches them, but does not feel them; he exists only in himself and for himself alone. And if on these terms there remains in him a sense of family, there no longer remains a sense of society.
ALEXIS DE TOCQUEVILLE, *DEMOCRACY IN AMERICA*

In what follows I argue that a concentration of value-oriented institutions and voluntary civic and community associations, combined with public service institutions (e.g., education), constitutes the seed that—planted in mixed-use, higher-density environment—will grow into a public realm. It is a realm that would be decentralized at varying scales but structured to provide the basis for communal expression as public space. The mission of these institutional centers would address the social, cultural, political, and environmental issues endemic to modern urban settlements. These concentrations of institutional infrastructures must be promoted by public policy and investment and guided by the active participation of citizens.

The sense of an ordered society was once the precondition for the creation of the public realm and its manifestation in intensely shared public space. So far, democratic culture in the United States has produced few such places. Their survival in Europe and, to a lesser degree, in eastern American cities is the result of weakened tradition shored up by a physical armature of space inherited from the past. This older public realm is the expression of clear, though autocratic, political and economic arrangements, supported by once-shared institutional and religious values.

The democratic impulse for freedom of personal expression, and the consequent proliferation of interest groups, is linked to the privatization of experience aggravated by the fear of change and the loss of control. Fundamentalist movements in politics and morals, the effort to reassert conservative values and reroot experience, are a compensating social reaction whose impact is further to disturb progressive social action across a broad spectrum. These processes are further destabilized by increased immigration and the proliferation of multiethnic populations.

> If we recognize a global breakup of customary forms or rural life as the main feature of twentieth-century politics, then all the competing ideologies and rival power alliances of our time can be seen as experiments in the management of populations that have been emancipated from customary constraints and that do not know what to expect under radically changing circumstances. Promises of deliberately accelerated progress and development, especially economic development, have an obvious appeal for land-hungry peasants and ex-peasants who have migrated to cities in search of jobs. . . . Yet there is a contrary current, also very strong, that aspires instead to restore the sense of community and shared values that economic development weakens or destroys. This took secular forms in inter-war nationalist and fascist movements, but became theological after World War II, when religious revivals—Jewish, Moslem, Christian, Hindu, and even Buddhist—began to play important roles in world politics. . . . Tension between secular universalism and religious sectarianism thus pervades the human response to risk and novelty inherent in the breakup of traditional orderings of society.[29]

Neither governmental reform nor private initiative operating through the market alone can be relied on to restore a valid sense of community. Instead, we must look to an enhanced role for the voluntary associations that Tocqueville identified as a distinguishing characteristic of the American Revolution.

> I have often admired the extreme skill with which the inhabitants of the United States succeed in proposing a common object for the exertions of a great many men and in inducing them voluntarily to pursue it. . . . Among Democratic nations . . . all the citizens are independent and feeble; they can

do hardly anything by themselves, and none of them can oblige his fellow men to lend him their assistance. They all, therefore, become powerless if they do not learn voluntarily to help one another. If men living in democratic countries had no right and no inclination to associate for political purposes, their independence would be in great jeopardy, but they might long preserve their wealth and their cultivation: whereas if they never acquired the habit of forming associations in ordinary life, civilization itself would be endangered. A people among whom individuals lost the power of achieving great things single-handed, without acquiring means of producing them by united exertions, would soon relapse into barbarism.[30]

Those civic and community agencies supported by the focused intellectual resources of our universities and foundations can operate in the policy twilight between the powerful and well-funded single-purpose authorities and state, county, and local government. They are also uniquely suited to operating in the contingent realm of interethnic relations, housing, education, citizen participation, and the environment and to participating in a variety of public policy debates. A whole new class of not-for-profit institutions is beginning to promote socially beneficial innovations in education, community-based policing, and environmental coalitions.

In the Southern California region, the threats to the existing social order that may give impetus to collective public action through the voluntary sector may be summarized as follows. First, the most serious problems facing the viability of the region are interconnected, yet the agencies devised to address them are autonomous, fragmented, and organized around a single mission. Issues of transportation, land use, air quality, waste management, and housing are related yet are never addressed as a system. As a result, agencies cross-plan, cross-regulate, and neutralize each other's initiatives. The friction arising from these inefficiencies also diverts large amounts of public funds that might otherwise be put to good use.[31] Complex bureaucracies often cannot process funds allocated for large public works efficiently—leading to large unexpended reserves. Part of the public justification for the creation of authorities is the complex and technical nature of the problems being addressed (e.g., construction of mass transit) and the necessity of operating over time and across different political jurisdictions. The issue then becomes one of accountability. Civic associations, furnished with technically sophisticated advice from universities and elsewhere, are in the best position to represent the interests of the general public in holding these agencies accountable and advocating integrated planning among competing bureaucracies.

Second, environmental necessities will increasingly become a coercive force in the organization of public institutional strategies and complicate debates over economic restructuring and job production. Regulatory issues and litigation associated with environmental impact reports threaten to

compromise environmental quality by disturbing economic growth and stability. At the same time, research is likely to broaden our understanding of
the connection between pollution and public health and further intensify
the debate. Voluntary agencies offer the best hope of managing a dispute
resolution process among the interested parties with the degree of disin-
terested sophistication necessary to make the process work. Gore Vidal has
called the environment the "green god" of the twenty-first century. Spiritual convictions arising from survival instincts will give compelling force
to the social, economic, and political restructuring caused by environmental imperatives.

Third, the regional economic restructuring now under way involves the
internationalization of the economy, the adjustment of the U.S. economy
to competition, the impact of immigration, and the reductions in standards
of living that have in part promoted the mass entry of women into the
workforce. Public reaction takes the form of tax revolts, term limits, and
an attack on bureaucracies and their costs, which have been inflated by
regulatory inefficiencies and the complexity of the problems they have to
address. All these factors combine to create an environment in which there
is less funding for public purposes. The voluntary sector will be compelled
to expand and coordinate its activities far more closely with government to
enhance the impact of expenditures and promote economic growth.

Fourth, the social problems facing the region have now twice erupted
in civic violence at very substantial cost to the region as a whole. The nature
of the conflicts underlying these disturbances is complicated by racism, police brutality, homelessness, the interaction of multiple ethnic cultures, the
pattern and timing of immigrations, persistent and widening poverty, the
decreasing spatial isolation of the poor from the middle class (and in some
cases from each other), and the thrombosis in public education. The sensitivity and intimacy required to address these problems could arise from
community-based organizations working with more broadly based civic institutions and universities to effect public policy and concerted private expenditures.

Finally, fragmentation and privatization, however deeply rooted in our
culture, however amplified by the fear of change and reduced economic
circumstance, must not prevent the emergence of compensating social purpose. The urgent threats to the public welfare are understood at some level,
although tax revolts, term limits, the initiative process, and low voter turnouts are not productive ways to address the problem. Alternative forms of
participation are offered through the enhanced role of voluntary institutions, environmental advocates, community housing corporations, cooperative banks and credit unions, adult education centers, dispute resolution
services, and private social services networks. These offer the best hope for
establishing some elements of a binding consensus, of a community of

trust, which permits public business to go forward without the proliferating litigation that is the most destructive expression of private protectionism. If there is hope in the intractable problems faced by regional communities around the nation, it lies in the edge of desperation most citizens feel and in the collective fear of threats to our well-being as a community. Some will retreat behind privatized fundamentalist barricades; others may exercise their instinct for survival through participation and communal action.

The yearning to reestablish the public realm, as it was once understood to exist in Europe, is impossible without a return to the coercive politics and religious privileges we renounced as a nation. The shape of public space in European capitals is the result of policies that suited the political strategies of an aristocracy or military or religious oligarchy.

Yet these preoccupations and defining cultural purposes, emphasizing individual freedom of choice as the goal of government and then identifying choice with mobility, do not lead to a pattern of urbanization from which the physical representation of the public realm naturally emerges. The densities necessary to animate public realms—streets, squares, boulevards, and parks—are still antithetical to the American public, although New York and Boston are representative of the few exceptions. At present, when left to its own preferences, the overwhelming, essentially free choice is for the extended city.

The presence of a variety of civic associations, schools, and cultural facilities in space provided by the community would introduce value-oriented behavior and the essential identification with place needed to enrich a scene that would otherwise be dominated by convenience-oriented consumption and themed development. The strong institutional, cultural, and educational presence in these communities could do much gradually to integrate across class and ethnic divisions through public programs and employment and the natural linkages that would occur over time with the surrounding business community.

THE MORPHOLOGY OF A PUBLIC REALM

What survived of that early vernacular culture was its nobility, its adaptability, its preference for the transitory, the ephemeral. Our vernacular landscape has unparalleled vitality and diversity, but it . . . [is detached] from formal space. . . . [It is indifferent] to history . . . essentially utilitarian, conscienceless [in its] use of the environment.

J. B. JACKSON, *DISCOVERING THE VERNACULAR LANDSCAPE*

The character of public space associated with these proposed transformations will not follow historical models. Something approaching the scale of a village, or a loose collection of villages, would seem a more appropriate

American scale. J. B. Jackson has captured the essentials of the democratic vernacular in an emergent marketplace culture, where the strength of the national economy has been able to support a huge privatized middle class. The goal of this society has been to free itself from constraint, and in the pursuit of individual self-determination this drive has come to be expressed through consumption. The structure of our vernacular landscape symbolizes and promotes this activity, embodies the energy of these pursuits, and organizes for selection a diversity of choices, constantly changing. A natural consequence of the obsession to discover new pleasure and comfort is to treat the whole as inconsequential—to glory in invention, novelty, fashion, and shock (if not schlock), to make a culture out of opportunism, of seizing the future through innovation. Convenient motion through space increases the opportunity for choice, whether by car through a strip or on foot through a shopping mall, naturally resulting in the detachment from formal space of which Jackson speaks. (These are themes also explored by Robert Venturi and Denise Scott Brown in *Learning from Las Vegas*.) The freeway system elevates this kind of activity to its ultimate expression at a regional scale.

But the culture of unlimited choice and unconstrained growth, movement, and inflated freedoms now faces the prospect of being radically altered by the restructuring of the national and international economy, by the migrations of people from less developed nations, by population growth, and by environmental limits. These developments constitute a new basis for the spatial expression of a collective impulse—the precondition of the public realm.

Our public spaces will not naturally take the shape of pure geometric form, implying a perfect, impossible consensus or, alternatively, a singular authority unconstrained by democratic opinion. Instead, public space would take an opportunistic, pragmatic (convenient) shape, patched together from leftover spaces and negotiated contributions from private and public owners, compromised with messy edges, imperfect, surprising in idiosyncrasy, mixing solids and voids in ambiguous relation, but nevertheless possessing a public character through shared, connected space, coherent greenery tied to gardens, enhanced public circulation, public places to sit, and the penetration of these spaces into the body of private and institutional buildings, through courtyards and glass-covered passages. Private or commercial frontages on public space should be permeable, presenting surfaces hollowed out at a public scale or projecting in pavilions to diminish the sense of uniform order, providing both an expression of the personal and an expression of the private deferring to public necessities. Behind and above a shared, differentiated, mixed-use public base, private space should be allowed security and identity. Institutional buildings would be given prominence of position and treatment. A variety of institutions that address the needs of continuing education, job training, and day care would be provided with subsidized locations.

Without social programs to address the needs of disadvantaged populations, however, such mixed-use centers will attract the homeless and the poor and promote the perception, if not the reality, of increased crime. Should this be the case, and should it pass tolerable limits, the market for these emerging activity centers will decrease. The potential for an illusive public realm will disappear, in favor of themed public activities based on pulse densities (intense evening or weekend use). Users of public space would be filtered by sophisticated security strategies catering to homogeneous populations and homogenized, prepackaged experience.

The overwhelming presence of environmental necessities and constraints must also have a central metaphorical presence in the communities we build and in the way we build them, providing an architectural principle analogous to the organizing presence of the church in European public space. These constraints will increasingly have an impact on built form, institutional and political mission, and the poetic imagination. Space should therefore be provided for the transformation of the public green of our colonial village heritage into playing fields, gardens, and community agricultural space, reflecting an understanding that we must live with nature in reciprocal balance through cultivation, rather than stand in awe and ecstasy or dominate in conquest and spoilation.

These urban villages and boulevards will be distinct from the prevailing interstitial tissue of the region that will remain hinterland and incubator, too vast in size and complexity to permit considered intervention. This geography will receive the first impact of immigrations, suffer from interethnic tensions, and represent a relatively unstable, even volatile social condition. In those places of enhanced activity supported by transit, the sense of security will be provided, in part, by "eyes on the street" and by the influence of benign value-oriented institutions with a communal mission and communal experience. It is these voluntary institutions that will increasingly mediate among ethnic subcultures and move between the political and private sectors to reduce social conflict, improve education, and articulate and promote the commonalities of interest that bind the citizenry to a sense of common purpose. From these settlements, civic colonies can be established in the hinterlands and the industrial mulch where waste, decay, change, innovation, and new growth begins.

If civic institutions, the third sector, emerge to claim a larger share of the public debate, they may alter the new American landscape but will never entirely displace the deep contradictions in our culture that continue to show through the mask that commerce has thrown up between our violent selves and nature, between a moral commonwealth and a commonwealth of self-enrichment. We may someday transform the new American cities we have built to bring them more nearly in phase with our better selves, but they will never have an authentic connection to the historic models of the European city that continue to haunt the imagination of our urbanists.

CONCLUSION

Uncertainty and danger have become so linked in the privatized, extended city that freedom—certainly the freedom of opportunity and hope—has for many been extinguished. The despair thus engendered, and the violence with which it has become associated, now threatens the freedoms of the privileged.

The changes associated with action, thought, and opportunity will always produce anxiety, if not fear, and change will provide growth in some places at the expense of decline and decay in others, but "so precious all these freedoms that the citizens judge the city's squalor as a fair price for its promise."[32] The present condition of Los Angeles is characterized by too much squalor with far too little promise and by intolerable levels of fear that perpetuate misery and isolation. Uncertainty and change will continue to be a persistent reality and will continue to produce an urban fabric of growth and decay. In between these extremes and constituting much of what we are and use will remain a tissue in a state of dissolution and melting toward waste, before the cycle begins anew. This dissolving urban substance can become, and probably already is, the fertile ground for small entrepreneurial enterprise. The villages and boulevards proposed here are intended to create a middle ground, a spatial zone protected from the fearful extremes of privileged isolation and squalid misery (nourished by unbounded, unstable hinterlands of small-scale industrial activity), where common purposes may be pursued by a mixture of people with just tolerable levels of risk. These purposes include education, recreation, health care, cultural activity, participation in government, and the ordinary round of shopping and service consultations. It is the role of the third sector institutions, those voluntary social service, environmental, civic, and cultural institutions, and the universities with a substantially expanded presence to cultivate this mixture through the diversity of their natural constituencies that exist across lines of race, class, and ethnicity.

A kind of uncertainty principle should affect the attitude of urban designers and planners as they approach the problems of the extended city and its characteristic matrix. For to gain influence over a part of the built environment, we must leave the rest of it to other influences that are moved by social and economic forces we little understand reeor have little power to control. Experience has taught that the dreams of urban paradise breed monsters and that sometimes in wishing to eliminate what is messy, perceived as ugly, or despised as the consequence of greed, to eliminate poverty and injustice, or rather to rely solely on a rational system premised on an idealized concept of man, produces results even more terrible than the circumstance that at first inspired comprehensive reform.

A democratic, pluralistic society generates imperfect partial plans. A necessary uncertainty is structured into the process, as a consequence of necessary compromise. As it is impossible to address social ills comprehensively, they will be addressed according to what is perceived as most urgent, within a context of competing alternative needs. Therefore, there will always be an unstructured, uncertain, ambiguous context of opportunity and despair in which specific action takes place. There will be a changing, imperfect, structural matrix that persists, whose behavior will occasionally produce a benefit we may secure and amplify or a misery too urgent to be ignored. Beneficial changes are most likely to occur when policy is able to focus both these transforming energies around an existing potential, enhanced by transit, to produce a new social circumstance, restructured institutional arrangements, and the physical correlative with which they interact and through which they are reinforced and a public realm established.

These places would express the inclination toward common purpose repressed in the structure of the extended city by the force of individual self-determination that separated us from Europe and its history. These beginnings will first exist within a larger fabric still compelled to take its shape from the idea of nature, privatized human settlement, and the practical, empirical imagination. Released by scientific inquiry and its technological successes to result in the conquest of a continent, we have elevated self-enrichment over a moral commonwealth and promoted the dominance of convenient, private choice at the expense of social and community values.

Compensating adjustments must begin to be made to this system of culturally determined inclinations and the physical frame for our lives, which is its built expression. Nature itself and our social constructions have begun to rebel against its operation; even the practical genius of our people is confounded by the uncontrolled complex interactions of its autonomous competing systems. Increasing social, economic, and environmental constraints will necessarily limit, are already limiting, the very freedom of action and dreams of self-fulfillment that attracted us west to this terrible and yet still compelling and sometimes still beautiful place.

NOTES

1. Leo Marx, *The Machine in the Garden: Technology and the Pastoral Ideal in America* (New York: Oxford University Press, 1964), 6.

2. Reyner Banham, *Los Angeles: The Architecture of the Four Ecologies* (New York: Pelican Books, 1978), 238.

3. Marx, *Machine in the Garden,* 301.

4. Lewis Mumford, in introduction to Robert Fishman, *Bourgeois Utopias: The Rise and Fall of Suburbia* (New York: Basic Books, 1987).

5. Robert Matson, *William Mulholland: A Forgotten Forefather* (Stockton, Calif.: Pacific Center for Western Studies, 1976), 30.

6. See Michael Pollan, *Second Natures: A Gardener's Education* (New York: Laurel, 1992), 87.

7. Ralph Waldo Emerson, excerpt from "Self-Reliance," 1841, in *Selected Writings of Ralph Waldo Emerson* (New York: Modern Library, 1950), 87.

8. Emerson, "Self-Reliance."

9. Richard Weiss, "The American Myth of Success, 1865 to the Present: A Study in Popular Thought" (Ph.D. dissertation, Columbia University, 1966), 3.

10. William James, "Is Life Worth Living," in *The Will to Believe and Other Essays in Popular Philosophy* (Cambridge: Harvard University Press, 1979), 59.

11. Weiss, "American Myth of Success," 161.

12. Santayana, cited in Weiss, "American Myth of Success," 167.

13. Robert M. Fogelson, *The Fragmented Metropolis: Los Angeles, 1850–1930* (Cambridge: Harvard University Press, 1967), 69.

14. Joel Garreau, *Edge City: Life on the New Frontier* (New York: Doubleday, 1991), 113.

15. George Grant, cited in E. C. Relph, *Place and Placelessness* (London: Pion, 1976), 144.

16. Karal Ann Marling, "Disneyland 1955: Just Take the Santa Ana Freeway to the American Dream," *American Art* 5, no. 1–2 (Winter/Spring 1991): 187.

17. From "An Interview with John Cage" (New York, 1993), Oral History Transcript by Thomas S. Hines, UCLA Music Collection.

18. Marling, "Disneyland 1955," 201.

19. Charles Moore, *Perspecta: The Yale Architecture Journal* 9–10 (1965): 65.

20. Grady Clay, cited in Relph, *Place and Placelessness,* 132.

21. Relph, *Place and Placelessness,* 117.

22. Marshall Berman, *All That Is Solid Melts into Air: The Experience of Modernity* (New York: Simon & Schuster, 1982), 247.

23. Frank Lloyd Wright, *The Living City* (New York: Horizon Press, 1958), 168.

24. Berman, *All That Is Solid,* 245.

25. Elias Canetti, *Crowds and Power* (New York: Farrar, Straus, Giroux, 1984), 208.

26. Berman, *All That Is Solid,* 239–240; quoting Bucher.

27. Ibid., 95.

28. Cited in Carey McWilliams, *Southern California: An Island on the Land* (New York: Duell, Sloan & Pierce, 1946).

29. Robert McNeil, "International Alliances," in *The Phenomenon of Change,* ed. Lisa Taylor, 56–57 (New York: Cooper-Hewitt Museum of the Smithsonian Institution; distributed by Rizzoli, 1984).

30. Alexis de Tocqueville, *Democracy in America,* vol. 2 (New York: Alfred A. Knopf, 1966).

31. As much as $4.5 billion in Southern California alone has been estimated. John Kirlin, "Toward Government Simplification, Accountability and Efficiency: Financing Regional Policymaking," Technical Report, August 1992.

32. Lewis Lapham, "City Lights," *Harpers,* July 1992, 4.

THREE

Hetero-Architecture and the L.A. School

Charles Jencks

What makes Los Angeles architecture so distinctive, so recognizably itself? Is it the background sprawl, or the foreground Pop, or the open-air living, or some combination of these? Most visitors are struck by an intangible quality that defines Los Angeles as a place, some elusive feeling that makes it different from its mid-American cousins such as Houston. It certainly is not the downtown cluster of forty-five skyscrapers, or the ten or twelve smaller such clusters that have sprung up on former urban villages. These, as many have said, are reproduced all over America, and now the Far East. Nothing distinctive there.

What makes Los Angeles unusual, if not unique, is that it is the primary example of what I have called a heteropolis, a new form of urban agglomeration that thrives on difference.[1] How can we define the heteropolis? The shortest definition might be a global city of more than eight million with a high concentration of multinational corporations and having a variety of economic sectors, multiplying lifestyles, and a diversifying ethnic population heading toward full minoritization. Most important, it is a place where heterogeneity—of culture and even of flora and fauna—is enjoyed.

Because of the breakup of the Communist empire and the mass migration of a global population—up from twenty to one hundred million in the last five years according to a UN census—many cities are headed the way of Los Angeles, and some like Berlin, London, and Tokyo are just beginning to confront the same problems and opportunities.[2] At a certain point heterogeneity in itself becomes a positive cause of economic and cultural growth—a reason for moving to the city or, if one fears the attendant problems, a reason for leaving.

The architects I discuss here quite evidently enjoy and exploit variety, difference, plurality. They are heterophiliacs who show a way beyond the usual politics of confrontation. They make an ad hoc art form including opposite forms, languages, and discourses. Their hybrid styles are, as a result, informal and more welcoming than the usual abstract languages of the classicists or modernists. Their buildings also epitomize the variety of the city as a whole, the most varied urban agglomeration anywhere.

ULTIMATE HETEROGENEITY

The evidence that Los Angeles is the ultimate urban bouillabaisse exists on entirely different levels (economic, political, social, aesthetic), and the wealth of this ontological difference is itself a mark of maturity. There are 18 urban village cores, more than 140 incorporated cities, and 13 major ethnic groups that create three different kinds of layers, and the 86 languages spoken in its schools cut up the cultural territory even further.

Economic diversity increases the difference: Los Angeles is the nation's largest manufacturing location and possesses the greatest concentration of high-technology industries (at least until the military-industrial establishment retreats) and, paradoxically, artisanal industries such as jewelry making, furniture, clothing, and movies. Sectoral divisions also fragment the population: Los Angeles is the major Pacific center of postindustrial and post-Fordist production. Like a well-balanced ecosystem, no single industry dominates. The economy is totally mixed (shall we say, following the ecological paradigm, it has a climax economy?).

This heterogeneity, at all levels, is at once excessive in Los Angeles and typical of the world city. London, Rome, and Tokyo are also hybrid agglomerations that allow their originating village structure to remain an imprint for later diversity. But none, it seems to me, is so characteristically heteroglot. Even New York City, with its 2,028 city blocks, each one dedicated to its own "mania," as Rem Koolhaas calls these fabricated identities,[3] seems homogeneous by comparison. If the 1940s mayor, Thomas Dewey, called New York not a "melting pot" but a "boiling pot," then that makes Los Angeles, as a form of food, a simmering, spread-out pizza with all the extras. As we will see with the L.A. School of architects and with such restaurants as Rebecca's, eating places constitute a leading building type.

With the Justice Riots of 1992, or whatever they should be called, it is evident that extreme heterogeneity can amplify conflict. The blacks and the Koreans, like other ethnic groups in Los Angeles's past, compete for territory, jobs, and power, and this continuous struggle directly affects the architecture. It not only leads to a defensive, inward-looking building, but, stylistically, it shapes architecture in two ways: either toward greater and greater heterogeneity and eclecticism or toward more and more subtly articulated abstraction. Either way, the polyglot reality is a pressure on building, forcing the L.A. School toward its two main modes, what I will call "analogous" and "representational" modes of heterogeneity (see fig. 3.1).

The city's status as a mosaic of mostly Third World cultures is well known but needs summarizing. It has the largest Korean metropolitan district outside Korea, the largest Mexican metropolitan area outside Mexico, the largest Filipino district outside the Philippines, and the largest Vietnamese district outside Vietnam, and it is second in such ratios with the Chinese and the Japanese populations. Beyond this, it has major concentrations of Salvadorans, Indians, Iranians, and Russians.[4] With Latinos, Jews, and WASPS the largest minorities in this minoritized place, it is more fitting to see the area as a set of countries—like Europe—than as a traditional, unified city. An ethnic map alone gives it the crazy-quilt pattern of a simmering Europe before World War I. And ethnic divisions are almost equaled in potency by lifestyle differences.

If one adopts the cluster categories of market research companies such as Claritas, which divide Americans into forty lifestyle consumption groups, yet another set of divisions and enclaves emerges, somewhat overlapping with ethnicity. Beverly Hills, with its cluster termed "Blue Blood Estates," at 81.40 percent, dominates "Gray Power," at 18.13 percent, and the two together make this area the quintessential wealthy enclave.[5] Many Americans even know it by a zip code, that of the television program called "90210." There are several other ethnically mixed cluster areas—Bel Air, Palos Verdes, Mission Viejo—and a few—such as Rolling Hills—are even gated communities with armed guards. But whether the identity comes from inherited ethnicity or chosen lifestyle, the effect is to divide Los Angeles into village-sized fragments, what I would distinguish as enclaves of exclusion (Rolling Hills) from enclaves of desertion (the black area of Watts). In addition, there are two more distinct cultural types, what I would call "multiclaves" to signify their heterogeneous identity. There are mixed multiclaves of transitory activity, such as Culver City, or semipermanent balance, such as Westwood or downtown L.A.

It is worth emphasizing, because the heterogeneity suddenly increases after 1960, that Los Angeles has been diverse since its foundation as a pueblo in 1781. The forty-four who took the site over from the Gabrieleno Indians numbered 2 Spaniards, 2 blacks, 11 Indians, and 29 mulattos or mestizos.[6] Ever since then there has been a struggle for power and ownership, with the land divisions first formed by the fifty-five ranchos (ranches). These cuts were followed, more or less, by the townships and main roads and then later by the ethnic and lifestyle clusters. It is instructive to compare the maps of ethnicity, lifestyle, and township with what could be called "identity areas" (the Barrio, Watts, Koreatown, Little Tokyo, Little Philippines, Little Saigon, Little Guatemala, the Gay District, University Town, Beverly Hills, Chinatown).

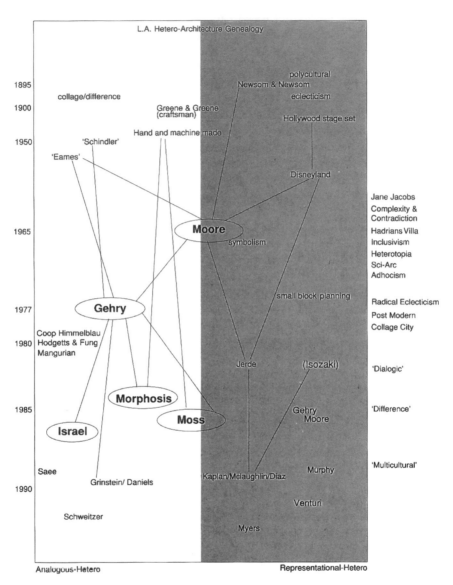

Figure 3.1. Los Angeles hetero-architecture and its genealogy. Architects on the left side tend to convey heterogeneity by analogy, through juxtaposed materials and images, while those on the right use more direct representational techniques.

This shows what our intuition tells us: Los Angeles is a combination of enclaves with high identity and multiclaves with mixed identity. Taken as a whole, it is perhaps the most heterogeneous city in the world. If we could measure and add to this the variety of businesses, building types, and ecologies, it would be confirmed as the most varied. If a city is a mechanism for sustaining difference, then, in terms of population, Los Angeles is on a par with New York and far beyond it in terms of ecological variation.

ARCHITECTURAL IMPLICATIONS: PERIPHERY AS CENTER

There are strong architectural consequences that flow from this heterogeneity. Negatively, it means that no one style will, at least for long, dominate the city as a whole and command widespread assent—the Spanish Mission revival notwithstanding. Reyner Banham ended his 1972 book on Los Angeles with a chapter entitled "The Style That Nearly . . . " made it: the ultra-thin, lightweight Case Study version of the international style, the mode of Pierre Koenig, Charles Eames, and Craig Ellwood. This proto-high-tech seemed ready to conquer L.A. and the world in the early sixties and then suddenly fell out of favor. Why? It seemed too reductive, pristine, and minimalist for the average L.A. temper, and architects such as Frank Gehry found it too hard to detail and build, especially in a climate of approximate craftsmanship.

Funk architecture, the self-built "art of the woodbutcher" that had sprung up in the early 1960s in such places as Woodstock, New York, or the boathouse community of Sausalito—the natural style of the surfers and body-builders and those whose appreciation of Miesian details was, well, primitive—was much more to the point in Los Angeles. Improvisation, creativity, incongruity, and iconic imagery—buildings shaped like castles, hot dogs, or cameras—were locally valued more than the cerebral abstraction of modernism.

And yet Los Angeles, being the inclusive city that it is, developed in opposed directions at the same time: the downtowns, Wilshire Boulevards, and Century Cities grew along late modern lines, while the peripheries went their own heteromorphic way. This sixties split established what has now become two architectural codes: Mies for the classes and hetero-architecture for the masses. What Gehry and others call the "establishment" transforms the downtown with a clutch of skyscrapers—forty new ones where there were only five in 1976—that could have been built in any modernizing city at any time over the last fifteen years.[7] Architectural modernism, in its socially acceptable late and neo forms, becomes the natural expression for modernization, as "safe" architects from the East, such as I. M. Pei and Kohn Pederson Fox, are brought in to design their signature buildings (notable ironically for their impersonality). It's a sad story, repeated in every American city: as building commissions get bigger, more expensive, and closer to the center of action, they become predictably duller, safer, more modernist. The dominant culture expresses this law of conformity with as much regularity as did the Romans, and the only exceptions are corporate headquarters where, very occasionally, someone tries something interesting.

"I'd rather be good than interesting," Mies van der Rohe said at the height of his corporate success in the early sixties, and the inversion of this proposition is almost the dictum of the L.A. School of architects with its love of the botched but fascinating joint. Yet such oppositions are too simple with postmodern movements. The main architects of this movement— Charles Moore, Frank Gehry, Morphosis, Frank Israel, and Eric Moss—do have an interest in craftsmanship and perfecting details; but in very personal ways. These architects and their associates in heteromorphism, such as Craig Hodgetts, Michele Saee, and Brian Murphy, have developed a very recognizable approach deserving the name "school."

Such a quasi-institution actually formed and broke up twice in the 1980s, perhaps an ironic indication that individualism and difference—as cultural forms—often refuse to be organized and protected. In 1982, George Rand and I brought together one incarnation of the so-named L.A. School, and a late, new version persists informally as the L.A. Museum of Architecture Project.[8] It was a successor to the Silvers and L.A. 12, previous groups that also failed to last for more than a year and a few meetings. In spite of its disorganization and individualism, the L.A. School has a coherent architectural approach that is clearly recognizable to anyone who lives outside the city. For those inside the maelstrom, the mutual identity is far from clear, and it is noteworthy that the very center of the movement, Frank Gehry, often disclaims an influence on his followers. Again ironic observation is in order. In the book summarizing recent developments, *Experimental Architecture in Los Angeles* (1991), the editors and publishers claim the experimental tradition three times as the Gehry-schule, or "The Gehry Kids," and three times Gehry disclaims paternity.[9] In conversation Gehry told me why he regards the "third generation" more as followers of Morphosis than himself: they present pieces of buildings, an aggregate of chunks and aggressive contraptions, rather than a whole. But while this may have some truth, it overlooks the larger, broader commonality.[10] From outside Los Angeles, the School appears as a coherent whole, with an identifiable attitude toward heterogeneity and a common realist aesthetic even if, from the inside, it may fall apart. The first meeting of the L.A. School at the Biltmore Hotel in 1981 was punctuated by acrimony and the exit of one member in jealous despair. Responding to the press notoriety on Gehry's recent house for himself, he muttered, while leaving, "What do you expect me to do, put a house inside a house?" The L.A. School was, and remains, a group of individualized mavericks, more at home together in an exhibition than in each other's homes. A culture of difference may preclude self-conscious organization. There is also a particular self-image involved with this non-school that exacerbates the situation. All of its members see themselves as outsiders, on the margins challenging the establishment with an informal and demanding architecture, one that must be carefully read.

But, as Leon Whiteson points out in *Experimental Architecture*, "this is a cultural environment in which the margin is often central."[11] The ultimate irony is that in the architectural cultures of Los Angeles, where heterogeneity is valued over conformity and creativity over propriety, the periphery often is the center. This the establishment knows, the developers and the *Los Angeles Times* know, because the media never let them forget it. It produces the paradox that the architects who make L.A. unique are precisely the ones the establishment refuses to hire for important jobs.

At least until Gehry won the competition for the downtown Disney Concert Hall, in 1988, the paradox was true: L.A. architecture prospered with its establishment marginals, its professional outcasts, its conventional iconoclasts. These oxymorons are perhaps the supreme expression of the heterogeneous background, suggesting that such a distinctive approach could only have grown in a city that quite naturally tolerates difference, inconsistency, and contradiction. In this sense there is a continuum of culture, from the all-accepting beach scene of Venice to the eclectic conversion of a warehouse. Everyone, except perhaps an Angeleno, can tell "The Style That Really . . . " has arrived, because it is open, dynamic, and tolerant (at least until one ethnic group, or individual, frustrates another). It is also why many of the architects settled here in the first place.

PRECURSORS

The antecedents of hetero-architecture are not only the diverse pueblo settlers of 1781 but subsequent invasions by different ethnic groups and individuals looking for a place in the sun. The story of this runaway development is too well known to need recounting, but less familiar—even to the architects themselves—is that an informal eclectic style (incidentally calling itself "modern" and "more up-to-date than Paris") surfaced in the nineteenth century.[12] The Newsom brothers, willing to take on any mode but particularly committed to the most variegated of styles, the Queen Anne revival, constructed some of their most creative and hybridized work in the city. On Carroll Street and along Bonnie Brae Street, both near downtown, they built their ingenious amalgams in wood and shingle, taking up the local flora and fauna in their ornament and making an identifiable Southern Californian language of decoration out of sunbursts, orange clusters, fish scales, waves, and other regional images. The explicit representation may be too obvious for most of the L.A. School (except Moore and Gehry), but there are also more implicitly local themes. Particularly the handling of free space, the multiple sliding partitions, and the verandas accessible by large windows. These were the inventive usages of the time that challenged East Coast decorum and the homogenization of taste. Today, when Thom Mayne attacks the standardization of modernism with complexity and difference, he really is an heir to the Newsom brothers, no matter if he finds their work too pretty.[13]

More obvious, and known as influences on the L.A. School, are the Greene brothers, Charles Eames, and Rudolph Schindler. These are the acceptable eclectics whose pedigree is modernist enough for mainstream critics and architects to overlook their lapse into radical heterogeneity. Greene and Greene made an architecture from plumbing fixtures, rain pipes, and exaggerated tie joints, just as Morphosis and Moss were later to do. They would continue this Arts and Crafts commitment (what Mayne and Moss call "authenticity") with allusions to Europe and the Far East, without worrying about unity and all the canons of exclusion that typify classicism and modernism. With the Newsoms and the Greenes inclusion becomes an implicit goal, a subliminal assault on the idea of a single integrated language and even a unified culture. By the early 1900s, Los Angeles architects have tacitly understood the importance of "heteroglossia," which Mikhail Bakhtin finds at the heart of certain art forms such as the novel, an idea to which we shall return.

Without explicitly defending it, because his main goals were elsewhere, Rudolph Schindler became the next exemplar of eclecticism and pluralism, at least in his handling of materials and the free plan. While consciously focused on geometrical planning, structure, and more purely abstract architectural ideals, his free use of building elements that are at hand is particularly striking, especially in his last works of the late forties and early fifties. Here we find an opportunistic ad hoc use of any available material, on a par with Gehry's chain link or Moss's sewer pipes. It is said that Schindler improvised because his clients were broke, and he was not much concerned with materials. As long as the spatial/geometrical idea was clear, it could be made from "crudboard," (as Banham described such high-maintenance material). In any case, Schindler's free handling of cheap, varied construction was to become a key point in the later "cheapskate aesthetic," the style of adhocism, where different systems of building are allowed their autonomy, to be celebrated as different.

Charles Eames, in his own Case Study house, pulled together an entire building from a catalog of industrial parts, showing that modernization did not have to lead directly to purism and the International Style. So Schindler and Eames, along with the funk architects and Pop artists of the sixties, became precursors to an informal approach that would soon turn into an L.A., even world, style.

FIRST FORMULATIONS, 1970S

In naming this style one encounters inevitable problems: there is more than a single one; it changes; architects have a constitutional dislike of style (they would rather it be a by-product of method, or personality), and there are already too many labels about. But there is no escape. If I try not to name the L.A. Style, it will slip out as a synonym, because the form-language of architecture abhors a vacuum. The only cure for one inadequate classification is another one. Accepting these limitations one can recall the names attached to this moving target without fixing on any of them; it was variously described in the 1970s as the woodbutcher's art, adhocism, radical eclecticism, postmodernism, inclusionism, technomorphism, the shed aesthetic, and monopitch-coal-town.

The last set referred particularly to Charles Moore's work at Sea Ranch on the Northern California coast, a picturesque assemblage of dark redwood sheds grouped like a little hamlet around a central court. This construction of 1965 had an industrial-vernacular flavor like an old mining town and a romantic feeling because of its extraordinary site perched over the Pacific, but what made it catch on among architects—and be repeated across the state—was its ingenious handling of space, imagery, and wood technology. Bright supergraphics contrasted with soft bearskin rugs and exposed flying beams in a new informal aesthetic that was at once relaxed, authentically vernacular, and spatially dynamic. The L.A. Style was born five hundred miles north of the city.

A little later Moore and one of his many partners, Donald Lyndon, were to formulate a theory of place-making, current among architects at the time but distinctive in its emphasis on inexpensive materials and using elements ad hoc, out of context, in an improvisational way. "The first purpose of architecture is territorial. . . . [T]he architect sets out the stimuli with which the observer creates an image of 'place'. . . . To build such places, often on a low budget, we like to, and must, build simply with readily available techniques."[14] The use of "readily available techniques" is the key idea, a notion derived from Eames. But Moore's usage was much more robust and open than the fastidious method that this modernist had formulated, which is why Gehry and Moss picked it up.

When Moore moved from New Haven to Los Angeles in the 1970s, he adapted the shed aesthetic to larger houses and produced a series of buildings that had his strange, slightly awkward, signature—the wandering, all-encompassing, monopitched roof. The two most successful were the Burns

House (1974) and a condominium (1978) in which he lived, both very inventive transformations of the stucco box, the minimalist "readily available technique" essential to L.A. mass building. That such modes and materials could lead to very rich spaces—painted in the Burns House seventeen different shades to bring out the layering of walls—was a lesson quickly learned by other architects, and a complex, postmodern spatial typology developed full of surprise and controlled ambiguity. It is a small step from here to Gehry's wraparound house for himself.

Moore's other contribution was his accepting attitude toward other people's tastes, notably those of the client. Because of his avuncular personality—self-deprecating where other American architects were aggressive—Moore could make contact with different communities and gain their confidence to participate in design. Like Gehry, who followed him in this way, he was relaxed, even casual, and occasionally whimsical. This manner, new in a profession prone to machismo, was somewhat a facade, but it did allow him to institute new methods of collaborative design wherein people felt they could enter into expert discourse without being intimidated.

A case in point was the Episcopal Church of St. Matthew in Pacific Palisades, the replacement for a previous structure that had burned down in one of the typical fast-moving L.A. canyon fires.[15] The congregation was divided, ideologically and by taste, into two basic groups—high and low church. Moore, Ruble, and Yudell introduced into this pluralist community various methods of participatory design, which allowed different groups to gain confidence in expressing their particular viewpoints. Some formed centralized plans, others preferred more formal Latin cross planes, while most liked the informal feeling of Alvar Aalto's Imatra Church in Finland (one of many shown in slide presentations that gauged the different tastes).

Four all-day workshops, spaced about a month apart, were set up. The first was devoted to picking the site, the next to making models of the church the parishioners wanted, the third to manipulating a kit of parts brought by the architects, and the fourth to picking details and establishing an overall ambience. Inevitably this participation resulted in a complex, yet consensual, whole. Contradictions were taken as a spur to design. For instance, the low ground-hugging outside reflected those who wanted a simple parish church, while the large-scaled center reflected those who wanted a noble, almost cathedral-like, space. Dormer windows were round like the traditional rose window, but their formality was lessened by the penetration of simple vertical mullions, an echo of the wooden studs that hold up every stucco box. The most creative result of these contradictions was the hybrid plan—a half-ellipse giving a centralized feeling, allowing parishioners to be as close to the altar as possible—and a modified Latin cross with long dormers for gables (fig. 3.2).

It is worth contrasting this motivated form-giving with the gratuitous

Figure 3.2. Moore, Ruble, and Yudell, St. Matthew's Parish Church, Pacific
Palisades, 1982–1984. Charles Moore and parishioners discussing the design for
the church, which is a heteromorphic combination of central and longitudinal
plans, Aalto and aedicules, exposed studs and stucco, and low and high tastes.

"ornamentalism" rampant at the time and other vacuous formalisms including even some work of Moore himself (such as his Beverly Hills Civic Center,
much compromised by the client, which is basically a police station and
bureaucracy done up as Verdi's Aida). Participation gave St. Matthew's a
seriousness and depth of form, and, as a result, the building has been appreciated and looked after by the parishioners. Heteroglossia, anchored in
real social difference, is a precondition for meaning in a pluralist society.

Gehry learned as much from Moore's methods and carefully careless
approach as he did from the world of Pop Art and his many artist friends—
Chuck Arnoldi, Billy Al Bengston, Larry Bell. In the late seventies and with
his own house conversion, he suddenly forged his second style, the one for
which he is known and the fundamental basis of the L.A. style. Previous to
this some elements of the synthesis were present in his Davis House, but it
is only with the freedom that came from being his own client and the impetus of other forces (such as constructivism and the Daydream houses of
L.A.) that he makes the breakthrough and attains a synthesis. Here, to
summarize the influences, is the "wraparound ruin" of Louis Kahn, the
exposed studs and woodbutcher detailing of Charles Moore, the spatial lay-

ering and complexities of Robert Venturi, the pink-vernacular and white-picket-fence of West Hollywood, the deconstructions and excavations of SITE, the tough materialism of modern architects—and his very own—cheapskate aesthetic, the corrugated siding and chain-link fence used as flying wedges. They sectioned the old house like a butcher slices a chicken.

Architecture would not be the same after this, in Los Angeles or elsewhere. The building as a calculated manifesto was taken up immediately because it corresponded to a shift in mood—toward the informal and expressionist. Even the mainstream *Time* magazine understood the point and amplified what, by now, had become a media event—leading to that rancorous outburst I have mentioned. With this building the L.A. School fell apart at the very moment it coalesced into an identifiable style.

Gehry has commented on his curious relationship to other Angeleno architects, both in *Experimental Architecture* and in conversation. As someone who was overlooked or slighted by the previous generation of architects and critics, such as Ray Kappe and Esther McCoy, and someone who never developed friendships with his followers, such as Thom Mayne, he could only find deep appreciation, oddly enough, from an unlikely ally on the East Coast.

> When I began to find my style there simply wasn't much of a support system [in L.A.] for anyone trying to do something different. There weren't a lot of people I could talk to. The established firms jealously guarded their turf and considered the few of us who were trying to innovate as interlopers who threatened their sense of security.
>
> The man who did most to change this mean situation nationally was Philip Johnson.[16]

Johnson and Tim Vreeland toured the Davis House, and since that point, in the middle seventies, Johnson has been a tireless champion of Gehry and his so-called *schule*.

While his own house marked the real breakthrough in design, Gehry's most radical heteromorphic architecture was to come. There were several projects in the early 1980s, such as the Whitney House, that fractured a single commission into many separate pieces—each in a different material, color, and image. These amalgams looked as if they belonged to different architects, all sharing the same funk aesthetic. The most successful built works of this period were the Loyola Law School, Wosk Penthouse, Temporary Contemporary, Aerospace Museum, and Norton House, most of them additions to and transformations of existing buildings.

This is one of the great strengths of the L.A. School and hetero-architecture in general: its ability to work with and against the existing context at the same time. Virtually all the best work of Morphosis, Israel, Moss, Saee, and company is a conversion—typically, of a warehouse. Some architects

Figure 3.3. Frank Gehry, Loyola Law School, Los Angeles, 1981–1984. An informal combination of Mediterranean building types, none of which is explicitly represented: The ultimate in suggested heterogeneity by analogy. Unfortunately, for security reasons, the scheme turns its back on the street and cuts itself off from the reality of city life with a wall of metal. Visually and symbolically, however, it relates to the adjacent towers of the downtown as well as the local neighborhood.

are at their best with an impossible site and an existing structure to modify, the typical conditions prevailing on the margins of Los Angeles practice. A greenfield site and tabula rasa, the ideal conditions for modern architects, does not often bring out their creativity. Instead, interacting with an existing structure and a strong client produces very personal, rooted architecture.

A case in point is the Loyola Law School addition (fig. 3.3), built over a long period. Because classical law provided the pretext, Gehry could modify the Greek temple, Roman palazzo, and Romanesque church to give a veiled equivalent of classical, legal precedent. Placing several such forms in opposition, building them from cheapskate materials and without the customary ornament, he managed to fit in both with the adjacent slum and with the fastidious skyscrapers of downtown Los Angeles. In the center of his scheme, an open-ended piazza, punctuated by different volumes, creates the public realm. In some respects this is the most public architecture recently built in Los Angeles, for it provides a pedestrian precinct in a variety of modest but expressive modes, and one with which the varied population—Hispanic, black, Anglo, Jew, and certainly those from Mediterranean cultures—can identify.

Familiar cultural and ethnic signs are almost, but not quite, present, thus allowing the user a certain latitude of interpretation and appropriation. This is not the universal grammar of modernism, the idea that we can only unify a pluralist culture by speaking in abstractions. Rather, it is a subtle form of eclecticism in which particular voices can find a response. The difference between these two positions over the question of difference is the key. The first holds that multiculturalism must lead to the equivalent of Esperanto, or else a zero-degree neutrality, the second that heterogeneous cultures can be acknowledged through analogues of difference, and even traditional meanings where they are sufficiently veiled and transformed.

REPRESENTATIONAL HETERO-ARCHITECTURE, THE 1980S

An indication of where the debate on representational architecture had reached in the early 1980s is Arata Isozaki's Museum of Contemporary Art (MOCA), built after an interesting power struggle between artists, architects, and patrons.[17] Placed in the center of a downtown redevelopment megaproject of stunning banality—the cynical L.A. triumph of greed and uptight taste over culture—it was born through a loophole fathered by creative financing and the mandatory "1 percent for Art." The rest of the megaproject, the other 99 percent, was expensive and dull enough to warrant building a museum to take people's eyes and minds off the sordid background and the method by which it "won" a limited competition. Fittingly, the bankrupt architecture has been followed by the bankruptcy of the architect, who left the country in a hurry.

The controversy over the museum itself concerned whether it should be a neutral shed for art—Gehry's Temporary Contemporary for MOCA showed how fitting this could be—or something more challenging. In the event, Isozaki produced an understated essay in postmodern representation, fusing recognizable pyramids, Renaissance garden and Palladian windows with veiled allusions to garden trellises (in the green steelwork), and the Southwest (in the rich red sandstone, actually from India, but it looks Arizonan). In plan and section he included veiled allusions to Eastern and Western mystical traditions, but no one would know this unless he or she had been told. The significance of the building was in the masterful control of spatial surprise and the fact that a major architect had finally been chosen for a prime downtown commission, and, for my argument, the fact that representational allusions had been carried through with enough finesse to inspire and validate more.

The major visual problem Los Angeles architects have faced is brought on by stereotyping and exaggeration. Hollywood and the brash Pop known as "vernacular California crazy" set the dominant tone and then Disneyland turned it into a formula, watering it down in the process. All these set such a powerful standard of cliché that it made understatement more welcome than usual. In fact, architects such as Moore and Isozaki tried to continue overstatement and ambiguity in a new way, and Moore defended Disneyland for its urban creativity in an article published in Yale's *Perspecta*, "You Have to Pay for the Public Realm."[18] His own Disnoid public realm for the Beverly Hills City Hall is disappointing partly because the public does not give it the intense use it needs, and its imagery is overblown; but the formula—the commercialized pedestrian precinct—has achieved a few notable results. The most authentic, architecturally, is Gehry's Santa Monica Place (1979– 1981), which has more recently been complemented by Johannes Van Tilburg's Janss Court, next door.

Undoubtedly the master of commercial eclecticism is Jon Jerde, who has made mid-ersatz into a high/low art. The popular Horton Plaza in San Diego (1986) established his practice as an international leader in turning shopping centers into eclectic urban places. After his Westside Pavilion in Los Angeles, and a few less successful malls elsewhere, he formulated a strategy known as "urbanopolis," the not surprising idea that people like to walk in tight streets and squares while they shop and the fact that this truth can reurbanize the most powerful building type of the last twenty years, the shopping mall.

Up and down the flatlands of Los Angeles one can find versions of this new building type trying to be born. There are mini-malls trying to be theme parks and village streets; and theme parks, such as Knotts Berry Farm, trying to be shopping centers. All of them are attempting to be something else, and exulting in this otherness and phoniness. At Knotts Berry Farm, as at Disneyland, stucco facades are constructed with preaged cracks and spalling surfaces, thus memorializing the Spanish Mission crumble, while anticipating what is known as the Big One, the great earthquake to come. I once stumbled across a real wedding ceremony there with rented guests [*sic*] dressed up in nineteenth-century finery.

If an outsider, Isozaki, opened the door to postmodern representation, then another one, Robert Venturi, again showed that it could be carried through at a high level. His Medical Research Laboratories for UCLA very skillfully transforms the adjacent vernacular—the heavy dumb box dedicated to health—into something urbane and amusing (but nonetheless strict and rational). Here finally is a building that plays with multicolored brick, stone, and concrete—the grammar of the campus—in a new way (fig. 3.4). The volume expresses its utilitarian packaging in its repetitive, flat-chested window wall, making a new visual virtue out of the flush detailing, and then, when necessary, inflects at the corner to allow a walk-

Figure 3.4. Venturi, Scott-Brown, MacDonald Medical Research Laboratories, UCLA, Westwood, 1989–1992. The huge medical building of the campus is modulated urbanistically into three parts and a garden and corner walk-through. A second research lab will enclose the garden court. The typical anonymous medical factory, the loft building, is articulated rhythmically with UCLA colors and signs, the slight variations signifying differences in labs versus offices, window seat areas, and special corner rooms. A large-scale ornamental arch—appropriate to the road and distant view—contrasts with the small-scale limestone ornament and colonnettes, meant to be perceived up close when the second building is complete. The building has the heroic straightforwardness of an industrial loft combined with the delicate touches of a palazzo.

through. Here is a building that makes the workplace into an aesthetically charged location—as we will see, a prime characteristic of the L.A. School.

THE L.A. STYLE: EN-FORMALITY

While a representational eclecticism, of semispecific elusiveness, was camping up mini-malls all over Los Angeles with gables and colorful peaked hat "à la Aldo Rossi," the fractious L.A. School turned more ascetic and difficult and tortured in response. The former were day-glo and effulgent with their architecture of "Have a Nice Day," so the latter became more sullen with their architecture of heavy metal and chain link. Ironically, the style Thom Mayne christened "dead tech" became the mode for eating out and actually enjoying oneself, as if one's taste buds were sharpened by raw concrete and rusting steel.

Dead Tech, that is, high-tech after the bomb, or ecological catastrophe, signified a new, sophisticated attitude toward modernism coming out of Sci Arc (Southern California Institute of Architecture), the avant-garde school of architecture that Mayne's partner, Michael Rotondi, took over in the 1980s. Whereas modernists had a faith in industrial progress, signified by the white sobriety of the International Style, the postmodernists of Sci Arc had a bittersweet attitude toward technology. They knew it brought pollution, knew that progress in one place was paid for by regress in another, but nevertheless still loved industrial culture enough to remain committed to the modernist impulse of dramatizing technology. "Technomorphism," Aaron Betsky called it, reminiscent of the same phrase used about 1960s Pop artists and technophantasts such as Archigram.[19] But whereas Archigram was still, like the modernists, optimistic about a liberating technology, the L.A. School conceived it in more ambivalent terms, sometimes celebrating its sadomasochism (the trussed-up heavy metal construction glorying in its gusset plates), other times lamenting its transience (the melancholic rusting steel member exposing its dark red fragility to the outside street).

Morphosis (Mayne and Rotondi) started this tradition with their 72 Market Street, a Venice restaurant finished in 1985, and developed it further with their Angeli's Restaurant (1985), Kate Mantilini's Restaurant (1987), and Club Post Nuclear (1988). Some called this the "post-holocaust" style (after Ridley Scott's *Blade Runner,* 1982), and it is once again appropriate to connect films, stage sets, and social attitudes to Los Angeles architecture. For some reason the style caught on for those serving the healthiest and most exotic California cuisine—that mixture of French cuisine minceur, simple Japanese tastes, and eclectic add-ons from India and Mexico. Punk architecture usually meant smart food. David Kellen designed the FAMA Restaurant (1989) and, with Josh Schweitzer, the City Restaurant (1989), in an expressionist version of the Gehry aesthetic; Schweitzer himself darkened its mood with the black and rust-crated Border Grill (1990); Elyse Grinstein and Jeffrey Daniels inflected it in ethnic directions with their Chaya restaurants (late 1980s) and toward a Pop constructivism with an eat-in-billboard for Colonel Sanders; and Michele Saee became the master of the genre with his Japanese Restaurant (1989), Angeli Mare (1990), and Trattoria Angeli (1987). Saee, who worked for Morphosis, continues what he calls the "rustic and elegant" in his restaurants, and such a combination should remind us that the L.A. Style is not all Sturm und Drang with sheet metal.

The mood conveyed by such buildings is an ambiguous mixture of aggression and hedonism, sadism and restraint, functionality and uselessness, self-promotion and withdrawal—a calculated informality that I call "en-formality." It is hardly as simple or straightforward as it appears, and it has appeared in so many buildings, not to mention restaurants, that we can really speak of a new convention, a shared aesthetic and attitude. At first approximation it looks close to the well-known Japanese philosophies and aesthetics of *wabi* and *sabi,* those systems of being that tea masters and Zen monks have developed over the centuries. Emphasizing the common and rough over the fussy and decorated—poverty over luxury, silence over loquacity, restraint over ostentation, spareness over ornamentation, serendipity over planning—it was appropriated by the modernists Bruno Taut and Walter Gropius in their appreciation of the Japanese Sukiya style. But, as Kisho Kurokawa has argued, wabi and sabi are always double encoded and include their opposite—display, luxuriance, ornament—as an undertone.[20] They are emphatically *not* the simple, reductive styles that foreign interpreters have made them.

In like manner, the L.A. Style, or en-formality, is complicatedly informal, rough, and ascetic: these qualities do predominate, along with the heavy metal contraptions, but behind them is another mood altogether. The architecture is friendly, outgoing, open, and accepting. Indeed this is the central focus of hetero-architecture: the ability to absorb other voices into a discourse without worrying too much about consistency or overall unity. That such an approach should reach consciousness with Frank Gehry and then self-consciousness with subsequent members of the L.A. School shows a maturity rare at a time of quick change. The information world usually dissolves these movements of shared sensibility as soon as they are formed, in a blitz of media attention, but here a common attitude has managed to develop, perhaps because of the background culture of Los Angeles. It too mixes a sunshine gregariousness, an openness to new experience, with a tough, sadistic streak.

Morphosis has been instrumental in forging this melancholic style, as much in their drawings, models, and personae as in their built work. Aloof, austere, downbeat, often unshaven, like characters in an MTV skit, they give the impression of being on the run, of living on the edge of sanity. How much this is simply the style of a whole generation, which shops at Esprit and finds in heavy metal a complete metaphysic, remains a question, but there is no doubt that the young find Thom Mayne's call to authenticity and sincerity—words of the romantic period—a welcome alternative to historical pastiche. What he means by authenticity is a "return to basic sources," a "presence within materiality," a "description in the process of making," all values evident in the thoughtful details of the work.[21] Whether it is a chair, a table, a lighting fixture, a door handle, a window blind, or an electric meter, the construction element is exaggerated in its material presence, much as Anthony Caro foregrounds his steel armatures.

Morphosis, in their refurbished block for the Salick Health Care Company, breaks down a preexisting homogenized volume into smaller fragments that lean this way and that, jostling like crowded spectators for more space (fig. 3.5). Modernism always privileged similarity over difference, Mayne insists, as he cuts up its surfaces and contrasts materials and joints.[22] Yet the awkward juts of the curtain wall, the obtuse angles and collisions, are as premeditated as any classical composition. Once again it is high architecture reflecting the heterogeneity, not actual street life itself (security guards see to that). Mayne even concentrates on the traditional architectural values: the way the building touches the earth and sky, how it turns the corner and is layered in section. The drawings and models convey this commitment. So what appears at first as another essay in deconstruction is, on second glance, a sophisticated attempt at articulating difference: cutting up one building into two and then further fracturing the elements so they symbolize heterogeneity.

BACK TO WORK, THE 1990S

Aside from en-formality, the L.A. School has made one other contribution to the architectural world that has also been taken up in other cities: the workplace as urban village, the office as a small city turned inside out. Several other postmodern architects have contributed to this new paradigm. There is the neoexpressionist NMB bank in Amsterdam, the hanging gardens of the Landeszentral Bank in Frankfurt, and Hiroshi Hara's office village in Tokyo, but these are all new buildings on a bulldozed site. The Los Angeles architects—Frank Israel, Morphosis, Eric Moss, and Frank Gehry—have instead developed the art of converting large warehouses into internalized streets and squares. Part of the reason is economic and pragmatic: these externally disguised, informal types turn their back on the real, hostile street for security reasons, and they retrofit an old structure because it is cheap. Nonetheless, the art of en-formality is a high art for office work,

Figure 3.5. Morphosis, Salick Health Care, Inc., Beverly Hills, 1990–1992. Mayne speaks of "the notion of the way the building touches the earth and sky, . . . how it defines the edge, . . . how it ends ambiguously at the top and is layered, . . . how the masonry starts heavy and terminates as billboard [and] part of the wall escapes to define the corner, literally describing the cutting process. . . . One building is woven together as two, a dialogue with a missing line, defined as a peel" (from a lecture at UCLA, April 1992).

in many ways much more suitable than the totally new building. An office, where most of the labor force in the First World will spend most of its time, must be more than a one-dimensional factory for work—much more. During the electronic revolution, when many people find it more attractive and functional to telecommute, it must incorporate other building types, for example, the home and place of relaxed entertainment. Already Los Angeles has more office-at-home space than other cities. Whereas most metropolitan areas have twenty square feet of office space per person (New York has twenty-eight), the electronic cottages of L.A. have reduced in-town office space to fifteen.[23] The place of work must become ambiguous, domestic, and heterogeneous to survive.

Israel has converted several warehouses into offices and understands the genre as much as his fast-moving clients—advertising agencies, design companies, film and record businesses, all typical of the postindustrial labor force. I find his transformation of the old Eames Studio the most successful of these, because the interaction between the present and past, figure and ground, is most balanced. One approaches this former warehouse and modernist studio by way of two tough billboards, one of gray sheet metal, the other a triangle of glass brought to a very aggressive point at the entrance. After these and other acknowledgments of a hostile environment, one enters a tiny village turned inside out. The arrival space is a yellow tower of stucco open to the sky, with jutting balconies of—what else?—gray sheet metal (fig. 3.6). From this inverted Italian campanile one is shunted through a dark sheet metal tunnel, to arrive at the third building within a building: the conference room in the shape of an inverted cone. To the right one finds the main avenue of the village, with private streets and offices, placed under the grid of the exposed trusses. As in all these conversions, metal gusset plates, wooden beams, and hanging ductwork are polished up to become essential icons of work and regular markers of space. Farther on the avenue widens slightly to form a curved piazza, and then the space constricts before opening out to end in a large open area.[24] The plan reveals all the conventions of postmodern space that have been current since Venturi and Moore developed the tradition in the sixties: the juxtaposition of skewed and distorted figures, positive and negative reversals, ambiguity, collage, and paradox. But it is all done with a sensibility and handling of detail that is particular to L.A. and Israel.

Among the many workplace conversions that have created the distinctive L.A. type, two stand out as supreme examples of the ad hoc art. One is by Eric Moss, a quintessential Los Angeles character. A sometime weight lifter who looks like Barry Manilow crossed with an intellectual, Moss accentuates certain aspects of the straightforward and idiosyncratic, perfect character traits for converting dumb warehouses into sensual enigmas. A didactic strain runs through his work—like James Stirling, he cuts up and explodes parts of his building to show what they are made of, knowing this appeals to the mind—but it also comes from his teaching at Sci Arc. He calls this didactic exposure "the railroad car theory" of beauty—the idea that "the erogenous quality of machinery," most evident in railroad cars, can be conveyed when buildings are "dissected" and "understood rationally . . . in a scientific sense."[25] But it is not the perfectly working machine aesthetic of modernism he is interested in: "The railroad car in this discussion has grease on the wheels, and sometimes goes off the tracks. It's like the helicopters Jimmy Carter sent to Iran that didn't work because they got sand

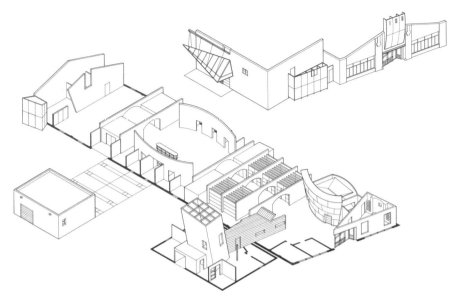

Figure 3.6. Frank Israel, Bright and Associates, Warehouse Conversion, Venice, 1988–1990. The axonometric shows the sequence of heteromorphic spaces: leaning cube, perspectival tunnel, semicone, triangle, arched offices, curved piazza, and open space.

caught in the propellers. It's that kind of machine."[26] Grease in the wheels, exposed gears, wires, chains, garage doors that sport their clunky mechanisms—a series of fetishistic images that every now and then slips into the rubber and chain cult. Moss has been crowned by Philip Johnson, in his own monograph no less, the "Jeweler of Junk."

Johnson sees him in an alternative tradition of Arts and Crafts modernists from Louis Sullivan to Tobias Scarpa, and while this has some truth, it carefully overlooks the much more obvious, local line: from the Newsoms to the Greene and Greene plumbing fixtures as architecture, from the machine adhocism of Eames and Schindler to the chain-link and sheet metal of Gehry, that is the real pedigree. And it makes Moss, to my mind, the ultimate Los Angeles designer, a true critical regionalist. He excavates preexisting structures in order to cut out and accentuate their qualities, he orients to the freeways and other local points he can find, and he elevates the L.A. funk aesthetic to an ugly/beautiful level.

Some of his work is overlabored and self-indulgent, but the modestly titled "8522 National Boulevard" (1988–1991) in Culver City is, to my mind, a masterpiece. It is the conversion of five light industrial warehouses that date from the 1920s into the near-perfect "office" environment. The plan reveals once again the office-village with its central street—in the shape of an *L*—and two public piazzas and four semipublic spaces, conference rooms or juncture points, within the separate office areas.

Hollywood is never far away from the L.A. School, but the mood could not be further from "Have a Nice Day." Actually some of the arts and design groups that inhabit this tiny village might work for Hollywood, and Moss and his developer, Frederick Smith, are quite consciously trying to cut across boundaries of taste and ideology.

> The definition of an intelligible building—the kind into which accountants, lawyers and film makers can go—is changing. You can put on a Brooks Brothers suit and go into 8522 National Boulevard and sell your stuff and be totally comfortable. (You don't have to be the hippest guy on the street.) The owners of such projects will exploit that; it allows them to move into areas that are a little less costly. . . . [Frederick Smith] is ready to let his conceptions—or the architect's conception—direct the selling, as opposed to letting the selling direct the architecture. . . . He's very unusual in that he takes the consequences of the risk.[27]

In such descriptions Moss conveys what is evident in his work: the intention to be both ordinary and idiosyncratic, further contraries that constitute en-formality.

A monumental space that is most successful at mixing heterogeneous codes is a conference room at the end of the interior street. This room, an elliptical cone of plywood, provides a very pleasing enclosure while parts of the old building—a brick wall, a pier, a window and skylight—are allowed to break into this figure (fig. 3.7). The effect of these interlocking codes really is magical, even disorientating in a convivial way, and, as with magic, it is perhaps better not to understand how the trick is done; but it has something to do with tilting a regular shape, the elliptical cone, with dimensions that are both bigger than the original floor and smaller than the roof. Such spaces, and their colliding skylights, penetrate what is in effect an informal but intricate urban tissue. The language cuts across categories, tastes, and time frames in a way that is canonical to postmodern literature—that of Umberto Eco, John Barth, and Salman Rushdie—and it is no surprise that Moss is an admirer of James Joyce.[28] For Joyce's Dublin we have Moss's Culver City, a near-perfect reflection of this area's heterogeneity caused by transitory activity, the mirror image of the fast-changing "exclave."

Just as heteroglot in its nature is Main Street, Venice, where Gehry has designed another converted and new office-village, along with 8522 an exemplar of the new genre. This one consists of an older warehouse conversion in back and a new set of buildings in front for the advertising agency Chiat/Day/Mojo. The context is as mixed as it can be: Main Street commerce and up-market restaurants hit beach bums and dossers' pads hidden

Figure 3.7. Eric Owen Moss, National Boulevard, Culver City, 1988–1991. Tilted cone and frieze of studs stand in counterpoint to the existing brickwork and piers—the dialogue of different periods and tastes.

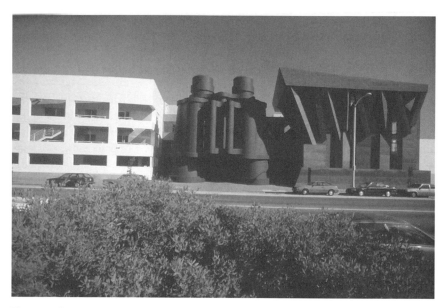

Figure 3.8. Frank Gehry, Chiat/Day/Mojo Office, Venice, 1989–1991. White boat (or a fish), binoculars, and copper trees—images for Main Street and the Pacific Rim—are placed in front of a converted warehouse.

in the bushes—looking straight at the executive conference room of Chiat, right into the binoculars (fig. 3.8).

Across the street to one side is a classical Corinthian arcade brought to a full stop by Jonathan Borofsky's Hermaphroditic Clown (its unofficial title), a running man-woman with ballerina legs and a mustache, while to the other sides are dumb stucco boxes, dingbat apartments, and the usual assortment of sheds and warehouses. To a certain extent Gehry's collection of small-scale fragments summarizes the spirit of the place, mixing ordinary, anonymous boxes with slightly veiled images—a white boat or fish to the left and copper trees and tree trunks to the right. The metaphors are understated, ambiguous, and somewhat appropriate, either to the context near the ocean or to the function (the tree branches serve as sun screens). Even the most explicit image, the binoculars designed by Claes Oldenburg and Coosje van Bruggen, serves appropriate functions, as a triumphal archway to the parking lot and a sardonic emblem for an ad agency.

But its relevance consists in the small-block planning and office-village layout. As the plans reveal, we again have the satisfying ratio of foreground to background, image to abstraction, of about one to five. Like a Renaissance palazzo the front is for show, the back to fill out the lot and form positive leftover space. There is the customary mixture of informal and regular layout that we have come to expect: the workstations organized on a grid, the conference rooms placed in a more free-form shape, and surface cores or piazzas punctuating the fabric. In the refurbished warehouse in back a relaxed urbanity prevails, created by a grid of major avenues, minor streets, and monuments set into the fabric.

Here the sting is taken out of the modern office slab with its typical open planning and utilitarian regimentation. *Burolandschaften,* office landscaping meant to increase security and control of the workforce, is asserted and subverted at the same instant: the workstations are open to view, but partially veiled behind screens of studs that form the streets. Another factor that mediates the central control is the crossing of categories. Because it is an ad agency where the owners collect art and display some of the products they have featured, one walks through a strange forest of symbols and signs. A real car is on the "street" (does the Mini work, or is it a present to the owners?); a basketball net is next to a sculpture and painting (is it for playing or looking?). One conference room is a Gehry fish (or is it merely a conveniently curved room formed by the cheapest of L.A. techniques, the exposed stud wall?). It is all an interesting interweaving of meanings, inclusive of the different voices that make up the corporation or the city.

Finally, in one part of the office-village is a place set apart from the noise and bustle of the city and workplace—an inner sanctum, something akin to a sacred or contemplative space, a room constructed of cardboard and corrugated paper. This is another magical place, as original and peaceful as those of Eric Moss, but one inflected more toward silence and thought: it cuts down the sound and reverberation to nothing. It is like being in an anechoic chamber, so silent you can hear your heart beat. With its interior oculus allowing a shaft of California light to move through the conical dome, it is reminiscent of other sacred spaces, such as the Pantheon in Rome. The comparison may sound far-fetched, but the idea is not so absurd as it appears, for why shouldn't a large office—the equivalent of a village—have one area given over to silence and contemplation?

The main point of hetero-architecture is to accept the different voices that create a city, suppress none of them, and make from their interaction some kind of greater dialogue. Bakhtin, who has formulated the idea of heteroglossia and dialogic, shows their possibilities for creativity.[29] Dialogic underlines the double nature of words that always entail two different attitudes at the same time: that of the speaker and that of the listener about to become a speaker. The dialogue is thus equally determined by at least two different codes, by words shared by addresser and addressee. And if this is true, then it is fundamentally open and oriented toward a future world, for no one can determine the outcome of a true dialogue, which might go in any direction.

Gehry and the L.A. School, particularly in these warehouse conversions for the workplace, combine many texts, many voices. Dialogues between the formal and informal, the present and the past, the industrial and the vernacular, and the animal and the mechanical. There is even an understated, half-suppressed, dialogue between the utilitarian and the spiritual: Israel, Moss, and Gehry, time and again, take a conference room, put it in a formal shape, juxtapose it with exposed beams and mechanical ducts, and then give it an ethereal skylight that turns it into a small chapel.

The opposite of hetero-architecture is not homo- but mono-architecture; that is, building that is reduced, exclusive, overintegrated, perfected, and sealed off from life and change. Mies van der Rohe's architecture, minimalism, most classicisms, most corporate and academic building—that is, most professional architecture—is monological and limited by definition and legal contract. After the drawings are made, the bids are sealed, and the specifications are written, it is a deterministic affair, with nagging ambiguities and changes to be disputed in court. With the L.A. School, particularly Gehry and Moss, it is often not clear, when, or even if, the building is ever finished; what can be taken away, or added, or punched through.

It is this improvisational, heteroglottic nature that is so characteristic of Los Angeles as a whole and the L.A. Style in particular, a mode that, because of the information world and similar conditions, can be found in several cities around the globe. Just as the office-village has become a prototype to be shared, so perhaps will the peculiar Los Angeles workplace, with its mixture of categories, functions, and voices. If America must reinvent more adequate attitudes to work in the nineties and reestablish a public realm, then convivial models can be found here. As an informal mode that articulates difference in a supraethnic way, it is the natural style for Los Angeles: it does not condescend to, or exclude, minorities. It is not uptight, intimidating, or associated with any particular group or ruling class. Rather, its relaxed humor and provocative sensuality open out in different directions with an inclusive gesture of transcendence. No wonder Gehry has been chosen as the designer of the Disney Hall and chosen to adapt the mode for a building at the heart of the establishment in downtown L.A. The periphery, and style of minoritization, has moved to the center.

NOTES

I would like to thank Tulasi Srinivas and Robert Lerner for their help in preparing this paper, for figures 3.2 and 3.3, and many conversations on Los Angeles and its architecture.

1. Charles Jencks, *Heteropolis: Los Angeles, the Riots and the Strange Beauty of Hetero-Architecture* (London and New York: Academy Editions, 1993).

2. See Raphael Salas, *The State of the World Population* (New York: The Fund, 6 July 1993), which estimates 100 million international migrants (these figures refer to 1991, pre-Bosnia).

3. Rem Koolhaas, *Delirious New York* (New York: Oxford University Press, 1978), 13. For Koolhaas, each of the 2,028 New York City blocks democratically fosters a different style, group, interest, or "mania."

4. Such observations became, in the 1980s, the repeated wisdom of articles on Los Angeles; see, for instance, Charles Lockwood and Christopher B. Leinberger, "Los Angeles Comes of Age," *Atlantic Monthly* (January 1988); 91.

5. Claritas is a research corporation that specializes in marketing information. They have kindly provided us with information for the maps and a description of "lifestyle clusters," a creation of theirs which they use as a marketing tool. A general review of the field can be found in Michael J. Weiss, *The Clustering of America* (New York: Harper & Row, 1988).

6. For this information, see Richard S. Wurman, *L.A./ACCESS* (Los Angeles: Access Press, 1981), 113.

7. Both popular and architectural critics see the undistinguished nature of downtown skyscrapers; for a recent view, see Mike Davis, "Chinatown Revisited?" in *Sex, Death and God in L.A.*, ed. David Reid (New York: Pantheon, 1992), 27, and for an older one, Reyner Banham, *Los Angeles: The Architecture of the Four Ecologies* (Harmondsworth: Penguin, 1971), 208–211.

8. The original "L.A. School" was initiated by George Rand and myself, had its first meeting at the Biltmore Hotel under the auspices of Gene Summers, and included, if memory is correct, Roland Coate, Peter De Bretteville, Frank Gehry, Craig Hodgetts, Coy Howard, Eugene Kupper, Tony Lumsden, Thom Mayne, Robert Mangurian, Charles Moore, Cesar Pelli, Stephanos Polyzoides, Michael Rotondi, Tim Vreeland, and Buzz Yudell. The L.A. Museum of Architecture Project started in 1989, was initiated by Nancy Pinckert and myself, and includes a much wider group of Los Angeles architects. There have also been other loose groupings, including that of Aaron Betsky's and Christian Hubert's Los Angeles Forum for Architecture and Urban Design, mostly for younger, more radical architects.

9. Los Angeles Forum for Architecture and Urban Design, *Experimental Architecture in Los Angeles,* introduction by Frank Gehry, essays by Aaron Betsky, John Chase, and Leon Whiteson (New York: Rizzoli, 1991). The back cover and pp. 47–48 and 88 refer to the Gehry-schule; Gehry denies it three times on p. 10.

10. Conversation with Frank Gehry, April 1992. It is true that there are important differences between Gehry and his followers, and they concern an emphasis on parts, details, fragments, and mechanical contraptions, which the followers get more from Morphosis, as Gehry insists. Nevertheless, still present are common attitudes toward material, en-formality, adhocism, hybridization, and, above all, heterogeneity.

11. Leon Whiteson, "Young Architects in Los Angeles: Social, Political and Cultural Context," in *Experimental Architecture in Los Angeles,* 84–89; quote on p. 88.

12. The Newsom brothers made these claims in their promotional brochures, published in San Francisco, 1890. This work was finally brought to public attention by the historians David Gebhard and Robert Winter. *Samuel and Joseph Newsom: Pic-

turesque California Homes; A Volume of Forty Plates, Plans, Details and Specifications of Houses. Originally self-published (San Francisco 1884). Reprinted, Los Angeles: Hennessey & Ingalls, 1978.

13. Thom Mayne has not made this point and is not acquainted with the Newsoms' work, but, judging from his remarks on other architects, like Gehry, Moss, and others in the L.A. school, he would find their work too cloying.

14. Charles Moore, quoted in Robert Stern, *New Directions in American Architecture* (New York: George Braziller, 1969), 70.

15. See Charles Moore, "Working Together to Make Something," *Architectural Record* 172, no. 2 (February 1984): 102–103.

16. Frank Gehry, in *Experimental Architecture in Los Angeles*, 9.

17. The museum saga is a long and complex one. Suffice it to say, first, that the "competition" was "won" by a Canadian developer—"bought" would be a better term—over the superior urban scheme of Robert McGuire's team. Then Isozaki's museum project, the best part of the Canadian scheme, was disputed by a group of artists and an architect, Coy Howard, who wanted a background design. After much dramatic maneuvering, using the press, Isozaki was able to regain design control and produce the building; a donor, Max Pavlevsky, then withdrew his gift.

18. Charles Moore, "You Have to Pay for the Public Realm," *Perspecta 9–10* (1965): 57–97.

19. Aaron Betsky, *Violated Perfection* (New York: Rizzoli, 1990), 183–203.

20. Kisho Kurokawa, *Rediscovering Japanese Space* (New York and Tokyo: Weather Hill, 1988), 70–77; *Intercultural Architecture* (London: Academy Editions, 1992), 19–27.

21. Thom Mayne, lecture at UCLA, April 1992; and unpublished manuscript, 6 April 1992.

22. Ibid.

23. See Mayne, Lecture, 1992, p. 36.

24. For an analysis of Frank Israel's Bright and Associates, see Sylvia Lavin, "Creativity Begets Creativity," *Designers' West* (September 1990): 68–75.

25. *Eric Owen Moss, Buildings and Projects*, preface by Philip Johnson, introduction by Wolf Prix (New York: Rizzoli, 1991), 14.

26. Ibid., 15.

27. Ibid., 13.

28. Ibid., 12, 15.

29. For Mikhail Bakhtin's notions of dialogic and heteroglossia, see Michael Holquist, *Dialogism, Bakhtin and His World* (London and New York: Routledge, 1990); Tzvetan Todorov, *Mikhail Bakhtin: The Dialogical Principle* (Manchester: Manchester University Press, 1984).

FOUR

In the City, Time Becomes Visible

Intentionality and Urbanism in Los Angeles, 1781–1991

Michael Dear

The Vision to See, the Faith to Believe, the Courage to Do
COMMEMORATIVE PLAQUE, UNION STATION,
LOS ANGELES, 1939

Los Angeles is a city without a past. It has constantly erased the physical traces of previous urbanisms and failed to produce a flow of historical studies that match and typify other national metropolises (e.g., Chicago and New York City). These conditions may explain why L.A. continues to be regarded as an exception to the rules of U.S. metropolitan development, despite Joel Garreau's warning that "every single American city that *is* growing, is growing in the fashion of Los Angeles."[1] In this essay, I will not argue that L.A. is unique or is a prototype of future urban developments, even though both viewpoints are at some level demonstrably true. I shall instead make a more modest claim: that L.A.'s peculiarities invite us to think differently about aspects of contemporary urbanism, both in Southern California and in the nation as a whole.

My interest is in land use planning. And instantly, Los Angeles presents us with a paradox. On one hand, L.A. appears as an intensely privatized, anarchic vision of urban growth; on the other, the city has a long history of formal planning (including the nation's earliest experiments with zoning and regional planning). L.A. landscapes are obviously a direct consequence of the constant interplay between the former and the latter—between the intentionalities of the private realm and those of the public sphere. In this discussion, I hope to demonstrate that significant consequences flow from this simple, noncontroversial beginning. Let me begin by suggesting the outline of my argument.

Since its inception, agents of change in Los Angeles have insisted on the need for collective action but have simultaneously resisted such intrusion. Urban outcomes have consequently been the product of a *public/private dialectic* in which the hegemony of either sector has periodically shifted according to specificities of time and place. Yet although patterns of dominance have shifted, there has through it all been a consistently identifiable "civic will," a series of broad alliances that have guided the city through its many phases of urban growth; very explicit forms of intentionality underlay L.A.'s urbanism for most of its two centuries of existence. This inherent rationality has created a "landscape of modernity" in Los Angeles, albeit a fragmented landscape unlike the more monumental modernities associated with (for instance) New York City.[2] Now, Los Angeles is no different from other U.S. cities in that it is the product of the public/private dialectic that characterizes urbanization in a capitalist society.[3] But L.A. provides a special opportunity to analyze what some regard as the emergence of a *postmodern* urbanism, in which past traditions and intentionalities have collapsed and previous verities have been suspended.[4] Certainly, residual modernities persist, in (for example) the built environment and the land use planning apparatus; but the rest of the city—its social, political, and economic fabric—has shifted irrevocably. Today, postmodern Los Angeles finds itself saddled with a relict planning apparatus characteristic of a period of high modernism, unable to mobilize the civic will necessary to legitimize formal urban development schemes. Postmodern Los Angeles challenges us to consider the origins and ramifications of a potentially radical break: that land use planning, as it has been practiced for most of this century, is now defunct, irretrievable, and that new legitimacies and intentionalities must be sought if L.A.'s urban development is to be channeled away from a dystopian future.

To examine this proposition, I have divided my essay into two broad themes: the first explores the theoretical dimensions of a putative shift from a modernist to a postmodern urbanism; the second offers an interpretation of six pivotal periods in the history of intentionality and land use planning in Los Angeles. I conclude with some reflections on the nature of L.A.'s postmodern urbanism.

FROM MODERN TO POSTMODERN

The state of theory, now and from now on, isn't it California? And even Southern California?

JACQUES DERRIDA, "SOME STATEMENTS AND TRUISMS ABOUT NEOLOGISMS, NEWISMS, POSTISMS, PARASITISMS, AND OTHER SMALL SEISMISMS"

The phrase "In the city, time becomes visible" is, of course, Lewis Mumford's. It suggests *avant la lettre* the possibility of examining the text of the city for insights into existing and emergent urban rationalities. My focus in this essay is on the texts of land use planning as evidence of intentionality in the production and reproduction of the built environment. This is, as I hope to show, a matter of considerable theoretical and practical consequence.

The essence of the problematic of postmodern urbanism can be captured, in an entirely serious way, by placing Babar the Elephant alongside Mickey Mouse. These two cartoon figures provide provocative exemplars of past and future urbanisms. In her study of the politics of design in French colonial urbanism, the architectural historian Gwendolyn Wright shows how powerful were the myths of colonial order by examining Babar's 1931 design for the construction of Célesteville, a city of elephants in Africa.[5] Behind a harbor, standardized shuttered huts for native peoples were arranged in neat rows below a hillside dominated by two monumental buildings: the Palais du Travail and the Palais des Fêtes. The vision of Babar's creator (de Brunhoff) was one of "social hierarchy, orderly growth, a thriving economy, and effective political authority." All this was to be accomplished by the colonial masters (needless to say) without effacing the indigenous African social fabric.

Contrast Babar's world with that of Mickey Mouse: a vision of the city as a collage of theme parks, best exemplified by the various Disneylands and, in particular, by the postmortem archetype, Los Angeles. The emergent reorientations invoked by the postmodern city are nowhere more evident than in Michael Sorkin's edited collection, *Variations on a Theme Park*. In his introductory remarks, Sorkin observes that "the city has historically mapped social relations with profound clarity, imprinting in its shapes and places vast information about status and power."[6] However, in Sorkin's "recombinant" city, this earlier modernist legibility has been obscured and dramatically manipulated: the phone and the modem have rendered the street irrelevant; social hierarchies, once fixed, have become "despatialized"; and space itself is "departicularized."[7]

Let us, for the moment, grant that this is so. That between the rigidities of modernist planning (in Babar's colonial guise) and the departicularized places of postmodernity (in Disney's theme parks), there is a world of difference. My question is, how? How are modernist legibilities being transformed and the peculiar spatialities of postmodernity being created? I can best respond to these questions by successively examining the origins of land use planning in the United States, the principles of modernist city planning (as exemplified by Brasília), and the particularities of the shift to a postmodern urbanism (following the arguments of Marshall Berman). I conclude the first part of this essay by placing Los Angeles urbanism squarely in the era of postmodernity.

The Origins of Rationality in American Urbanism

The rationalities of American urban land use planning were established somewhere between the end of the nineteenth and the beginning of the twentieth centuries. The end of the nineteenth century was a period when people searched for "an instinct for improvement."[8] The key reformist language of this era referred to such notions as *uplift, harmony,* and *instinct.* By the beginning of the twentieth century, a few decades later, an emergent land use planning discourse had appeared, emphasizing *unity, control,* and *expert skills.*[9] According to M. Christine Boyer, this new disciplinary order had as its goal the use of surplus capital for civilizing and socializing purposes. It required state intervention, a revised municipal politics, and the production of a category of experts.

The emergent social rationality grew out of the post–Civil War turmoil, when reformers worried how to discipline and regulate the urban masses and how to control and arrange the spatial growth of cities.[10] As happened in previous eras, a host of urban ills were attributed to industrialization and urbanization, and an intense antiurbanism was reinvented. A new relationship between the urban public and social science knowledge was forged, which by the end of the nineteeth century had called forth a process of city planning. Capitalists joined reformers to address social and economic needs: environmental reform was promoted as a remedy for the social pathologies of urban areas; and public health legislation was closely followed by the design of model tenements intended to improve the quality of life in urban areas. There was also a need for centralized, supervised operations by some form of institutional authority, especially to contain what some perceived as ill-distributed relief.[11] Around this time, for example, Charles Mulford Robinson, a journalist who identified himself as a "city improver," remarked on the strange evil of excessive urban generosity.[12]

The new "totalization of poverty" required an expanded chain of information. A concept of the "curative whole" emerged, reflecting the linkage between pathologies of the individual and pathologies of family, neighborhood, and city.[13] As a consequence, attention shifted to new spatial categories and to new environmental causes. The search for spatial order was principally directed through nature and classical architecture. Robinson was an important figure in the search for municipal art, reflecting the influence of Baron Georges-Eugène Haussmann when he wrote,

> It has been found that often there is no better way to redeem a slum district than by cutting into it a great highway that will be filled with through travel of a city's industry. Like a stream of pure water cleansing what it touches, this tide of traffic pulsing with the joyousness of the city's life of toil and purpose, when flowing through an idle or suffering district, wakes it to larger interests and higher purposes.[14]

The birth of a planning mentality meant a new spatial order in American cities, but planning documents quickly zeroed in on the minutiae of the built environment. A concern with physical detail became increasingly abstracted from the motives and conflicts that led to the production of the urban landscape, and civic improvements were recommended without consideration of those vested interests that led to the production of city form. In short, the process of capitalist urbanization was overlooked while an idealized/utopian planning theory developed and a bureaucratic maze regulated the practice of development control. Planning practice thus created its own totalization; for detailed plans to be constructed, an extensive fact file was needed to organize the physical, social, economic, and legal/administrative fabric of the city.[15]

Building the Modernist City

The verities of modernist land use planning and the consequences of separating the capitalist process from planning theory and practice are succinctly revealed in the anthropologist James Holston's account of the construction of the city of Brasília.[16] Holston notes that the city's modernist plan was founded on the principles of the Athens charter and the philosophy of the Congrès Internationaux d'Architecture Moderne (CIAM). The CIAM philosophy concentrated on four functions of the city: housing, work, recreation, and traffic; it later added the administrative function to this list. Most important, Holston reveals how the modernist city managed to harness mutually antagonistic social and political programs to a single architectural program:

> Brasília was planned by a left-center liberal, designed by a communist, constructed by a developmentalist regime and consolidated by a bureaucratic authoritarian dictatorship each claiming an elective affinity with the city. Precisely because the CIAM model manages to unite such dissident interest, its brand of modernism has come to dominate development projects worldwide.[17]

The CIAM city was a city of salvation. It was intended to solve the urban and social crises attributed to maladies caused by unfettered private interests. The most important exponent of CIAM principles was the architect Le Corbusier. (His groundbreaking text, *The Radiant City*, includes the following epigraph: "This work is dedicated to authority.") The rationalist metropolis that resulted was a city that dehistoricized the particular; it was a city distilled into a universal model. The plan was sketched initially by Lucio Costa and executed by Oscar Niemeyer. Their view was one of the harmony of the whole.[18] Brazil's totalitarian President Jucileno Kubitschek de Oliveira was committed both to modernism and modernization; he was also a utopianist, who envisaged the architecture of Brasília as a prescription for social change. But how could capitalists and Communists simultaneously find their visions signified by the same set of symbols? The answer, according to Holston, lies in the *polysemous* nature of architecture: each group could identify with the break with a colonial past and the leap into the future implied in the plan.[19] Moreover, no priority could be established among the competing ideological claims represented in the plan.

There is, however, another condition beyond architectural ambiguity that explains how a single representation could absorb the multiple significations implied by its Communist and totalitarian supporters. The peculiar genius of the modernist city plan lies in its "empty vessel" quality; anyone can pour identity or signification into it. The abstract ahistoricism and aspatiality of modernist thought allowed a split to occur between the material side of modernism and its spiritual side. It is this division that has given modernist thought its remarkable resilience—a chameleonlike ability to satisfy all persuasions at once. At the same time, however, the qualities of ahistoricity and aspatiality betray modernity's greatest flaw, that is, its separation of the political economy of modernization from the culture and spirit of modernity. Thus the rationalities of production and reproduction in capitalist urbanization have been divorced from the utopian ideals of planning thought as well as from the minutiae of planning practice. This is a recipe for impotence. And somewhat predictably, the particular dynamism of Brazilian society conspired to destroy the plan's utopian dreams. *Even as the physical design persisted,* albeit in a mutated form, the practices of everyday life preempted the modernist logics that underlay it.[20]

From Modernity to Postmodernity

In his examination of the culture of modernity, Marshall Berman captures the essence of the separation I have just described.[21] Let me use some of Berman's definitions to clarify his terminology. *Modernity* is the experience of contemporary life that has been fed by numerous movements including science, industrialization, demographic change, urban growth, mass communication, nation-states, social movements, and the rise of a worldwide capitalism. *Modernization* refers to a state of perpetual becoming, a process that brought modernity into being. *Modernism* is a discussion about changing visions and values that accompany modernization.[22] According to Berman, the essence of the twentieth century is the dialectic between modernization and modernism. The process of modernization has engorged the world, and the developing global culture of modernism has achieved much in art and social thought; but as the modern public expanded, it shattered into a multitude of fragments speaking incommensurable private languages. Thus fragmented, modernity loses much of its capacity to organize and give meaning to people's lives. As a result, we find ourselves today in the midst of a modern age that has lost touch with its roots. As Berman puts it,

> To be modern . . . is to experience personal and social life as a maelstrom, to find one's world and oneself in perpetual disintegration and renewal, trouble and anguish, ambiguity and contradiction: to be part of a universe in which all that is solid melts into air. To be a modernist is to make oneself somehow at home in the maelstrom, to make its rhythms one's own, to move within its currents in search for the forms of reality, of beauty, of freedom, of justice, that its fervid and perilous flow allows.[23]

The consequences for a disoriented, decentered society are profound. According to Berman, a dynamic new landscape has been created through which we experience modernity. A radical flattening of perspective has occurred, accompanied by a shrinking of the imaginative range. The twentieth century has lurched toward rigid polarizations and flat totalizations; open visions have been supplanted by closed visions (for example, *both/and* is replaced by *either/or*). The iron cage of a capitalistic, legalistic, and bureaucratic framework has closed around us, giving rise to a state of "total administration." And finally, the kind of person constructed by the new modernity is Herbert Marcuse's "one-dimensional man"—one who recognizes himself solely through his consumption of commodities.[24]

Using the examples of Charles Baudelaire, Le Corbusier, Robert Moses, and Jane Jacobs, Berman reveals how the burgeoning dualism between modernization and modernism diminishes our understanding of the ways materialism and spiritualism invade each other.[25] The early Baudelaire portrayed a pastoral vision of modernity, celebrating modern life as a fashion show, a carnival. The later Baudelaire constructed a counterpastoral vision that poured scorn on the notion of progress and modern life, suggesting that the concept of indefinite progress must be the cruelest and most ingenious torture ever invented. It is important that the historical context for Baudelaire's work was the modernization of Paris by Haussmann on behalf of Napoleon the Third. Through Haussmann, Paris became a unified physical and human space, especially via the construction of the boulevards. Baudelaire's description of life on the boulevard shows how new private and public worlds came into being through the re-creation of the cityscape. Berman quotes Baudelaire's primal modern scene: "I was crossing the boulevard, in a great hurry, in the midst of a moving chaos, with death galloping at me from every side.[26] The archetypal modernist is a pedestrian thrown into the maelstrom of modern city traffic, contending against an agglomeration of mass and energy that is heavy, fast, and lethal. The street and traffic know no spatial or temporal bounds; they spill into every urban place and impose their tempo on everybody's time, transforming the entire environment into a moving chaos. The boulevard thus becomes a perfect symbol of capitalism's inner contradictions: rationality exists in each individual unit, but an anarchic irrationality in the social system results when all these units are brought together.[27]

Berman argues that the creation of modernist urban space required that collisions and confrontations do not occur. He extends Baudelaire's example to Le Corbusier's discovery of traffic. After fighting his way through the congestion, Le Corbusier makes a sudden daring leap, identifying totally with the forces that have just been bearing down on him:

> On that first of October 1924, I was assisting in a titanic rebirth of a new phenomenon: traffic. Cars, cars, fast, fast! One is seized, filled with enthusiasm, with joy . . . the joy of power. The simple and naive pleasure of being in the midst of power, of strength. One participates in it, one takes part in the society that is just dawning. One has confidence in this new society: it will find a magnificent expression of its power. One believes in it.[28]

From being the familiar man in the street dodging the snarling traffic, in the next moment Le Corbusier's viewpoint has radically shifted, so that now he lives and moves from within. He has gone from fighting traffic to joining it. His is the perspective of "the new man" in the automobile—a paradigm for twentieth-century modernist urban planning. Such a paradigmatic shift implies the death of the street.

In his search for a revitalized modernism, Berman draws a distinction between Robert Moses and Jane Jacobs. The Moses myth was founded on a conflation of progress and people's rights. He was able to orchestrate the release of millions of federal dollars following the initiation of several important New Deal agencies, in particular, the Federal Housing Administration and the Federal Highway Program. Subsequently, he constructed new and imaginative public places, parkways, and bridges within the New York City area. But Berman suggests that just as the construction of Moses's cross-Bronx Expressway was completed, "the real ruin" of the Bronx began; the fundamental results of his intervention were suburbanization of the metropolitan fringe and abandonment of the inner city. For her part, Jacobs recognized that everyday street life nourished modern experiences and values. She brought the opinions and perceptions of women into the discourse of modernist urbanism, recognized that streets are places of twenty-four-hour detail, and drew attention to the ecology and phenomenology of the sidewalk. Jacobs argued that for the sake of the modern, we must preserve the old and resist the new, and her writings were instrumental in provoking a wave of community activism to protect neighborhoods from further destruction by expressways and other forms of urban redevelopment.

The differences between the Moses megaproject and Jacobs's focus on the quotidian raise the question of modernist morality. Returning to the Bronx to recover what was good about his old neighborhood, Berman discovered a contradiction. One resident claimed that the moral imperative of the Bronx was to *get out* of the neighborhood in order to achieve advancement. Berman generalizes this sentiment, recognizing that the American way to overcome contradictions has generally been to drive away from them.[29] The important change that occurred sometime in the 1970s was that economic recession meant that modern societies lost much of their ability to blow away their past; they were forced to remain, to confront their modernism by remembering instead of forgetting: "At a moment when modern society seemed to lose the capacity to create a brave new future, modernism was under intense pressure to discover new sources of life through imaginative encounters with the past."[30]

Those who are awaiting the end of modernity can be assured of steady work, according to Berman. But

> if modernism ever managed to throw off its scraps and tatters and the uneasy joints that bind it to the past, it would lose all its weight and depth, and the maelstrom of modern life would carry it helplessly away. It is only by keeping alive the bonds that tie it to the modernities of the past—bonds at once intimate and antagonistic—that it can help the moderns of the present and the future to be free.[31]

But, I must add, the loosening of fetters feared by Berman *has already occurred;* modernism *has* floated away, loose, weightless, and depthless. This has already happened; this is what postmodernity is.

Unraveling the Postmodern Time–Space Fabric

By now, it is commonplace that postmodern sensitivities require new ways of seeing.[32] Questions of *difference and representation* are uppermost in the minds of those who would rehearse the break with modernity. It is certainly evident that urbanists seeking to understand the postmodern metropolis have increasingly turned away from traditional manufacturing cities and the conventions of the Chicago school in their search for explanations of Los Angeles, São Paulo, and Mexico City, or Atlanta, Seattle, and Phoenix.[33] Understanding the intentionality of postmodern urbanism requires a different kind of geographic imagination, one that not only allows Sorkin's departicularization of space but also focuses on the particularization of place. There is every reason to assume that postmodern society is just as profoundly imprinted in its urban places; it is simply that the manner of inscription, and the consequent urban forms, will likely differ from that of modernist conventions.

The social construction of space is at the core of the geographer's agenda, and uneven spatial development has long been understood as capital's way of overcoming the contradictions inherent in its "progress." Berman recognized that the American way to overcome contradictions is to leave them behind, to continually create new places representative of the unfolding American dream. Fredric Jameson goes further, identifying a new postmodern "hyperspace" characteristic of our era but so vast and complex that no one can as yet imagine its time-space coordinates.[34]

The search for postmodern landscapes has taken Jameson (and many others) to the urban edges, especially those of Southern California; here, they have discovered a "flattened" landscape, characterized by what Sorkin describes as a "repetitive minimum."[35] The consequent accumulation of enthusiasms for Southern California is impressive. I have already mentioned Garreau who, in his study of "edge cities" (concentrations of retail, commercial, and residential activities on freeway-accessible urban peripheries), asserts that every growing American city is following the trajectories set by Los Angeles.[36] In describing "postsuburban" California (i.e., Orange County), Mark Gottdiener and George Kephart claim to have identified "a new form of settlement space—the fully urbanized, multinucleated, and independent county. . . . As a new form of settlement space, they are the first such occurrence in five thousand years of urban history."[37] Somewhat less apocalyptic, and ultimately more persuasive, is Ed Soja's vision of Los Angeles as a gigantic agglomeration of theme parks, a lifespace composed of Disneyworlds that are

> divided into showcases of global village cultures and mimetic American landscapes, all-embracing shopping malls and crafty Main Streets, corporation-sponsored magic kingdoms, high-technology-based experimental prototype communities of tomorrow, attractively packaged places for rest and recreation all cleverly hiding the buzzing workstations and labor processes which help keep it together.[38]

In what follows, I shall examine the proposition that Los Angeles is the archetype of an emergent postmodern urbanism, as evidenced in the texts of the past, present, and emergent built environments. My historical analysis should reveal a progressive erosion of the rationalities of unity, control, and expert skills that characterized the newborn planning profession at the turn of this century. It should portray the preeminence of a totalizing discourse that facilitated the production of a modernist landscape, favoring urban abstractions (plans as empty vessels) that were capable of accommodating multiple ideologies, but ill-suited to the exigencies of socioeconomic and political change. My analysis should also uncover a constant renegotiation of the public/private dialectic in the city and the emergence of a fragmented metropolis characterized at once by centralizing administrative tendencies and tensely developed local autonomies. Postmodern Los Ange-les should be a city that has lost contact with the heritage of its past mod-ernisms and (free-floating) betrays a new depthlessness. The intentionali-ties guiding previous urbanisms will either be discarded or renegotiated; at a dysfunctional extreme, outmoded and obsolescent intentionalities may still remain to impede an urban process that has long since superseded them.

THE MAKING OF LOS ANGELES

My purpose in the remainder of this essay is to examine the historical rec-ord for evidence of a "postmodern turn" in the intentionalities that underlie urban development in the City of Angels. Before I begin, let me underscore the obvious: what follows in no way purports to be a compre-hensive urban history. I simply identify six pivotal moments from two cen-turies of urban growth to examine the proposition that L.A. provides sig-nificant insights into an emerging postmodern urban society. Each of these six periods provides examples of strikingly different rationalities in the creation of the built environment—intentionalities sometimes dominated by private interests, at other times by the public interest, most usually an alliance between public resources and private profiteering. But on every occasion, the deliberate intentionality that (re-)creates the urban environ-ment is backed by a clearly demonstrable collective civic will (even though, on occasion, the collective spirit turns out to be kinder to some groups than to others). In the conclusion of this essay, I shall consider the consequences of the atrophy of civic will implied by the emergence of the postmodern city.

Colonial "Beginnings," 1781–1846

Look carefully at the places and ports where it might be possible to build Spanish settlements without damage to the Indian population.
CITY PLANNING ORDINANCE NO. 5, LAWS OF THE INDIES OF
KING PHILIP II OF SPAIN (1573)

On 2 August 1769, a Spanish land expedition was making its way from San Diego to Monterey under the command of Gaspar de Portolá. It stopped at the site where, twelve years later, the pueblo of Los Angeles was to be founded.[39] In a contemporary diary, Father Crespi noted the advantages of the site: it had "all the requisites for a large settlement," including "a large vineyard of wild grapes," "an infinity of rose bushes in full bloom," and soil "capable of producing every kind of grain and fruit."[40] He recorded that a number of the Indians who "live in this delightful place among the trees on the river" brought the visitors gifts, and some old men "puffed at us three mouthfuls of smoke."[41] The Indians who met the Spanish army were the Yang-na (or Yabit); they were Shoshonean in speech and had settled an area close to the present-day City Hall. The Portolá party named the local river Nuestra Señora la Reina de Los Angeles de Porciúncula.[42]

In April 1781, Felipe de Neve, governor of Spanish California, arrived at the Mission San Gabriel to prepare for the settlement of a pueblo on the river.[43] De Neve had in mind to establish a new kind of settlement, located at an inland river site, to be primarily agricultural rather than military or missionary. In this way, he hoped to make the *presidios* less dependent on Mexico for food supplies.[44] As part of his colonial armory, de Neve had at his disposal a set of city planning ordinances—the so-called Laws of the Indies—that had been issued by King Philip II in 1573 (themselves a compilation of previous land use planning edicts issued since the beginning of the Conquest).[45] Based on Roman city planning principles, the 148 ordinances dealt exhaustively with every aspect of site selection, city planning, and political organization. The ordinances effectively "reinforced the unilateral objectives of conquest, emphasized the urban character of Spanish colonization, and specified clearly the physical and organizational arrangements that were to be developed in the new cities of America. Above all, the ordinances stressed a Christian ideology and a cultural imperialism."[46] Following a royal request to update settlement legislation in California, de Neve used his newfound autonomy to significantly modify the existing ordinances. His detailed regulations—the *Reglamento*—received royal assent in 1781. Among other things, they shifted power from the church to the state, paid settlers a salary, and encouraged Indians to continue living in villages apart from the missions.[47] Fifty years later, this shift in authority would ultimately culminate in the secularization of the missions.[48]

On the evening of 4 September 1781, forty-four settlers arrived at the site chosen by de Neve, accompanied by four soldiers who had escorted them from the Mission San Gabriel.[49] The new settlement was called El Pueblo de Nuestra Señora la Reina de los Angeles de Porciúncula; it was situated not far from present-day Olvera Street. The site was systematically surveyed according to regulations.

> The original pueblo consisted of four square leagues or 28 square miles, the center of which was a plaza 275 ft. by 180 ft. Building lots 55 ft. by 111 ft. were plotted around this plaza and assigned to the eleven families that constituted the settlement, a population of 44 persons. There were 12 of these building lots, 4 on the northwesterly side, 4 on the southeasterly side, 2 on the northeasterly side and one each on the northerly corner and the easterly corner. The southwesterly side was reserved half for public buildings and half for open space. Two streets 27 1/2 ft. in width extended through the building lots on each of the long sides of the plaza and three on the short side. A

short distance away 36 fields, each containing about 7 acres, were laid out and each settler was allowed two for cultivation. Beginning in 1875 the governor granted ranches of large tracts of land outside the pueblo, some of which are owned today by the descendants of the original grantees.[50]

The pueblo prospered beyond expectations, and by the 1830s, it ranked first in size among California settlements. But the Spanish army and Christian religion were to prove disastrous for the aboriginal inhabitants of the pueblo and California as a whole. As Robert M. Fogelson observed, "For the aborigines, slavery in this world was a prerequisite for salvation in the next."[51] By the time of the Mexican-American War (1846–1848), a sizable Indian population lived "in misery and squalor" at the pueblo.[52] When California came under American control, the city council was prompted to take action against Indian squatters. The council required all individuals with Indian servants to keep them inside "to check their excesses"; and those Indians without employment were to be granted lots at the edge of the city.[53] Between 1770 and 1832, the aboriginal population in California declined from 130,000 to 90,000.[54]

American Rationality, 1846–1853

After 1860, with surveys complete, land parcels could be bought and sold in the normal American manner.
H. J. NELSON, *THE LOS ANGELES METROPOLIS*

Once California had been ceded by Mexico to the United States, the former Spanish-Mexican system of land tenure did not long survive. The conquerors promptly imposed their own values and institutional arrangements, including political structures, taxation, and landownership.[55] These replaced more traditional methods of trading agricultural products and land titles (including the subdivision of ranchos) that characterized Mexican Alta California. Long-standing problems associated with the absence of a competent land survey were resolved when Lt. Edward O. C. Ord was dispatched in 1846 to survey Los Angeles. The imposition of "American order" was one of the primary tasks of the new authorities, and it was understood that "the permanent prosperity of any new country is identified with the perfect security of its land titles."[56] Ord mapped all the lands then under cultivation, thus enabling city authorities to understand what they were governing and to sell land parcels to benefit the city treasury.

In 1853, pueblo lands beyond Ord's original survey were extensively mapped by Henry Hancock. Local business interest sought to incorporate as much land as possible into the survey so that it could be sold at city prices.[57] In 1848, gold was discovered in California, and this triggered the first of many spectacular development booms in Southern California (this time based in beef production for the gold town markets in the north).[58]

Emergence of the Entrepreneurial State, 1880–1932

And so came into being a great American city destined to become the great American city.

L. L. HILL, *LA REINA: LOS ANGELES IN THREE CENTURIES*

Between 1880 and 1932, Los Angeles grew from a town of 10,000 people covering roughly 29 square miles to become the country's principal western metropolis with 1.2 million people and a territory of 442 square miles. During this period, L.A. transformed itself from a small entrepreneurial growth regime to a state-centered growth regime in which public infrastructure projects (most notably in water, power, and harbor development) and influential local bureaucracies shaped the region's development.[59]

L.A.'s early entrepreneurial regime, from 1880 to 1906, was composed of a hegemony of business interests with primary emphases on boosterism and real estate speculation to produce growth.[60] The business community, dominated by the Southern Pacific Railroad, created and controlled what was essentially a small caretaker local state.[61] The Southern Pacific treated Southern California as a colony and effectively constrained local economic development. But as the century drew to a close, its stranglehold was increasingly challenged by a locally based commercial, financial, and real estate elite, who did not share the vision of a railroad-dominated L.A.[62] For Harrison Gray Otis (of the *Los Angeles Times*) and his partners in the newly formed L.A. Chamber of Commerce, the 1888 collapse in the land boom had revealed the weakness of a regional economy founded on real estate. They firmly believed that industrialization was the the key to the region's growth.[63] Otis and the chamber envisioned L.A. as the commercial and manufacturing center of the West Coast, and they challenged the Southern Pacific over the matter of L.A.'s harbor.[64] While the Southern Pacific was promoting Santa Monica Bay as the preferred site for harbor investment, L.A.'s broad business coalition countered with a proposal for a municipally owned harbor at San Pedro (which would also bring in the Santa Fe Railroad to challenge the Southern Pacific's monopoly). The eventual selection of San Pedro as the site for massive federal investment in harbor development signaled the beginning of the shift in balance of power to local business and away from outside corporate influence over the region's political economy.

But it was potable water, not a harbor, that fundamentally limited Southern California's regional growth. At the turn of the century, the Los Angeles River and nearby artesian wells could sustain a population of only

300,000. Fresh from its harbor victory, the *Times* and its business allies brought the privately owned Los Angeles City Water Company under public control by organizing a special election enabling voters to approve the city's 1899 bond issue to purchase the existing private waterworks.[65] A political reform movement followed, and the railroad's hegemony was squashed. By 1906, an activist, progressive city council had replaced the caretakers and begun the task of building the public infrastructure deemed necessary for the region's growth. Two actions by the growth-oriented local state were harbingers of things to come: territorial expansion to link the city with the new harbor and a $23 million Los Angeles Aqueduct bond issue (which in turn paved the way for public provision of cheap power).[66]

In 1906, voters approved the so-called Shoestring Addition, a narrow sixteen-mile-long strip of annexed land linking Los Angeles with San Pedro and Wilmington. The land thus acquired expanded the city's area by almost 50 percent and became the prototype for L.A.'s subsequent campaign of infrastructure-based territorial expansion.[67] Though the newly formed L.A. Board of Harbor Commissioners lacked an actual harbor in 1907, they successfully formed bond campaign committees to raise the needed funds and thereby emerged as a formidable bureaucratic apparatus. By 1932, the Port of Los Angeles was the most important on the Pacific Coast and third in the nation in terms of total tonnage handled.[68]

While the harbor commission had pursued a collaborationist strategy with the local business community (and enjoyed its continuous support), the Department of Water and Power (DWP) faced major business opposition.[69] Announced in 1905, the Los Angeles Aqueduct was opened in 1913, bringing sufficient water for two million potential consumers (at the behest of City Water Engineer William Mulholland) from the Owens River Valley on the eastern slopes of the Sierra Nevada to the San Fernando Valley.[70] Mulholland vigorously lobbied to make annexation a precondition for receiving aqueduct water, thereby expanding the city's bonding capacity. In over seventy separate annexation elections between 1906 and 1930, the city's administrative area grew dramatically from 43 to 442 square miles.[71]

Los Angeles's new aqueduct also generated low-cost steam and electricity. The DWP used these resources between 1909 and 1932 to raise public capital to expand the Owens River system, to purchase L.A.'s private utilities, and to secure water and power from the federal Boulder Canyon Dam project.[72] Because power dominated the political agenda, the DWP moved to center stage in local politics during this period. The DWP bureaucrats Mulholland, William B. Matthews, and Ezra Scattergood were instrumental in securing congressional passage of the Boulder Canyon Project Act, a federal water project that ultimately permitted the city to grow beyond two million inhabitants. L.A.'s electrical power rates became the lowest of any major city in the nation and acted as a magnet for eastern industries.

Domesticating Land Use Planning, 1900–1941

The problem offered by Los Angeles is a little out of the ordinary.
C. M. ROBINSON, "THE CITY BEAUTIFUL"

City and regional land use planning emerged out of Los Angeles's post-1900 progressivism. The progressives' complaints about the negative consequences of uncontrolled development focused on "private enterprise's single-minded devotion to profits and public authority's exclusive dedication to material progress."[73] Their advocacy led in 1915 to the creation of the Los Angeles City Planning Association and ultimately (in 1920) to the legally constituted City Planning Commission. The president of the latter announced candidly that the commission was not a conservative branch of city government but would "Dream dreams and see Visions."[74] In reality, the burgeoning land use planning apparatus was promptly preempted by real estate interests. A business ethos was clearly evident in the contemporaneous priorities set by one planning practitioner: "A city plan should be prepared from the economic standpoint first, the social or human standpoint second, and the aesthetic viewpoint last."[75] From his perspective on a century of transportation planning in Los Angeles, David Brodsly concluded that "planners on all levels have consistently tried to play down their active role in public policy . . . [and] had to guard against being considered utopian visionaries."[76]

Zoning was first introduced into the United States by a 1904 experiment in Los Angeles that separated residential and industrial land uses.[77] Interest in land use planning was intensified when Charles Mulford Robinson (a renowned advocate of the City Beautiful movement) visited L.A. and prepared a series of grand designs for the city's future. In an inspiring conclusion to his report, Robinson wrote,

> I have tried to show what I thought should be the municipal ideal toward which Los Angeles should develop. . . . Not to be simply big; but to be beautiful as well. Not to be content with narrow, crowded streets, with meanness of aspect and a modeling after cities where lives must be spent indoors; but to be spacious, handsome, as a capital city, the streets alluring one out of doors, and offering so many drives and giving one so much to do that tourists will not pass through Los Angeles. They will stay here, in a real "Paris of America"—a summer city, when the East is swept by wind and snow; and they will find a gay outdoor life where other cities are stamped with the grime and rush of earnestness that knows not how to play. It is a beautiful, enviable role.[78]

Despite these lofty thoughts, the practicalities of day-to-day zoning occupied the minds of many Angelenos. The Los Angeles Realty Board (LARB) campaigned on behalf of the first citywide zoning law in 1908 and pushed to establish the County Regional Planning Commission in 1923—the first in the country—to "facilitate suburban growth and circumvent the need for involvement by the City of Los Angeles in land-use regulation, infrastructure and service provision, and property taxation."[79] However, the intervention of the LARB should not be understood as a naive or homogeneous instrumentality on the part of its members. The board was frequently divided over issues, some members wanting to use zoning to promote speculation, others favoring protecting districts from sprawl and thereby stabilizing land values.[80] On other occasions, smaller landowners often found themselves at odds with large holders of land, the former generally resisting any and all controls on land and property development.[81] The subsequent growth and development of L.A.'s land use planning apparatus was inextricably linked with the interests of the LARB. For example, the collapse of the local real estate market in 1907 and the weak market associated with the 1914–1915 nationwide depression led the LARB to press (successfully) for new zoning regulations.[82]

In other cities, the conflicting objectives of planners and private developers frequently developed into a classical standoff, a constantly shifting dialectic between progressive visions and economic imperatives. But in L.A., successive rushes of spectacular urban development erased most utopian overtones from a dialogue on the urban future. In 1918, 6,000 building permits were issued in Los Angeles; by 1923, the peak year of the boom, the number had climbed to 62,548 with a total value of $200 million. By the end of 1925, L.A. had no less than 600,000 subdivided lots standing vacant; the city had already parceled out enough land to accommodate seven million people, fifty years before the reality of demographic growth would catch up with the realtors' speculative appetite.[83] These consistently high rates of expansion are often cited as a principal reason for planning's subservient role with respect to business. In addition, the city's planning department was usually chronically understaffed and almost exclusively concerned with zoning.[84] During the 1920s, for instance, zoning matters occupied 80 percent of the department's and the commission's time,[85] while in the first nine months of its operation, the Regional Planning Commission was obliged to review over eight hundred proposals for tract development in unincorporated territories.[86]

Fogelson claims that "nothing in Los Angeles demonstrated the tenacity of private development as convincingly as the course of public planning."[87] Indeed, there is little doubt that city planning was generally consonant with the ambitions of developers and residents alike. Los Angeles developers "fully understood the need for planned infrastructure to support their realty projects, and they were quite willing to utilize government for such purposes."[88] The potential of planning was thus effectively reduced to the exigencies of zoning practice,[89] which "merely sanctioned the preferences of private enterprise."[90] Brodsly underscores the confluence of convenience and conscience implicit in these alliances.

> Los Angeles' history has been one continuous real estate enterprise, with land speculation a driving force for its never-ending growth. . . . [The] metropolis began to take shape, not according to any plan but rather at the subdivider's discretion.[91] . . . Los Angeles' urban form has been, perhaps to an unprecedented degree, a reflection of choice.[92]

Whose choice? According to Fogelson: "In all essentials, the planners shared the populace's suburban ideals, and the populace agreed with the metropolitan aspirations."[93]

After a half century of truly unprecedented urban growth, in 1942 Los Angeles prepared for the long postwar boom. The prospects facing the city's planning apparatus at this time were succinctly summed up by a planning commission member, William H. Schuchardt: "The present situation of the City of Los Angeles, from the standpoint of the city planner, may be couched in one word: Chaos."[94]

Transportation Palimpsest, 1941–1954

[The] freeway system in its totality is now a single comprehensible place, a coherent state of mind, a complete way of life.
R. BANHAM, *LOS ANGELES: THE ARCHITECTURE OF THE FOUR ECOLOGIES*

The chaos of postwar planning was a consequence of staggering rates of demographic growth in Los Angeles during the preceding decades. Total population in Los Angeles and Orange counties rose from under one million to over 2.3 million during the decade of the 1920s. A further 1.4 million was added during the 1940s, and 2.3 million in the 1950s. The population was already ethnically and racially diverse and highly segregated into separate neighborhoods.[95] To complicate matters, the early Angelenos began early their love affair with the car. In 1915, L.A. County's 750,000 residents had over 55,000 cars—the highest ownership rates in the nation. By 1918, vehicle registrations rose to 110,000, and to over 400,000 by 1924.[96]

Transportation has always played an important role in Southern California's sprawling suburbanism. The architect Reyner Banham characterized the region as a "transportation palimpsest," by which he meant that it was a huge tablet of movement, constantly being revised by successive generations.[97] The first railroads defined the major infrastructural axes for the burgeoning multicentered settlement pattern, even though they themselves had followed routes that were used by Indian and colonial settlers, which in turn were a reflection of the region's topography.[98] However, the birth of the fragmented metropolis was made possible, in a most dramatic way, by Henry Huntington's Pacific Electric Railway Company, which (by 1925) gave L.A. the largest electric interurban railway system in the world.[99] The millions of newcomers streaming into Southern California (particularly from the Midwest) rode the streetcars in search of their suburban ideal.[100] Thus, despite L.A.'s popular image as the "automotive city," Southern California's signature urban sprawl *originated* as a dispersed polycentric system of electric rail lines.[101]

The chief effect of the automobile was to provide an unstoppable impetus to the decentralization imperative.[102] Streetcars had facilitated suburbanization primarily along clearly defined linear corridors; the car, however, permitted urban development in any area where a road could be cleared. Congestion levels rose. The first major step in establishing public control of automotive transport was undertaken via the 1924 report, "A Major Traffic Street Plan for Los Angeles," by Frederick Law Olmsted, Harland Bartholomew, and Charles H. Cheney.[103] Fundamental to this plan was the notion that the "promiscuous mixing of different types of traffic" was harmful and that all streets should be divided into three use classes: major thoroughfares, parkways or boulevards, and minor streets.[104] Although little of immediate practical consequence flowed from the Olmsted report, important seeds for future freeway planning were thus planted. During the 1920s, there was a significant change in patterns of public transportation patronage. Suburban routes were cut, and in the 1930s they began to be replaced by bus lines. The Great Depression had a catastrophic effect on transit operator revenues. What happened to rail in L.A. was no different from what was happening to urban streetcar systems elsewhere in the country. Despite the popularity of a "conspiracy theory" that blamed General Motors for the demise of public transit, Angelenos had simply come to dislike congested streetcars and to prefer the convenience of the private car.[105]

It did not take long for highway planning to develop quickly and effectively in Southern California. The Regional Planning Commission's 1941 report, "Master Plan of Highways," codified plans that it had been accumulating since 1923; the Automobile Club of Southern California published its freeway plan in 1937; the Arroyo Seco Parkway (later the Pasadena Freeway) had been opened in 1938; and the highly influential "Transit Program for the Los Angeles Metropolitan Region" was issued in 1939. This last was essentially adopted wholesale into the City Planning Department's "Parkway Plan for the City of Los Angeles and the Metropolitan Area" in 1941.[106] However, planning highways was to prove easier than building them, largely as a consequence of the absence of funds. But once state and federal monies were allocated, the freeway system was rapidly implemented. In 1947, California's Collier-Burns Highway Act accelerated freeway construction in Los Angeles and was given further impetus when the National System of Interstate and Defense Highways was launched in 1956. Most of the region's major freeways were begun during this period.[107] Brodsly commented on the "perceived lack of real alternatives" in contemporary road transportation planning documents.[108] He notes that highway planning could proceed confidently, assuming (usually correctly) that the public supported the plans and that the "science" of traffic engineering had substituted for the political process.

For many years, the local land use planning apparatus basked in the successes of the highway planners. A 1941 city charter amendment authorized expansion of the Department of City Planning.[109] Staffing levels doubled during the wartime expansion,[110] and several significant project initiatives were undertaken. For instance, the Comprehensive Zoning Ordinance became effective on 1 June 1946; in 1948, Mayor Fletcher Bowron established the Community Redevelopment Agency of Los Angeles (CRA), an institution that was to have a major impact in later decades; and in 1954, Mayor Norris Poulson approved the first redevelopment plan in the state of California (the Ann Street Redevelopment Project).[111] It seemed that the 1930 prophecy of L.A.'s City Planning Commission had at last come true: "City planning is rapidly developing into an exact science."[112] Planning had arrived, polished and glistening, confident in its modernist regalia.

High Modernism, 1956–1991

It is then . . . the peculiar overlap of future and past . . . the resistance of archaic feudal structures to irresistible modernizing tendencies . . . that is the condition of possibility for high modernism. . . . [The] postmodern must be characterized as a situation in which . . . the archaic has finally been swept away without a trace.
FREDRIC JAMESON, *POSTMODERNISM, OR THE CULTURAL LOGIC OF LATE CAPITALISM*

It did not take long for the sheen to become tarnished. A 1956 report by the consultant firm of Adams, Howard and Greely was highly critical of the L.A. City Planning Department. While acknowledging the enormity of the tasks facing the staff, the report pointed out that Los Angeles was still without a comprehensive master plan despite the mandate given by the 1941 city charter revision. It also highlighted problems of inadequate staffing, the absence of background research, excessive bureaucracy, and the lack of coordination between different branches of city government.[113]

The city responded to these complaints by searching for new technical and organizational rationalities that could improve the department's performance. In January 1959, Stanford Optner and Associates submitted a report to the City Planning Department, "Feasibility of Electronic Data Processing in City Planning." Insisting on the increasingly technical and complex nature of planning, the report incorporated then-fashionable systems concepts into what was termed a "theory of planning through electronic data processing."[114] Two years later, in 1961, the ever-expanding planning department received yet another report, "Analysis of Land-Use Planning in Large Metropolitan Regions," this time from UCLA's Department of Engineering. The report had two objectives: "to examine the technique of master planning for a large metropolitan region . . . and to examine possible applications of high speed computers to the planning task."[115]

The continuing search for "science" and the "master plan" was to dominate the decades that followed the hegemony of the highway planners. For instance, in the early 1960s, three reports in the "Los Angeles Centropolis, 1980" series were issued. With a focus on downtown L.A., the series analyzed the local economy, planning principles to guide future development, and transportation options. The reports were intended to provide the basis for a comprehensive plan for the central city area.[116] Then, in 1969, the City Planning Department, under the leadership of Calvin Hamilton, issued the Centers Concept, a master plan emphasizing the polycentric nature of the metropolitan region. The Centers Concept's view of relative equality among the many competing centers was rejected the following year by the downtown L.A. Central City Association, which commissioned its own plan to deal with the post-Watts riot realities of Los Angeles. In 1971, the so-called Silver Book plan for downtown Los Angeles was published, ushering in two decades during which the city's Community Redevelopment Agency became the dominant force in urban redevelopment schemes throughout the city, especially in the downtown and most spectacularly in Bunker Hill. For a brief moment, Mayor Tom Bradley shifted the emphasis away from downtown L.A. when, in 1988, his corporate-dominated blue-ribbon committee produced a strategic plan for all of Los Angeles, entitled *LA 2000*.

POSTMODERN CONSEQUENCES

The essence of Los Angeles was revealed more clearly in its deviations from [rather] than its similarities to the great American metropolis of the late nineteenth and early twentieth centuries.

R. M. FOGELSON, *THE FRAGMENTED METROPOLIS*

The roots and precepts of modern urban planning lie deep in the history of modernity, especially the rationalities characteristic of the Enlightenment and the hegemonies of science. Thus it is not difficult to reach back beyond the twentieth century for evidence of appeals to unity, control, and expert skills in the history of urbanization in Southern California. In the *origins* of Los Angeles, we have witnessed an essentially colonial rationality inspired by the material and spiritual imperatives of the Spanish conquerers, bolstered by a thoroughly systematic code of city planning principles (handed down to the Spanish by the archrationalists, the conquering Roman Empire). An equally imposing example of early intentionality was the introduction of a market rationality following the U.S. takeover of Alta California in the mid-nineteenth century. The Ord and Hancock surveys created an urban land and property market where there was as yet scarcely a city, thus enabling trading in the normal American way.

The *maturation* of a distinctly modernist urban planning in Los Angeles can be seen in the successive emergence of entrepreneurial and state-centered growth regimes at the turn of the century. During this time, an aggressive local boosterism promoted massive public infrastructure investment that pushed Los Angeles to the forefront of national urban consciousness. It was also a period when a fundamental split occurred between the material and the spiritual in modernist thought—when the modernist/modernization dialectic was sundered and an idealized utopian planning theory was divorced from the localized processes of capitalist urbanization. The most consequential practical manifestation of this fracture was the subordination of the land use planning apparatus to the exigencies of local capital. In the ensuing instrumentality, planning practice created its own micro-level totalization in the form of detailed information-gathering and regulatory mechanisms. Although city and regional planning had been born from progressive ideas (which persisted, albeit as a muffled chorus), most utopian discourse was henceforward drowned in the sheer scale of the development tsunami in Southern California.[117]

The *apex* of twentieth-century modernist urban planning in Los Angeles is perhaps best represented by the freeway-building era. Transit rationality was replaced by a freeway rationality (the reverse appears to be true in the 1990s) as freeways and roads provided an unstoppable impetus to a decentralization that existing rail lines had only prefigured. The freeways ultimately created the signature landscape of modernist Los Angeles—a flat totalization, uniting a fragmented mosaic of polarized neighborhoods segregated by race, ethnicity, gender, and class.

The *transition to postmodernism* begins in the period of high modernism, when social, political, and economic structures begin to remake themselves against the backdrop of obsolescent institutional frameworks. The clash is evident in many ways: when the freeway rationality is confounded by Jane Jacobs's shout from the street; or when the Bronx imperative (still present as an escape to edge cities) is challenged in Los Angeles by an uprising—in 1965 and again in 1992—by those left behind, unable or unwilling to uproot themselves to the new frontier. New social contracts are being written in Los Angeles. The postmodern hyperspace appears to be upon us though we remain uncertain about what it will look like. In *postmodernity*, we seek ways to understand these new spaces—the texts of an untamed, incongruous urbanism. A postmodern way of seeing abandons, finally, the obsolete canons of modernist thought, replacing them with new conditions of knowing.

So what is Los Angeles, the postmodern archetype, trying to tell us?[118] In social terms, postmodern L.A. is a city split between extremes of wealth and poverty, in which a glittering First World city sits atop a polyglot Third World substructure.[119] Economically, it is an emergent world city that is undergoing a simultaneous deindustrialization and reindustrialization.[120] Politically, it is witnessing a fundamental political realignment as the Bradley era becomes a distant memory and old elites are replaced by place-based coalitions forged from the politics of racial and ethnic tribalism.[121] Postmodern L.A. is the homeless capital of the United States, and the scene of this century's worst urban riots.[122]

One of the most characteristic themes of postmodern urbanism is fragmentation. This finds expression in Los Angeles not only in NIMBY (not-in-my-backyard)-induced slow-growth/no-growth movements and the preponderance of isolated (often gated) communities but also in patronage-driven development opportunities opened up by the collapse of government oversight. Paradoxically, such fragmentation simultaneously encourages the proliferation of intense local autonomies and the rise of informal politics. Related to this is an emergent privatism; during the 1980s the reassertion of individual rights over community obligations resulted in an atrophy of community. This is evidenced in myriad ways: from the debates over family values through the epidemic of crack cocaine to the collapse of the formal welfare state (its place taken by a privatized nonprofit- and voluntary sector-based "shadow state").[123] Land use planning, too, has become privatized, in a reversal of a century-long trend in which the profession has been progressively absorbed within the apparatus of the state. The residual modernisms of conventional land use planning are of course still evident in the postmodern built environment, for example, the residential townscapes of Orange County or downtown L.A. redevelopment schemes. But such schemes are essentially mausoleums of the modernist imagination.

There is now, to my mind, a clear nonconformity between Los Angeles's persistently modernist urban planning and the emergent postmodern urbanism of Southern California.[124] Yet the modernist verities of U.S. land use planning are still practiced in L.A. For instance, in 1991, the Los Angeles Community Redevelopment Agency commissioned a new downtown strategic plan to replace the 1971 Silver Book; at the same time, about forty other plans pertinent to downtown and its adjacent districts already existed; and although money for freeways has long dried up, a multibillion-dollar investment in rapid transit promises to reintroduce a transit-based rationality in the 1990s. Thus it appears that late-twentieth-century land use planning has detached itself from the spirit of the postmodern age. Free floating, it becomes a relict apparatus with only the most tangential relationship with the emergent postmodern city.

In 1961, John E. Roberts, who joined the L.A. City Planning Department in 1939 and became its director in 1955, issued this appeal:

> It is our objective to plan for the kind of City that the people of Los Angeles must prefer, for it is the people who make the City; it is the people who are the City. With the continued support of all civic-minded citizens, Los Angeles will steadily enhance its position as a truly Great City.[125]

The central irony in this appeal to "the people" who make Los Angeles a "truly Great City" is that it is no longer possible to identify *the* people of Los Angeles. This polycentric, polarized, polyglot metropolis long ago tore up its social contract and is without even a draft of a replacement. There is no longer a single civic will or a clear collective intentionality behind L.A.'s urbanism; and the obsolete land use planning machinery is powerless to influence the city's burgeoning social heterodoxy. *This* is the insistent message of postmodern Los Angeles: all urban place-making bets are off; we are engaged, knowingly or otherwise, in the search for new ways of creating cities.

NOTES

I am grateful to Gregg Wassmansdorf for his research assistance and to Tom Jablonsky and Jennifer Wolch for critical comments, none of whom should be held responsible for errors this essay may contain.

1. Joel Garreau, *Edge City: Life on the New Frontier* (New York: Doubleday, 1991), 3. In this essay, I shall use the designation "Los Angeles" or "L.A." to refer loosely to the urbanized region of Southern California, most especially the City and County of Los Angeles. When precision is necessary, an appropriate qualification will be included in the text.

2. See, for example, David Ward and Oliver Zunz, eds., *The Landscape of Modernity* (New York: Russell Sage Foundation, 1992).

3. Michael Dear and Allen J. Scott, eds., *Urbanization and Urban Planning in Capitalist Society* (London: Methuen, 1981).

4. Recent studies of Southern California urbanism include Edward W. Soja, *Postmodern Geographies: The Reassertion of Space in Critical Social Theory* (London: Verso, 1991); Mike Davis, *City of Quartz: Excavating the Future in Los Angeles* (London: Verso, 1990); Rob Kling, Spencer Olin, and Mark Poster, eds., *Postsuburban California: The Transformation of Orange County since World War Two* (Berkeley, Los Angeles, and Oxford: University of California Press, 1991); Michael Sorkin, ed., *Variations on a Theme Park: The New American City and the End of Public Space* (New York: Noonday

Press, 1992); Sharon Zukin, *Landscapes of Power: From Detroit to Disney World* (Berkeley, Los Angeles, and Oxford: University of California Press, 1991).

5. Gwendolyn Wright, *The Politics of Design in French Colonial Urbanism* (Chicago: University of Chicago Press, 1991), Introduction.

6. Sorkin, *Variations on a Theme Park*, xii. Also see Soja, *Postmodern Geographies*.

7. Sorkin, *Variations on a Theme Park*, xiii.

8. M. Christine Boyer, *Dreaming the Rational City* (Cambridge: MIT Press, 1986), 3.

9. Ibid.

10. Ibid., 9.

11. Ibid., 13–26.

12. Ibid., 27.

13. Ibid., 28–33.

14. Quoted in Boyer, *Dreaming the Rational City,* 54.

15. Boyer, *Dreaming the Rational City,* chap. 4.

16. James Holston, *The Modernist City: An Anthropological Critique of Brasília* (Chicago: University of Chicago Press, 1989).

17. Ibid., 40.

18. Ibid., 91.

19. Ibid., 95.

20. Ibid., 98.

21. Marshall Berman, *All That Is Solid Melts Into Air: The Experience of Modernity* (New York: Penguin Books, 1982).

22. Ibid., 16.

23. Ibid., 15.

24. Ibid., 18–28.

25. Ibid., 133–332.

26. Ibid., 159.

27. Ibid. A similar logic underlies the essays in Dear and Scott, *Urbanization and Urban Planning in Capitalist Society.*

28. Berman, *All That Is Solid,* 166.

29. Ibid., 328.

30. Ibid., 332.

31. Ibid., 346.

32. The consequences of postmodernism are discussed in, *inter alia*, Steven Best and Douglas Kellner, *Postmodern Theory: Critical Interrogations* (New York: Guilford Press, 1991); Michael Dear, "The Postmodern Challenge: Reconstructing Human Geography," *Transactions of the Institute of British Geographers* 45, no. 3 (1988): 262–274; Barry Smart, *Postmodernity* (London: Routledge, 1993); Soja, *Postmodern Geographies.*

33. The entire issue of *Society and Space* 4, no. 3 (1986) is devoted to an understanding of Los Angeles.

34. Fredric Jameson, *Postmodernism, or the Cultural Logic of Late Capitalism* (Durham: Duke University Press, 1991), chap. 1.

35. Sorkin, *Variations on a Theme Park*, introduction.

36. Garreau, *Edge Cities.*

37. Mark Gottdiener and George Kephart, "The Multinucleated Metropolitan Region: A Comparative Analysis," in Kling, Olin, and Poster, *Postsuburban California,* 51.

38. Soja, *Postmodern Geographies,* 246.

39. See Dora P. Crouch, Daniel J. Garr, and Axel I. Mundigo, *Spanish City Planning in North America* (Cambridge: MIT Press, 1982), 7. Full information on the early planned settlements of the American West is contained in John William Reps, *The Forgotten Frontier: Urban Planning in the American West before 1890* (Columbia: University of Missouri Press, 1981). The standard history of Southern California is Carey McWilliams's *Southern California: An Island on the Land* (Salt Lake City: Peregrine Smith Books, 1973).

40. William Wilcox Robinson, *Los Angeles from the Days of the Pueblo* (San Francisco: California Historical Society, 1959), 12. The southern California coast had been "discovered" by Juan Rodriguez Cabrillo in 1542 and more thoroughly explored by a merchant contractor, Sebastian Vizcaino, during 1602–1603.

41. Robinson, *Los Angeles from the Days of the Pueblo,* 12.

42. Ibid.

43. Crouch, Garr, and Mundigo, *Spanish City Planning,* 156.

44. Ibid.

45. Ibid., xviii.

46. Ibid., 2.

47. Ibid., 157. See also Robinson, *Los Angeles from the Days of the Pueblo,* 17; Los Angeles Department of City Planning, "City Planning in Los Angeles: A History" (1964); L. L. Hill, *La Reina: Los Angeles in Three Centuries* (Los Angeles: Security Trust and Savings Bank, 1929), 13; and John William Reps, *Town Planning in Frontier America* (Princeton: Princeton University Press, 1969), 63–64.

48. Crouch, Garr, and Mundigo, *Spanish City Planning,* 157.

49. Robinson, *Los Angeles from the Days of the Pueblo,* 5.

50. Ibid.

51. Robert M. Fogelson, *The Fragmented Metropolis: Los Angeles, 1850–1930* (Cambridge: Harvard University Press, 1967), 5.

52. Crouch, Garr, and Mundigo, *Spanish City Planning,* 167.

53. Ibid., 167–168.

54. Fogelson, *The Fragmented Metropolis,* 6.

55. Crouch, Garr, and Mundigo, *Spanish City Planning,* 162.

56. Ibid.

57. Ibid., 164.

58. Ibid., 171–172; Robinson *Los Angeles from the Days of the Pueblo,* 49–50; Fogelson, *The Fragmented Metropolis,* 15–16.

59. This history is cogently presented in Steven P. Erie, "How the Urban West Was Won: The Local State and Economic Growth in Los Angeles, 1880–1932," *Urban Affairs Quarterly* 27, no. 4 (June 1992): 519–554; and in Davis, *City of Quartz,* chap. 2.

60. Erie, "How the Urban West Was Won," 521. An integral component of this early speculative era were the boulevards of L.A.: see D. R. Suisman, *Los Angeles Boulevard* (Los Angeles: Los Angeles Forum for Architecture and Urban Design,

1989). An intriguing pictorial history of one important subdivision, Hollywood, is contained in G. Williams, *The Story of Hollywoodland* (Los Angeles: Papavasilopoulos Press, 1992).

61. Erie, "How the Urban West Was Won," 525. For a full discussion of the "local state," see Gordon L. Clark and Michael Dear, *State Apparatus: Structures and Language of Legitimacy* (Boston: Allen & Unwin, 1984).

62. Erie, "How the Urban West Was Won," 526–528. The emergence of the Progressive Era in California is described in George E. Mowry, *The California Progressives* (Berkley and Los Angeles: University of California Press, 1951). See also Kevin Starr, *Inventing the Dream: California through the Progressive Era* (New York: Oxford University Press, 1985).

63. Fogelson, *The Fragmented Metropolis,* chap. 6.

64. Erie, "How the Urban West Was Won," 530–531; Davis, *City of Quartz,* 110–114.

65. Erie, "How the Urban West Was Won," 532.

66. Ibid., 534. Also see Fogelson, *The Fragmented Metropolis,* chap. 10, on the politics of the Progressive Era in Los Angeles.

67. Erie, "How the Urban West Was Won," 534.

68. Ibid., 538.

69. Ibid., 538–540.

70. The story of water and Los Angeles has been told many times; see, for example, William A. Kahrl, *Water and Power* (Berkeley, Los Angeles, and London: University of California Press, 1982). The remarkable career of William Mulholland is recounted in Margaret L. Davis, *Rivers in the Desert: William Mulholland and the Inventing of Los Angeles* (New York: HarperCollins, 1993).

71. Erie, "How the Urban West Was Won," 540. Also useful is Richard Bigger and James D. Kitchen, *How the Cities Grew: A Century of Municipal Independence and Expansion in Metropolitan Los Angeles* (Los Angeles: Haynes Foundation, 1952).

72. Erie, "How the Urban West Was Won," 541–547. For a discussion of Harry Chandler's leading role in this latter period, see Davis, *City of Quartz,* 114–120.

73. Fogelson, *The Fragmented Metropolis,* 247.

74. Ibid., 248; Gordon Whitnall, "Tracing the Development of Planning in Los Angeles," in Los Angeles Board of Planning Commissioners, *Annual Report, 1929–30,* 38; Los Angeles Department of City Planning, "City Planning in Los Angeles," 8–9.

75. Fogelson, *The Fragmented Metropolis,* 249.

76. David Brodsly, *L.A. Freeway: An Appreciative Essay* (Berkeley, Los Angeles, and London: University of California Press, 1981), 134.

77. Los Angeles Department of City Planning, "City Planning in Los Angeles," 2–3; H. E. Smutz, "Zoning in Los Angeles," in Los Angeles Board of Planning Commissioners, *Annual Report,* 58.

78. Charles Mulford Robinson, "The City Beautiful," Report to the Mayor, City Council, and Members of the Municipal Art Commission, Los Angeles, California (1907), 31. For Robinson's role in the City Beautiful movement, see William Henry Wilson, *The City Beautiful Movement* (Baltimore: Johns Hopkins University Press, 1989).

79. Marc Weiss, *The Rise of the Community Builders* (New York: Columbia University Press), 1987, 80–81. Similar chapters in New York City's urban planning history are recounted in Ward and Zunz, *The Landscape of Modernity*. See also, Los Angeles Department of City Planning, "City Planning in Los Angeles," 10; G. Whitnall, "Tracing the Development of Planning," 43.

80. Weiss, *The Rise of the Community Builders*, 79–80, 100–101.

81. Ibid., 80.

82. Ibid., chap. 4, "The Los Angeles Realty Board and Zoning." In 1939, the LARB also attacked the administration of zoning in L.A., focusing on corruption and the "zoning variance racket."

83. Kevin Starr, *Material Dreams: Southern California through the 1920s* (New York: Oxford University Press, 1990), 69–70.

84. Fogelson, *The Fragmented Metropolis*, 257.

85. Los Angeles Department of City Planning, "City Planning in Los Angeles," 13.

86. Brodsly, *L.A. Freeway*, 132.

87. Fogelson, *The Fragmented Metropolis*, 271.

88. Weiss, *Rise of the Community Builders*, 79.

89. According to W. L. Pollard (in 1930), the LARB's planning and zoning attorney, "planning as it is generally known in Los Angeles consists of zoning"; ibid., 105.

90. Fogelson, *The Fragmented Metropolis*, 257.

91. Brodsly, *L.A. Freeway*, 132.

92. Ibid., 136. The spectacular urban design of the 1930s was one consequence of this confluence of interests; See David Gebhard and Hariette von Breton, *Los Angeles in the Thirties: 1931–1941*, 2d ed. (Los Angeles: Hennessey & Ingalls, 1989).

93. Fogelson, *The Fragmented Metropolis*, 250. While agreeing with the importance of the automobile, Fishman emphasizes that the "suburban idea" predated the automobile era; see Robert Fishman, *Bourgeois Utopias: The Rise and Fall of Suburbia* (New York: Basic Books, 1987), chap. 6, "Los Angeles: Suburban Metropolis."

94. Los Angeles Department of City Planning, "City Planning in Los Angeles," 25.

95. Brodsly, *L.A. Freeway*, 89, 109; Fogelson, *The Fragmented Metropolis*, 79–84.

96. Brodsly, *L.A. Freeway*, 82.

97. Reyner Banham, *Los Angeles: The Architecture of the Four Ecologies* (Harmondsworth: Penguin, 1971), chap. 4, esp. p. 75.

98. Brodsly, *L.A. Freeway*, 2–3, 64.

99. Ibid., 69.

100. Ibid., 69.

101. Ibid., 80. Something of the effect of the region's burgeoning decentralization is conveyed in the relative decline of downtown Los Angeles as a center of urban activities. By 1930, the central area was already the slowest-growing part of the metropolis (ibid., 91).

102. Peter Hall, *Cities of Tomorrow: An Intellectual History of Urban Planning and Design in the Twentieth Century* (New York: Blackwell, 1988), chap. 9.

103. Brodsly, *L.A. Freeway*, 85. See also Fogelson, *The Fragmented Metropolis*, 250;

and Scott L. Bottles, *Los Angeles and the Automobile: The Making of the Modern City* (Berkeley, Los Angeles, and London: University of California Press, 1987), esp. chap. 4.

104. Brodsly, *L.A. Freeway*, 85.

105. Ibid., 93–94; Bottles, *Los Angeles and the Automobile*, chap. 1; and Fogelson, *The Fragmented Metropolis*, chap. 8.

106. Brodsly, *L.A. Freeway*, 96–106.

107. Ibid., 115–116; Bottles, *Los Angeles and the Automobile*, 232–233.

108. Brodsly, *L.A. Freeway*, 136.

109. Los Angeles Department of City Planning, "City Planning in Los Angeles," 23.

110. Ibid., 26.

111. Ibid., 28–33.

112. Ibid., 46.

113. Adams, Howard and Greely, "Los Angeles City Planning Department," Report to the Board of City Planning Commissioners (1956); see Los Angeles Department of City Planning, "City Planning in Los Angeles," 36–42.

114. Los Angeles Department of City Planning, "City Planning in Los Angeles," 48–48.

115. H. W. Case, B. Campbell, R. Brenner, W. W. Mosher, Jr., and R. B. Sheridan, "Analysis of Land-Use Planning in Large Metropolitan Regions," Department of Engineering, University of California at Los Angeles (1961), 1; Los Angeles Department of City Planning, "City Planning in Los Angeles," 51–52.

116. Los Angeles Department of City Planning, "City Planning in Los Angeles," 57–59.

117. See especially Paul Greenstein, Nigey Lennon, and Lionel Rolfe, *Bread & Hyacinths: The Rise & Fall of Utopian Los Angeles* (Los Angeles: California Classic Books, 1992); also see Davis, *City of Quartz*, prologue.

118. The search for answers to this question is, of course, a principal dynamic behind all the essays in this book.

119. Recent examples of an increasingly rich literature on non-Anglo Los Angeles include Lynell George, *No Crystal Stair: African-Americans in the City of Angels* (New York: Verso, 1992); Davis, *City of Quartz;* Rubén Martínez, *The Other Side: Notes from L.A., Mexico and Beyond* (New York: Vintage, 1993); David Reid, ed., *Sex, Death and God in L.A.* (New York: Pantheon, 1992).

120. Allen J. Scott, *Metropolis: From Division of Labor to Urban Form* (Berkeley, Los Angeles, and London: University of California Press, 1988); Soja, *Postmodern Geographies.*

121. Davis, *City of Quartz*, esp. chap. 2–3; Raphael J. Sonenshein, *Politics in Black and White: Race and Power in Los Angeles* (Princeton: Princeton University Press, 1993); Ty Geltmaker, "Queer Nation ACTS UP," *Society and Space* 10, no. 6 (1992): 609–650.

122. Institute for Alternative Journalism, *Inside the L.A. Riots* (New York: Institute for Alternative Journalism, 1992); Jennifer R. Wolch and Michael Dear, *Malign Neglect: Homelessness in an American City* (San Francisco: Jossey-Bass, 1993); Mike Davis, "Fortress Los Angeles: The Militarization of Urban Space," in Sorkin, ed., *Variations.*

123. Jennifer R. Wolch, *Shadow State* (New York: Foundation Center, 1990).

124. I have discussed the particular issues that comprise a "postmodern planning" in Michael Dear, "Postmodernism and Planning," *Society and Space* 4, no. 4 (1986): 367–384, and in Michael Dear, "Privatization and the Rhetoric of Planning Practice," *Society and Space* 7, no. 4 (1989): 449–462. On postmodern urbanism, see Michael Dear, "The Premature Demise of Postmodern Urbanism," *Cultural Anthropology* 6, no. 4 (1991): 538–552.

125. Los Angeles Department of City Planning, "City Planning in Los Angeles," 65.

FIVE

The Evolution of Transportation Policy in Los Angeles

Images of Past Policies and Future Prospects

Martin Wachs

Cities are known by their symbols. Just as the Eiffel Tower defines Paris and the Statue of Liberty symbolizes New York, the freeway is the universal icon by which Los Angeles is described. The freeway network, in addition to being an important transportation system, is considered the world over a symbol of Los Angeles, and what a dramatic metaphor it is for life in a modern complex metropolis. The freeway is a tangible facility that is also a flexible path through a maze. It is a pathway that encourages purposeful interaction between far-flung but interconnected communities; yet it contributes to the sense of placelessness noted by so many critics of this region. An invitation to unfettered motion at high speed in a shiny black limousine or a sexy convertible; and at the same time the source of tedium and frustration that comes from endless delays in traffic jams. Inviting people to experience ocean, mountain, and desert within minutes of one another, it is a major source of the smog that makes them invisible. It is a lifeline by which millions are supplied with their daily sustenance, yet it can be a place of carnage and police chases.

Like the freeway itself, our collective understanding of the evolution of transportation in Los Angeles is filled with confused, partial, and competing images. Informed by snippets of information repeated in the popular media and reinforced by questionable sources like the movie *Roger Rabbit*, millions state with conviction that a perfectly good rail rapid transit system was destroyed by General Motors in a conspiracy to sell cars and that the freeways encouraged and gave rise to a low-density, sprawling single-family region.[1] By purchasing controlling interests in urban railways in many cities, including Los Angeles, General Motors and other large corporations are alleged to have replaced perfectly good streetcar lines with diesel buses, thereby guaranteeing a market for their own products. These generalizations are, of course, partly true, but they are gross oversimplifications. The reality of Los Angeles is difficult to discover beneath the glib platitudes and movieland images; and it is far more complex than any of the popular images. This is also true for the transportation system that helped make this metropolis what it is and what it is always in the process of becoming. Frequently at the center of the region's bitter political struggles, the transportation network of Los Angeles is both the product of and the means by which we have acted out our images of modernity and by which those with muscle have exercised their political power.

In this chapter, I explore how the transportation network of the Los Angeles region has for over a hundred years consistently reflected these two themes. In each era, major innovations in transportation policy were presented as paragons of "modernity," packed with metaphors of innovation, technological change, and futurism. At the same time, however, the imagery of modernity has been consistently manipulated by politically powerful interests to suit their goals for economic and spatial domination of the region. Thus the metaphor of modernity has been used to justify a series of transportation plans and programs, few of which have ever been fully implemented. Rather, new proposals favored for reasons of political expediency have replaced their predecessors in a succession of plans put forth as absolutely necessary to promote the progress of the Los Angeles region. And today, though the metaphor of modernity continues to dominate the rhetoric of transportation policy makers, the Los Angeles transportation system actually consists of an accumulation of poorly integrated elements representing different concepts of political expediency, each of which in its day was presented as a symbol of progress and technological achievement.

PUBLIC TRANSIT IN THE EARLY
DEVELOPMENT OF LOS ANGELES

After it was first settled in 1781, Los Angeles remained a sleepy and relatively unimportant town until it was linked to a growing national rail network a hundred years later. The census of 1870 showed that Los Angeles had a population of 6,000, but that was before the Southern Pacific completed a line between San Francisco and Los Angeles in 1876 and completed a more direct route between Los Angeles and the East in 1881. People poured in looking for economic opportunity and adventure. In 1885, the Santa Fe offered competition to the Southern Pacific, and a fare war invited even more westward migrants. By 1890, the city's population exceeded 50,000 and the county's was more than 100,000.

Railroad construction led to Los Angeles's growth, and similar technology helped give it form. Between 1870 and 1910 urban transit technology was advancing rapidly. In eastern cities, entrepreneurs were replacing horse car lines with cable, steam, and electric traction street railways, and similar technologies were part of the original development of Los Angeles during its initial growth spurt. The timing of the growth of Los Angeles resulted in a significantly different pattern of development than was typical in Boston, New York, or Philadelphia. Those cities had developed to considerable size before the advent of streetcars, and because walking was the primary mode of transportation, they were characterized by areas of extremely high population density. By connecting the outskirts with the downtown business center, the advent of public transit technology enabled those cities to add new residential suburban communities on the fringes of those already dense central areas.[2] Real estate developers were the principal stockholders in the new street railways, and the increased accessibility that those railways gave to their landholdings made that land much more valuable.[3] Often, the transit companies stood on shaky foundations, yet they facilitated substantial profits in real estate development.

In Los Angeles real estate development held out similar prospects for quick and large profits, especially because of the rapid growth the region was experiencing, just as the new streetcar technologies became available. But the large core city of walking scale that was well developed in Boston, New York, Philadelphia, and Chicago did not yet exist in Los Angeles, so the transit-oriented "suburbs" of Boyle Heights, Burbank, Glendale, and others sprang up around a much smaller downtown than was the case in those older eastern cities. Between 1870 and 1910, as the population exploded from under 5,000 to over 320,000 people, the new cable, steam, and electric urban and interurban railways made residential development possible at substantial distances from the urban core and at relatively low densities that have come to be the characteristic form of Los Angeles.[4]

Despite many financial crises and even bankruptcies among the privately owned rail lines during the early years of this century, the rapid population growth and vigorous real estate activity led to the development in Los Angeles of what most transportation historians refer to as the largest system of interurban electric lines in the country. The Pacific Electric system, assembled and extended by Henry Huntington from seventy-two separate companies, by 1923 offered service on its Red Cars over 1,164 miles of track extending over 100 miles from end to end. Balboa was connected to San Bernardino and Pasadena to Santa Monica by his interurban network, and the Los Angeles Railway's Yellow Cars plied an additional 316 miles of track, mostly providing local service on the streets of Los Angeles. Spencer Crump observes that "unquestionably it was the electric interurbans which distributed the population over the countryside during the century's first decade and patterned Southern California as a horizontal city rather than one of skyscrapers and slums."[5] By so distributing the population, the trans-

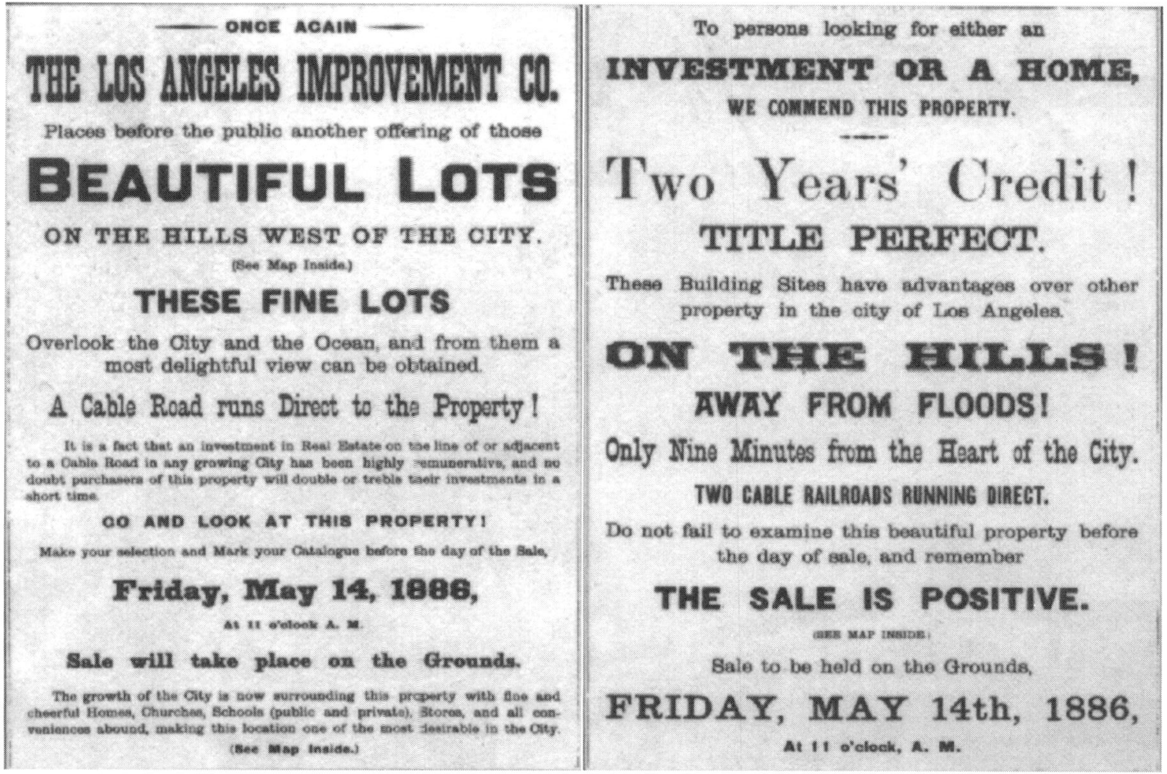

ONCE AGAIN

THE LOS ANGELES IMPROVEMENT CO.

Places before the public another offering of those

BEAUTIFUL LOTS

ON THE HILLS WEST OF THE CITY.

(See Map Inside.)

THESE FINE LOTS

Overlook the City and the Ocean, and from them a most delightful view can be obtained.

A Cable Road runs Direct to the Property!

It is a fact that an investment in Real Estate on the line of or adjacent to a Cable Road in any growing City has been highly remunerative, and no doubt purchasers of this property will double or treble their investments in a short time.

GO AND LOOK AT THIS PROPERTY!

Make your selection and Mark your Catalogue before the day of the Sale,

Friday, May 14, 1886,

At 11 o'clock A. M.

Sale will take place on the Grounds.

The growth of the City is now surrounding this property with fine and cheerful Homes, Churches, Schools (public and private), Stores, and all conveniences abound, making this location one of the most desirable in the City.

(See Map Inside.)

To persons looking for either an

INVESTMENT OR A HOME,

WE COMMEND THIS PROPERTY.

Two Years' Credit!

TITLE PERFECT.

These Building Sites have advantages over other property in the city of Los Angeles.

ON THE HILLS!

AWAY FROM FLOODS!

Only Nine Minutes from the Heart of the City.

TWO CABLE RAILROADS RUNNING DIRECT.

Do not fail to examine this beautiful property before the day of sale, and remember

THE SALE IS POSITIVE.

(SEE MAP INSIDE.)

Sale to be held on the Grounds,

FRIDAY, MAY 14th, 1886,

At 11 o'clock, A. M.

Figure 5.1. Advertisements for land subdivisions in Los Angeles illustrating the prominence of railway access in the promotion of real estate.

Figure 5.2. In eastern cities like New York, new transit technology was added to densely developed communities.

Figure 5.3. In Los Angeles the Pacific Electric was used to develop low-density, outlying areas. Highland Park, 1910.

portation system was also participating prominently in the establishment of a spatial distribution of political power and influence that was far more dispersed than was typical in other American cities at the time and that would later bear heavily on the outcome of important political struggles over the shape and form of the transportation system.

THE ARRIVAL OF THE AUTOMOBILE

During the period of expansion and consolidation of the rail transit lines that made low-density residential development possible in Southern California, the automobile was being introduced and improved. At first it was available only to the wealthy, and before 1920 most autos were open to the elements and extremely uncomfortable in rain, snow, and cold weather. Early cars were difficult to operate where there were few paved roads, especially when winter weather turned unpaved roads into quagmires. Not surprisingly, in comparison with eastern cities, Southern California turned early and with enthusiasm to the automobile. The mild, dry climate was ideally suited to driving, and the predominantly low density pattern promoted by the street railways was extremely inviting to automobile ownership and use. Single-family lots provided space for the storage and maintenance of cars which was simply unavailable in dense urban residential quarters in the East, and the dispersion of destinations gave people reason to buy and use cars. Lower densities also made the personal storage and handling of gasoline—very important in the early days of autos—just a little safer than it was in the crowded quarters of eastern cities.

By 1920 the citizens of Los Angeles had one automobile per nine people, by far the highest rate of automobile ownership in any major American city, and growth was accelerating. Between 1910 and 1920 William Mulholland completed the great aqueduct providing a reliable supply of inexpensive water from the Owens Valley, oil production was growing, and voter-approved initiatives provided funding for the development of harbor facilities at San Pedro and Wilmington. During the decade that followed the First World War, Los Angeles grew very rapidly, automobile acquisition peaked, and the orientation of the region toward single-family homes and low densities was reinforced. This had important consequences for regional politics and for the future of the transportation system.

Between 1920 and 1930, the population of the City of Los Angeles grew from 577,000 to 1,240,000; and that of the county grew from 1,238,000 to 2,200,000.[6] This remarkable increase was described by a perhaps overly exuberant historian of the time as "the largest internal migration in the history of the American people."[7] By 1930, although two-thirds of all Americans lived in the states in which they were born, only 20 percent of the residents of Los Angeles had been born in California, which had a larger proportion of middle-aged and older residents than the country as a whole. Median income was high, in part because the growth rate in employed workers substantially exceeded the growth rate in population. The proportion of workers employed in manufacturing declined from 28 percent in 1920 to 20 percent in 1930, and Los Angeles came increasingly to be known as a "white collar town, with employment in real estate, finance, and tourism growing most prominently."[8]

During the first wave of dispersal, between roughly 1880 and 1910, residential suburbs grew up in outlying areas as bedroom communities in response to the provision of interurban and street railways. The larger wave of growth after 1920 was characterized by a decentralization of a great deal of business and commercial activity as well as the continued expansion of suburban residential communities. Between 1906 and the mid-1950s, a Los Angeles law limited building height to 150 feet, with the single exception of the 1928 City Hall high-rise building, and that limitation may have been another factor in the continued dispersion of many land uses. Some believe that the height limitation was due primarily to a fear of earthquake damage, and its enactment had followed fairly quickly on the heels of the great San Francisco earthquake. But a review of newspaper comment from the period also reveals a preference for low-density cities, which are described in terms of images of modernity and contrasted to the high density of New York tenements. Los Angeles would not repeat the "mistakes of the past" and would instead be kept a "city in a garden," and thus a suitable environment for the raising of children and enjoyment of good health.[9]

The public transit operators at first benefited from the dispersed growth of the early twenties. Annual rail passenger boardings increased from 74 million in 1919 to more than 109 million in 1924, an increase of 47 percent in only five years.[10] This was, however, a much smaller rate of growth than took place in automobile ownership and use, and after 1924 rail transit patronage fell steadily as the popularity of the automobile grew ever greater. Between 1919 and 1929, for example, the number of automobiles registered in the county rose from 141,000 to 777,000,[11] a rate of growth that far exceeded population growth, so that on the eve of the Great Depression in 1929 there was already one car per three people in Los Angeles.

Even when the public transit system was at the peak of its annual ridership, a cordon count revealed that in 1924 fully 48 percent of those entering the central business district of Los Angeles came in automobiles, and by 1931 that proportion had risen to 62 percent, a proportion that is essentially equal to the results of a cordon count conducted in 1980. Thus the relative extent of the reliance on automobiles by downtown commuters had not changed significantly for fifty years. Mark S. Foster reported that in 1933 during the twelve hours of daylight some 277,000 cars entered downtown Los Angeles, a dramatically large number when compared with other

Figure 5.4. The suburban residential community of Los Angeles in the twenties.

American cities. At the time, Chicago's central business district was the destination of 113,000 automobiles per day, Boston's central area received only 66,000, and St. Louis's some 49,000.[12]

This rapid growth of automobile ownership and use during the early twenties had two important impacts. First, it increased congestion on the streets, especially of the inner city, much more quickly than street widenings and new street openings could accommodate. In the process, it elevated the status of traffic congestion to a major public and political concern. Second, the growth in automobile traffic had a devastating effect on the street railways, which had already been in dire financial straits prior to the twenties. The automobile first cut into streetcar revenues by robbing the transit system of weekend excursion trips to the beaches and mountains. Later, as the country slowly converted from a six-day workweek to a five-day workweek, another one-sixth of the transit work trips were eliminated and replaced largely by Saturday automobile shopping trips and family social excursions. While work trips continued to be made in large numbers on the Pacific Electric and Los Angeles railways, weekend automobile excursions replaced the transit trips to the beach or amusement park, and this reduced the already marginal operating profits to near zero.

Since most of the transit tracks had been laid in the streets, increasing automobile traffic slowed the transit vehicles and caused them to have great difficulty meeting their schedules. More and more riders gave up on them and switched to autos, accelerating the vicious circle of ridership decline and deficit growth. As more and more autos criss-crossed the trolley tracks, serious accidents between trains and autos rapidly grew in number, and the payment of injury and damage claims further weakened the finances of the rail operators. In an effort to meet rising operating costs, the transit operators repeatedly asked for permission to raise fares, and their customers testified that fares should not be raised for dirty vehicles, slow service, and trains that were always late. The Public Utilities Commission repeatedly denied requests for fare increases, and this in turn led to service reductions, which led to even more unhappy travelers who continued to switch to private autos. Thus long before General Motors, Firestone, Mack Truck, and Chevron acquired stock in the street railways and converted the trolley cars into bus operations, the competition between the transit lines and the automobile was being won by the latter, and transit operators were obviously losing their ability to stay in business at all. Annual ridership on the Pacific Electric fell from about 109 million in 1924 to 100 million by 1931.

CHOOSING BETWEEN TRAINS AND CARS IN THE TWENTIES

The decline of public transit and the rise of the automobile in the twenties had much to do with images of modernity associated with these different

Figure 5.5. Traffic congestion in downtown Los Angeles. Spring Street, circa 1920.

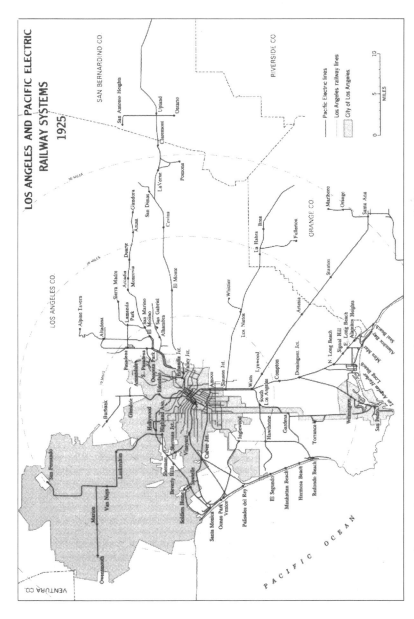

Figure 5.6. Map shows the major streetcar and interurban transit routes serving Los Angeles in 1925.

transportation modes and also with the balance of political power within the Los Angeles area. There is no doubt that public policy shifted in the twenties toward accommodating the automobile at the expense of public transit, and today many environmentalists and activists retrospectively label the policies of the twenties as mistaken. Nevertheless, those policies must be understood in the context of their era, and it must be understood that those who today label the decisions of the 1920s mistakes are measuring them according to criteria of modernity that prevail today and that are in some cases diametrically opposite those of the twenties.

In the 1920s, despite the fact that much of the population remained dependent on public transit, the transit operators were generally the object of public hostility, derision, and contempt. The transit companies were privately owned by wealthy tycoons who were known for their extravagant lifestyles and magnificent mansions. As their transit holdings became less and less profitable, the condition of the cars deteriorated and trains ran late. Whenever fare increases were sought, ostensibly for the purpose of improving service and upgrading capital equipment, citizens flocked to hearings to decry the audacity of the transit operators. Because service was poor and the vehicles rickety, they were seen as being unworthy of fare increases; they were privately owned monopolies, and fare increases were seen as attempts by millionaires to make more money at the expense of working people. As profits fell and owners cut service and reduced maintenance, hatred of transit management grew in intensity, and this made it virtually impossible for city councils and public utilities commissions to approve even sound business proposals needed to keep the street railways operating.

In contrast, and spurred on by automobile advertising, the private car was counterposed to public transit as the epitome of modernity and stylishness. An automobile provided an individual with freedom of choice, was an object of conspicuous consumption, and could carry four people for the same price as one, something public transit surely could never do. Finally, as Scott Bottles argues, the automobile engendered populist feelings that welled up against the transit operators. Using a private car, in addition to being modern and stylish, was also a way the working man could strike a blow against monopoly capitalism, which was personified by the owners of the transit systems. While Henry Huntington was portrayed as a villain, Henry Ford was seen as a savior, and his profits were to a far lesser extent the object of derision by popular activists.[13] Thus, while today some critics maintain that the demise of the Red Cars was a major public policy mistake that should not have been allowed to happen and that destroyed an otherwise efficient transit network,[14] editorial comment and letters to the editor in every leading newspaper of the period lead to the conclusion that most citizens felt the transit system was anything but efficient. The view of most citizens of the day was that the trains were late, the cars were filthy and stifling in summer, the drivers were always insolent and sometimes drunk, and the owners were tyrants and monopolists. And while today General Motors is portrayed as the corporate giant that destroyed an otherwise efficient public service, at the time these events were actually unfolding, the symbolism associated with expanding auto use at the expense of transit was quite different. Autos were new, exciting, powerful, fast, and increasingly financially accessible. Best of all, they provided an alternative to reliance on the infamous street railways for mobility in the city of Los Angeles.

In the early twenties Los Angeles embraced the growing national movement to establish formal institutions to plan the future of the city and region. In 1920 a city planning commission was established by the City of Los Angeles, and in 1923 the county established its Regional Planning Commission. According to Robert M. Fogelson, the new commissions were dominated by members who favored a dispersed, low-density community in conscious reaction to eastern cities. He states, "From their conception of congested eastern and midwestern metropolises, the planners assumed that the great city was no longer the most pleasant place for living or the most efficient location for working. They proposed, as an alternative, residential dispersal and business decentralization."[15] This view was reinforced by the appointment of real estate agents, bankers, and land developers to the commissions. They directed the staffs of the agencies to concentrate on two principal activities: the rationalization of land subdivision activity and the provision of adequate streets and highways, primarily through negotiated agreements with land developers. This view was consistent with the widely stated notion that Los Angeles, at the time, devoted a far smaller proportion of its land area to streets and highways than any other leading American city and that traffic congestion could best be addressed by increasing the availability of paved streets and boulevards.[16]

The Automobile Club and a voluntary association of civic leaders calling itself the Los Angeles Traffic Commission set about the task of presenting to the public for adoption on behalf of the city a comprehensive auto-oriented street and highway plan for the Los Angeles area. Each member of the commission donated money, and together they retained Frederick Law Olmsted, Harland Bartholomew, and Charles H. Cheney for the purpose of producing the "Major Traffic Street Plan for Los Angeles," which was delivered in 1924. The plan provided for the widening, extension, and straightening of many streets and the provision of a network of major streets or boulevards. It proposed the first grade-separated parkway, following the Arroyo Seco from Pasadena to Los Angeles, modeled after the suburban parkways of the New York metropolitan area. The report advocated the separation of different classes of traffic: through traffic from local traffic, streetcars from automobiles, and so forth. Viaducts, tunnels, and other forms of grade separation were proposed in addition to the straightening and widening of many existing streets. The plan is reflective of an "engineering approach," in that it emphasizes efficiency and provides an enormous number of details by which the street system was to be improved. Design elements resemble those later incorporated into the freeway network, but the scale of the proposed highways is more humane than that of the freeway network: parkways and boulevards seem much more integrated with the communities of this region than do the freeways that were eventually built.

The plan received widespread support and endorsement from civic and political leaders, automobile club representatives, suburban land developers, and others. It was even endorsed by the street railway executives, who thought that relief of traffic congestion would benefit their operations by allowing streetcars to operate at faster speeds. The city council of Los Angeles quickly voted to place the plan on the ballot in November 1924 for endorsement and also included a bond issue to provide $5 million for its implementation. A combination of general revenues, bond issues, and local assessments of affected property owners was perceived to be a fair approach to the implementation of the plan. Home owners' groups joined in supporting the ballot propositions, despite some limited opposition that argued that schools were more important than roads and that the program was too costly. Both propositions were approved by wide margins, and the taxes were raised later in the twenties to speed the implementation of the plan. When the depression hit in 1929, only a modest start had been made at implementing the plan, but the consensus remained that the street and highway system was the core of the emerging regional transportation system and that it was worthy of continued support and systematic implementation.

THE RAPID TRANSIT PLAN OF THE TWENTIES

The future of rail transit was to be much more bumpy. While virtually everyone agreed that the automobile was the key to the future prosperity of Los Angeles, few believed that rail rapid transit would not also play a critical role. Support for the highway plan was based in part on the increased level of transit service it would provide, along with the improved automobile traffic flow. Yet public sentiment remained very critical of the railway companies, and newspaper articles continued to document the inefficiency and poor service they provided. While one subway tunnel was under construction in the early twenties which would permit streetcars to avoid the growing congestion on surface streets downtown, city charter revisions in 1924 included a provision stating that further rapid transit construction should await the adoption of a citywide transit plan, and in 1924 the council and the county board of supervisors agreed to share the cost of hiring the Chicago firm of Kelker, DeLeuw, and Co., to prepare a regional transit plan.

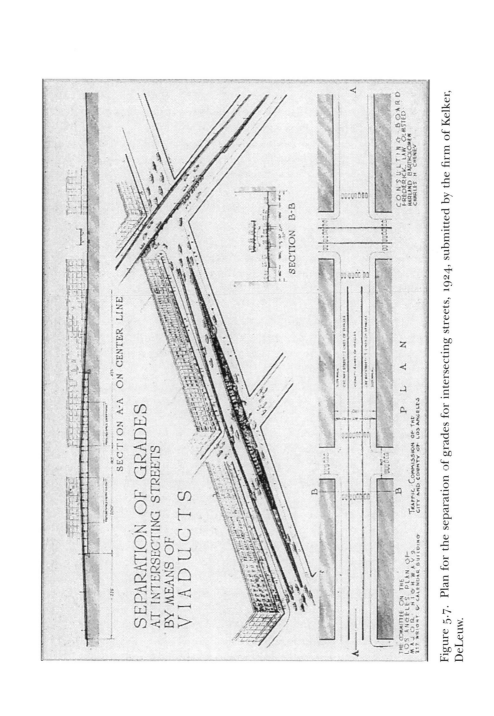

Figure 5.7. Plan for the separation of grades for intersecting streets, 1924, submitted by the firm of Kelker, DeLeuw.

In 1925 they submitted the *Report and Recommendations on a Comprehensive Rapid Transit Plan for the City of Los Angeles.*

The proposal called for construction of 26 miles of subways and 85 miles of elevated routes over a ten-year period, plus an extensive network of feeder bus lines and bus routes in outlying areas. The capital cost of the proposal was estimated to be $133.4 million. It recommended that the city levy special assessments at the station sites that would benefit from the increased accessibility and that the city participate in the accumulation of value that would flow from the rail lines by purchasing vacant property near the station sites for eventual development. Finally, and perhaps fatally, the report acknowledged that a fare increase, probably from five to eight cents (a 60 percent increase!) would be needed to cover the costs of the construction.

Most of the support for the proposal came from central city businesses and real estate interests, which had begun to realize that traffic congestion was putting the central city at a disadvantage with respect to the outlying areas and that a radial transit system would give downtown businesses a competitive advantage in recruiting both a workforce and customers. To be sure, representatives of some suburban employment centers also supported rail transit, but, ironically, the suburban residential communities that had grown up in response to the streetcar system were the source of most of the opposition. Why should substantially higher fares and taxes be approved to create noisy systems that cast shadows and create dust? Reports appeared in the local press of depressed property values in the vicinity of elevated railways in New York, Chicago, and Philadelphia, and elevated lines were portrayed repeatedly as "Chinese Walls," which divide communities and create blight. The automobile and the motor bus were presented as environmentally superior to the rail proposals, a concept that must surely be puzzling to today's advocates of clean air through vigorous controls on the automobile, but the public's notion of what constitutes environmental blight has obviously changed considerably over the years.

It was inevitable that the politics of rail transit in Los Angeles came to be tied up with ongoing efforts to force the major railways serving Los Angeles (the Santa Fe, Union Pacific, and Southern Pacific) to abandon their separate downtown terminals and to finance jointly a single or "union" station located near the plaza at which the city was supposedly founded. The railroads preferred to maintain their own individual terminals, in part because a union station would undoubtedly have to be open to competition from additional railroads that could not break into the Los Angeles market because each railroad refused them access to their rights-of-way and terminals. A major political battle ensued which lasted throughout most of the twenties. The *Los Angeles Times* led the fight for the Union Station at the plaza site, undoubtedly because the Chandlers owned land near the site that would increase in value should the terminal be built. Several other newspapers supported the position of the railways. The railway tracks at ground level on the east side of downtown were constraining the growth of the central area and contributing substantially to traffic congestion. These tracks were in practical and symbolic terms a brake on the future development of the central business district.

In an effort to head off growing support for the union station, the railroads finally offered to elevate the tracks approaching their several stations, thereby reducing interference with surface automobile and truck traffic, and they offered to allow the Pacific Electric interurban passenger trains to use the elevated tracks. The opposition depicted elevated tracks as an environmental blight on the city that would forever make it unattractive for capital investment and that would move it backward rather than forward on the path toward becoming "a city in a garden." And while the railroads had once wielded an enormous amount of political power, the decentralized population they helped to create felt detached from the railroads and the central city and very loyal to a lifestyle of open space and quality residential communities.

In the election of 1926 two ballot propositions finally decided the issue. Asked on the first proposition to approve the concept of a union station, the voters overwhelmingly approved the proposal by a margin of 61 to 39 percent. The second proposition asked whether to locate the union station at the plaza site, and it also passed, though by a smaller margin. The defeat of the railroads' position was widely interpreted as a defeat for elevated rail transit in Los Angeles, and as the depression arrived the city council could not seriously consider the Kelker-DeLeuw plan, nor had it promoted any alternative rail transit plan. The image of the existing rail transit system continued to deteriorate, and the operators gradually, with the permission of the Public Utilities Commission and the concurrence of the city council, replaced expensive, worn-out, and poorly patronized transit routes with diesel motor coach routes.

COMPETITION BETWEEN BUSES AND TRAINS

While it is often repeated that General Motors and others conspired to destroy the Pacific Electric, there is ample evidence that motor buses provided serious competition to rail lines for many reasons, and that they did so much earlier. And, given the extent of public hostility toward the operators of the street railways and the widespread displeasure with their services, it is not surprising that the motor bus became a symbol of modernity in contrast with the hated streetcar. Eli Bail points out that the Pacific Electric opened its rail line to San Bernardino in 1914 but that the existence of an excellent paved road nearby permitted a profitable organized bus competitor that went into service only three months later, offering an alternative that was fast and cheap.[17] Beginning in 1917, the Pacific Electric itself operated bus lines, in some cases buying out competitors, in other cases initiating bus feeder routes to its rail stations, and finally replacing some of its own more expensive rail lines with more flexible and less expensive bus routes. During the twenties and thirties the bus was seen by many commentators as superior to rail lines in many respects. Lawrence R. Vesey and Carl W. Stocks both wrote of the fact that bus operations could be much less expensive than rail and boasted that "de luxe" bus service was considered far more attractive than trolley cars by the riding public.[18] While buses were first used as feeders from residential subdivisions to rail stations, direct bus service eliminated the time-consuming modal transfers, and buses were in many instances able to provide quicker door-to-door service. In the early thirties, buses were repeatedly described as cleaner, quieter, faster, more flexible, and more maneuverable than rail vehicles. A. T. Warner pointed out that when faced with heavy traffic congestion, buses could be rerouted around the traffic jams while trolleys were doomed to be stuck in traffic because they were confined to the rails.[19] Buses were reported to earn higher profits than streetcars for several reasons: their operating costs were lower; their flexibility and speed led to higher utilization; and their speed, quietness, smooth rides, and convenient routing led them to be more popular with commuters. Whether or not they were completely true, stories in transit industry publications described cases in which the introduction of buses recaptured for transit many former trolley users who had forsaken the streetcars for private automobiles.[20] By 1926 the Pacific Electric was serving 15 percent of its passenger miles in buses, and by 1939, one year before the alleged conspiracy involving General Motors and others took place, the Pacific Electric had itself increased bus service and decreased rail service to such an extent that 35 percent of its travelers were served by buses. Throughout the thirties and forties, buses were in the ascendancy, they were considered the wave of the future, and rail transit was slowly declining in terms of use, status, and quality.

A MULTIMODAL TRANSPORTATION PLAN FOR LOS ANGELES

By the late thirties, continuing decline of transit and growth of automobile use, coupled with innovative new regional transportation plans in Chicago and San Francisco, led Los Angeles to undertake another regional transportation planning effort, and its outcome is reflective of the image of regional planning that was current in its day. This plan formed the basis for the first and largest metropolitan freeway system built in the United States,

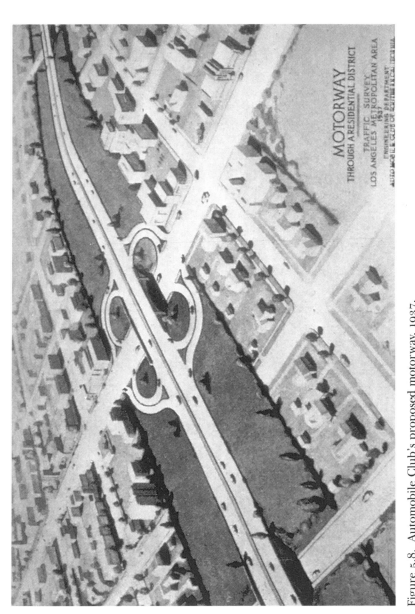

Figure 5.8. Automobile Club's proposed motorway, 1937.

yet in many important ways the plan was different from the freeway system that was eventually implemented. It is instructive because of both the similarities and the differences between the current system and the system that was planned in the late thirties.

The plan was prepared by Lloyd Aldrich, then chief engineer of the City of Los Angeles, who submitted it on behalf of the city's Transportation Engineering Board, which he chaired. It incorporated many principles that were included in earlier and similar plans developed for other cities by Miller McClintock, who advocated networks of "limited ways" that were grade separated from the surrounding streets and that permitted operating speeds well in excess of forty miles per hour. The centerpiece of Aldrich's plan was a regionwide expressway and transit system that linked the downtown area of Los Angeles with many outlying suburbs. The expressways had several functions. Radials focused on the downtown and gave it enhanced access; circumferential routes enabled through traffic to bypass the congested center; and "direct interdistrict" routes recognized the growth of traffic between the many new outlying centers. Expressways, incidentally, were not exactly of the scale at which the Los Angeles freeways were eventually built. They were to be partly grade separated rather than completely so; they did permit traffic signals at some intersections, while others were on overpasses and underpasses, and the expressways consisted most typically of four-lane roadways. While a number of parkways built in other cities had emphasized landscaping along the routes, the expressway plan emphasized integration with the existing street and highway system through transitional roads and integration with neighboring residential and commercial facilities, for example, by having exit ramps directly serve the parking areas at activity centers.[21]

Aldrich's plan was also explicitly multimodal, in that it provided for a variety of public transit modes as well as high-capacity highways. In the introduction to the report, Aldrich wrote,

> As far as mass transportation is concerned, the ultimate solution of the rapid transit problem in a large and densely populated area can be found only in rail rapid transit, and there is no doubt that such a solution will eventually be necessary in portions of the Los Angeles Metropolitan Area. In the intermediate stage, while population densities are still moderate and financing of rail rapid transit facilities difficult, a satisfactory alternative is available, for the provision of express highways and the operation of express buses thereon makes it possible to provide the desired rapid transit simultaneously for both private and public types of transportation.[22]

In keeping with this concept, the plan included provision for bus transfer stations at the intersections of major expressways, and it also provided for grade separation of rail lines in subways at some locations and in medians of the expressways at other locations.

The 1939 expressway plan for Los Angeles was remarkable in many respects. It was a quantum leap beyond the earlier street plan in providing for high-capacity channels of movement, yet it was rather sensitive to the integration of land use with both highways and public transit, treating transportation facilities consciously as elements of urban design. Brian Taylor notes that the plan was assembled by people who were politically astute and sensitive to the needs of many interest groups.[23] He observes that most expressway planners did not want to damage the popularity of their proposals by including private transit, which still suffered from great unpopularity. Yet, recognizing that transit would continue to be an important source of mobility for a large proportion of the population, Aldrich seems to have consciously put together a plan that included something for every constituency: downtown business interests and transit users liked the ring-radial plan, and exclusive transit rights-of-way promised to relieve downtown congestion, benefiting both transit users and auto drivers; the automobile club and its members were impressed by the outlying parkwaylike facilities; land developers in outlying areas noted that the new bypass and interdistrict roads would open up new land to development potential; and city and county officials finally came to like the plan because they believed it would have lower cost and was in many ways more practical than green-belted parkways, which were popular at the time and under construction in other cities.[24]

Despite its widespread popularity, implementation of the 1939 plan required resources that were not available to Los Angeles in the last years of the Great Depression and continued to be unavailable during the Second World War. The Arroyo Seco Parkway (later known as the Pasadena Freeway) was under construction since 1937, and land acquisition had started for what later became known as the Hollywood Freeway, but Taylor calculated that at the rate of annual highway spending that prevailed in 1939, it would have taken over one hundred years to implement the entire plan, which included some 612 miles of expressways and transit facilities.[25] Slowly, in search of the needed resources, Los Angeles turned to the state and federal governments for funding and started a process that led to the construction of the Los Angeles freeways according to design criteria different from those that were emphasized in the 1939 plan.

LOS ANGELES FREEWAY PLANS

During the 1930s the federal Bureau of Public Roads, influenced by the high-speed road network that Hitler conceived of for Germany, had begun to plan for a safe, efficient, and high-speed national network of highways. Intercity highways, however, were designed to meet a completely different set of needs from intracity expressways. Quite naturally, intercity roads paid little or no attention to integration with public transit, and because they were designed to traverse rural terrain, they were designed without much concern for their integration with adjacent land uses. Local traffic congestion was addressed, for example, only insofar as it inhibited the free flow of intercity traffic. The system under consideration, which eventually became the Interstate Highway System, was designed to connect communities at great distances from one another and to get the farmer out of the mud. To facilitate high speeds and safety, the roads were planned to be straight or to employ very gentle curves and to have minimal grades and broad protective shoulders. Early in the evolution of the program it was the plan of the federal authorities to build this system of high-speed roads only to the city boundaries, with internal road improvements to be made primarily in the form of locally planned networks like Aldrich's plan for Los Angeles. In the urban areas, in all probability, lower design speeds were adequate, uses of traffic signals were appropriate, steeper grades and sharper turns were appropriate to allow the road to blend into the existing urban fabric.

Several influential national planning reports recommended building such a national system of rural and intercity roads but noted that traffic demand was not yet established to such a level as to justify the necessary capital investment. Eventually, to demonstrate that there was a "need" for a national highway system, federal officials began to advocate that what they had previously envisioned as a rural highway system should in addition penetrate metropolitan areas in order to serve the central business districts. It seems clear that the motivation for these urban segments of the national highway system was not really to accommodate intraurban traffic but rather resulted from the recognition that the vast majority of traffic flowed within cities and that inclusion of more heavily traveled routes in a national highway system would help to justify the expenditure of national resources needed to build it. President Franklin D. Roosevelt asked the Bureau of Public Roads to delete the urban portions of the proposed federal system, leaving them to be dealt with by local engineers and planners; but the bureau made its proposals to Congress for a system that included the urban segments, undoubtedly because they felt the national road system could not otherwise be justified.

In 1944, the Roosevelt-appointed Interregional Highway Committee, whose seven members included a number of the most prominent planners and engineers in the country, advocated the building of a system of 39,000 miles of intercity highways, connecting nearly all cities in America having populations over 100,000. Interestingly, their report advocated that uniform design standards be employed in rural areas, yet it specified that about half of the mileage of highways within metropolitan areas should be left to be studied and determined by local planners and elected officials.

> Once the routes enter the environs of the city . . . they become a part of the sum total of urban transportation facilities, and as such must bear a proper relation in location and character to other parts of the street system. . . .
> How near they should come to the center of the area, how they should pass it or pass through it, and by what course they should approach it, are matters for particular planning consideration in each city.[26]

In sum, the emerging federal plan for a national network of highways provided sufficient leeway for a variety of highway designs and for flexible design standards that would allow urban highways to be treated explicitly as elements of urban design within their varying urban contexts. And the Aldrich plan seemed to provide Los Angeles with a highway concept that accomplished these objectives specifically within the context of that city. Yet the freeway system that emerged in Los Angeles ended up having a character very different from the system advocated by Aldrich, and, predictably, this occurred because of the need to compromise in order to obtain the funding needed to undertake construction.

In the 1940s the Interstate system was adopted by Congress, but because of the national war effort the system was adopted without any federal funding. At the same time, the City of Los Angeles was proceeding at a very slow pace toward implementation of the Aldrich plan. The state became the instrument of implementation of the federal plan, and in California the legislature decided to raise highway user fees (primarily gasoline taxes) in order to implement a statewide highway plan that included intraurban highways in Los Angeles. In doing so, the legislature made the critical decision that the expressway plan would be implemented by the state highway department, thus preempting the authority of the Los Angeles Bureau of Engineering and making the freeways the domain of state engineers and planners, under whose management they remain today. In the 1950s the exigencies of securing funds for the national road system again dominated the determination of urban freeway routes. Contrary to the recommendations of the Interregional Highway Committee, the Bureau of Public Roads, in an effort to secure the votes of urban members of Congress for its national system of interstate highways, published the intended routes for every mile of urban routing included in the system. Second, in order to give the utmost priority to the construction of roads on the Interstate system, the traditional federal highway funding formula, providing for equal sharing of the costs by state and federal governments, was replaced by a funding formula that had the Federal Highway Trust Fund paying 90 percent of the costs and states bearing only 10 percent of the costs of the interstates. When the 1956 Highway Act was passed, it made available an enormous

Figure 5.9. Harbor Freeway under construction near Santa Barbara Boulevard in the 1940s.

amount of federal gasoline tax revenue for the construction of the Interstate system, and the availability of nine federal dollars for each state dollar
spent was simply irresistible.

Thus when construction of the Los Angeles freeway network went into
high gear in the late 1950s, the Aldrich plan, which was sensitive to local
conditions and urban design principles, was sacrificed. The routing followed was that of the federal legislation, which in fact bears much similarity
to the routing included in the Aldrich plan. Terrain and traffic patterns
have caused most highway system proposals for Los Angeles to be broadly
similar to one another. More significant to the urban form of Los Angeles
is that California state highway engineers and the Bureau of Public Roads
adopted uniform freeway design standards that were applied consistently
to freeways planned throughout the state. These design standards specified
the number and width of lanes, clearances, radii of curves, widths of shoulders, and spacing of on- and off-ramps. The standards were adapted from
rural highway practice, serving design speeds of sixty or seventy miles per
hour. The urban design principles included in the Aldrich plan were set
aside. To thread the proposed expressways more effectively through an already densely built urban fabric, they would have permitted design speeds
of fifty miles per hour and would have allowed for sharper curves, occa-
sional use of traffic signals, and narrower and fewer lanes, medians, and
shoulders. The system that was built, however, incorporated far less sensitivity to local street networks, far less integration into the urban fabric of
the communities through which they passed, and far less accommodation
of mass transit. As the Los Angeles freeway system was built, some freeway
alignments, such as the Hollywood Freeway, initially included the Pacific
Electric right-of-way in the median strip, but as transit patronage fell and
auto traffic exceeded the projected volumes, the rail routes were removed
to permit enhancement of the highways' capacity.

Many have observed that the freeways of Los Angeles are terribly destructive of a sense of community, that they cut swatches out of the urban
fabric and provide barriers to community cohesion by creating enormous
discontinuities throughout the city, especially in inner-city minority communities. It is not clear that the Aldrich plan would have avoided all of the
social disruption and alienation that we have come to associate with the
construction of the freeway system, but it is clear that the plan had different
goals and priorities, which on the surface seem to imply that Los Angeles might be a significantly different place had that plan been fully implemented. It even appears probable that the land acquisition costs of building
the regional freeway system might have been lower had the uniform statewide design standards not been adopted, but as is so often the case, the
immediate availability of funds was valued over long-term full social costs,

and the financial exigencies of the construction program caused these long-term considerations to be set aside.[27]

THE LONG STRUGGLE TO BUILD
RAIL TRANSIT IN LOS ANGELES

Despite the long, steady decline of public transit patronage and widespread dissatisfaction with existing service, there continued to be a loyal following of supporters who felt that public transit would remain an essential service and that it was in need of renewal and expansion. During World War II, when gasoline was rationed and new autos were unavailable, transit ridership experienced a temporary resurgence of substantial proportions, but after the war, ridership returned to its familiar pattern of steady decline. As the war was ending, the Metropolitan Traffic and Transit Committee of the Los Angeles Chamber of Commerce formed the Rapid Transit Action Group (RTAG), which worked aggressively toward the upgrading of public transit in Los Angeles. In February 1948, after consulting with leading transportation engineers and planners for several years, the group sponsored a meeting to which no less than eight hundred business, civic, and political leaders were invited, at which they unveiled their proposal: *Rail Rapid Transit—NOW!* The proposal borrowed from the Aldrich plan in providing for rail rapid transit in the median strips of several of the radial freeways being planned to serve downtown, and it also advocated upgrading a number of the remaining Pacific Electric rail lines to the status of true rapid transit. The upgrading would involve the construction of tunnels in the downtown area and the systematic elimination of grade crossings throughout their length.

The report explicitly addressed the importance of constructing rail rapid transit in a diversifying, expanding low-density region. It conveyed the notion that the population would be increasing in coming decades and that ever larger numbers of people would be living in suburban areas and attempting to reach the downtown area. To keep downtown healthy, it would be necessary to invest in high-capacity, high-quality, high-speed transit links to those communities. Unstated, but certainly implied in the report, was the fear that unless a radial system were built serving the central hub, the downtown would suffer in the competition for jobs and for development capital with the rapidly growing suburban communities. They urged that a special unit of government—a transit district—be created to ensure the rapid transit system they were advocating. Sy Adler reports that the proposal met with mixed reactions, gaining strong support from downtown businesses and City Hall, their political allies in the construction and downtown development businesses, and the newspapers based in the downtown area.[28] There was also, however, clear opposition, primarily from property owners, real estate developers, and community leaders in outlying communities that had already established significant levels of offices and retail in their communities. Commercial interests in Long Beach, Santa Monica, Pasadena, and elsewhere stated that the plan provided relief for downtown taxpayers at the expense of their communities. These groups were upset with the radial orientation of the rail system, which, like a substantial portion of the freeway network, centered on the downtown area of the City of Los Angeles.

They were equally concerned that the creation of a transit district would result in a unit of government with special powers that would be dominated by downtown representatives. Owners of property in the Wilshire District also opposed the proposals, arguing that it was "socialistic" to create a public transit district, when transit had always been a private industry. They argued that rail rapid transit was in decline in New York and Philadelphia, cities with far higher population densities, so it could certainly never be successful in Los Angeles.

Interestingly, the proposal to form a new transit district and to upgrade transit operations was also opposed by the Los Angeles Transit Lines (LATL; formerly the Los Angeles Railway) and the Southern Pacific, which had acquired the Pacific Electric from Henry Huntington because it gave them important trackage for their freight operations. Starved for capital, the LATL was attempting to sell its rights-of-way, buildings, and tracks to the city in order to obtain needed cash and was offering to operate those lines for a fee once they were owned by the public. They feared that a new transit district would compete with them for patronage and public funding. The Southern Pacific was finding freight operations more profitable than passenger service, and it favored a strategy of converting passenger operations to buses, which would interfere less with their potential to move profitable freight trains on their tracks. They feared that the rail rapid transit plan would make it less likely that they could implement their freight strategy. When faced with this opposition, the RTAG decided to advocate rail transit and creation of a transit district but to insist that one proposal was not a requirement for the other and that other transit plans could also be studied.

After intense debate, in 1948 the Los Angeles City Council voted by a narrow margin of 8 to 6 against the creation of a special district to overhaul transit, the power of the outlying areas having prevailed over the central city interests. The L.A. Chamber of Commerce, smarting from its defeat, devoted its energies to attempting to ensure that the freeway system included many radial routes, which would provide the downtown area with an accessibility advantage similar to that which would have been provided by improved rail transit. A map of the Los Angeles freeway system indicates that they were successful to a large extent. While there are, of course, many freeways that do not directly serve the central area, downtown is the clear focus of a set of radials that, given its small share of regional employment, provide it with a surprising accessibility advantage in comparison with other centers of economic activity throughout the region. In the late forties and throughout the fifties, the Pacific Electric and LATL repeatedly petitioned the Public Utilities Commission for permission to substitute bus for rail service and to abandon some services entirely, and over time an increasing proportion of their requests was granted.

Between 1950 and 1980, a large number of rail transit proposals were placed on the public agenda by a variety of groups, and in fact the state legislature did create the Los Angeles Metropolitan Transportation Authority in 1952, which in 1964 became the Southern California Rapid Transit District, whose legislative mandate specified that rail rapid transit was to be undertaken and had the authority to levy sales taxes for the purpose of rail system construction if a successful vote of the public could be obtained. After several bond measures failed to achieve the required two-thirds vote of the populace, the legislature amended the requirement so that a simple majority would be needed, yet the sales tax and bond measures that followed this amendment also failed.

In 1976, impatient with these earlier legislative creations for their failure to initiate rail system construction, the state legislature acted again by creating the Los Angeles County Transportation Commission, with a mandate to seek funding through ballot propositions. Between 1948 and 1980, however, at least six different plans that included some form of rail transit were placed before the citizens, and all failed to be enacted. Some died without making it onto the ballot, while others were defeated at the polls. Among the most notable were a proposed monorail that would have run along the Los Angeles River and another that would have connected Van Nuys with Los Angeles International Airport, running above Interstate 405 (the San Diego Freeway). Another distinctive proposal was made vigorously by County Supervisor Baxter Ward. He promoted his proposed system aggressively, under the rubric of the "Sunset Coast Line," which promised many more miles of rail service at lower cost than other proposals by using existing rights-of-way and freeway medians. Ward believed that several earlier proposals had failed because their benefits were limited to so few areas that only a minority of the voters would have anything to gain from the proposals. His proposal, unabashedly configured to attract more votes, would do so by maximizing the miles of rail right-of-way and thus bringing more voters' residences within the rail service area. His Propositions R and T (for "rapid" and "transit") would have provided a half-cent sales tax for capital funding and another half cent for operating subsidies, but they, like the three other sales tax measures placed on the ballot between 1968 and 1978, were both defeated. So large a proportion of the region's voters lived at low and moderate densities and worked outside the central business district that it was repeatedly proving impossible to muster sufficient support to implement a regional rail system that would primarily benefit central business interests.

In the San Francisco Bay Area, a fragile and sometimes stormy consensus held downtown and suburban interests and construction companies together in support of a regional rail system. When BART trains were already running in the seventies, the central city of Los Angeles simply could not get together as comprehensive and lasting a coalition as was needed to gain local, state, and federal funding for any of the rail proposals. In large part this may be due to the fact that a larger share of regional employment, capital investment in real estate, and political influence reside in the central city of San Francisco, while in Angeles the central city lost ground to the suburbs at a faster pace. Even today, for example, downtown San Francisco provides in excess of 15 percent of its region's jobs, while the central city of Los Angeles provides less than 10 percent of its region's employment opportunities.

Federal support for transit capital investment first became available in 1964, and the availability of federal funds grew throughout the sixties and seventies, with Congress often earmarking the transit capital investment funds for projects in particular cities: Atlanta, Baltimore, Buffalo, and, of course, Washington, D.C. Despite this potentially lucrative source of funding for a rail system and Los Angeles's growth to a position of national leadership and prominence, its many efforts to undertake a rail construction program faltered. Since most of the rail proposals emphasized radial lines serving the downtown area, some felt that there was no reason to grant downtown a special benefit of accessibility; others focused their energies on the completion of the freeway network; others felt that the low densities of Los Angeles were better served by buses on busways; still others felt that rail would provide benefits, though not sufficient to justify its high costs and too localized to warrant a general sales tax increase. The El Monte Busway was built in the seventies in the median of the San Bernardino Freeway at much lower cost than rail transit would require, and the fact that it was perceived as a success weakened the arguments of the supporters of rail transit. Federal officials, including then U.S. Secretary of Transportation Drew Lewis, visited Los Angeles on several occasions and embarrassed the local business and professional communities by pointing out that the main reason federal funding for rail was not flowing into Los Angeles, as it was into other cities, was the failure of Los Angeles rail proponents and politicians to "get their act together." Eventually, however, several conditions changed which enabled a political consensus to be built.

BUILDING A SUCCESSFUL RAIL TRANSIT STRATEGY

Slowly, through the seventies and eighties, insightful analysis of the earlier failures, changing political conditions, and a complex set of tactics in pursuit of various self-interests led to a strategy that finally emerged as successful in obtaining both local and federal financial support and a broad local consensus to build rail transit in Los Angeles.

As had been the case for freeway construction earlier, a critical ingredient was the potential availability of federal funding at favorable matching ratios, reaching as high as 75 percent at some points in the 1980s. This meant that for each local or state dollar made available for rail construction, potentially as many as three federal dollars could be obtained. Added to this was the irritation that local officials felt when they realized that income taxes paid by Los Angeles area citizens were being used to build subways in other cities, while Los Angeles was not receiving its "fair share" of the national transit construction pie. Even if one preferred busways, it was hard to resist the argument that taxes collected in Los Angeles were being used to provide construction jobs in other cities but that Los Angeles was not getting its share of the resources. This situation gave impetus to renewed efforts to construct a political consensus that would finally lead to the adoption of a plan that could succeed in the political arena.

Second, coupled with the availability of federal funding for public transit was dramatically declining revenue for highway construction. While the state gasoline tax had been raised six times between 1947 and 1963, it was not increased at all between 1963 and 1982.[29] Although increased automobile ownership and use resulted in higher gasoline tax collections during those years, inflation reduced the real value of those collections, and increases in the costs of road construction and maintenance substantially exceeded the general rate of inflation. By the late seventies and early eighties, federal fuel economy standards were resulting in more and more vehicles that traveled over twenty miles per gallon of gasoline consumed, in comparison with earlier vehicles that attained mileage ratings between nine and twelve miles per gallon. This change substantially reduced state and federal gasoline tax revenues, which were all levied on a per-gallon basis. A vehicle that attains a rating of twenty miles per gallon produces as much congestion and roadway wear and tear but only half the gasoline tax revenue per mile of driving as does one rated at ten miles per gallon. Taken together, all of these factors meant that by the late seventies highway construction programs were being starved as miles of new road construction decreased dramatically from year to year. Construction contractors and unions were looking for greener pastures. Naturally, the federal transit capital investment funds did not escape their notice, and slowly groups that had previously been occupied in the provision of new highways began to see reasons to promote transit projects as well.

Third, it is important to note that by the 1970s images of modernity in transportation had changed dramatically throughout American society and especially in Los Angeles. While the bus had once eclipsed the rail car as the epitome of modernity, and the automobile had for sixty years been the ultimate symbol of individuality and material success, rail transit began to have a new and far more favorable public image. Buses were now seen as slow, dirty, crowded, polluting, and crime ridden, while rail transit was becoming symbolic of progress and municipal accomplishment. In addition, growing concern with energy conservation and air pollution gave transit an aura of public spiritedness and environmental conservation. Trains and monorails thus became symbols of technological advancement and environmental sensitivity, and proponents of rail transit investments began to market these images vigorously to the public.

Fourth, regional business and political leadership became far more sophisticated in dealing with the ongoing disagreements over priorities for transportation planning in Southern California. The perception became widespread that failure to reach a consensus on transportation priorities for the region was resulting in a failure to obtain federal funds. This led many participants in transportation policy making to set a higher priority on the goal of reaching a consensus. Slowly, more and more parties to transportation policy making realized that the best way to reach consensus was to broaden the object of that consensus to include within a single plan elements that were critical to different players. While many rail proponents had been favoring a regional system of between five and seven corridors of rail service, they were for tactical reasons willing to support a "consensus" plan that specified one starter line along the Wilshire corridor, clearly committed to following the starter line with other elements of the preferred regional plan. While many preferred express bus rapid transit on freeway "high-occupancy vehicle lanes" and others preferred capital investments in rail, participants in the policy debates decided that consensus was more important than choosing their preferred option; thus a plan was devised which included both rail and bus rapid transit. And to gain the support of the citizens in South Los Angeles and Long Beach, and in clear recognition that the southern sector had powerful political representatives, including, for example, County Supervisor Kenneth Hahn and Congressman Glen Anderson, who chaired the powerful House Public Works and Transportation Committee, all parties were asked to endorse a plan that included a light rail line from downtown Los Angeles through South Central Los Angeles, ending in Long Beach. Since energy conservation and air pollution were rising higher on the public agenda, a transportation demand management or ride-sharing component was also added to the plan.

In the late 1970s, a four-part transportation plan was agreed to by many downtown and outlying area interests: a heavy rail starter line (the Red Line), a light rail to Long Beach (the Blue Line), express buses on freeway high-occupancy vehicle (HOV) lanes, and transportation demand management or ride-sharing. This plan enabled all transportation policy interests in Los Angeles to tell federal and state funding authorities that indeed a regional consensus finally existed and that a regional program could now be undertaken with state and federal financing along with some local taxation. In 1980, the Los Angeles County Transportation Commission placed on the ballot a proposal called Proposition A, which would provide the local funding necessary to complete the package, especially because federal officials were increasingly demanding larger local shares in funding as a condition for granting federal support. Knowing that voters had previously defeated six separate transportation taxing measures, the framers of the proposition carefully crafted a measure that would, like the consensus plan, appeal to a broad cross section of voters. Proposition A asked voters to approve a half-cent sales tax and promised bus users a three-year rollback of fares from 85 cents to 50 cents. The proposition was also designed to appeal explicitly to those who favored rail transit for Los Angeles. In the booklet presenting the proposition to the voters was a map showing several potential rail corridors for future expenditure of funds. The map featured extremely broad lines so that nearly every neighborhood in the city was shown as being served by or accessible to the rail service. In an effort to obtain the support of local politicians throughout the county, the proposition also provided that some of the proceeds of the tax would be returned to each of the eighty-four cities in the county for use on transportation projects they favored. Carefully crafted to appeal to multiple interests, this proposition was approved by the voters in 1980, and Los Angeles finally was able to mobilize for the construction of a rail transit system.

Over time, as California voters approved a statewide gasoline tax increase in 1990, along with two bond measures to raise capital for transit projects, and as county voters approved in 1990 a doubling of the local transit sales tax, the transit plan has grown to include rail and HOV elements, bus electrification, suburban commuter rail services (Metrolink), and related plans that will collectively cost over $180 billion over the coming thirty years. From being unable to reach consensus on a single rail project prior to 1970, the Los Angeles region has again turned transportation politics on its head and is now pursuing the most vigorous transit capital investment program of any metropolitan area in the country, perhaps in the world. Many critics believe that the program is too ambitious and that it will eventually be truncated just as the freeway network was reduced during its thirty years of construction. Many believe that the rail network will, in the end, do little to alleviate air pollution and traffic congestion in a sprawling, low-density, auto-dependent region, unless land use patterns are changed dramatically to create high-density corridors of residences and businesses along the transit routes. Nevertheless, the dramatic reversal of transportation policy in Los Angeles is an impressive political accomplishment and an instructive lesson in public policy making.

CRITIQUE OF THE CURRENT REGIONAL TRANSPORTATION PROGRAM

A regional transportation planning policy that emphasizes the construction of a costly rail network, HOV lanes on highways, and the reduction of peak-hour work trips through transportation demand management (TDM) will surely result in the reduction of some trips that would otherwise be made by singly occupied automobiles. But as long as these approaches remain at the center of our regional policy, they will cumulatively have small effects and large costs. Traffic congestion will not increase as much as it would without these measures, but it will not improve nearly as much as it could under alternative policies. More people will use transit, carpools, and vanpools as a result of these programs, but at very high financial costs, and each year the increase in single-occupant auto trips will be far greater than the number of trips captured by these alternative modes. In other words, as these programs increase the numbers of transit riders and ride-sharers in absolute terms, they will still continue to lose ground to the automobile in relative terms. Unfortunately, the small absolute gains for transit and ride-sharing come with an enormous price tag of public subsidy, and it is clear that these programs cannot be cost effective within the current policy environment.

The Regional Rail Program

The Blue Line cost nearly a billion dollars of capital investment, and even when the amortization of those capital costs is excluded, the fares paid by its riders cover only 11 percent of the operating costs. This facility now serves slightly more than 30,000 riders per day, and about half of those riders previously made the same trip using the bus. For the former bus users, the prior mode required smaller public subsidies and accommodated their trips in shorter travel times. Overall, local buses in Los Angeles cover close to 40 percent of the costs from fares paid, and some crowded, inner-city routes manage to cover nearly 90 percent of their operating costs through their revenues. Presumably, the purpose of building the rail line was not to attract people from buses but rather to draw them out of automobiles. Thus, the 16,000 or so daily riders who previously made their trips by automobile are the real measure of the contribution of the Blue Line.

This is a tiny fraction of the forty million daily trips made in the Los Angeles Basin, and the total annual subsidy per new daily rail rider is in excess of $20,000.

The new Metrolink suburban commuter rail system is even more dramatic and photogenic, but it is extremely expensive in relation to the benefits it is providing. During the opening week, when rides were completely free and when some travelers were being further encouraged to use the train by free (public subsidized) taxi rides from the stations to their offices in the San Fernando Valley, the daily ridership reached as high as 7,500, or about as many people as are carried by one freeway lane in three hours at a tiny fraction of the public cost. When the "fare-free week" was over, however, ridership quickly dropped off to about 3,000 daily boardings, a few more than the number of people served by one freeway lane in ninety minutes. Of course, the "steady state" ridership remains to be seen. To achieve this level of ridership, taxpayers spent money on refurbishing three railroad rights-of-way, acquiring dozens of attractive bilevel rail cars and locomotives, and building or renovating eighteen rail stations despite the fact that there are roughly 200 daily boardings per station in the system. There is no doubt that as the Red Line and Green Line are added to the rail system, ridership will increase. But the most optimistic outcome will result in annual ridership of the combined system of rail lines of something less than one year's increase in the number of automobile commuters in this region, though it will have taken over a decade and more than $10 billion to build.

There are several reasons for this dilemma. First, in a region as extensive as Southern California and characterized by low and moderate population densities, even hundreds of miles of rail right-of-way can provide stations within reasonably comfortable distances (on foot, or by car, bus, or cycle) of only a tiny fraction of the homes of the region's residents and of the workplaces of only a tiny fraction of the region's employed workforce. For example, the Blue Line, Red Line, and Metrolink all provide improved access to the Los Angeles Central Business District (CBD), yet downtown jobs represent less than 5 percent of regional employment, and that share is steadily decreasing as suburban "edge cities" capture more and more of the employment in the region. In addition, because of the low-density development pattern of the Los Angeles region, many users of the new rail system must drive to the stations, and this discourages rail system usage: as long as one is in the car and driving, the marginal effort and cost of continuing to the destination are small in comparison with the effort of using a park-and-ride lot and paying to board the train.

Second, the rail rights-of-way in many cases, including the Blue Line and Metrolink, have been chosen because of their availability and not because

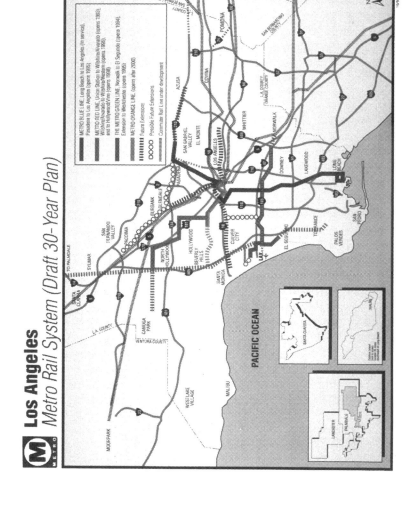

Figure 5.10. Draft of the thirty-year plan for the Metro Rail System.

they are located in corridors of heavy travel volume. Since they do not all serve the established corridors of traffic flow in the region, they can appeal to only a small segment of the travel market.

Third, even at subsidized prices, it is difficult for these services to compete with the cost of the automobile in a region in which more than 90 percent of workers are provided with free parking at work. For example, the monthly fare on Metrolink between Simi Valley and Union Station, though subsidized, is $176. This is surely significantly less than the total monthly cost of driving between Simi Valley and downtown, but among inner-city workers more than half of the cost of the auto trip is attributable to the monthly cost of parking. Where employers provide for free parking spaces having a market value in excess of $120, few commuters will forgo that benefit in exchange for the opportunity to pay for their own monthly rail ticket. Fortunately, under municipal and state legislation, employers are increasingly being required to offer their employees contributions to transit commuting in lieu of free parking spaces, and for some commuters this might begin to make a difference.

Fourth, many people forgo the train because they need to make use of their automobiles in the course of their daily work. Others couple trips for child care, education, and recreation with their daily work trips.

An unfortunate aspect of the high cost of rail services in relation to the low patronage is the fact that other transit alternatives are being forgone which could be more cost effective in Southern California. While costs for both rail routes and busways vary considerably depending on local conditions, one recent study estimated that the cost of a single mile of heavy rail construction was approximately equal to the cost of 3.2 miles of light rail line, or 13.3 miles of elevated busway.[30] In a region of low density, thirteen miles of busway would certainly provide far more public benefit per dollar of expenditure than one mile of underground subway. The opportunity to expend funds on busways, however, is limited by the extent of the commitments to the rail network.

Similarly, the financial resources expended on the rail network are providing dramatic improvements in expensive transit service for a relatively small number of suburban middle- and upper-income commuters. Alternative uses of the funds, however, could provide a much larger quantity of less expensive service for lower-income inner-city dwellers who are far more dependent on public transit and who use the service regularly. While uncrowded and heavily subsidized suburban trains are being expanded, packed inner-city buses that require far less subsidy are passing up crowds at inner-city bus stops. In an effort to prove that rail transit can be safe, regional transit authorities are expending more per year on the security of the Blue Line than they are on security for the entire regional bus system, despite the fact that ridership surveys indicate that fear of crime is the single most important factor deterring bus ridership.[31]

The current policy incorporates many inequities and is over time making the poor increasingly worse off in relation to the rich. The sales tax that is used to finance a major portion of the program falls disproportionately on the poor. The emphasis on suburban rail service transfers benefit to rich suburbanites, results in higher fares on the basic inner-city bus services on which the poor depend, and results in fewer inner-city local bus service expansions, which might provide greater benefits for the transit-dependent population.

The Regional Transportation Demand Management Program

The second dimension of transportation policy that was part of the regional consensus plan was transportation demand management. Southern California is today engaged in a far-reaching experiment in TDM aimed at reducing commuters' reliance on the single-occupant automobile for the journey to work. So far, the most tangible impacts on commuters have occurred through actions of the South Coast Air Quality Management District (SCAQMD). The severe air quality problem in the Los Angeles area has given rise to the district's Regulation XV. An important element of the region's air quality management plan, it requires employers to take responsibility for encouraging workers to consider alternatives to driving to work alone, including public transit, carpooling, vanpooling, walking, telecommuting, and cycling. Regulation XV was adopted by the board of the SCAQMD in October 1987, and its implementation began on 1 July 1988. It requires that public and private employers (firms, government agencies, schools, hospitals, etc.) having one hundred or more workers at any work site complete and file a plan for that site by which they intend to increase the average vehicle ridership (AVR) to a specified level within one year of the SCAQMD's approval of its plan. AVR is determined by surveying the workforce and is defined roughly as the quotient of the number of employees reporting to work between 6:00 and 10:00 A.M., divided by the number of motor vehicles driven by these employees. Employment sites in the central area of Los Angeles are assigned a target AVR of 1.75, and employers in low-density, outlying areas are expected to aim for a target AVR of 1.3. Intermediate areas, which constitute most of the area and most of the sites covered by the regulation, have AVR targets of 1.5. The SCAQMD anticipates that a regional AVR of 1.5 will be reached by the mid-1990s. The regulation also requires every covered work site to have a trained employee transportation coordinator (ETC), and it requires the employer to implement the plan once it has been approved. The South Coast Air Quality

Management District estimates that there are about 6,200 firms, agencies, and institutions that employ one hundred or more workers at individual sites and are subject to this regulation. Together they employ approximately 3.8 million workers.

The regulation is having a measurable impact on the travel patterns of the affected work sites. For a panel of 1,110 work sites that have completed one full year of implementation, overall average vehicle ridership, as defined by the SCAQMD, has increased from 1.22 to 1.25, a statistically significant increase, with an average increase among all the work sites of 3.4 percent. For a smaller sample of 243 work sites at which the regulation has been implemented for two full years, the AVR continued to rise in the second year to 1.30. Of the 1,110 employment sites included in the full panel, about 69 percent experienced increases in AVR during the first year, with just about 20 percent of the employment sites experiencing increases of more than 10 percent in their AVRs and half of the sample having increases of up to 10 percent. At another 31 percent of the work sites, AVR decreased during the first year of program implementation.[32]

Among the 1,110 employment sites in the full sample, the proportion of workers driving to work alone decreased from 75.7 percent in the first survey to 70.9 percent in the second. Among the smaller sample of 243 work sites for which data are available for two years, the proportion of workers driving alone declined by the end of the second year to 65.4 percent. The largest shift in mode was toward carpooling, and vanpooling also increased significantly. The public transit share and the proportion of workers walking and cycling, however, did not increase significantly. There was great variation in the extent to which employment sites are meeting the goals of Regulation XV, and many firms have done much more poorly than others. In general, the greatest improvement in AVR was found among employers whose initial AVR values were among the lowest, and, interestingly, the size of the workforce at a given site was not statistically associated with the extent of improvement in its AVR.[33]

The purpose of Regulation XV is to reduce auto emissions by reducing peak period travel, which is usually measured in terms of total vehicle miles of travel (VMT). Accurate calculation of VMT reduction would require identification of the particular employees who changed mode and the mode to which each changed. Employee information is not available, and VMT reduction must thus be estimated based on the overall number of trips reduced. Expanding this calculation to the population of companies subject to Regulation XV to generate the regional VMT impact yields an estimate of 1.3 million daily VMT, or a reduction of 0.4 percent of annual VMT. Since work trips constitute roughly a quarter of all trips, and only half of all work trips in the region are taken by employees of work sites having one hundred or more employees, it is not surprising that even the successful outcome of the regulation noted so far has resulted in an extremely small shift away from singly occupied automobiles when viewed in the context of all of the travel taking place in the region.

Very important to the evaluation of Regulation XV is an estimation of the costs it imposes on the regulated work sites. Many critics of expensive regional capital investment programs in rail networks cite transportation demand management as a much more cost-efficient alternative, so cost is an important dimension on which to evaluate the Regulation XV program to date. Unfortunately, it is extremely difficult to come up with authoritative cost estimates in which we can have a great deal of confidence. In a survey of 182 ETCs who were asked to estimate how much their employers were spending on Regulation XV programs, an extremely wide variation in estimates was obtained, probably reflecting the difficulty of properly accounting for costs. However, the mean estimated annual expenditure on implementing Regulation XV was $31 per employee, and the median was $20 per year per employee. The maximum value was $250 per employee per annum, and the standard deviation was $39.[34]

Case studies of five companies were also conducted. The case studies included a detailed examination of Regulation XV costs. These ranged from $12 to $263 per peak employee per year and excluded the costs of any ride-sharing activities that preceded the Regulation XV plan. The accounting firm of Ernst and Young conducted a detailed survey of employment sites subject to the regulation for the purpose of estimating the cost of trip reduction through TDM. Their survey of 5,763 regulated sites concluded that the average reported annual cost of Regulation XV was $105 per regulated employee and that the cost to the regulated community of removing one vehicle trip per day has been around $3,000 per year, or $11.76 per daily trip removed from the road.[35]

On the basis of the best available evidence in Southern California, then, it would appear that efforts to remove automobile trips from the road and to replace them by either rail transit or, through TDM, carpools, vanpools, or buses as well as trains can produce results that involve modest shifts away from singly occupied automobiles and toward alternative modes. However, in both cases these approaches produce modest numbers of changes in trips, and they result in costs to private employers and public agencies that are disappointingly high per trip shifted. It would seem on the basis of results summarized here that by themselves the strategies of increased investment in rail transportation and transportation demand management cannot provide large shifts in travel patterns at acceptable costs. It is probably not in the public interest to expand programs that have such high public and private costs per unit of benefit, and if the costs of these programs were widely understood by the public, political support for them might quickly erode. Approaches must be sought to either increase the cost-effectiveness of these approaches or find other ways of accommodating growth in travel in this region that are more cost effective than the policies that are currently being pursued.

ALTERNATIVE TRANSPORTATION POLICIES FOR SOUTHERN CALIFORNIA

Since the two major strategies for controlling traffic congestion and reducing the environmental consequences of widespread automobile dependency are likely to produce only modest successes at high social costs, transportation policy makers must consider alternative strategies that could produce more satisfying results in a more cost-effective manner. In the following sections, I consider policies that discourage growth in the use of the automobile by levying higher charges against it in an effort to come closer to recouping its full social costs through charges paid by drivers. In addition, I consider policies that attempt to reshape urban form so that land use patterns and the spatial distribution of activities will be more compatible with greater reliance on alternative modes of transportation. Finally, I consider the encouragement of entry into the transportation market of a wide range of alternative forms of transit service, including jitneys and cars for hire.

Pricing the Automobile Appropriately

One major reason for the modest shift of travel from the automobile to alternative modes, despite extensive investments in rail systems and despite expanding requirements for transportation demand management, is the fact that the automobile is so heavily subsidized through direct and indirect policies of the national, state, and local governments. The long list of subsidies to the automobile surely includes the exclusion of roads and highways from the local tax rolls, the support of traffic police and medical emergency services by property and sales taxes, and the setting of gasoline taxes and vehicle use fees that do not recoup the economic value of the "externalities" created by the automobile in the form of air pollution, energy resource depletion, and time losses due to congestion. Many workers are provided with additional direct subsidies for the use of automobiles in the form of free or highly subsidized parking spaces at their workplaces, reimbursement of automobile operating expenses when cars are used in the course of work, and the use of employer-owned or leased automobiles for work-related purposes and personal benefit. With the automobile priced so far below its full social cost, we are all encouraged to make greater use of it than we would if its price reflected its true costs to society. And it is extremely difficult to encourage people to use rail transit, buses, carpools, vanpools, or bicycles or to walk as long as the direct and indirect subsidies to the automobile are so high. Transportation policy incorporates enormous inefficiencies by, on one hand, encouraging profligate use of the automobile through numerous subsidies and, on the other, enacting regulations to require use of alternative modes or by attempting to encourage travelers to abandon their automobiles by providing even heavier subsidies to alternative modes. Undoubtedly, if the automobile were charged something closer to its full social cost, greater use of transit and ride-sharing modes would occur, and those modes would require lower levels of direct public subsidy in order to survive.

There are several ways in which public policy could levy more realistic charges against the automobile, but all would be difficult to enact under current political circumstances. Perhaps most obvious would be substantial increases in gasoline taxes. It is well known that European gasoline taxes are much higher than those in the United States and that Europeans continue to drive more fuel-efficient cars and to use transit for a larger share of their trips than do Americans, even though the use of the automobile in Europe is now actually rising at a faster rate than it is in the United States.[36] In some countries, gasoline prices exceed $4 per gallon, with the largest share of the selling price being the fuel tax. Many have advocated higher fuel taxes in the United States for the purpose of both recouping more of the social costs of automobile use and simultaneously encouraging the use of alternative modes. Major objections, of course, are from large users of fuels and from advocates for the poor, who believe that automobile fuel taxes would be regressive. Gasoline consumption is, however, clearly income related, and the regressiveness of higher gasoline taxes must be judged in relation to the very large recent increases in sales taxes (which are also regressive) to support transportation programs.

One of the most intriguing proposals involving gasoline prices would be to shift the burden for paying for part of our automobile insurance to the form of a per-gallon charge at the pump. While allowing automobile users to carry additional insurance beyond this minimum, such a plan would have several benefits. First, it would respond to the problem of uninsured motorists in Southern California, where it has been estimated that approximately 25 percent of automobiles on the road are in violation of the law requiring insurance. Second, such a program would add an element of equity to the system of charging for insurance, which is now based largely on geographic location of residence rather than use of the vehicle. Finally, the insurance premium in the form of a gasoline surcharge, by raising the unit cost of driving rather than treating insurance as a fixed cost, would contribute to the increased attractiveness of alternative modes in relation to the singly occupied automobile. Other policy options by which the social costs of the automobile might be more fully charged to those who benefit from automobile use include revisions to the annual vehicle registration fee structure. Present vehicle taxes are structured to be roughly proportional to the value of the vehicle. As an alternative it has been proposed, for example, that we rebase annual automobile registration fees so that they would be inversely proportional to their fuel efficiency. Registration charges would be lower for low-emission vehicles and higher for gas guzzlers. Such a fee structure would encourage the purchase of fuel-efficient vehicles and would thus use pricing mechanisms to encourage more socially responsive patterns of ownership and use.

A final policy option involving the cost of motor vehicle use would be the adoption of a system of congestion pricing, sometimes called road user charges. Proposed in one form or another for decades, congestion pricing might provide a way of aligning the charge for automobile use with the social cost of travel. Congestion pricing involves charging drivers more to travel at times and at locations at which congestion is heavy and less to travel at times and locations that are uncrowded. The goal of such charges is to encourage people to avoid traveling at the most congested times and places by using alternative modes (including carpooling), by shifting to less crowded routes, or by deferring travel to a time period at which the roads are less crowded. In theory, the charge for travel can be continually readjusted to eliminate congestion. While the total cost of owning and operating an automobile would appear to increase under a system of congestion pricing, substantial reductions in delay and improvements in travel times certainly have value to individual travelers and would result in far more efficient use of the existing transportation network. In principle, congestion pricing is similar to the form of pricing used by telephone companies to encourage calling in the evenings and on weekends and by airlines to encourage weekend flying.

Congestion pricing has two basic forms: area charges and facility charges. Area charges are today in use in Singapore and Trondheim and are being planned in detail for an increasing number of European and Asian cities to control traffic and increase revenue for transportation programs. A cordon line or border is set up around a congested area, and during defined periods of heavy congestion admittance to the area is granted only to vehicles paying an entry fee. Facility charges are tolls, more like traditional bridge or highway tolls, which are levied when a traveler uses a particular roadway segment during congested periods. The charges may be levied on a per-trip basis, or recorded electronically in an account for which a bill is sent weekly or monthly.

Some objections to congestion pricing arise over the administrative complexity of collecting the fees and the potential invasion of privacy that comes with certain systems of billing travelers for their charges. These problems have recently been substantially minimized by new communications technology. Automatic vehicle identification and debit card systems have been combined to provide convenient and efficient charging without violating the privacy of the driver.

More serious objections to congestion pricing deal with the impacts of such charges on the poor. Certainly, under normal circumstances, richer people will have a larger number of options available to them than the poor, and richer people will generally be less sensitive to tolls than poorer people. While this is true, there are approaches to congestion pricing that can mitigate potential negative impacts on the poor. Congestion tolls would generate large amounts of revenue (a recent Southern California case study suggests annual fee revenue of $3 billion) that could be used in part to offset losses to the poor. For example, if the revenues from the congestion tolls were used to fund improvements in public transit, the poor, who use transit in much larger numbers than the rich, would benefit directly from such a policy. In addition, it is possible to structure the congestion prices so that there is a lifeline rate available, just as there is for telephone service. Finally, income tax credits could be granted to poor people for their payments of congestion fees.[37]

There is also concern that if the major response to congestion pricing should be the rerouting of traffic to other areas or facilities, congestion could worsen in those areas even as it is lessened in the areas subject to the charges. In addition, some worry that the levying of a congestion charge in some areas may put them at an economic disadvantage in competition for tenants and customers, while others argue that the alleviation of congestion might well counterbalance the charge in the minds of potential customers and tenants.

Despite the fact that congestion pricing is receiving a growing amount of attention internationally, a great deal of political opposition will have to be overcome before the concept is adopted on a significant scale in California. Citizens will naturally be unsupportive of a system requiring them to pay for the use of roads that were in the first place built using the proceeds of taxes: it would be akin to charging twice for the same service. In addition, citizens do not trust planners who assure them that in exchange for the charges travelers will obtain the benefit of less congested highways.

Because of widespread skepticism regarding congestion pricing, several demonstration projects that do involve congestion fees will constitute important proving grounds for the concept in Southern California. On Route 91 in Orange County, for example, two lanes are being added to the median by a private corporation. Costs of construction and of operating the facility will be covered by tolls. Current plans call for varying the toll with traffic conditions and vehicle occupancy. Vehicles with three or more occupants will be exempt from the tolls. This will provide an important initial test of commuter acceptance of highway pricing in Southern California. Other demonstration projects are being planned, funded both by Caltrans and by the federal government under the Intermodal Surface Transportation Efficiency Act (ISTEA).

Influencing Transportation by Policies Affecting Urban Form and Land Use

The urban form of Southern California—large expanses of low- and medium-density residential and commercial activities punctuated by moderate- to high-density activity centers or "edge cities"—is considered by many to be the major cause of our steadily increasing travel volumes and the ultimate source of our traffic congestion, automotive air pollution, and inefficient energy consumption patterns. It is argued, therefore, by many urbanists and environmentalists that policies should be pursued which will lead to the "densification" of the metropolitan area, especially at transportation nodes such as rail transit stations. Higher-density areas, especially of mixed land uses, provide opportunities for people to satisfy their needs by traveling shorter distances and thus result in fewer trips per capita. Quite a few architects and urban designers are attempting to incorporate this principle into plans for new developments, such as the massive Playa Vista project near Los Angeles International Airport. This development is one of several that incorporate the concept of "neotraditional town planning," including higher densities, more diverse mixes of residential and commercial land uses in close proximity to one another, and the provision of higher than typical levels of transit service within the developed areas.

These proposals are extremely interesting, yet their prospect for alleviating traffic congestion remains largely unproven. Among the important reasons for skepticism is the fact that built form changes very slowly over time, so this approach can yield only marginal results in the short term. At least two-thirds of the existing built environment was in place fifty years ago, and even if we were to adopt a strategy of promoting higher densities and mixed uses in many new developments over the coming decades, the effect of these policies would have to be phased in over fifty years or more. In addition, land use is regulated by local governments that jealously resist the centralization of control over land use at the regional level and that treasure the low-density patterns of their own communities. For this approach to have a noticeable impact on urban form and travel behavior, hundreds of local jurisdictions would have to change their land use development regulations, and the existing population would in many instances resist such change because they would perceive these approaches as threatening to the lifestyles they have consciously chosen when they made their residential location decisions.

It is clear that most advocates of densification are located disproportionately in Los Angeles County, which, of course, is already developed to a greater extent than the rest of the region. Some cynics and some realists point out that advocating densification is merely a strategy to ensure that Los Angeles County will capture an increasing share of future growth in comparison with the recent trend of suburban expansion and that the strategy may be motivated by a desire for the fiscal returns from growth rather than from the reduction of traffic congestion. In outlying areas there is no evidence whatsoever that residents or commercial investors prefer moderate- or higher-density development patterns in comparison with those that have recently prevailed.

It is very important to note that while traffic reduction by density increases has become increasingly popular among environmentalists and urban reformers, many scholars have demonstrated that low-density development patterns do not necessarily result in heavier traffic congestion, and there is little empirical evidence that this approach is fundamentally sound. While authors like Peter G. Newman and Jeffrey R. Kenworthy demonstrate that higher-density cities generate fewer trips and lower energy consumption per capita than lower-density cities, they accomplish this by comparing different cities at one point in time rather than by tracking particular cities over many decades.[38] Thus Los Angeles is compared with Hong Kong or New York in order to reach the conclusion that density can make the intended difference, but there is no guarantee that the adoption of such densities in Los Angeles would result in the intended outcome. In fact, most of the high-density cities that are cited as examples were major metropolises long before the coming of the automobile, and over time they are becoming less dense as lower-density suburbs are added at their peripheries and as higher rates of automobile ownership occur in response to rising incomes. Traffic congestion in New York and Hong Kong and other high-density cities is, if anything, increasing more rapidly than congestion in Los Angeles And, in contrast, scholars who have studied metropolitan areas like Los Angeles over time note that development at the fringe is not increasing trip volumes or trip lengths substantially in lower-density metropolises.[39]

It is possible to reconcile these views, which might seem on the surface to be in disagreement with one another. While it is true that higher-density areas do generate fewer automobile trips *per capita* or *per dwelling unit* because their residents can walk, cycle, or use transit to accomplish more of their travel needs, it is obvious that higher-density areas are by definition also characterized by higher populations and larger numbers of dwelling units *per unit of area* than are lower-density communities. While they may be more "efficient" by generating fewer auto trips and vehicle miles of travel per capita, their higher densities result in a larger number of total trips. Thus while New York has higher population densities than Los Angeles and a greater jobs-housing balance than Los Angeles, and New Yorkers consequently make higher proportions of their trips by walking and using public transit than do Angelenos, the fact that there are more New Yorkers per square mile still yields very high levels of traffic congestion on the streets of that city. Anyone who has visited New York or Hong Kong must be skeptical of proposals to reduce congestion here by increasing densities, because congestion levels in those cities are at least as great as congestion levels here despite the fact that more trips are made there by transit and on foot.

Would it be good policy to adopt a program to make Los Angeles more like Hong Kong or New York in the face of congestion levels in those cities and evidence that over time those cities are becoming more like Los Angeles? And would the citizens of Los Angeles support policies to encourage much higher densities here? The answer to these questions is not obvious, but should be left to the land market and to policy choices that are based on more complex sets of issues than traffic congestion alone. It may well be true that many citizens in this region would prefer to live at higher densities in "neotraditional neighborhoods" than do so presently, and this may be the result of land use policies that have restricted higher densities in regions like this one. For that reason we might encourage more diversity in our built form and more experiments like Playa Vista which would provide a wider range of choices for citizens among a greater variety of built environments and which might produce more efficient travel patterns even while increasing traffic volumes beyond their current levels.

In addition, it may be rational and appropriate to encourage higher densities and greater mixes of land uses at locations that are well served by public transit. In fact, as noted above, the ongoing commitment to increasing the extent of the rail network in Los Angeles constitutes a commitment to an extremely high-cost form of urban transportation, which will in all likelihood garner very little patronage in relationship to its capacity and cost. Thus it would seem essential to encourage higher densities at the station sites in order to produce greater patronage and thereby to avoid a financial disaster that could flow from the need for ever-increasing subsidies if we are determined to keep the rail system operating over the coming decades. Rather than needing rail to alleviate traffic congestion due to growth, this region may actually need higher densities at the station sites in order to minimize the costs of the adopted transportation system. But even substantial commitments to greater mixing of land uses and to higher density at the station sites will make only a marginal change in the overall travel patterns of this region for decades to come, and it is difficult to accept policies jointly advocating rail construction and higher density as "the solution" to growing traffic congestion over time. The BART impact studies and several studies of the Washington, D.C., Metro have demonstrated that mixed-use land developments in the vicinity of the station sites have resulted in increased traffic congestion in those areas. We must be careful to acknowledge, therefore, that whatever benefits may flow from increased density, reductions in traffic congestion—especially local reductions—are not likely to be among the primary justifications for aggressive mixed-use development at the station sites.

A Wider Range of Mass Transportation Choices

If we accept the notion that mass transit consists of a wide range of transportation modes that can function as alternatives to the singly occupied automobile, we can envision many opportunities to increase the efficiency of the local transportation system which are far more cost effective than the policies presently in place. For example, if we consider carpooling, vanpooling, shared ride taxies, jitney services, local buses, and employer-operated buspools as examples of mass transportation modes, in combination these modes can improve mobility substantially within a future transportation system that remains dominated by the automobile.

The most successful transit options will be those that compete most closely with the automobile, and that means that they should be able to connect many low-density communities, provide relatively immediate response times, and overall door-to-door costs and travel times that approximate those of the automobile. As automobile subsidies are reduced, a larger range of such alternative services become economically feasible. In many parts of the world, the private sector is providing a wide range of such options, and they might have a significant role to play in the future of Los Angeles. In Queens, New York, thousands of Caribbean immigrants have started operating vans that take commuters from residential communities to Manhattan workplaces at fares slightly higher than those charged by the urban transit system, and they are doing a booming business. The success in Los Angeles of the airport shuttle vans provides another example of a system that moves large numbers of people and reduces congestion in comparison with the automobile. Rather than requiring heavy capital investments like rail systems, these alternatives require very little public investment. In combination with modern communications technology and the availability of increasing numbers of HOV lanes, such services can offer quick response, lower-cost travel options for the citizens of this region. Furthermore, if barriers to entry into businesses of this type were lowered, and if the automobile were priced at levels closer to its true social costs, such options would occur without major public expenditures and would provide jobs for many more workers in the transportation sector. But when heavy capital investments are made in centralized transportation networks, there is a tendency to retain regulations that eliminate private van services and jitneys from competition with the public system and thereby to protect the integrity of the public system by guaranteeing it monopoly status.

In addition, if heavy investments of capital in rail transit were reduced, it would also make funding more readily available to increase local bus services that are today overcrowded and that are given too little attention by public authorities. Transit deficits would be reduced by increasing bus services on heavily traveled inner-city local routes that are the backbone of the transit system, that require the lowest subsidies per passenger served, and that provide essential services for the poor, carless, elderly, and disabled populations. If these improvements were coupled with adaptive improvements to the street network, such as the provision of exclusive bus lanes on more city streets, traffic signal priority for buses, and bus turnouts and off-street loading facilities, higher volumes of bus traffic could be accommodated without a worsening of street traffic congestion.

Finally, if employers were to take some of the money they now invest in subsidies for single-occupant automobiles and redirect it into subsidies for vanpools and company-operated buses, a wider range of transit options would be available for the workforce to choose from.

A ROLE FOR TECHNOLOGICAL IMPROVEMENTS

Many look to technological breakthroughs to enhance the future transportation network, and it is extremely dramatic, large-scale innovation that receives the most attention. Magnetic levitation vehicles and high-speed trains capture the imagination of the press and the citizens, though they hold open the prospect for benefiting only a relatively small number of people. Almost unacknowledged are other technological improvements that have actually contributed much more to the progress of the transportation system. Recent improvements in automobile fuel economy and decreases in automobile emissions have actually been very dramatic and have substantially improved well-being in the Los Angeles region. There is reason to expect technological progress in the coming decade which will continue to improve access to and increase the efficiency of the transportation system.

Communications technology is advancing very rapidly, and we can soon expect travelers to be able to receive a great deal more information on their travel options than is presently available. For example, within a very few years, using telephones or computer terminals, travelers will be able to be informed of the location of the next bus on a certain route and its expected arrival time at a certain point. This technology is already in use in a few test locations in Europe, and it is functioning quite well. In addition, we are very close to having available what transportation officials refer to as a "universal fare medium," a transportation "smart card" that employs microchip technology to allow its holder to pay different fares—depending on mode, trip length, and time of day—using a single device very similar to a credit card.

While not likely to see application in the immediate future, automated vehicle control systems are actively being developed which will enable higher volumes of travel on existing roadways by permitting vehicles to move at higher speeds and at closer spacing than is now possible. Although such technologies are not likely to be applied to general automobile traffic during the coming decade, they will be applied to bus transportation and possibly to HOV lanes in the near future. Technological contributions of these sorts are likely to make marginal but significant contributions to transportation system efficiency and effectiveness in the coming decade and will become increasingly more salient in the early decades of the coming century.

CONCLUSION

The history of transportation policy in Southern California is complex and politically charged. Politics is the art of oversimplification, and very few citizens of this region understand the complexity of its transportation history. Instead, we repeat simple platitudes that are widely agreed on by lay persons and political leaders. Over time, many have argued that an automobile-dominated system or a rail-dominated system is necessary for the future well-being of the region. It has been noted less often that to a great extent the investments made in highways and rail lines have complemented one another in creating the low-density, multicentered region. In many instances, proposals were presented using populist language intended to mobilize citizen support for one proposal by associating a competing concept with monopoly capitalists; in earlier days the villains were the railroads, which perpetuated terrible service, and more recently the villain was General Motors, which destroyed an allegedly wonderful system. In each era, a particular approach to providing transportation in Los Angeles was portrayed as an environmental savior and as a successor to an environmental disaster associated with an earlier age. In each period, a particular transportation plan or technology was presented to the public as the epitome of modernity and inventiveness, though often the favored technology was state of the art. In each period, large-scale plans—some for highway networks and some for rail transit lines—were adopted but never fully implemented because costs rose beyond what had been forecast, because funding was not available for their completion, and because public enthusiasm for the whole system declined after part of it was built. Often, this decline in public enthusiasm resulted from the fact that system plans promoted in different periods of time were vastly oversold as panaceas for traffic congestion, while the negative social and environmental impacts of each plan or proposal were hardly mentioned until they were experienced by many unsuspecting citizens.

Today, Los Angeles has embarked on an enormous capital investment in a regional rail system, which is envisioned over the coming decades to have many corridors and extensions. There is also currently a strong commitment to transportation demand management, the effort to encourage behavioral shifts away from the use of singly occupied automobiles. The history reviewed in this essay provides a very good guide to the likely future of these recent policies. It is already clear that the capital investment needed to complete the current rail plan will be much higher than the estimates that have been presented to the public. As several transit routes go into operation, I believe they will carry fewer passengers than have been forecast and that land use changes hoped for in the vicinity of the station sites will occur far slower than the proponents of the system anticipate. Similarly, public opposition to transportation demand management on the basis of its limited results at fairly high cost is already building. Traffic congestion on the freeways will hardly be affected by the presence of the rail system and the modest successes of TDM, since even optimistic forecasts indicate that the rail system will carry only a tiny fraction of the region's trips and that TDM will serve a reasonably small clientele. As more communities are disrupted by subway construction, the public will undoubtedly tire of the promises of environmental benefits and congestion relief. As costs rise to complete the system, later elements of the proposed rail network will be deleted, as were many of the elements of the proposed freeway network of Los Angeles. Similarly, TDM benefits are already looking small in comparison to their costs and their restrictions on individual freedom of choice. Looking back at the 1990s from the perspective of 2030 or so, we will describe this era as being quite like the period of rail construction in the period 1910–1920 or the highway building of the 1950s: it was a period of action and change, but the plans were not fully implemented for lack of funding, because the political consensus that resulted in their implementation was transitory and because the concept of modernity in urban transportation was a shallow notion based on fad and fashion, which changed during the implementation of the current plan.

Melvin M. Webber argues eloquently that increased mobility by citizens of Los Angeles is not a social, environmental, or economic problem. Indeed, people should have the opportunity to travel more than they do now, rather than less. Mobility means access to opportunities for employment, health care, recreation, and social interaction, and the goal of transportation policy should continue to be to increase those opportunities rather than to restrict them.[40] The challenge before us is to find ways of increasing mobility while avoiding its negative consequences—congestion, air pollution, and the inefficient use of energy. The complexity of the urban area, of individual decision making about residential and work location and travel, and of American politics makes it difficult to conceive of a single policy or technology that can promise an immediate increase in mobility while decreasing the negative impacts of the transportation system.

Automobile users must be assessed the social costs they are imposing on the urban system. Policies that achieve this will have a positive effect on the local economy and quality of life. In the presence of appropriate accounting for the social costs of the automobile, a wide variety of transportation alternatives are both feasible and efficient; in the absence of that policy, the construction of high-capacity systems having high capital costs is inadequate to counter the effects of deep and varied subsidies supporting ever-increasing automobile ownership and use. It is doubtful that any single policy aimed at recasting urban form in service of transportation policies can have a salient effect on the future of the region, but a wider variety of urban forms can respond to appropriate social pricing of the automobile to increase future choices of living environments as well as of travel modes.

NOTES

1. Scott L. Bottles, "Bad Rail Service Began LA's Auto Obsession," *Los Angeles Times,* Opinion Section, 13 September 1987, 3.

2. Sam Bass Warner, *Street Car Suburbs: The Process of Growth in Boston, 1870– 1900* (Cambridge: Harvard University Press and MIT Press, 1962).

3. K. H. Schaeffer and Elliot Sclar, *Access for All: Transportation and Urban Growth* (Harmondsworth: Penguin, 1975).

4. Martin Wachs, "Autos, Transit and the Sprawl of Los Angeles," *Journal of the American Planning Association* 50, no. 3 (1984): 297–310.

5. Spencer Crump, *Ride the Big Red Cars: How Trolleys Helped Build Southern California* (Corona del Mar, Calif.: Trans-Anglo Books, 1962), 96.

6. Wachs, "Autos, Transit and the Sprawl of Los Angeles," 298.

7. C. Warren Thornthwaite, *Internal Migration in the United States* (Philadelphia: University of Pennsylvania Press, 1934), 18.

8. James Clifford Findley, "The Economic Boom of the Twenties in Los Angeles" (Ph.D. dissertation, Claremont Graduate School, 1958).

9. Mel Scott, *American City Planning Since 1890* (Berkeley, Los Angeles, and London: University of California Press, 1971), 189–190.

10. Crump, *Ride the Big Red Cars,* 251.

11. Mark S. Foster, "The Decentralization of Los Angeles During the 1920s" (Ph.D. dissertation, University of Southern California, 1971), 143.

12. Ibid.

13. Scott Bottles, *Los Angeles and the Automobile: The Making of the Modern City* (Berkeley, Los Angeles, and London: University of California Press, 1987).

14. Bradford C. Snell, "American Ground Transport: A Proposal for Restructuring the Automobile, Truck, Bus, and Rail Industries," report presented to the Subcommittee on Antitrust and Monopoly of the Committee on the Judiciary, U.S. Senate, 26 February 1974.

15. Robert M. Fogelson, *The Fragmented Metropolis: Los Angeles, 1850–1930* (Cambridge: Harvard University Press, 1967), 250.

16. Bottles, *Los Angeles and the Automobile,* 99.

17. Eli Bail, *From Railway to Freeway: Pacific Electric and the Motor Coach* (Glendale, Calif.: Interurban Press, 1984).

18. Lawrence R. Vesey, "The Pacific Electric Railway Company, 1910–1953: A Study in the Operations of Economic, Social and Political Forces upon American Local Transportation," unpublished manuscript, 1953, available through the library of the Los Angeles County Metropolitan Transportation Authority; Carl W. Stocks, "Improving the Bus to Increase Its Usefulness," *Electric Railway Journal* (June 1930): 387–390.

19. A. T. Warner, "Development of the Bus for Mass Transportation," *Electric Railway Journal* (December 1930): 745–746.

20. Jonathan E. D. Richmond, "Transport of Delight: The Mythical Conception of Rail Transit in Los Angeles" (Ph.D dissertation, Massachusetts Institute of Technology, 1991).

21. Transportation Engineering Board, City of Los Angeles, *A Transit Program for the Los Angeles Metropolitan Area,* 7 December 1939.

22. Ibid., vi.

23. Brian Deane Taylor, "When Finance Leads Planning: The Influence of Public Finance on Transportation Planning and Policy in California" (Ph.D. dissertation, University of California, Los Angeles, 1992), 24–25.

24. David W. Jones, "California's Freeway Era in Historical Perspective," paper prepared for the California Department of Transportation, Institute of Transportation Studies, University of California, Berkeley, 1989.

25. Taylor, "When Finance Leads Planning," 24–25.

26. Quoted in Taylor, "When Finance Leads Planning," 38.

27. Taylor, "When Finance Leads Planning," 38.

28. Sy Adler, "Why BART but No LART? The Political Economy of Rail Rapid Transit Planning in the Los Angeles and San Francisco Metropolitan Areas, 1945–57," *Planning Perspectives* 2 (1987): 149–174.

29. Taylor, "When Finance Leads Planning," 130.

30. Russell Driver, "Transit Construction Costs," unpublished manuscript, Graduate School of Architecture and Urban Planning, UCLA, 1992.

31. Maritz Marketing Research Incorporated, "Bus Operations Study," report prepared for the Southern California Rapid Transit District, 30 September 1991.

32. Genevieve Giuliano, Keith Hwang, and Martin Wachs, "Employee Trip Reduction in Southern California: First Year Results," Transportation Research 27A, no. 2 (1993): 125–137.

33. Ibid.

34. Martin Wachs and Genevieve Giuliano, "Employee Transportation Coordinators: A New Profession in Southern California," *Transportation Quarterly* 46, no. 3 (1992): 411–427.

35. Ernst and Young, "South Coast Air Quality Management District Regulation XV Cost Survey," Los Angeles, August 1992.

36. John Pucher, "Urban Travel Behavior as the Outcome of Public Policy: The Example of Modal Split in Western Europe and North America," *Journal of the American Planning Association* 54, no. 4 (Autumn 1988): 509–520.

37. Kenneth Small, "Using the Revenues from Congestion Pricing," *Transportation* 19 (1992): 359–381.

38. Peter G. Newman and Jeffrey R. Kenworthy, "Gasoline Consumption and Cities: A Comparison of U.S. Cities with a Global Survey," *Journal of the American Planning Association* 55 no. 1 (Winter 1989): 24–37.

39. Peter Gordon, Harry W. Richardson, and Myung-Jin Jun, "The Commuting Paradox: Evidence from the Top Twenty," *Journal of the American Planning Association* 57, no. 4 (Autumn 1991): 416–419.

40. Melvin M. Webber, "The Joys of Automobility," in *The Car and the City: The Automobile, the Built Environment, and Daily Life,* ed. Martin Wachs and Margaret Crawford, 274–284 (Ann Arbor: University of Michigan Press, 1992).

SIX

How Eden Lost Its Garden

A Political History of the Los Angeles Landscape

Mike Davis

In March 1930, the most distinguished citizens committee in Los Angeles history submitted its final report to city and county authorities. A letter of transmittal, signed by Mary Pickford, John O'Melveny, J. B. Lippincott, Irving Hellman, and others warned of a situation "so disquieting as to make it highly expedient to impress upon the public the present crisis in the welfare of Los Angeles."[1]

With nearly one-fourth of the city out of work in that grim depression year, it might be presumed that the report's urgency was focused on unemployment relief or soup kitchens for the hungry. In fact, the attention of the 162 prominent members of the Citizens' Committee on Parks, Playgrounds and Beaches was riveted on the "park and recreation crisis." This was less strange than it might seem.

As the report's authors, the renowned urban design firm of Olmsted Brothers and Bartholomew and Associates, pointed out, accessible open space was the foundation of an economy capitalized on climate, sports, and outdoor leisure. But the region's scenic beauty was being eroded on all sides by rampant, unregulated private development. Los Angeles's future prosperity was directly threatened by the increasing discrepancy between tourists' buoyant expectations and their disillusioning experiences in the Land of Sunshine.

> The widely-advertised attractions of climate and scenery bring thousands to the Los Angeles Region every year. They find the climate fully equal to expectations but the facilities by which the out-of-doors may be enjoyed prove a surprise and disappointment. . . . The beaches, which are pictured in the magazines to attract eastern visitors, are suffering from the rapid encroachment of private use; the wild canyons are fast being subjected to subdivision and cheek-by-jowl cabin construction; the forests suffer annually from devas-

tating fires; the roadsides are more and more disfigured by sign boards, shacks, garages, filling stations, destruction of trees.[2]

Frederick Law Olmsted, Jr., and Harland Bartholomew further observed that "the things that make [Los Angeles] most attractive are the very ones that are the first to suffer from changes and deteriorate through neglect." Although Los Angeles spent more than other cities to advertise its charms, it paradoxically invested less to preserve or enhance them. The deficiency of parks was "positively reprehensible" and the region fell "far short . . . of the minimum recreation facilities of the average American city." Moreover, as the authors acknowledge, "all this has been realized for years."[3]

Indeed, Charles Fletcher Lummis, editor of *Out West* and impresario of the "Arroyo Culture," had thundered against Los Angeles's Victorian elites for "impoverishing the future" through their reckless alienation of the original pueblo lands.

> As late as 1856 the city owned eighty per cent of its area of some 17,000 acres. It gave this priceless heritage away—generally for nothing, and altogether for next to nothing—without even once getting an equivalent or a good bargain. . . . We would have the finest parks in the world, and the finest public buildings—and all endowed beyond the dreams of avarice. As it is, nothing was left in the city but the Plaza and some riverbed when we began to take notice.[4]

By the early 1900s, moreover, even this residual public domain was under threat, as the once arcadian landscape of the Los Angeles River was transformed into a sewer for the city's expanding industrial district. The Rev. Dana Bartlett, planning advocate and settlement house pioneer, battled the corporate "Octopus" of the Southern Pacific Railroad (the largest floodplain landowner) in an unsuccessful crusade to reclaim the riverbed as a nature preserve and playground for the children of the "congested areas" east of downtown.[5] Meanwhile local leaders of the Progressive movement indicted Los Angeles's meager and poorly maintained parks as the "shame of the city." "Some of our parks," they complained, "are filthy to the grade of a public nuisance and should have been condemned long ago."[6]

It was in this context that Charles Mulford Robinson, the famed apostle of the City Beautiful, included a comprehensive plan for parks, boulevards, beautification of the Los Angeles River, and a civic acropolis on Bunker Hill in his 1907 report to the Los Angeles Municipal Art Commission.[7] In order to finance his heroic proposals, he urged the city to "grasp the big idea" and become a land developer in its own right.

> There will be great gain if the city can obtain that authority which the cities of Pennsylvania and Ohio have already secured, and by which the great municipal improvements of Europe and South America have been financed— the right to acquire property on the edge of a public improvement, in order

to protect that improvement, and to recoup the cost of making it by the resale
of the property at the enhanced value which the improvement bestows.[8]

He cautioned that "the tourist metropolis of the country . . . simply cannot
afford to stand still, or, rather, with your increasing population . . . to go
from bad to worse in congestion, in city discomfort and ugliness." Robinson
hinted that if Los Angeles wavered in its commitment to public space, other
"more beautiful" cities would usurp its destiny (was he already thinking of
Seattle?).[9]

By the time Olmsted and Bartholomew surveyed the same problem
twenty years later, the equivalent of the population of Philadelphia (nearly
two million people) had moved to the Los Angeles region. Their 1930 report was, first of all, a stinging critique of the giddy twenties boom that,
after its collapse in the oil scandals of 1927–1928, left 175 square miles of
vacant, unsold lots on the city's fringes, but only a few hundred acres of
new parkland.[10] Developers had stubbornly ignored official pleas to dedi-
cate parks for their subdivisions, and thus, as the population soared, per
capita recreation space drastically decreased. By 1928, for example, parks
comprised a miserable 0.6 percent of the surface of the metropolis and
barely half an inch of publicly owned beach frontage was left for each citizen of Los Angeles County.[11]

With considerable acuity Olmsted and Bartholomew analyzed why public
investment in open space had lagged so far behind the growth of population and regional income. In the first place, new tax revenues were swallowed up by aqueduct bonds and the high infrastructure costs of the low-
density, often scattered-site, subdivisions that were officially identified with
the region's unique semirural quality of life.[12] Powerful homeowners' associations, meanwhile, opposed every attempt to pass specific assessments for
parks or recreation. A selfish, profit-driven presentism ruled Southern California. As Olmsted and Bartholomew paraphrased the dominant attitude,
"The benefit of parks brought now will accrue largely in future years and
even to future generations. We can get along without them a while longer,
anyhow. And if land at those prices is a good purchase, we would rather
use our money to get lots on speculation for personal profit than give it up
in taxes for our share of a park system."[13]

Indeed, speculation—"excessive and fictitious prices for raw land"—was
the crux of the landscape crisis. The "high capitalization of future rental
values" in even the most marginal or hazardous terrain made a comprehensive program of park building prohibitively expensive.[14] Ironically, the
entire inflationary process was subsidized by local government. Olmsted
and Bartholomew were especially critical of the costly public outlays (e.g.,
roads, sewers, fire protection, flood control, etc.) that encouraged promoters to subdivide scenic canyons, streambeds, and foothills.

It costs so much in the long run to adapt rough mountain lands satisfactorily to ordinary intensive private uses that their real net value as raw materials for such use is generally far less than their value for watershed protection and for public recreation. Unfortunately in the local speculative land market this fact is often ignored and subdivision sales are made which commit the community to extravagant wasteful private and public expenditures for converting a good thing of one kind into a poor thing of another kind.[15]

The Gordian knot of land speculation, however, could be cut with a single, decisive blade: *hazard zoning.* Since the "burden of wrong development does not fall on the purchase alone, and scarcely ever on the vendor, but most heavily on the community at large," the municipality could justifiably invoke its powers to exclude speculative development from floodplains and hillsides (as well as, by implication, from surficial earthquake fault zones and chronic wildfire corridors).[16]

Together with radically enlarged public ownership of ocean frontage, the redemption of Los Angeles's riparian landscapes was the key to Olmsted and Bartholomew's elegant design for a unified regional system of beaches, parks, playgrounds, and mountain reserves. At their 1924 conference, Los Angeles County regional planners had already recognized the crucial role of river courses as the "easiest and often the shortest connection between the mountain and the beach playground areas." In addition to advocating public ownership of the oceanfront, the conference recommended "that all principal natural drainage channels be acquired and controlled by the community for the highest public use."[17] In their elaboration, Olmsted and Bartholomew demonstrated how greenbelts (or "pleasureway parks" in their slightly awkward terminology) could simultaneously solve problems of flood control, recreation, and traffic congestion. Using hazard zoning to force land values downward and "stop the ill-directed spread of the population," they proposed to transform the major flood channels and associated wetlands into a 440-mile network of multipurpose parkways reminiscent of Frederick Law Olmsted's famous 1887 design for Boston's Back Bay fens.[18]

The report further stressed the importance of embedding regional highways in attractive, tree-lined park corridors screened from adjacent industrial and residential developments.[19] "Parkways should be greatly elongated real parks . . . several thousand feet in width," parallel to broad natural flood channels and offering a variety of recreational experiences. Parkways thus conceived would reinforce the role of natural hydrology in dividing up the otherwise monotonous coastal plain into attractive, well-defined community landscapes. Finally, Olmsted and Bartholomew's plan explicitly redistributed park and open-space resources to the advantage of the neglected working-class districts south and east of downtown: "Those of lower incomes generally live in small-lot, single-family home districts, and have more children and less leisure time in which to go to distant parks and recreational areas. These families comprise 65 percent of the population, and they should be given first consideration."[20]

KILLING THE LOS ANGELES RIVER

The 1930 report is a window into a lost future. A heroic culmination of the City Beautiful era in American urban design, it was also the final fruit of Olmsted Brothers and Bartholomew's intense, decade-long involvement in California landscape planning. (The firm also prepared master plans for Los Angeles County highways, the state park system, and the preservation of watershed in the East Bay hills and designed the acclaimed suburb Palos Verdes Estates.)[21]

Frederick Law Olmsted, Jr., and Harland Bartholomew were quiet, conservative reformers whose personal utopia was park-rich Minneapolis, not Soviet Russia. Yet if their proposals had been implemented, the results would have nonetheless been virtually revolutionary. The existing hierarchy of public and private space in Los Angeles would have been fundamentally overturned. A dramatically enlarged Commons, not the private subdivision, would have become the commanding element in the Southern California landscape. Preserved natural ecosystems (Olmsted was a passionate proponent of native flora) would have imposed clear boundaries on urbanization. The speculative real estate market would have been counterbalanced by a vigorous social democracy of beaches and playgrounds. Needless to say, such extravagant conceptions of public space alarmed guardians of Los Angeles's reputation as the capital of antiradicalism and the open shop. (One of the major local events of 1930 was the LAPD's brutal attack on a peaceful May Day rally at Pershing Square.) The *Los Angeles Times,* in particular, disdained proposals to municipalize almost 100,000 acres of private land and to triple the area of public beach frontage. The Chamber of Commerce (which originally sponsored the 1930 report), as well as leading members of the Citizens' Committee, also took their distance from Olmsted and Bartholomew's bolder planks.

But even if an encompassing civic consensus had existed, neither the city nor the county had the wherewithal, in the bleak early days of the depression, to undertake a massive park-building program.[22] Only Washington, D.C., had the requisite resources. Ironically, when New Deal agencies finally came to the fiscal rescue of Los Angeles, local government used federal capital to pave over the wetlands and streams that were so central to Olmsted and Bartholomew's vision. The death of the Los Angeles River, in particular, was a dismal portent of the future role of government in reshaping and degrading the regional environment.

The Army Corps of Engineers has often reminded its critics that Los Angeles, sited in an alluvial plain at the foot of a rugged, unstable mountain range, has the worst flood problem of any major Northern Hemisphere city. But, as Olmsted and Bartholomew emphasized in their report, flood control could be accomplished by different combinations of land use planning and public works. Their preference, of course, was to strictly limit private encroachment within the fifty-year floodplain. They wanted to conserve broad natural channels for multiple use as spreading grounds, nature preserves, recreational parks, and scenic parkways. Olmsted and Bartholomew eloquently criticized the false economy of investing in a linear, strictly mono-purpose infrastructure: "Where flood control alone is dealt with in computing the size of anticipated floods, there is a natural tendency to curtail the area of land to be acquired. . . . Such a policy defeats itself. It compels large outlays for costly construction on narrow rights of way which would not be necessary on wider rights of way."[23]

The opposing solution was to deepen and "armor" (pave) a narrow width of the channel in order to maximize potential industrial development within the floodplain. Although beneficial to large landowners, this strategy would entomb the natural river in a concrete straitjacket—effectively destroying the riparian landscape. Not surprisingly, this latter camp was initially organized and financed by Paul Shoup of the Southern Pacific Railroad, the major floodplain landowner. Beginning with the bitterly contested special election of February 1917, Shoup's so-called Flood Control Committee portrayed the river as a virtually apocalyptic threat to the city's "humble home-builders": "It should be remembered that prior to 1824, the Los Angeles River, when in flood, flowed southwest through the present location of the city into Santa Monica Bay. If we had another flood like that of 1889, and a bridge fell into the river and dammed it, this might happen again, causing a calamity equal to that of Johnstown or Galveston."[24]

Unprecedented losses of life in the great deluge of 1938, which turned 300,000 acres of the San Fernando Valley and Orange County into inland seas, seem to ratify the flood control lobby's worst-case scenario. There was broad agreement that the urban-riparian interface had to be reconstructed to take account of the huge population explosion of the 1920s. (Urbanization inexorably magnified the flood menace by reducing the porous surface area available to absorb runoff.) But Olmsted and Bartholomew's greenbelt alternative, with its explicit assertion of communal sovereignty, was never seriously debated. Nor did anyone seem to pay much attention to the new State Planning Board, appointed by Democratic Governor Culbert Olson, when it echoed the Olmstedian proposition that it was cheaper to keep property away from floodplains through zoning than to keep floods away from property through vast public works.[25]

A decisive new factor, moreover, was the promise that flood control construction would generate thousands of temporary jobs for the unemployed.
Fletcher Bowron, the reform mayor installed in the famous recall election
of 1938, was under tremendous pressure from his trade union allies to coordinate with Washington in expanding public works employment. Thus
local New Dealers, as well as the city's traditional Republican elite, campaigned for the comprehensive plan that Congress eventually approved as
the Flood Control Act of 1941. The Army Corps of Engineers was authorized to reshape the county's natural hydrology into a monolithic system of
concrete storm sewers. The Los Angeles River—the defining landscape of
the nineteenth-century city—was sacrificed for the sake of emergency work
relief, the preservation of floodplain land values, and a merely temporary
abatement of the flood problem.[26]

In the same period the city also came perilously close to killing Santa
Monica Bay. Since the citrus revolution of the 1880s, most Southern California towns had recycled their sewage to farmers as valuable irrigation
water and fertilizer. Los Angeles, by contrast, in 1894 began discharging its
raw sewage into the ocean through an outfall at Hyperion Beach. A primitive screening process was finally introduced in the early 1920s after a storm
of protest against the unspeakable pollution of nearby beaches. But waste
treatment was unable to keep up with population growth, and, with the
huge wartime immigrations, the system broke down entirely. As a result,
thousands of swimmers and picnickers contracted bacillary dysentery. To
forestall the more lethal threats of full-fledged typhoid and poliomyeli-
tis epidemics, the state Board of Health in 1943 declared a "gross public
health hazard" and closed ten miles of fetid beaches.[27]

Indeed, a decade after Olmsted and Bartholomew's report, the "parks
and recreation crisis" had become a comprehensive environmental crisis.
With biblical implacability, floods and sewage spills were accompanied by
massive beach erosion (from improper groining and breakwater construction), land subsidence (from oil drilling), and saltwater intrusion into the
underground water supply (from overdraughts). The first smog attack in
1943—an eerie "darkness at noon" over the Los Angeles Basin—caused
almost as much consternation as Pearl Harbor.[28]

In a historic symposium of the region's leading architects and planners
on the eve of the Second World War, Ralph Cornell lamented that "no other
metropolitan center has been so effective . . . in the obliteration of the natural beauty of its site, in the mutilation of its scenic resources." Clarence
Dykstra, who had just left UCLA to become president of the University of
Wisconsin, warned that "the disintegration has begun. . . . [W]e have come
to the time when old values are being destroyed faster than new ones are
being created."[29]

THE BATTLE OF THE VALLEY

This same 1941 symposium also included a remarkable contribution from Richard Neutra, the architectural representative on the new State Planning Board. "Was this metropolis a paradise," he asked, "or did there exist here a type of blight which fitted none of its classical descriptions?"

In answering his own polemical question, Neutra denounced the reckless disfigurement of the hillsides, the dispiriting uniformity of most subdivisions, and, above all, the corrosive impact of extreme privatism. "Beautiful and broad views from individual dwellings," he argued, "can hardly atone for the lack of a comprehensive and convincingly landscaped neighborhood design and for lost communal opportunities." Large-scale government housing projects, rather than private developments, offered the best opportunity for integrated community design.[30]

Neutra's derisory attitude toward private homes in the hills rings odd today since it is precisely for such projects that he and other first-generation Los Angeles modernists are most popularly remembered. Yet between the beginning of Lendlease and VE Day domestic architecture scarcely made an appearance in (L.A.-based) *Arts and Architecture* magazine. The war mobilized an unprecedented coalition of architects, planners, and New Deal reformers committed to a common vision of regional planning, slum clearance, social housing, and environmental conservation.

Thus the famous Case Study Houses of 1945–1947 were preceded by the even more important, if less well remembered, "case study communities" of the early 1940s. In a score of federal war-housing projects, as well as in several exemplary private subdivisions, Southern California's leading modernists attempted to crystallize a new urbanism based on medium-density bungalows and garden apartments grouped around dramatic common spaces. If Neutra's Channel Heights project is justifiably remembered as the finest single design of the period, then Baldwin Hills Village has been the most successful as an enduring community.

Completed between 1939 and 1942 after a long struggle to obtain federal financing, the Village was an evolutionary advance on the Radburn garden city ideal. Six hundred thirty row houses and apartments, in five styles, were arranged in a continuous *S* plan around garden courts opening onto three large greens connected by tree-shaded malls. Uniquely for Los Angeles, automobile traffic was confined to the project's periphery, while the center was an oasis of pedestrian serenity. At every level of organization, the Village's design sustained a superb dialectic between private and communal space. After more than a half century, it remains one of Los Angeles's most vibrant, as well as integrated and ungated neighborhoods.

In its original context, moreover, the Village was envisioned as a proto-type "democratic community" for the postwar era, an alternative urban building block to the automobile-dominated private subdivision. One of the most influential contemporary advocates of this new urbanism was Robert Alexander, a member of the architectural team that created the Village and a future partner of Richard Neutra. Appointed to the Los Angeles City Planning Commission at the end of the war, Alexander boldly attempted to use agricultural greenbelts—much in the spirit of Olmsted and Bartholomew—to deflect postwar suburbanization into a new design path, based on the commons-centered, pedestrian-scaled examples of Baldwin Hills Village and Channel Heights.[31]

Alexander foresaw that the voracious postwar demand for housing, if left to the speculative marketplace, would simply repeat the 1920s boom on a larger and more destructive scale. The remaining agricultural areas of coastal Southern California, especially the San Fernando and San Gabriel valleys, would be transformed overnight into a monotonous mosaic of tract homes and vacant lots. The orchards and truck farms that formed the historical matrix for suburban garden cities would be uprooted and new development would coalesce into a shapeless amoebic mass.

Furthermore, Alexander and City Planning Director Charles Bennett recognized that the San Fernando Valley, already under tremendous pressure from real estate speculators, would be the first and most decisive battlefield. Accordingly, they proposed a zoning strategy that opened the valley to hundreds of thousands of house-hungry ex-GIs and aircraft workers, but concentrated new development at medium-density levels around sixteen existing suburban nodes permanently separated by eighty-three square miles of citrus and farm greenbelts.

> The planning department staff prepared a master plan for each of the sixteen town centers. . . . Each plan formed a small, compact, self-sustaining community, surrounded and separated from other country towns by agricultural greenbelts. To provide a transition, each urban area was separated from the agricultural zones by a suburban zone in which truck gardening, chickens, rabbits, bees and incidental domestic animals were permitted.[32]

Implicitly, Alexander theorized a *virtuous circle* where open-space zoning simultaneously preserved landscape integrity, promoted clustered housing, reduced the costs of school and utility provision, and ensured sufficient population densities to sustain rapid transit systems (the existing Red Car system as well as a proposed downtown-to-valley monorail). This new urban fabric, moreover, would be especially conducive to strong neighborhood identity and democratic participation—key values in the New Deal paradigm of planning.[33]

Greenbelt zoning for the valley was actually passed into law by the city council at the end of the war, but, as Alexander vividly details in an unpublished memoir, it lacked the broad political support to survive the relentless counterattack of developers and landowners.

> With a vast pent-up demand and a sure market, it would have been quite profitable for developers to buy undeveloped lots in any of the existing town centers. They could even acquire adjacent unsubdivided land, applying for changes in zone from R-A suburban to R-1, but nothing would satisfy their greed. Instead, they obtained options for practically nothing to buy the cheapest land zoned for agricultural use and applied for changes in zone to R-1. Sometimes accompanied by a veteran wearing an American Legion hat, they found willing cooperators in the planning director and four of the commissioners who needed no urging to respond to the hysteria of the housing shortage. They gained untold riches as they converted "greenbelts" to densely packed urban town lots.[34]

As politically naive planners were soon shocked to discover, other layers of government were active accomplices in the destruction of Los Angeles's agricultural periphery. The county tax assessor, for example, increased the pressure on farmers to sell out by reappraising their land as prime residential real estate—"a self-fulfilling prophecy which spread like wildfire."[35] The Federal Housing Administration, already notorious for its tolerance of racially restrictive covenants and white-only suburbs, refused to lift a finger to preserve natural landscapes or to discourage leapfrog development.

As a result, Alexander's virtuous circle was inexorably transformed into the *vicious circle* that he had warned against: total loss of horticultural landscape, an excessive number of vacant lots, expensive utility and school provision, a dramatic imbalance of homes and jobs, minimal community cohesion, and a low-density population pattern transportable only by private cars. By the early 1960s, instead of a "balanced self-sufficient constellation of communities" bordered by greenbelts, the San Fernando Valley had become a paved-over "undifferentiated slurb" of nearly one million people.[36]

ECKBO VERSUS THE URBAN DESERT

In 1958, the sociologist William Whyte, author of *The Organization Man*, had a disturbing vision as he was leaving Southern California. "Flying from Los Angeles to San Bernardino—an unnerving lesson in man's infinite capacity to mess up his environment—the traveler can see a legion of bulldozers gnawing into the last remaining tract of green between the two cities, and from San Bernardino another legion of bulldozers gnawing westward." When he reached New York he wrote a famous article for *Fortune* magazine, describing the insidious new growth-form he called "urban sprawl."[37]

TABLE 6.1   East San Gabriel Valley Changes
in Land Use Inventory, 1940–1960

Land Use Type	1940 (%)	1960 (%)	1940–1960 change (%)
Residential	1.3	15.5	+14.2
Agricultural	72.4	19.5	−52.9
Vacant	19.4	42.4	+23.0
Other	6.9	22.9	+16.0

SOURCE: Regional Planning Commission, *East San Gabriel Valley* (Los Angeles, 1956), 12.

TABLE 6.2   Urbanization of the Santa Monica
Mountains (west of Cahuenga Pass only)

Year	No. of Dwellings
1930	3,000
1940	5,000
1950	12,000
1960	21,000

SOURCE: Adapted from David Weide, "The Geography of Fire in the Santa Monica Mountains" (M. A. thesis, California State University, Los Angeles, 1968), 145.

After the debacle in the San Fernando Valley, there was little political or bureaucratic opposition to the obliteration of the rest of Southern California's picture-postcard landscapes. Although Los Angeles County paid homage in its 1941 master plan to the "major importance" of protecting choice agricultural land from subdivision, its actual land use policies encouraged sprawl. In a 1956 report on the eastern San Gabriel Valley, for example, the Regional Planning Commission confirmed that all the remaining orchards in what had once been the world's largest citrus forest would be soon subdivided. The commission's only concern was that "this transition to urban uses should be encouraged to take place in an orderly manner" that minimized the "dead period" between land clearance and home construction.[38] As table 6.1 demonstrates, however, the speculative home-building frontier of the 1950s produced the same excess of subdivision—"ghost towns in reverse"—that so shocked Olmsted and Bartholomew during the 1920s.

For a decade, meanwhile, at least one thousand citrus trees were bulldozed and burned every day. Between 1939 and 1970, agricultural acreage in Los Angeles County south of the San Gabriel Mountains (the richest farmland in the nation according to some agronomists) fell from 300,000 to less than 10,000 acres. One of the nation's most picturesque and emblematic landscapes—the visual magnet that had attracted hundreds of thousands of immigrants to Southern California—was systematically eradicated.[39]

Hillside and canyon environments, meanwhile, fared little better. Both Olmsted and Neutra had denounced the privatization of hillside vistas, and Olmsted had urged public ownership of key tracts in the Santa Monica Mountains. The 1945 County Citizens Committee—reminding political leaders that the quality of recreational landscape was "the goose that lays our golden eggs"—proposed extensive open-space conservation in the Palos Verdes, Baldwin, Montebello, Puente, San Raphael, and Verdugo hills. But, as table 6.2 shows, the postwar demand for "view lots" was virtually unquenchable. Within Los Angeles County as a whole, more than 60,000 house sites were carved out of the mountains and foothills during the 1950s and early 1960s.[40]

While park building once again lagged far behind growth, the automobile devoured exorbitant quantities of prime land. By 1970, more than one-third of the surface area of the Los Angeles region was dedicated to car-related uses: freeways, streets, parking lots, and driveways.[41] What generations of tourists and migrants had once admired as a real-life Garden of Eden was now buried under an estimated three billion tons of concrete (250 tons per inhabitant).[42]

Southern California sprawl eventually became a national scandal. Thanks again to the crusading efforts of Whyte, federal responsibility for the "exploding metropolis" was subjected to unprecedented scrutiny and debate. Despite fierce opposition from the National Association of Home Builders, the Kennedy administration officially acknowledged the social costs of sprawl and introduced legislation in 1961 to support the conservation of urban open space.[43]

Back in California, the legislature was prodded by the Sierra Club and California Tomorrow into authorizing a major study of the state's "open-space crisis." The consultants were the eminent San Francisco firm of Eckbo, Dean, Austin and Williams (EDAW), which dominated environmental planning in California during the 1960s and 1970s in the same way that Olmsted and Bartholomew had hegemonized park design in the 1920s. Although Edward A. Williams wrote the final report for the State Office of Planning in 1965 (reissued in 1969 and updated in 1972), the overarching influence of Garrett Eckbo in this and subsequent studies was obvious, and a few words need to be said about the background of the firm's most prominent partner.

Eckbo is justly regarded as a pioneer of modernism in American landscape architecture. "A green Californian from the frontier," he arrived at Harvard University in the late 1930s just as Walter Gropius was starting a mini-revolution in the architecture department. But the Bauhaus has been only one of many fertile influences in the evolution of a complex personal philosophy. In equal measures he has also been a regionalist, an ecologist, and a radical social democrat who has conspired to turn the aristocratic inheritance of landscape design on its head. Since his early days with the Farm Security Administration designing yards and gardens for farmworker housing, Eckbo has been preoccupied with "the contradiction between social relations and individual land use, . . . between the interests of ordinary citizens and those free enterprise elements who see no values beyond their own private profit."[44]

Thus in his postwar manifesto for the new environmental design, *Landscape for Living* (1949), Eckbo decried the "sordid chaos" of "general commercial speculation" and argued that it was "no more than democratic Americanism to say that such forces can be analyzed, exposed and placed under proper public control." Rejecting the reservation of the lushest landscapes for the rich, he evoked the "truly democratic organization of our general community tree patterns" which would replace "the sterile formality of authority" with the "tremendous tree symphony of the future." Indeed, as authentic democracy began to achieve "cultural expression in the landscapes . . . the present scale of landscape values will tend to reverse itself."

> Instead of moving from the ugly city toward the peak of wilderness beauty, it will be possible to move from the wilderness through constantly more magnificent and orderly rural refinements of the face of the earth, to urban communities composed of structures, paving, grass, shrubs, and trees, which are rich, sparkling, crystalline nuclei in the web of spatial relations that surrounds the earth—peak expressions of the reintegration of man and nature.[45]

The *Urban Metropolitan Open Space Study* submitted to Governor Pat Brown in 1965 as the keystone of a proposed state development plan was resonant with the bold values and motifs of *Landscape for Living*. Indeed, to the ears of some Sacramento bureaucrats, EDAW must have sounded almost as radical as the contemporary firebrands in Berkeley's Sproul Plaza. Consider, for example, Williams's treatment of individual property rights:

> The traditional view toward private ownership of property that permits the temporary owner a proprietary interest has been outmoded by new knowledge of man's relationship to nature and to the community. This knowledge demands a new attitude toward ownership of land, substituting the concept of trusteeship for exploitation.[46]

The study warned that all of California's remaining Mediterranean valleys and foothills, including the exquisite Santa Barbara–Ventura coast as well as the famed vineyards of Sonoma and Napa counties, were threatened with the same fate as Los Angeles's citrus belt. It condemned county governments for the "weak, timid and unimaginative" use of zoning powers and denounced a tax system that rewarded land speculators and punished farmers. It also emphasized the profound causal relationship between landscape-destroying sprawl at the urban edge and neighborhood decay at the center.[47]

"One of the most significant findings," moreover, was that "a clearcut crisis situation exists in the Southern California urban-metropolitan area." Postwar suburbanization had entirely outpaced the production or conservation of public space. At minimum, Los Angeles County was facing a 100,000-acre shortfall of regional parks. At the municipal level the recreation crisis was frequently much worse. Indeed, the open-space situation throughout the Los Angeles Basin—"1,500 square miles of low grade, monotonous suburban construction"—was so hopeless that the study focused instead on stopping sprawl at its periphery.[48]

In 1965, significant farm and foothill belts still defended Ventura-Oxnard, San Bernardino, Riverside, and San Diego from engulfment by Greater Los Angeles. Although local environmentalists had targeted the Santa Monica Mountains as the most important conservation area, the study emphasized instead the San Jose, Puente, and Chino hills, which separated the San Gabriel Valley from the suburbanizing west end of San Bernardino County and the Chino Plain from northeast Orange County. As "the center of the greatest population pressure within the region . . . they should become the most highly prized and zealously protected open-space resource."[49]

The second regional priority was "from Conejo to Hidden Hills, between Los Angeles and Ventura, an area of beautiful rolling hills and valleys, peculiarly vulnerable to destruction by careless and indifferent development, yet peculiarly pregnant with possibilities for rich and imaginative design." Other crucial battlegrounds were the undeveloped parts of the Palos Verdes Peninsula, the Oxnard Plain, the Elsinore-Temecula corridor in southwest Riverside County, and the coastal mesas and valleys between San Diego and Vista.[50]

The study also briefly, but prophetically, surveyed the dismal results of urban overspill in the Mojave and Colorado River deserts. "The entire desert seems to be subdivided and covered with a gridiron of graded street; such development destroys the desert as landscape and as open space, replacing them with nothing but the empty wasteland of ex-urbanism." Moreover, the elaboration of community designs suitable to the desert environment appeared to be simply "beyond the capability of [existing] planning processes."[51]

THE SCANDAL OF COUNTY PLANNING

These theses were amplified in subsequent articles and reports by EDAW. In 1966, for example, Eckbo was asked by *Cry California* magazine (the publication of California Tomorrow) to comment on the issue that the study had deliberately sidestepped: how to expand open-space resources within the congested and overdeveloped Los Angeles Basin. After observing that "no comparable urban region in the nation even remotely approaches the basin's inadequacy [in parkland]," Eckbo made a characteristically audacious proposal for "greening the urban desert." He suggested that the county could redevelop suburbs into parks by relocating 10 percent of the population ("from various income groups") into new higher-density housing. Estimated cost: seven to nine billion dollars.[52]

Six years later, in 1972, EDAW produced another major open-space survey, this time an exhaustive study of the Santa Monica Mountain coastline for the California Legislature. Saluting Olmsted and Bartholomew, they reminded readers that the problem of sprawl first had been recognized in the landmark 1930 report, which had also recommended massive public land-banking in the Santa Monicas. Yet two generations later, 95 percent of "the last major open space resource remaining in the greater Los Angeles metropolitan region" was still in private hands, mostly in large, speculative parcels.[53]

As previously in their 1965 study, EDAW insisted on the need to shift land use analysis from traditional market-centered criteria toward new social and ecological values. In their view, there was a fundamental epistemological conflict between the conception of the mountains as an abstract land unit and as a complex natural environment. They urged the legislature to "treat the area as a total system of air, land and water relationships, not simply as real estate to be developed."[54]

Given the Santa Monicas' incalculable recreational and landscape value, they expressed incredulity at a general plan projection of a buildout population of 405,000 in the environmentally sensitive Malibu area.[55] They pointed out that Malibu, apart from major problems with earthquakes, flooding, and landslides, also had a fire history "unique in intensity, devastating in effect, and heightened during Santa Ana wind conditions." (The October 1993 firestorm merely followed the twentieth-century pattern of a major Malibu area fire every *four* years on average.) Again echoing Olmsted and Bartholomew, EDAW decried the ease with which developers in high-risk areas shifted the costs of fire and flood protection onto the taxpayers at large.[56] They proposed a stringent permit system to keep new construction at a minimum while the legislature evaluated options for expanding public ownership in the Santa Monicas.[57]

The EDAW reports were critical moments in the renaissance of regional planning and landscape conservation. The 1965 draft of *Open Space* was followed the next year by two landmark environmental polemics: Raymond Dassmann's *The Destruction of California* and Richard Lillard's *Eden in Jeopardy*. Californians were suddenly forced to confront the cultural and ecological costs of their postwar "golden age," and, from Eureka to San Diego, they were shocked by what they saw.

In the Bay Area, a unique heritage of Brahmin conservationism provided Nob Hill support for successful efforts to protect the bay's wetlands and create a regional open-space conservancy in the foothills. People for Open Space (POS), with 16,000 subscribers to its newsletter, united the followers of John Muir and Lewis Mumford—environmentalists, planners, and philanthropists—in a common defense of San Francisco's great natural beauty. With the help of the Ford Foundation, POS developed the first comprehensive "anti-sprawl" plan for any American metropolitan area. Soon afterward, California Tomorrow, with the assistance of the architectural senior statesman Nathaniel Owings, produced a detailed strategic outline for statewide land use planning emphasizing the preservation of agricultural landscapes and the intensive regulation of the suburban fringe. Both documents reproduced or elaborated core ideas in the Olmsted-Alexander/Neutra-EDAW tradition.[58]

Within Southern California, meanwhile, counterpart movements crusaded to stop flagrant tract development in the Santa Monica Mountains and other foothill and coastal areas. The successful passage of the Coastal Initiative in 1972 finally codified the principles of public access and controlled beach development that Olmsted had advocated back in 1930. *Ralph Nader's Study Group Report on Land Use in California* included a shocking account of the planning system's total breakdown in regulating speculative development in the Antelope Valley.[59] At the same time, environmental groups sued the county to force it to protect the endangered remnants of Los Angeles's (last) "significant ecological areas."

The Los Angeles County Regional Planning Commission was theoretically the chief custodian of the regional landscape. Yet as critics charged in their lawsuit, the commission had historically functioned as "expediters for fringe growth" whose planning documents had seldom been more than "blueprints for sprawl." (The League of Women Voters independently claimed that the commission had done little more to "preserve the Santa Monicas than color the vacant land green on its master plan.")[60] After soliciting environmental development guidelines from a distinguished panel of natural scientists (Los Angeles County Environmental Resource Committee) in 1970, the commission brazenly discarded them in order to double the area of land targeted for urbanization. In response, the Coalition for Planning in the Public Interest organized a successful legal campaign to block the county's 1973 master plan.[61]

At stake were the remaining fragments of those key open spaces identified by Williams and Eckbo in the 1965 study: the fringes of Santa Clarita; the Ventura Freeway corridor beyond Calabasas; the Hacienda Heights, Rowland Heights, and Diamond Bar areas of the Puente and Chino hills; and Quartz Hill between Palmdale and Lancaster. The commission proposed to feed hungry developers another million acres of priceless agricultural and foothill landscape, while the coalition argued that population growth should be accommodated by infill and densification within the existing urban fabric.

In his withering critique of the master plan, Judge David Thomas accused the commission of concealing staff reports that showed that 99 percent of the additional urban expansion area consisted of endangered habitats or vital watershed. Its environmental impact report, moreover, was "no more than a sterile declamation of unsupported generalities almost entirely failing to convey any factual information." He temporarily enjoined the commission from authorizing new fringe development.[62]

In 1979, this controversy over open-space management suddenly erupted into full-fledged public scandal. A grand jury investigation—based on muckraking evidence from the Center for Law in the Public Interest—dramatically exposed the inner workings of a regional planning system dominated and corrupted by development interests. As critics had long charged, and Commissioner Robert Meeker now acknowledged, county officials paid "little more than lip service to restrictions on land use." Indeed, key planning officials had advised developers in the Santa Monica Mountains and the Antelope Valley how to circumvent public hearings and environmental regulations by illegally partitioning their property among relatives and dummy corporations. An astounding *13,000* individual cases of fraudulent lot division were alleged.[63]

Similarly, when planning staff recommended against environmentally destructive projects in Diamond Bar and Santa Clarita, they were summarily overruled by the commission majority. Planning Director Norman Murdoch, moreover, routinely refused to acknowledge memos from Carolyn Llewellyn, the sole critic on the commission. The independent-minded Mrs. Llewellyn was regularly shouted down by the commission chairman, Owen Lewis—himself a developer appointed by another developer (Supervisor Peter Schabarum).[64]

Although public outrage eventually forced the resignation of Chairman Lewis and other members of the commission, it was a very modest, even Pyrrhic, victory for the environmental movement. The brief light focused on corruption within the Regional Planning Commission was never allowed to illuminate the more fundamental conflicts of public and private interests within the Board of Supervisors (the "five little kings" who are the most powerful and least accountable local officials in the United States). Moreover, once the commission reformed its most egregious practices, the steam went out of the (largely legalistic) battle to stop the fringe development juggernaught. To appease Judge Thomas, the county was finally forced to officially designate some sixty-two "significant ecological areas" (SEAs), but no legislation was enacted to ensure their preservation.

The SEAs, in fact, currently lack any zoning or land use designation within the General Plan, and there is no penalty provided for development that ignores so-called SEA Design Compatibility Criteria. On the contrary, the plan offers a series of loopholes that makes it possible, for example, to totally destroy one of the last intact oak woodlands (Towsley Canyon in the Santa Susanas) for the sake of a new "essential use" garbage dump. The Regional Planning Department, moreover, does not monitor development in the SEAs and doesn't even know "which areas are intact or degraded." To rub salt in the wounds of environmentalists, the majority of members of the technical body monitoring the SEAs are full- or part-time consultants to developers.[65]

As a result, suburbanization has devoured each of the crucial open-space buffer zones prioritized by Williams and Eckbo. Small environmental gains here and there—notably by the Santa Monica Mountains Conservancy— have been parried and checked by relentless subdivision. Even the most endangered and highly prioritized ecosystems—like the Ballona wetlands or the Diamond Bar oak savannah—have been raped by new development. Unlike the Bay Area, there have been no unqualified victories for open-space preservation, just the accumulation of worthless environmental impact reports and toothless development guidelines.

In part, this must be attributable to the different political cultures and power structures of California's two major metropolitan regions. County government in Southern California is so hopelessly captive to the land development industry that sweeping electoral reforms, comparable to California's Progressive revolution of 1911, are probably the prerequisite for overthrowing the "new Octopus" and transforming land use priorities.[66]

Yet 1970s environmentalism in Los Angeles County was also compromised by its own parochialism and historical amnesia. In contrast both to the Bay Area's People for Open Space and, especially, to local precedents from Olmsted to Alexander and EDAW, the mainstream Los Angeles environmental groups fell short of a coherent vision of stabilized city-nature equilibrium. There was little discussion, in the spirit of regional modernists like Neutra or Eckbo, of the role of parks and open space as the "functional skeleton of the community." More often than not, environmental battles were fought piecemeal (and usually on the turf of Westside concerns) without consideration of overall strategy or coalition with other constituencies. The social justice dimension of recreational planning and open-space conservation was pointedly ignored. Ecology, in other words, stopped short of the more subversive, but utterly necessary, politics of urban design.

FROM LANDSCAPE TO VIRTUAL REALITY

In his eloquent 1966 jeremiad, *Eden in Jeopardy,* Richard Lillard warned that it was already one minute before midnight in the battle to save Southern California's most precious natural and historic landscapes. That was nearly thirty years ago. Where are we now?

All the old battles, of course, are still being fought at the megalopolitan frontier. But the bulldozers that so troubled William Whyte are now halfway across the Mojave, and developers uproot Joshua trees with the same mindless zeal with which they once cut down the citrus empire. Suburban sprawl has grown another hundred miles broader in circumference, and Los Angeles smog blights the view at the Grand Canyon. Meanwhile, Los Angeles's inner-city neighborhoods and blue-collar suburbs, swollen with two million new immigrants, continue to suffer the long drought of recreational and green space. Public action mitigates the environmental crisis primarily for the top 10 percent of the population who benefits from the conversion of wetlands into marinas and from hidden subsidies for hillside living. Even in the maw of the worst recession since the 1930s, Lillard's "profligate meddling with nature" is unabated, and Southern California remains radically unplanned, undesigned, and out of control.

How much natural landscape actually remains in Southern California? Thirty-five years ago, the Berkeley geographer Homer Aschmann used aerial photographs to estimate the "persistence of wild landscape" in a cross section of terrains from the ocean to the Colorado River. My update in table 6.3—roughly calculated from a Landsat panorama—assesses the further erosion of natural environments in the coastal climate belt of Southern California, exclusive of the high mountains.

Table 6.4 attempts to periodize the order of landscape loss and ecosystem decline. Together with Aschmann's wild landscapes, it includes canonical cultural landscapes, like the citrus empire, as well as more distant ecologies, like Owens Lake and the Colorado Delta, destroyed by Los Angeles's water-and-power infrastructures.

There are, of course, further ironies to the fate of landscape under the current dictatorship of the Hyperreal. Since several hundred acres of orange groves were cut down in the mid-1950s to make way for Disneyland, theme parks and special effects environments have inexorably supplanted natural and horticultural landscapes as the chief destinations of tourists

TABLE 6.3   Persistence of Wild Landscape (Aschmann Updated)

	Percentage in Aboriginal Wild Landscape		
Ecological Zone	Landscape One (1769)	Landscape Two (1959)	Landscape Three (1995)
A. Coastal	11	3	1
B. Valleys and Hills	50	8	3
C. Interior Uplands	39	22	12
I. *Wild Landscape*	100	33	16
II. *Urban Landscape*	0	67	84

SOURCE: Based on Homer Aschmann, "The Evolution of a Wild Landscape and Its Persistence in Southern California," in *Man, Time and Space in Southern California: A Symposium*, ed. W. C. Thomas, Jr., *Annals of the Association of American Geographers Supplement* 49, no. 3 (1959): 2:55.

arriving in Southern California. Postcards—that neglected archive of the changing ideology of sightseeing—vividly illustrate this transformation.[67]

Before 1940, the most common postcard image of the Los Angeles region was a sunny panorama of orange groves at the base of snowcapped Mount Baldy. Often a mission or Mission revival residence was included in the foreground. The scene's huge popularity undoubtedly derived from its unification of three classical landscape ambiences: the "wilderness sublime" of the wild mountain, the "Hesiodic idyll" of the well-ordered orchard, and the "romantic nostalgia" of the medieval ruin (or, rather, its local equivalent, the mission).

By the mid-1960s, however, the citrus–and–Mount Baldy motif had totally disappeared from the postcard racks. In its place, the most popular postcard view of Southern California had become (and remains today) an image of Mickey Mouse cavorting along Disneyland's Main Street. Old Baldy—now obscured by smog for much of the year—has been replaced by a stucco replica of the Matterhorn. The new scene merely unified the infantile and the spurious into the mawkish.

Yet the very extinction of Southern California's golden era scenery may ensure its eventual resurrection and ghostly afterlife within a theme park microcosm. Two recent news items illuminate the weird dialectic in question. A half-paragraph in the Orange County *Register* (17 October 1994) announces that the Anaheim city council is preparing the way for the transformation of the city's last remaining orange grove, planted in 1892, into a seven-acre parking lot. The other, an undated blurb from the Disney Corporation, explains that their proposed billion-dollar Westcot addition to Disneyland will be themed around images of fin de siècle Southern California, at the height of the citrus boom. Disney insiders, meanwhile, claim that

TABLE 6.4   Lost Landscapes

19th century	native grasslands/oak savannahs
1900s–1930s	Owens Valley Colorado River Delta Hollywood and Repetto hills
1940s–1950s	riparian ecosystems: Los Angeles, Rio Hondo, San Gabriel, and Santa Ana rivers; Ballona and Coyote creeks tidal marshes and coastal dunes Coachella Valley "Pentagon desert"
1950s–1960s	citrus empire and prime farmland Palos Verdes open space Santa Monica Mountains and coastline
1960s–1970s	valley foothills: Santa Susana, Verdugo, San Jose, Puente, Merced, etc. Calabasas and Oxnard Plain Simi and Newhall valleys southern Orange County
1970s–1980s	Antelope and Victor valleys Cucamonga Fan San Jacinto Basin I-15 corridor
1990s–2000s?	remaining tidal marshes and coastal sage scrub San Raphael Hills lemon belt in Santa Clarita Valley Fort Tejon open space

the secret content of the new expansion will be spectacular virtual reality amusements. Like a virtual orange grove, perhaps?

NOTES

For Kurt Meyer, mentor and friend.

1. Olmsted Brothers and Bartholomew and Associates, *Parks, Playgrounds and Beaches for the Los Angeles Region* (Los Angeles: Olmsted Bros. and Bartholomew and Associates, 1930), xiv.

2. Ibid., 23.

3. Ibid., xiii, 1–3.

4. Charles Fletcher Lummis, *Los Angeles and Her Makers* (Los Angeles: 1909), 244–245.

5. Dana Bartlett, *The Better City* (Los Angeles: Neuner Co. Press, 1907), 33–35. As Bartlett later explained to a national audience, "We feel that we must work not for a commercial city, and industrial city, primarily, but for an out-of-doors city,

typical of the life of the Southwest." See "Remarks by the Official Representatives from Several Cities," *Proceedings of the Fourth National Conference on City Planning* (Boston, 1912), 5.

6. Judge Silent quoted in the *Los Angeles Herald,* 1 March 1910.

7. Robinson's proposal for weaving the city's parks into a continuous greenbelt system was later amplified by Park Commissioner J. B. Lippincott, who envisioned magnificent, intersecting park corridors from Westlake (today's MacArthur Park) to Silverlake and from Elysian to Griffith parks. (See *Los Angeles Express,* 27 May 1911.)

8. Charles Mulford Robinson, *The City Beautiful: Report to the Municipal Art Commission* (Los Angeles, 1909), 32. This advice retains its full cogency today. By allowing private speculators to reap super-profits from the inflation of land values adjacent to subway stations, parks, and other public improvements, Los Angeles's redevelopment and transit agencies have squandered a major stream of potential revenue.

9. Ibid., 3.

10. Nearly one-half million vacant lots imposed huge social costs on depression era Los Angeles. Olmsted and Bartholomew estimated that the carrying charges alone amounted to $100 million per year. For a more extended discussion, see Constantine Panunzio, "Growth and Character of the Population," and Clifford Zierer, "The Land Use Pattern," in *Los Angeles: Preface to a Masterplan,* ed. George Robbins and L. Deming Tilton, 38–39, 56–59 (Los Angeles: Pacific Southwest Academy, 1941). Also see Works Progress Administration, *Land Use Survey of Los Angeles County,* Los Angeles, 1938 (original maps and worksheets in Huntington Library, San Marino).

11. Testimony of Frederick Law Olmsted, Jr., to Citizens' Committee, *Los Angeles Times,* 22 Feb. 1928; and Los Angeles County, Regional Planning Commission, *Preliminary Report on Existing County Parks* (Los Angeles, September 1928), iv. The commission pointed out that "most neglected are neighborhood parks and playgrounds within walking distance of the masses" (p. iii).

12. According to the Los Angeles County Regional Planning Commission, the metropolis possessed "infinite expansion space" and thus could avoid such "curses of urban congestion" as narrow lots and row houses. "May we never suffer this affliction! If we are to attract Easterners to our communities we must not offer them their own ills" (*Report on Lot Sizes* [Los Angeles, 1928], 10).

13. Olmsted and Bartholomew, *Parks, Playgrounds and Beaches,* 5.

14. Ibid., 11.

15. Ibid., 10.

16. Ibid., 14–16.

17. Regional Planning Conference, *Minutes of the 1924 Session* (Los Angeles, 1924), n.p.

18. Olmsted and Bartholomew, *Parks, Playgrounds and Beaches,* 14–16.

19. The 1928 report of the Regional Planning Commission contained a beautiful prototype design for a parkway/linear park along the Rio Hondo near the historic Gage adobe. (Regional Planning Commission, *Report* [Los Angeles, 1929], 27.)

20. Olmsted and Bartholomew, *Parks, Playgrounds and Beaches,* 22.

21. See Frederick Law Olmsted, Jr., Harland Bartholomew, and Charles Cheney, *A Major Traffic Street Plan for Los Angeles* (Los Angeles, 1924); Olmsted Brothers and Ansel Hall, *Proposed Park Reservations for East Bay Cities* (Oakland: 1930); and Frederick Law Olmsted, Jr., "Palos Verdes Estates," *Landscape Architecture* 17 (July 1927). In its organization of land use, Palos Verdes Estates (1923) was intended as a model for Southern California. It dedicated 25% of its surface area to recreational and natural landscapes as compared to the mere 2% in most contemporary Los Angeles neighborhoods.

22. The translation of the 1930 report into a county master plan for parks and recreation was a Sisyphean effort that eventually took two generations. Resumed in 1939, after a nine-year hiatus, the planning process proceeded at a snail's pace through the war years. A new Citizens' Committee on Parks, Beaches and Recreation was convened in 1945 to consider how to save "the [recreational] goose that lays our golden eggs." Confessing that it lacked time and resources to reconsider the detailed proposals of the Olmsted Plan, it urged regional planners to make that "their immediate priority." A master plan of parks was finally completed in 1948 but was widely judged to be inadequate. In 1952, the Regional Planning Commission ordered a restudy, which was finished in 1958. Virtually obsolete on publication, it was superseded in 1957 by "preliminary work on aspects of regional park planning" that was finally completed a decade later. (See Regional Planning Commission, *Annual Reports* [Los Angeles: 1932–1968]; and County Citizens Committee, *Parks, Beaches and Recreation Facilities for Los Angeles County* [Los Angeles: Haynes Foundation, 1945], 3–4.)

23. County Citizens Committee, *Parks, Beaches and Recreation Facilities*, 16.

24. *Flood Control Advocate*, a four-page tabloid distributed by the Flood Control Committee before the 20 February 1917 election. The major issue in the election was whether flood control works would be financed by a special assessment of floodplain landowners (the position of opponents, including the Progressives and Socialists) or by general revenue bonds (the self-serving position of proponents, like Shoup and the committee). The heavily promoted bond measure passed.

25. Seldom-used provisions of the California Subdivision Ordinance of 1938 were designed to legalize hazard zoning and "control individuals whose selfish interests might endanger the human or financial resources of others." A comprehensive case for floodplain zoning as an alternative to pharaonic public works was submitted to Governor Olson shortly before his reelection defeat in 1942. See Ralph Wertheimer, *Flood-Plain Zoning: Possibilities and Legality with Special Reference to Los Angeles County* (Sacramento: California State Planning Board, June 1942), esp. pp. ii and 40.

26. The Los Angeles County flood control system—one of the largest public works in world history—was finally completed in 1969 after nearly thirty years of continuous construction. In the late 1980s, however, a comprehensive "restudy" by the Army Corps of Engineers revealed that the system could no longer deal with the "fifty-year flood event" that it was designed to control. In particular, the postwar suburbanization of the formerly agricultural eastern San Gabriel Valley has increased storm runoff beyond the detainment capacities of the system. For a brilliant reflection on the quixotic quest to manage natural forces with single-purpose mega-

engineering, see "Los Angeles Against the Mountains" in John McPhee's *The Control of Nature* (New York: Farrar, Straus, Giroux, 1989).

27. See Elmer Belt (president, California State Board of Health), "Sanitary Survey of Sewage Pollution of Santa Monica Bay," *Western City* (June 1943): 17–22.

28. A strikingly similar conjunction of environmental disasters reoccurred in *annus horibilis* 1987–1988. See my *City of Quartz: Excavating the Future in Los Angeles* (London: Verso, 1990), 196–203.

29. Ralph Cornell, "The Importance of Appearance," and Clarence Dykstra, "The Future of Los Angeles," in *Los Angeles: Preface to a Masterplan,* ed. George Robbins and L. Deming Tilton, 5–6, 220–224 (Los Angeles: Southwest Academy, 1941).

30. Richard Neutra, "Homes and Housing," in Robbins and Tilton, *Los Angeles,* 189, 194–195.

31. A slightly later (1947) "case study community" in the same vein was Gregory Ain's and Garrett Eckbo's Mar Vista project: 52 small houses with a common green, private gardens, and continuous campuslike planting.

32. Robert E. Alexander, "The San Fernando Valley" (unpublished manuscript, 1990), 80. Cf. Charles Bennett, "Planning for the San Fernando Valley," an address intended for the war-canceled convention of the Urban Land Institute, November 1944 (in John Randolph Haynes archives, UCLA Special Collections); and Los Angeles City Planning Commission, *Accomplishments—1944* (Los Angeles, 1945), 5–12.

33. Shortly before his death in 1992, I had an opportunity to talk with Alexander at some length about the social and environmental implications of his 1945 San Fernando Valley zoning plan.

34. Alexander, "The San Fernando Valley," 82.

35. Ibid.

36. Ibid.

37. William Whyte, "Urban Sprawl," *Fortune* 57 (January 1958): 302.

38. Los Angeles County Regional Planning Commission, *Master Plan of Land Use* (Los Angeles: Regional Planning Commission 1941); and *East San Gabriel Valley* (Los Angeles: Regional Planning Commission, 1956).

39. See Mark Northcross, "Los Angeles County: Biting the Land that Feeds Us," *California Tomorrow* 36; and Raymond Dassmann, *California's Changing Environment* (San Francisco, 1981), 81.

40. County Citizens Committee, *Parks, Beaches and Recreational Facilities;* and Richard Jahns, "Seventeen Years of Response by the City of Los Angeles to Geologic Hazards," *Geologic Hazards and Problems: Conference Proceedings,* ed. Robert Olson and Mildred Wallace (Santa Rosa: Office of Emergency Preparedness, Region Seven, 1970), 266.

41. Donald Coates, ed., *Environmental Geomorphology and Landscape Conversation.* vol. 2: *Urban Areas* (Stroudsburg, Pa.: 1974), 273.

42. Calculated by the architect Christopher Wegscheid (Southern California Institute of Architecture, 1994) using data that I supplied on historical aggregate (sand and gravel) production in Los Angeles County.

43. At the same time, the Scottish-born landscape architect Ian McHarg was reacquainting a new generation with the greenbelt philosophies of Geddes, Mum-

ford, and the Olmsteds. His influential *Design with Nature* (New York: John Wiley, 1992) challenged the postwar notion of open space as mere residuum. On the contrary, he argued that good city making begins with the identification and preservation of vital natural systems, especially streams and rivers. Like Olmsted and Bartholomew in 1930, he advocated the rigorous exclusion of development from fifty-year floodplains and from slopes steeper than twelve degrees. See also his "The Place of Nature in the City of Man," *Annals of the American Academy of Political and Social Sciences* 352 (March 1964): 1–12.

44. Garrett Eckbo, *Landscape for Living* (New York: Architechtural Record, with Duell, Sloan & Pearce, 1950), 27, 245.

45. Ibid., 45, 111–112.

46. Edward A. Williams (Eckbo, Dean, Austin and Williams), *Open Space, the Choices Before California: The Urban Metropolitan Open Space Study* (San Francisco: 1969), 21. See also Eckbo, Dean, Austin and Williams, *State Open Space and Resource Conservation Program for California* (Sacramento: California Legislature Joint Committee on Open Space Lands, 1972).

47. Williams, *Open Space,* 22–23.

48. Ibid., 15, 24.

49. Ibid., 41.

50. Ibid., 42.

51. Ibid., 45.

52. "Parklands in the Urban Desert" (originally published in *Cry California,* 1966), reprinted in John Hart, ed., *The New Book of California Tomorrow: Reflections and Projections from the Golden State* (Los Altos: 1984), 150–53.

53. Ventura–Los Angeles Mountain and Coastal Study Commission, *Final Report to the Legislature,* prepared by Eckbo, Dean, Austin and Williams (6 March 1972), [6.1], [12B15.1]. Unfortunately, latifundist ownership, descended from Mexican land grants, had prevented the incorporation of the Santa Monicas into the Angeles National Forest in the 1890s.

54. Ibid., [11.2].

55. The egregious Malibu case was not unique. Nineteen-sixties–era general plans in Southern California—following the hyperbolic estimate by the (Pat) Brown administration of 50 million Californians by 2000—almost universally zoned foothill and mountain land for maximum subdivision. Los Angeles and Glendale city plans, for example, projected nearly 75,000 new residents in the Verdugo Mountains. Although settlement at this density ultimately proved infeasible, the Verdugos—the key open-space resource in the eastern San Fernando Valley—were punctually raped and pillaged. For an exemplary analysis, see Claremont College, Program in Public Policy Studies, *Verdugo Mountains: Planning in Conflict* (Claremont: Program in Public Policy Studies, 1972).

56. *Final Report,* [9.2]. In their 1972 update of *Open Space,* EDAW decried the failure of authorities to use hazard zoning—*pace* Olmsted and Bartholomew—to prevent development in "areas of high fire risk, slide areas, areas subject to subsidence, steep lands and tsunami zones." "Though studies about restricting the use of these areas had gone on for decades, virtually nothing has been done to solve the problems raised" (p. 32).

57. *Final Report,* [12B3.1]. Until 1930, the Malibu coast was an inaccessible Shangri-la owned by the reclusive and eccentric Rindge family. The failure of county officials to acquire the bankrupt Rancho Malibu when it was offered in exchange for $1,100,000 in delinquent taxes must count as one of the greatest environmental and planning mistakes in California history.

58. Thomas Kent, Jr., *Open Space for the San Francisco Bay Area: Organizing to Guide Metropolitan Growth* (Berkeley: Institute of Government Studies, University of California, 1970); and Alfred Heller, ed., *The California Tomorrow Plan* (Los Altos: W. Kaufmann, 1972). Owings, one of the top corporate architects in the nation, was the epitome of an aristocratic environmentalist. He was an early leader in conserving Big Sur, and his San Francisco office (Skidmore, Owings and Merrill) designed a model "green community" in the Carmel Valley.

59. Robert Fellmeth (proj. dir.), *Politics of Land: Ralph Nader's Study Group Report on Land Use in California* (New York: 1973), 436–455.

60. League of Women Voters of Los Angeles County, *Open Space in Los Angeles County* (Los Angeles: The League, November 1972), 33. The league also emphasized that the county supervisors and planning commissioners contemptuously ignored their own recreation and open-space plans, making no effort to restrict development in targeted areas (p. 22).

61. For a concise account, see W. David Conn, "Environmental Management in the Malibu Watershed: Institutional Framework" (Washington, D.C.: Environmental Protection Agency, 1975).

62. See *The Coalition for Los Angeles County Planning in the Public Interest v. Board of Supervisors, Los Angeles County,* Superior Court: C-63218 (12 March 1975).

63. *Los Angeles Times,* 3 April 1979.

64. Ibid., 16 May and 9 July 1979.

65. For bleak assessments, see *Los Angeles Times,* 2 December 1990; and Betsey Landis, "Significant Ecological Areas: The Skeleton in Los Angeles County's Closet?" in *Interface Between Ecology and Land Use in California,* ed. J. E. Keeley, 112–113, 116 (Los Angeles: Southern California Academy of Sciences, 1993).

66. For a more detailed view of latifundism Southern California-style, see *Politics of Land,* as well as my *City of Quartz* (chap. 2). If large developers dominate county politics, city government on the suburban fringe is frequently a "republic of realtors." Until last year, for example, all ten council members in the cities of Palmdale and Lancaster were realtors!

67. I benefit here from discussion with local postcard collectors and dealers.

SEVEN

Bounding and Binding Metropolitan Space

The Ambiguous Politics of Nature in Los Angeles

Margaret FitzSimmons and Robert Gottlieb

The control of nature involves the constitution of political and technological spaces within which this control is to be imposed. These spaces are not primordial, or naturally given—though spatial attributes/aspects of nature are often appropriated to delineate, legitimate, and bound them. The spaces within which the control of nature appears arise out of social spatiality as well as natural variation. They construct access and exclusion, rent surfaces, and the transfer of value from one locality to another, as well as a transformed biophysical environment.[1] In the process of construction of these political-natural spaces, the terrain itself becomes political, though the political choices involved may be naturalized, disguised by the attribution of political boundaries to the politics of "natural order."

Metropolitan Los Angeles has been a laboratory for institutional strategies of environmental control—and thus for the formation and bounding of "natural" spaces—since its founding as a Spanish agricultural pueblo in 1781. The Spanish explorers were impressed by the water wealth of the region and brought that water to the new settlement and its fields through a network of canals, the first stage in what was to become an immense water supply bureaucracy. A hundred years later, after the surrounding mountain ranges had been deforested to supply timber and fuel for the new city (and the gold mines that helped to capitalize it) so that the rivers that those forests had metered had begun to regularly flood in winter and run dry in summer, city leaders turned to the new federal institution of national forest reserves to bound the growing metropolis with public land whose rational reforestation, it was hoped, would restore the regional water economy.

Attending to the intersection of nature and Los Angeles forces us to notice both historical and geographical ironies: the ironies of history—utopian Los Angeles become an environmental dystopia—intersect the ironies of geography—the oasis city become the city in the desert, the city whose climate and clean air drew settlers from across the continent become a world symbol of urban pollution. The deep, well-watered agricultural soils that—with the climate and access to cheap labor—made Los Angeles County once the richest agricultural county in the United States now are covered and governed by coalescing cities. In a region whose continuous sunshine encouraged early innovations in solar power, the huge (but diminishing) pools of petroleum and natural gas that lie below the metropolis provide only a portion of the fossil fuels whose combustion poisons what remains of the mountain vegetation and reduces the life expectancy of those who live in the region. At the same time, institutions built to constitute, define, and manage nature in Los Angeles have become an arena of political control behind the scenes, naturalizing political and spatial metropolitan integration by writing it onto a constructed and naturalized landscape.

This is not a story of environmental defeat. In 1900, the Los Angeles metropolis had a population of 325,000 and drought was thought to be imminent; the Metropolitan Water District (MWD) now provides water to more than 15,000,000 people. At the end of World War II, air pollution loomed disastrously over the region; metropolitan population has since multiplied four times, and industrial growth, expansion of the city, and miles traveled have increased accordingly, but the level of air contamination today is below that of 1970. Though often presented as an example of the calamitous environmental consequences of modern urban growth, Los Angeles should also be seen as a locus of successful innovations in environmental management. Over time, these innovations have created a complex of specialized agencies managing local and imported water, air quality, and other regional environmental problems.

Though these agencies have had substantial successes, they remain the focus of controversy. In recent years, two questions have dominated the discussion of regional environmental management for the Los Angeles metropolis.

- Does the very number of these agencies and their overlapping and intersecting powers and roles constitute an important part of the problem? Would regional consolidation lead to more effective environmental management for the metropolis, while reducing the cost?
- How can agencies that provide resources and manage pollution minimize their costs to the regional economy? Would the development of markets for resources (and pollution permits) substantially improve environmental compliance and reduce the economic burden, when compared with historical practices and policies?

Each of these addresses the intersection between regional environment and regional economy, between demands for a safe environment and the challenge of continuing economic growth.

In this chapter, we first review the complex initiatives that led to the establishment of the current structure of environmental governance in metropolitan Los Angeles. Then we address the questions of regional integration and of environmental markets. Finally, we examine the political and planning choices that link environmental management, economic growth, and political participation in Los Angeles. We suggest that what appears now in Los Angeles is likely to appear elsewhere as well.

LOCAL INITIATIVES AND NATIONAL AGENDAS: THE INTERSECTING ORIGINS OF THE CURRENT REGULATORY STRUCTURES

Los Angeles has a long history of local initiative in addressing environmental problems. Many Southern California agencies are now mandated to implement compliance with state and federal environmental laws, but the agencies themselves (or their precursors) originated first out of local concerns. They reflect two distinct political impulses: local elite concerns about limits to local economic growth and popular concerns about quality of life. Particular agencies sprang from one or the other impulse, but most must now accommodate compromises between elite and popular claims.

The division of planning and regulatory activities by environmental medium—the separate institutional treatment of water, air, sewage, waste disposal, open space and natural resource conservation, and land use planning—also developed incrementally as ad hoc responses to the problems and limits of urban and industrial growth in Southern California. Public concern about each new problem led to a new agency, often with new and unique regulatory boundaries, to manage that specific problem. This institutional and spatial fragmentation of environmental issues has established a complex institutional division of labor in Southern California. Though in this chapter we refer primarily to the two largest and most powerful of these agencies (the South Coast Air Quality Management District [SCAQMD] and the MWD), by one observer's count there are currently seventy-two agencies in the Southern California area with significant permitting roles in environmental regulation.[2]

Existing environmental agencies are responsible primarily for either infrastructure development or pollution control. The basic structure of the infrastructure agencies antedates World War II, while the pollution control agencies result from the surfacing environmental problems of rapid urban growth and industrial expansion during and after the war.

The Infrastructure Agencies

In the prewar period, as Los Angeles rapidly expanded its industrial, commercial, and residential base, municipal and regional resource agencies and utilities were formed to construct infrastructure that would support and direct that expansion. The story of water resource development is relatively well known.[3] Los Angeles' Water Department (later the Department of Water and Power) was formed to rationalize the local, then privately dominated, water supply system and to plan and construct the Los Angeles Aqueduct, bringing water from the eastern Sierra. This new water supply stimulated Los Angeles's annexation of other local cities and of undeveloped land but also precipitated an intense resistance to annexation in some local communities, which defended their political autonomy, leaving a complex patchwork of municipal boundaries across the local terrain. As a result, the next stage of integrated infrastructure development required a new institution, the multicity, multicounty Metropolitan Water District of Southern California, formed in 1928 to bring water from the Colorado River to land outside the Los Angeles municipal boundaries, thus opened to further urban growth and development.

Two aspects of this infrastructure development should be noted. Each agency funded imported water primarily by taxes and charges against the largely residential already developed land base, thus assigning the costs of these huge capital projects primarily to home owners, rather than to the industrial and land development leaders who sought further growth. At the same time, the changing service area of each agency had strong effects on the municipal and regional political geography of the metropolitan region.

Imported water also had a powerful and negative effect on the management and conservation of local water supplies. Rapid growth in Orange County and parts of Los Angeles County outside the city, later spilling over into Riverside and San Bernardino counties, both stimulated excessive groundwater withdrawal and contributed to growing contamination of aquifers by industrial wastes. The management districts established to protect water rights holders in the basin areas dealt with the problems of urban expansion not by managing growth but by contracting for additional imported water from the MWD. This addressed immediate overdraft problems and allowed expansion to continue unimpeded, but it undercut any potential for managing water use or water quality, for conjunctively storing imported water in groundwater basins as reservoirs, or for containing demand.[4]

At the same time, the new regionally oriented electric utilities, notably Southern California Edison and the city's power department, encouraged the local development, siting, and expansion of a rapidly growing manufacturing base. Here also municipal bond-based funding of construction, regressive pricing policies,[5] and an aggressive search for new external energy sources[6] characterized agency policy. The strategy of securing huge external sources of water and power well in advance of local demand and of subsidizing industrial and land development by assigning capital and operating costs differentially to residential users culminated in the "Grand Plan" after World War II.[7] In this, Southern California utilities allied with southwestern (and later Pacific northwestern) utilities and industries to establish an interregional power grid to facilitate the intense growth of the postwar years. These alliances, like the Colorado River Compact that allocated that river's water, articulated growth in the Los Angeles region with much of the rest of the western United States; the entrepreneurial cities now jointly managed their huge common hinterland with a shared agenda of urban economic growth.

The Pollution Control Agencies

As metropolitan growth continued even more rapidly after the war, significant—and visible—environmental problems threatened to seriously affect the patterns and dynamics of such growth. Popular concern about these problems led to the formation of new agencies. Water supply and sewage treatment and disposal, air pollution and transportation systems, land development and waste disposal were set up as separate issues. To address sharp increases in sewage outflow into Santa Monica Bay, for example, in the early 1950s Los Angeles constructed its Hyperion sewage treatment facility, which discharged sludge through a seven-mile-long outfall to the ocean floor.[8] The plant was soon discovered to be inadequate; the city had failed to plan for future growth or to anticipate the nature and volume of sewage flows and had overlooked the environmental contamination from the discharge of sludge into the bay.[9] Though the MWD ensured coordination of the regional water supply, there was no parallel regional coordination of sewage treatment and disposal.[10] Nor was there an institutional connection between growth and its environmental consequences.

In the same period, air pollution and land contamination problems also began to tax the region severely. The first major episode of visible air pollution was the 1943 "Black Monday" smog attack; smog events became frequent in the early 1950s. Intense public concern led to quick response from the County Board of Supervisors, immediately complemented by the Chamber of Commerce Smoke and Fumes Commission.[11] The chamber lobbied to limit the extent and severity of regulation, favoring an "educate and persuade approach over "command and control." But some local leaders broke with the chamber's attempts to limit direct regulation; the *Los Angeles Times*'s support of a state bill to establish a countywide Air Pollution Control District (APCD) in 1947 overran business opposition.[12] Still, local regulators were encouraged to consider only stationary sources of air pollutants. The first interventions included elimination of all incinerators (and development of a solid waste disposal system at the county level) and smokestack and engineering controls on industry, particularly oil refineries. The unwillingness of the APCD to regulate autos led the state to set up the Motor Vehicle Pollution Control Board. Cars were then blamed, by the APCD, for 80 to 90 percent of basin smog.[13]

This differentiation of stationary and mobile source regulation continues today. The South Coast Air Quality Management District is the regional successor to the County Air Pollution Control Board and regulates stationary sources primarily; the State Air Resources Board (successor to the Motor Vehicle Pollution Control Board) and its regional offices address the problem of mobile sources of air contamination.

Stationary source restrictions, begun from the hypothesis that air pollution resulted from the engineering weaknesses of backward or careless plants and industries, tended to focus on pollutant by pollutant regulations. Regulatory separation of industrial and mobile sources of pollution discouraged attention to the relationship between air pollution and land use patterns: industrial siting and transport and long-distance individual commutes from the growing suburbs. The construction of freeways continued to encourage peripheral growth.

Problems of waste disposal, linked to residential and industrial expansion and to changes in the composition of the commodity stream, also escalated dramatically. Sanitation officials focused on accommodating the growing waste stream, treating waste issues only as disposal questions. New strategies abandoned previous practices of sorting and recycling municipal waste and relied exclusively on the development of new landfill sites at the urban margin. Industrial hazardous waste disposal was also located outside developed areas, but rapid suburbanization quickly brought these facilities, like the BKK site in West Covina, into the residential suburbs. These landfills then became contested by adjacent communities and by those who claimed the mountain canyons as ecological and recreational resources.

Waste disposal, air quality, and sewage problems continue to plague the region. Each, when defined as public responsibility to accommodate the effects of unrestrained private actions, outruns public resources as the costs and dimensions of that responsibility grow, unconstrained. Agency strategies have managed but only slowed, not reversed, the release of contaminants. Continued definition of regional environmental questions as a set of discrete media-specific issues, where each agency has had jurisdiction over only one segment of a particular environmental flow and where agencies are under pressure not to interfere with unabated industrial and residential expansion, makes these problems extremely difficult to resolve.

State and National Environmental Mandates   By the 1970s, many of these environmental problems were coming to be defined as national in scope, requiring new national forms of public intervention. The federal environmental laws of the 1970s sought to accelerate and restructure the process of environmental mitigation and treatment, by setting national pollutant standards (discharge and emission limits) and by stimulating the development and use of add-on or "end-of-pipe" pollution control technologies. Nearly all the federal laws mandated state and regional or county implementation, thus establishing an entirely new set of responsibilities for local and regional agencies. New state laws also established new agencies and new roles for existing agencies in the management and protection of specific resources, such as groundwater or air. California enacted particularly rigorous environmental laws.

Together, this set of state and federal initiatives led to a complex and intricate pollution control system, now pressed forward by changing federal legislation and mandates. The system was designed primarily to control flows of pollutants at a regional level (defined in terms of air basins, groundwater basins, land areas, surface and bay waters, etc.) on a pollutant by pollutant basis through industry- and media-specific technological controls and (primarily) technology-derived standards. Environmental problems, though increasingly recognized as derivative of the industrial fabric and spatial construction of a region, were regulated only as externalities requiring better engineering. Because environmental policy was developing in the absence of industrial or regional economic policy, the environmental agencies operated without direct guidance on economic issues other than the arguments of the industries they were charged with regulating. Agencies accepted the dominant models of economic development and growth and tried to accommodate them, while meeting specific mandates about pollutant levels. Given an economic status quo ante—a mix of industries and technologies developed without industry responsibility for reducing environmental problems—environmental agencies regularly failed to meet deadlines and targets for pollutant reductions, defended themselves by questioning the value of such targets, and became subject to growing criticism from community and environmental groups.

The infrastructure agencies and utilities had helped to organize the spatial patterns of industrial and residential expansion, but the new pollution control bureaucracies separated the problems of environmental pollution from directing regional growth, addressing each problem narrowly and incompletely. The two sets of agencies thus often acted against each other.

Community Resistance to Agency Initiatives   The perceived bias of the agencies toward encouraging growth brought the agencies under serious attack during the 1970s and 1980s at the community level. Regional growth and integration distributed economic and environmental costs and benefits unequally and unevenly. Communities fought the siting of landfills, the construction of new treatment facilities, the delayed cleanup of waste sites, and continuing failure to control the flow of pollutants into groundwater basins, bays, or air basins. Some opposition arose from established environmental groups active at the state and federal level, but many new opponents were rooted in their neighborhoods, involving constituencies new to environmental policy and planning issues.

During the late 1970s, the Los Angeles Bureau of Sanitation sought alternative disposal strategies for residential solid waste as home owner groups and environmentalists blocked the city's plans to expand landfills into new sites in the Santa Monica Mountains. This shift led to plans for three large regional solid waste incinerators, collectively known as the Los Angeles City Energy Recovery project (LANCER). The first LANCER project was to be built in South Central Los Angeles where opposition, Bureau of Sanitation officials assumed, would be nonexistent. A dramatic campaign by the newly mobilized Concerned Citizens of South Central blocked LANCER and enlarged the debate about solid waste management policy. Similar struggles occurred in places like Glen Avon in Riverside County (where a local community group, Neighbors in Action, challenged the cleanup strategies for the Stringfellow Acid Pits Superfund site) and East Los Angeles (where a community group, Mothers of East LA, successfully fought a planned hazardous waste incinerator and raised larger questions of environmental equity and "negative land uses" in poor communities).

In the San Gabriel Valley, residents concerned about the cleanup of contaminated wells organized to challenge long-entrenched water agency boards and their ties to land development and industry.[14] In westside communities of Los Angeles, coastal residents established Heal the Bay, an organization that demanded Los Angeles's compliance with Clean Water Act restrictions on marine discharges. Similarly, the Coalition for Clean Air sued the SCAQMD to force its plan for industry compliance with the Clean Air Act. Beyond specific pollution issues, a number of groups pushed for growth constraints in their communities, primarily through ballot initiatives. These slow growth movements, defining their concerns in terms of quality of life, focused on the failure of local governments to address the impacts of residential and commercial expansion on local infrastructure.

These extraordinary mobilizations involved local residents with no prior activist history. They challenged specific issues of environmental compliance or resource policy and proposed new strategies to restructure the regulatory framework and to establish new agency priorities. Intense community opposition to solid waste landfills and incinerators, for example, helped generate the political momentum that led to the 1989 passage of AB 939, which established recycling mandates for local governments and a focus on reducing household hazardous wastes. As a result of the passage of AB 939 and the defeat of the LANCER project, the City of Los Angeles set up a new agency (the Office of Integrated Solid Waste Management) to encourage recycling and reduction efforts.

In the area of toxics and hazardous waste policy, mobilization at Stringfellow and the city of Vernon near East Los Angeles pushed policy makers away from a disposal and treatment focus toward the concept of pollution prevention or toxics use reduction.[15] The rapid growth of Heal the Bay, which combined lobbying and litigation with protest and mobilization, quickly translated into successes on sewage and storm drain issues.[16] In response, the sanitation agencies began to consider sewage reduction at the pretreatment stage (including the direct linkage between water use and sewage flow). Heal the Bay also helped draft new ordinances addressing the structural causes of urban runoff pollution, through "good housekeeping" and toxics use reduction as well as by maximizing the on-site percolation of runoff.[17]

The agency most directly challenged by community and environmental criticism, the SCAQMD, was also the agency whose regulatory activities had the highest-profile environmental and economic implications.[18] In the district's revised Air Quality Management Plan of 1989, the agency appeared to extend the parameters of regulatory intervention. The new plan included changes in rule-making procedures, stricter standards and pollutant reduction targets, specific product bans, an emphasis on clean technologies (such as gasoline substitutes and electric vehicles), and strategies to change behavior (e.g., Regulation XV, which required firms to address employee vehicle use). But the SCAQMD approach was ultimately limited by two crucial conceptual choices: spreading the blame for pollution to consumers and small firms (promoted by large emitters such as the oil refineries) and accepting industry assumptions about the prerequisites of economic growth, a justification of the market-oriented RECLAIM program (discussed in more detail below).[19]

Thus uncertainty about appropriate regional environmental policy seems today to be greater than ever, particularly with regard to the ways that environmental and economic policy intersect. Community and environmental movements have forced agencies to modify treatment and control strategies and have challenged their growth biases. Yet most agencies have failed to redefine their missions or to alter the premises of regulation fundamentally. Community groups lack coordination. Perhaps most important, many community groups still fail to address *industrial policy* directly, in relation to the need for jobs, the search for clean technology, and the articulation of strategies for urban sustainability.[20]

RECONCILING FRAGMENTED AND DIFFERENTIATED SPACES

By the mid-1980s, the existing structure of environmental management in metropolitan Los Angeles was under attack from several directions. Community groups throughout Los Angeles had taken up their cudgels to try to drive the agencies toward more aggressive intervention and were beginning to form coalitions at the regional scale; at the same time, the most-regulated industries (particularly land development and the petrochemical industries) were challenging the structure of environmental governance, arguing that regulatory gridlock as a result of multiple and redundant regulatory and permitting agencies was chilling the regional economy. New leaders of the major agencies also recognized that their mandates required coordinated efforts—that the existing fragmentation of responsibility left each agency inadequate to its task and vulnerable to its critics.

Pressure to reconsider the existing structure of agency responsibilities and boundaries thus appeared from all sides. Theorists of land use regulation argued that the administrative blockage caused by municipal autonomy in land use decisions had to be—and was being—set aside[21] (though critics pointed out that land use management at the new regional scale was closely related to the rise of regional-scale land development firms).[22] The stage was set for the play of agency reorganization that would further metropolitan integration.

Though regionalization seemed to be the answer, there was little agreement on the question. Los Angeles was in the throes of what Daniel Press has described as the great conflict of agendas of environmental regionalization: the antinomy between administrative regionalism and what Press calls bioregionalism (a broader term would be ecological regionalism). Administrative regionalism, Press suggests, "seeks to increase policy implementation and effectiveness by consolidating environmental management functions in region-wide agencies. . . . [A]dministrative regionalism redraws jurisdictional boundaries in ways that inevitably alter the balance of power over policy. . . . [P]roposals for regional administration attempt to bridge different media (e.g., water, air, land), management functions (planning, enforcement, zoning, monitoring), and political boundaries."[23]

Though Press contrasts administrative regionalism to bioregionalism, a conception that in its extreme moments has little concern for the future of urban areas and their residents,[24] administrative regionalism can also be contrasted to contemporary more-urban struggles over the environmental circumstances of everyday life.[25] In Los Angeles in the mid-1980s as now, the developing popular movement for a democratic environmental regionalism displayed some of the oppositional characteristics Press identifies: pressure for popular participation in setting goals, standards, and decision rules and for negotiations with affected communities and a general preference for action from the bottom up. Popular urban environmentalism in the mid-1980s had stimulated some substantial innovation: Proposition 65, the California Safe Drinking Water Initiative of 1986, had begun in popular action under arguments of "community right to know" and allowed for citizen suits against polluters and for criminal charges against public officials who were shown to know of toxic releases they had not reported to the public.[26] Community action groups like Mothers of East LA and Concerned Citizens of South Central raised claims for environmental justice in concert with their claims for environmentally sound investment in their impoverished communities. But the agendas of popular regionalism were very different from those of administrative regionalism.

Earlier Moments of Regional Integration

The natural environment as a regional commons has been employed as a communicative metaphor to justify arguments for integrated regional planning for the Los Angeles metropolis at various times in this century. Agendas for the centralization and coordination of otherwise fragmented municipal and economic power have intersected professional arguments for rational comprehensive planning and public administration in several periods. At each moment, advocates of centralization have had to confront the concerns of those who argue for the primacy of local autonomy in municipal politics. Where integrative agencies have been successfully established, such integration has been justified on the basis of the environmental commons.

Resistance to the growing power of municipal Los Angeles limited the prospects for formal regional planning in the 1920s and 1930s, though Southern California planners led the national movement for regional planning.[27] Tension between the efficiencies of regional integration and the desire for local municipal autonomy led to the creation of a number of special districts that together make up the complex institutional structure of the infrastructure agencies introduced above. In the 1920s, progressive attempts to establish regional planning succeeded with regard to the County Sanitation District and the Metropolitan Water District and to transportation, airports, and beach development; other attempts to coordinate at the county/regional level failed. Though the county set up the Regional Planning Commission in 1922, the commission had limited powers to regulate land use and deferred to the cities within municipal boundaries.

Local reformers and public citizens continued to support regional integration and progressive governmental forms. One powerful figure was J. R. Haynes, a wealthy doctor and municipal reformer who in 1925 organized the Direct Legislation League, which supported the Progressive agenda of referendums, initiatives, and recalls of elected officials, in concert with other groups such as the League for Better City Government.[28] Haynes's agenda was continued by the John Randolph and Dora Haynes Foundation, which promoted rationalization of metropolitan government by funding research that examined the potential for metropolitan rationalization from the 1930s until the present.[29]

In addition to projects initiated or supported by the Haynes Foundation, other arguments for regional environmental integration have appeared regularly. One, which offers an informative contrast to the conflicting agendas that surfaced in the mid-1980s, was the Los Angeles Region Goals Project of the late 1960s. In their report, *Environmental Goals for the Los Angeles Region,* the architects and planners who met to develop this agenda agreed on two premises: "environment must be thought of and conceived in its physical and cultural forces together" and any agenda for Los Angeles must engage "the whole metropolitan area."[30] This commission focused on the experience of everyday life in the metropolis. Its report is written in an architectural language and is concerned primarily with the integration of built form, at the urban scale, into the natural environment. In contrast with the issues of efficiency, rationality, and power that characterize the Progressive legacy of regional integration, this return to the concerns of the City Beautiful movement from within the Los Angeles of the late 1960s conveys an apparent innocence. The problem they address is alienation (the lack of human interaction, a loss of the potential aesthetic, the increasing remoteness of people from each other in the face of rapid development, suburbanization, etc.). Though concerned with everyday life in the experience of relatively privileged people, this study has some connection with the popular environmentalism that was to follow it.

This innocence was gone twenty years later, when the City of Los Angeles again convened a community of professional and public citizens to consider regional integration. The period of the 1970s and 1980s had seen increasing public challenges to the functioning of the various regional environmental management agencies. After the 1965 Watts riots, issues of race and class informed antigrowth sentiment among many of the multiple communities of Los Angeles, from the affluent west side to the increasingly impoverished South Central region and East Los Angeles. People felt the loss, not just of quality of life, but of a healthy environment, and recognized that that loss was differentially distributed.

Administrative Regionalism

The claim for spatial integration that became, in the mid-1980s, the primary focus of elite agendas for regionalization such as the Los Angeles 2000 process or the developing collaboration between the SCAQMD and the Southern California Association of Governments (SCAG) clearly fit the arguments for administrative regionalism that Press describes. Though the large regional environmental regulation, resource, and planning agencies—SCAQMD, MWD, and SCAG—were on the front lines with respect to managing the regional environment, they themselves were plagued with problems of accommodation (to federal and state agencies and their changing standards and agendas) and coordination (among themselves and with the multiple smaller or less powerful agencies that also acted within the regional regulatory environment). Their abilities to address the regional environmental questions with which they were concerned were limited by media-specific and changing mandates from above and by sometimes-insurgent and chaotic agendas from below. As the most locally conspicuous occupants of the regulatory front line, they were held responsible by both industry and the citizenry for the limitations of a regulatory process over which they had incomplete control. Increasing challenges to the complex practice of environmental management, derived from the politically uncertain process of an increasingly contested social dilemma now the locus of struggle from the national to the most local scale, impeded their agendas and restricted their opportunities for effective action.

Each agency also faced specific frustrations. The MWD had been formed to manage the water infrastructure of the region behind the scenes of the apparent local autonomy of its member agencies and had based its *pax aquatica* on a compact, the Laguna Doctrine, that guaranteed its supremacy as the regional manager of water resources in return for its promise to its members and clients that local growth would never be constrained by limitations in water supply. The MWD now found itself confronted by a prolonged drought, by the court reallocation to Arizona of water it had traditionally taken from the Colorado River, and by a statewide movement (Proposition 9, the anti-Peripheral Canal referendum) that successfully opposed the further transfer of water from Northern to Southern California. The SCAQMD, which had managed to contain the increase in air pollution in the South Coast air basin despite extraordinary regional urban and industrial growth, could not achieve compliance with federal standards set without consideration of the particular circumstances of the region it was to manage and faced a revolt of its most regulated industries, which insisted that they had done their fair share and that the regulatory finger should point elsewhere. SCAG, headed by a new director who was committed to regional planning as a strategy of effective environmental management and who worked intensely to encourage regional institutional innovation to bridge the contradiction between environmental regulation and economic growth, had only an advisory, not a regulatory, role.

The leading industries of the region also supported the integration and rationalization of environmental planning and management. ARCO, the Times-Mirror Corporation, and the Bank of America,[31] as well as other regional economic leaders directly and through the Los Angeles Chamber of Commerce, joined with the major environmental agencies in encouraging reconsideration of the regional organization of environmental issues.

The impetus for this new coalition was twofold: real concerns for the increasing complexity of environmental management and its associated rapidly rising costs to both industry and government; and a desire to preempt the growing popular opposition to further growth. Out of the intersection of these concerns came a new blue-ribbon committee, LA 2000, whose members were drawn from among the most prominent business people and public citizens of the region.

The questions submitted to this overall committee were first assigned to goals committees charged with a series of topical areas: livable communities (growth management, housing, transportation, safe neighborhoods), environmental quality (environmental management, air, water, waste, energy, earthquakes), individual fulfillment (education, literacy, human services), enriching diversity (economic development, arts), and crossroads city (economy, seaports, airports, transportation). Participants in the goals committees were solicited from government agencies, local universities and colleges, industry and business, and community and public interest groups. Most committees met regularly over a period of more than a year.

The discussions of the environmental quality goals committee reflected the common concerns of its membership, which included the general manager of the MWD, the executive director of SCAG, the former chair of the state Air Resources Board (ARB), members of the board of the SCAQMD, and representatives of public interest groups and major local businesses, including manufacturing. Many issues were openly discussed; only a few, such as the question of whether the region required additional sources of imported water, were set aside as unproductive for discussion, because committee members had already taken opposing, firmly held positions.

Committee discussions covered a wide range of topics in substantial detail. Members and consultants prepared straw plans for discussions in a number of specific areas, such as sewage treatment and disposal, water conservation, energy, and the management of solid and toxic wastes, but these specific discussions were used mostly as a foundation for more general discussion of the problems of integrated environmental planning. Particular themes emerged in these discussions and were carried over to the committee's final summary straw plan.

- *The ecosystem of Southern California is fragile.* Economic expansion and residential growth put increased pressure on the environment and the agencies charged with its management, and current mandates to these agencies "treat growth as a given that must be accommodated." Resource supplies, environmental hazards, and environmental contamination are difficult to manage where growth is unregulated and each is treated as a separate issue.
- *Environmental problems are interconnected.* Contaminants move among environmental media, and end-of-pipe strategies of pollution control move contaminants from one medium to another. The federal legislation, where it is media-specific, severely limits the abilities of responsible local agencies to control this environmental shell game.
- *Source reduction is the best strategy.* The best way to control contamination is not to produce it in the first place. Technological developments based on end-of-pipe controls have achieved most of what they can; the next stage is to improve processes and products so that fewer pollutants are generated.
- *The burden of costs and benefits should be fairly distributed.* Regulators must extend emission standards to smaller firms but recognize that these firms face greater difficulties in compliance. Impacts of environmental contamination should be fairly shared among communities. Financial incentives might help with both small-firm compliance and community fair share.
- *Trade-offs should be local and accountable.* The current agency structure forces land use planners to treat resources for meeting environmental standards as unlimited and separates responsibilities and powers among the various environmental management agencies. There is no lead agency and therefore no clear structure of accountability.[32]

The specific examples given to support each of these points reflect the contrasting concerns of the committee's membership, but the principles expressed were shared.

The language of the straw plan addresses the implications of environmental regulation for business and the regional economy, pointing out the negative economic effects of perceived environmental problems, the need to recognize the importance of small firms and subcontracting relationships, the particular problems small firms face in meeting environmental goals, and the difficulties of multiagency regulation. It suggests that effective environmental regulation requires a better understanding of the regional economy and sensitivity to its complex structure. The straw plan also focuses on an issue that many of the discussants agreed was central to the problem of regional environmental management: the inflexibility of the mandates imposed on regional agencies by state and federal regulation. Most members of the committee agreed that more effective regional coordination and management would require negotiating new agreements with supervising state and federal agencies to allow regional agencies to address trade-offs between environmental media, to consider the question of growth directly in relation to accumulating environmental problems, and to address the issue of the distribution of costs and benefits of environmental contamination and environmental regulation. This need to renegotiate the roles of the primary regional agencies, *though the agencies themselves need not be consolidated into a single regional environmental management agency,* was one of the unexpected outcomes of the committee's discussions. The committee found the primary constraints to improving environmental regulation in the restricted powers agencies had to fit the rules to local situations, not in the multiplicity of agencies themselves. Many committee members agreed that it was necessary to decentralize environmental decisions where possible, to allow general public participation and to ensure accountability about decisions; some felt that consolidation would reduce access and participation. The goals committee did not recommend the creation of a single regional environmental agency.

The recommendations of the various goals committees were passed to the governance committee and then to the Los Angeles 2000 Committee itself. In late 1988, the committee released its final report, *LA 2000: A City for the Future.* This public report carries over much of the discussion of the earlier drafts, with one substantial difference: it recommends the creation of a single regional environmental management agency, connected to and subordinated to a new growth management agency with the power to control land use decisions across the region. The terms in which the responsibilities of this growth management agency are discussed are revealing: it is to replace (and subordinate) the SCAQMD in addressing jobs-housing balance, transportation corridors, airport expansion, and facilities siting. It is also to have the power to overrule municipalities in order to site locally unwanted facilities. It is to have superior powers—to regulate land use without oversight by the courts or delays caused by the problems of environmental compliance. It is, it appears, to free land development and industry from the challenges posed by local communities and by the growing regional claim for better environmental management.

The proposed growth management industry represents administrative regionalism carried to the extreme. Its purpose is the subordination of environmental management, social and political autonomy, and the claims of local communities to a rationale of regional efficiency centered on freeing, not constraining, land use change and land development. This is clearly revealed in the paragraph that precedes the discussion of this agency:

> The Committee notes the emergence of strong community-based organizations. United Neighborhood Organization, South Central Organizing Committee and homeowner associations are examples of this trend. The Committee also notes and commends the establishment of the community advisory boards to participate in the revision of the City's community plans. We must create in Southern California an environment that nurtures the involvement of all residents in public policy issues at every level of government. *Neighborhood activists should understand their community within the larger context of city, county, and regional concerns.*[33]

This larger context is not, in the end, the environmental commons—because those who addressed the environmental commons did not advocate this administrative centralization. Instead, it is power over land use, over the profits of land development and the exigencies of industrial siting, within the region that stands revealed as the central agenda of regional consolidation in this case.

The Los Angeles 2000 process and its internal contradictions suggest that the use of environmental issues to justify administrative regionalism is not always successful. When it is not, the real interests involved must be stated more baldly. While some might argue that a committee that included senior agency managers was unlikely to resolve to consolidate those agencies, the discussions of the participants in the Environmental Goals Committee were not that self-interested. Faced with a problem of effective and fair management of what all participants agreed were pressing regional problems, the committee chose to put regional autonomy and the need for those who knew the locality to be free to address its problems flexibly, rather than regional integration, first. Though administrative rationalization could not, at the end of the LA 2000 process, enlist all of the participants in a consensus for the need for integrated environmental management, the issues of environmental regulation continued to serve its successor, the 2000 Partnership, in its attempts to reorganize regional governance.

Agency consolidation, to reduce the effects of regulation on regional business, was still clearly on the agenda for Southern California. This agenda was shared by other areas of the state. The publication, in 1989, of an Assembly Office of Research study recommending regional planning throughout the state complemented this metropolitan agenda, and the issue briefly stimulated the introduction of bills to support regionalization by the Speaker of the Assembly and other powerful legislators. However, these initiatives are not now the center of legislative attention. The 2000 Partnership continues to lobby for regional planning powers in Sacramento and Washington,[34] but their early success in interesting powerful legislators has eroded as issues such as term limits, general problems of the California economy, and the looming controversies about immigration and crime claim primary attention.

The strategy of reducing the regulatory burden on Southern California business has shifted to a new technique: the establishment of environmental markets.

LOOKING CRITICALLY AT ENVIRONMENTAL MARKETS

In the same period that Los Angeles 2000 was considering the question of regional planning integration, the rules and practices of environmental management at state and federal levels were also in play. In the period from 1980 to 1992, the federal government undertook a critical examination of its practices of environmental regulation in the name of regulatory reform.

As the wide-ranging federal environmental legislation enacted in the 1970s entered the rule-making stage, federal agencies began to formalize their decision-making processes to defend and justify their interventions. This required the development of a new language of environmental principles and an arsenal of new decision rules. Federal agencies were required to establish uniform standards and to employ objective measures if their rule making was to stand up against legal challenges. Initial standards were technology based, reflecting the statutory language of "best available technology" or "best practicable technology." But as opponents to this new arena of federal engagement mobilized their forces and arguments to challenge the economic effects of this regulation and defenders of the regulations entered the lists to force the federal agencies to proceed with rule making and enforcement, economic tools and standards also came to be employed by all sides.

The initial use of economic tools in the review of federal regulations emphasized the application of benefit-cost analysis.[35] This new requirement had several effects: it substantially delayed and impeded new environmental rule making, and it brought hordes of economists into the various executive agencies, not just the Office of Management and Budget, as the agencies struggled with the president's staff to get their rule making approved. The economists who took up these new staff positions were trained in neoclassical economics and convinced of the usefulness of formal microeconomic tools. Many were to become ready conscripts in the war for regulatory reform and advocates of the usefulness of environmental markets (the preferred tools of these economists) to replace technology-based standards (the preferred tools of environmental scientists and engineers).

The Struggle over Rational Regulation: The National Debate

The regulatory reform movement has consolidated an argument for the use of economic analysis in assessing the effects of environmental regulation. This movement appears to have begun in the Environmental Protection Agency (EPA) during the Carter administration, with the rapid growth of the community of economists housed in the EPA Office of Planning and Management and their increasing role, in concert with other executive economic oversight groups, in the debate over the best strategies of environmental regulation.[36] These various groups have made strong claims for the need for the use of economic tools—cost-benefit analysis, cost-effectiveness analysis, and so on—in evaluating proposed regulations and in developing a regulatory structure that limits government intrusion into decisions about production technology. They have sought to substitute "environmental markets" for the established "command and control" strategy of regulation, which set technological and emissions standards to control industrial emissions in the workplace and into the ambient environment.

Environmental markets, it is argued, increase the efficiency with which given overall regulatory goals are met by allowing firms to trade emissions reductions within a particular regional (or regulatory) environment. Thus firms that can easily reduce their emissions below mandated levels ("surplus reductions") can bank them and sell them to other firms whose production processes are more difficult to rework or who require additional permitted emissions capacity to support plant expansion or new plant development. This flexibility, it is suggested, benefits both the firms involved and all participants in a particular regional economy, since it allows market processes to allocate the most efficient strategy of emissions reduction. It thus better manages the presumably otherwise negative effects of environmental regulation on economic growth.

The economic theory on which these arguments are based is strongly microeconomic. It starts from the position of firms that argue that they themselves are better at finding strategies of emissions reductions than are regulators external to the firm. It also treats economic regulation as a new cost of doing business, differentially imposed by location and industry and forcing regulated firms to increase their costs of production (and change their mixes of inputs and operating costs). From this, it supports the argument that environmental regulation is bad for business because of the forced incorporation of previously external costs for some firms while competitors (particularly offshore) are not forced to internalize these costs. Firms often cite environmental regulation as a reason for plant closures and plant relocations.[37]

These two points—the microeconomic question about the economic efficiency of environmental regulation and the more basic question about the economic effects of regulation—have led to a common conception of the problem as one that opposes environmental regulation and regional economic well-being and growth. But this analysis suffers substantially from the absence of a more macroeconomic model based on tools of regional economics. If we look at the question of environmental regulation and economic growth in a more sophisticated and nuanced way, we are much more likely to be able to discover whether environmental safety and improvement necessarily carries costs in jobs and economic well-being.

Sectoral Effects and Industry Structure   Microeconomic analysis does help us work out the immediate effects of environmental regulation within the firm. Environmental regulations force firms to invest in pollution control strategies: equipment, industrial process changes, better hygiene, and trade-offs among production processes and between production and other polluting firm-related activities (e.g., transport, worker transport, etc.). Command and control regulations, as they have come to be called, specify specific process emission standards or particular control technologies as the ways in which firms must do this; in recent years, a number of more flexible alternatives have been developed within the regulatory community, including the bubble concept.

These regulations allocate costs differently among, and differently disadvantage, large and small producers in a given industry. Within an industry, firms' costs in response to environmental regulation include compliance costs, reporting costs, and litigation and lobbying costs. The effects of each set of costs for a particular firm depend in part on its position in the complex of firms in its industry, all competing (more or less) in the market for their particular goods or services. Reporting costs are likely to be a much more significant burden, per unit output, for small firms, since they cannot afford the development of specialized staff and administrative structures to meet these requirements. Compliance costs within an industry are also likely to have uneven effects across firms: smaller firms, with more difficulty in gaining access to capital and technical assistance to meet emissions or production standards, are more pressured by these requirements; to the degree that they are already marginal within the industry, they may be forced out. Where smaller firms and marginal firms tend to be more labor-intensive than their larger competitors in the production of a particular good, this then accentuates the job-loss problem associated with regulation. Reporting and compliance requirements also tend to force smaller firms into more specialized, less diversified, production activities—technological simplification to avoid multiple moments of regulation. They are then potentially more vulnerable to shifts away from their particular goods or services.

One countervailing effect of environmental regulation, which may increase the number of smaller firms, occurs where larger firms choose to shed particular production activities to small subcontractors. Since most regulations address the factory, rather than the product, larger firms can subcontract regulated activities (painting and metal plating, plastics forming, etc.) to avoid regulation and liability. This practice of subcontracting in response to regulation substantially increases the regulatory costs to government, since it increases the number of firms with which regulators must deal. It also increases the aggregate commitment of resources to regulation, counting both agency and firm costs, as a result of the overall increase in transaction costs.

Therefore, within a given industry and its associated suppliers and subcontractors, environmental regulations have complex but generally predictable effects. Marginal and smaller firms are likely to be differentially displaced, except where they take on a subcontracting relationship to larger firms. Environmental regulations oriented toward the factory, rather than the product, have encouraged both industrial concentration and the expansion of networks of subcontracting in many industries.[38]

Intersectoral Effects of Environmental Regulation   The intersectoral effects of environmental regulation are more complex to describe and are complexly interrelated with geographic variations in regulation. Firms have argued that more stringent local regulation (this may be "local" to the region, the state, or the nation—in contrast to other production locations) places them at a competitive disadvantage and, in the long run, forces industrial relocation, or runaway firms. The degree to which this actually occurs is disputed. Factors that influence the locational decisions of firms are highly complex, and firms in different industries are differentially mobile.

Factors that affect mobility include fixed capital investment, the need for particular input factors (raw materials, a particular labor force, or access to particular information), particular market relationships (marketing and merchandising patterns that arise both out of uneven patterns of consumer demand and as an institutional result of particular patterns of regional agglomeration), and the cost of information about and within potential alternative locations. Mobility also needs to be understood in terms of the product- (or profit-) cycle position of the industry: rapidly expanding new industries are making large numbers of new location decisions within which environmental location may take a role.[39]

Mature industries are typically making many fewer new location decisions. Their production operations are complexly embedded in the particular regional economies that their own earlier growth and development has created; these regional economies have complex and segmented labor markets and complex networks of input manufacturers and tend to persist over long periods. They are redefined and renegotiated only in major periods of industrial restructuring. Steel, autos, and oil refining are all examples of such industries. Competition in these industries is mostly for market share of existing products: they rise and fall on the fortunes of the industries (auto, high-rise construction, etc.) for which they produce inputs. If we look at the steel industry as an example, restructuring has been related to reduced demand for the industry's products as inputs to other manufacturing processes (autos, etc.) due to reduction of use within commodities and also of market share of their usual customers. Technological change in the auto industry has reduced the steel needed for each car; at the same time, American manufacturers have lost market share to external competitors and have relocated their sources of components into foreign sites. If General Motors produces or purchases most components of its cars in Mexico, its purchase of inputs is also likely to shift away from American steel. The chemical industry, closely connected to petrochemical refining, has maintained a very high rate of profit by a constant high rate of product innovation and is expanding—but still selects relatively few new locations within already developed economies—except for formulation and fabrication plants (and firms) for which the big refineries produce inputs.

For these firms, the imposition of new environmental regulations with their associated capital, operating (administrative, reporting, and surveillance), and lobbying and litigation costs may lead the firm to decide to close an already marginal and moribund plant sooner than it otherwise would have done. However, the possibility of allocating marketable pollution permits to firms now emitting criteria pollutants may encourage firms to keep plants open, in the hope of reaping a last-minute capital windfall through a new property right, if they feel that the potential sale of that right in the regional manufacturing and services economy will more than offset the net cost of keeping the plant operational for a short time. Empirical work needs to be done on this, but such analysis is difficult, of course, since these choices are internal to the firm and are normally treated as industrial secrets for obvious political reasons.

The initial conception of environmental regulation in the 1960s and early 1970s itself depended on market forces to work out the effects of environmental problems. This conception sought to force, through command and control, the internalization of the environmental costs of production and then to let the market work out the structural implications of these real costs. It has no doubt influenced intersectoral shifts and capital withdrawal in particular industries and locales. However, the magnitude of this effect is difficult to determine given the dynamic forces of competition, along a number of different parameters, that have manifested in these sectors in the same period. Most firms that close major plants now cite regulatory burdens as the reason. However, in previous periods of restructuring, without such regulatory burdens, firms have still closed marginal plants and industries have still restructured.

Macroeconomic Effects of Environmental Regulation within Regions The smaller the geographic scale, the easier it is to estimate the potential economic effects of environmental regulations. Complex patterns of industrial shares and the effects of potential choices on the regional economy as a result of changes in input and output markets and in wage packets, all with associated regional multipliers, give us a basis for this estimation. The simplest model of this estimation is the market efficiency criterion that lies behind the argument for marketable pollution permits, but this model is too simple and excludes supplier and subcontracting linkages and other multiplier effects too completely to be used to address the effects of regulation on the well-being of any particular region or on growth in a particular regional economy.

This becomes particularly important when we consider the potential economic effects of new regulatory strategies (marketable pollution permits, etc.) that allow intersectoral trading in emission reduction credits. The economic effects of this for the regional economy, in wages earned and spent locally and in profits and taxes paid by regional suppliers, depend on the gain and loss of economic activity in particular sectors. They are not well estimated by simple measures of greater efficiency of compliance.

Thus one necessary component of understanding the effects of environmental markets for various commodities/services is a careful analysis of the structure of the space economy within which these markets are to be placed. Abstract arguments about the functioning of theoretical markets are relatively useless in real-world situations, where markets encounter the realities of industrial structure in space. Environmental markets are necessarily spatial and often regional; those who seek to purchase environmental goods or services are seeking access to scarce resources that are scarce in part because of local/regional natural *and* social conditions and that are managed (made available to the market) through regional institutions.

Market strategies have been recently proposed in Southern California as ways to govern access to both water and air. The implications of the proposals to establish a marketlike allocation mechanism in each of these two environmental goods are very different, because the circumstances of each are different in both their physical and historical bases. However, comparison of the two potential markets supports some general statements about the implications of market regulation of natural resources or environmental contaminants and offers some insights that may clarify the relationship between environmental planning and the functioning of regional economies, in Los Angeles and elsewhere.

The Question of Water Markets   Water is available to prospective users in the Southern California metropolitan area as a result of both natural endowments and a huge public expenditure. The Southern California water system is embedded in a complex institutional base of water law, water agencies, and political tradition. Old alliances between Southern California land developers, urban water agencies, and agricultural users in the Central and Imperial valleys built a massive system of water transport that relocates precipitation from a hinterland of over 250,000 miles. The history of development of these alliances has left 80 percent of developed water in California committed to agricultural uses, under current social and economic conditions, a disproportionate share of a major natural resource.

Continuing growth in demand for water for urban, industrial, and agricultural uses under conditions of fluctuating rain- and snowfall has compromised these alliances, but proposals to enable transfers of water among the various current users offer benefits to each group. To the degree that water markets can allocate water to meet changes in demand without requiring the development of new supplies, there are environmental benefits. Indeed, new policies of water allocation can include commitments of water to maintain natural systems threatened by current practices.

There are several issues in water policy that need to be considered in evaluating proposals for water markets. The greater ability of urban users to pay for water should not in itself be used to justify large-scale reallocation of water from rural to urban uses. Agricultural uses of water are important to the state's economy, to farm communities, and to those who consume California's myriad agricultural products. Urban uses of water are often wasteful and carry substantial environmental costs, overloading sewage and waste treatment systems and carrying environmental contaminants into sensitive ocean and wetlands environments. A simple market for water, unconstrained by a careful concern for the effects of urban growth and growth in urban water consumption, will not resolve the environmental issues in which the water system is implicated. However, it is clear that there is room for improvement in water policy and that voluntary transfers of water entitlements among users offer substantial benefits when compared to the alternative of new source development.

Though water is an essential resource for California agriculture, there is substantial room for water conservation in many current agricultural practices. Water entitlements established by agricultural users can be considered an asset, as well as a resource. More efficient use of water in farming can free water for urban and industrial use and for restoring environmental systems, and the differential relative value of a given quantity of water across these different users can fund farmers to invest in more water-efficient technologies and crops. Though problems of risk and uncertainty in agriculture are substantial, and some farmers see any loss of water security as an unacceptable additional risk, other farmers have joined metropolitan water agencies and their urban and industrial clients in seeking change in the existing strict structure of entitlements to allow flexibility (from year to year) in transferring water to adjust to new patterns of demand and higher-value uses.[40]

The water "markets" currently in development are highly imperfect, but they may allow greater flexibility and resilience in what is otherwise a stressed system of resource allocation. Water transfers must accommodate the basic problem of water management in California, increasing demand that intersects huge year-to-year variations in supply. Current strategies of impoundment and conservation reserves manage this variation somewhat, but in the long run flexible transfers of water from agriculture offer the most likely source of additional and dry-year supplies. Coupled with incentives for demand management and better conjunctive management of local and distant resources, water markets that transfer water from agricultural to urban uses offer an expanded supply at costs substantially less than those to develop new distant sources. Where the agencies engaged in these market negotiations are responsible and accountable to their publics, water markets can provide substantial public benefits and improved efficiencies of resource use, at relatively low cost.

The natural, social, and economic impact of the transfer of water from rural to urban uses varies with the situation. The impact of Los Angeles's capture of the entire water supply of the Owens Valley is quite different than that of MWD's "purchase," from the Imperial Irrigation District, of Colorado River water already in transit to the Imperial Valley and which would otherwise be lost, unproductively and destructively, in percolation from leaking unlined canals. Similarly, the impact of transfers of water from Central Valley agriculture to metropolitan (or environmental) uses will differ depending on whether that water would otherwise be employed to irrigate (1) permanent crops that support relatively small-scale farming and relatively continuous employment for local farmworkers, processing, and shipping workers or (2) annual crops, like cotton, that are already in surplus and whose continued production offers little in terms of multiplier effects to the local economy.

Markets for transfer of water can be established with relative ease in California because the institutional precursors for such innovation are already established. Such precursors include the establishment of water rights as formal property rights, the development of agencies of water management, and the physical construction of an infrastructure capable of transporting water from seller to buyer. Property rights in water (through a complex set of institutions tied to landownership or membership/entitlement in some agency that manages water resources) are well developed and relatively accepted. The establishment of markets for water transfer requires some redefinition of these rights, particularly where use of a particular water reserve is shared (as with unadjudicated groundwater basins or riparian rights shared among all landowners along a particular watercourse). However, pressures on the water resource base in California have gradually led to the establishment of quantified rights in most cases; where this has occurred the next transition, to the right to sell the water for use off the land from which the right is initially derived, is not a great one.[41] There is no requirement that the water delivered to the buyer is the actual physical water released by the seller, since water is treated as a standardized commodity. The existing physical infrastructure of storage and transport of water in California already provides the transfer of water over long distances and from multiple sources; since what is normally to be traded in this proposed market is entitlements to already developed water, rather than newly captured water, no substantial new issues of water quality are involved. Hence many of the capital and transaction costs required by a water market are already being paid, so that the benefits of market-based transfers of water appear convincing.

The water markets proposed at present are fictions in another sense. While the decision to sell water entitlements may, in some cases at least, be made by individual farmers, the decision to buy is not made by the final consumers. This is likely to have environmental consequences. The prime movers and potential purchasers of this impetus toward marketed water in California are the large urban water districts and, most centrally, the MWD, which was formed to provide imported water to the Los Angeles metropolis and has expanded to provide water to a six-county area stretching from Ventura to San Diego as well. The power of the district's management and board in setting water policy for Southern California, given the MWD's specific role as a purveyor of imported water and its continued distance from other water-related issues, biases the regional discussion of water and water quality issues toward imported water as the solution to all water problems. Water transfer arrangements—markets or not—that recruit additional water to Los Angeles will not help to resolve the pressing and closely related regional problems of demand management, groundwater quality, conjunctive use of local ground- and surface water, and sewage and waste treatment and wastewater disposal. In abstracting the question of water supply from the whole problem of water management, markets fail to close the ecological/environmental loop. The benefits of water markets are not measured against these costs.

Water markets must be seen, then, as a mechanism for compensating farmers for releasing water needed to meet urban demand, a device that may stimulate the willing release of water to which farmers have already established rights. We should not assume that water markets necessarily bring about greater efficiencies of use, that they in themselves resolve environmental problems, or that they in themselves create benefits in which all share fairly.[42] Allocation in much more perfect markets is not neutral with respect to disparities in wealth and power; any use of remunerated water transfers must acknowledge that the rural systems of California employ and feed many people who will have little voice in this decision to shift water from the rural to the urban environment.

What is needed, in both rural and urban areas, is a better sense of what F. Lee Brown and Helen M. Ingram call the community, not the commodity, value of water.[43] Markets cannot be presented as resolving the complex questions of fairness involved in water allocation entirely and in themselves, because the property rights on which markets are based do not allow all who are affected to have a voice in these decisions. Compensated water transfers may induce the willing release of water from farmers or irrigation districts and yet leave behind a landscape without jobs or local communities. They may also, in establishing a right to transfer water between regions, have disastrous effects on the environment of the sending region. Markets for water may make good servants, but they are sure to be bad masters.

A Regional Market for Air?   The questions we have raised about the institutional advocacy of markets for water appear, even more clearly, in the proposal to use markets to manage air quality. The advantages cited for marketable permits, as a way to manage trade-offs between production and environmental control, include (1) the opportunity such permits would give firms to establish innovations themselves for reducing emissions, rather than responding to command and control decisions from regulatory agencies not as capable of discovering opportunities for emission control within the industrial processes of a particular firm or industry; (2) the reduction in surveillance costs for regulatory agencies, to the degree that firms themselves police their competitors so as to protect the benefit of their own property rights; (3) the reduction in adversarial relationships between firms and regulators and in the costs of such relationships in litigation, and so on, both to firms and to regulatory agencies.[44] But marketable pollution permits do not address several important aspects of the effect of regulation on regional economies. They focus on the relationship between the regulatory agency and the firm, or between the agency and large regulated firms in general. They do not directly consider the regional environmental effects of production in particular sectors.

To do this, we need to turn to measures that examine the relative contribution of firms (and industries) to the regional economy, such as the multiplier effects associated with local employment, investment, and purchasing. Here, we may discover that the apparent contradiction between environmental regulation and economic growth is made more understandable if we look at the employment effects of regulation as one primary criterion of regulatory choice. This criterion would require that we seek to maximize pollution control relative to jobs lost as a result of that intervention. Local employment supports local provision of consumer goods and services; local sourcing of inputs supports expanded local employment. The cumulative effects of this, as dollars from wage packets associated with both direct and indirect employment circulate through the regional economy, are a higher rate of regional economic growth and a more diverse regional economic base.

The Southern California regional manufacturing economy encompasses one of the major manufacturing regions of the world.[45] It is highly diversified, but rapid growth in federal defense spending in the 1980s followed by rapid reduction after 1989 has significantly stressed the stability of its defense-related components. The restructuring of the 1980s also involved the withdrawal of most fixed investment in the traditional, Fordist, industries and included the closure of the Kaiser steel plant at Fontana and the General Motors assembly plant at Van Nuys, among others. Of the major Fordist industries, only the petrochemical industry remains important in the regional economy. The growing industries within the regional manufacturing economy are those whose industrial organization has been described as post-Fordist;[46] that is, they function through complex networks of interfirm interaction, including various kinds of subcontracting, just-in-time inventory, and high rates of technological and product innovation. Production within post-Fordist industries involves complex networks of larger and smaller firms, not immense oligopolistic firms with largely internalized production activities.

This is a very different form of economic structure from that envisioned by the strategy of environmental regulation institutionalized in the federal environmental legislation of the 1970s. The implications of firm-by-firm regulation become intolerably complicated when industries are complexly and externally organized, made up of intricate networks of interrelated firms. Under these circumstances, the transaction costs of firm-by-firm regulation are overwhelming for the firms themselves,[47] for the regulatory agencies mandated to address their environmental problems, and for the regional economy. At the same time, certain aspects of federal environmental law encourage subcontracting and the externalization of particularly hazardous, or particularly regulated, production activities.[48]

The historical practice of regulation of industrial air emissions in Southern California began with local and state regulatory initiatives. Because of their major contribution to the release of pollutants of primary concern, the petroleum refining, petrochemical, and utilities industries were targeted for regulation from early in this period. However, by the mid-1970s, federal legislation had preempted local concerns. Federal legislation and associated rules established national standards for "criteria air pollutants." These criteria pollutants included hydrocarbon emissions (reactive organic gases), oxides of nitrogen and sulfur, carbon monoxide, and particulates— all (in part) by-products of the combustion of fossil fuels by both mobile and stationary sources, by transportation and industrial manufacturing. EPA set national standards for pollutant concentrations, which amalgamated pollutants emitted by mobile and stationary sources.[49] This required the two Southern California air agencies to work in concert to achieve compliance with EPA standards.[50]

Stringent end-of-pipe regulation of emissions from utilities and the petrochemical industry achieved some reductions; application of the bubble concept (by which regulated firms could find emissions reductions anywhere within a fictive "bubble" visualized as covering all of their operations, not just from end-of-pipe controls) encouraged further reductions. Stringent standards for vehicle engineering and maintenance also had an important impact. However, it became clear that Southern California could not comply with EPA standards based on these regulatory strategies alone. In 1989, the SCAQMD released a new plan that promised to bring Southern California into compliance with federal standards by 1996 for nitrogen dioxide, by 1997 for carbon monoxide, and by 2007 for ozone and regulated particulates.[51] The 1989 air plan was a collaborative effort of the SCAQMD, the ARB, and SCAG (which contributed plans for regional transportation, growth management, and land use controls). Without the formation of a single regional environmental agency, these organizations had succeeded through collaboration in combining their interests and powers to connect urban form and environmental controls.

The 1989 air plan placed stringent requirements on a number of formerly more loosely regulated industries and economic activities. It also imposed restrictions on the manufacture and use of substances contributing substantially to the region's air quality problem, regulating a whole complex of substances and activities not previously the focus of regulation. Most visible were restrictions on the use of solvents and coatings that emitted a substantial share of the reactive organic gases entering the regional atmosphere. The regulation of these materials was intended to force reformulation of these commodities, to regulate the paints and coatings industries not just by containing their manufacturing processes but by demanding that they manufacture a much cleaner product.

The plan went further, regulating consumer products such as aerosol sprays and underarm deodorants and commercial activities such as restaurant grills and barbecues. The focus of the plan was on reducing emissions of reactive organic gases, an ozone precursor, to achieve EPA standards for ozone concentrations in the difficult climatic circumstances of Los Angeles by 2007.

The plan stimulated immediate controversy. Where earlier air regulations had focused on relatively concentrated and capital-intensive industries such as petrochemicals, autos, and utilities, these new regulations reached broadly across firms and into consumer products. At the same time, the new regulations were seen as putting substantial regulatory pressure on important local industries, particularly furniture and electronics. These industries were complexly organized and made up of relatively large numbers of smaller firms. They also employed large numbers of minority workers. Many firms in these industries were facing other economic pressures and reacted to the imposition of new regulations on the products they used as a significant threat. Popular fears of unemployment, issues of disparate impact on people of color, and consumer fears of the loss of customary goods, transportation practices, and commercial services all supported a challenge to the new plan.[52]

The inclusiveness of the regulatory impulse of the 1989 air plan strengthened the position, and the constituencies, of the utilities and petrochemical firms. These industries had pushed the SCAQMD to extend stringent regulation of emissions to smaller firms using a "fair share" argument—that they had already achieved significant emission reductions and the same standards should be applied to all firms. They now took advantage of the new broader fear of SCAQMD regulation among smaller firms, workers, and consumers to strengthen their arguments against command and control regulations as a strategy. The SCAQMD board backed down.

SCAQMD staff was directed to pursue the alternative of marketable pollution permits. The shift to marketable pollution permits, rather than command and control, pleased the two apparently distinct constituencies from which the board faced the most concentrated pressure: the heavily regulated major emitters and the regulatory reformers at EPA. EPA, in the clasp of the regulatory reform movement, was pleased to use Los Angeles as a laboratory for permit markets. Rather than continue to struggle to apply command and control regulation to the nation's most intransigent air problems, the SCAQMD would turn responsibility over to a market in rights to emit.

This market was initially supported by many across the region. Firms, large and small, saw it as an opportunity to respond flexibly to the requirement of overall emissions reductions, by selling emissions rights if they could reduce their own emissions, by buying rights if they could not. Environmental groups also supported the early concept because it promised a gradual reduction in emissions (each transaction was to require a reduction from the previously permitted emissions) and because it offered the opportunity for public bidding to retire emissions permits and thus achieve more rapid reductions. The SCAQMD and its allies argued that the marketable permit program would have very limited effects on the regional economy, leading to a small loss of jobs in the aggregate (though there might still be significant job loss in some industries).

However, as planning for a marketable permit program proceeds, the scale, scope, and potential benefits of this new institutional strategy have become significantly reduced. Participation has been limited to a relatively small number of firms, the largest emitters in the most concentrated industries. The program now offers less regulatory relief and fewer opportunities for broad participation. SCAQMD has been reduced to constructing a new institution whose primary effect is to confirm the current emission practices of its oldest client/antagonists. Observers and SCAQMD staff agree that the RECLAIM program will have limited effects on the region's economy. As Kelly Robinson states,

> There are several reasons for this. First, compliance costs under either CAC [command and control] or RECLAIM remain a relatively small part of overall production costs for most industries, and many of the investments that are required have already been made. Second, the universe of sources covered under RECLAIM represents only a fraction of those facilities subject to pollution controls in the basin. Third, the cost savings attributable to the program are concentrated in just a few industries, and these tend to be industries producing for local markets. This makes it less likely that cost savings will translate directly into enhanced competitiveness for the region.[53]

The benefits that might appear with a more extensive market for emissions in a complexly structured and diverse regional economy are absent when emissions trading rights are limited to the largest, most concentrated industries. These industries are capital intensive, have relatively limited labor forces, are purchasing few local inputs, and are stable or declining in the region. The RECLAIM program offers little advantage for firms in those industries that make up the growing segments of the region's industrial base.[54]

Turning the Model Upside Down   To rethink our practices of environmental regulation with respect to the economic effects of this intervention, we must ask again which industries should be regulated. Initially, agencies identified these industries heuristically, based on the criterion of their proportional contribution to total emissions of criteria pollutants. More recently, agencies have acceded to the claims of those now heavily regulated industries that regulation should be a general, not a specific, burden—that the Fordist industries have done their fair share and new regulatory pressures should be spread across the regional economy. In the absence of a more theoretically informed and dynamic sense of the relationship between environmental regulation and a healthy regional economy, agencies are relatively defenseless against these claims. In asking what is the economic effect of each regulation, as they currently do, agencies overlook the role of environmental regulation as a constituent of industrial policy. The industries they regulate do not.

The tool that SCAQMD employs to estimate the regional economic effect of proposed regulation is a regional economic model, the REMI model, which is widely used in such situations and which has been carefully investigated.[55] As a result of the development of historical practices of regulation that began with command and control of emissions technology and then looked, defensively, at the economic effects of particular proposed regulations, the district first identifies practices and activities subject to regulation and then, using the REMI model, estimates the economic effects of these proposed regulations. As a consequence, the process of identifying the best opportunities for emissions control begins at the wrong point, if environmental planning is to seriously engage the relationship between environmental protection and economic growth.

Tools like the REMI model are used to estimate effects in employment and sales, aggregated at the regional scale. These tools might also be used to look for the most efficient points of intervention in regional economies. The following scenario would apply. An agency could ask, where can we get the maximum emissions reduction for each potential job lost? for each local wage dollar? How can we comply with federal standards and achieve the most constructive outcome for the regional economy? That strategy would directly engage the relationship between environmental and economic gains. It would also bring to the surface the currently hidden connections between environmental regulation and economic change, opening the choices that must be made to a more democratic, participatory public debate.

ENVIRONMENTAL PLANNING AND DEMOCRATIC PRACTICE

In conclusion, we address the question of regional integration. Suggested initiatives toward regional environmental planning would shift the power to regulate environmental issues (and thus, under current institutional circumstances, the power to regulate the industrial, land use, and social choices within which those issues appear) from municipal and county agencies to decision makers beyond the domain of municipal and county politics. This is for some the purpose of this initiative, to free firms from the constraints imposed by local political opposition. Such disenfranchisement of local communities (even the huge City of Los Angeles) would create an immense problem of public participation and political accountability, under the guise of rational comprehensive planning. It is also likely to exacerbate current inequities of income and power, unless some effective structure of political participation and local control is tied to the rationalization of the policy and permitting process from the start.

The problem of democratic participation should be taken seriously. It is too easy for those of us accustomed to life in Los Angeles to forget that the Southern California metropolitan region contains one out of every twenty people living in the United States. More than sixteen million people live within the MWD service area, and the population affected by the actions of the SCAQMD is only slightly smaller. The Los Angeles metropolitan region is larger, in population and at times in area, than the countries of Eastern Europe that are struggling so hard to establish democratic forms. It is also much more diverse. It is not legitimate to consider constructing a form of government, through integration of regional environmental planning, that makes crucial policy choices affecting the everyday lives of every resident of this metropolis but that is not subject to accountability through mechanisms of democratic participation and consent.

At the same time, some sort of regional integration is necessary. The question is, how is it to be composed? Environmental planning, like all collective action, takes place in a complex and differentiated social space in which many conflicting interests are vested. Administrative strategies of regionalization seek to rationalize the management of that space from the top down and usually reflect the concerns of, and struggles among, the most powerful actors in the region. Agencies must act in ways that inevitably redistribute environmental and economic costs and benefits, but they must acquire the tools to understand the consequences of their actions and to identify the actions they should take. These tools must be able to grasp the complex realities of the region, its economic structures, and its distributions of power, and they must, if they are to be democratic, consider issues of social justice and open participation.

What we suggest is integration and disintegration, coordination and concentration of agencies, and, at the same time, devolution of their powers to make choices about policy and location to elected representatives of the communities their choices affect. To be effective, environmental planning must be based in communities as well as agencies. Social choices about the difficult issues of environmental and economic risk and uncertainty must be submitted to popular approval if they are to be legitimate and effective.

The relationship between environmental and industrial policy in these issues should be brought to the surface. All participants in the debates about Nature in Los Angeles agree that they want a strong regional economy with growing employment. But the connection between employment growth and environmental regulation is complex and needs full investigation and public discussion. The representations of the regulated and subsidized industries are necessarily self-serving; they cannot provide the only source of information and the only appraisal of the choices involved in constructing economic growth and environmental quality.

The Los Angeles regional economy is changing; it is being restructured by changes in the global economy and in national policy as well as by the limited effects of local regulation. A discussion that begins with the assertion that we want to stimulate the growth of an environmentally sound industrial base, with good employment practices, high rates of innovation, and effective protection for worker, community, and consumer health and safety and quality of life, comes to a different conclusion than one that sees the role of the planning agencies as protecting vested industries with low employment rates and high environmental costs.

We should allow local communities a strong role in setting planning and regulatory agendas. The role of the regional environmental planning agency might be to centralize information gathering and to develop and provide scientific and technical information, but decisions about environmental policy must have effective citizen representation and accountability. Centralization of some planning activities must be complemented by constructing a structure that allows for community-level as well as subregional and regional planning and general popular participation. Space, location, participation, and power are intimately related. The most crucial mission effective environmental planning can have is the charge to stimulate and incorporate creative ideas, innovation, and responsible action from all participants, in reconciling the metropolis and its natural environment. When dealing with nature, space is problematic but cannot be ignored.

NOTES

We would like to acknowledge Julie Roque's contribution to our analysis in the course of several years' discussions of environmental issues in Los Angeles. We would also like to acknowledge that this argument would have been inconceivable without finally learning to understand what Ed Soja keeps telling us about space. Any errors or omissions are our own.

1. This point is very well made by two otherwise quite disparate observers of the urban scene. See David Harvey, "Rent, Finance and the Urban Revolution," in *The Urbanization of Capital* (Baltimore: Johns Hopkins University Press, 1985; and John McPhee, "Los Angeles against the Mountains," in *The Control of Nature* (New York: Farrar, Straus, Giroux, 1989).

2. Letter from Roy Anderson, Chair, Los Angeles 2000 Partnership, to Governor Pete Wilson, 4 May 1992.

3. See Steven P. Erie, "How the Urban West Was Won: The Local State and Economic Growth in Los Angeles, 1880–1932," *Urban Affairs Quarterly* 27, no. 4 (June 1992): 519–554.

4. See, for example, William A. Kahrl, *Water and Power: The Conflict over Los Angeles' Water Supply in the Owens Valley* (Berkeley, Los Angeles, and London: University of California Press, 1988); Robert Gottlieb and Margaret FitzSimmons, *Thirst for Growth: Water Agencies as Hidden Government in California* (Tucson: University of Arizona Press, 1991); Erie, "How the Urban West Was Won."

5. On the question of imported water as a peaking source, see James H. Krieger and Harvey O. Banks, "Ground Water Basin Management," *California Law Review* 50 (1962): 57; see also Albert Lipson, *Efficient Water Use in California: The Evolution of Groundwater Management in Southern California* (Santa Monica: Rand Corporation, 1978), CA R-2387/2-CSA/RF.

6. Particularly, sharp declining block rates, which meant that large industrial users paid much less per unit than households.

7. Initially associated with water supply infrastructure, as in the hydroelectric generators of the Los Angeles Aqueduct and Hoover Dam on the Colorado; later with the development of coal resources on the Kaiparowitz Plateau.

8. The term "Grand Plan" was first introduced by a DWP official in the early 1950s. See Peter Wiley and Robert Gottlieb, *Empires in the Sun: The Rise of the New American West* (Tucson: University of Arizona Press, 1985).

9. On the background to the development of the Hyperion plant, see Winston W. Crouch et al., *Metropolitan Los Angeles: A Study in Integration. V. Sanitation and Health* (Los Angeles: Haynes Foundation, 1952).

10. As industry grew, the technical problems associated with combining residential and industrial sewage increased, chemical use became more common, and industrial discharges frequently killed the bacteria employed to digest residential wastes.

11. Though the Los Angeles County Sanitation District provided parallel sewage treatment and disposal services for some new municipalities and their rapidly growing population, other areas constructed local treatment plants and infiltrated their effluent into the ground overlying the groundwater pools.

12. Marvin Brienes, "Smog Comes to Los Angeles," *Historical Society of Southern California* 58, no. 4 (1976): 525–532.

13. Jeffrey Fawcett, *The Political Economy of Smog in Southern California* (New York: Garland, 1990).

14. Ibid., 84.

15. The term of preference for community and environmental groups; see Mark Rossi, Michael Ellenbecker, and Kenneth Geiser, "Techniques in Toxics Use Reduction: From Concept to Action," *New Solutions* 2, no. 2 (Spring 1990): 25–32.

16. One Heal the Bay activist became the president of the Board of Public Works (overseeing both the solid waste and sanitation bureaucracies) and, subsequently, regional administrator of the U.S. Environmental Protection Agency.

17. See, for example, the City of Santa Monica 1992 ordinance on storm drain runoff, drafted in conjunction with Heal the Bay staff members, approved 11 August 1992.

18. Challenges to the SCAQMD primarily took the form of litigation.

19. The SCAQMD's activities symbolize the uneven nature of agency response

to the community challenges. In the toxics area, for example, pollution prevention has become a new buzzword for local governments and agencies but has failed so far to translate directly into a shift in regulatory direction.

20. It should be noted, however, that several of the groups, ranging from Concerned Citizens of South Central and Mothers of East LA to the Silicon Valley Toxics Coalition in the Santa Clara area and the Los Angeles-based Labor/Community Strategy Center have begun to explore some of the questions related to the link between environmental and industrial policy.

21. Fred Bosselman and David Callies, *The Quiet Revolution in Land Use Control* (Washington, D.C.: U.S. Government Printing Office, 1972).

22. Richard Walker and Michael Heiman, "Quiet Revolution for Whom?" *Annals of the American Association of Geographers* 71, no. 1 (1981): 67–83.

23. Daniel Press, "Environmental Regionalism and the Struggle for California," *Society and Natural Resources* 8, no. 4 (1995): 289–306.

24. One active bioregionalist announced to us, at a meeting we had organized in 1986, that "after nuclear war bioregionalism would come into its own."

25. See Robert Gottlieb, *Forcing the Spring* (Washington, D.C.: Island Press, 1993), for a review of the long history of urban environmental struggles in the United States.

26. Margaret FitzSimmons and Robert Gottlieb, "A New Environmentalism," in *Reshaping the U.S. Left: Popular Struggles in the 1980s,* vol. 3 of *The Year Left,* ed. Mike Davis and Michael Sprinker, 114–130 (New York: Verso Books, 1988).

27. See Judith Norvell Jamison, "Coordinated Public Planning in the Los Angeles Region," *Studies in Local Government,* no. 9, Bureau of Governmental Research, University of California, Los Angeles, June 1948.

28. For a detailed discussion of this period of Los Angeles history, see Robert Gottlieb and Irene Wolt, *Thinking Big: The Story of the Los Angeles Times, Its Publishers, and Their Influence on Southern California* (New York: Putnam, 1977). See also Erie, "How the Urban West Was Won."

29. The authors wish to acknowledge the support of the Haynes Foundation for their research for the book *Thirst for Growth.*

30. Environmental Goals Committee, Los Angeles Region Goals Project, "Environmental Goals for the Los Angeles Region," Southern California Chapter, American Institute of Architects (1967), i.

31. The Bank of America had recently relocated its headquarters to Los Angeles from San Francisco.

32. Los Angeles 2000 Environmental Quality Committee, Summary Straw Plan (revised), 6 November 1987.

33. Los Angeles 2000 Committee, *LA 2000: A City for the Future,* 1988, p. 70. Emphasis added.

34. Roy A. Anderson, president of the 2000 Partnership, wrote to Governor Pete Wilson on 4 May 1992 to make the following points:

> The primary theme of The 2000 Partnership is governmental simplification, efficiency, and accountability. We seek the consolidation of the planning functions of single purpose regional agencies. . . .

Analyses undertaken for The 2000 Partnership have demonstrated that single-focus agencies are spending over $5 billion in the Southern California region. There is substantial evidence that they now operate sometimes at cross purposes and sometimes in ignorance of each other in ways that increase costs. Those increased costs are borne not only directly by taxpayers but also by businesses and individuals whose activities are subject to uncertainties, delays, and sometimes, perverse decisions.

We note with considerable concern the number of local, State, and Federal agencies involved in environmental, water quality, hazardous waste, solid waste, and air quality issues that affect the Southern California region:

	Total	Local	State	Federal
Agencies that issue environmental permits	72	27	32	13
Agencies with water quality authority	38	14	18	7
Agencies with hazardous waste authority	38	17	13	8
Agencies with solid waste authority	14	7	6	1
Agencies with air quality authority	17	6	6	5

We will continue to work with your staff and state legislators, as well as with Southern California officials, to realize the simplification and efficiency needed. The current economic climate and the need to assist business in an environmentally responsible way would seem to call for bold and decisive action.

35. Richard N. L. Andrews, "Economics and Environmental Decisions, Past and Present," *Environmental Policy under Reagan's Executive Order,* ed. V. Kerry Smith, 43–85 (Chapel Hill: University of North Carolina Press, 1984).

36. For useful discussions of this movement and its origins, see Brian J. Cook, *Bureaucratic Politics and Regulatory Reform: The EPA and Emissions Trading* (New York: Greenwood Press, 1988); and Robert K. Raufer and Stephen L. Feldman, *Acid Rain and Emissions Trading: Implementing a Market Approach to Pollution Control* (Totowa, N.J.: Rowman and Littlefield, 1987). The authors, in both instances, are advocates of and participants in the movement for regulatory reform.

37. Though empirical investigation of particular locational controversies (Dow Chemical's proposed plant in the Sacramento–San Joaquin Delta, the SOHIO terminal at Long Beach Harbor, etc.) finds other factors (chairing competitive environments for labor, etc., and market reorganization) to better explain these firms' withdrawal from their proposed projects.

38. This is true not just of environmental regulations but of much recent regulation of industry. Worker health and safety regulations and the requirement that employers pay benefits such as social security, pension contributions, and health care also have encouraged the development of subcontracting relationships—here the subcontracting of the employment of labor.

39. Though in these industries the literature suggests that the influence of environment on new plant siting depends more on the positive effects of environmental amenities for their skilled labor force than on the negative effects of environmental regulation as a component of production costs at new facilities; they also may separate production and R&D facilities in competing for skilled R&D workers,

leaving R&D facilities in high-amenity locations while relocating production facilities into lower-amenity, lower-wage, and less-unionized locales.

40. For an extended discussion of the history of development of these initiatives and their implications, see Gottlieb and FitzSimmons, *Thirst for Growth.*

41. These implications are closely related to the structure of governance of the particular irrigation district. Where voting rights within the district are weighted by amount of land owned, smaller farmers individually or collectively may have little voice in the district's decision. See Merrill R. Goodall, John D. Sullivan, and Timothy DeYoung, *California Water: A New Political Economy* (New York: Allanheld, Osmun, 1978), for a discussion of the differing structures of governance of irrigation districts in California. See Patricia Ballard, "And Conflict Shall Prevail: Reclamation Law, Water Districts and Politics in the Kings River Service Area of California" (M.A. thesis, UCLA, 1980), for a critical examination of the implications of these structures for smaller farmers.

42. It should be noted here that agricultural uses are not fully consumptive uses in the way in which urban uses are consumptive. Irrigation water not captured by the plant or evaporated from the soil percolates into underlying groundwater and is an important source of groundwater recharge in many agricultural areas. Where that water is instead exported from the basin, such recharge is lost and the groundwater resource may be more rapidly depleted.

43. F. Lee Brown and Helen M. Ingram, *Water and Poverty in the Southwest* (Tucson: University of Arizona, 1987).

44. See discussion of implications of marketable permits in Kelly Robinson, "The Regional Economic Impacts of Marketable Permit Programs: The Case of Los Angeles," in *The Cost-Effective Control of Urban Smog,* eds. Richard K. Kosobud, William Testa, and Donald Manson, 166–188 (Chicago: Federal Reserve Bank, 1993); see also staff reports of the South Coast Air Quality Management District, Marketable Permits Program Working Papers nos. 1–5, 1991–1992.

45. Edward Soja, Rebecca Morales, and Goetz Wolff, "Urban Restructuring: An Analysis of Social and Spatial Change in Los Angeles," *Economic Geography* 59 (1983): 195–230.

46. The primary work on this issue has been done by Allen Scott and his associates and students. See, for example, Allen Scott, *Technopolis: High-Technology Industry and Regional Development in Southern California* (Berkeley, Los Angeles, and London: University of California Press, 1993); and Allen J. Scott, *New Industrial Spaces* (London: Pion, 1988).

47. Many of these are too small to comfortably internalize the technical and reporting costs of environmental compliance.

48. For example, defense/aerospace contractors such as Rockwell had begun to bring metal-plating activities into their own production lines, where quality could be more closely controlled. The advent of Superfund (CERCLA) led these firms to return to subcontracting metal plating and coating in order to shed the liability associated with this hazardous process and its wastes.

49. Uniform national standards of air quality (like many other federal uniform environmental, and social, policies) are an attempt to establish a level playing field, to avoid pressures on states and regions to trade off local conditions in an attempt

to attract investment. Federal environmental law often allows states to set more, but not less, stringent standards. California has led the country in setting emission standards and mandating emissions control technologies for private cars and has justified this on the basis of the particular difficulties of controlling air pollution in the state's urban environments.

50. The division of labor between the two agencies has become somewhat blurred as both have sought solutions to this intransigent problem; though the Air Resources Board remains focused on reducing motor vehicle emissions and ensuring compliance with stringent standards of emission control and vehicle maintenance, SCAQMD had also taken up the problem of mobile sources through its Regulation XV, which requires large employers to seek emissions reductions through reducing overall travel to and from work and allows firms to include the emissions reductions that result in their reported emissions reductions.

51. For a summary of this complex plan, see SCAQMD, "The Path to Clean Air: Attainment Strategies," El Monte, SCAQMD, May 1989.

52. See Robin Bloch and Roger Keil, "Planning for a Fragrant Future," *Capitalism Nature Socialism* 6 (New York: Guilford Publications); see also Eric Mann, *LA's Lethal Air* (Los Angeles: Labor/Community Strategy Center, 1991).

53. Robinson, "Regional Economic Impacts," 166.

54. Ironically, the SCAQMD's new plan has again been diverted by new circumstances from within and without the metropolitan region. Under the Clinton administration and in response to the loss of a lawsuit that claimed that EPA had not adequately enforced its own rules, EPA has now stepped directly into the process of planning to bring Los Angeles into compliance with federal standards. How this new EPA agenda would articulate with the SCAQMD's continuing activities in developing the RECLAIM market while also implementing the tier I rules of the 1989 plan was not yet clear at the time of writing.

55. See Karen R. Polenske, Kelly Robinson, Yu Hung Hong, Xiannuan Lin, Judith Moore, and Bruce Stedman, "Evaluation of the South Coast Air Quality Management District's Methods for Assessing Socioeconomic Impacts of District Rules and Regulations," report prepared for the SCAQMD by the Multiregional Planning Staff, Department of Urban Studies and Planning, MIT, 1992; see also S. Lieu and G. I. Treyz, "Estimating the Economic and Demographic Effects of an Air Quality Management Plan: The Case of Southern California," *Environment and Planning* A, no. 24 (1992): 1799–1811.

EIGHT

L.A. as Design Product

How Art Works in a Regional Economy

Harvey Molotch

Using Los Angeles as a case study, I investigate how local aesthetics—the way people draw, shape, and play, fantasize, concoct, and socially explore—affect what businesses produce and market. Local art is a factor of production, well beyond and perhaps even more important than the usual "cultural" considerations of worker discipline, management style, or information infrastructure now part of discourse on productivity.[1] I try to show how the cultural-material outputs, in turn, change not only the region of Los Angeles but also modes of expression and economic production globally. I argue that local aesthetics, broadly construed, are as important to the business climate or "industrial atmosphere" as any other element. Art counts for far more than the volume of sales in galleries or the urban renewal a museum may stimulate. Although I focus on the Los Angeles region (grandly defined as the urbanized zone from Santa Barbara south to the Mexican border), I strive to show how art *works* as a general matter, and at all geographic scales, including nations.

HIGH AND LOW: INTERSECTING ARTS

Every designer's hand, whether a teen's use of found objects to structure a day's outfit or a sophisticated studio's rendering of a new car model, draws from the surrounding currents of popular and esoteric arts and modes of expression—verbal, literate, and plastic—that make up everyday life. These interpenetrations of daily rounds and high culture, ways of life and circulating beliefs, are raw materials of what can come from place. They are factors of distinctive production and consumption, part of the "anthropology of goods" that characterizes all societies.[2]

All the forms of indigenous creativity intersect—fine art and folk sentiment, kitsch and camp, freeway-sign tagging and garden tool design. The

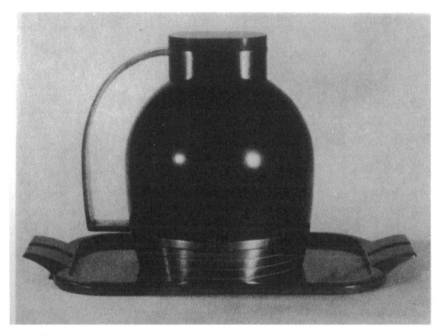

Figure 8.1. Pitcher with tray designed by Henry Dreyfuss for American Thermos Bottle company, 1935.

culture of a place, as Arthur C. Danto remarks, "is really all of a piece, though it takes time for ghetto forms to reach high culture, as break dancing entered ballet, or commercial culture, as rap music has succeeded in doing—or, in the opposite direction, the way the highly mannered poses of *Vogue* photographs by Irving Penn or Richard Avedon emerge in East Harlem as a special dance form, 'voguing.' "[3]

I add in commercial products. Some merchandise is directly taken from popular culture (e.g., the Mickey Mouse watch and a line of furnishings using TV comedy Simpsons themes). Other designs may have museum art as their more obvious progenitors. The design historian Penny Sparke links the design of a thermos by the pioneer American industrial designer Henry Dreyfuss (fig. 8.1) to "the abstract forms of a sculptor like Archipenko" (fig. 8.2).[4] L.A.-based Harry Bertoia credited his now-classic steel-rod chair (fig. 8.3) to the inspiration of an artist: "I wanted my chair to rotate, change with movement, like the body in Duchamp's 'Nude Descending the Staircase' " (fig. 8.4).[5] Working in the other direction, Duchamp had notoriously proclaimed the American urinal as art object;[6] Miró meticulously drew hardware as study exercises before reforming them into his abstract shapes.[7] Now plumbing manufacturers put out products mimicking the

Figure 8.2. Alexander Archipenko, *Femme Assise*, bronze, 1912.

likes of his finished works or Picasso's; spigots and knobs curve like a Jean Arp sculpture and fire hydrants have a Brancusi look.

Many successful commercial designs (measured by retail sales and export figures) were from people acclaimed as artists in other realms or were directly influenced by avant-garde art figures, as for example the Bauhaus designers' (Marcel Breuer, Mies van der Rohe) relations with cubist and minimalist painters. Duchamp inspired Bertoia and Bertoia set off mass imitations, as in a popular wire-backed 1950s dinette set made by Virtue Brothers of California (see fig. 8.5). Elite acceptance of the high art-inspired products continuously leads to mass market knock-offs. It doesn't matter that even elites often don't "understand" the art they hang on their walls and admire in museums,[8] the fact that they accept and circulate it prepares the ground for wider dissemination of its motifs in other types of

Figure 8.3. Harry Bertoia's steel rod chair, 1952, influenced by Duchamp.

art and merchandise. Museums do little to clarify these relations between fine art and everyday stuff because they segregate art from artifact (if they collect or display artifact at all). Even the Museum of Modern Art's extraordinary 1990 exhibition, *High and Low: Modern Art and Popular Culture,* gave scant attention to merchandise; instead it focused on the relation between high art and the "low" in graphics (e.g., cartoons, graffiti, advertising).[9] Only exhibits of preliterate or otherwise exotic cultures mix the genres, usually in natural history museums where curators accentuate interactions across media, from paintings and sculpture to utilitarian objects.[10]

That museums fail to show the connection doesn't mean that populations fail to make it. The image of places comes from the sense people have—local people and those far away—of the cultural-material interactions within them. And this reputation of place becomes another aspect of

Figure 8.4. Marcel Duchamp, *Nude Descending a Staircase, No. 2,* 1912.

local economic structure, a part of its geographic capital. People desire goods associated with a specific place because they want, at a distance, the place itself. We cannibalize a place—take in some of its social and cultural power, its cachet—by consuming the objects from it. The admired human relations that adhere in its products can be appropriated through the material acquisitions. Paris was the scene of the opera, Chevalier, and the avant-garde (*civilization*—"a model of enlightened consumption")[11] as well as the charm of the waif. It had great fashions, and the glamour became generalized such that what went on there among designers, clients, and commentators created, in itself, an export market for products attributed to its milieu. The demand for Swiss watches, made by a people imagined as precise and workmanlike, likely goes beyond any inherent superiority of the products. The positive connection of product image to place yields a

Figure 8.5. Dinette set by Virtue Brothers of California, circa late 1950s, influenced by Bertoia.

kind of "monopoly rent" that adheres to places, their insignia, and the brand names that may attach to them. Their industries grow as a result, and the local economic base takes its shape. Favorable images create entry barriers for products from competing places.

Sometimes, of course, outsiders steal the image and mislead that a product comes from a place it does not. Detroit routinely put California marques on Detroit-designed and manufactured cars (e.g., Chevrolet Bel Air and Malibu, Pontiac Ventura), just as they also exploited the French (Cadillac de Ville, Buick Riviera). Southern California markings appear on a lot of sportswear and equipment made in Asia, sometimes by indigenous or European-owned companies. Ice cream stands in Paris have banners that say "The Famous American Flavors" and "Direct from USA," with graphics showing an obviously Southern California beach scene (tropical palm trees) coupled with the words "San Francisco California." But even the mistakes spread the association between the good life and the Southern California lifestyle. This enhances the market space for an authentic local product.

THE L.A. PROFILE

To discover the L.A. expressivity in merchandise, we need to set forth a version of what L.A. as a culture looks like. Then we can go "find it" in goods. My serious and noncondemnatory treatment of L.A. (as well as of its merchandise) runs against intellectuals' frequent portrayal of Los Angeles as a mindless, narcissistic, and know-nothing wasteland. American reactionaries, in their version, rail against L.A.'s satanic infidelity to traditional values. The less vituperous worry "there are no seasons" to structure proper work or family cycles. In its sybaritic valleys and on its cliff tops and seashore, life is shallow; Jean Baudrillard echoes the description of it as "the world centre of the unauthentic"[12]—not, in his case, as sincere derision, but to signal appreciation for so fine an example of postmodern ennui. Hollywood is "the illusion factory,"[13] so described by the avant-garde French poet Blaise Cendrars from his 1930s sojourn, prefiguring Baudrillard's later simulacrum-toting version. Cendrars was also able to spot the "hyperreal," noting that in Los Angeles, truth and fantasy came together, and in ways not easy (or taken by locals as necessary) to distinguish. With good command of later Southern California shtick, Cendrars remarked that L.A. was a place where "anyone who gets around on foot is a suspect." Bertrand Russell was not nice at all: "Los Angeles represents the ultimate segregation of the unfit."[14] Clever visitors go back quite a way, come back still again, and in their writings amplify certain images that, however unintended, seem to only boost an L.A. appeal.

There are, of course, many L.A.'s to present to the world—variations that, at base, come from the diverse migrations that displaced the indigenous peoples. One 1913 journalist reported the local scene as "rural pietist obsessed with the spirit of village fellowship, of suburban respectability, . . . overrun with militant moralists, connoisseurs of sin, experts of biological purity."[15] In a more general account, it was the end of the great heartland migration: "as New York was the melting pot for the peoples of Europe, so Los Angeles is the melting pot for the peoples of the United States."[16] Compared to most other receiving zones of large migrations, California in general, and Southern California in particular, really was a *chosen* land. At least for portions of its history, the L.A. region's migrants were affluent compared to those who usually make great treks. The dust bowl desperados notwithstanding, Southern California's prospects for excitement, health, and creativity have played a special role compared to dire necessity in explaining who came.

Besides its WASP nativist element, Southern California's migrants included Europeans and Asians, resulting in separate little Germantowns, Danishtowns, Little Tokyos, and utopian settlements (foreign born and domestic) to fulfill visions of socialism, physical health, or religious salvation. A large Mexican population, continually replenished through immigration, predates statehood. The more recent movements of Third World peoples into L.A. from Central America and Asia spins out images of the new global city, alongside the significant but no longer growing African-American population.[17] The image on a postcard printed and sold in England (see fig. 8.6), with its central figure a far cry from ingenuous blond surf-guy, may presage a new L.A. mystique in the making—still sexy and young, but now presented in sullen Man of Color (with girl).

The cultural bent of L.A.'s immigrants and sojourners—of whatever language, skin color, or demeanor—shapes the economy and culture. Without naively falling in with local mythologies, these streams really did contain, besides an element of voluntarism, a distinctive ethic of experiment and openness. Besides the economic deprivations that "push" people out of one location and the job opportunities that "pull" them to another, there is also a selective migration based on cultural leanings—a factor usually ignored by demographers.[18] Besides being more risk receptive in general, the footloose likely have cultural and personality differences that allocate them to different kinds of destination settlements. Southern California has long held a special appeal to certain subculture types: those seeking health restoratives, including very unconventional ones, religious experiences of unusual sorts, both the spiritual new age (or "new thought" as it was called in an earlier incarnation) and sects of various fundamentalist pioneers (e.g., Aimee Semple McPherson, Billy Graham, and Robert Schuller's drive-in church and Crystal Cathedral).[19] Southern California offers zones of sexual freedom, including gay liberation. Many Protestant conservatives of Orange County have had trouble, during the 1980s and 1990s, swallowing the regressive cultural orientations of the heartland Republican party.

The distinctiveness of L.A. migrations, combined with the physical ambience and its life patterns, forms a sort of "national character" on which almost all accounts agree. Whether as accolade or complaint, whether from writings of visitors or comments by informants I interviewed for this essay, the saying is (and, appropriately, it is a song lyric as well) that in Southern California "anything goes."

Not *anything* goes (the temptation to overstate does go with the territory). There are in L.A., like anywhere else, civil proprieties that must be observed and, perhaps more than most places, a police force with a long list of proscribed behaviors, sometimes brutally enforced among those on the

Figure 8.6. "Freeway Entrance," a postcard printed in England and purchased in Paris.

wrong side of the class and racial divides. But in ways that help create a distinguishing profile, people are free to invent. This is less through principled questioning of convention as a directness—alternately joyful, thoughtless, or contrived—to carry on with less regard for how things are usually done. Rather than being a place without a culture, one of the brickbats often tossed, "the apparent culturelessness of the place, the endless process of willfully sweeping aside what has gone before, whether in technology, history, or the arts, *is* the culture."[20] In contrast to Baudrillard's sentiment, *real things* happen as a result. As we look for L.A. in product, the anything goes theme remains a clue, expressed through the somewhat distinctive nature of those who, regardless of their migratory stream, settled in long enough to matter.

HOW ART WORKS: SELECTED PRODUCTS AND INDUSTRIES

L.A.'s playfulness becomes one important aspect of its productivity, an aspect that, if history is a guide, should not be a surprise. The eminent historian of technology Cyril Stanley Smith gives a lot of examples of how "play domains"—like toys and sports—led to massively important material changes. Playing with pets "probably gave the knowledge that was needed for purposeful animal husbandry"; recreational fireworks gave birth to explosives; the block and tackle was invented to lift animals from underground storage pits to the game floor of the Roman Coliseum.[21] Flower gardening preceded food agriculture.

Some of the L.A. versions are still waiting for their big-time application, but meanwhile they are, in themselves, important elements of the local economy. The Frisbee, introduced in 1957 by San Gabriel–based Wham-O (initially under the name Pluto Platter) replaced the pie tins flying on California beaches at least as early as 1940. There are also toys from El Segundo's Mattel, including Barbie, the first doll to have breasts, followed by Ken (lacking a penis, but having a suggestive bump). Departing from conventional baby doll images, these constantly evolving human character playthings mimic shapes and life roles idealized in the movie and TV studios. Now thirty-four years old, Barbie has outsold any commercial toy in history, with 1992 sales at $1 billion (American girls own an average of eight Barbies each). Disney products are another of Mattel's "Global Power Brands," the term it uses in its annual reports.[22]

Southern California's athleticism also translates into significant dollars. Compared to other places, individualistic sports (rather than those team-based) garner local enthusiasm: surfing, bicycling, swimming, snowboarding, Rollerblading, skateboarding, wind surfing, Frisbee throwing. Other Southern California–made merchandise, including entertainment itself, is also leisure oriented. Most of these products, precisely because of their favored lifestyle connotations—and most stuff does not do this—spawn other consumer goods. These collateral products include clothing, luggage, dishware, furniture, radios, toys, bed linen, school supplies, candy, and watches, linked to the core merchandise through insignia, logos, and other artistic referents rather than by function (e.g., as opposed to the way a computer "needs" a compatible printer).

By 1990, L.A. had almost matched New York in the number of people employed in what Sharon Zukin calls the "creative occupations"—designers, theater and movie people, authors, architects, and artists of various sorts.[23] Whereas in 1980 New Yorkers in these job categories numbered about 97,500 compared to L.A.'s 70,000, the gap had almost closed a decade later (New York had 114,000 compared to L.A.'s 109,000). More than other spheres in which the two cities could be compared, Los Angeles made enormous gains.

Some think there is an identifiable L.A. region "feel" across products of all sorts. In *Business Week*'s breathless version, Southern California designs are distinctively "exuberant, warm, optimistic, and playful, . . . part California, part Japanese, a brash expression of Pacific Rim confidence in the 90's. Think myth, metaphor, humor, and color."[24] In its special issue on innovation, the magazine heralded Los Angeles as "the capital of this new design aesthetic," a "Cali-sushi" that contrasts with the "Eurostyle" of Bauhaus-inspired plain surface and crisp detail (as in Braun appliances), yet oriented to the disciplined simplicity of Japanese tradition. One design commentator refers to this "amalgamation" as "the L.A. centered California movement, emphasizing the cool, unusual, and above all, individual."[25]

An important art critic praises Mike Kelley's paintings for their "gleeful use of adolescent metaphors" that simultaneously embrace and reject "the hot-rodding, anti-intellectual, surfer-boy high jinks that, in the 1960's, shaped the founding ethos of art in Los Angeles."[26] As in the paintings of Ed Kienholz and his group, it is "hedonism according to a blueprint."[27] Two New York critics observe in L.A. "a certain cool . . . bemusement at all the self-righteous 'struggling'and huffing" of the New York art scene.[28] Often it is ironic and self-mocking, as in the British expatriate David Hockney's straight-on paintings of swimming pools and apartment houses.[29] In the vein of songwriter Randy Newman, those who say "I Love L.A." distance their sincerity with wink or sneer. People who sing and talk of leaving their hearts in San Francisco or of New York as "a wonderful town" (which they love in June) seem provincially naive by contrast. Products of such sensibilities lack the L.A. twist.

Part of it is also Southern California's interaction with Zen, as in the "light and space" art of Robert Irwin and the profound iconoclasm of native son John Cage, who treated the mind as itself the "canvas" that the artist opens to the surrounding world of light, ambient sound, and human buzz. Irwin explicitly praises both the meteorological and social aspects of the L.A. climate for freeing him from obligation to service artistic "schools" and allowed him to make art as moments of life experience rather than things to hang on walls.[30] These are elements of the aesthetic spirit behind L.A.'s transformation, in the words of the *New Yorker* art critic Adam Gopnik, "from a provincial backwater to an artmaking capital equal to New York."[31] Whatever its substance—whether in swiggles and swaggles of bright color or Zen-like embrace of the ordinary as divine—art and artifact play loose with the canon.

Certain technology and product trends may be giving special opportunities to the Southern California way. In an age of plastics and miniaturization, products that formerly had their shape, weight, and bulk defined by the mechanisms that filled them (viz., telephone shells once had to accommodate bells, gears, dials, and wiring) have now become "dematerialized." What is necessary inside is small and light compared to what can go on the outside. Shape can follow whimsy, mimic icons, and enhance visual and tactile experience. Production runs can be short and tailored to idiosyncratic cultural niches. This revisits a California architectural tradition in which buildings, especially but not only the movie palace, were constructed as castle or tepee and temples of the Mayans, Egyptians, and Chinese. There was little regard for "the truth" of their function or internal configuration. Restaurants, shops, and gas stations were made into shapes evoking the product for sale—not the actual activity within. Hot dogs were sold from a structure that *was*, in stucco, a hot dog; a tamale stand was a tamale, an ice cream store could be an igloo. Form and function were utterly divorced, except in a playful and immediately accessible symbolism ("programmatic architecture," David Gebhard calls it).[32] As manufactured products approach this type of interior-exterior juxtaposition, L.A. design gains an edge.

Again, I don't want to overdo it. There are other leading design sources in the world, including those that emanate from Northern California's innovative powerhouse of Silicon Valley and the design sophistication of San Francisco—never mind the ongoing hypercreativity from New York and Boston. On a global scale, Milan, Barcelona, Paris, and Tokyo are the hot scenes.[33] But while L.A. may not be the whole place, it is an important one, and one with a record. The trick is to show just how, in this mixed and contradictory L.A. habitus, these ways of making and seeing lives becomes a mundane economic force in the larger U.S. and world setting. Beyond hoopla and Frisbee, we explore for several major industries just how L.A. expression comes to market.

The Movie-Industrial Complex

The most obvious export that rises from L.A. aesthetics is commercial entertainment, a sector with obvious relations to art worlds—popular as well as fine painting, sculpture, photography, music, poetry, and prose. "The industry" is the ninth-largest sector of the L.A. industrial base, involving over three thousand businesses.[34] It also provides a stock of skills and workers used in other fields; set designers end up in industrial product design, costumers conceive and even manufacture lines of clothing, graphic artists and writers work in advertising, packaging, and printing businesses. All sorts of entertainment workers, including again writers, graphic designers, and special effects artists, are the ones who create, staff, and service tourist complexes like Disneyland.[35] They are available for other creative tasks, whether for an hour, a week, or a lifetime. The result is a unique form of cultural agglomeration; in Reyner Banham's words, "Hollywood brought something that all other fantastists needed—technical skill and resources in converting fantastic ideas into physical realities."[36]

Show business creates an army of highly skilled lumpen wanna-bes who can work only sporadically at their chosen craft. In some of the Hollywood trades, fewer than 10 percent of those paying union dues are at work at any given time.[37] Their persistence is made possible by a kind of motivated calling found in culture industries and the arts more generally, ironic given Max Weber's use of the trait to explain ascetic capitalism. People who can't make it in, say, auto spark plug production, don't hang around; they move on to another town, another sector, another career. But there's no business like show business—and its related spheres—either in what people will go through "to get that extra feeling" or in the types of economic agglomerations they produce. Workers establish their arts identity not through paid wage (low and intermittent) but through the places in which they hang out, the clothing they wear, how they eat, and what and who they know.[38] Meanwhile they take "day gigs" that often turn into life projects, including significant businesses. Culture people do even ordinary types of work in a different way than others would. "Theatrical" restaurant waiters provide a distinctive twist; as Zukin remarks, "the accents and appearance of waiters affirm distinctions between restaurants as surely as menu, price, and location."[39]

The entertainment milieu also builds economy through its rapidly growing product tie-in and licensing sector. Sales of such items can come to a goodly sum; caps and other paraphernalia (100 different products) related to Spike Lee's 1992 *Malcolm X* went to about $100 million, a figure that James Dean licensed products continue to generate *annually*.[40] The Batman movie spawned product sales of $1 billion, $100 million of which were racked up by L.A.-based Kenner Toys.[41] *Star Trek*, the project of L.A.-born Gene Roddenberry (once an LAPD sergeant) has also sold more than $1 billion in books, videos, and paraphernalia, with no end in sight.[42] Products are now developed specifically for a movie with the tie-in part of the advanced planning. The kids' backpack, tape recorder, and Monster Sap foam soap used by the central child character in the movie *Home Alone 2* were, at their inception in the plot line, meant to be part of a larger merchandising program.[43] *Jurassic Park* was a monster. Because its CEO worried that "things don't happen by accident," Disney employs a fifty-member Synergy Department to exploit potential connections.[44]

These include tie-ins with the rapidly expanding video and computer game industry (1992 industry sales at $4.5 billion) because game software increasingly uses actual footage from Hollywood movies and video. The games application now is being built into the production process from the outset,[45] enlarging, in turn, markets for the films or—going round still again—stimulating more movies or TV series based on the game. Along with the games, home sales and rentals make movie impacts more durable than before; domestic home-market sales and rentals now run threefold the dollar volume of the box office.[46] A given entertainment product enjoys an open-ended life span and economic future. Educational video emerges as another blockbuster industry, one that relies on entertainment techniques and, at times, stock entertainment footage. A *Business Week* cover story has proclaimed the coming of "the entertainment economy": "The entertainment industry is now the driving force for new technology, as defense used to be."[47]

The industry has always prospered through diversity, providing L.A. and the country with a regional elite distinct from the Anglo-Protestant establishments that more completely ruled in other locales. Jews from Europe and the U.S. East created the studios and produced and directed many of the movies (and are still a well-represented part of what Mike Davis calls the "West Side Mafia").[48] The Hollywood moguls had the exuberant chutzpah to put America's (and much of the world's) modern fantasies on the screen; they gave audiences access to their own sentiments, fears, and dreams, blown up big-screen, big-time, in excess. Jewish comedy infused scripts and performances, as in Charlie Chaplin, the Marx Brothers, and Milton Berle. It comes into other realms like advertising jingles, slogans, and thirty-second TV spots. Immigrants from all over Europe, many from the higher circles of literature and the arts, wrote screenplays and musical scores and advanced the art of cinematography. The country's rural and urban hinterlands stocked the studio stables with celebrities and glamour. African-Americans and U.S. Latinos, however anonymously, were a main source of the sounds and choreography (jazz and the "Latin beat"). Increasingly they also fueled the music, images, and locution of the global entertainment machine.

The immigrants helped make production relevant to a diverse and global audience; a nation of nations provides a test market for the world. In commenting on the fact that Americans "are all foreigners," Alfred Hitchcock said that "whatever frightens the Americans frightens the Italians, the Rumanians, the Danes, and everyone else from Europe."[49] L.A. thrives on the rich and conflictful "ethnoscape"[50] of its employees and residents, along with tourists, business visitors, and still-flowing immigrants and seekers from across the world. In the 1980s, it gained more foreign immigrants than any U.S. city. Given the mix, being in L.A. provides a competitive advantage for industries dependent on accessing world sensibilities. Echoing the maxim that "California sets the cultural agenda for the world," a Coca-Cola executive explained his firm's hiring an L.A. talent agency to manage its worldwide marketing campaigns, thus tipping a healthy slug of advertising commissions away from its traditional New York City base.[51]

Entertainment is a billboard for local products. Southern California has had celebrities for so long, and has been a backdrop for their interesting and glamorous lives, that it has become, in itself, a *celebrity space*. In Carey McWilliams's words of over forty years ago, the concentration of so much of the world's popular entertainment in one city "has made possible the distillation of a pure essence, Hollywood, . . . to sell clothes, real estate, ideas, books, jewelry, furniture, cold creams, deodorants, and perfume."[52]

Some of these products owe both their initial development and their production to the entertainment sector. The cosmetics industry was transformed by Max Factor who, after migrating from Estonia, became wig maker to the stars. From wigs, Factor moved into greasepaints and dominated that market worldwide. But greasepaint (and other forms of makeup) fared poorly in Technicolor (greasy faces reflected set colors), leading Factor to develop a new kind of cosmetic, applied by dabbing moist sponges on solid, caked-up product. The result was "pancake," and, decoratively encased, it became the world's makeup, valued in the mass market because it made skin appear more natural than liquids or salves.

Factor's other "Hollywood glamour secrets" included the first mass marketing of eye shadow and eyebrow pencils, the invention of lip gloss and lip brush, waterproof makeup, human-hair wigs and eyelashes, and the "color harmony" concept in which hair, lip, eye, and skin color products are coordinated—"the principle upon which the beauty industry still functions."[53] Before becoming part of Procter and Gamble, the Max Factor company was operating in 190 countries, with words like "California," "Hollywood," and the endorsements (gratis) of virtually every movie star as the basis of its promotions. The man who reorganized beauteous Marlene Dietrich's eyebrows could, as is sung in "Hooray for Hollywood," even "make a monkey look good."

The localness of entertainment, its dependence on a particular confluence of cultural skills and expressivity, make it a business that cannot go offshore, cannot be imitated abroad, and cannot be branch planted. It is a "transaction rich" network of firms,[54] and the nature of that transaction system has an idiosyncratic localness. The Japanese and Europeans must buy existing corporations in place to gain market share (allegedly at inflated prices), lock, stock, and barrel. In ways not always appreciated, L.A.-based entertainment is a secure U.S. profit center that radiates benefits for California products in particular and U.S. output in general.

Tourism

Tourism, of course, benefits from even corrupted associations; California and Los Angeles grew from the beginning through the images created of it and by it. The very word *tourist* (as opposed to "traveler," for example) first gained currency in the United States, says McWilliams, to designate a certain type of visitor to Southern California—a species of unusual sojourners who were "explorers and discoverers, butterfly catchers and health seekers."[55] Although the various governments and chambers of commerce associated with the region still advertise its assets widely (L.A. got its start as the most advertised city in the world),[56] these are now trivial compared to the free hype that comes with the designs and logos on the clothes, graphics, and products that reach across the globe (as well, of course, from the movies). Unusual in that it came early in the city's industrial development (compared, for example, to San Francisco, but not Miami), tourism remains big, with annual revenues at $7.2 billion, second only to the category of business and management services as the L.A. region's largest industrial sector.[57] Even after the police brutality on Rodney King and its aftermath of mayhem and recrimination, tourism grows.[58] For a variety of reasons—including the advertising and visiting that tourism generates— " 'real' cities . . . have developed behind a tourist front."[59]

One important component of the tourist draw, indeed the basis for a new version of tourism, is the invention of the modern theme park, Disneyland. Along with the area's other big-scale regional theme parks (four of them) and Universal Studios, it innovates spatial management and social relations. Crowds are channeled to specific destinations, with little need for instructions, policing, or even signs. Disneyland practice and training materials refer to workers as "actors" and "actresses," their uniforms as "costumes"; and they are expected to speak from "scripts" that will deliver "the same consistent show." The park is divided into "onstage" (spaces where "guests" and "audience" are present) and "backstage" (e.g., workrooms and employee cafeterias). The worker is performer whose mind, body, and friendly soul are part of the act, and so are the customers who, regarded as incipient actors themselves, are cued from scene to scene, moved along with props and characters through the park, and encouraged in every way to play an active role in creating their own contentment. Disneyland represents, in a spokesperson's words, "a new industry with happiness as its principal product."[60] Camouflaged authorities quickly whisk out of sound and sight any obstreperous human or litter. Main Street has no crime; urban strangers can assume the good intentions of one another in the most violent of all modern societies. In multiple ways, the park invites and gets "the same suspension of disbelief required of moviegoers."[61]

At the other end of the spectrum from ineffable fantasy, Disneyland has always been in interaction with the entertainment and engineering prowess of the larger region.[62] Disney characters emerged, of course, out of the film cartoons that preceded the parks and the merchandise. The Disney rides, life-size animations, and other attractions utilized techniques and personnel from the region's aerospace-military complexes. And these complexes, in turn, owe something to the local fantasy infrastructure; the space shuttle program modeled certain elements around imageries from *Star Trek* (which was also the imaging source for the cellular phone and "bio-comp"-like medical monitoring equipment now in use).[63] The very origin of the first big aerospace companies grew from Southern California fun; they reflect an "early flowering of a culture of amateur aviation in the region" from the likes of Glenn Martin, Donald Douglas, and John Northrop.[64] Hughes Aircraft was established as a service facility for its CEO's air racing activities;[65] Lockheed was inspired by its Santa Barbara founders' kite-flying enthusiasm.[66] Only on the surface are institutions like Disneyland and the U.S. war machine and space programs opposites. The benign weather and open spaces of Southern California had something to do with their common point of beginnings. But so was the L.A. social climate of fantasy and exploration, equally applicable for searching the stars, amusing the folks, or targeting a missile.

Eating

Beyond the popularization of health foods and vitamins, Southern California has altered the mores and organization of the way people eat. Los Angeles is likely the birthplace of what may be the earliest fast-food institution, the commercial cafeteria. The first was opened in 1905 by Helen Mosher ("All Women Cooks—Food that Can be Seen," was the slogan).[67] The L.A. cafeterias emulated "a sort of indoor picnic" in the sense that customers pass along a line of assorted foods and choose for themselves what they want (railroad worker chow lines are a poorer model because they don't offer choice). Indeed, the early cafeterias are said to have been filled with plants and to have large skylights and outdoor themes, with names like Fern Cafeteria,[68] not unlike "a kind of concentrated form of nature," in the phrase used to later describe Disneyland's "Hollywood jungles."[69] Southern California was referred to by the writer Leon Wilson, in 1923, as "Sunny Cafeteria."[70] The cafeterias may have been popular because they emulated the picnics regularly held by the "state societies" (associations of migrants from the same U.S. state) and the foreign immigrant association picnics then common in Southern California. They also make it easier for people who do not speak the language or have familiarity with cuisines on offer. Unlike restaurants, cafeterias choreograph people through a continuous line to pick up their own food and carry it to their tables (although not to clear their own dishes—that was to come later). Cafeterias lend themselves to informality because once past the cashier, customers are untended and can join others, change tables, and sit as long as they like.[71]

Other types of eating establishments arose from Southern California's car culture, including the coffee shop designed to be noticed by drive-by customers making their restaurant choice from behind auto windshields ("billboard architecture"). The L.A. style of coffee shop—glass walls, boomerang roofs, and elaborate tropical landscaping (the Hollywood jungles again)—is sometimes called "googie," connoting its somewhat offbeat adaptation of the modern style. Interiors feature bright lighting, open kitchens, and "floating seats" at the counter (the stool's base was angled out from above the floor) to enable mopping even while the customer eats (informality again). Many designed by the L.A. firm of Armet and Davis, these places defined the genre,[72] particularly as L.A.-area clients Bob's Big Boy and Denny's went national (the latter to become the country's largest coffee shop chain). In upmarket versions, employees introduced themselves on a first-name basis to their "guests" ("Hi, my name is _____ and I'll be your . . . "). Whether in fast-food or some other business, the employee doesn't just haul product but "is responsible for managing impressions"—the "moment of truth" that helps constitute the novel aspect of the product.[73]

It was the drive-in that was to truly launch a thousand stores. The White Log Taverns, sheathed in "concrete logs," were a chain of sixty-two California drive-ins by 1937.[74] McDonald's, itself born in 1948 as a San Bernardino drive-in, went on to introduce modern fast food. "Speedee" service (as McDonald's first merchandised it) bypasses traditional mealtime ritual, eliminates preparation and cleanup activities, and provides a way for people to eat on their way to other tasks. The original McDonald brothers undersold competitors, limited the menu, quickened the service, and—relative to their time—standardized product and store look. Chicago-based Ray Kroc, who began in 1953 as the firm's national franchise agent, refined and greatly elaborated all these elements. The McDonald regimen precisely controlled cooks' creations to a degree that was probably a worldwide departure for those who make food. The grand design meshes employees' movements with the automated cooking and serving processes and trains customers to prepare their order while in queue and clean up after they eat.[75] Even after McDonald's headquarters was moved to Illinois, innovations still came from Southern California, such as the first McDonald's Playland (Chula Vista, 1971) and the first McDonald's breakfast (the Egg McMuffin, Santa Barbara, 1973). Fast food became a three-meal-a-day possibility; by 1986 one of every four U.S. breakfasts eaten outside the home came from McDonald's.[76] We are dealing with an "industrialization of the service sphere"[77] in the unlikely sector of food preparation and service.

The original McDonald's inspired other chains, an outcome enhanced by the McDonald brothers' laid-back sharing of their practices with potential competitors. A frequent customer at the San Bernardino store opened a clone, but one that added tacos to the burger list to become Taco Bell (now a PepsiCo subsidiary). Another visitor, on examining the McDonald brothers' operation, created a smaller chain called Hamburger Handout[78] that evolved into the now-international Sizzler chain. San Diego–based Jack in the Box combined speedy service with the drive-in (and a bit of mechanical toy fantasy) to produce the "drive-thru" restaurant, in turn emulated by still other chains.

These innovations are quintessential American, and more specifically, Southern Californian; a lack of hardened custom facilitates breakdown of previously established institutional behaviors. American fast-food chains now dominate globally; non-Americans appreciate them as much for their "real U.S." style and mode of operation as for the food itself. French customers of McDonald's rank the interior environment, particularly the visibility of the kitchen action systems, as the prime attraction of the place, rather than the food, price, or service.[79] With a sense of "anything goes," fast food has emerged as a major U.S. profit source from Southern California—"the center of contemporary restaurant innovation."[80]

The path of inventiveness continues with L.A. restaurants that serve kosher burritos, tandoori pizzas (marketed by California Pizza Kitchen restaurants, now going national), and blueberry bagels. Foods of the East and West meet in French-Japanese restaurants and the whole concept of California cuisine means melding the style of French nouvelle with fresh fruits and vegetables, and the flavorings of any national tradition whatever. To be sure, this is a global trend, not just found in L.A., but as in other instances, L.A. leads. Sometimes the innovation becomes a base industry as in the frozen foods merchandised by Del-Mar's Jenny Craig, promoted with health and lifestyle hoopla as are the cookies of exercise personality Richard Simmons. Packaging that used to bring the likes of dowdy Betty Crocker into the kitchen instead announce movie star Paul Newman (a Connecticut resident but Hollywood-made) or Wolfgang Puck, Austrian transplant to Malibu.

Apparel

In terms of U.S. clothing manufacture, Los Angeles has passed New York as the largest producer (San Francisco comes third);[81] apparel and textile manufacture rank as the L.A. area's eighth-largest employer (second only to aircraft in manufacturing employment).[82] L.A.'s strength is in "street wear" and sports clothing, as opposed, for example, to tailored suits, formal wear, or sleep clothing.[83] Southern California tends toward lighter colors, bold and unusual configurations, and the "beach-active look," today a global taste.[84] Leaders include Guess? in downtown L.A., Bugle Boy in Simi Valley, Rampage in Vernon, and Carole Little south of downtown. The head of the California Mart, which is L.A.'s dominant clothing showroom center, says, "The industry in Southern California has always been the trendsetter for the country, a little way out, a little kooky."[85] The major Los Angeles rule, according to Rosemary Brantley, head of fashion design at Otis-Parsons Design School, is to "break the rules."[86] If you go into a good Los Angeles restaurant at dinner, "you can find *anything*," says Brantley, from wingtips to running shoes, tuxedos to jeans. That won't happen in New York or Milan, or even San Francisco to the same extent. The analogous sentiment of playful mixing is in a given outfit or even a single piece of clothing. California clothes also tend toward comfort, with elastic waistbands on skirts and pants to provide easy fit and to do away with belts that can pinch people who, in Brantley's words, "drive around in cars all day."

The entertainment industry plays a role in creating, not just reflecting, clothing tastes. As did painting and sculpture in a prior era, films influence popular canons of beauty and fashion.[87] As early as 1910 and through the 1940s, fashion shows were incorporated into feature films, however awkward for the plot line. Such interludes gave mass audiences access to the filmmaker's sense of couture and glamour. Because movies show people in motion, movie clothes must allow motion to be seen, and this provoked styles, beginning after about 1920, with less overall fabric volume on the body and the use of textiles and designs that looked right on a moving form.[88] The coming of talkies discouraged fabrics that made noise, like the rustle of taffeta.[89] Official censorship (the Hays Commission) promoted clingy satins and silks to "expose" women's breasts, otherwise banished from view. Whatever their origin, movie designs were quickly copied, especially those worn by the main characters. The New York Macy's sold fifty thousand copies of a big-shouldered Joan Crawford dress from a 1932 film. Manufacturers sometimes linked the stars' names to a specific garment (e.g. "the Ida Lupino").[90] Fashion often overruled character, with bar girls (like the one played by Bette Davis in a 1937 Warner Brothers picture) dressed to the nines. Edith Head's sarong for Dorothy Lamour in *The Jungle Princess* (1936) "was widely adapted as playwear."[91] To save money, some fashion magazines used publicity stills from the Hollywood studios to illustrate stories on latest trends, even those described as coming from Paris.[92]

More recent films that set off changes in mass style were *Saturday Night Fever, Flashdance, Bonnie and Clyde,* and *The Boyfriend.*[93] Just as Douglas Fairbanks brought tennis whites and blue blazers into widespread vogue in the 1920s, the Ralph Lauren–designed wardrobe for the film version of F. Scott Fitzgerald's *The Great Gatsby* set off a twenties revival of that fashion (as remembered) fifty years later.[94] No one better capitalized on the trend then Lauren himself with his lines of "Polo" clothing, home furnishings, and retail outlets.

The Hollywood stars are the world's common royalty, usually with the bodies and stances to showcase garments whose appeal they enhance through the emotion-laden characters they portray in precisely ideal-ized settings. The clothing industry, particularly in L.A., pays attention to "screen style"—an effort helped along by a regular fashion column in the *Los Angeles Times* by that name. These columns describe in detail the cloth-ing, jewelry, and eyeglasses worn by characters in movies in production.

Part of the Hollywood influence over clothing comes from the organiza-tional exigencies of the film industry. Attempts to glamorize contemporary characters can't go overboard or the film product will be out of date when seen in theaters, sometimes two or three years after wardrobes are fixed. For this reason, Hollywood tended not to emulate the excesses of French and Italian fashion houses, and instead "attempts were made to evolve a style of designing which would appear fashionable but would be at the same time dateless."[95] Fashion commentators call this simplification of continen-tal styles the "American look." Even when Americans did go for couture, at least in the postwar era, it was for the "acceptably Parisian alternative" of Chanel's simplicity rather than the "antics" of the likes of Schiaparelli.[96]

Of course, the American movies have promoted all sorts of looks that owe little to high fashion, but instead have as their provenance the cocktail lounge, the gym, the streets, and science fiction. Levi's jeans, worn by John Wayne and Gary Cooper in early forties westerns, surely owe their popular-ity to the movies. These masculinist associations laid the basis for Levi's as the appropriate fetish for "rebels without a cause" and other errant youth in pictures like *The Wild One, East of Eden,* and *Blackboard Jungle.* They were to surface as the uniform of the sixties counterculture (including its enter-tainment heroes). Young gay men, themselves a trend-setting force, eroti-cized the Levi's 501 (the tight-fitting "classic"). Eventually, the generic jean became "Regular Guy garb from Hong Kong to Hounslow to Houston," however at odds the potbellies and big buttocks were with the young James Dean and Brando bodies they mimicked.[97] The jeans worn 'round the world are the core of Levi Strauss, now the largest clothing manufacturer on earth. The fabric comes originally from Nimes, France ("de Nimes"); the company is in San Francisco, the products are made worldwide, but the concept is Los Angeles.

Music videos may be more important today than the movies in sell-ing clothing; music television carries style across the globe at a much faster rate than films or conventional television ever did. Hollywood produces music videos within the same time frame as the CDs from which they are drawn (sometimes even in advance of the CD).[98] While the largest operator, MTV, runs out of New York, most of the stars and much of the product are from L.A. Video music approaches an integrated global circuit with few distributional delays. The audience of MTV alone now includes 210 million people in seventy-eight countries (with other music video networks like VH1 bringing in millions more).[99]

Particularly when it comes to video, the big-city streets initiate style change, and the L.A. streets likely count most because those are the streets the performers and video fashion designers walk, stalk, and slouch on. Although the African-American neighborhoods of other cities were equally part of the early 1990s "hip-hop" look—long chains and oversized baggy shorts—L.A. (and New York) took it to the world. After a video premieres on TV, young designers mimic *the next day* what was shown.[100] Even the surf wear designers brought "inner-city styles" into their clothing lines.[101] Youth fashion changes at hyperspeed through the video medium, with the young and those otherwise not very privileged having strong impact. These styles migrate throughout the fashion system, including upwards to boutique and couture.

Another part of the entertainment industry spinoff are out-of-work people with modeling know-how, individuals who know how to walk, pose, strut, smile, and pout. By virtue of location and social circle, they are au courant as to just what *attitude* of stance, grimace, and gait goes with precisely which type of clothing and market niche. Even though Miami, for example, shares with L.A. the presence of a large low-wage labor force (in Miami, drawn from Haiti, Cuba, Central America, and the indigenous African-American population), there has not been much of a youthful glamour base to support its fledgling clothing industry. But now, notes *Women's Wear Daily,* the rise of hip South Miami Beach (the "art deco district") provides stylishly attractive young people for modeling. Their presence will also spark inventiveness.[102]

Southern Californians' propensity for sports and its athletes' fame have an impact on the clothing industry. At the Seoul Olympics, California (mostly the Southern portion, although data are reported by state) had five times as many entrants as did New York State; the Barcelona games' comparison was 168 to 36. The California total represents better than one-fourth of all U.S. athletes. The state has produced half the top swimmers *in the world.* As the veteran track and field star Bill Toomey was quoted as saying, "There's a spirit of adventure here, less inhibition, room for dreaming and for scheming. . . . I would not have made the Olympic team if I had stayed anywhere else."[103] Clothing makers use athletes' names as well as the colors, styles, and logos that imply the active life. L.A. is headquarters for Speedo, Cole, and Catalina, all big in swimwear. Individualistic sports—for which L.A. is the center, as opposed to team sports—more easily lend themselves to "civilian" spillover because the athletes do not usually wear uniforms. The clothing they do wear can become, with some modification, lines of sportswear for other life realms—for example, tennis shoes, sweats, socks, pullovers. Jackets and shirts can become wardrobe basics; volleyball and surfer shorts can be shorts for any type of use. Professional football, as a contrasting example, has little to transfer.

Still another of Southern California's cultural currents to enter the cloth-ing business, sometimes perhaps cynically, is environmentalism. Marketers in New England (L. L. Bean, EMS) and Northern California (REI, Sierra, White Face) are pioneers, but the L.A. region also leads. Patagonia—the Ventura maker of fashionably rugged outdoor wear—links environmental-ism to every aspect of its activities, including marketing, which advertises earth fragility. It uses green-friendly raw materials and production tech-niques. One percent of gross revenues goes to environmental causes. This way of doing business generates top prices for its goods. L.A. was hip to the "hot news" from the fashion press of "nontoxic muted colors" derived from berries and herbs[104] and natural fibers in dresses (a full-page *Women's Wear Daily* advertisement headlines "Fit for the Environment").[105] Camarillo-based (just northwest of L.A.) Freestyle Watch Company, oriented toward the surfer world, is a leader in environmentally friendly packaging. Recycle Revolution, east of Santa Monica, turns tires and other waste products into handbags, belts, and vests under the motto "Because Everyday is Earth Day." The L.A. retailer Fred Segal houses specialty shops called Fred Segal for a Better Ecology Center and Terra Verde to market globe-friendly fashions and housewares, from buttons made of nut shells to bedsheets woven of organically grown cotton.

Beyond its role in manufacturing, producers manage much offshore clothing production from Southern California. The Pacific Rim location obviously helps; the confluence of propinquity and style savvy makes South-ern California an appropriate base. Why don't California firms make *all* their clothing offshore? Local production puts designers and producers in close proximity. By paying the domestic labor cost premium, manufacturers can execute fresh designs in half the time needed for production offshore, important in so fickle a market as that for clothing fashions of the sports-wear, youth market variety.[106] Because L.A. has style, some production stays there.

Residences and Furniture

Architecture and furnishings have always reflected art and expressivity. Ar-chitecture began as settings for rituals and ceremony, particularly necropo-lises for the dead;[107] significant structures likely arose, not to serve func-tional need, but to express the symbolic. Houses and their furnishings have been called "temples in disguise; we may not be aware of it, but they are sacred objects, and as such they are able to provide us with something of greater value than mere shelter."[108] Even the most basic item of interior furnishings, the bed, is anthropologically odd: "where it exists, its readily traced ancestor is the throne." Chairs are unusual among world peoples, most of whom prefer to squat or sit flat on the ground. In Europe during the medieval era and in sub-Saharan Africa up to the modern period, chairs were not designed or used for comfort but to denote authority.[109]

Migration to Southern California, whether to work or retire, often turns on visions of living in a California house. To the degree that lifestyle drives migrants and the enterprises they come to create, the specific conditions of residential life are a force in growth and economic development. In California, says Brendan Gill, "houses are dreams that have come true." The Southern California way of doing up houses conforms to the California way of doing most things: lighter on the orthodoxy, heavy on whim, including mimicry of any architectural setting or period (French Regency, English Tudor, Spanish colonial, etc.) or combination thereof. A regional specialty is "Spanish style," which borrows from Spain, Morocco, Mexico, New Mexico, and Italy, mixed with U.S. architectural idiom and some modern materials. Southern California was also the "epicenter" of the Craftsman (Arts and Crafts) movement that reacted against Victorian gingerbread, with results still omnipresent in the peak-roofed, wide-eaved, wood-sided bungalows that line street after street in L.A.[110] Little about this style really suits Southern California's climate or topography, but its use reflects, in still a different way, an antitradition ethos. Southern California tiles used in Craftsman houses incorporated a "freer use of color" then those made elsewhere.[111] Its pottery, less effete than the Eastern versions, "glorifies the rustic beauty and the natural colors of California [bringing it] one step closer to a true definition of Arts and Crafts."[112] California versions of Craftsman furniture ("Mission style") form the basis of Clint Eastwood's contemporary line of furniture, albeit manufactured in North Carolina.

The openness of Southern California also made it open to the modern International Style of the 1920s through 1960s, but in a way that "brilliantly synthesized European and American modernism." R. M. Schindler, probably the key figure, was an Austrian immigrant who married Bauhaus to the naturalism of Frank Lloyd Wright. While Schindler's "compromise" prevented him from gaining full recognition from the rigid New York modernists who controlled the canon,[113] his sometime friend, L.A. collaborator, and fellow Austrian, Richard Neutra, enjoyed a larger success. As with many Southern California migrations, Neutra's began with a poster—in his case, a German one, reading "California Calls You"; he reported that for several years he repeated the words, "in a kind of commando tone . . . over and over again."[114] After his arrival, he, Schindler, and others of like mind, formed an L.A. circle of experimental modernism. Neutra made extensive use of post, beam, and glass favored by the European modernists, but now dramatically and a bit playfully applied in L.A. residences, where topography and sunlight could be put to stunning use. His clients were frequently Hollywood intelligentsia and other nonconformists; the commission for the now-famous Lovell House came from the antidrug physician who was a leader of the natural health movement. Neutra's buildings have been called "the first mature example of the International Style in America";[115] he gave credit to "Southern California [where] I found what I had hoped for, a people who were more 'mentally footloose' than those elsewhere, . . . where one can do most anything that comes to mind and is good fun."[116] This "California school" preceded the famous modernist buildings of Mies and Gropius in the East.

Neutra's influence on ordinary housing and the rest of the country occurred, in part, through distribution of his house plans by *Better Homes and Gardens* (a "Bildcost House") and *Ladies Home Journal,* as well as his participation in the "Case Study houses"—an L.A. demonstration program of house prototypes, actually built, by leading modernists (e.g., Charles Eames and Eero Saarinen). Linked to the "California lifestyle" at a popular level, home designers all over the country imitated the L.A. modernists with the glass-walled, slider-to-the-patio, single-story "ranch house" built in suburbs everywhere, as well as larger-scale "motel-modern" emulations. The architecture created markets for materials like aluminum and glass as well as kindred interior furnishings.

L.A.'s architects are today again a strong force with personages like Frank Gehry, Frank Israel, and Thom Mayne designing buildings around the world—distinctive enough to be called the "L.A. School."[117] Numbers of other Southern California architect and landscape architect firms take up major commissions in Europe and Japan. Gehry attributes inspiration to the artists he knew, including Jasper Johns and Frank Stella. He saw them making art from junk and cheap materials, giving him the idea of using similar mundane stuff in the underbudgeted remodels and house additions of his early career.[118] Out of this came the Gehry style of deliberate incorporation of inexpensive materials into even major buildings (and furniture), juxtaposed in quasi-makeshift and untraditional configurations. The more commercial Jon Jerde (a major project: "CityWalk" for MCA Entertainment) is iconoclastic in a different way, dedicated to designing interesting experiences for "the space between buildings" while letting the buildings more or less take care of themselves. His theatrical spirit yields some of the highest grossing per-square-foot sales in the world.

In terms of Southern California furniture, the single most important force over the years was the husband-wife team of Charles and Ray Eames. Migrating to L.A. from Detroit's Cranbrook Academy (where they worked with Saarinen), Eames and Eames invented new film techniques (e.g., "multivision"—simultaneous projection, in a single environment, on screens of many shapes and sizes) as well as wide ranges of furniture and other artifacts. The Eameses' forms were rounded and organic, simple yet somewhat fantastic, akin to the art of Miró, Arp, and Calder.[119] As with Schindler and other L.A. modernists, they parted from the severe austerity of Bauhaus,

Figure 8.7. Charles Eames, plywood chair, 1946, and "Dax" fiberglass armchair, 1949.

utilizing organic forms of plywood, plastic, and fiberglass accessed from local aerospace technologies. Themselves a strong commercial success, the Eameses' chairs (fig. 8.7) and other pieces have been variously imitated, becoming a mainstay in U.S. furniture manufacture. One of the most simple and spare was so omnipresent and influential, it has been called "a cultural monument."[120] More sumptuously, Charles Eames first created a leather upholstered easy chair and ottoman (still on the market at $3,000 each) as a gift for the movie maker Billy Wilder, whose house Eames also designed; it has sold well over 100,000 units (fig. 8.8). Although Herman Miller of Zealand, Michigan, marketed most of the Eames pieces, many were made in Los Angeles whose higher-tech manufacturers (e.g., Zenith Fabricators) could handle the untraditional shapes and materials. The Eameses' forms migrated from furniture into other types of consumer goods (including electric appliances and office equipment) and inspired car designs, the trend-setting Pontiac Firebird for one.[121] During the war, the Eameses molded plywood leg splints for the military, with the assistance of a sculptor, Marion Overby, and a theatrical designer, Margaret Harris.[122]

Besides the Case Study houses, another effort to link product and art

Figure 8.8.   Charles Eames, lounge chair and ottoman, 1956. Designed for Billy Wilder.

came through the efforts of Eudorah Moore, curator of the Pasadena Art Museum, who organized "California Design" exhibitions from 1962 to 1976. The exhibitions included both decorative art and mass-production pieces and helped launch small companies. Moore "went round the garages looking for surfers and climbers, the real innovators," in what has been called "the first generation of the New Crafts Movement. It was their technical mastery and profound knowledge of materials that made possible sensitive applications of high technology" in art, surfboards, snowboards, furniture, and other durables.[123]

California furniture designs partake of certain practical elements of the local lifestyle. Because people wear less, designers avoid sticky surfaces, ones that could be cold in winter, or fabrics that work poorly with sweat, like velvet. In terms of wood furniture, a small movement has been toward alderwood because it can be "made to look like almost anything," important given the local "penchant for mixing and matching styles, even within a single piece."[124] Alderwood, because it lacks a predominant grain pattern, can provide finishes appropriate to French, German, English, Japanese, and Chinese styles and simulate walnut, cherry, or mahogany. Like the ubiquitous exterior stucco, the indigenous alderwood serves any period fantasy (a design tendency that may help rain forests survive the makers of bedroom suites).

There is a blurring of inside and outside. The concept of "outdoor rooms" means that coffee tables, sofas, and even desks move to the patio—a marketing move pioneered by L.A.'s Brown-Jordan Company, one of the country's biggest makers. Outdoor metal furniture also comes inside in the form of tables, chairs, and canvas upholstered goods otherwise appropriate for withstanding inclement weather. The Brown-Jordan firm was the first furniture company to use aluminum for commercial, not just military, purposes, resulting in pieces that could duplicate classic designs and reflect new ones at lower costs than with iron or steel.[125] Use was made of both the materials and technologies of the region-based war industries.

As part of the informality and experimentation in L.A. furniture, chairs may have only one arm; a sofa may have only half a back or no back at all. The furniture varies in this way because its use is left open; chairs can be curled into, they can be sat on "sideways" with legs hanging over an arm; a sofa is designed to be laid on like a chaise longue. There is also a history of multipurpose designs (some silly), including easy chairs with radios built into the arms and combination shelving/table units, including those of refined Eames design. L.A. furniture has tendencies toward multiple use and informal incorporation into daily life, as with the chaise longue that can be inside or outside, used as a place to eat, sleep, watch TV, or work.

Such versatility is not completely a California or even an American invention; in eighteenth-century England, allowance was made "for the grand gesture, the leg drawn up, the arm thrown out over the back . . . [and] the broad armchair that allowed a variety of positions."[126] But what was "grand" in the mannered eighteenth century (paintings "often show men and women sitting sideways or leaning across the chair back")[127] shifts in modern times into a greatly evolved mass style of expression. Furniture becomes an extension of the body, a vehicle for self-display and comportment. Entertainers exhibit the playful use of furniture as they are photographed in their houses for magazines or on studio sets. As with the way they wear clothes, these people can make such informality especially appealing; they can place their limbs in unusual configurations and yet avoid awkward appearance. As a furniture designer told me, "They look great doing it; they know how to use their bodies, even on my pieces" (see fig. 8.9, Candice Bergen "sits" on a chair, as displayed in *Vanity Fair*). Fred Astaire, it should be recalled, danced on the ceiling.

The movie industry sometimes figures directly in furniture manufacture; a documented instance is the Monterey-style furniture pieces created for the 1929 movie *In Old Arizona*. The furniture was then mass produced by the local Mason Furniture Manufacturers through the 1940s (sold through Barker

Figure 8.9. *Vanity Fair*, December 1992, featuring Candice Bergen.

Bros.), with later versions by two other L.A. area firms, Jaeger Company and Brown-Saltman.[128] Because Universal Studios set designers had a standing contract to buy every piece manufactured by Brown-Saltman, the original *Arizona* pieces came full circle back into movie sets.

Southern California houses are distinctive in the way their residents use them, their importance in daily life, and the effort and expense to which people go to acquire them. By the mid-1970s, Southern California housing began its hyperinflation to become the most costly on the continent (along with the Bay Area). Speaking of those wealthy enough to purchase, an L.A. designer observes, "People live in their homes here, they have more fun with their homes, they change their homes more often. . . . [I]t keeps us inventing."[129] Even modest Southern California dwellings are large compared to their counterparts in eastern cities and certainly in Europe. In the extravagances of the late 1980s, L.A.'s rich were building houses of huge scale (25,000 square feet was not uncommon). Big proportions induce the big-scale furniture of the L.A. look—"works generous in size and spirit," in the words of *House Beautiful*'s special issue "Big Style Directions from California."[130] Prominent L.A. designer and manufacturer Mimi London, for example, had a success with actual tree trunks as the verticals for her canopy bed (fig. 8.10), designed and manufactured locally. Big scale is also evident

Figure 8.10. Mimi London, log bed, circa 1992.

in upholstered pieces with chair backs and armrests almost as wide as a seat might be in more "normal" furniture (see fig. 8.11). Southern California furniture tends toward deep and wide seats, in one case, including the "chair and a half," actually 50 percent larger in width than the same producer's usual product.[131]

The Los Angeles five-county area[132] now produces more furniture than any other part of the United States, except for the state of North Carolina. Most of it serves markets within the state and western region. But especially beginning in the 1970s, California furniture caught on in many parts of the country, including where it was inappropriate. Just as Californians can occasionally furnish their beach houses with Williamsburg reproductions, L.A.-inspired overscaled furniture crowds the small living rooms of New Jersey apartments. Easterners who have captured the "California look" with

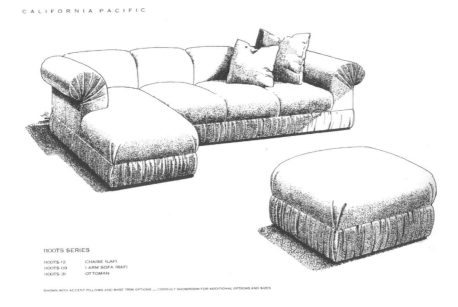

CALIFORNIA PACIFIC

1100TS SERIES

1100TS-12   CHAISE (LAF)
1100TS-09   1 ARM SOFA (RAF)
1100TS-31   OTTOMAN

SHOWN WITH ACCENT PILLOWS AND BASE TRIM OPTIONS ... CONSULT SHOWROOM FOR ADDITIONAL OPTIONS AND SIZES

Figure 8.11. Typical large-scale "California style" furniture.

"picture windows" overlooking urban street scenes and sliding glass doors to rarely used patios desire California pieces compatible with their imported architecture.

Although the bulk of L.A. area furniture production is at the lower end, L.A. possesses a strong group of furniture designers for the high-style and avant-garde markets. One writer portrays them as marked by "artistic minds" sometimes inspired by "nostalgia for the past . . . or a concern for the future of the planet." One L.A. designer (Alwy Vischedyk) uses ecologically correct eucalyptus wood, fast growing and abundant in California, but heretofore unsuccessful as a workable material. Some say California designs have a special "sense of fantasy and wit" and "invented histories."[133] L.A. dwellings mix cutting-edge with the old junk circulated from omnipresent yard sales and the large number of secondhand stores dotting the business districts. Again, as with clothing, L.A.-designed pieces land on magazine covers and travel the world in popular films and music videos. The leading home furnishings magazine, *Architectural Digest,* publishes from Southern California.

In the more utilitarian realm of office furniture, there tends toward a California-specific product. California customers favor stronger colors and "daring" departures like floral prints and geometries on office chairs.[134]

They prefer clean and contemporary pieces rather than European period or Early American imitations. Beyond surface difference, California informality translates into group-oriented office systems. Workers have individual spaces ("caves" in the trade), but arrayed around a "common" containing an open conference arena or specialized equipment. The hardware to support such an environment includes low walls and furniture less designed to display hierarchy (e.g., oversized executive chairs with high backs and massive desks) than to facilitate and *show* adaptability to changing work tasks. As the work-group office concept continues to grow in other markets, firms already making the appropriate furniture will have "first-mover" advantage. This was the rationale behind American Seating's acquisition of Condi, a high-end California manufacturer of such "caves and commons" furniture.[135]

As in the apparel industry, some companies manufacture their L.A.-designed furniture locally despite lower wages and weaker environmental restrictions across the border and offshore. Again, they want control. Furniture is frequently made in small batches, sometimes custom for specific clients or at least modified with a specific client in mind, including institutions (restaurants, hotels, airports) or a decorator representing an individual end-user. In some instances, a design may "grow" from a piece on the showroom floor, modified to a client's specification. Instructions to the factory must be carried out precisely and quickly. A piece developed in this way can become the basis for still another line of furniture that must again "turn on a dime" in response to changing preferences. Close relations develop between decorators or designers and the factory they use. This assures the finished product will be correct (e.g., the right mix of fabrics and specific details of tucks and fringes, tufts and thicknesses, levels of gloss on a finish). Frank Gehry insisted that the small factory established by Knoll International to make his furniture be adjacent to his existing Santa Monica architecture practice so that he could "stop in on short notice."[136]

Automobiles

Like the house and its furnishings, the body and its coverings, cars do more than fill a function. No less a scholar of stuff than Roland Barthes remarked, in admiration for a particular model of Citroen, "I think that cars today are almost exactly the equivalent of the great Gothic cathedrals: I mean the supreme creation of an era, conceived with passion by unknown artists, and consumed in image if not in usage by a whole population which appropriates in them a wholly magical object."[137]

Besides its tradition of freeways, hot rods, drive-ins, cruisin' song lyrics, and other appurtenances of "auto-mania,"[138] L.A. was once a major production center (second only to Detroit in the U.S.). But design is the Southern

California thing. While Henry Ford launched and dominated the mass market through his assembly line, the rise of General Motors was propelled by design concepts from Los Angeles. L.A.'s Harley Earl founded the first automobile styling department for a car company (at GM); he had earlier achieved fame customizing cars for movie stars. Earl and "his taste for 'Hollywood styling' "—as General Motors President Alfred P. Sloan, Jr., approvingly called it—reflected these entertainment roots. Earl and his father were close to the center of the Hollywood social scene.[139] When brought to Detroit, Earl inaugurated annual design changes, the use of coordinated color on both exteriors and interiors, and deliberately used fashion to create and occupy market niches. The cars outsold Ford's, and at the higher prices that people showed themselves willing to pay for "style." Thus was Henry Ford's staid philosophy of "any color you want as long as it's black" overturned and with it his company's dominion over the car market. In the late 1940s, GM and the other car companies were moving toward what the art historian Edson Armi calls "more irregularly sculpted cars [that] have more in common with the automatism of postwar expressionist painters and their biographic fantasies.[140] GM reached its apogee with its 1957 flagship Cadillac—with "Duchamp, Gropius and Marinetti all commingled in the tail fin,"[141] an auto part to become icon of the age.

GM was to lose its edge to foreign producers, especially the Japanese who were the first car makers to "come back" to L.A., with the establishment of design studios in Southern California. Toyota took the lead with its wholly owned Calty Design Center in 1973; the first Detroit company took a decade to follow suit. There are now eighteen auto design studios in Southern California, including the major Japanese producers, Hyundai (Korean), Mercedes-Benz, Volvo, BMW, and Volkswagen. This design presence has not in itself significantly increased the regional industrial base; car design will not show on any list of Southern California's major industries (Toyota's staff numbers 48; the others are smaller still). The long lead time of car production, compared to clothing and furniture, has meant that design and production could be geographically separated (although even here perhaps not optimally).[142] But these studios strengthen the region's general capacity for product development in other realms; their employees take on work for other types of products and spin off other types of design firms.

Those in California auto design disagree among themselves on what, if anything, may be the basis for the region's special design role. For Hiroaki Ohba, executive vice president of Toyota's Calty Design, the company's Orange County location is particularly stimulating, among other reasons because "Newport Beach is a museum for automobiles and an idea place for the automobile designer." He says, in his halting English, "We see many antique cars in Newport Beach."[143] Cars last a long time in the California weather. There are also more exotic cars on the streets of a place like New-port Beach (Porsches, Ferraris), more, according to Ohba, than one would find in Germany or Japan. The youth of California have for generations been great style experimenters. One auto design leader told me that the fashions on Melrose Avenue, a 1990s hot strip of boutiques and high-end junk shoppes for the affluent young, influence car designers.[144] The shapes and colors of jewelry, the textures and combinations of outfits, all may end up in design details like knobs and fittings, upholstery, and even overall body outlines. Even if not consciously inventorying "the trends," designers are alert to such messages from the streets and shop windows. The GM California studio chief says he likes to take "a few of our guys and drive along the beach . . . to see what people do on weekends with their vehicles."[145] The Chrysler vice president for design explains his company's presence in Southern California as taking "advantage of the local culture there, even the air they breathe." His Ford counterpart says California is "a totally different environment, . . . a melting pot of automotive design, from low-riders and dune buggies to some very sophisticated European products. It's a very exciting environment for a designer—the architecture, the culture and the pace of life. You're bound to get a different viewpoint on design."[146]

Others are more skeptical that the local milieu means that much, although no one seems to dismiss it altogether. Toyota-Calty's studio director, David Hackett, thinks the main issue is that good design will be more likely to come from people who are happy with their life situation, and California provides contentment. If a designer was happy living in Detroit (and he speaks without implying Detroit designers could not be), then Detroit would also make for good design.[147] Another important auto design figure, Charles Pelly, expressed the view that global media, travel, and circulation of objects themselves create an international design aesthetic.[148] Even for Pelly, however, there was a California difference—not so much in a specific look to the end product as in the kind of designers attracted to the region (better ones) and the spirit that encourages them to innovate. I have interviewed many L.A. designers who resigned or turned down Detroit "dream jobs" because they "couldn't handle the culture."

Another aspect of Southern California's design significance is its design education centers, Cal State University Long Beach, Cal Arts, and the Art Center College of Design in Pasadena. The latter institution, the first in the world to establish an auto design program (in the 1930s), ranks as the country's "premier training ground for tomorrow's designers," especially in cars, but also in other fields.[149] Among its alumni are many of the world's top designers, including Japan's postwar design leader, Kenji Ekuan, the adviser on design policy to MITI (Ministry of International Trade and Industry) and himself creator of many familiar products, including the Kikkoman soy sauce bottle. Art Center trained ten of the California auto design studio heads as well as an estimated half of the professional car designers practicing in the United States.[150] A veteran member of its faculty, Strother MacMinn, served as the primary design consultant when Toyota established its first California studio. He was another Detroit escapee ("I would have turned into a vegetable").[151] His trajectory somewhat parallels that of Richard Hutting, an ex-Detroiter hired out of the Art Center faculty to set up Ford's California studio.[152]

The California auto design centers traditionally played the role, for both the domestic and foreign makers, of "advanced design." This contrasts with "production design." Advanced design means coming up with early concepts rather than specifications for actual production. It means that the California studios were used as idea sources, as "inspirations" (Ohba used that word) or "blue sky" for the larger corporate apparatus. California conceptions were heavily screened, first through the design departments in Detroit or Tokyo and then, by engineers and nondesign-oriented executives. A designer's complaint is that "designers design it, engineers compromise it, then accounting does it in."

One reason the U.S. makers have been at such a disadvantage compared to their foreign competitors, according to one informant,[153] is that the Detroit executives simply will not accept the judgment of their own (excellent) local design teams, much less the "far-out" California studios. More than their Japanese counterparts, it has been the Detroit companies that have used California merely as "a playpen"[154] and "listening post."[155] Detroit designers have been subject to autocratic top-down dictum. Lee Iacocca walked through Chrysler's design studios and made changes to his taste; he insisted on the boxy look and vinyl roofs that made most of his company's cars the design duds (and poor sellers) of the late 1980s. The opposite approach is to provide "a heavyweight team of people with absolute freedom," an explanation an academic business expert has provided for the success of the Ford Taurus series and the 1993 Chrysler LH car line (the latter an Iacocca-free design, heavily shaped by the California studio's advance design for the Portofino, Millenium, and Eagle Optima).[156] Design is now regarded as having "saved" Chrysler Corporation, with the LH series not only providing sales growth of its own but also creating a new image that sells other company products as well.[157]

The California studios of the Japanese companies have played the critical role in the design of many more production models. The Miata sports car is one well-told case of an immediately successful vehicle, designed at the California Mazda studio in Irvine (a very Californian vehicle in function and aesthetic, including its retro imageries of the British-made Lotus line of the 1950s). Other Southern California–bred models include a series of cars from Nissan's San Diego studio: the 1986 Hardbody Truck, the Jeep-like 1987 Pathfinder, the 1987 Pulsar NX, the Infiniti J30, and the 1992

Altima.[158] All these cars come from a studio headed by the former chief designer of Buick who says he left Detroit because "it represented everything I loathed about American design, the aesthetics of excess."[159] Other cars in which the California studio played the decisive role include Isuzu's Trooper and Amigo as well as Toyota's Previa van, Celica (in 1975), and Lexus.

In the Toyota case, each design team is bicultural in its constitution, being made up of three professionals, always including one Japanese—"the best of both worlds." Not one to shun conventional stereotype, Toyota's Ohba says the Americans are good at designing the overall car, the Japanese "at details and quality." The California designers taught the Japanese, among other skills, how to make presentations. This is no minor task given that a decision to produce a model can rise or fall on how well the designers communicate their conception in graphics, models, and talk—that is, on art of another sort. The Japanese had used only sketches of cars while the Californians used models. In originating the Lexus, the design work began by hand molding clay into aesthetically pleasing sculptural shapes of what vaguely might be portions of a car (fenders, hoods), rather than the sketching or mocking up of a complete vehicle. The designers photographed the shapes, and when the images were projected on screen, the screen was turned and the images stretched as part of still other design experiments. They deliberately worked with exaggerated forms, knowing they had "a car in there." This process of working clay with hands, prior to even a preliminary auto sketch, had been used a generation earlier in the design of U.S. cars (by Gordon Buehrig)[160] but was abandoned under Harley Earl's two-dimensional design dictates at GM. This sculptural system was thus new (again) to car design and was exported to Tokyo for use in Toyota's studios there.

The car is now treated as art not only within the design studios but also in the marketplace. While U.S. makers once advertised their cars using sex symbols, family scenes, elegant couples, or hearty hunters, they now let the physical form of the car itself sell the product (see figs 8.12–8.15). A prominent case was the campaign for the Lexus, displayed as though a work of art on a plinth. Advertisers used the same technique for marketing even low-priced cars, making it virtually a universal tactic by the mid-1990s.[161]

AESTHETIC IN PRODUCT: LESSONS FROM L.A.

Images of fruits and nuts have made Southern California, clearly a major industrial force, a sometime target of ridicule.[162] But as I have tried to show, fruits and nuts sustain. They innovate. They win awards in numbers of creative fields, including industrial design. About one-fourth of the 1990 Industrial Design Society of America's gold medalists are California residents (al-

Better ideas make a better wagon. A man's wagon.

A man shouldn't have to treat people like baggage, Mercury figures.
So we put a Dual-Action Tailgate on our Mercury wagons. It swings open like a door for people. Down like a platform for easy cargo handling. Crafty.
See are the side panels on the Colony Park, above, that look like yacht deck walnut—but there's the strength of steel underneath.
And the choice of third-seat options, either rear-facing or dual center-facing (see left): so kids get their own built-in playroom and aren't breathing down your neck.

A man needs man-sized room. The Colony Park takes 4-ft.-wide loads without scraping either side. The 2-seat model neatly hides

11.7 cu. ft. of gear in below-decks storage space that's lockable.
Other man-pampering features: power rear window. Power front disc brakes. See your Mercury Man, your Mercury dealer.

Ford | MERCURY
LINCOLN

Mercury, the Man's Car.

Figure 8.12. Car advertisements before the 1990s placed the car within an idealized social context—a sexy woman, a happy family, as in this one for a Mercury Colony Park wagon.

beit, both Northern and Southern).[163] L.A. firms won the top CLIO awards for advertising in 1994. Despite the "laid-back" imageries, I know of no evidence that Southern Californians, of any social stratum, work fewer hours or less intensely than those of other regions. The industrial designer Charles Pelly said, "Orange County may be the epitome of this; they wear white shoes but boy they work long hours." The entertainment industry is notorious as a nonstop world of twelve-hour days, seven days a week. That people "do lunch" is semantic evidence that eating is marginal to the work that goes on. Southern California university faculties are productive. Nor does the La-La land image acknowledge even the presence of the working classes who have always and still do carry out the unromantic chores that

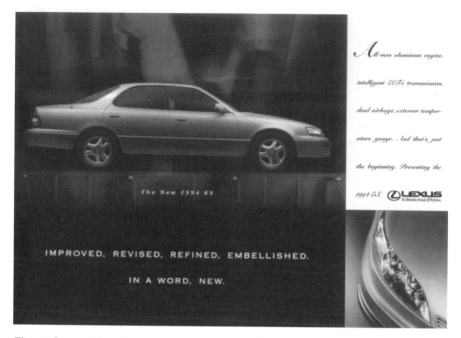

Figure 8.13. Advertisement for 1993 Lexus, displaying the car as a piece of sculpture, without humans.

lie behind all production systems. In Southern California all of this—including the cauldron of racial, ethnic, and cultural variation—combines and recombines into image and product that the world buys.

The L.A. region tests rigorously, not only in sports where the best are demonstrably up against the best, but also in goods consumption. As in Japan—that other hotbed of consumption, waste, and innovation—Southern California is notorious for its lack of consumer loyalty; people will switch from Nissan to Toyota, just as they led the nation's switch originally from U.S. brands to foreign ones. Political party loyalty has always been weak. Even in religion, there is less stability and more niche marketing; people pick and choose denominations like they were dealing with competing brand names on the shelves. Indeed, new churches obscure their linkages with larger denominations (if they have them) using names like Shepherd of the Hills, Horizon Christian Fellowship, Celebration Center, Saddleback Valley Community Church.[164] The toughness of the indigenous clientele may help make Southern California designs better ones.

While they are choosy and fickle, L.A.'s indigenous immigrants from everywhere act as a proxy for world taste as well as sources of creativity. The open spirit capitalizes on generic human playfulness, coincident in this

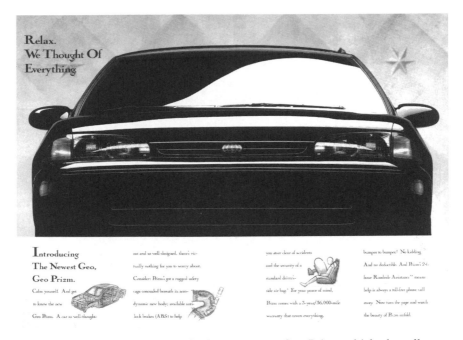

Figure 8.14. Advertisement for the low-cost 1993 Geo Prizm, which also sells the car as a sculptural element.

century with the vast expansion of technologies that can carry pleasure products to the world. The absence of stultifying tradition means that output is not restricted to specific cultural tastes. Nor, whatever else its failings, has L.A. ever been reluctant to risk being what some might see as low-brow—a production virtue given that such brow is not only at times exactly what the world wants, but also because what is lowbrow at one moment may be reincorporated as highbrow in the future. While the Japanese may succeed in developing successful products in diverse areas by opening an "outpost" (as they did with car design in the U.S.), the L.A. honchos appear less deliberate, more innocent. Hollywood did not succeed in the world by first test-marketing in global branches. Instead the moguls went global by doing what, for them, came naturally.

Designs can be wonderful by the lights of certain art currents, but not able to succeed in mass or diverse markets. The right touch means being ahead, but not irrelevant. The advantage of an open agenda means not only that specific individuals can invent but also that the system can *collectively* offer up a continuous stream of innovations. So, in a way parallel to the failure of so many who try to make it in show business, the real design asset for a place is not that every concept works but that enough new stuff hap-

Figure 8.15. In an oft-repeated formula, advertisers showed luxury cars, such as this Cadillac Sedan de Ville, with the beautiful "luxury people" who purchased them.

pens that some of it will. Doing things for fun produces just such a bountiful harvest; a small number of big successes become more likely with a large selection.

The mistake is always to bracket art from production, and to think of the artistic, whether in material form or human, as defining the opposite of the practical. All this is consonant with the historical record of how playfulness and aesthetics have worked themselves into economy over history. As Cyril Stanley Smith points out in stressing how children's toys have led to large-scale industrial change, it may take generations: "all big things grow from little things, but new little things will be destroyed by their environment unless they are cherished for reasons more like love than purpose."[165] Chandra Mukerji stunningly shows how English taste for calico floral prints stimulated first the spinning jenny and then Awkwright's water wheel, thus generating the English cotton industry and, more than plausibly, the industrial revolution itself.[166] Decorative etching for plaques and jewelry in the latter eighteenth century "led directly to the most important single scientific discovery in metallurgical history!"[167]—the basis of modern steel production. Decorative plating presaged the electrical generator.[168] Military camouflage was developed by Cubists working for the French military; the molded concrete formations of the Maginot line were also developed by avant-garde architects.[169] Most profoundly of all, it was the search for spice and useless glitter that made the world go round.

At the individual cognitive level, according to more than one scientist, "There is no doubt that nonscientific, even nonverbal, thought plays a crucial role in all invention, including that of engineers."[170] "Thinking in pictures" is fundamental—whether in regard to particular machining problems or the development of "a new paradigm of production" like the assembly line.[171] Designers are sensors of emerging needs, tastes, and cultural patterns, as well as—if they are completely good—the kinds of production apparatus that can make their stuff efficiently. They may be dreamers, but people's needs and engineers' principles inflect their dreams ("blueprint hedonism," again). The Sony Walkman, one of the world's consumer breakthroughs, was initiated by the design department rather than by the marketing or production division.[172] The idea to make watches mere palettes for artistic and fashion design allowed the Swiss to withstand Japanese and Asian competition with the Swatch. Design orientation means not just acute awareness of color and line, but of changing preferences and emerging niches.

In late modernity, images flow with great speed across social and political borders, causing some to think locality has become irrelevant. But place differences still exist, and just as God is in the details,[173] the success or failure of a cultural form and a commercial product turn on very small differences. In this as in other realms, *the worldwide does not abolish the local.*"[174] Precisely because of the relative homogeneity of world places, audiences read with increasing subtlety and consume using ever-finer distinction. Globalism places even greater premium on place, proximity, and the efficiencies that only face-to-face interaction and in situ cultural absorption can provide. As worldwide marketing makes things more alike, it raises the rewards to those who can produce the small differences the world wants. If the designers of successful products quote from the present, the production edge goes to those who are where, indeed, it is happening.

Retarding innovation from the creative margin holds back the center.

Although not frequently linked, the inner decay of the Soviet system was accompanied by a doctrine of command aesthetics that destroyed a buoyant postrevolutionary modern art movement ("constructivism"), once making a brilliant mark on graphic design, housewares, and architectural plans. The lesson should not be lost on those who would censor the arts, including those aspects of Hollywood anathema to the politically correct or the politically Neanderthal. Industrial design, as a profession, was invented in the United States by exploiting the modernist art movements led by Communists, anarchists, homosexuals, nudists, nihilists, and drug users as well as styles from those on the devalued end of the cultural stick. Product design and the arts with which it is inextricably linked have forged the Southern California economic base and had an impact on the cultural and material circumstances of people far afield. L.A.'s world leadership of today's entertainment economy clearly shows aesthetics as a force. But wit, dreams, and beauty—including dangerous beauty—are the important factors of production everywhere just as they have always been the staff of life. They arise through the cultural yeast in given places at certain times more than others. Los Angeles, I have tried to show, has been an important site—and sometimes, although by no means always—for the better. It and the art at its heart need to play a larger role in discussions of what makes up places and their economies.

NOTES

I especially thank the following: Richard Appelbaum, Edson Armi, Howard Becker, Deirdre Boden, Gray Brechin, Avery Gordon, Betty Klausner, Michael Kimmel, Magali Larson, Margit Mayer, Thomas Spence Smith, Bruce Spear, Glenn Wharton, Arlene Zeichner, and Sharon Zukin. Daniel Gibbons, Hugh Louch, and Elisabeth Jordon provided able research assistance.

1. Ash Amin and Nigel Thrift, "Neo-Marshallian Notes in Global Networks," *International Journal of Urban and Regional Research* 16, no. 4 (1992): 571–587.

2. Mary Douglas and Baron Isherwood, *The World of Goods: Towards an Anthropology of Consumption* (New York: Basic Books, 1979).

3. Arthur C. Danto, *Beyond the Brillo Box: The Visual Arts in Post-Historical Perspective* (New York: Farrar, Straus, Giroux, 1992), 134. For a discussion of the links between high culture and popular culture, see Herbert Gans, "American Popular Culture and High Culture in a Changing Class Structure," in *Art, Ideology, and Politics,* ed. Judith H. Balfe and Margaret Jane Wyszomirski, 40–57 (New York: Praeger, 1985). An early, and highly elitist, classification of societies in terms of the linkage between utilitarian and the artistic expressions is C. Stumpf, ed., *Richard Payne Knight Expedition into Sicily* (London: British Museum Publications, 1986).

4. Penny Sparke, *An Introduction to Design and Culture in the Twentieth Century* (New York, Harper & Row, 1986), 100.

5. Interactive computer program at London Design Museum, accessed 4 April 1993.

6. Under an anonymous name, Duchamp wrote that "the only works of art America has given are her plumbing and her bridges." "The Richard Mutt Case," *The Blind Man,* no. 2 (1915): 1; quoted in Kirk Varnedoe and Adam Gopnik, *High and Low* (New York: Museum of Modern Art, 1991), 277.

7. Varnedoe and Gopnik, *High and Low,* 306.

8. I thus disagree on this point with Halle's interpretation of his very useful data. See David Halle, *Inside Culture: Art and Class in the American Home* (Chicago: University of Chicago Press, 1993).

9. When goods do arise, the stress is on how merchandise influenced the artist, not the other way around. See, e.g., Varnedoe and Gopnik, *High and Low,* 270.

10. Perhaps the distinctions don't matter as much when dealing with cultural products less valued in any aspect. It may not be as imperative to impose the mystique of an autonomous artistic sensibility among such peoples.

11. Rosalind Williams, *Dream Worlds: Mass Consumption in Late Nineteenth-Century France* (Berkeley, Los Angeles, and London: University of California Press, 1982), 8.

12. Jean Baudrillard, *America* (New York: Verso, 1989), 104.

13. Blaise Cendrars, *Hollywood: Mecca of the Movies,* trans. Garrett White (Berkeley, Los Angeles, and Oxford: University of California Press, 1995) (French edition, 1936).

14. Quoted in Carey McWilliams, *Southern California: An Island on the Land* (New York: Duell, Sloan & Pierce, 1946), 181.

15. Willard Wright, writing in *The Smart Set,* quoted in McWilliams, *Southern California,* 157.

16. Sarah Comstock, quoted in McWilliams, *Southern California,* 232.

17. Ironically, this L.A. of blacks, Latinos, and Asians became most visible through the upheavals following the first Rodney King verdict: "With its cameras pointing at itself for 80 hours straight, Los Angeles in chaos was more comprehensible than it is in calmer times." See Richard Reeves, "L.A. Story," *Travel and Leisure* (July 1992): 32–34, on p. 34.

18. But see Saskia Sassen, *The Mobility of Labor and Capital* (New York: Cambridge University Press, 1988). She attributes much contemporary global migration to cultural forces that connect disparate world locations.

19. For a description of the early California migrants and their cultural variants, see Kevin Starr, *Americans and the California Dream, 1850–1915* (Oxford: Oxford University Press, 1973), and *Inventing the Dream: California Through the Progressive Era* (Oxford: Oxford University Press, 1985). For an informative account of California religion, see Eldon G. Ernst (with Douglas Firth Anderson), *Pilgrim Progression: The Protestant Experience in California* (Santa Barbara: Fithian Press, 1993).

20. The quote is from Britisher Bill Moggridge, head of the California design firm IDEO, as cited in Hugh Aldersey-Williams, *Nationalism and Globalism in Design* (New York: Rizzoli, 1992), 158.

21. Cyril Stanley Smith, *A Search for Structure: Selected Essays on Science, Art, and History* (Cambridge: MIT Press, 1981), 329.

22. Mattel, Inc., Annual Report, 5 March 1993, 4.

23. Sharon Zukin, *The Cultures of Cities* (Cambridge, Mass.: Blackwell, 1995), 148.

24. "California Design, Funk Is In: Brash, Passionate Newcomers are Taking on Austere Eurostyle," *Business Week,* Special Bonus Issue (1990): 172–177.

25. Daniel Wood, "Predicting the Future of Product Design," *Christian Science Monitor,* 26 November 1991, 10–12.

26. Christopher Knight, "Mike Kelley, at Large in Europe," *Los Angeles Times Calendar,* 5 July 1992, 70. Ed Kienholz and the group of painters formed around him are exemplars (Scott Lash and John Urry, *Economies of Signs and Space* [London: Sage, 1994], 166).

27. p. 97, Adam Gopnik, "Diebenkorn Redux," *New Yorker,* 24 May 1993, 97–100.

28. Varnedoe and Gopnik, *High and Low,* 154.

29. This discussion owes much to conversations with the artist David Legare.

30. Lawrence Weschler, "In a Desert of Pure Feeling," *New Yorker,* 7 June 1993, 81–90.

31. The art critic Robert Hughes wonders why New York, the place where more art is *sold,* is a place where relatively less is inspired and produced. See Robert Hughes, "The Decline of the City of Mahogany," *New Republic,* 25 June 1990, 27–38.

32. David Gebhard, Introduction to Jim Heimann and Rip Georges, *California Crazy: Roadside Vernacular Architecture* (San Francisco: Chronicle Books, 1980).

33. For a view of American design that pays little respect to Southern California, see Hugh Aldersey-Williams, *New American Design* (New York: Rizzoli, 1988); for a rejoinder, see Martin Smith, "Designing Profits," *California Business* (October 1988): 46–48.

34. California Employment Development Department; U.S. Bureau of the Census (taken from "What is Southern California? How Do the Pieces Fit?" Los Angeles Area Chamber of Commerce (n.d.), D.10, p. 19. See also *Los Angeles Annual Report* (Los Angeles: Benchmark, 1992), 65.

35. John Findlay, *Magic Lands: Western Cityscapes and American Culture after 1940* (Berkeley, Los Angeles, and Oxford: University of California Press, 1992), 68.

36. Reyner Banham, *Los Angeles: The Architecture of the Four Ecologies* (New York: Penguin, 1971).

37. Sharon Zukin provides this data in regard to musicians in New York City. See also "High Culture and 'Wild' Commerce: Redeveloping a Center of the Arts in New York City," in Hartmunt Haussermann and Walter Siebel, *New York: Strukturen Einer Metropole* (Frankfurt: Suhrkamp, 1993), 24.

38. Bernard Beck, "Reflections on Art and Inactivity," in *Culture and the Arts Workgroup,* CIRA Seminar Series Monograph, vol. 1 (May 1988): 43–66 (Evanston, Ill.: Center for Interdisciplinary Research in the Arts, Northwestern University).

39. Zukin, *The Cultures of Cities,* 155.

40. David Wharton, "What Becomes a Legend Most?" *Los Angeles Times,* 17 November 1992, E1.

41. Bruce Horovitz, " 'Jurassic Park' Faces Tough Obstacles to Beat 'Batman' in Retail Sales," *Los Angeles Times,* 1 June 1993, D1, D6.

42. David Gates, "Wagon Train to the Stars," *Newsweek,* 4 November 1991, 56.

43. Bruce Horovitz, "New Twist in Tie-ins: 'Home Alone 2' May Redefine Merchandising," *Los Angeles Times,* 12 November 1992, D1, D5.

44. Charles McGrath, "Rocking the Pond," *New Yorker,* 24 January 1994, 50.

45. Jonathan Weber, "Video Games Go to the Movies," *Los Angeles Times,* 21 March 1993, D1, D8.

46. James Bates, "Video Sales, Rentals Top $17 Billion in '92," *Los Angeles Times,* 9 January 1993, D1.

47. *Business Week,* 14 March 1994, 60, as cited in Zukin, *The Cultures of Cities,* chap. 1.

48. Mike Davis, *City of Quartz: Excavating the Future in Los Angeles* (London: Verso, 1990), 73,124.

49. "Alfred Hitchcock on His Films," *The Listener,* 6 August 1964, 189–90. Reprinted in Sidney Gottlieb, ed., *Alfred Hitchcock on Film: Selected Writings and Interviews* (Berkeley, Los Angeles, and London: University of California Press, forthcoming).

50. Appadurai, "Disjuncture and Difference in the Global Cultural Economy," *Theory, Culture and Society* 7 (1990): 295–310.

51. Alan Citron and Bruce Horovitz, "Coke Makes Consulting Deal with Ovitz's Agency," *Los Angeles Times,* 5 September 1991, A1.

52. Carey McWilliams, *Southern California: An Island on the Land* (Salt Lake City: Peregrine Smith, [1946] 1973), 339. See also p. 341.

53. Wall copy, 29 May 1993, Max Factor Museum, Hollywood, California.

54. Michael Storper and S. Christopherson, "The City as Studio, The World as Black Lot: The Impact of Vertical Disintegration on the Location of the Motion Picture Industry," *Society and Space* 4 (1987): 305–320.

55. McWilliams names the source as Robert J. Burdette, but provides no other details. See McWilliams, *Southern California,* 143.

56. McWilliams, *Southern California,* 157. A 1913 *Examiner* account calls "advertising, ballyhoo, publicity, the most ancient of California's professions" (28 February 1913); quoted in Robert M. Fogelson, *The Fragmented Metropolis: Los Angeles, 1850–1930* (Cambridge: Harvard University Press, 1967), 191.

57. The dollar figures comes from *Los Angeles Annual Report* (Los Angeles: Benchmark, 1992), 61. See also California Employment Development Department, U.S. Bureau of the Census, "What Is Southern California? How Do the Pieces Fit?" D. 10/p. 18.

58. Los Angeles Convention and Visitors Bureau.

59. Zukin, *The Cultures of Cities,* 273.

60. Findlay, *Magic Lands,* 75.

61. Ibid., 68.

62. See Findlay, *Magic Lands.* See also Allen J. Scott, *Technopolis: The Geography of High Technology in Southern California* (Berkeley, Los Angeles, and London: University of California Press, forthcoming).

63. Yvonne Fern, *Gene Roddenberry: The Last Conversation* (Berkeley, Los Angeles, and London: University of California Press, 1994).

64. Scott, *Technopolis.*

65. Ibid.

66. Barney Brantingham, "Those High-Flyin Loughead Brothers," *Santa Barbara News Press,* 27 December 1992, B2.

67. Steve Harvey, "Only in L.A.," *Los Angeles Times,* 28 September 1993, B2. McWilliams says the country's first was L.A.'s Boos Brothers cafeteria. In conflict with both claims, Pillsbury says New York's Childs was "certainly" the first but gives no date and provides no documentation. Richard Pillsbury, *From Boarding House to Bistro* (Boston: Unwin Hyman, 1990), 61.

68. McWilliams, *Southern California,* 171.

69. Randy Bright (first quotation) and Anthony Haden-Guest (second quotation), both cited in Findlay, *Magic Lands,* 71.

70. McWilliams, *Southern California,* 172.

71. Contemporary cafeterias may still function this way (see Mitchell Duneier, *Slim's Table: Race, Respectability, and Masculinity* [Chicago: University of Chicago Press, 1992]). For an account of the contrasting effort to achieve privacy within restaurants, see Robert Thorne, "Places of Refreshment in the Nineteenth-Century City," *Buildings and Society: Essays on the Social Development of the Built Environment,* ed. Anthony D. King, 228–253 (London: Routledge and Kegan Paul, 1980).

72. Amy Wallace, "Coffee Shops Modern," *Los Angeles Times,* 1 April 1993, B1, B4.

73. Both quotes are from Zukin, *The Cultures of Cities,* 63.

74. David Gebhard, Introduction, 20.

75. Robin Leidner, *Fast Food and Fast Talk* (Berkeley, Los Angeles, and London: University of California Press, 1994). For histories of McDonald's, see John Love, *McDonald's: Behind the Arches* (New York: Bantam Books, 1986), and Ray Kroc, *Grinding It Out: The Making of McDonald's* (Chicago: H. Regnery, 1977).

76. *McDonald's History Listing* (Oak Brook, Ill.: McDonald's Corporation, n.d.), n.p.

77. The phrase is from Theodore Levitt, "The Industrialization of Services," *Harvard Business Review* 54 (1976): 63–74.

78. Pillsbury, *From Boarding House to Bistro,* 93–95.

79. Rick Fantasia, "Fast Food in France," *Theory and Society,* forthcoming.

80. Although Pillsbury is here referring to California generally, the innovations of economic consequence are from Southern California. Of the chains, only faltering A&W emerged from Northern California.

81. *Women's Wear Daily,* 1 June 1992, 2.

82. California Employment Development Department, U.S. Bureau of the Census (culled from "What Is Southern California? How Do the Pieces Fit?"). The vast majority of the five-county employment is in L.A. County.

83. The lack of strength in formal wear is paralleled by L.A.'s weak reputation in the jewelry business; it may be that the informality of the local environment hinders the development of a high-fashion industry using precious gems. For an account of L.A.'s status in jewelry, see Allen J. Scott, "Variations on the Theme of Agglomeration and Growth: The Gem and Jewelry Industry in Los Angeles and Bangkok," unpublished ms., Lewis Center for Regional Policy Studies, UCLA.

84. Interview, 11 October 1991, conducted by Richard Appelbaum and Edna Bonacich at Bugle Boy. I am grateful for access to these materials.

85. Corky Newman, president of the California Mart. See Vicki Torres, "Bold Fashion Statement: Amid Aerospace Decline, L.A. Garment Industry Emerges as a Regional Economic Force," *Los Angeles Times*, 12 March 1995, D1.

86. Interview, 6 July 1992. Otis-Parsons is a leading center of fine arts training; alumni include Jackson Pollock, Robert Motherwell, Philip Guston, Robert Irwin, and John Baldessari.

87. Anne Hollander, *Seeing Through Clothes* (New York: Viking, 1986).

88. Ibid., 154.

89. W. Robert LaVine, *In a Glamorous Fashion: The Fabulous Years of Hollywood Costume Design* (New York: Charles Scribner's, 1980), 35.

90. Martin Battersby, *The Decorative Thirties*. Revised and edited by Philippe Garner (New York: Whitney Library of Design, 1988), 216.

91. Annette Kuhn with Susannah Radstone, eds., *Women's Companion to International Film* (London: Virago Press, 1990), esp. pp. 144, 145, entries by Mary Beth Haraolovich.

92. Battersby, *The Decorative Thirties*, 216.

93. Penny Sparke, Felice Hodges, Anne Stone, and Emma Dent Coad, *Design Source Book* (Secaucus, N.J.: Chartwell QED, 1986), 188; Witold Rybczynski, *Home: A Short History of an Idea* (New York: Penguin, 1986), 3.

94. *New York Times*, 17 April 1973, 46, in Rybczynski, *Home*, 3. The Fairbanks influence is mentioned by Starr, *Inventing the Dream*, 338.

95. Battersby, *The Decorative Thirties*. Edith Head says a film she designed had to be canned because the costumes were out of date by the time of a delayed release (interview with Rosemary Brantley, 6 July 1992).

96. Valerie Steele, "Chanel in Context," in *Chic Thrills: A Fashion Reader*, ed. Juliet Ash and Elizabeth Wilson, 118–126, on pp. 125, 126 (Berkeley, Los Angeles, and Oxford: University of California Press, 1993). Chanel spent a year in Hollywood; she dressed Gloria Swanson, among others.

97. Neil Spencer, "Menswear in the 1980s," in Ash and Wilson, *Chic Thrills*, 40–48, on p. 42.

98. Interview with Tori Metzger, Creative Artists Agency (CAA), 1 April 1992.

99. The influence of MTV in creating global product is also emphasized by a Bugle Boy informant (interviewed by Richard Appelbaum and Edna Bonacich, 11 October 1991); see also Ken Wells, "Global Ad Campaigns Bring Record Sales, but Minefields Remain," *Wall Street Journal* X, no. 45 (1992): 1, 4.

100. Brantley interview, 6 July 1992.

101. Chris Woodyard, "Surf Wear in Danger of Being Swept Aside by Slouchy, Streetwise Look," *Los Angeles Times*, 21 June 1992, D3.

102. Georgia Lee, "Miami Makers Enjoy a Place in the Sunshine," *Women's Wear Daily* 163, no. 121 (22 June 1992): 1, 6, 7.

103. Richard Hoffer, "The Golden State," *Sports Illustrated*, 22 July 1992, 36–40, on p. 40.

104. Pamela Sellers, "Fabric Trends Take Their Cue from the Environment," *California Apparel News* 48, no. 26 (26 June–26 July 1992): 1:5.

105. 3 June 1992, 13.

106. Interviews by Richard Appelbaum and Edna Bonacich of garment industry informants, 11 October 1991. Although L.A. labor costs are higher than in the Third World, they are not that much higher, as little as 50 cents on a blouse.

107. Brendan Gill, "California: Hats, Beds, and Houses," *Architectural Digest*, May 1989, 36–44, on p. 42.

108. Ibid.

109. Rybczynski, *Home*, 26; Shelly Freirman, "Seats of Power," *Metropolis*, October 1994, 66.

110. David Gebhard and Robert Winter, *A Guide to Architecture in Los Angeles and Southern California* (Santa Barbara: Peregrine Smith Books, 1977), 18. The California bungalow was mimicked by the likes of Gustav Stickley in the East, not invented there. See John Jackson, "Craftsman Style and Technostyle," in *Ornament*, ed. Stephen Kieran, 57–62 (Philadelphia: Graduate School of Fine Arts, 1977).

111. Riley Doty, comment on *The Arts and Crafts Movement in California* Oakland Museum show, published in *Arts and Crafts* 6, no. 2 (August 1993): 27–28.

112. Caro Tanner MacPherson, comment on *The Arts and Crafts Movement in California* Oakland Museum show, published in *Arts and Crafts* 6, no. 2 (August 1993): 28–29.

113. Joseph Giovanni, "Back to the Future," *Art in America* (December 1992): 57.

114. Thomas S. Hines, *Richard Neutra and the Search for Modern Architecture* (New York: Oxford University Press, 1982), 28. Depressed at one point by a dull job and bitter cold, Neutra wrote that he wished he "could get out of Europe and get to an idyllic tropical island where one does not have to fear the winter, where one does not have to slave but find time to think, or even more important, can have a free spirit" (p. 28).

115. Hines, *Richard Neutra*, 78.

116. Ibid.

117. Charles Jencks, *Heteropolis: Los Angeles, the Riots and the Strange Beauty of Hetero-Architecture* (Los Angeles: Academy Editions, 1993).

118. Frank Gehry interview by Charlie Rose, Public Broadcasting System, 5 January 1993.

119. The Eameses were not, of course, the only alternative force to the Bauhaus; the whole thrust of Italian design as early as the 1930s represented a break with the severe modernist aesthetic. See, e.g., Sparke et al., *Design Source Book*, 148.

120. Arthur J. Pulos, *The American Design Adventure* (Cambridge: MIT Press, 1990), 80.

121. C. Edson Armi, *The Art of American Car Design: The Profession and Personalities* (University Park: Pennsylvania State University Press, 1980), 95.

122. Charles Gandy and Susan Zimmermann-Stidham, *Contemporary Classics: Furniture of the Masters* (New York: McGraw-Hill, 1981), 136.

123. Paola Antonelli, "Economy of Thought, Economy of Design," *Arbitare* 329 (May 1994): 243–249.

124. Ann K. Nicknish, "California Classics Make a Lasting Impression," *FDM: Furniture Design and Manufacturing* (November 1991): 62–64, on p. 63.

125. Lee Fleming, "Remaking History," *Garden Design* 11, no. 4 (September/October 1992): 34–36.

126. Rybczynski, *Home,* 97.

127. Ibid.

128. W. Robert Finegan, *California Furniture: The Craft and the Artistry* (Chatsworth, Calif.: Windsor, 1990), 64, 65.

129. Carla Simi, "Manufacturing Success in California," *Perspectives: Newsletter of Pacific Design Center,* 4.

130. "Big Personality Pieces," *House Beautiful,* February 1987, 70.

131. Ibid., 72.

132. Los Angeles, Orange, Riverside, San Bernardino, and Ventura counties.

133. Barbara Thornburg, "Sitting on Top of the World," *Los Angeles Times Magazine,* 11 October 1992, 42.

134. Interview, David DeMarse, Director of Marketing and Business Planning, American Seating Co., 17 June 1992.

135. Ibid.

136. Martin Filler, "Frank Gehry and the Modern Tradition of Bentwood Furniture," in *Frank Gehry: New Bentwood Furniture Designs* (Montreal: Montreal Museum of Decorative Arts, 1992), 102.

137. Roland Barthes, *Mythologies,* quoted in Varnedoe and Gopnik, *High and Low,* 318.

138. This is a term from the pre-1920 era. See Gebhard, Introduction, 11. Southern California was the site of the first organized drag race, at Muroc in 1938 (now part of Andrews Air Base). See Kristine McKenna, "Revving Up the Rat Fink," *Los Angeles Times,* 20 December 1993, F1.

139. Armi, *The Art of American Car Design,* 1.

140. Ibid., 53.

141. Varnedoe and Gopnik, *High and Low,* 407.

142. Michael Schwartz and Frank Romo, *The Rise and Fall of Detroit,* forthcoming.

143. Hiroaki Ohba, "Automotive Design in the Fast Lane," lecture at the Pacific Design Center, West Hollywood, Calif., 2 July 1992 (notes made from my transcription of the tape).

144. Interview, Marty Smith, Art Center, 8 March 1992.

145. Paul Lienert, "Detroit's Western Front," *California Business* (December 1989): 55.

146. This and the previous quote from the Chrysler executive come from Lienert, "Detroit's Western Front," 38.

147. Response to a question after his talk at the Pacific Design Center, 2 July 1992.

148. Interview with Charles Pelly, President of Designworks/USA.

149. *Business Week,* Special 1990 Edition on Design, 174. The *U.S. News and World Report* college rankings place it among the country's three top schools in the arts (along with Juilliard and the Rhode Island School of Design).

150. *Business Week,* Special Issue, 184.

151. Preston Lerner, "One for the Road," *Los Angeles Times Magazine,* 9 February 1992, 33.

152. Paul Lienert, "Detroit's Western Front," 41.

153. Interview, Martin Smith, Art Center, 8 March 1992.

154. Telephone conversation with C. Edson Armi, 10 October 1992, based on his interviews in the early 1980s.

155. J. D. Power and Associates, "General Motors' California 'Skunk Works' Leads the Way," *California Report* (June 1989): 8.

156. The quote is from Kim Clark of the Harvard Business School in "Fast Action Is Viewed as Key to G.M.'s Success," *New York Times*, 2 November 1992, C4. Iacocca's willingness to let his personal taste dictate design decisions is repeated again and again in the business press; see, e.g., "Surge at Chrysler," *Business Week*, 9 November 1992, 89; and Alex Taylor III, "U.S. Cars Come Back," *Fortune*, 16 November 1992, 64. The influence of the California studies on the LH "cab-forward" configuration was confirmed, in conversation with Steve Harris, Executive Director, Chrysler Public Relations, 23 March 1994.

157. Interview with Harris, 23 March 1994.

158. According to the head of American operations, headquarters told California the Altima would "make or break" Nissan's North American business: "it would be the most important car we would ever design in the history of this company." Patrick Boyle, "The Sun Also Sets," *Los Angeles Times Magazine*, 10 January 1993, 16.

159. Larry Armstrong, "It Started with an Egg," *Business Week*, 2 December 1991, 142, 146.

160. C. Edson Armi, conversation, 6 May 1993.

161. Industrial designers now create their products with such advertising in mind, and strive to play a role in how the advertising will be handled.

162. For years national TV networks ended the nightly news with a feature from Southern California's offbeat lifestyles as segue into the sitcoms and other light fare of prime time. See Jason Epstein, *News from Nowhere* (New York: Random House, 1973).

163. "The Importance of Design to California's Economy," unpublished circular, Art Center College of Design, Pasadena (n.d.).

164. Ernst, *Pilgrim Progression*. See also Philip Hammond, *Religion and Personal Autonomy: The Third Disestablishment in America* (Columbia: University of South Carolina Press, 1992).

165. Smith, *A Search for Structure*, 331.

166. Chandra Mukerji, *From Graven Images: Patterns of Modern Materialism* (New York: Columbia University Press, 1983).

167. Smith, *A Search for Structure*, 210.

168. Ibid., 215, 230.

169. Stephen Kern, *The Culture of Time and Space, 1880–1918* (Cambridge: Harvard University Press, 1983).

170. Terry Smith, *Making the Modern: Industry, Art, and Design in America* (Chicago: University of Chicago Press, 1993).

171. Eugene S. Ferguson, "The Mind's Eye: Nonverbal Thought in Technology," *Science* 197 (August 1977): 827–836.

172. Penny Sparke, *Introduction to Design and Culture in the Twentieth Century*, 189.

173.   The fastest-growing U.S. magazine in men's clothing fashion, with a circulation of a half million in 1994, is called *Details*. See Patrick Reilly, "Condé Nast Taps a New Publisher to Lift Vanity Fair," *Wall Street Journal,* 9 June 1994, B3.

174.   Henry Lefebvre, *The Production of Space* (Oxford: Basil Blackwell, 1991), 330. Leonard Nevarez highlighted this passage for me.

NINE

High-Technology Industrial Development in the San Fernando Valley and Ventura County

Observations on Economic Growth and the Evolution of Urban Form

Allen J. Scott

Southern California is in many ways *the* archetype of a high-technology industrial region. Well before the emergence of Silicon Valley as a major manufacturing center, Southern California had already acquired a significant complement of aircraft, missile, and electronics industries, and today it is indisputably the largest high-technology industrial region in the world. It is, indeed, made up of a multiplicity of discrete industrial districts (some of which are individually comparable to Silicon Valley in terms of size and rapidity of growth) scattered over its entire geographic extent. Each district contains large numbers of individual manufacturing establishments clustered together in geographic space in search of the many different sorts of economic benefits that flow from such agglomeration. Among these benefits, the cost reductions and dynamic innovation effects associated with the formation of diversified local pools of labor and dense networks of inter-establishment transactional relations are of major importance.[1]

In this essay, I will investigate the logic and dynamics of high-technology industrial district formation in the northwest quadrant of the greater Los Angeles region—an area that corresponds more or less to the San Fernando Valley and Ventura County. The area is of special interest because it has been almost entirely overlooked in prior discussions of the geography of high-technology industry in the United States, and yet in this one small segment of the region alone is to be found a significant portion of the nation's high-technology industrial capacity. It also represents a sort of microcosm of the temporal and spatial process of high-technology industrial development across the whole extent of Southern California. In the decades since the end of World War II, the area has gone through several phases of industrial district formation, and a thorough analysis of its changing fortunes tells us much about the wider pattern of industrial and urban development in the entire metropolitan region.

BACKGROUND

The seeds of high-technology industrial development were planted in Southern California in the 1920s and 1930s when a number of major aircraft assembly firms began to make their appearance in the region. The industrial landscape of Los Angeles at this time was composed of a central manufacturing district arranged in the form of a collar around the downtown area, with a few large aircraft producers scattered around what were then the suburbs. With the advent of World War II, the region's aircraft industry expanded apace as massive government orders poured in.[2]

By the time the war had come to an end, two new industrial districts had sprung up in Los Angeles, while the central manufacturing zone had now started to decline as industry moved from expensive inner-city locations to cheaper land in the urban periphery. One of these newly developing districts was located to the west and southwest of Los Angeles, encompassing the communities of Santa Monica, Culver City, El Segundo, Hawthorne, and Inglewood. Firms such as Douglas, Northrop, North American Aviation, and Hughes Aircraft were to be found in this area, together with a large number of subsidiary parts suppliers and subcontractors. The other district was located to the northwest, in Burbank, Glendale, and North Hollywood (i.e., at the eastern extremity of the San Fernando Valley); it was focused above all on the great Lockheed aircraft assembly plant that had been established in Burbank in the 1920s and that had now become one of the largest aircraft manufacturers in the world.

The outbreak of the Korean conflict in 1950 marked the beginnings of the long cold war and of an ever-growing stream of Department of Defense demands for high-technology weaponry. These demands created round after round of additional industrial growth in Southern California and stimulated a constant process of high-technology industrial innovation and diversification. By the early 1950s, missiles and defense electronics were added to the manufacturing capabilities of the region. This growth induced further proliferation of high-technology industrial districts, with each new district, as it sprang into existence, appearing at a yet more distant location from the center of Los Angeles. In this manner, each district in turn came to function as the core of a new outer city in the expanding suburbs of Los Angeles.[3] Thus, in the mid-1950s, a major high-technology industrial district started to develop in Orange County immediately to the south of Los Angeles, and by the early 1960s, an analogous growth was occurring to the northwest of Los Angeles in the western reaches of the San Fernando Valley around Chatsworth and Canoga Park. These two industrial districts became the dominant high-technology centers of the entire region over the 1970s and 1980s. Further industrial district formation occurred in the 1980s, as northern San Diego County and Ventura County both began to expand rapidly, thus diverting some of the growth from the now-maturing complexes in Orange County and Chatsworth–Canoga Park. Beyond these latest cases of high-technology industrial district formation in San Diego and Ventura counties, it is possible to decipher something of the earliest stages of the same phenomenon in Santa Barbara County and perhaps, too, in parts of Riverside and San Bernardino counties.

To be sure, as the cold war came to an end in the late 1980s, the entire high-technology industrial complex of Southern California began to falter, and since 1987, employment in the basic aerospace-defense industries of the region has actually declined in absolute terms. Should there be a reignition of high-technology industrial growth in the region, however, this will surely be associated with a recurrence of the same process of episodic outward expansion and localized industrial development. One of the distinctive features of this historicogeographic process of industrial growth in Southern California is its expression in a leapfrog pattern of land development. As a consequence, the spatial arrangement of the region's high-technology industrial districts at any given moment in time conforms to a sort of distorted radial-sectoral motif. My objectives here are to describe this process in empirical terms by means of a detailed study of high-technology industrial development in the San Fernando Valley and Ventura County and to sketch out some foundations for a theoretical understanding of its main contours. In this manner, I hope to be able to make some modest contribution to our understanding of the complex relations between economic growth and the evolution of urban form, and thus of some of the important forces that have shaped the Los Angeles metropolitan region over time.

PATTERNS OF GROWTH AND DEVELOPMENT, 1950–1990

The geographic setting and layout of the San Fernando Valley and Ventura County are displayed in figures 9.1 and 9.2. This general area contains three generations of high-technology industrial districts, namely, (1) a decaying original cluster in Burbank-Glendale-North Hollywood, (2) a major center that has now probably passed its developmental apogee in Chatsworth–Canoga Park, and (3) an incipient complex in Ventura County that has grown particularly fast over much of the 1980s. Interwoven with this mass of high-technology industrial enterprise in the study area is a considerable amount of other economic activity in both the manufacturing and the service sectors.

In parallel with the preceding discussion, three main developmental episodes since World War II can be distinguished.

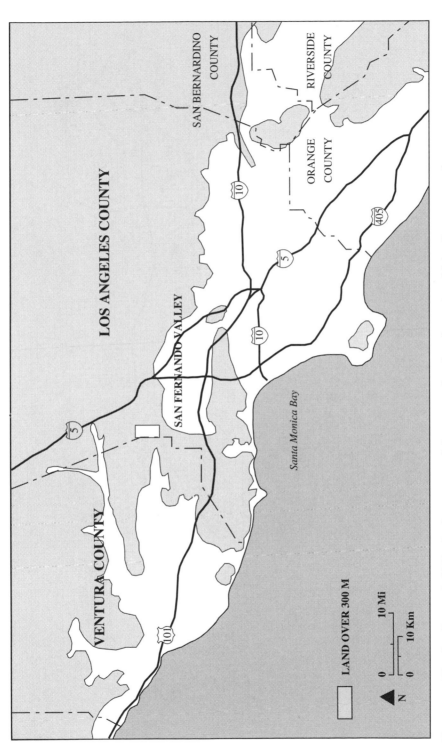

Figure 9.1. The San Fernando Valley in the context of the greater Los Angeles region. Major freeways are shown.

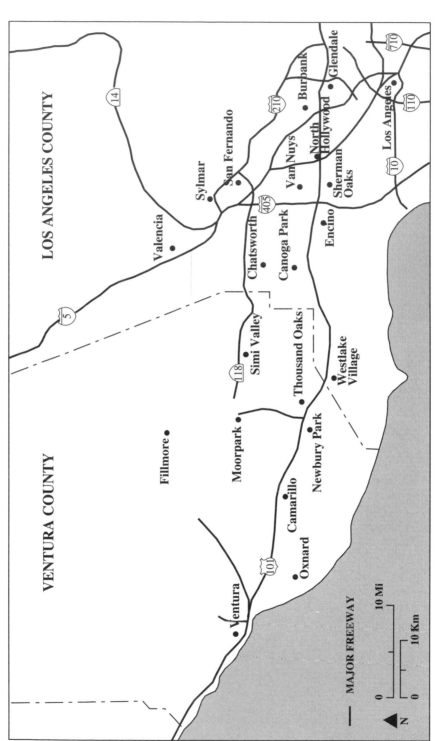

Figure 9.2. The San Fernando Valley and Ventura County.

The Immediate Postwar Years

In the late 1940s, the San Fernando Valley held a wide variety of land uses and levels of development. At its easternmost extremity lay the then-burgeoning industrial district in and around Burbank, surrounded by largely low-income neighborhoods. This gave way in the west to more well-to-do residential subdivisions in communities like Sherman Oaks and Encino. Still farther west, the pattern of land uses faded into farmland and scattered commuter settlements.[4] Figure 9.3 delineates the spatial distribution of the population of the valley in 1950; it clearly reveals the main concentration of population in the east (coinciding with the communities of Burbank and Glendale) and the highly dispersed distribution farther west. According to one count, the population of the entire valley at this time was 403,000.[5]

By the early 1950s, the Burbank-Glendale-North Hollywood industrial district was growing rapidly. There was, in particular, a major resurgence of manufacturing activity at the Lockheed aircraft assembly plant and at the many local plants providing it with various inputs. Other major aerospace-electronics producers in the same area at this time included Bendix Aviation, Collins Radio, Grand Central Aircraft, Menasco, and Weber Aircraft and, in the then-extensive margins of urban development in Van Nuys, Marquardt, Radioplane (a division of Northrop), and RCA.[6] By the end of the decade, an advance guard of large defense-oriented systems houses such as Rocketdyne, Litton Industries, and TRW had established themselves even farther to the west in Canoga Park. In addition, the entire industrial apparatus of the area was spatially and functionally interpenetrated by many small firms providing different kinds of subcontract services and input supplies, such as aircraft parts, customized electronics components, and molded metal and plastic products. Figure 9.4 shows the distribution of high-technology industrial establishments in the valley in 1955 when the original Burbank-Glendale-North Hollywood agglomeration was still the dominant focus of high-technology industry in the northwest section of Los Angeles County.[7]

One important side effect of the rapid growth of the San Fernando Valley in the early 1950s was the emergence of a form of intracommunity political conflict whose main lineaments have subsequently been played out several times over in the recent history of Los Angeles. With the pressures of development making themselves sharply felt, major confrontations erupted between those who were concerned to maintain the valley as a relatively undisturbed suburban-rural environment and those who wanted more jobs, population, and economic progress.[8] Although the former group was able to mobilize significant political energies in pursuit of

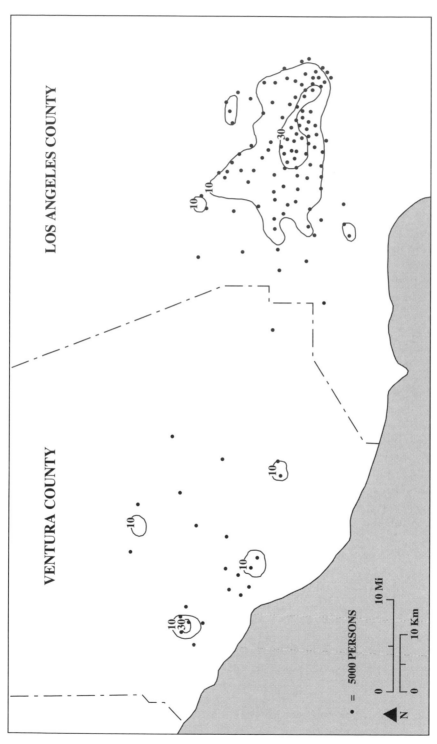

Figure 9.3. Distribution of population in the San Fernando Valley and Ventura County, 1950. Isolines represent gravity-potential measures for total population.

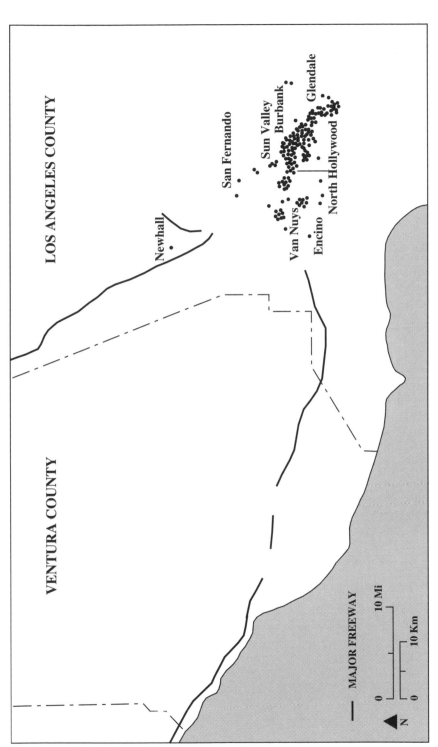

Figure 9.4. High-technology industrial establishments in the San Fernando Valley, 1955. Freeways are shown as of 1955.

its ends, it succeeded only temporarily in holding back the winds of change. In fact, the valley was by this time in the grips of a process of industrial and demographic growth that over the next few decades would sweep steadily westward, transforming in its course every locale and neighborhood that it encountered.

Growth and Consolidation, the 1960s and 1970s

By the time of the 1960 census, the population of the San Fernando Valley had increased to 841,000.[9] The 101 Freeway through the valley was now completed, which helped to open up more distant locations farther west and to make them accessible to firms and households fleeing from rising land prices, congestion, and expanding immigrant communities closer to the urban core.[10] The distribution of population in the valley and in Ventura County in 1970 portrayed in figure 9.5 reveals a striking spread and intensification of residential land use in the area compared to the situation in 1950. In addition, over the 1960s, immigrant Hispanic workers were being absorbed at a rapid rate into the valley's economy; this was especially marked in the small sweatshop industries (in such sectors as plastics molding, electronics assembly, and printed circuit board production) that were now springing up in large numbers in and around all the high-technology industrial districts of Southern California. By 1970, Hispanics had become a very significant presence indeed in the social fabric of the valley, especially at its eastern end (see fig. 9.6).

The geographic arrangement of high-technology industry in the San Fernando Valley and Ventura County in 1973 is depicted in fig. 9.7.[11] The early 1970s was a time when the Burbank-Glendale-North Hollywood agglomeration was just past its peak moment of development and when a new complex of high-technology industry was emerging strongly in Chatsworth–Canoga Park around the large systems houses that had been established in the late 1950s. With its intermixture of systems houses and many small producers and subcontractors, the Chatsworth–Canoga Park agglomeration was (and is) a parallel development to the flowering of the northern half of Orange County as a center of high-technology industry. A further parallel can be found in the role of land development companies, which in both areas created industrial parks, shopping centers, and residential subdivisions (e.g., the Warner Center in Chatsworth and the ongoing Porter Ranch project in Canoga Park), though there is little or nothing in the Chatsworth–Canoga Park area to compare with the grandiose development schemes of the Irvine Company in Orange County. Still farther west, in Ventura County, lay the outermost frontier of industrial development, with a handful of pioneering establishments in 1973, as shown in figure 9.7.

Just as in Orange County this form of outer-city development seemed to

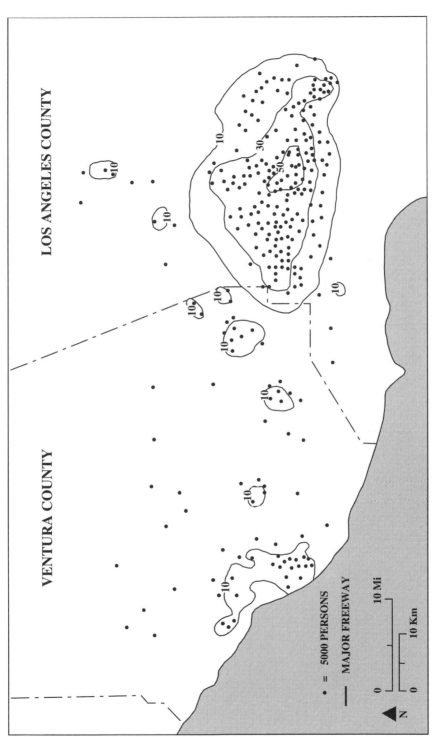

Figure 9.5. Distribution of population in the San Fernando Valley and Ventura County, 1970. Isolines represent gravity-potential measures for total population.

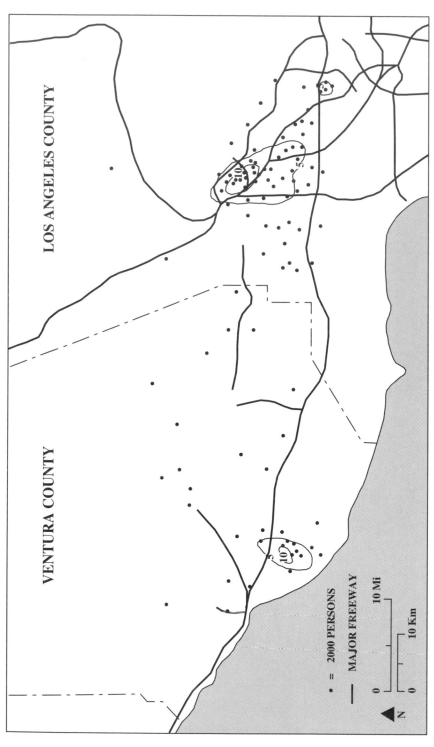

Figure 9.6. Distribution of Hispanic population in the San Fernando Valley and Ventura County, 1970. Isolines represent gravity-potential measures for total Hispanic population. Freeways are shown as of the early 1970s.

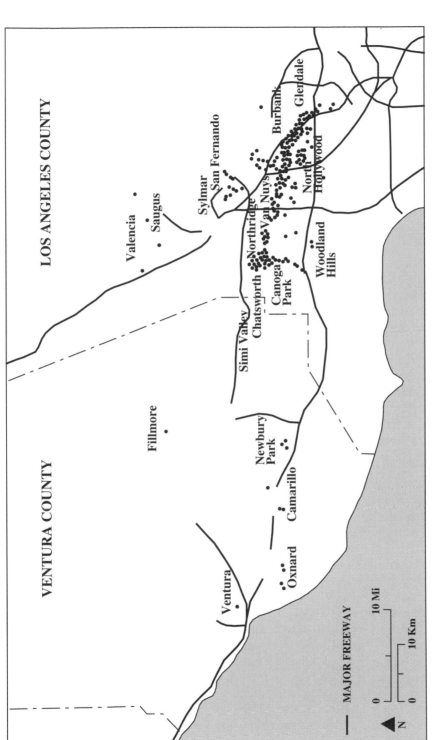

Figure 9.7. High-technology industrial establishments in the San Fernando Valley and Ventura County, 1973. Freeways are shown as of 1973.

be conducive to political conservatism, and the more well-to-do communities of the San Fernando Valley now too became important centers of resistance to liberal agendas and breeding grounds of what was shortly to become the Reagan revolution. Over the 1970s, the home owners associations of these communities functioned as political lightning rods for tax revolt and opposition to school busing. Indeed, the Sherman Oaks home owners association was one of the most vocal proponents of Proposition 13, which after its passage by the electors of the state in 1978 effectively reduced the powers of local authorities to tax property owners, thereby sparking off a fiscal crunch whose effects are still reverberating through the state.

The 1980s and Beyond

The 1980s were a period of rapid growth for high-technology industry in Southern California at large, though the downturn in Department of Defense procurements after 1987 caused a sharp reversal in this trend.[12] The decade also witnessed rapid population growth throughout the region and a continued influx of immigrants, particularly from Latin America and East and Southeast Asia.

In the San Fernando Valley and Ventura County, this growth was associated with an accentuation of the trends already described above. By 1990, the resident population had spread throughout the valley, and a great wave of population was now also moving across Ventura County (see fig. 9.8). The Hispanic population of the area also grew rapidly and continued to consolidate its hold over the eastern portions of the valley, particularly North Hollywood and San Fernando (fig. 9.9). In addition, a significant Asian presence (much of it Korean) was evident by 1990, especially in neighborhoods just to the west of the main Hispanic concentration (fig. 9.10). These trends have made the valley considerably more cosmopolitan than it once was, though it is a cosmopolitanism composed for the most part of segregated neighborhoods, not of evenhanded residential intermixture. Ventura County remains a bastion of the white middle class, with the exception of the Oxnard area whose intensive agriculture serving the Los Angeles market employs large numbers of Hispanic day laborers.

The geography of high-technology industry in the San Fernando Valley and Ventura County in 1991 is shown in figure 9.11.[13] By the early 1990s, the original Burbank-Glendale-North Hollywood high-technology industrial cluster was rapidly losing establishments and employment (as it had been over much of the 1980s), and even the major Lockheed aircraft plant in Burbank was closed and its main assembly operations shifted to Georgia. Through much of the 1980s, the decline of the Burbank-Glendale-North Hollywood cluster was counterbalanced by the enormous expansion of the Chatsworth–Canoga Park agglomeration, which now came to form the

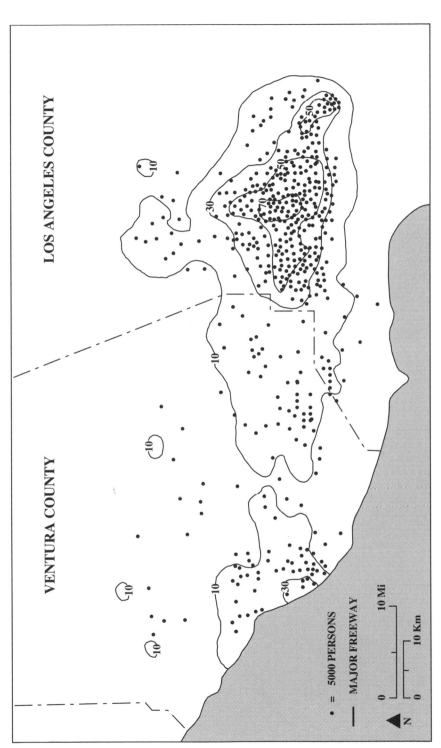

Figure 9.8. Distribution of population in the San Fernando Valley and Ventura County, 1990. Isolines represent gravity-potential measures for total population.

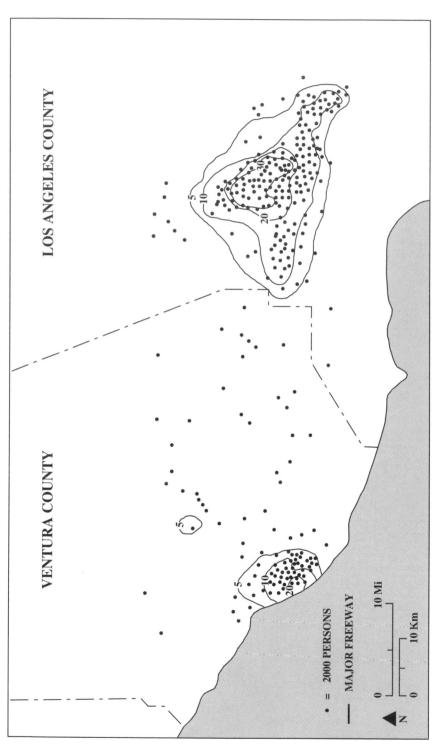

Figure 9.9. Distribution of Hispanic population in the San Fernando Valley and Ventura County, 1990. Isolines represent gravity-potential measures for total Hispanic population.

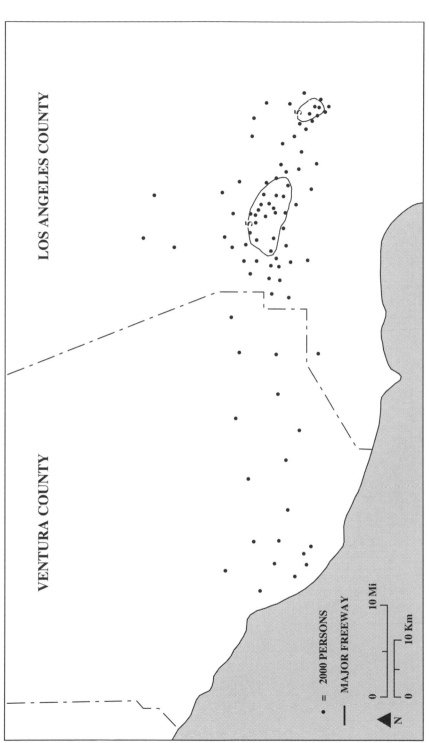

Figure 9.10. Distribution of Asian population in the San Fernando Valley and Ventura County, 1990. Isolines represent gravity-potential measures for total Asian population.

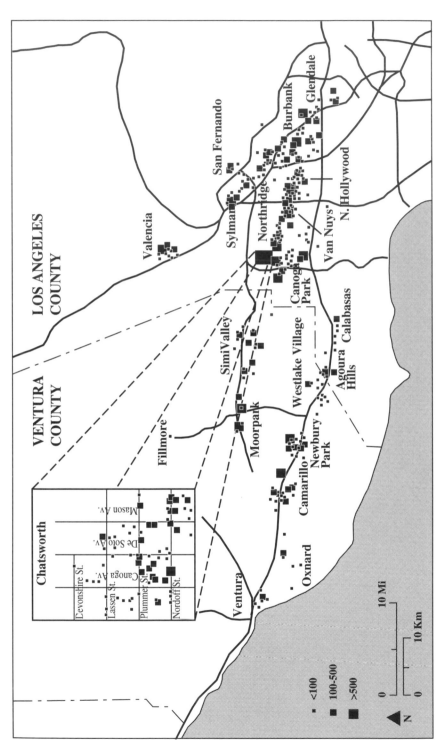

Figure 9.11. High-technology industrial establishments in the San Fernando Valley and Ventura County, 1991.

major focus of high-technology industrial development in the area. Here could be found the usual blend of large manufacturing plants (e.g., Hughes Aircraft Missile Systems Group, Micropolis, and Rocketdyne) together with a host of small and medium-sized establishments, though significant losses of industrial capacity and employment occurred as the defense downturn intensified over the early 1990s. In Ventura County, an additional high-technology industrial complex also began to emerge over the 1980s, with its main locational axes corresponding to the 101 Freeway corridor (with major developmental nodes at Westlake Village, Newbury Park, and Camarillo) and with a smaller parallel formation along the 118 Freeway through the Simi Valley.

Even in the recent climate of defense cutbacks and job loss, Ventura County's economy has demonstrated a remarkable resilience compared to many other parts of the region. Moreover, as Ventura County, in its turn, is swallowed up by the expanding industrial-urban frontier, it faces the same political stresses that communities to the east faced in earlier periods. Accelerated economic growth is bringing to the county the usual symptoms of suburban sprawl, traffic congestion, environmental degradation, and so on, and slow-growth movements have accordingly mushroomed.[14] In tune with the ethos of the 1980s and the 1990s, these movements have not been slow to add the cachet of environmentalism to their banner. The proponents of slow growth in Ventura County compare the condition of the county today to that of Orange County and the western San Fernando Valley in the late 1950s, when the latter were quiet suburban and agricultural backwaters about to be overwhelmed by large-scale development. This comparison seems apt, and if industrial growth in Southern California should revive again in the near future, Ventura County's slow-growth advocates will face a very daunting task indeed in their attempts to turn the tide of development, just as their predecessors in other parts of Southern California did at previous times of economic expansion.

INDUSTRY AND URBAN FORM: ELEMENTS OF A STATISTICAL ANALYSIS

We can visualize the expansion of the Los Angeles metropolitan fringe as proceeding on two main fronts. In the first place, population spreads more or less continuously outward in a sort of endless wave as increasingly more peripheral residential subdivisions are opened up. In the second place, industry seems to shift outward in a rather more episodic or staccato rhythm in which development is temporarily concentrated on a particular set of locations forming distinctive industrial districts. There is always observable, to be sure, some degree of peripheral industrial sprawl, but this phenomenon is of secondary importance compared to the emergence of identifiable agglomerations close to but always contained within the margins of residential settlement. This leapfrog pattern of industrial land use change is not, of course, the only possible form of industrial-urban development, nor is it characteristic of all urban places at all times. It has been a feature of the outward expansion of high-technology industry in the Los Angeles region since the Second World War, but it was conspicuously absent from many of the large manufacturing cities of the Northeast during the crisis years of the 1970s and early 1980s when much industry simply dissolved away or dispersed to the far national and global peripheries. With this proviso in mind, the pattern has nonetheless been sufficiently recurrent at various times in and around major world cities that it merits some attempt to conceptualize its mainsprings.

The analysis below proceeds in two phases. First, I provide some fragments of a statistical investigation into the underlying processes linking industrial development and urban form in the San Fernando Valley and Ventura County. Unfortunately, the absence of a reasonably rich and ample data base imposes limits on the degree of closure obtainable in this phase of analysis. Second, I develop an explicitly theoretical synthesis of these same processes, drawing on the evidence adduced for the case of the San Fernando Valley and Ventura County but generalizing far beyond the peculiarities of this specific instance.

Employment Structures and Interindustrial Linkages

Previous research suggests that industrial districts typically form in response to the external or agglomeration economies that flow from both densely developed local labor markets and the gathering together of many interlinked producers in one particular locale. We may ask, how are labor markets and linkages structured in the cases of the high-technology industrial districts of the San Fernando Valley and Ventura County, and do they vary in any systematic way from one part of the study area to another? An attempt was made (with only partial success, however) to address such questions as these by means of data collected in a mail questionnaire survey of high-technology manufacturers in the study area. To facilitate execution of the survey, only producers of electronics systems and subsystems were sent a questionnaire. The specifications and results of the survey are described in the Appendix to this chapter, along with a series of statistical analyses of the data collected. Here, I shall present only a broad sketch of the main results.

In total, thirty-five establishments sent back usable questionnaires. These establishments employ 156.0 workers each on average, a figure that appears to be rather larger than the average for manufacturing plants in the study area generally, though the discrepancy can no doubt be accounted for by reference to the internal scale economies that usually characterize electronics systems assembly operations. Of the total workers employed by surveyed establishments, 15.4 percent are qualified engineers; 25.7 percent are Hispanic and 13.4 percent Asian; in addition, 39.5 percent of all workers are female.

The same establishments have average annual sales of $22.9 million, and they subcontract work to the value of $1.6 million a year on average. Sample establishments purchase 18.6 percent of their inputs from their immediately surrounding area (defined as all points within a twenty-minute drive of the respondent's location), and they purchase 52.7 percent of their inputs from Southern California as a whole. As we might expect (since the sample consists for the most part of original equipment manufacturers who tend to market over a wide geographic area), sales are much less localized than purchases (see table 9.1). Moreover, if we recompute these spatially defined purchase and sales statistics on a weighted average basis (relative to total employment), the values are consistently lower than their simple average counterparts, a result that is consistent with the familiar finding that small production units are usually much more closely bound to the local area than large ones.

The subcontracting linkages of sampled establishments are even more closely confined to a narrowly circumscribed area than general sales and purchases. Table 9.2 shows average subcontract linkages for five different forms of work that are commonly subcontracted out by the types of electronics establishments under consideration here. These are printed circuit board fabrication, printed circuit board assembly, plastics molding, sheet metal work, and machine shop work. Note that the numbers of reporting units are low compared to the numbers given in table 9.1, for not all surveyed establishments have a need for all of the designated tasks, whether in-house or on a subcontract basis. For the five designated tasks, establishments award from 36.2 to 62.3 percent of the work that they subcontract out to firms located within a twenty-minute drive, and from 59.1 to 67.8 percent to firms in Southern California as a whole. The weighted averages are again in general smaller.

This brief profile conveys a picture of high-technology industry in the study area in which establishments are (1) on average medium-sized with an admixture of many small producers and a handful of large plants; (2) marked by a rather segmented labor force with distinctive ethnic and gender variations; and (3) endowed with well-developed linkages to other plants in the region, especially for various subcontracting activities.

Moreover, these features of electronics producers in the San Fernando Valley and Ventura County area are modulated in interesting ways in rela-

TABLE 9.1   Percentage of All Purchases and Sales (by Value) Made by Surveyed Establishments over Given Geographic Ranges

	Simple Averages		Weighted Averages		Number of Reporting Units	
	(a) Within a 20-minute drive	(b) Within Southern California	(a) Within a 20-minute drive	(b) Within Southern California	Topic (a)	Topic (b)
Purchases	18.6	52.7	11.9	43.2	32	33
Sales	7.9	25.2	1.3	7.9	32	34

TABLE 9.2   Percentage of Five Different Kinds of Work Subcontracted Out by Surveyed Establishments over Given Geographic Ranges

	Simple Averages		Weighted Averages		Number of Reporting Units	
	(a) Within a 20-minute drive	(b) Within Southern California	(a) Within a 20-minute drive	(b) Within Southern California	Topic (a)	Topic (b)
Printed circuit board production	53.1	59.1	57.3	67.7	18	17
Printed circuit board assembly	42.5	50.4	20.8	23.0	12	13
Plastics molding	36.2	66.5	8.5	54.6	13	13
Sheet metal work	62.3	60.8	47.1	52.3	17	20
Machine shop work	55.3	67.8	43.1	44.4	19	18

tionship to location. Two main points now need to be made. First, as we have already seen, the labor force of surveyed establishments contains a high proportion of Hispanics and females; that said (as equations [1] and [2] in the Appendix suggest), the proportional representation of Hispanic workers at places of employment *decreases* as we move from east to west whereas the representation of females *increases* as we move in the same direction. These findings suggest that non-Hispanic suburban women and Hispanic men may to some degree be substitutes for one another in the labor force, depending on their relative accessibility to worksites. A parallel attempt was made to assess variations in the proportion of Asians in the labor force at different locations in the study area, but without any success. Second, equation (3) in the Appendix tells us that the proclivity of surveyed establishments to subcontract out work declines as we move farther and farther into the urban field and as the age of establishments increases. This observation is consistent with the notion that with decreasing access to subcontractors, producers find it more economical to internalize many production tasks; it also implies that older and more stable establishments are more successfully able to internalize production tasks than younger establishments, especially as the latter often have comparatively volatile technological and organizational configurations so that it is often more efficient for them to subcontract out work than to make fixed capital investments.

The Special Case of Ventura County

Figure 9.12 reveals that whereas total manufacturing employment in Ventura County grew rapidly and consistently (though relative to a small base) over the 1970s and 1980s, manufacturing employment in Los Angeles County reached its maximum in 1979 and has tended to decline ever since. If we consider only high-technology industry (which accounts for approximately one-third of manufacturing employment in both counties), employment trends in the two counties are more closely correlated (see fig. 9.13).[15] Again, however, Ventura County has expanded with much greater rapidity in recent years than has Los Angeles County. Thus, from 1979 to 1987, high-technology industrial employment grew at an overall rate of 82.4 percent in Ventura County, but in Los Angeles County, the rate was only 10.1 percent over the same period. Since 1987, both counties have lost high-technology employment, with Ventura County losing 18.5 percent between 1988 and 1992 and Los Angeles County losing 28.0 percent over the same period.

These differing patterns of industrial development in the two counties are, in part, a reflection of their contrasting mixes of manufacturing activities, with Ventura County having a much larger share of new, dynamic, and competitive firms than Los Angeles County; and, in part, they are a consequence of the differing industrial milieus. In particular, whereas Los Angeles County has a large number of aging systems houses (especially in aircraft assembly) that have been very negatively affected by recent Department of Defense cutbacks, high-technology industry in Ventura County has a more flexible structure with relatively many more small establishments (see fig. 9.14). With the eventual revival of economic growth in Southern California, these small, flexible producers (many of them increasingly dependent on civilian markets) are doubtless more likely to spring back to

Figure 9.12. Total manufacturing employment in Los Angeles and Ventura counties, 1972–1990.

vigorous life than the old and large aerospace-defense establishments of Los Angeles.

Give or take a number of idiosyncrasies, Ventura County's state of development today resembles that of other incipient agglomerations in Southern California at earlier periods. It bears a particularly close resemblance to Orange County as it was in the late 1950s and early 1960s. Thus Ventura County's population in 1990 was 666,800, while Orange County's population in 1960 was 703,925. In 1992, Ventura County had a total manufacturing labor force of 31,600; for Orange County in 1959, the equivalent figure was 38,673. In addition, the average size of all manufacturing establishments in Ventura County in 1992 was 35.0 employees, and in Orange County in 1959 it was 47.4. In the latter county, however, there was shortly to be a massive expansion in the number of large high-technology systems houses, a turn of events that seems unlikely to recur in Ventura County given current changes in the international defense environment.

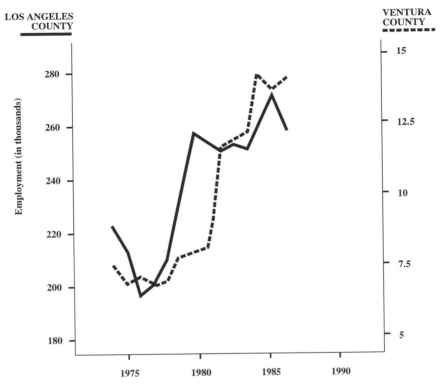

Figure 9.13. Employment of high-technology industry in Los Angeles and Ventura counties, 1974–1987. Note that changes in SIC definitions in 1987 make later data noncomparable with the data presented here.

THE LOGIC OF INDUSTRIALIZATION AND URBANIZATION RECONSIDERED

A Theoretical Synthesis

Certain elements of a possible theoretical synthesis of the interrelations between economic growth and urban form seem now to be in place. Even so, the conceptual argument laid out below is highly schematic and speculative, and much research needs to be devoted to the development of further refinements and to the tasks of systematic empirical verification. The framework draws on observations and ideas that have been broached at earlier stages in this chapter, as well as on various preexisting accounts of the geography of factor costs within metropolitan areas.[16]

Let us start with the supposition that we are observing a large metropolitan area (analogous, say, to Los Angeles in the early 1950s) with a vigorous

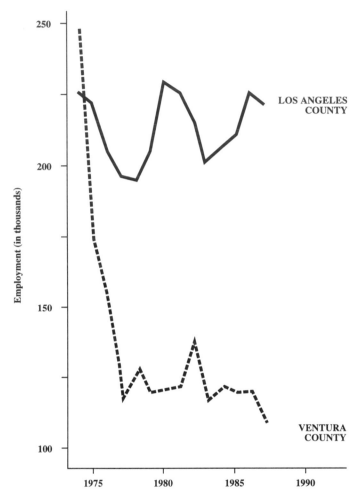

Figure 9.14. Average size of high-technology industrial establishments in Los Angeles and Ventura counties, 1974–1987. Note that changes in SIC definitions in 1987 make later data noncomparable with the data presented here.

industrial district or agglomeration located toward the origin of any geometric sector radiating out from the core of the metropolis. This agglomeration will thrive under the usual conditions where localized external economies are being created via the endogenous dynamics of local labor market development, industrial differentiation, transactional interchange, and so on. Individual producers will make a decision to locate inside or outside the agglomeration depending on the variation of different costs and benefits within and around it.

- First, land rents will tend to be relatively high toward the center of the agglomeration, and they will decline with distance out toward the urban periphery (though there may be upward kinks in the surface at discrete subcenters).
- Second, wage rates as paid at the job site will also tend to decline from the agglomeration outward in response to relatively high demands for labor at the center.[17]
- Third, because of the concentration of producers in the agglomeration, local transaction costs of all kinds will tend to be relatively low at that location and to increase with distance outward.
- Fourth, a stream of localized external economies will flow from the labor market activity and transactional interchange in and around the agglomeration. A wide assortment of additional external economies will be available too, for example, as a consequence of public investment in infrastructural services.

We can now incorporate these different costs and benefits in two separate functions of distance, namely, (a) a function designated $\alpha(d)$ which identifies a set of costs that *decrease* with distance, d, from the center (i.e., land costs and labor costs), and (b) a function designated $\beta(d)$ which identifies all costs that *increase* with distance (transactions costs in particular). Illustrative cases of these two functions are depicted in figure 9.15. Note that the shaded area in the first graph is meant (very schematically) to represent the effects of agglomeration economies as such; up to the distance δ from the center, these economies more than cancel out any costs in the function $\beta(d)$, but at and beyond d, rising transaction costs eliminate any positive benefits to producers. By summing the two functions, we obtain $\alpha(d) + \beta(d)$ as shown in figure 9.15. This composite function clearly reveals that under these cost and benefit conditions, the best (i.e., minimum cost) location for producers is at the center.

With the passage of time and with continued industrial growth within the central agglomeration, a number of changes are likely to come about. Land prices will rise ever upward at the center under the pressures of development, as will wages due to the increased demand for workers. While agglomeration economies may for a time continue to increase, they are also at a certain stage likely to decline as a consequence of negative overspill effects such as congestion, overbuilding, pollution, rising noise levels, and labor shortages. All of this will slow the growth of the central agglomeration and induce some producers to adopt locations outside of the center. To begin with, a significant proportion of these producers may be expected to have relatively high levels of vertical integration and thus to be comparatively insensitive to spatial variations in transactions costs (see equation [3] in the Appendix). As decentralization proceeds, however, transactions costs

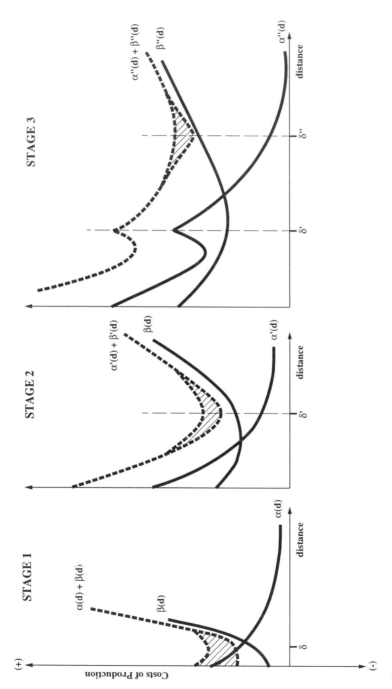

Figure 9.15. Locational costs for interrelated industries as a function of distance from the city center. The shaded area represents agglomeration economies.

at noncentral sites will tend to fall because of the co-location of increasing numbers of producers, and this will intensify the outward flow of establishments by making it feasible for more disintegrated producers to relocate.

Eventually, a situation may be reached as represented by stage 2 of figure 9.15, where aggregate costs are minimized at the distance δ' from the center. All else being equal, the location of the minimum point on the aggregate cost curve is likely to migrate continuously and monotonically away from the central industrial cluster. However, the emergence of agglomeration economies will tend to stabilize the location of the minimum point over a definite period of time. Thus, as the locational variate, δ', attains some sufficiently large distance from the original agglomeration, and as decentralization moves forward, δ' will also begin to emerge as a subsidiary center of gravity of industrial activity. This new center will be a locus of incipient agglomeration economies. The advantageous cost conditions together with the presence of agglomeration economies at δ' will induce more producers to locate in the immediately surrounding area, and in a typical process of cumulative and circular causation a secondary agglomeration will now materialize (as represented, for example, by the development of the Chatsworth–Canoga Park high-technology industrial agglomeration in the 1960s). Growth of the agglomeration will be enhanced by localized investments in infrastructural artifacts, including the upgrading of transportation routes and provision of commuter services focused on the new center. At the same time, many workers employed at the center will shift into surrounding neighborhoods and an intensification of residential land use is likely to take place. Significant socioeconomic changes may also occur as low-wage and unskilled workers move into the local employment shed. This spatial refocusing of local labor markets is well illustrated by figure 9.16, which shows the location of Rocketdyne in Canoga Park and the spatial distribution of the residences of its workers. The pattern of residences fully envelops the place of employment, which, however, at the time of its creation, was on the very edge of the metropolitan built-up area and thus presumably had to draw most of its labor from neighborhoods located to the east. In these different ways, the new agglomeration will condense out in geographic space, thus creating—for a time—a collectively immobile complex of interrelated production and labor market activities.

However, precisely the same sequence of events described above may now be repeated yet farther out in the urban field, with $\alpha(d)$ rising upward at δ' and $\beta(d)$ beginning to decline with distance from the same point. The net result is likely eventually to be a situation as described schematically in stage 3 of figure 9.15. Note that in stage 3, the distance-dependent cost functions $\alpha''(d) + \beta''(d)$ are such that total costs at δ' are now relatively high, and δ'' is the minimum-cost production site. Accordingly, δ'' is potentially

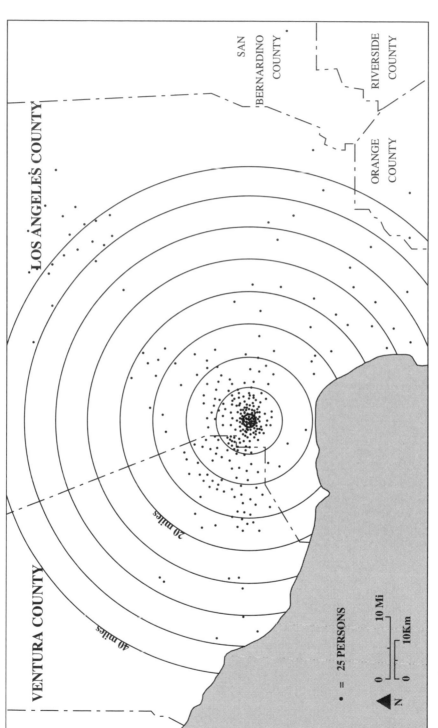

Figure 9.16. Residential locations of workers employed at Rocketdyne, Canoga Park, 1988.

a site at which intense agglomeration economies may begin to make their historical and geographic appearance. Should a new agglomeration in fact take root at this point, the dynamic of cumulative and circular causation will once more begin to push it to a high level of development.

So long as industrial production and employment in the whole urban system continue to grow, and so long as this growth creates and re-creates industrial complexes with a propensity to industrial district formation, the space-time structuring of industrialization and urbanization will tend to proceed as described above. This process involves the reconstitution of new industrial agglomerations farther and farther out in the urban field, while older agglomerations closer to the urban core will decompose as a result of the shifting structure of factor costs. The key mechanism is one of *spatial lock-in*, where, for a time, agglomeration economies freeze the location of the dominant pivot of growth. This scenario of growth and decomposition surely captures something of the historical and geographic experience of the San Fernando Valley and Ventura County over the last several decades. However, we must also interject a warning about the error of turning this descriptive scenario into a sort of teleology. In fact, any significant change in the basic underlying dimensions of the process (whether it be in forms of industrial technology, labor demands, markets, or whatever) could potentially undermine the economic logic sketched above and set the industrial-urban system on an altogether different evolutionary course.

A Forward Glance

In spite of this last caveat, the process of outer-city industrial development described above seems to have been commonly in operation in many major American metropolitan areas in recent decades. It has assuredly been at work throughout Southern California over the entire period since the Second World War: each successive round of economic growth and suburban expansion has been associated with a series of newly developing high-technology industrial subcenters and, nowadays, service subcenters too. Each time in the past that one of these subcenters has risen to importance, a fairly predictable train of events has been set in motion: rising land prices, a property boom, intensifying congestion and increasing commuting times, changes in local socioeconomic character and ethnic composition, environmental deterioration, and so on. Orange County is perhaps the most dramatic recent example in Southern California of this syndrome, but it is fully evident in the Chatsworth–Canoga Park area, and it is also starting to become apparent in Ventura County. These events typically create tensions and conflicts between those who advocate growth and development and those in favor of slow growth, environmental preservation, and community stability.

Southern California's high-technology industrial development has been driven over most of the postwar period by enormous Pentagon demands for aircraft, missiles, and defense electronics. These demands have been declining at a rapid pace in recent years, and further declines are foreseeable over the remainder of the 1990s. Thus much of the region's high-technology industrial base is now under threat, and the threat is sharpened by a rising tide of foreign competition in exactly those products in which Southern California has hitherto enjoyed a virtually unchallenged supremacy. In the worst-case scenario, it is conceivable that the region's past history of growth and outward expansion may be displaced by a contrary trend to shrinkage and implosion. However, there are numerous indications that the region may still find a way through the current crisis; in particular, a number of new high-technology industries serving civilian markets (such as biotechnology, medical instruments, environmental control devices, artificial intelligence, and communication systems) are beginning to establish themselves at diverse locations throughout Southern California. It is possible, too, that the region may acquire a thriving electric car industry and other advanced transportation technology industries in the foreseeable future.[18]

Several of these emerging sectors already show signs of re-creating earlier patterns and paradigms of industrial-urban development in the region, though their scale of operation tends to be smaller than was the case with many of the older defense-oriented industries. They are certainly much given to network forms of interaction, and accordingly, their future success will most likely depend in part on their continued ability to form specialized industrial agglomerations and to reap the advantages of spatially dependent external economies. These external economies constitute an asset that is held jointly by all participants in the local economy. They accrue, of course, from individual efforts, talents, and skills; but they also exist as synergies that grow out of the forms of collective order that always characterize local industrial systems: stocks of formal and informal technological knowledge, the acquired human capital of the labor force, networks of social interaction and information exchange securing the bases of new entrepreneurial opportunities, and so on. They are thus legitimately, if not inescapably, an object of public policy; and if Southern California is to survive industrially in the new global economic order now coming into existence, it must assuredly set to work on the task of building institutional infrastructures that can deal effectively with this increasingly urgent public policy imperative.

CONCLUSION

The historical-geographic patterns of high-technology industrialization and urbanization in the San Fernando Valley and Ventura County are of interest and significance in their own right, but they also represent an exemplary case that reproduces much of the recent experience of other parts of Southern California and, indeed, of many other Sunbelt cities. I have tried to set up an analytical framework for the comprehension of the peculiar leap-frog dynamic that has characterized the spatiotemporal development of high-technology industrial districts in Southern California. As I have argued above, this dynamic can be in large degree deciphered as an outcome of the complex interplay between land prices, wages, transactions costs, and agglomeration economies in a growing metropolitan system.

I have also intimated that Southern California as a whole is now at a turning point in its developmental pathway. Unlike the older manufacturing cities of the Northeast, Southern California has never in the past had to confront a really traumatic crisis of industrial restructuring. It is clear that the local economy is now, however, going through major disruptions, and it is certainly the case that the old military-industrial complex that formed the base of so much of the region's prosperity in the postwar decades is now breaking down. In spite of this state of affairs, it seems unlikely that the region will turn into another Rust Belt, at least for the foreseeable future. As the case of Ventura County so strongly suggests, a more resilient and more entrepreneurial high-technology industrial apparatus seems currently to be making its appearance in Southern California, and this may eventually help to pull at least selected parts of the region out of the present crisis.

That said, the way forward remains fraught with dangers. If Southern California is to withstand the many assaults that now so strongly menace its high-technology (and other) industries, it needs to put into place effective policy initiatives that can help these industries climb once more to mastery of world markets. The idea here is not to establish a regional command economy but to create a framework for building a series of new coalitions and partnerships involving business, labor, community groups, and local government in the interests of securing and enhancing Southern California's competitive industrial advantage on wider national and international markets.

APPENDIX

Early in 1992, a mail questionnaire survey was sent out to 343 electronics manufacturing establishments in the San Fernando Valley and Ventura County. The addresses of these establishments were taken from a variety of industrial directories. To achieve some degree of homogeneity in the survey, an effort was made to direct questionnaires only to establishments engaged in producing complex electronics assemblies, that is, those classified as belonging only to SIC 357 (computer and office equipment), SIC 366 (communications equipment), and SIC 381 (search and navigation equipment).

Out of the 343 questionnaires dispatched, 73 (i.e., 21.3%) were returned. However, 38 of the returns were found to be void for various reasons, including the fact that the respondent was not a bona fide electronics manufacturer. Thus, in total, 35 valid questionnaires (filled out in varying degrees of completeness) were received from producers in the core target group. Of these, 27 are located in the San Fernando Valley proper, and 8 in Ventura County. The questionnaire survey is unsatisfactory in many respects, and no claims are advanced as to its representativeness or reliability. The data analysis that follows is thus presented only as one of several investigative way stations, each of which is quite limited in its meaning and value, but all of which collectively appear to point in some fairly consistent directions.

First, we look at a couple of equations describing certain variations in employment structures among sampled establishments as a function of location (i.e., distance from the core of Los Angeles). The equations are

(1) $H_i = 1/[1 + 0.0022\exp(2.1354\log D_i)]$,
$$(0.6636)$$
$R^2 = 0.25, \quad \text{d.f.} = 31;$

and

(2) $F_i = (1/[1\ 79.9738\exp(-0.8582\log D_i - 0.0409H_i)]$,
$$(0.4196) \qquad (0.0080)$$
$R^2 = 0.48, \quad \text{d.f.} = 29.$

Here the terms H_i and F_i signify, respectively, the proportion of the ith establishment's labor force that is Hispanic and the proportion that is female; and D_i is the distance of the establishment from downtown Los Angeles. These two equations are presented as logistic regressions in order to preserve the status of the dependent variables as genuine proportions. The first equation suggests that Hispanic (male and female) representation in any establishment's labor force declines as we move westward, which is no doubt simply a reflection of the concentration of Hispanic neighborhoods in the eastern part of the study area. The second equation tells us that the proportion of females in the labor force is positively related both to distance and to the proportion of Hispanics. Taken together, the two equations imply that (as far as the Hispanic and female segments of the labor force are concerned) workplaces located toward the central part of the study area are characterized by a mix of Hispanic male and female workers, whereas more peripheral workplaces are characterized by non-Hispanic female workers. The implication here is that there seems to be substitution occurring (depending on location) not just between non-Hispanic females and Hispanic females but also between non-Hispanic females and Hispanic males.

Second, we examine the subcontracting behavior of surveyed establishments via the equation

$$(3) \quad \ln S_i = 4.4621 - 2.6180 \ln D_i - 0.0960 A_i,$$
$$\qquad\qquad\qquad (0.7971) \qquad (0.0382)$$
$$\qquad R^2 = 0.36, \quad \text{d.f.} = 22.$$

In this equation, S_i is the total dollar volume of work subcontracted out as a ratio of total sales at the ith establishment, and A_i is the age of the establishment in years. Evidently, subcontracting activity (in proportional terms) tends to decline toward the spatial margins of the study area, just as it declines with the age of the establishment. These findings are consistent with the notions (a) that establishments tend to reduce subcontracting activity as their accessibility to subcontracting services declines, and (b) that young establishments (with changing internal technologies and organizational structures) tend to be more prone to subcontract out work than older, more stable establishments.

Each of these three equations is very significant in a statistical sense, even though values of R^2 are small. The latter circumstance can be accounted for in part by the fact that here the observations are individual behavioral units (i.e., manufacturing establishments), whereas in cases where the observations are aggregates of data (e.g., census tracts, cities, or states) the impact of large individual error terms and extreme values is mitigated by the very process of data aggregation.

NOTES

1. See Allen J. Scott, *Metropolis: From the Division of Labor to Urban Form* (Berkeley, Los Angeles, and London: University of California Press, 1988); and Michael Storper and Allen J. Scott, "Work Organisation and Local Labour Markets in an Era of Flexible Production," *International Labour Review* 129 (1990): 573–591.

2. Allen J. Scott, *Technopolis: High-Technology Industry and Regional Development in Southern California* (Berkeley, Los Angeles, and Oxford: University of California Press, 1993).

3. Mike Davis, *City of Quartz: Excavating the Future in Los Angeles* (London: Verso, 1990); Joel Garreau, *Edge City: Life on the New Frontier* (New York: Doubleday, 1991); Rob Kling, Spencer Olin, and Mark Poster, "The Emergence of Postsuburbia: An Introduction," in *Postsuburban California: The Transformation of Orange County since World War II*, ed. R. Kling, S. Olin, and M. Poster, 1–30 (Berkeley, Los Angeles, and Oxford: University of California Press, 1991); Edward W. Soja, *Postmodern Geographies: The Reassertion of Space in Critical Social Theory* (London: Verso, 1989).

4. Lawrence C. Jorgensen, "Subdivisions and Subdividers," in *The San Fer-*

nando Valley: Past and Present, ed. L. C. Jorgensen, 136–153 (Los Angeles: Pacific Rim Research, 1982).

5. Security First National Bank, *The Growth and Economic Stature of the San Fernando Valley* (Los Angeles: Security First National Bank, Research Department, 1960).

6. Alex E. Izzard, "The Factors Influencing the Agglomeration of the Electronics Industry in the San Fernando Valley" (M.A. thesis, University of California, Los Angeles, 1961).

7. High-technology industry in 1955 is identified—in terms of the Standard Industrial Classification (SIC) then in force—as SIC 19 (ordinance and accessories), SIC 366 (communications equipment), SIC 372 (aircraft and parts), and SIC 382 (measuring and controlling devices).

8. Fred E. Case and James Gillies, "Some Aspects of Land Planning: The San Fernando Valley Case," *Appraisal Journal* 23 (1955): 15–31.

9. Security First National Bank, *Growth and Economic Stature.*

10. Davis, *City of Quartz.*

11. High-technology industry in 1973 is defined as SIC 357 (office and computing machines), SIC 366 (communications equipment), SIC 367 (electronic components and accessories), SIC 372 (aircraft and parts), SIC 376 (guided missiles, space vehicles, and parts), and SIC 382 (measuring and controlling devices).

12. Economic Roundtable, *Los Angeles County Economic Adjustment Strategy for Defense Reductions,* a report to the Community Development Commission of Los Angeles County (Los Angeles: Economic Roundtable, 1992).

13. High-technology industry in 1991 is defined as SIC 357 (computer and office equipment), SIC 366 (communications equipment), SIC 367 (electronic components and accessories), SIC 372 (aircraft and parts), SIC 376 (guided missiles, space vehicles, and parts), SIC 381 (search and navigation equipment), and SIC 382 (measuring and controlling devices).

14. Ventura County Economic Development Association, *Directory of Business and Industry Economic Report* (Ventura: VCEDA, 1991).

15. Note that figure 9.13 is a based on a different data source from figure 9.12. This is because the Employment Development Department of the State of California (the source of the data used in fig. 9.12) does not publish complete historical statistics on high-technology employment in Ventura County.

16. See, for example, Peter J. Bull, "Intra-Urban Industrial Geography," in *Progress in Industrial Geography,* ed. Michael Pacione, 82–110 (London: Croom Helm, 1985); Glen B. Norcliffe, "Nonmetropolitan Industrialization and the Theory of Production," *Urban Geography* 5 (1984): 25–42; Scott, *Metropolis.*

17. Allen J. Scott, "The Spatial Structure of Metropolitan Labor Markets and the Theory of Intra-Urban Plant Location," *Urban Geography* 2 (1981): 1–30.

18. Rebecca Morales, Michael Storper, Miriam Cisternas, Carlos Quandt, Allen Scott, John Slifko, Ward Thomas, Martin Wachs, and Samira Zakhor, *Prospects for Alternative Fuel Use and Production in Southern California: Environmental Quality and Economic Development,* Working Paper no. 2, University of California, Los Angeles, Lewis Center for Regional Policy Studies, 1991.

TEN

Income and Racial Inequality in Los Angeles

Paul Ong and Evelyn Blumenberg

The arrest of a young African-American man on the streets of Los Angeles ignited the frustrations, hostilities, and tensions of the city's residents. Days of urban unrest took the lives of many; numerous others sustained serious injuries; and the daily routines of millions of Southern Californians were temporarily disrupted. The outburst of protest scarred the face of the city, leaving behind charred facades, stores emptied of their contents, and a precarious quiet. In the aftermath, the mayor formed a commission to "rebuild Los Angeles" and appointed a leader believed able to elicit private investment to the war-torn city.

What exactly is being described here? Short-term memory will bring to mind Los Angeles in 1992 and the reaction to the acquittal of four Los Angeles police officers in the brutal beating of Rodney King. But the scenario described above could easily be Watts in 1965. The details may differ, but the events are analogous—an arrest, an outraged reaction in the form of burning and looting, and, when the violence settled, efforts to attract primarily private resources to replace what had been destroyed. In both instances, the arrest precipitated a violent response, but the fundamental cause of unrest had been building for years—a desperation born out of racism, growing economic inequality, unfulfilled political promises, and a repressive judicial system.

This essay focuses on economic inequality and poverty, which have been persistent and growing realities of life in Los Angeles. The City of Angels, the city of sunshine, palm trees, suburban living, and movies with happy endings, has an underside—declining wages and rising poverty. We are not suggesting that Los Angeles today is as it was in 1965; this would not be an accurate portrayal. Over the last two decades, Los Angeles *has* changed. In the aftermath of the 1965 riots, a coalition of African-American and Jewish voters replaced the white, conservative Mayor Sam Yorty with Tom Bradley, Los Angeles's first African-American mayor. Accompanying the change in political guard was continued economic expansion. With help from the new mayor, commercial developers reshaped downtown, attracting corporate headquarters and creating over one hundred thousand new jobs in the downtown area alone.[1] Not only did Los Angeles's skyline change, but so too did the composition of its residents. Primarily a non-Hispanic white city in 1970, the Los Angeles of the 1990s is a multiethnic, multicultural metropolis, where non-Hispanic whites no longer comprise a majority of the city's residents. Projections by the County of Los Angeles show that by 1995 Latinos will become the single largest ethnic group represented in the metropolitan area.[2]

Despite, or perhaps because of, these significant changes in the Los Angeles social landscape, economic inequality remains a deeply embedded facet of Los Angeles life. The disparity in income between rich and poor continues to widen with the increase in the percentage of low-wage workers and the steady rise in the poverty rate.[3] Not surprisingly, economic inequities often coincide with racial and ethnic divisions, leaving African-Americans, Latinos, and Asians disproportionately represented at the bottom of the economic ladder. Therefore, while many residents bask in the well-celebrated Los Angeles charms, others, the poor of Los Angeles, survive in impoverished inner-city neighborhoods, the very same neighborhoods that exploded into violence on 29 April 1992.

To understand the economic roots of social unrest in Los Angeles, we examine the conditions prior to the 1992 riots. The analysis relies on data from both published and unpublished sources, including information from the decennial censuses and the Current Population Surveys. Although these sources are subject to inherent biases resulting from the undercounting of minorities and the poor, the data nonetheless provide useful insights into the nature and scope of inequality in Los Angeles. We are as interested in changes over time in economic inequality as we are in a cross-sectional portrait of inequality. Furthermore, to minimize the influence of business cycles, we present statistics for peak business years when possible (i.e., 1969, 1979, and 1989). We include some comments on the potential effects of the current recession in the concluding section.

DECLINING FORTUNES: ECONOMIC RESTRUCTURING AND GROWING INEQUALITY IN THE UNITED STATES

The economic problems facing Los Angeles are not unique; they are part and parcel of the crisis facing this nation as a whole. Income inequality and poverty are unfortunate realities, deeply embedded in our social and economic structures and a product of both historical and contemporary forces.

Income and wealth have never been equally distributed in the United States.[4] In popular parlance, the United States has always been divided into haves and have-nots. While the notion of "class" distinctions in the U.S. remains vague, the growing gulf between rich and poor has been widely acknowledged.

It may be an unrealistic expectation to believe that we can completely eliminate inequality and poverty in our lifetime; however, in previous decades, this nation demonstrated an ability to improve the conditions of those at the bottom of the economic hierarchy both absolutely and relatively. For nearly a quarter of a century after World War II, the United States gradually moved toward greater income equality as robust growth and an expanding economic pie enabled the bottom to advance without threatening those at the top. This progress toward equality continued well into the 1960s. Between 1959 and 1969, the population living below the official poverty line fell from 22.4 to 12.1 percent of the total population, and from 39.5 million persons to 24.1 million persons. The poverty figures reached a low in 1973 when only 11.1 percent, representing 23 million persons, lived in poverty.

Progress toward income equality stalled during the 1970s as the United States suffered some of the consequences of an emerging global economy. Since the early 1970s, the United States has undergone a protracted period of economic turmoil, characterized by stagnation and uncertainty in the 1970s and massive restructuring of work and production in the 1980s. Enormous price shocks in the form of unstable and higher prices for energy and raw materials rocked the U.S. economy. At the same time, increased foreign competition threatened the survival of numerous domestic industries. In turn, these global forces contributed to inflation, economic dislocation, and a slowdown of growth in productivity. For workers, these new economic conditions meant heightened suffering in the form of lower wages, lost jobs, and growing poverty.

The economic crisis of the last two decades was remarkable when compared to the rising standard of living during the prior two decades. For example, real hourly compensation from 1948 to 1969 increased by 98.9 percent in the private sector, extending the purchasing power of workers.[5] In contrast, real hourly compensation from 1969 to 1989 increased by a relatively meager 14.5 percent. At the same time, unemployment levels increased secularly.[6] Between 1969 and 1979 (both peak business years), the unemployment rate grew from 3.5 to 5.8 percent. Following this period, the United States experienced the highest levels of unemployment since World War II, the back-to-back recessions of 1981 and 1982. Economic recovery in the late 1980s brought down the unemployment rate to 5.3 percent, yet this level of unemployment was still considerably higher than that in previous peak business years, including 1969.

The economic misfortunes of the 1970s and 1980s reversed the distributional progress made in previous decades, polarizing the wages of workers. In an extensive analysis of data for the years from 1963 to 1986, Bennett Harrison and Barry Bluestone find that the distribution of wages grew more equal during the first part of this period but became increasingly unequal in the period after 1975. By 1986, the level of inequality was no better than it had been in 1969. More recent analysis indicates a slight improvement in the late 1980s, but nonetheless wages were considerably more evenly distributed in the late 1960s than in the late 1980s.[7]

A major factor contributing to the growth of wage inequality was an increase in the relative and absolute number of low-earning workers as measured by statistics for full-time/full-year (FT/FY) workers. From 1969 to 1989, the number of low-earning FT/FY workers grew from 39.3 million to 53.3 million, from 14.4 to 16.3 percent of the FT/FY labor force.[8] The absolute and relative growth of low-earning FT/FY workers was particularly evident in all three major racial groups (non-Hispanic white, African-American, and Hispanic origin), and as the economy plunged into a recession beginning in 1990, the number of low-earning workers has increased concomitantly.

Another indication of the growth of inequality can be seen in the distribution of family income.[9] In 1969, 10.9 percent of all families had annual incomes at least twice as high as the median. Two decades later, 14.7 percent fell into this category. At the same time, the numbers of families with annual incomes less than half the median grew from 17.9 to 22.1 percent. Clearly, not all families suffered equally over the last two decades; as the rich became richer, the poor became poorer. Growing income inequality translated into increasing poverty rates. In 1973, the poverty rate stood at 11.1 percent, but by 1989, it jumped to 12.8 percent.[10] In absolute numbers, the ranks of the poor grew from 23 million to 31.5 million, with more and more people falling below the poverty line as the current recession continued unabated.

A VIEW FROM LOS ANGELES:
ECONOMIC GROWTH AND RESTRUCTURING

Unquestionably, the fortunes of Los Angeles depend, in part, on the economic prospects of the nation; however, with its distinctive mix of industries, natural resources, and other endowments, Los Angeles has been uniquely affected by global and national economic restructuring. The attributes of regions affect their vulnerability to international competition and their ability to take advantage of new sets of economic conditions. For example, while northeastern manufacturing states were devastated by higher energy costs and increased foreign trade, creating what is now called the Rust Belt, other energy-rich states profited from higher oil prices, contributing to the rise of the "Sun Belt." Of course, as history reveals, neither regional depression nor regional expansion is a permanent phenomenon. Some Rust Belt manufacturing states have responded to economic threats by creating new economic bases while, with the collapse of the OPEC cartel, the fortunes of oil and gas states have fallen.

During the 1970s and 1980s, changes in Los Angeles were rapid and extensive as well.[11] Like many other industrial centers, a good segment of manufacturing in Los Angeles came under increased competitive pressures. By the late 1960s, Los Angeles had emerged as a major industrial center, with 30 percent of its workforce employed in manufacturing, a considerably higher percentage than for the country as a whole. Major segments of Los Angeles's industrial sector, particularly the defense-related aerospace industry, have been sheltered from direct foreign competition.[12] However, Los Angeles was also the center of West Coast smokestack manufacturing, which was as vulnerable to market forces here as in other regions of the country. Even the quintessential movie industry, long concentrated in the Los Angeles region, came under attack from overseas competitors and from other U.S. regions.[13]

Yet, unlike many other areas of the country, Los Angeles was well situated to take advantage of the new international economic order, to capitalize on trade with the Pacific Rim. Los Angeles became a principal gateway to the United States, emerging as the second-largest customs district and the busiest port in the nation, with most goods coming from and going to Japan and the newly industrializing Asian countries.[14] Moreover, in the midst of these transformations, Los Angeles became the second-largest banking center in the country, surpassing its old rival, San Francisco.[15] Los Angeles also benefited from the influx of capital and labor from abroad. Using the funds accumulated from its trade surplus, the Japanese invested heavily in local real estate.[16] To a lesser extent, Los Angeles received capital from Korea and Hong Kong.[17] Equally important was the massive influx of immigrant labor from both Asia and Latin America. In 1990, there were more than 858,000 persons in Los Angeles who had entered the United States during the late 1980s and another 668,000 who entered in the early 1980s.[18] The impact of immigration can be seen in the dramatic change in the ethnic and racial composition of the region's population. Los Angeles's population has shifted from being predominantly Anglo (non-Hispanic white) to a new majority composed of African-Americans, Latinos, Chicanos, and Asians, a transformation that is discussed below.

Both the emergence of Los Angeles as America's major urban center on the Pacific Rim and the influx of capital and labor to the area have

TABLE 10.1   Employment Trends in Three Major Metropolitan Areas

	1959	1969	1979	1989
Manufacturing (in 000s)				
New York	1,040	921	611	437
Chicago	874	983	852	560
Los Angeles	744	881	925	892
Nonmanufacturing (in 000s)				
New York	2,744	3,246	3,106	3,704
Chicago	1,581	2,044	2,362	2,604
Los Angeles	1,406	2,019	2,660	3,331
Unemployment Rate				
New York	n.a.	3.4	8.1	5.4
Chicago	n.a.	2.5	5.2	5.5
Los Angeles	n.a.	4.1	5.5	4.7
United States	n.a.	3.4	5.8	4.2

SOURCE: United States, Bureau of Labor Statistics, *Employment and Earnings* (Washington, D.C.: Government Printing Office, various years).

enabled Los Angeles to plot a course unlike any other major urban area in the United States. Los Angeles did not deindustrialize during the 1970s and 1980s but rather continued to generate new manufacturing jobs. This anomalous trend can be seen by comparing the fortunes of America's three largest metropolitan areas (see table 10.1). By the 1960s, New York had already passed its peak as an industrial center, with manufacturing jobs declining by 11 percent during the decade. The trend accelerated in the 1970s, with the loss of 310,000 jobs, a decline of 34 percent, and continued into the 1980s, with a loss of another 174,000 jobs. Chicago, in contrast, grew during the 1960s and eventually eclipsed New York to become the largest industrial center in the United States. But this was a short-term triumph, as Chicago's employment base declined in the 1970s and 1980s, losing 131,000 and 292,000 manufacturing jobs in these years, respectively. Unlike the other two areas, Los Angeles experienced secular growth in manufacturing jobs throughout the 1960s and 1970s. By the late 1970s, this increase in manufacturing combined with the decline in manufacturing employment elsewhere transformed Los Angeles into the largest industrial center in the United States.[19]

While in aggregate Los Angeles did not deindustrialize, manufacturing production did experience tremendous internal restructuring. A more detailed analysis of sectors indicates that industrial growth was not uniform. Similar to the rest of the country, traditional durable industries, such as

TABLE 10.2   Industrial Employment, United States and Los Angeles

	Number of Jobs (in 000s)		Percent of Total		
	1969	1989	1969	1989	Growth
United States					
Total	70,384	108,413			54.0
Mining	619	700	0.9	0.6	13.1
Construction	3,575	5,200	5.1	4.8	45.5
Durable mfg	11,862	11,422	16.9	10.5	−3.7
Nondurable	8,304	8,004	11.8	7.4	−3.6
TPU*	4,442	5,648	6.3	5.2	27.1
Trade	14,705	25,851	20.9	23.8	75.8
FIRE*	3,512	6,724	5.0	6.2	91.5
Other service	11,169	27,096	15.9	25.0	142.6
Government	12,195	17,769	17.3	16.4	45.7
Los Angeles					
Total	2,899.8	4,220.6			45.5
Mining	11.6	8.7	4.0	0.2	−25.0
Construction	108.9	154.4	3.8	3.7	41.8
Durable mfg	619.7	570.5	21.4	13.5	−7.9
Nondurable	260.8	315.8	9.0	7.5	21.1
TPU*	176.8	213.6	6.1	5.1	20.8
Trade	626.1	961.3	21.6	22.8	53.5
FIRE*	160.6	288.4	5.5	6.8	79.6
Other service	528.6	1,186.1	18.2	28.1	124.4
Government	406.7	521.8	14.0	12.4	28.3

SOURCE: U.S. Bureau of Labor Statistics, *Employment, Hours, and Earnings, 1909–1990*; California Employment Development Department, *Annual Planning Information* (1991).
*TPU and FIRE represent transportation and public utilities and finance, insurance, and real estate, respectively.

steel, rubber, and automobiles, lost jobs locally. The growth sectors were heterogeneous and include high-technology industries, such as aerospace, communications equipment, and electronics, as well as labor-intensive industries, such as textile, apparel, and furniture. Los Angeles, therefore, simultaneously underwent both industrial contraction and expansion (see table 10.2).

The protection of some sectors of Los Angeles's economy was thought to play a role in maintaining the region's industrial base. Protection did safeguard some industries; a much talked about example is the aerospace industry. Aerospace developed with the military expansion of the Reagan administration and was protected from foreign competition by federal laws that limited government procurement to domestic suppliers. During the military buildup, employment in this industry grew from 124,000 in 1983 to 144,000 in 1988, a 16 percent increase. Other unprotected industries suffered the fate of their counterparts in other regions of the country. The closure of branch plants in the auto and tire industries occurred as part of a process of geographic reconsolidation, a direct response to increased foreign competition.

However, "protection" was not the sole determinant of economic survival. Both nondurable production such as apparel and high-technology industries such as microelectronics competed in open markets and expanded their employment base. From 1969 to 1989, Los Angeles's apparel industry expanded to 132,000 employees.[20] A similar story can be told for microelectronics. Once sheltered by America's technological lead, high-technology industries have recently become internationalized; yet in Los Angeles the microelectronics industry has continued to expand. Industrial expansion in the competitive sectors of the Los Angeles economy is both intriguing and pertinent to an understanding of growing inequality because it is these same industries that have developed at the expense of the region's low-wage immigrant workforce.

Los Angeles's economy also benefited from the rapid growth in the service sector. In relative terms, as measured by the percentage of the total labor force, Los Angeles became less industrial; a growing percentage of jobs was concentrated in the service industries. From 1969 to 1989, employment in all nongovernmental services expanded by 85 percent, a smaller increase than that for the nation but impressive nonetheless. Consequently, the service sector increased its dominance, from 45 percent to 58 percent of all jobs, making Los Angeles a more service-oriented economy than the nation as a whole, as indicated in table 10.2.[21] Service sector jobs are varied and include high-paid positions in the financial sector as well as low-wage jobs as janitors. A good share of the growth in the service sector was linked to changes in manufacturing both locally and globally.[22] The recent trend toward vertical fragmentation of industries transferred some white-collar activities that had once been within manufacturing firms to service firms and allowed for a greater spatial separation—even to the global scale—between production and nonproduction functions. Moreover, much of Los Angeles's employment growth was linked to the emergence of the region as the financial and corporate center for the Pacific Rim. The growth in banking pushed employment in finance, insurance, and real estate (FIRE) from 161,000 in 1969 to 288,000 in 1989, a 79 percent increase over two decades. Overall, sectoral shifts to a service economy indicated a significant transformation in the organization of production as well as the emerging international prominence of Los Angeles.

TABLE 10.3   Income and Poverty in Los Angeles

	Los Angeles			United States		
	1969	1979	1989	1969	1979	1989
Per capita income	15,492	17,363	19,906	12,549	14,754	17,592
Median family income	37,072	36,081	39,035	32,740	34,139	35,225
Income ratio	11.8%	9.7%	7.8%	13.8%	12.5%	10.3%
GINI	.368	.401	.444	.349	.365	.396
Poverty rate	10.9%	13.4%	15.1%	13.7%	12.4%	13.1%

SOURCE: Per capita income statistics derived from the Bureau of Economic Analysis, U.S. Department of Commerce; median family income and poverty rates are taken from the decennial census; national income ratios and GINI coefficients are taken from published reports based on the Current Population Survey; L.A. income ratios and GINI coefficients are calculated from census data.

NOTE: All income statistics are in 1989 dollars.

LOS ANGELES'S UNDERSIDE:
ECONOMIC POLARIZATION AND GROWING POVERTY

Despite employment growth, Los Angeles has not escaped the problem of increasing income inequality. This is not to argue that growth has not benefited the region in aggregate. As the averages in table 10.3 show, Los Angeles maintained higher average family incomes and per capita incomes than the nation as a whole. However, over the two decades, income was more unequally distributed in Los Angeles than in the United States as a whole.

Economic growth in the 1970s and 1980s was not synonymous with rising wages. Figure 10.1 depicts the dramatic drop in median earnings for male full-time, full-year workers (in 1989 dollars).[23] From a two-decade high of $32,700 in 1975, male earnings plummeted to a 1989 low of $25,000. It is not surprising, therefore, that the collapse in male earnings translated into a polarization of income. The percentage of male FT/FY workers earning less than $15,000 a year more than doubled, from less than 7 percent of all workers in 1969 to approximately 19 percent of all workers in 1990 (see fig. 10.2).[24] As of 1989, approximately 267,000 FT/FY men earned less than $15,000, and approximately 76,000 of them earned less than $10,000 per year. Conversely, the percentage of workers in the middle-income categories, from $30,000 to $44,999, declined from 38 to

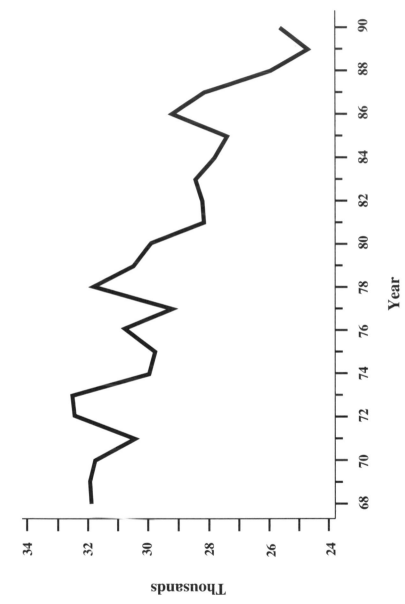

Figure 10.1. Median annual wages in 1989 dollars for male full-time workers.

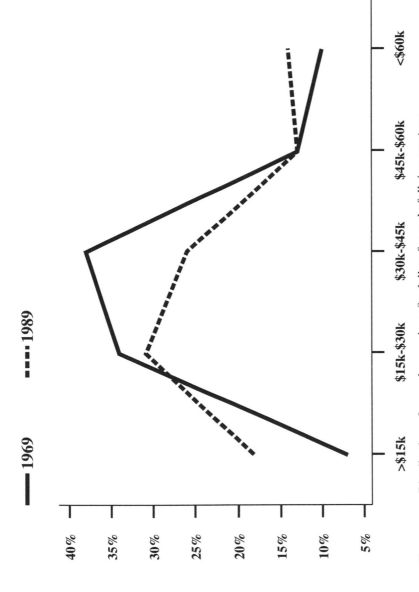

Figure 10.2. Distribution of annual wages in 1989 dollars for male full-time workers.

26 percent. At the upper end of the wage distribution ($60,000 plus), the percentage of male workers rose from 10 to 13 percent.

In Los Angeles, broad structural changes in the economy appear to have played a minor direct role in altering the distribution of earnings. At the national level sectoral shifts explained one-fifth of the growing inequality in the wage distribution between 1963 and 1986.[25] However, their finding is not supported by data for Los Angeles in which only 5 percent of the increase in low-wage work is attributed to sectoral restructuring.[26] Moreover, data for the United States and Los Angeles may understate the effect of economic restructuring on low-wage work by their failure to capture the growth in low-wage jobs within, not just across, sectors of the economy. Finally, the restructuring process may influence the earnings distribution more indirectly in Los Angeles, through supply-side changes such as a recomposition of the labor force. In Los Angeles, changes in the gender and racial composition of the Los Angeles workforce explained 40 percent of the increase in low-wage work, with racial changes being the single most important predictor.[27] We will return to the role of race below.

Not surprisingly, the bifurcation of the wage distribution and the growth in low-wage workers translated into growing income inequality and rising poverty rates. Patterns of inequality can be measured by the income going to the poorest fifth of all families as a percentage of the income going to the richest fifth. For all three years, this percentage was lower in Los Angeles than in the nation (see table 10.3). For Los Angeles, the decline in this percentage took place during the 1970s, whereas the decline for the nation occurred throughout the 1970s and 1980s. The GINI coefficients, also contained in table 10.3, replicate this same overall pattern of inequality.[28]

Rising poverty accompanied growing income inequality. In 1969, the poverty rate for Los Angeles was 2.8 percent lower than that for the United States. This quickly changed as Los Angeles's poverty rate continued to creep upward and the poverty rates for the nation dropped. By 1979, the poverty rate for Los Angeles was 1 percent higher than that for the nation. And as of 1989, Los Angeles's poor had grown to account for more than 15 percent of the population.

Popular images of the poor focus on the single welfare mother; however, the empirical reality for Los Angeles reveals a poverty population notable for its diversity. Men made up 43 percent of the poor in Los Angeles. And although female-headed households were more likely to be poor than other types of households, they constituted a small proportion of all families. Moreover, despite the image of the welfare mother, most families in poverty were not dependent on government assistance for their survival. According to data from the Current Population Survey, only a minority of the adult poor in Los Angeles collected any form of public welfare assistance, including income from such programs as Aid to Families with Dependent Children, General Assistance, and Medi-Cal.

These economic changes and rising poverty were related, but in a complex and dynamic fashion. A substantial proportion of those in poverty can be classified as the working poor. In 1989, 42 percent of the poor adults worked some amount over the previous year, with 9 percent working full-time and full-year. Among males, the corresponding percentages are 63 and 14.

The working poor suffered from both the lack of education and job skills (what has become known as "human capital") and diminishing employment opportunities. Certainly, the entry of unskilled immigrants with little formal education contributed to rising poverty levels. Unfortunately, as studies have demonstrated, human capital investments are necessary but not sufficient in alleviating poverty. Poverty, like the increase in low-wage work, was also driven by broad shifts and fluctuations in the economy. The significant decline of the middle-wage sector established a new labor market structure with fewer avenues of upward mobility. In previous decades, some individuals could eventually move into better-paying jobs; however, more recently, many avenues for upward mobility have been closed.

Economic restructuring during the 1970s was, perhaps, more extensive in Los Angeles than in the rest of the United States as the dual process of deindustrialization in the high-wage sector and reindustrialization in the low-wage sector shaped the industrial structure of Los Angeles. Contrary to expectations, secular growth did not lower the poverty rate. As history reveals, economic growth did not necessarily lead to rising average incomes when it was accompanied by an increasingly unequal distribution of income. Since the early 1970s, the poverty-reducing factors of growth were overpowered by changes in the income distribution. Such has been the trend in Los Angeles.

THE RACIAL DIVIDE

The Los Angeles of the 1970s and 1980s was not only segmented by rich and poor but was also plagued by significant and lasting racial and ethnic divisions. Racial inequality was not a recent phenomenon in Los Angeles; Asian, Latino, and African-American migrants to Los Angeles had long experienced low wages, poverty, and racism.

Lured by the prospect of gold, Chinese immigrants migrated to California and by 1852, constituted 10 percent of California's population. In the next three decades some 335,000 Chinese immigrated to working the mines, the railroads, and the fields. By 1890, 4,424 Chinese immigrants resided in Los Angeles County, the largest concentration outside of San Francisco and the largest immigrant group in Los Angeles.29 Following this

TABLE 10.4   Population by Ethnicity for Los Angeles

	1970	1980	1990	2000
Persons (000s)				
Anglo	4,885	3,849	3,619	3,385
Black	747	929	993	1,070
Latino	1,024	1,918	3,230	4,805
Asians	234	645	1,021	1,664
Percent				
Anglo	70.9	52.4	40.8	31.0
Black	10.8	12.7	11.2	9.8
Latino	14.9	26.1	36.4	44.0
Asians	3.4	8.8	11.5	15.2

NOTE: The Asian category for 1970 and 1980 includes a small number of individuals who were classified as non-Latino "Other."
SOURCE: 1970 and 1980 statistics are estimated from the Public Use Microdata Samples of the U.S. Census; the 1990 numbers are taken from Summary Tape File 1A of the U.S. Census; 2000 Projections are drawn from the Urban Research Section, Los Angeles County (1992).

first wave of Chinese immigration to California were Mexicans driven from their homes by political unrest and drawn to the economic opportunities they saw across the border. The number of Mexicans in California tripled during the 1920s, growing to 368,000, with 40 percent settling in Southern California.[30] African-Americans were the last major ethnic group to migrate to the region. Until World War II, African-American migration to Southern California was small; however, from 1941 to 1945, a booming war economy pulled African-Americans to Los Angeles, where many acquired well-paying employment in the skilled trades. The number of African-Americans jumped from 124,000 in 1941 to almost half a million in 1945. By the early 1940s, all three ethnic groups were represented in Los Angeles in significant numbers.

While the presence of ethnic minorities in Los Angeles predates the 1970s, it was only during the last two decades that Los Angeles emerged as a majority nonwhite city (see table 10.4). The demographic metamorphosis of the region during this period was as dramatic and far-reaching as its industrial restructuring. In 1970, 71 percent of the city's population was non-Hispanic white or Anglo; the remaining 29 percent of the population was divided among Latinos (15%), African-Americans (11%), and Asian Pacific Islanders (3%). By 1980, the non-Hispanic white population dropped to 53 percent; in 1990, it had dropped to 41 percent. Large-scale immigration from Latin America and Asia coupled with a moderate growth in the African-American population expanded the numbers of Latinos, Asians, and African-Americans throughout the 1970s. Immigration continued to reshape the demographics of Los Angeles into the 1980s as the percentage of Latinos and Asians swelled.[31] By 1990, Latinos comprised 36 percent of the city's population; African-Americans and Asians constituted 11 percent, respectively. The demographic revolution of Los Angeles is not over; if current trends continue, by the end of the century Anglos will fail to make up even a plurality of the region's population.

Los Angeles's evolution into a multiethnic world city was built on ethnic and racial inequality. Minorities were consistently pulled into the region to fill the growing supply of low-wage jobs, jobs often dismissed by white workers for their lack of status, their dangerous work conditions, and their low pay. Over the last few decades, minority workers were disproportionately employed as agricultural workers, as domestics, as operators in low-wage, nondurable manufacturing industries, and in the growing service industries as janitors, busboys, and so on. Only African-Americans made some occupational progress, gaining access to higher-wage manufacturing and government service jobs.

The occupational positions of racial and ethnic minorities translated into enduring earning disparities (see table 10.5). Although the earnings gap between African-Americans and their non-Hispanic white counterparts persisted into the 1990s, it consistently narrowed over this period. By 1989, African-American men earned 69 percent of the median earnings of non-Hispanic white men and African-American women earned 91 percent of non-Hispanic white women's median earnings.[32] For Latinos, the unfortunate story was one of growing inequality. The income of Latinos steadily dropped so that by 1989, Latino men and women earned 46 and 50 percent, respectively, of the median earnings of non-Hispanic white males and females. Referring back to the distribution of wages for male FT/FY workers (fig. 10.2), we find that 66 percent of all male workers earning less than $15,000 were Latino, and 83 percent of all those making $60,000 or more were non-Hispanic white.

Some of the decline in relative income can be attributed to the influx of unskilled immigrant labor to the region; traditionally, immigrants have entered the bottom tier of the labor market. In previous decades, the entry of immigrants into the labor market had only a temporary effect on the income distribution as immigrants eventually moved into better-paying jobs.[33] However, more recently, economic mobility for Latino immigrants, in particular, has diminished. Recently arrived Latino men earned 13 percent less in 1980 than in 1970.[34] Opportunities for advancement among Latinos who had lived in the United States for five to ten years grew worse; this group of men earned one-third less in 1980 than in 1970.[35] During the 1970s, labor market integration slowed for Latinos.[36] By 1980, recently arrived Mexican men earned 50 percent less than Latinos who had immigrated more than twenty years ago; moreover, these new arrivals took longer to catch up to the earnings of their more assimilated counterparts.

TABLE 10.5   Labor Market Outcomes by Race, 1990

	Anglo	Black	Latino	Asian
Labor Force Participation Rates				
Male	89%	77%	90%	87%
Female	72%	68%	61%	68%
FT/FY Employment Rate				
Male	72%	61%	55%	62%
Female	56%	57%	46%	56%
Education (at least a B.A.)				
Male	32%	18%	7%	43%
Female	30%	16%	5%	38%
Median Annual Earnings*				
Male	$35,000	$24,000	$16,000	$25,000
Female	$22,000	$20,000	$11,000	$18,000

SOURCE: Estimates are from the 1% 1990 PUMS.
NOTE: All data are for persons ages 25–64.
*Income in prior year for those with a minimum of 100 hours of work.

Immigration alone cannot explain growing racial disparities; U.S.-born minorities made little economic progress during the 1960s and 1970s.[37] Economic differences between minorities and non-Hispanic whites were the outcome of variations in human capital (age, education, work experience) and the persistence of labor market discrimination. Regression analysis isolates the independent effect of both of these factors on earnings in 1989. (See Appendix for details.) The results clearly show that investments in education and labor force experience can have a significant effect in increasing earnings. Holding constant these two factors, the model indicates that among males, being African-American lowers earnings by 31 percent, virtually identical to the 30 percent in 1969. Affirmative action programs of the 1970s aimed at reducing discrimination against African-Americans appeared to have had little appreciable effect on closing the racial gap; on the contrary, the numbers suggest that discrimination among African-Americans is persistent. The regression analysis also reveals that U.S.-born Latinos and Asians face labor market discrimination; they earned 13 and 11 percent less, respectively, than their Anglo counterparts.[38] Interestingly, the effects of race among females are less pronounced, with Latinos and African-Americans earning less (2% and 6%, respectively) and Asian-Americans earning more (7%) than their Anglo counterparts. These smaller racial differences (relative to those among males) may be due to the overall effect of sexism in compressing earnings among all female workers.

Inequality is not only expressed in earnings; it is also reflected in terms

TABLE 10.6   Poverty Statistics for Los Angeles

	Persons Below Poverty (in 000s)			Poverty Rate (%)		
	1969	1979	1989	1969	1979	1989
Total groups	753	985	1301	11.1	13.4	15.1
Anglo	378	288	229	7.8	7.5	6.6
Black	180	215	203	24.2	23.2	21.2
Latino	169	388	744	16.6	19.2	22.9
Asian	26	94	125	11.2	14.6	13.2

SOURCE: The statistics for 1969 and 1979 are estimates from the Public Use Microdata Samples. The Asian category for these two years includes a small number of persons who were classified as non-Latino "other." The statistics for 1989 are from the 1990 census, with estimates for the Anglo population derived by subtracting the number of estimated white Latinos.

of household income. As of 1989, the median income of African-Americans was 62 percent that of non-Hispanic whites. Latinos fared slightly better than African-Americans due to a larger number of wage earners per household. The median family income among Latinos was 67 percent that of non-Hispanic white families. At 94 percent, Asian-Americans fared by far the best, and this was achieved by having both relatively larger numbers of workers per households and relatively high levels of educational attainment.[39]

Race and ethnic inequality is further highlighted with the variation in poverty rates among groups (see table 10.6). Despite the attention placed on the poverty status of African-Americans, in recent years, Latinos have been the fastest-growing ethnic group among the poor. Historically, the poverty rate among African-Americans has dwarfed that of all other ethnic and racial groups. However, sometime during the 1980s, this ceased to be true, as Latino poverty climbed and as poverty among African-Americans declined slightly. An overwhelming 58 percent of the poor are Latino, 20.5 percent are non-Hispanic white, and 13.4 percent are African-American. These numbers reflect not only the growth in the number of Latinos in Los Angeles but also the rapid increase in Latino poverty.

THE FUTURE IN LOS ANGELES

Since the early 1990s, the economic woes facing Los Angeles have grown with a deep, prolonged recession that has driven unemployment to double-digit levels. The economic contraction is driven by both a national cyclical downturn and long-term forces such as the decline of military spending, increased international competition, and the flight of businesses to escape local regulations and taxes. The estimated unemployment rate jumped from a low of less than 4 percent in March 1989 to more than 11 percent in July 1992. Los Angeles did not experience economic recovery until 1993, well after improvements in the national economy; but even by the summer of 1995, the unemployment rate remained over 8 percent.[40] Along with falling incomes and higher unemployment, the poverty rate has been rising. Based on estimates from the March 1994 Current Population Survey, 23 percent of the population lived below the poverty line in 1993, which is over seven percentage points higher than in 1989. A percentage point may not seem like much, but each additional point is equal to approximately ninety thousand persons. The hardships are reflected in an unprecedented increase of the welfare rolls as laid-off workers either have no unemployment benefits or have exhausted their benefits. At the beginning of 1989, roughly 0.9 million persons received some type of public assistance in Los Angeles County, but by the end of 1992, the number stood at 1.6 million.[41]

For the poor in the inner city, their problems have been compounded by the riots and uprising of 1992. According to California's Employment Development Department, between 5,000 and 6,000 persons qualified for unemployment benefits as a direct consequence of the urban unrest.[42] One unfortunate outcome of the uprising is the destructive effect it had on an already underdeveloped economic base in poor inner-city neighborhoods. Those adversely affected by the uprising either directly or indirectly probably number in the tens of thousands. Many workers lost their jobs to the fires and have failed to qualify for benefits; other individuals feel the multiplier effect as the initial loss of earnings places a drag on the local economy; and jobs in the tourist industry are lost as Los Angeles's reputation for unrest draws fewer visitors. These are only a few examples.

If anything positive can come from the 1992 uprising, it may be a renewed concern and commitment to alleviate inequality in Los Angeles. In the wake of the violence, local politicians and a broad segment of the public have demonstrated an interest not only in rebuilding the inner city but also in remaking Los Angeles so that the least fortunate among us can enjoy better economic opportunities. This latter concern is certainly not new. One need only look back to the months after the 1965 Watts riots to find a similar public discussion about poverty and inequality.

The economic problems were already apparent two years before the 1992 riots. Even as the region was enjoying economic growth in 1989, the editors of the *Los Angeles Times* wrote,

> The economic boom of the past decade has obscured an alarming acceleration of income disparity. If it is not arrested, we confront a future in which an affluent, overwhelmingly white minority assumes the privileges and opportunities of a permanent ascendancy, while the nonwhite, non-Anglo mass

of working people are relegated to the status of hereditary bondsmen, left to scavenge in the bleak wastes between the drudgery of dead-end jobs and the misery of utter destitution.[43]

In response to the inequality and poverty, the editors called for "major public investments in nutrition, shelter, health care, education and training" and stated that "providing every man and woman with the means to achieve a decent livelihood and a healthy and humane environment in which to enjoy it are the only goals worthy of a great city."[44]

In a 1989 *Los Angeles Herald Examiner* article that would later prove to be a harbinger of events in 1992, the unidentified writers stated,

No healthy society can long survive with the kind of grotesque and socially destabilizing income inequalities regions like Los Angeles have developed. Waging a war on this kind of poverty calls for concerted and sustained efforts by local, state and federal officials, backed by active private-sector initiatives. . . . Winning this struggle won't be easy. But everyone, not just the poor, will lose if we fail.[45]

The costs have indeed proven to be high.

The preriot concerns about poverty and inequality were not limited to the media. In Mayor Bradley's 1989 inaugural address in his unprecedented fifth term, he stated that "Los Angeles cannot permanently exist as two cities—one amazingly prosperous, the other increasingly poor in substance and in hope."[46] Included in the agenda for his new term was a promise to end the growing economic disparities. Some questioned the sincerity of this pledge, pointing to the possibility that the mayor was merely attempting to divert attention away from the growing political and financial scandal that plagued him. Mayor Bradley's real goal may be immaterial. The unfortunate truth, however, is that during the two years following his pledge, conditions in Los Angeles grew worse, and a growing sense of economic hopelessness and social alienation added fuel to the 1992 uprising.

Ending inequality and poverty is not a new goal for Los Angeles. The question today is whether the soul-searching and concerns expressed by politicians, public agencies, private corporations, and untold numbers of individuals will establish a new agenda able to reverse the two-decade-old trends discussed here. Much attention has been given to promoting the economic recovery of the riot-affected areas—to helping some businesses reopen, to securing pledges of new private investments in poor neighborhoods, and to creating jobs. These objectives are appropriate immediate responses to the crisis. Unquestionably, each rebuilt building, each new store, and each additional job help residents. Yet we should not expect that this "rebuilding" approach will solve Los Angeles's problems; a much larger effort is needed. Yet in this recessionary period, Los Angeles does not possess the required private and public resources to make a noticeable dent in solving the problem of growing inequality. Nor is it realistic to expect much help from Washington, D.C. The first round of national support targeted to Los Angeles will give way to fewer and fewer resources as other urban areas facing the same set of economic conditions lay claim on available monies. Moreover, regardless of who is president into the 1990s, the federal government will be constrained by the enormous and growing national deficit. In light of these realities, we should view each rebuilt or new building and each additional public or private dollar as important symbols of the efforts to rebuild and transform Los Angeles. The danger is that such actions will only be symbolic if the root causes of inequality and poverty are left unattended.

Los Angeles will not be able to reverse its fortunes without addressing the more fundamental issues of racism, decaying public institutions such as the schools and the judicial system, and the weakening of social and community institutions; these issues are crucial to long-term viable economic development. Unfortunately, working on these problems is far less glamorous than the immediate physical rebuilding efforts; they afford fewer photo-opportunities and fewer opportunities to make the headlines. On the bright side, some Los Angeles residents are taking up this larger challenge, particularly within community-based organizations. Our hope is that Los Angeles will address some of the fundamental roots of inequality; it is only through such an effort that the city will make genuine progress toward equality.

APPENDIX: REGRESSION ANALYSIS

Annual earnings are modeled with the following formula:

$$Y = b_1 + b_2 \text{GRADE} + b_3 \text{EXP} + b_4 \text{EXPSQ} + b_5 \text{BLACK} + b_6 \text{CHICANO} + b_7 \text{ASIAN}$$

where Y is some measure of earnings; GRADE is the number years of formal education; EXP is the potential years of labor market experience measured by age minus the number years of education; EXPSQ is experience squared; and BLACK and CHICANO are dummy variables to capture the effects of race and ethnicity on earnings. The model is estimated for three types of dependent variables: EARNINGS, total annual earnings from wages and self-employment income; Ln(EARN), the natural log of annual earnings; and Ln(WAGE), the natural log of the hourly wage, which is estimated by dividing EARNINGS by total hours worked. The sample includes U.S.-born persons between the ages of 17 and 64 with at least $1,000 in earnings. The estimated coefficients are as follows:

Males	*Earnings*	*Ln(Earn)*	*Ln(Wage)*
Intercept	−52286***	7.400***	0.668***
Grade	4552***	0.120***	0.096***
Exp	2356***	0.101***	0.055***
Expsq	−3687***	−0.171***	−0.082***
African American	−11564***	−0.313***	−0.225***
Chicano	−4982***	−0.131***	−0.108***
Asian	−6396***	−0.113***	−0.058***
Adj R-Sq:	0.231	0.330	0.255

Females	*Earnings*	*Ln(Earn)*	*Ln(Wage)*
Intercept	−25736***	7.366*	0.566***
Grade	2619***	0.116*	0.099***
Exp	1201***	0.071*	0.040***
Expsq	−2206***	−0.134*	−0.071***
African American	−2372***	−0.018	−0.049***
Chicano	−1802***	−0.060***	−0.048***
Asian	1015***	0.069*	0.070**
Adj R-Sq:	0.157	0.183	0.180

significance levels:	***$p < .01$	**$p < .05$	*$p < .1$

NOTES

This chapter is based, in part, on research that was included in the report *The Widening Divide: Income Inequality and Poverty in Los Angeles* (Graduate School of Architecture and Urban Planning, University of California, Los Angeles, 1989). The research for this report was directed by one of the authors of this chapter, Paul Ong. Where appropriate, new, updated, or revised data are included. We are indebted to the researchers who contributed greatly to the development of many of the ideas and findings included in this chapter. This research was partially funded by grants from the Ford Foundation and the Poverty and Race Research Action Council. We alone are responsible for the contents of this paper.

    1. Mike Davis, "Chinatown, Revisited? The Internationalization of Downtown Los Angeles," in *Sex, Death and God in L.A.*, ed. David Reid (New York: Pantheon Books, 1992).

    2. Los Angeles County, "PEPS92 Population Model," unpublished memo. (Urban Research Section, 1992).

    3. Nationally, these findings were reported by Bennett Harrison and Barry Bluestone in their book *The Great U-Turn* (New York: Basic Books, 1988); they were replicated for Los Angeles by Paul Schimek in "Earnings Polarization and the Proliferation of Low-Wage Work," in *The Widening Divide: Income Inequality and Poverty in Los Angeles* (Graduate School of Architecture and Urban Planning, University of California, Los Angeles, 1989), 27–52.

    4. For evidence of this, see Anthony B. Atkinson, *The Economics of Inequality*

(Oxford: Clarendon Press, 1983), and Lester Thurow, *Generating Inequality: Mechanisms of Distribution in the U.S. Economy* (New York: Basic Books, 1975).

5. Unless otherwise noted, national statistics cited in this chapter are taken from the Council of Economic Advisors, *Economic Report of the President* (Washington, D.C.: Government Printing Office, various years).

6. A secular movement is the underlying trend after accounting for the effects of business cycles.

7. See W. Norton Grubb and Robert H. Wilson, "Trends in Wage and Salary Inequality, 1967–88," *Monthly Labor Review* (June 1992): 23–39.

8. These figures are reported in U.S. Bureau of the Census, *Workers with Low Earnings: 1964 to 1990,* Current Population Reports, Series P-60, no. 178 (Washington, D.C.: Government Printing Office, 1992), 3. The definition of a FT/FY, low-earning worker is a person who earns less than $12,195 in 1990 dollars. The Bureau of the Census used the CPI-U-X1 index, which shows a lower rate of inflation than the CPI-U index, to adjust current dollars to constant dollars.

9. These figures are reported in United States, Bureau of the Census, *Trends in Relative Income: 1964 to 1989,* Current Population Reports, Series P-60, no. 177 (Washington, D.C.: Government Printing Office, 1991).

10. These figures are reported in United States, Bureau of the Census, *Poverty in the United States: 1964 to 1989,* Current Population Reports, Series P-60, no. 175 (Washington, D.C.: Government Printing Office, 1991).

11. For a discussion of some of these changes, see Ed Soja, Rebecca Morales, and Goetz Wolff, "Urban Restructuring: An Analysis of Social and Spatial Change in Los Angeles," *Economic Geography* 59 (April 1983): 195–230; and Allen J. Scott, *Metropolis: From the Division of Labor to Urban Form* (Berkeley, Los Angeles, and London: University of California Press, 1988).

12. Although the defense-related industries have been sheltered from foreign competition, employment in this sector has not been any less volatile because of fluctuations in federal spending. Moreover, the federal cuts in defense spending have led to a serious decline in employment in these industries. For a discussion of federal cuts in the defense industry, see Janis Breidenbach, "The Employment Effects of Military Spending in Los Angeles County" (master's thesis, Graduate School of Architecture and Urban Planning, University of California, Los Angeles, 1987); and Paul Ong and Janette R. Lawrence, "The Unemployment Crisis in Aerospace," Report Series (Urban Planning, University of California, Los Angeles, 1993).

13. For an analysis of Los Angeles's film industry, see Michael Storper and Susan Christopherson, "The Effects of Flexible Specialization in Industrial Politics and the Labor Market: The Motion Picture Industry," *Industrial and Labor Relations Review* 42, no. 3 (April 1989): 331–347.

14. Discussions of the linkages between Los Angeles and the Pacific Rim appear in two reports, one by the Los Angeles Area Chamber of Commerce entitled "The Los Angeles Area, Dimensions of a World-Class Market" (Los Angeles: Los Angeles Chamber of Commerce, 1985) and a second by the Pacific Rim Task Force of California's Economic Development Corporation entitled *California and the Pacific Rim: A Policy Agenda* (1986).

15. See Christopher Payne, "Restructured Labor Markets in Commercial Bank-

ing: A Comparative Study of Los Angeles and San Francisco" (master's thesis, Graduate School of Architecture and Urban Planning, University of California, Los Angeles, 1989).

16. Yuko Aoyama, "Japanese Real Estate Investment in Downtown Los Angeles" (master's thesis, Graduate School of Architecture and Urban Planning, University of California, Los Angeles, 1988).

17. This topic is examined by Ivan Light and Edna Bonacich in *Immigrant Entrepreneurs: Koreans in Los Angeles, 1965–1982* (Berkeley, Los Angeles, and London: University of California Press, 1988) and Michael Goldberg in *The Chinese Connection* (Vancouver: University of British Columbia Press, 1985).

18. These figures are based on data from the 1990 U.S. Census. Because a large number of undocumented aliens were not counted, these immigrant counts underestimate the number of recent immigrants.

19. There is a note of caution here. Los Angeles may be entering a stage of development similar to New York in the 1960s and Chicago in the 1970s. During the 1980s, manufacturing employment in Los Angeles fell moderately. It is too early to determine if the modest decline in manufacturing is a harbinger of the deindustrialization of Los Angeles in the 1990s.

20. These figures are reported in *Annual Planning Information* (California Employment Data and Research Division, 1991). According to this same source, garment employment has continued to expand during the 1990s, rising to 138,000 in 1991.

21. Basic employment data come from United States, Bureau of the Census, Bureau of Labor Statistics, *Employment and Earnings* (Washington, D.C.: Government Printing Office, various years). Unfortunately, the 1969 information for Los Angeles contains only the total employment for all manufacturing. We estimate the employment in the two broad industrial sectors according to the ratio of the employment in durable to the employment in nondurable calculated from data published by the California Department of Employment (1970).

22. Saskia Sassen, *The Mobility of Labor and Capital: A Study in International Investment and Labor Flow* (Cambridge: Cambridge University Press, 1988).

23. We focus here on the wages of male, full-time, year-round workers. This approach avoids the argument that income polarization is the outcome of the recent entry into the labor market of low-wage female workers. The annual series is estimated from the March Current Population Survey, which reports income data for the prior year. For the 1968–1988 survey years, we used data extracted from the Current Population Surveys: Uniform March File, which was constructed by Robert D. Mare and Christopher Winship and distributed by the Inter-University Consortium for Political and Social Research.

24. The distributions were estimated with data from the 1 percent Public Use Microdata Samples for 1970 and 1990. All males working full-time, full-year with at least $1,000 in annual wages (1989$) were included. For 1970, no averages were reported for the number of hours worked per week in 1969, so the averages reported for 1970 were used.

25. Harrison and Bluestone, *The Great U-Turn.*

26. Paul Schimek, "Earnings Polarization and the Proliferation of Low-Wage

Work," in *The Widening Divide: Income Inequality and Poverty in Los Angeles* (Research Group on the Economy, Graduate School of Architecture and Urban Planning, UCLA, 1989).

27. Ibid.

28. The GINI coefficient is a widely used measure of income distribution in which the larger the value, the greater the level of inequality. The measure is equal to twice the difference between the observed distribution of family income defined by the Lorenz curve and the hypothetical curve obtained if income were absolutely equally distributed.

29. Department of Interior, Census Office (1895), *Report on Population of the United States of the Eleventh Census: 1890* (Washington, D.C.: Government Printing Office), 437.

30. For historical figures on migration, see Thomas Muller and Thomas J. Espenshade, *The Fourth Wave: California's Newest Immigrants* (Washington, D.C.: Urban Institute Press, 1985).

31. The African-American population experienced a net increase of only 50,000 people during the 1980s. Increasing out migration of African-Americans since the 1960s has reduced the level of net immigration. See James H. Johnson and Curtis C. Roseman, "Increasing Black Outmigration from Los Angeles: The Role of Household Dynamics and Kinship Systems," *Annals of the Association of American Geographers* 80, no. 2 (1990): 205–222.

32. One of the growing problems for African-American men has been their declining labor force participation. In 1990, African-American men were twice as likely not to be in the labor force as any other male racial group.

33. See Rebecca Morales and Paul Ong, "Immigrant Women in Los Angeles," *Economic and Industrial Democracy* 12, no. 1 (1991): 65–81.

34. These figures are reported in Ann Forsyth, "Immigration and Economic Assimilation," in *The Widening Divide: Income Inequality and Poverty in Los Angeles* (Research Group on the Los Angeles Economy, Graduate School of Architecture and Urban Planning, University of California, Los Angeles, 1988), 101–128.

35. Ibid.

36. Ibid.

37. See Holly Van Houten, "The Cost of Not Being Anglo," in *The Widening Divide: Income Inequality and Poverty in Los Angeles* (Research Group on the Los Angeles Economy, Graduate School of Architecture and Urban Planning, University of California, Los Angeles, 1989), 81–100.

38. The smaller coefficients for the race variables in the Ln(Wage) regressions than in the Ln(Earn) regressions for males indicate that some of the differences in annual earnings are due to minorities having lower total hours of employment.

39. The median household income was $40,500 for Anglos, $25,000 for African-Americans, $25,000 for Latinos, and $38,000 for Asian-Americans. These estimates were derived from the 1 percent PUMS based on the race/ethnicity of the head of the household.

40. See *UCLA Business Forecast for the Nation and California* (Los Angeles: John E. Anderson Graduate School of Management, June 1992).

41. These numbers were reported by Paul Fast of the L.A. County at the AFDC

Caseload Conference, sponsored by the Estimates Bureau, California Department of Social Services, 26 August 1993, Sacramento.

42. This estimate is based on a 1992 interview with Vicky Johnsrude of California's Employment Development Division, Local Labor Market Division.

43. Editorial, "Bradley's Major Assignment," *Los Angeles Times,* 30 June 1989, 8.

44. Editorial, "The Poor Get Poorer," *Los Angeles Times,* 21 June 1989 and 30 June 1989, II, 6.

45. Anonymous, "High Cost of Poverty," *Los Angeles Herald Examiner,* 21 June 1989, A10.

46. Bill Boyarsky, "Bradley Vows Help for Poor in his 5th Term," *Los Angeles Times,* 1 July 1989, II, 6.

ELEVEN

A City Called Heaven

Black Enchantment and Despair in Los Angeles

Susan Anderson

The first generation of black political leadership in Los Angeles was inadvertently launched on 19 January 1856 as the result of a fairly routine court case. In the First Judicial District of the State of California in the City of Los Angeles, Judge Benjamin Hayes manumitted a group of illegally held slaves. Sisters Hannah and Biddy and their children and grandchildren were granted "full liberty and discharge" under the Sheriff Special Guardian.[1] The younger sister, Biddy, would become one of the most prominent citizens in Los Angeles history, a wealthy property owner, philanthropist, and community leader.

However, on that January day, Biddy Mason stood between slavery and liberty. She and her family had accompanied their Mormon master, Robert Smith, from Mississippi to Utah and Southern California as part of the "Great Mormon Experience." In Los Angeles, Biddy was free. But her slave master planned to leave California and reenslave his captives in Texas. Biddy, Hannah, and their children were encamped with him in the Santa Monica Mountains. Captive, illiterate, even a woman of such remarkable resources as Biddy Mason could not act alone. In a drama indicative of the sophistication and dedication of the tiny black Los Angeles population, a businessman, Robert Owens, and a woman named Elizabeth Flake Rowen helped Biddy and her family escape from the canyons surrounding the city. Owens, one of the wealthiest men in the city, whose own descendants would later intermarry with Biddy's, produced the writ of habeus corpus that resulted in the liberty of the slaves.

The political leadership, particularly of the African-American middle class, has exercised an incalculable influence over the city. Biddy Mason learned the lessons of this leadership early: no one is empowered alone. Among her achievements was the founding of the First African Methodist

Episcopal (AME) Church—a pivotal institution, the base for political up-
start Tom Bradley in the early 1960s, and the site of contentious crowds the
night of the 1992 uprisings. She was eulogized as leading a life "filled with
good works" in her 1891 obituary in the *Los Angeles Times*.[2] A monument to
her now stands on the site of her former home on Spring Street downtown.

African-American institutions in Los Angeles are testaments to the community's faith in salvation as a "beautiful city of God." The urban ideal has
been potent in black culture. For generations, congregations have sung the
lyrics of the traditional hymn, "City Called Heaven,"

> I am a poor pilgrim of sorrow,
> I'm tossed in this wide world alone,
> No hope have I for tomorrow,
> I've started to make heaven my home
> Sometimes I am tossed and driven, Lord,
> Sometimes I don't know where to roam,
> I've heard of a city called heaven,
> I've started to make it my home.[3]

Rural life for blacks has meant, among other things, slavery, peonage, isolation, and terror. It is not surprising that the city, symbolizing escape from
the racist excesses of the Deep South, is an object of black enchantment.
But it is also a cause for despair as immigrants, even those early pioneers
like Biddy Mason, discovered, as all utopian searchers must discover, that
the beautiful city of God is not of this place.

Sometimes it does seem that Los Angeles is the promised "city called
heaven." Blacks in the early history of the city found an economic ease
unparalleled in the country. One hundred years later, black-owned firms
were responsible for California's 1990 title as the "home of the largest number of successful black entrepreneurs" in the nation, moving ahead of New
York on *Black Enterprise*'s top 100 list.[4] Census figures show Los Angeles
has the highest concentration of high-income African-Americans in the
country.

The ethnic diversity in the city allows blacks to participate in a cosmopolitan urban culture; it mediates the relations between blacks and white
power. As far back as 1905, one writer argued its benefits: "Perhaps the
presence in this section of the country in large numbers of the representatives of every nation on the globe, has much to do with the success that
has attended our men, as representatives of the so-called backward races;
they have no monopoly of the embarrassing attention and prejudice so
often directed mainly at them."[5] Then there is Los Angeles as that fictional
space, "Black Hollywood," which, like Hollywood itself, in the words of *City
of Nets* author Otto Friederich, "is really an imaginary city that exists in
the mind of anyone who has, in his mind, lived there."[6] In the city itself,

black stars preside at civic events; it was a point of note that Dionne Warwick sang at Bradley's first swearing-in. Even in the bedrock of community life, among the three hundred or so African-American churches, the most prominent and affluent vie for identification as the "church home" of Arsenio Hall, Magic Johnson, and other famous stars.

However, while Los Angeles has the highest concentration of high-income blacks in the country, it also has the highest concentration of low-income blacks. The celebrated ethnic diversity threatens to collapse into a "retreat into fortress identities" as the city divides along racial and ethnic lines. And the glowing imagery exported by Hollywood belies the fact remarked by the film director Charles Burnett that "the Los Angeles Police Department has more affirmative action than Hollywood."[7]

In the foreword to his novel of early L.A. life, Jess Kimbrough plaintively acknowledged what most blacks still know and feel about their city.

> Los Angeles is . . . a dream. . . . [I]t encompasses more of everything than the wakeful mind is capable of imagining. . . . No other group of people on earth has had such a varied cultural background to build upon. . . .
>
> But there is something more. On the outer fringe, well removed from the mainstream, the hand of fate has haplessly dropped the Negro, the unsolvable social headache with all of its accompanying tensions. . . . Yet in some vague way he, too, calls the city his home, and there was a time when he considered it a haven.
>
> . . . It is likely that the lush valley, walled in on the north by a mountain range which breaks the fierce wind, seemed a perfect place to rest . . . a fit habitat for heavenly angels.
>
> [But] . . . it appears that the eternities are definitely marked on the basis of color. All the redeemed of heart in heaven are white, and all the damned in hell are black. And with a background so firmly rooted in antiquity, it is not surprising that the same demarcation of color is a fact of life in the City of Angels.[8]

EARLY BLACK POLITICS

All great cities, to use Rainer Maria Rilke's words about Rome, have an abundance of pasts. In Los Angeles, an extraordinary period, just ended, has become one of the city's pasts. The period began with the convening of political and social forces that elected Tom Bradley to the city council in 1963, then made him the first black mayor of a large American city in 1973. It continued, for a generation, through the maintenance of tacit bargains and intricate relationships, to keep him there. It ended with the refusal of Mayor Bradley to run for reelection in 1992, the election of Richard Riordan, and the extraordinary events surrounding the succession, particularly the 1992 civil unrest. A change in mayor rarely can be considered one of the great events in a city's life. However, Bradley's election marked a rupture with history. Crucial to that change was the catalytic role of black Angelenos, as infiltrators of the city's political imagination, as heralds of its political transformation and shapers of its political edifice.

The powerful black influence in the events of the city helped to create a new ethos of political rule, opening city government to elites of racial, ethnic, and political communities that had previously been excluded. It also helped to bring the entire city around to facing black leadership's historical bedrock concerns: political representation and police brutality. In the post-Bradley setting, a major uncertainty is whether the diverse black community will continue to be as pivotal a force in the public life of the city and whether the prevailing ethos of the Bradley era will continue to inform city life.

Throughout its early history, the black community in Los Angeles had agitated for political power with scant success. By 1960, the *California Eagle* editor, Charlotta Bass, was forced to declare, "Los Angeles is one of the most laggard cities in the nation when it comes to entrusting public office to Negroes."[9] In a 1961 comparison of black representatives on the city councils of the nation's largest non-Southern cities, only Los Angeles, Cincinnati, and Boston had no black members. In contrast, New York had two out of twenty-five; Detroit, one out of nine; Cleveland, eight out of thirty-three; Chicago, six out of fifty; St. Louis, six out of twenty-nine; and Philadelphia, one out of seventeen. In 1960, the only black elected official from Los Angeles was Augustus Hawkins, who had been in the state assembly since the Great Depression. By this time, the black population comprised 13.5 percent of the overall population in 1960. With its growing numbers, and the added force of the Southern civil rights movement, grew a pent-up demand for political representation.

The exclusion of blacks from public office resulted from a variety of factors. There were deliberate tactics, such as gerrymandering. As part of the reform movement, district elections for city council had been established in 1925, eliminating at-large elections. Many cities around the country were forced to eliminate at-large elections by civil rights court challenges on the grounds that they diluted minority votes. In Los Angeles, district elections "did not prevent city leaders from purposely crippling Black political power. . . . [A]s far back as the 1930s, the city divided up Black districts that went naturally north-south and joined them to adjacent West Side white areas. When . . . Black westward mobility increased, the city then drew the lines north-south to prevent the creation of Black majority districts."[10]

Additionally, the political culture itself was a barrier to black participation. The odd admixture of reform policies and conservative civic sensibilities proved hostile to challenge. Reform efforts destroyed machine politics, which in other cities ironically functioned to include African-Americans, albeit with limitations, by taking advantage of the political base provided by segregation. At the same time, the civic culture in Los Angeles managed to exclude, violently at times, labor, the Chinese-, Japanese-, and Mexican-American communities, liberals, and Jews along with blacks. In fact, the history of Los Angeles politics is a history of animosity in the extreme toward each of these groups. When it came to blacks, the rude expression of this political culture altered over the years, but it was evident enough in a *Los Angeles News* editorial in 1867: "The soul of the Negro is as black and as putrid as his body. Should such a creature vote? He has no more capacity for reason than his native hyena or crocodile."[11]

It is also possible to argue that the caution of local African-American leadership contributed to the long years of exclusion. The black community here has been a "sober residential and business settlement," declared Bass.[12] From the nineteenth century until after World War II, perhaps the greatest preoccupation of the community was securing its economic status, not its political power. Indeed, despite segregation, the rates of home ownership for blacks in Los Angeles were higher than those for other minorities in the city and higher than those for blacks in other cities (for example, 36.1 percent compared with 2.4 percent in New York). Despite discrimination, the wages and occupational gains for Los Angeles blacks exceeded other cities. In 1920, it was observed that African-Americans made "a better adjustment in Los Angeles than any other American city."[13] This sense of well-being persisted for many generations and formed the ontological core of black experience from the city's earliest days.

THE GOLDEN ERA

From 1850 until the 1920s, with all its tenuous liberties, legal restrictions, and customary racism, life in Los Angeles proved an atypical, almost halcyon, urban experience for its growing black population. The numbers of blacks burgeoned in L.A., from 12 in 1850 to 15,579 in 1920, hovering under 3 percent of the population. That group lived an anomaly compared with their African-American compeers elsewhere. This period is characterized by the defeat of Reconstruction, terror, and persecution in the South and the privations of large-scale migration to the North. In Los Angeles, in dramatic contrast, these years have been referred to as "the golden era."

In those early years, black economic strength was predicated on a unique set of factors in the Los Angeles labor market and economy. The sheer diversity of industries here meant that black areas of employment included housing, construction, and transportation as well as domestic work. The wages available to skilled black artisans and semiskilled workers were

among the highest in the nation. In addition, Los Angeles was the first city
in the country to hire African-Americans on its police force and fire department, hence initiating an early black entry into the city's civil service.
Even L.A.'s largely open-shop factory employment, while noxious to trade
unions, meant wider opportunities for black workers because of the absence of the layer of preclusion practiced by white-run labor organizations.
Also, as the black newspaper *Liberator* crowed in 1904, "The colored people
are not all laborers and white washers. . . . [T]hey are evidencing a disposi-
tion . . . to go into business for themselves."[14]

In the early nineteenth century, California was optimistically seen by
African-Americans as "the western wilds . . . where the ploughshare of
prejudice has at yet been unable to penetrate the soil."[15] Actual experience
quickly mitigated this view and helped to stimulate the formation of several
early civil rights organizations and campaigns. These efforts were singularly
successful and include gaining the right to testify in court and participate
in juries in 1863, outlawing separate schools for "colored children" in 1890,
passing one of the first equal public accommodations laws in 1870, and
overturning a city ordinance mandating whites-only jitney buses as public
transportation. By 1921, the first black state legislator, Frederick Roberts,
was elected to the assembly in Sacramento from the Watts district. To protect and extend these gains, civic organizations and local chapters of national groups—Marcus Garvey's United Negro Improvement Associations,
the NAACP, and the Urban League—flourished in Los Angeles.

In politics, the long-lived Los Angeles Forum, founded in 1903, had what
the historian Rudolph Lapp called an "umbrella effect" over diverse black
organizations. Run by the sober burghers and business owners of Central
Avenue and meeting weekly in the E. 28th Street YMCA, the Forum set the
agenda for blacks in the city, while holding open meetings and providing services for newly arrived black migrants. The Forum, and later the
1960s Committee on Representative Government, while in no way reflecting monolithic black political sensibilities, did temper the infighting and
antagonisms that became prevalent in other cities such as Chicago and New
York and may have helped to create the long-standing, relatively peaceful
coexistence among Los Angeles's black political structures.

The NAACP held its first western convention in Los Angeles in 1928 in
the Dunbar Hotel, a just-built, elegant establishment (a product of black
money and fierce discrimination in the city's hotel industry—a not un-
profitable combination for the African-American entrepreneur) on the
bustling corner of 41st and Central, south of downtown. W. E. B. Du Bois
had already traveled to Los Angeles on behalf of the newly founded civil
rights group in 1913. In a graphic display of how middle-class comfort and
race protest have often been wedded in black life, Du Bois rode in a mo-
torcade of about ten cars and later posed for a photograph with the obvi-

ously prosperous motorcar owners. The contact with the cream of the Los Angeles black population stirred Du Bois to write in the August 1913 *Crisis,* "Los Angeles is wonderful. Nowhere in the United States is the Negro so well and beautifully housed, nor the average efficiency and intelligence in the colored population so high. . . . Out here in this matchless Southern California there would seem to be no limit to your opportunities, your possibilities." In the same issue, however, Du Bois couched a warning in his glowing words: "Los Angeles is not Paradise, much as the sight of its lilies and roses might lead one at first to believe. The color line is there sharply drawn."[16]

THE RISE AND FALL OF THE GHETTO

It wasn't long after Du Bois's observations were published that spatial restrictions on the black presence intensified, underpinning and facilitating social and economic discrimination. Nowhere was the color line more sharply drawn than in housing. Strict housing segregation, enforced by restrictive covenants, block agreements, law, custom, and violence, existed in all American cities. However, in Los Angeles residential segregation had not been typical of the African-American experience. When housing segregation emerged in Los Angeles it was swift and doubly cruel, representing a retreat from an almost unrestricted spatial dispersion for blacks.

From 1850 until the 1920s, in the words of one early inhabitant, "Negroes lived anywhere they could afford to live. Homes were rented to anyone who had money."[17] African-Americans, rather than being restricted to one or two primary residential areas, lived in the various neighborhoods of Boyle Heights, West Temple to Occidental between 1st and 3d streets, San Pedro to Santa Fe, 35th and Normandie, and Pico Heights, as well as other places. It was a point of pride that black residency was autonomous of the ghettos that had long formed in other urban areas. "The Negroes of the city," the *Liberator* boasted, "have prudently refused to segregate themselves into any locality, but have scattered and produced homes in sections occupied by wealthy, cultured White people, thus not only securing the best fire, water, and police protection but also the more important benefits that accrue from refined and cultured surroundings."[18]

With the large-scale migration of Southern blacks *and* whites by the 1930s, racial lines began to harden and a formidable array of forces had the practical effect of herding African-Americans into designated areas of the city. The factor of intense, forced residential segregation contributed more than anything else to the deterioration of the quality of black life in Los Angeles. The ghetto was created.

The black influx to Los Angeles was rapid and immense. In 1910, the black population was 7,599; in 1920, it was 18,738; in 1930, 30,893; in

1940, 75,209. By 1950, the black population was nearly 200,000, and it continued to increase through the 1960s. With the start of increased migration, the boundaries were set for black residency; by the early 1930s, 70 percent of all black Angelenos resided in one assembly district. That pattern continued until the Watts riots, which sparked the initial out-migrations from the crowded black neighborhoods described by *L.A. Times* literary editor, Robert Kirsch, in 1965 as "a kind of forgotten archipelago in the garish basin of the region."[19]

The early dispersal of the black population had not been complete; there were black neighborhoods, particularly around Central Avenue in the early part of the century, which have been called "spatial ghettos" because the only characteristic in common with the well-established ghettos in northeastern cities was that the inhabitants were African-American. These spatial ghettos, peculiar to Los Angeles, were almost uniformly composed of owner-occupied single-family bungalows. Moreover, although the bourgeois press rarely admitted their presence, so strenuous were its effort to demonstrate the worthiness of the black population, poor blacks often lived in the housing courts around railroad tracks or found themselves, along with other poor migrants from Mexico and China, in makeshift housing downtown. Also, Watts, variously known as Mudtown or Nigger Heaven, was a stark contrast to the urbane black existence in the central city and west side. As Arna Bontemps put it in his 1931 novel, *God Sends Sunday,*

> The small group in Mudtown was exceptional. Here, removed from the influences of white folks, they did not acquire the inhibitions of their city brothers. Mudtown was like a tiny section of the deep south literally transplanted. Throughout the warm summer days old toothless men sat in front of the little grocery store on boxes, chewing the stems of cob pipes, recalling the 'Mancipation. . . . [T]he women cooked over fireplaces in the yards and boiled their clothes in heavy iron kettles. There were songs in the little frail houses and over the steaming pots. Lilacs grew at every doorsep. In every house there was a guitar.[20]

These areas were exceptions. For the most part, in Los Angeles, blacks escaped wholesale involuntary residential segregation common to the rest of the country.

A study of residential title law alone would reveal the patterns and practices that distorted and segregated city life beginning in the 1920s. Popular white aversion to the growing black population was expressed in campaigns to "keep the neighborhood white," through block protective associations and use of individual deed covenants. Black and white realtors capitalized on these sentiments through the block-busting tactics long used in other cities. The extremes of this sentiment were acted out by the Ku Klux Klan whose activities "nearly always involved issues of homeowning and accommodations."[21] As late as 1940, the "hooded terror" marched through downtown Los Angeles from City Hall to Broadway and 8th Street and back again.

As with many political issues, black concerns over housing segregation were both an expression for racial justice and an indication of middle-class desires. As the *California Eagle* editorialized in 1940, "When the Negro property-owner buys in 'white' neighborhoods, it is usually because there is no section in the Negro district which can offer him a home honestly reflecting his economic position and cultural tastes. To be told that he cannot live in property bought outside the narrow confines of the accepted black belt, as though his presence contaminates the very atmosphere, is a biting humiliation."[22]

The fight against housing segregation became a preoccupation of the black movement. L.A. leaders were among those who welcomed the 1940 Supreme Court decision that ruled unconstitutional a property restriction that forced the wealthy Carl Hansberry out of his home in an exclusive area of Chicago. So profound was black concern over residential segregation that, before the decade was over, the issue became the turning point in the now-classic Broadway play, *Raisin in the Sun,* written by the daughter of the plaintiff in the Hansberry case. And Los Angeles would become "the nation's leading center for legal challenges to restrictive covenants."[23]

The case that provided the national rallying focus against housing segregation was known as the "92d Street Outrage." In 1939, Mr. and Mrs. Lee Lofton bought a home in the Good Year Tract along East 92d Street. The Good Year Tract extended south from Manchester Boulevard to 92d Street and west from Central Avenue to Hooper Avenue. The first African-American moved there in 1908 and left in 1935. In October 1939, the Lofton couple moved to the neighborhood with their children. By the summer of 1940, white neighbors sued the Loftons, saying the "use, lease, sale, or occupancy of the property to persons other than Caucasians" was prohibited. As their case against the injunction developed, the Loftons were the targets of racial harassment. Refusing to obey an eviction notice, the entire family went to jail. The arrest was a dramatic event; the Loftons were forcibly led off their property by the police as white neighbors jeered. The Loftons' own suit precipitated years of national litigation and became part of a set of similar cases brought before the U.S. Supreme Court. In 1948, the U.S. Supreme Court outlawed restrictive housing covenants, declaring them unconstitutional.

By the late 1940s, crowded, inadequate housing was a citywide problem and public housing was viewed as a response to the situation exacerbated in the post–World War II population boom. The real estate lobby, an intricate network of banks, property owners, and the *L.A. Times,* was able, however, through its considerable clout, to redbait and agitate the city into refusing to build the number of units needed. This defeat of public housing had a ripple effect throughout the region and in the loosely structured political culture of cities such as Dallas, San Antonio, Houston, Seattle, Akron, and Portland, which was "inspired" by the "success" of L.A.'s landed interests. As a consequence, Los Angeles led the country in the loss of federal funds for public housing. The local effect of this Pyrrhic victory was increasing overcrowding and inadequate housing in the inner city. In the meantime, white working-class and middle-income families, including the war veterans for whom public housing was also intended, took advantage of the suburban boom, departing the scene of the problem.[24]

The growth of the San Fernando Valley as an enclave long reserved for white home owners was directly dependent on the concentration of black renters in the city core. Real estate interests "worked hand in hand" with the federal government, to create residential segregation. Between the 1930s and 1940s, the federal program of mortgage loan guarantees "administered, advised and sometimes required developers of residential projects to draw up restrictive covenants against nonwhites as a condition of obtaining F.H.A.–insured financing. . . . [T]he policy closed almost all African Americans out of the federally insured mortgage market and excluded them from the new suburbs altogether." Even after restrictive covenants were outlawed, "between 1946 and 1959, less than 2 percent of all the housing financed with the assistance of federal mortgage insurance was made available to blacks."[25]

The slightest opening in housing provoked black flight from the inner city. Between World War II and 1960, the black population swelled to nearly 14 percent of the population—a high for L.A. but far behind other urban centers such as Chicago or Detroit where blacks made up half or more of the residents. It was during this time that the Supreme Court decision outlawed restrictive covenants. Black migration began out of the central and south central parts of the city into the west side.

By the 1980s, redlining replaced housing covenants as the main form of segregation. African-Americans are more consistently denied home mortgage loans than any other group. In addition, recent studies such as the 1993 Consumer Union's "The Thin Red Line: How the Poor Still Pay More" provide evidence that all low-income residents of Los Angeles, particularly blacks, live in areas where goods and services, from health care to food, cost more and provide less compared with middle-class communities. Again, in response to the newer forms of segregation, there has been large-scale flight. During the past decade alone, about 76,000 African-Americans left South L.A., heading past the San Fernando Valley into San Bernardino and Riverside counties and beyond. According to one report, "the African-American population of South Los Angeles actually decreased by 20 percent during the [1980s] while the African-American population in the rest of the City increased slightly. The African-American populations of Riverside and San Bernardino Counties . . . increased by 99 percent and 134 percent, respectively."[26] More than 60 percent of these migrants were considered "traditional" households: professional, two-parent families.[27] This flight from Los Angeles of working black families can be considered a long-term, quiet revolt with consequences far outweighing the city's outbreaks of violence in 1965 and 1992.

One consequence is that only 7 percent of black Angelenos live in "all-black neighborhoods" compared with 37 percent in other cities.[28] Most formerly black neighborhoods have become reintegrated: in South Central, by mostly poor Latin American immigrants; in west side neighborhoods, by gentrifying whites. As a recent L.A. United Way study suggests, "What we commonly knew of the Black community over the last twenty to thirty years was geographically presented, based on a cluster of neighborhoods with a concentrated majority of the city's black population. . . . However, as demonstrated by the impact of diversified population growth, the notion of a geographically determined black community is no longer correct or viable."[29] In other words, the ghetto no longer exists.

Those who remain concentrated in the areas once considered ghettos live in conditions described by demographers in the 1980s as "hypersegregation." Hypersegregation keeps residents "isolated from the resources that would help them escape the ghetto. . . . [R]esidents . . . would be very unlikely to come into regular contact with a member of Anglo society, except through participation in the labor force, an option that is denied to the . . . central-city blacks who are under or unemployed."[30]

The black population in Los Angeles is enormously kinetic, its patterns of movement a response to continuing patterns of housing discrimination. Importantly, these movements corresponded with differences in income and resources. The west side became the hub for an affluent stratum of blacks with an influence that could be compared to the early dons of Central Avenue. By 1960, after several waves of changing black residential patterns, there was enough concentration of population in the Eighth and Ninth city council districts for black voting strength to override the attempts to limit black political participation in the city. Significant, too, was the base of affluent blacks in the multiracial Tenth District. Together, these areas would launch the juggernaut that in one year elected Thomas Bradley, Gilbert Lindsay, and Billy Mills to the city council and reshuffled the balance of political power in the city.

A MEDIATING FORCE

It was not inevitable that Los Angeles would have a black mayor. While the number of blacks in the city was behind only New York and Chicago, the proportion of blacks in the overall population, especially among voters, was far behind many urban centers. Blacks alone could never have mustered the clout needed to put one of their own in citywide office. It took the combination of three conditions to elect Tom Bradley mayor and transform the political character of the city: an apt public persona, a new coalition of voters, and a sense of political urgency.

If a persona were to have been manufactured to fit the emerging exigencies of Los Angeles following 1960, it would have been Tom Bradley. First among his characteristics was his lifelong ability to maneuver between contested territories in the city, between black and white, Jew and gentile, police and populace, privileged and poor. Bradley acknowledged this trait in himself beginning as a student at Poly High where he successfully campaigned for offices formerly closed to minorities. There began, he said, "what was to become a whole pattern in my life, . . . working with and trying to serve as a mediating force among people of different backgrounds."[31] Before entering electoral politics, Bradley's public life was centered in networks of interracial, interreligious organizations, from the time of his student involvement in UCLA's campus Religious Conference to his formation of an ambitious LAPD community relations program while he was a police officer to his activities in the progressive California Democratic Council. By the time he was elected to the city council in 1963, he had a web of citywide contacts that would provide the infrastructure for seizing City Hall.

Once elected to the city council, representing the Tenth District in 1963, Bradley also proved his aptness as a citywide leader by establishing a reputation that both accommodated and defied traditional politics. In L.A.'s political cosmos, this meant being seen as independent of machines, fiscally conservative, and enamored of the distance between the city and Washington, D.C. Except for the latter, Bradley differed little from mayoral antecedents while on the council, voting separately from fellow black members Billy Mills and Gilbert Lindsay, resisting the established Democrats, and favoring spending cuts, including and foreshadowing sterner conflicts, in the LAPD budget. Conversely, Bradley instituted a public style perhaps unprecedented in the city. Not only did he hold regular monthly meetings in public places in the Tenth District; to the discomfiture of fellow council members, he also held meetings on issues he was concerned about in their districts. Not only did Bradley initiate this "characteristic of an accessible public official" in a city that had been virtually closed politically, he also increased his visibility among citywide voters and widened his network of contacts.

That Bradley had been a career policeman was also salient to his rise to mayor. In a city whose police force operated as a political leveraging force on the office of mayor and whose voters were still overwhelmingly white and conservative, no mayor could reign without the pleasure of the LAPD. Certainly, no black candidate, regardless of his other qualifications, would have been palatable to voters without strong, visible attachment to the police department. And it was Bradley's career in the LAPD that bolstered his early public critiques of the police force, particularly before and after the Watts riots. However, at the same time, it is questionable whether a black candidate could have been elected without criticizing the police, for the black vote hinged on this issue. And, following the Watts riots, police reform again emerged as a compelling theme for all voters in citywide politics.

The coalition that formed around Bradley expressed the pent-up aspirations of the elite representatives of those who had been traditionally and systematically excluded from political participation. A breakthrough had been made with Ed Roybal's election as the first nonwhite to the city council. Bradley and others participating in that campaign would later draw resources from the Roybal camp. However, when Roybal was elected to Congress in 1962, the vacuum remained in city politics, as glaring as ever. The Bradley coalition drew on Asian, Latino, and labor leadership. It drew great strength from liberal gentile and Jewish leaders. But the core of the coalition, the force that provided the others a rallying point, was African-American leadership.

African-American political leadership in L.A. has shown a remarkable calm and unity, compared with other cities. This has meant an absence of the destructive divisions experienced elsewhere. Black leadership here is characterized by sangfroid, the imperturbability personified by Bradley. But it has also produced a middling leadership, lacking the creative disunity that has been a hallmark of the black community. On a national scale, the antagonisms between black leaders provided the force behind a century of social and racial reforms: abolitionist Frederick Douglass fighting insurrectionist Henry Highland Garnett; socialist A. Philip Randolph contending with the Harlem elite; the black agitators of the Congress of Industrial Organizations upstaging the probusiness Urban League; the direct action movement of Martin Luther King vying with the litigious NAACP. In other cities, such antagonisms gave rise to memorable political leaders: the fiery militance of New York's Adam Clayton Powell, the labor clout of Detroit's Coleman Young, the civil rights credentials of Atlanta's John Lewis, the leveraging ability of the Black Panthers' Elaine Brown in Oakland. Los Angeles's primary contribution to the pantheon of black political leaders has been Tom Bradley, along with few others. Bradley was a precise reflection of a fundamentally conservative city and an African-American community that had as its origins a "sober business and residential settlement."

There were, however, serious divisions between Bradley and other forces in the African-American community. These fissures would have profound consequences for the city as the Bradley administration distanced itself from the very black neighborhoods whose massive dissatisfactions—ferociously expressed in the 1965 Watts riots—had supplied the urgency that propelled him into office in the first place.

First was Bradley's independence from what many progressive Democrats considered the Unruh machine. As a consequence, Jesse Unruh "reguiars" Mervyn Dymally and Julian Dixon, both eventual members of Congress, supported Bradley's opposition in both 1969 and 1973. Dymally was concerned that the mayor would not "lend his resources to develop black politicians" but instead would dilute his influence and be "mayor of all the people." This was a sentiment shared by some black voters, particularly in South Central neighborhoods, who felt a Bradley victory would not necessarily be a black victory, particularly not a black working-class one. One observer noted the class distinctions between the multiracial Bradley camp of "reformers" and the traditional Democratic "regulars," calling them "cotton socks vs. silk stockings."[32] But the momentum, exhilaration, and organizing ability of the Bradley campaign was impossible to withstand. Whatever fissures existed beneath the surface disappeared as Bradley captured an enthusiastic 91 percent of the black vote in his successful 1973 mayoral campaign.

During the time of Bradley's ascendancy, between 1967 and 1987, one national trend helped carve the emerging divide in black political leadership. The ranks of the middle class swelled as a result of an expanding economy and the successes of the civil rights movement, which opened up jobs and education. Black households with incomes of more than $50,000 grew by 350 percent. In California alone, the number of blacks in elected office went from one in 1960 to 300 in 1989. These gains contained the seeds of later disunity based on an unprecedented economic differentiation between blacks and growing class distinctions.

The Bradley coalition could not have survived without the successful mobilization of poor and working-class black voters. However, the Bradley coalition was built with an elite African-American leadership at its center. Bradley himself, though born poor, had rapidly ascended the hierarchy of the city's income ladder. He decided to attend Poly High rather than Jefferson, his South Central neighborhood school. He departed the church of his domestic worker mother, South Central's New Hope Baptist Church, to join the affluent First AME congregation. He purchased a home in upscale, west side Leimert Park when it was an all-white enclave; indeed, a white friend had to buy the house. Bradley was a creature of west side black affluence, and the coalition that formed around him was inspired by the leadership representing that sector of black life.

The Bradley administration was remarkable for being a force in history that opened City Hall to the excluded. Additionally, it initiated affirmative action in City Hall and developed ties to the federal government and access to federal funds, previously spurned by Los Angeles mayors. Under Bradley, redevelopment of commercial corridors around the city, production of high-income housing, and the publicly subsidized creation of a new downtown helped produce a new city environment and sensibility that was a far cry from the old conservative outpost. But the Bradley administration also presided over a city undergoing wrenching changes—massive migration, economic changes, political shifts—that were more easily overlooked than in other cities because of the economic boom that persisted throughout the 1980s. Where the transformations were being most painfully experienced was in poor neighborhoods throughout Los Angeles. But the administration itself did little to alleviate the explosion of poverty in areas such as South Central. For instance, the *LA Weekly* found that in the administration's final years, from 1988 to 1992, South Central received fewer "per-person-in-poverty" funds for economic development than better-off West L.A., fewer job training dollars per-person-in-poverty than West L.A. or the North Central area of the city, and only 29 percent of human services funds compared with 49 percent in the valley and 40 percent in West L.A.[33]

In postriot L.A., with redistricting, population changes, and the absence of a black figurehead at the top of city government, black political leadership is up for grabs. Tensions have already sporadically broken out in the wake of the Bradley administration. In a series of skirmishes between outgoing Mayor Bradley, City Councilman Mark Ridley-Thomas, and Congresswoman Maxine Waters, it appears that a realignment is in process. Before Bradley left office, these three represented distinct forces in Los Angeles who, nonetheless, had maintained, if not a common front behind Mayor Bradley, then a shared assenting silence. However, the realignment of African-American leadership will not occur as a result only of personalities. As in Bradley's time, the bedrock concerns of the community, not yet determined in postriot Los Angeles, will find expression in the political process itself.

Regardless of what the emerging issues will be, it is doubtful that Los Angeles will experience the kind of entropic rivalries common between African-American leaders in other cities. A likely scenario points to a lengthy transition period defined by three or four types of leadership in competition for representation of African-Americans: conventional, liberal, career politicians who will hold on to their seats as long as they can before Latino or Asian constituents emerge, isolationists who stand outside the political process vying for the political imagination of poor blacks and the race-conscious, more conservative voices whose critiques of big-city liberalism will resonate with black residents weary of such failures. Perhaps, though, Los Angeles will witness the rise of a new kind of leader.

Historically in California, black leaders "agitated only for their own group."[34] Black political sophistication far exceeded that of other "minority" groups, and many of the early black migrants to California were practiced abolitionists and public leaders. In the contemporary age, as economics and race and nationality newly commingle, black strategies will also rearrange themselves. The British writer Kevin Robins describes the tensions and tempations that arise as cultures directly confront each other in the new, multiethnic global cities: "Older certainties and hierarchies of identity have been called into question. Of course, they do not disappear. Cultural nationalism and patriotism are always posed to reassert themselves in a storm of jingoism and xenophobia. . . . How do we cope with the shock of confrontation? . . . This is perhaps the key political agenda in this era."[35] Richard Rodriguez speculates that because, in L.A., "African-Americans must live within a new kind of national complexity, alongside Russian Jews, Syrians, Mexicans, Armenians and Vietnamese," a black leadership might emerge here "different from any other in America."[36]

Any new black leadership that emerges in Los Angeles would have to undertake the burden of the failures of the civil rights movement as well. It was upon the problem of the poor in the cities that the black political movement stumbled, and Watts was its first stumbling point. When organizers of the 1963 March on Washington censored Student Nonviolent Coordinating Committee leader John Lewis's speech, the act presaged the movement's failures in the cities. "In good conscience," Lewis was to have asserted, "we cannot support the Administration's civil rights bill. . . . What is in the bill that would protect the homeless and starving people in the nation? What is there in the bill to insure the equality of a maid who earns $5.00 a week in the home of a family whose income is $100,000 a year?"[37] What was considered by civil rights leadership too divisive to be even uttered in official public discourse now seems obvious to the point of banality.

After the 1992 Los Angeles riots, now-Congressman Lewis confessed, "It was easier to go and sit at a lunch counter all day and let a lighted cigarette get put out in your hair. . . . It was easier to march across the bridge in Selma and get tear-gassed" than it is to bring equality to the poor in American cities.[38] Black leadership made its own contribution to the urban crisis with what scholar Gerald Horne calls "a de facto Faustian bargain."[39] This tacit agreement was a trade: racial concessions from the establishment at the expense of a programmatic critique of economic injustice. When the glittering evidence of this bargain was on worldwide display during Nelson Mandela's 1990 visit to Los Angeles, Horne argued that, as quiet as it was kept, civil rights leadership had forsaken the road taken by Mandela's African National Congress, which explicitly speaks of the redistribution of wealth as the basis of black equality in South Africa. Ironically, the Mandela visit provided, among other things, a virtuosic display of the mobilizing capabilities of the black elite, but that mobilization has stopped short of the population most in need. Los Angeles gang members interviewed by reporters did not even know who Mandela was.[40] As 60,000 spectators in the

Los Angeles Coliseum chanted "Free South Africa," one woman could be overheard devising her own slogan: "Free South Central." These incidents illustrate that poverty, as an issue for modern black leadership, has been utterly without glamour. Or, as one observer put it, "It's easier to think about sending money to Johannesburg than to think about . . . crack-addicted babies."[41]

"HOLD YOUR CLUBS FIRMLY"

The political fates of black Angelenos and the LAPD have been closely intertwined. Beginning in 1991, with the repeated airing of the videotaped beating of Rodney King, the warring personas of Mayor Tom Bradley and Police Chief Daryl Gates became the catalyst, as in a mythological conflict, for immense tragedy. The two men's personal enmity, however, was a symbol of the long-standing animus between black Angelenos and the LAPD. Ultimately, it expressed, as well, the central conflict at the heart of city governance: the historical antagonism between the Los Angeles Police Department and what the political scientist Raphael Sonenshein labeled its "extreme bureacratic independence" and the weak office of the mayor.

The first paid police officers were hired in 1869. Along with their badges and weapons, those officers were admonished to "keep your coats buttoned . . . and hold your clubs firmly."[42] By 1890, the city had a black police officer, said to be the first in the nation. Many cities throughout the nineteenth century, fearing a retaliatory urge in blacks for injustices done them, prohibited blacks from joining their police and fire departments. Additionally, these public jobs were typically protected for those favored by the local political machine. The turn-of-the-century hiring of a scattered few blacks into LAPD ranks bolstered black optimism about their "matchless" city. When a black officer, Robert Williams Stewart, posed for a photograph with fellow members of the department's "strong man" boxing and wrestling team, there were 85 officers for a city of 52,000, including 1,258 blacks.

From the start, the LAPD was a volatile, corrupt fortress that had sixteen police chiefs in the thirteen years after its founding. In its earliest years, the LAPD was known for two characteristics: graft and corruption and extreme aggression toward the Chinese population, the largest nonwhite group in the city. Indeed, the first occasion of Los Angeles making national headlines was following the lynching, on 24 October 1871, of nineteen Chinese residents. The mob violence was instigated by the LAPD breakup of a dispute in Chinatown. By 1890, the police force had "an obsession with downtown vice" and, under Police Chief J. M. Glass, concentrated its efforts on dismantling Chinatown "practically board by board."[43]

Perhaps the first major attempt at reforming the department's relationships with minority communities was the citizens committee appointed by

California Governor Earl Warren to investigate the Zoot Suit riots in 1943. By this time, the LAPD had been revamped according to the city charter of 1925. In the charter, still the foundation document for city governance, the mayor was removed from all citizens commissions, especially the police commission, to prevent political influence. The authority to appoint the chief of police was removed from the mayor to prevent corruption in the department. Even with these changes, the LAPD remained an unstable agency; it had twenty police chiefs between 1900 and 1933. By World War II, the Mexican-American community, which had become and would remain the predominant minority group in the city, was the target of "mass arrests, drag-net raids, and other wholesale classifications of groups of people based on false premises [that] tend to merely aggravate the situation," in the words of the Warren-appointed committee. This erupted in the 1943 skirmishes between Mexican-American youths and servicemen, riots, attacks against and mass arrests of Mexican-American youths called the Zoot Suit riots. The committee's recommendation that "law enforcement agencies should provide special training for officers dealing with minority groups" would be echoed again in responses to violence in the city.

By this time, the black population was on the rise in Los Angeles, forced by housing segregation into distinct areas of the city. Although never as large as the Mexican-American community, blacks began to become a special target of the LAPD. Tom Bradley had entered the police force in 1940, the end of the period during which, in the words of former LAPD Commander Homer Broome, "working conditions were extremely harsh for Black officers. Racial prejudice and discrimination were evident at all levels, assignments, and tasks. Most Black officers were assigned to work foot traffic beats on Alameda Street . . . and were assigned to Newton Division. . . . First and foremost, Black officers were always assigned to work together or alone. There was no integration."[44]

In the 1940s, Bradley became part of the first quartet of blacks to reach the rank of lieutenant. The department, in order to prevent them from commanding white personnel, established an all-black watch for them to command. As Bradley acknowledged, the LAPD attracted blacks because it "paid better than any civil service job, any other job generally available to blacks at the time." However, the strict discrimination in the department pushed Bradley and others to develop alternative careers, particularly in the law.

Despite its reputation for violence in minority communities and discrimination within its own ranks, the LAPD entered its heyday in the 1950s under Chief William Parker. The department achieved a mythical status, emulated and acclaimed around the country. In 1955, the International Managers Association annointed the LAPD "the most soundly organized large police department in the country."[45] The purported virtues of the

LAPD, toughness, efficiency, and a kind of L.A. cool, were insinuated into the mass psyche through the radio and television series, "Dragnet." Chief Parker coined the term "the thin blue line," which resonated throughout America's suburbs as an accurate description of the fragility of the force of order countervailing against urban threats. The department was considered an innovator, for its high-tech weaponry, special units replacing foot patrols, and autonomy from elected officials. Above all, its paramilitary style and practice appeared to distinguish it favorably from its counterparts in other cities. In television imagery, Los Angeles was conveyed through the crewcut dispassion of Jack Webb in "Dragnet." New York was portrayed by the anarchic buffoonery of "Car 54 Where Are You?"

Chief Parker symbolized the obliviousness of L.A.'s institutions to the eruptive, expansive nature of the city itself. In a 1955 address to the National Conference of Christians and Jews, Parker, unwittingly describing the very conditions that would feed subsequent violence in the city, asserted confidently,

> I refer your attention to Los Angeles. That city is, today, characterized by a quality of intergroup cooperation which renders it almost unique among our great cities. . . . If organized violence occurred anywhere, it should, by all socio-economic standards, have been Los Angeles. In the last decade, the city has nearly doubled in size; it has suffered the intense dislocation of adjustment to an industrial economy; it has been and still is the focus of one of the greatest migrations in this nation's history. . . . [It] is a melting pot of races, colors, creeds, and ideas. . . . The story of that city's freedom from strife is largely the story of the professionalization of its police department.[46]

Perhaps during the quiescent 1950s there was conceivable merit in such a statement. However, as late as 1965 in its 1964 Annual Report, the LAPD was claiming (in response to alarms by City Councilman Bradley and others) that "racial conflict would not occur in Los Angeles. Compatibility between the community and the police was well-established."[47] Chief Parker himself argued in a speech on crime and the Great Society six months before the Watts riots, "The progressive curtailment of existing police authority is destroying this nation's ability to protect itself against its criminals. . . . The law has lost its majesty and is treated by many with demonstrated contempt." He ended with a strangely anachronistic recitation of Rudyard Kipling's "The Recessional."

> If drunk with sight of power, we loose
> wild tongues that have not Thee in awe—
> Such boastings as the Gentiles use,
> or lesser breeds without the law—
> Lord God of Hosts, be with us yet,
> Lest we forget—Lest we forget![48]

When the Watts riots hit six months later, Parker replaced Kipling's polite, colonial "lesser breeds," calling Black rioters "monkeys in a zoo" and proclaiming "We're on top and they're on the bottom."

The well-known spark that ignited the Watts riots was the LAPD's long-standing abusive treatment of black and other minority residents, crystallized at the moment of the arrest of Marquette Frye. The McCone Commission, appointed by California Governor Edmund "Pat" Brown recommended police reforms already familiar to a city that had been scrutinized by the citizens commission report on the Zoot Suit riots twenty years earlier. The two motive issues in the Los Angeles black movement, political representation and police brutality, joined after 1965. But neither the election of Tom Bradley as mayor nor attempts at community policing under Chief Ed Davis mitigated the continuing hostilities between the LAPD and the inhabitants of the occupied territory its officers roamed.

In 1979, Bradley's sixth year as mayor and head of the city's ruling political coalition, the LAPD shooting of Eulia Love again aggravated tensions in the city. Two police officers shot Mrs. Eulia Love to death on her South Central front lawn in January. They had been summoned by the gas company after an employee had been threatened when trying to collect an overdue bill of twenty-two dollars. Subsequently, the district attorney refused to file criminal charges, the attorney general found no basis for prosecuting under the civil rights statutes, and the LAPD's own investigation found the officers involved "complied in all respects with Department policies concerning the use of firearms and deadly force." Only the police commission dissented from these exonerations, questioning the testimony and actions of the officers as well as the department's training and preparation. Again, recommendations were made to strengthen "community relations" and provide training for "assignment to minority areas."[49]

One of the ironies of the uproar that followed the shooting is that it occurred during a five-year decline of police shootings—from 208 in 1974 to 146 in 1979. Fatalities were decreasing as well. But the incident quickened black disaffection with the LAPD. A *Los Angeles Times* survey after the Love shooting showed black satisfaction with LAPD performance at only 30 percent, what the Police Commission called "a precipitous decline of 24 percent over a period of eighteen months."[50]

The feebleness of Bradley's response was caused by his own ambiguity concerning the LAPD and the limits of his office. It also highlighted the limitations of political representation for blacks, demonstrating that access to the highest municipal office was not the guarantee of redress that some in the leadership sought. During the Eulia Love crisis, one change, however, was evident. The involvement of established black leadership was institutionalized for the first time through the Police Commission Steering Committee "representing a broad constituency of the black community, with the aim of improving police-community relations in the 77th, Southeast and Southwest Divisions." Church leaders, too, were consulted and a series of public hearings held. During these, Mayor Bradley publicly rebuked Chief Gates, who, responding to the stinging reproofs of black ministers, said they were not representative of their community. In a display of the ambiguity and denial that characterized his public stance toward the LAPD, when asked if his defense of the black clergy caused problems in his relationship with the chief, Bradley answered, "Not at all. Not at all."

In 1991, by saturating the national consciousness with the images of the Rodney King beating, it seemed that television broke its own spell and, finally, helped demystify the LAPD. The nation voiced an outrage similar to what blacks had experienced and tried to convey. In the city itself, amid the fallout from the April 1992 riots, the public careers of both Mayor Bradley and Chief Gates were sacrificed. The appointment of the Christopher Commission was the last important act of the Bradley regime. The commission, its critical findings and recommendations, and the 1992 passage of the charter amendment to curtail the "extreme bureacratic independence" of the LAPD demonstrated that the historical indifference of the city had been ended. The city had finally been engaged by the remaining core preoccupation of black leadership: the need to transform intolerable practices of the LAPD. However, between the time of the beating of Rodney King and the passage of the police reform measure, it took the 1992 civil unrest to provide the most persuasive evidence of unacceptable police practices.

POLITICS BY RIOT

In the experience of the crowd, which has become our national culture, Americans shared hours around thousands of television sets in April 1992, watching the aerial helicopter views of uncountable buildings burning in Los Angeles. The grid of South Central and Mid-City streets resembled a well-laid, if shabby, garden exploding with black, sky-high blossoms. One passive crowd of television watchers observed the actions, or the consequences of the actions, of another, mobile crowd in the street. In the city, it was possible to drive west on, say, Manchester from Central Avenue and see block-long charred hulks of buildings that once were the area's signature ratty storefronts and strip malls with their jumbled signs and second-rate goods. The sooty broken frames now reached jaggedly skyward in some forlorn mockery of a cathedral. With the stench of arson yet fresh, the majestic Western notion that we can build our way to grace was itself just a ghostly irony.

By watching Los Angeles, the country was scrutinizing its own possible future, the likelihood that the facade of social cohesiveness everywhere would splinter as surely as any structure torched in the riots. The Police

Commission report on the civil disorder states, "When the unrest began on April 29, the City's Mayor and Chief of Police had not spoken to one another directly for more than a year"—since Bradley had publicly called for Gates's resignation after the Rodney King beating. The divisions in Los Angeles began at the top. They were so profound that for a few days the marines, national guard, sheriff's deputies, and the police department ruled L.A.'s neighborhoods like the Four Powers in the rubble of Vienna's inner city after World War II.

At the heart of the divisions is the breakdown of black unity. For thirty years Los Angeles has, unconsciously, relied for its peace on the relative accord among sectors of the black community. That unity was held together by the racial symbolism in the mayor's office and the tacit acceptance of the ruling political coalition of liberals, Jews, and labor. But the night of April 29, as Mayor Bradley presided over a nervous forum at First AME Church, where his political career was first launched, demonstrators outside expressed their rage toward those inside. Black unity dissolved and with it, the ruling coalition's power over the city.

Los Angeles has now become identified as the city whose contemporary history is bracketed by two violent, large-scale riots that have provided revelation of the plagues in America's social reality. This, perhaps, is L.A.'s perverse gift: the city as oracle, the prophetic urban place that utters a message no one wants to hear.

The 1965 Watts uprising predicted the subsequent economic degeneration of low-income black communities and the inability of national leadership to cope with the trends. When Martin Luther King spoke at the Westminster Neighborhood Center auditorium days after the riots, he was booed off the stage. Responding to Watts, Southern Christian Leadership Conference strategist Bayard Rustin was forced to examine the premise of the mainstream black movement and the liberal agenda attending it. "At issue," he wrote in *Commentary*, "is not *civil rights* strictly speaking. . . . [T]he Negro today finds himself stymied by obstacles of far greater magnitude than the legal barriers he was attacking before. . . . These are the problems which, while conditioned by Jim Crow, do not vanish upon its demise. They are more deeply rooted in our socio-economic order; they are the result of society's total failure to meet not only the Negro's needs, but human needs generally."[51]

That the 1992 outbreak is connected to the spread of the general condition of poverty and "society's total failure to meet human needs" appears undeniable. In South Los Angeles, the rate of poverty is above 30 percent—twice the overall city rate, three times the national rate, and higher than at the time of the Watts riots. More than half the population age sixteen and older is unemployed or out of the labor force altogether. The proportion of households on welfare increased from 19 to 25 percent, and welfare benefits are less than they were twenty-five years ago. South Los Angeles has the highest school dropout rate, 26 percent, in the county. And residents of South L.A. are hardest hit by high rents and housing shortages.[52]

Once, this litany of the immiseration of the population of South L.A. would have described "the Negro." In 1965, the area was 81 percent black. Today, it is at least 52 percent Latino. And the downward spiral of poverty in the city is hardly limited to the confines of once-black neighborhoods. The concentrated Central American community of Pico-Union, near MacArthur Park, compares with South L.A.'s desperate circumstances. Explaining the outbreak of looting and rioting in the area, a representative of the Central American Refugee Service Center said the reasons "are simple. . . . [T]here is an incredible amount of poverty, lack of jobs, shortage of housing. Add to that a gang and a drug problem and complete lack of response from the government and you have the recipe of social unrest."[53] The city was taken by surprise when it witnessed the new temperament among the immigrant poor. Less reminiscent of other immigrant experiences, they are more like the offspring of Southern black migrants to Los Angeles twenty-five years ago who were "unwilling to settle for the luxury of being an American and the token gestures of gradualism."[54]

The underside of what is optimistically called the New Majority is exposed in the high rates of poverty extending through all communities. Asians, including immigrants from Cambodia, Vietnam, Korea, and the Philippines, have, at 14 percent, a poverty rate twice that of whites.[55] Even those least associated with poverty in the public mind have had, in order to make a living, to scuttle at the bottom of the region's economy.

Extremes of poverty in Los Angeles rival the Third World; extremes of wealth flourish here, too. During the past decade, median household incomes in Los Angeles County outgrew the nation's by 19 percent; the number of California households with a yearly income of $75,000 or more increased 800 percent.[56] According to the United Nations, "the U.S. has the largest gap between wealth and poverty in the developed world and that ratio is widest in New York and Los Angeles, comparable to Karachi, Bombay, and Mexico City."[57]

The violent events in April belong—as nearly all else in Los Angeles—in a global context. Wrenching changes have permanently transformed the economy and, by doing so, have created a profound inequality in the lives of low-income Angelenos that is becoming increasingly characteristic of American cities. The brunt of this restructuring, which forcefully emerged in the 1970s, was felt in low-income black neighborhoods with plant closings, the loss of manufacturing jobs, and the disappearance of commercial neighborhood enterprises. Decreases in public funds exacerbated the losses. A UN analyst has described the riots as being part of "an urban revolution taking place on all six inhabited continents, brought on by conditions very similar to those in Los Angeles: crime, racial and ethnic tension, economic woes, vast disparities in wealth, shortages of social services and deteriorating infrastructure." Los Angeles has emphasized, according to the World Bank, that "urban poverty will become the most significant and politically explosive problem in the next century."[58]

The 1992 events in Los Angeles have ended the familiar "race riot" and its cycle: police provocation in a black neighborhood, bedlam, white fears, the restoration of "calm," the hurried assembly of an official report, and amnesia—until the next race riot. The police commission report said that "members of all racial groups were involved in the spreading physical assaults and looting. People of all ages and gender participated in the looting."[59] As the writer Tim Rutten put it, in Los Angeles the country experienced its first "multiethnic riot."[60]

The multiethnic inner cities of Los Angeles have yet to be included in conventional politics; political representation is again a motive issue in the city. Voter participation in inner-city council districts is so low that out of 1.4 million residents, only 37,000 voters participated. Rather than chaos, the violence in 1992 was, at least in part, a reaction to exclusionary local government, the crowd engaging in desperate political discourse with those in power. Writing of such outbreaks in early urban history, Eric Hobsbawm said, "This mechanism was perfectly understood by both sides."[61]

HOW TO SURVIVE

The raplike syllogism in vogue on the street during the April riot—"no justice, no peace"—could have been anticipated with any systematic attention to the Los Angeles contribution to rap music. So-called gangsta rap can be many things: racist and sexist, brutal and insipid, but it also can be a guidebook to the challenging terrain in the shifting neighborhoods once called ghettos.

Rapper Ice Cube asked, in the sound track of the film *Boyz N the Hood,* "How to survive in South Central?" A generation of residents have asked the same, as manufacturing shut down, working families fled, crack invaded, migration increased, and the government safety net was yanked out from under thousands. In April 1992, the country (as it is prone to do with irresistible black popular expression), found itself rapping, too: Indeed, how to survive in South Central?

New urban maladies have merged with the tragic proliferation of guns. The American fetish of gun-toting and gun-wielding is indulged in more intensely and more frequently in Los Angeles than anywhere else. The LAPD and its high-tech arsenal was perhaps the most obvious symbol of gun culture in the city. The population is armed as well: one in four homes in L.A. County has a gun, and, contrary to national trends, more people in Los Angeles are killed by gunfire than by traffic accidents. There are more licensed and unregulated gun dealers here than in any other county in the country, and one in six households was victimized by gun-related crime in 1991.[62]

In South Los Angeles, low-income residents, particularly African-Americans, are more likely to be victims of violent crimes than any other group, and a greater percentage of them perceive crime as among the worst problems in the city.[63] Accordingly, black residents, who make up the majority of voters in the wide sweep of South Central Los Angeles, voted twice during the 1980s to approve police taxes "by majorities topping 70%" as "these revenue-raising measures were shot down by conservative white districts."[64] Contrary to former Police Chief Gates, who repaid the pro-protection sentiment among black voters with what the world now knows is widespread harassment and brutality, Willie Williams, the new police chief here, will most likely find vast support among these voters, not only because he, too, is African-American, but because South Central residents deeply want peaceable conditions in their gun-scarred neighborhoods.

Black leaders generally promote the liberal argument that jobs are the missing ingredient in the stark postindustrial landscape that has produced L.A.'s "gangsta" culture. But the proposals for these deproletarianized youth are negligible. These young people are the most expendable of a black working class that is becoming obsolete. They could, in Marxist terms, be considered the shock troops of the unemployed reserve army of labor. But the difference between previous classes of unemployed and these postindustrial casualties is that they can no longer expect their fortunes to rise with the next economic tide. The inequalities for this generation, like the global metastasis of the economy, are permanent. Despite this, liberal politicians call for "job training" and welfare reform. These proposals display an extravagant cynicism for they pretend that jobs for these young people, like the dead souls in Gogol's story, exist.

Remarkably, following the April 1992 riots, the immediate product of the truce declared between the two major South L.A. gang cartels was a set of recommendations that went beyond a jobs program and addressed comprehensive community needs. This Crips/Blood document reveals a faith, amounting to an apotheosis, in the virtues of capitalism, the responsiveness of government, and the goodwill of the community. Flyers distributed by the gangs in neighborhoods hit by the riots declared gang members' good intentions. "We will clean up our community from graffiti and trash and prove to the media, police and everyone else that we are not outcasts just out to do wrong."[65]

The nine-page Blood/Crips document includes suggestions to fund a community face-lift and infrastructure improvement; an education program that will refurbish school buildings, supply computers, and reward high achievers in math and science; a community policing proposal; a plan for funding economic development that would hire local employees; a demand that welfare "be completely removed from our community and . . . replaced by state work and product manufacturing plants," and a proposal to clean up parks and increase hospitals. In exchange for nearly $4 billion requested to support these programs, the gang leaders offer to stop drug traffic and divert funds from the drug business into "business and property in Los Angeles." The irony in the reasoned demands for modest urban aid in the Blood/Crips proposal lies in the fact that there is no leadership prepared to meet it.

The children of the black working class face extraordinary challenges that a generation ago would have been unthinkable. They face a labor market unable to absorb them, a political system that has abandoned them, and a culture unwilling to embrace them—except as criminals. In postriot Los Angeles, following the repudiation of liberalism in the 1994 elections, participation seems again to be a key issue for black leadership.

At First AME Church—the establishment founded by ex-slave Biddy Mason, the launching ground for Tom Bradley—the Disney Corporation held interviews for two hundred summer youth jobs. It was June 1992; the effects of the riots were everywhere. A crowd of working-class kids materialized, wearing their Sunday suits and clothes. A *New York Times* photograph showed one of them, a seventeen-year-old girl, smiling with the combination of guilelessness and watchfulness that seems the province of the adolescent. The girl appeared slim and well attired. She seemed unaware that she represented, as James Baldwin put it, "a social and not a personal or a human problem" that brings to mind "statistics, slums, rapes, injustices, remote violence, . . . the beast in our jungle of statistics."[66] The newspaper described her background with its impeccable proletarian credentials: she is the daughter of a nurse and a disabled roofer; her brothers and sisters work in a school cafeteria, as a cashier at Dodger Stadium, as a mail carrier, as a bus driver, as a custodian. In the logic of newspaper fairy tales, she inevitably gets one of the summer jobs at Disneyland and is thrilled; this quite transcends her previous employment at McDonald's. When confronted with her and the rest of the crowd, a Disney spokesman admitted being "taken aback." The sight of several hundred presentable black youngsters eager to work seemed to stun him as he confessed, "We didn't know they were there."

NOTES

1. Delihah L. Beasley, "Slavery in California," *Journal of Negro History* 3, no. 1 (January 1918): 50–54, California Freedom Documents.

2. *Black Angelenos, the Afro-American in Los Angeles, 1850–1950* Exhibition, 11

June 1988–6 March 1989, Lonnie Bunche, curator, California Afro-American Museum catalog, p. 18.

3. *Songs of Zion* (Nashville, Tenn.: Abingdon Press, 1981), hymn 135.

4. "State's Black-Owned Firms Thrive," *Los Angeles Times,* 9 May 1990, D1.

5. *Black Angelenos,* 21–22.

6. Otto Friederich, *City of Nets: A Portrait of Hollywood in the 1940's* (New York: Harper & Row, 1986), xii.

7. Ella Taylor, *Mirabella,* September 1992, 48.

8. Jess Kimbrough, *Defenders of the Angeles: A Black Policeman in Old Los Angeles* (London: Macmillan, 1969), vii–ix.

9. Raphael J. Sonenshein, *Politics in Black and White: Race and Power in Los Angeles* (Princeton: Princeton University Press, 1993), 33.

10. Ibid., 34.

11. Homer F. Broome, Jr., *LAPD's Black History, 1886–1976* (Norwalk, Calif.: Stockton Trade Press, 1978), 5.

12. Charlotta Bass, "On the Sidewalk," *California Eagle,* 27 August 1940, front page.

13. Carey McWilliams, *Southern California: An Island on the Land* (Salt Lake City: Peregrine Smith Books, 1973), 325.

14. *Black Angelenos,* 22.

15. James A. Fisher, "The Political Development of the Black Community in California, 1850–1950," *California Historical Quarterly* 50, no. 3 (1971): 257.

16. Quoted in Rudolph Lapp, *Afro-Americans in California* (San Francisco: Boyd & Fraser, 1987), 39.

17. Melvin L. Oliver and James H. Johnson, "Inter-Ethnic Conflict in an Urban Ghetto: The Case of Blacks and Latinos in Los Angeles," in *Proceedings of the Conference on Comparative Ethnicity* (Los Angeles: Institute for Social Science Research, 1988), 68.

18. Lawrence De Graf, "The City of Black Angels: Emergence of the Los Angeles Ghetto, 1890–1930," *Pacific Historical Review* 39, no. 2 (August 1970): 333–334.

19. Jerry Cohen and William S. Murphy, *Burn Baby Burn! The Los Angeles Race Riot, August 1965* (New York: Dutton, 1966), 12.

20. Arna Bontemps, *God Sends Sunday* (New York: Harcourt, Brace, 1931), 118.

21. *Black Angelenos,* 36.

22. Charlotta Bass, "On the Sidewalk," *California Eagle,* 5 December 1940, front page.

23. Sonenshein, *Politics in Black and White,* 28.

24. Don Parson, "Los Angeles' 'Headline-Happy Public Housing War,' " *Southern California Quarterly* (1983): 251–267.

25. Dennis R. Judd, "Segregation Forever?" *Nation,* 9 December 1991, 740.

26. *The City in Crisis: A Report by the Special Advisor to the Board of Police Commissioners on the Civil Disorder in Los Angeles,* 21 October 1992, 36.

27. Miles Corwin, "L.A.'s Loss: Black Flight," *Los Angeles Times,* 13 August 1992, A1.

28. "Blacks Lead in Rejections for Home Loans," *Los Angeles Times,* 6 September 1992, A1.

29. *The Black Community of Greater Los Angeles: A Community in Transition,* Full

Study Report, Black Partnership Development Council, United Way of Greater Los Angeles, 16 October 1991, chap. 2.

30. "Hypersegregation Traps U.S. Blacks in Ghetto, Study Finds," *Los Angeles Herald Examiner,* 5 August 1989, A1.

31. Thomas Bradley, *The Impossible Dream,* interview by Bernard Galm, Oral History Program, UCLA, 1984, 27.

32. Sonenshein, *Politics in Black and White,* 57.

33. "Malign Neglect" and "Malign Neglect II," *LA Weekly,* 30 December 1988–5 January 1989 and 28 August–3 September 1992.

34. Rudolph Lapp, *Afro-Americans in California* (San Francisco: Boyd & Fraser 1987), 9.

35. Kevin Robins, "Global Times," *Marxism Today,* December 1989, 20–27.

36. Richard Rodriguez, "Multiculturalism with No Diversity," *Los Angeles Times,* 10 May 1992, M1.

37. Cited in Robert L. Allen, *Black Awakenings in Capitalist America* (Trenton, N.J.: Africa World Press, 1990), 24.

38. Jason De Parle, "The Civil Rights Battle Was Easy Next to the Problems of the Ghetto," *New York Times,* 17 May 1992, sec. 4.

39. Gerald Horne, "Mandela's Way: The Road Not Taken," *Los Angeles Times,* 27 June 1990.

40. "American Blacks Talk of Change as Main Legacy of Mandela Visit," *New York Times,* 1 July 1990, 1.

41. Ibid.

42. Broome, *LAPD's Black History,* 1.

43. Jack Webb, *The Badge* (Englewood Cliffs, N.J.: Prentice Hall, 1958), 293–294.

44. Broome, *LAPD's Black History,* 97–98.

45. Webb, *The Badge,* 244.

46. W. H. Parker, Chief of Police, "The Police Role in Community Relations," *Daily Training Bulletin,* Los Angeles Police Department, vol. 4, bull. 41, 5 July 1955.

47. Paul Jacobs, *Prelude to Riot, A View of Urban America from the Bottom* (New York: Vintage Books, 1968), 22.

48. "Crime and the Great Society," address delivered by W. H. Parker, Chief of Police, Los Angeles, California, 18 February 1965.

49. *The Report of the Board of Police Commissioners Concerning the Shooting of Eulia Love and the Use of Deadly Force* (Los Angeles: Board of Los Angeles Police Commissioners, 1980), Pt. I, p. 1.

50. Ibid., 22.

51. Bayard Rustin, "From Protest to Politics: The Future of the Civil Rights Movement," in *Problems and Prospects of the Negro Movement* ed. Raymond Murphey and Howard Elinson, 409, 412 (Belmont, Calif.: Wadsworth, 1966).

52. Shawn Hubler, "South L.A.'s Poverty Rate Worse than '65," *Los Angeles Times,* 11 August 1992, A1.

53. Ruben Martinez, "This Was About Something to Eat," *Los Angeles Times,* 18 May 1992, Op-Ed.

54. Martin Oppenhemier, "Riot Ideology among Urban Negroes," in *Riots and*

Rebellions, ed. E. L. Quarantellis and Russel Dynes, 428 (Beverly Hills, Calif.: Sage Publications, 1968).

55. "The Widening Divide, Income Inequality and Poverty in Los Angeles," Research Group on the Los Angeles Economy, Paul Ong, Director, UCLA, 1989, 8.

56. Frank Clifford, "Rich-Poor Gulf Widens in State," *Los Angeles Times,* 11 August 1992, A1.

57. Robin Wright, "L.A. Riots Called Symptom of Worldwide Urban Trend," *Los Angeles Times,* 25 May 1992, A1.

58. Ibid.

59. *The City in Crisis,* 23.

60. Tim Rutten, "A New Kind of Riot," *New York Times Review of Books,* 14 May 1992, 52.

61. Eric Hobsbawm, "Looting in Civil Disorders, An Index of Social Change," in *Riots and Rebellions,* 139–140.

62. David Freed, "Los Angeles County Found Armed, Dangerous," *Los Angeles Times,* 17 May 1992.

63. *Black Community of Greater Los Angeles,* chap. 3.

64. "L.A.'s Black Poor Demand Law and Order," *Wall Street Journal,* 23 May 1989.

65. "Gang Truce Brings Hope of Peace," *Los Angeles Sentinel,* 14–20 May 1992, 1.

66. James Baldwin, *Notes of a Native Son* (New York: Bantam, 1972), 18, 22.

TWELVE

Latino Los Angeles

Reframing Boundaries/Borders

Raymond A. Rocco

I think that probably the biggest change is that now we are everywhere. When I was growing up in East L.A. in the fifties, you knew where the Mexican areas were, and when you wandered out of those, you saw very few of us in places like Santa Monica and the west side. But now, it doesn't matter where I go in L.A., there we are. It feels so different now. When I was a kid sometimes my dad would take me with him on his deliveries over in Culver City, West L.A., Santa Monica, even Beverly Hills, and I would feel kind of funny, you know what I mean? I felt out of place; I wouldn't see any other Mexicans at all. But now, hell, I feel at home almost everywhere because I know there is going to be somebody that looks like me, that talks like me, no matter where I am.
ROBERT GONZALEZ

Robert Gonzalez grew up during the 1950s in Belvedere, one of the oldest Mexican neighborhoods in East Los Angeles. He is one of the participants in an ongoing UCLA-based study, "Latino Community Formation in Los Angeles," designed to examine the causes and dynamics of the development of Latino communities that have been established during the last twenty-five years. The above is his response to a question we posed regarding what he thought had changed most about Los Angeles during his lifetime.

What Gonzalez describes, the extensive growth in the size and location of Latino communities, is indeed one of the most basic features of the dramatic and rapid changes that have transformed Los Angeles. This "Latinization" of Los Angeles, as some commentators have referred to the growth in the Latino population, has been part of a wide-ranging process of structural transformation in the region: a reconfiguration of the structure of social location (racial, ethnic, class, gender), of the demographic composition and distribution of the population, of political alignments, political actors, and policy agendas, of economic and fiscal landscapes; and the expansion of spatial boundaries and the development of new, nearly self-contained residential communities far removed from the urban reality.[1]

As a result, Los Angeles is extremely fragmented or extremely diverse, depending on one's perspective or ideology.[2] What is clear, even to the casual observer, is that there is more than one Los Angeles, that these "multiple Los Angeleses" are a defining characteristic of the region. This is not, however, a phenomenon peculiar to Los Angeles, although it is probably more visible and basic here. Processes of fundamental economic and cultural changes have transformed most major urban regions in the United States, resulting in a recomposition of the populations and a new set of political and policy issues.

These processes have transformed the Los Angeles of Robert Gonzalez's youth from a city with relatively segregated Mexican communities into one where Latino presence is pervasive.[3] However, the analysis of this transformation needs to go beyond the abstractions promoted by some multiculturalist approaches that simply note the coexistence of many different nationalities and racial and ethnic groups as a context for the study of urban realities. The dimensions of social location that are so often used to identify—to "place," to "situate"—different groups in the city need to be construed as more than only conceptual categories or spatial metaphors. We need to view each "Los Angeles" as constituting a particular, specific, and concrete way of living in and through the city that is both bounded by and linked to other sectors by its particular configuration of factors such as race, class, gender, immigrant status, political access, and economic resources.

As these configurations are the result of dynamic processes and shifting tendencies, the growth in the Latino population in Los Angeles has to be seen as more than simply an increase in population statistics. What has to be understood is that these processes of change have resulted in the emergence of new Latino *communities* and the transformation of older ones. Thus this process of Latino community formation needs to be situated within and in interaction with the pattern of changes in the broader structural and institutional context of the region.

In this essay, I present a general interpretation of the Latinization of Los Angeles as both cause and effect of these changes. The analysis proposes one way of understanding what has been involved in the transformation that Gonzalez alludes to, identifying the processes leading to the creation of new Latino communities, indicating some of the ways these changes have been experienced and interpreted by different sectors of Latino communities, and delineating some of the political and policy consequences. The following observations and analysis are based on extensive ethnographic studies and life histories carried out during the last four years.[4] First, let me provide a general sense of how the Los Angeles region has changed in terms of the rise of these new Latino communities.

LATINO LOS ANGELES:
RECONSTITUTING BORDERS/BOUNDARIES

As Robert Gonzalez recalls it, the Los Angeles of his youth was one where Mexican-origin communities had fairly clear spatial boundaries/borders, with all that is implied by this type of segregation. The established barrios in the Los Angeles area in the 1950s included communities like East Los Angeles, whose neighborhoods included Lincoln Park, Belvedere, and Maravilla. Other important Mexican communities were located in San Gabriel, San Fernando, Wilmington/San Pedro, and a small barrio in the Venice area. The pattern of labor market segmentation, housing discrimination, and political marginalization that led to the restricted nature of these communities has been illustrated in works by Rodolfo Acuña and Ricardo Romo.[5]

However, this particular configuration of Mexican community boundaries has been neither a consistent nor an even one. The historian George Sanchez has shown that the type of segregation that formed part of Gonzalez's experience existed in the late nineteenth century but that between 1900 and 1940, Mexican residents were more widely dispersed throughout the Los Angeles area, with the exception of the west side.[6] But between the early 1940s and the mid-1960s, the Mexican population once again found itself in relatively cohesive and segregated residential communities.

This is important to note because it reflects the fact that the development patterns of the Mexican communities have been neither static nor linear but have consistently been affected in fundamental ways by broader structural patterns and tendencies. Thus in our effort to account for the dynamic of development underlying the creation of new Latino communities since the 1960s, it is necessary to frame the issues in terms of the contextual dimensions that provided the historical horizon for the specific strategies of adaptation, resistance, accommodation, and change adopted by the Latino population.

But first we need to provide some sense of the size and characteristics of the different Latino communities of Los Angeles. The official estimate of the 1990 census is that 3.3 million Latinos lived in Los Angeles County, 76 percent (roughly 2.5 million) of whom are of Mexican origin. The next largest group consisted of Central Americans, numbering about 453,000, over half from El Salvador. However, the Mexican American Legal Defense Fund (MALDEF) estimates that nearly 430,000 Latinos were missed in that census. So a more accurate number is likely to be over 4 million. Among some of the other Latino groups, the official estimate is that there are nearly 100,000 South Americans, mostly from Colombia, Peru, Chile, and Argentina, and another 90,000 Spanish-speaking people from the Caribbean countries. There has thus been significant change in the composition of the Latino population since the late 1960s. Prior to that time, nearly all of the Spanish-speaking population in California was of Mexican origin. Since then, Latino communities have become more diverse. As the figures indicate, a large number of people from Central America, particularly El Salvador and Guatemala, now make Los Angeles home. And smaller but significant numbers have immigrated from Peru, Cuba, Colombia, Puerto Rico, and Argentina.

These figures reflect a dramatic change in the population base of the region. Between 1980 and 1990, the total population of Los Angeles County grew by 1.38 million residents, of which 1.24 million, or 89 percent, were Latinos. At the same time, 360,000 Anglo residents left the county, while the African-American population increased by 20,000 and the Asian population by 490,000. Thus it is clear that the majority of those new to the workforce, to the schools, and to the health care system, those seeking to rent or buy homes and apartments, were likely to be Latinos. This influx is obviously one of the principal causes of the transformation of communities and the dramatic increase in the number and location of neighborhoods with Latino majorities.[7]

But these data do not reveal where these populations have established cohesive communities or neighborhoods that are integrated by a range of personal, economic, cultural, educational, service, and recreational networks. Both our ethnographic studies and a review of census tract data indicate that these populations are spread throughout the Los Angeles area. Entire neighborhoods have been transformed into Latino communities, in some cases within a year. Latino communities with at least a minimal set of interactive networks now exist in a large number of areas of Los Angeles that previously had a very small or no Latino presence. While some of these began to form during the mid- to late 1960s, others have developed only very recently or are in the process of establishing themselves. One area where the early stages of the transition to a Latino majority was visible by the late 1960s was in Southeast L.A., previously an area of predominantly white working-class residential neighborhoods. The rate of growth here accelerated quickly during the 1970s and 1980s, and these communities are now over 90 percent Latino. The largest concentrations of Latinos in that region are in Maywood, Huntington Park, Bell, Bell Gardens, South Gate, and Lynwood. A similar pattern of growth occurred in adjacent areas, such as Pico Rivera, Montebello, Commerce, San Gabriel, and Rosemead, to name but a few.

More recently, substantial and relatively new Latino communities have also formed west of downtown, extending from the Pico-Union area to Santa Monica. An extensive barrio has developed, for example, in the Culver City/Mar Vista area on the West side, concentrated in a corridor that runs along Inglewood Boulevard, Centinela, and Sawtelle. The population of South Central Los Angeles is now at least 50 percent Latino and growing. And the percentage of Latinos residing in and close to the city of Santa Monica has increased dramatically. Whole areas of the San Fernando Valley, such as North Hollywood, Van Nuys, and Canoga Park, have been transformed into Latino communities, adding to the older areas such as the city of San Fernando and surrounding Pacoima.

Our ethnographic research also revealed that the dispersion and residential mobility of Latinos throughout Los Angeles is so great that many of their social networks overlap in spatial terms. Thus, for example, while there are distinct Latino areas in Southeast Los Angeles, the social networks of many of the residents that constitute the basis of community linkages overlap and crisscross spatial boundaries, extending to sections of the San Fernando Valley, Hollywood, Orange County, and the San Gabriel Valley. Thus it is clear that the tendency to identify communities primarily or only in terms of physical spatial boundaries is of limited value. Rather, it is cultural space that seems to form the basis of community networks.

While the Mexican population continues to predominate in most of these areas, there are particular neighborhoods where significant numbers of the other groups have established an integrated system of social relations, networks, services, restaurants, stores, medical practitioners, cultural practices, and so on. Thus Salvadorans and Nicaraguans have established extensive networks in the Pico-Union area. Peruvians have created close-knit economic, social, and recreational networks in both South Gate and Hawthorne. Some of the businesses, whose clients are primarily Latinos, have been so successful that they have branched out into three and four locations. One Peruvian restaurant, Pollo Inka, has locations in Hawthorne, Torrance, Orange County, the San Fernando Valley, and Redondo Beach. A Cuban restaurant is flourishing in an otherwise Anglo community in predominantly Anglo Hermosa Beach, and yet the majority of customers are Latinos. Other businesses serving Latino customers are to be found throughout the city and in areas that as recently as two years ago had almost no Latinos. These businesses and service providers that cater to Latinos have been one of the important ways that we have used to identify the spatial location of new Latino communities.

Significant numbers and networks of Cubans, some of which control access to the distribution of Latin American music to retail outlets in Los Angeles, appear to be expanding very quickly. Colombian organizations sponsor monthly dances and get-togethers that in reality serve as a major mechanism for maintaining their social networks and also to help orient and incorporate recent arrivals into the new environment, very often by finding both temporary and permanent housing, furniture, and jobs. *Actualidad,* published by Peruvians, and *El Colombiano,* published by Colombians, are regularly circulated throughout the region through Latin American restaurants, nightclubs, record shops, and travel agencies.

Many of these types of activities that are the basis of communities in formation have been established in older Mexican communities for many decades. The publication of newspapers, a large network of voluntary and regional associations, cultural institutions, and networks that provided food, clothing, shelter, and job information for recently arrived immigrants were also part of the process of the growth pattern of Mexican communities going back more than a century in Los Angeles. In fact, many of the small communities of other Latino groups are spatially within or adjacent to Mexican neighborhoods. The pattern of interaction between the Mexican population and the other Latino groups is an uneven one, however, and in most cases that we examined was relatively limited. Culturally, Latino communities have flourished and have established associations to ensure that there is continuity between the culture of origin and both the form and content of the social relations that are established here.

The development of these new communities, however, was not an isolated phenomenon but part of a process of transformation in the spatial and social landscape of the Los Angeles region.[8] Thus as Latino immigrants moved into areas with large concentrations of African-Americans, such as South Central Los Angeles, Watts, and Compton, there was an out-migration of the latter group into sections of areas farther west, such as Inglewood and Hawthorne, previously populated by a majority of whites. There was also substantial movement south to previously predominantly white neighborhoods in the Long Beach area. Thus Latino migration into certain areas in turn resulted in many non-Latino residents moving to outlying areas. According to some of our non-Latino respondents, this was one of the factors in the development of new residential communities in areas such as Valencia, Saugus, and Newhall in the Santa Clarita Valley, as well as in other areas such as the Simi Valley, Calabasas, and even Oxnard.

What has driven these processes of expansion and creation of new Latino communities? We can begin to answer this question by returning to the observation made earlier that the development of new Latino communities has both transformed Los Angeles and been transformed by Los Angeles in fundamental ways. This has been part of a process of restructuring that occurred in the city since 1970 at several levels and along different axes.

ECONOMIC RESTRUCTURING

The basic dynamics of the economic restructuring that has occurred over the last twenty-five years have been presented in great detail in both general terms[9] and in the specific form it has taken in the Los Angeles area.[10] One of the most apparent changes in Los Angeles since 1970 is the dramatic increase in the size of the Latino immigrant population. And this growth has been a principal factor in promoting the pattern of Latino community formation beyond previously established Latino neighborhoods. What is not so apparent but is nevertheless made clear by the literature is that there is a direct relationship between the basic forces behind restructuring and the increase in immigration from Latin America and Asia. Of course, the connection is not a one-dimensional or simple one but is mediated through other factors as well. The restructuring process has been driven by policies adopted by capital since the late 1960s to change its relationship to labor. Clearly, this has not been a uniform process but has taken different forms and has occurred in different ways in particular countries.

The detailed analysis of this process that Saskia Sassen has carried out demonstrates that, quite ironically, the economic policies pursued by the United States, particularly through its role in the International Monetary Fund and the World Bank, have themselves been one of the major reasons for the rapid growth of large immigrant communities throughout the United States. As Sassen indicates,

> U.S. efforts to open its own and other countries' economies to the flow of capital, goods, services and information created conditions that mobilized people for migration and formed linkages between the United States and other countries which subsequently served as bridges for migration. . . . Measures commonly thought to deter emigration—foreign investment, or the promotion of export-oriented agriculture and manufacturing in poor countries—have had precisely the opposite effect. Such investment contributes to massive displacement of small-scale agricultural and manufacturing enterprises, while simultaneously deepening the economic, cultural and ideological ties between the recipient countries and the United States. These factors encourage migration.[11]

In addition to the displacement of traditional economic arrangements and the establishing of strong ties with the United States, it is also the case that the conversion to export-driven economies decimated the middle class and lowered the domestic standard of living in these countries, even as the overall economic output was increasing—most of it targeted for external markets. This contributed to the migration during the 1980s of well-educated, skilled labor, particularly from Mexico, Peru, Colombia, Chile, and Argentina.

The same international economic policies and processes that were promoting investment and the expansion of manufacturing jobs in low-wage countries also directly altered the nature of the demand for labor in the domestic economy of the United States. The domestic traditional manufacturing sector went through a process of deindustrialization—reindustrialization that greatly downgraded (or "downsized," as the current corporate language calls it) the labor demand, resulting in the growth of low-wage, semiskilled or unskilled jobs. Coupled with the job growth in the high-technology sector and the great increase in subcontracting (including sweatshops and home work), what resulted was an economy characterized by very distinct and different labor markets for immigrant labor and for middle-class, high-technology, and professional labor and by a highly polarized and fragmented social fabric. Thus the long-standing popular anti-immigrant sentiment tapped into by the disclosures last year that Cabinet nominees hired undocumented immigrants, and which has been given political expression in Proposition 187 and aroused such passionate divisions, is a situation set in motion by the United States itself.

Although the economic dimensions and consequences of the restructuring were fundamental in promoting migration from Latin America, in some cases there were other factors that played a significant role. For example, in the case of many immigrants from El Salvador, Nicaragua, and Guatemala, war, and the economic and other kinds of dislocations it caused, was a primary reason for leaving. Based on our interviews and ethnographic work, it appears that the economic and political motivations were often intertwined. As some of the Central Americans we talked with indicated, war ruined the economies in their countries and made economic survival even more problematic than before.

COMMUNITY TRANSFORMATIONS

While the analysis above details the changes occurring at the macroinstitutional level, it tells us little about how the social, cultural, and political life of the Los Angeles region has been affected.[12] What is the relationship between these forces and the nature and pattern of the everyday social practices and relationships that emerge as strategies in response to them? By trying to answer this, we can begin to understand why Latino communities have exploded throughout the region and we can trace the impact on the lives of families and households in the region, to see how social and spatial relations have been transformed and how race and class realities have reconfigured the political landscape and agenda of Los Angeles.

As it is not possible to analyze each of the relevant communities in Los Angeles, we will focus on a specific region, Southeast Los Angeles, as a case study. While not all of the types of changes discussed here are to be found in Southeast Los Angeles, the transformation of this region does illustrate how both the specific processes and the particular impact of restructuring have affected the growth in Latino communities.

The study was designed and based on a framework similar to that outlined by Louise Lamphere in a recent ethnographic study of immigration.[13] She offers a general approach that addresses the issue we have focused on: how to conceptualize and empirically examine the dynamic nature of the relationships between institutional, structural levels and the practices of everyday life. The argument is that only a combination of macrolevel data on the local political economy and microlevel qualitative observations can provide an adequate understanding of the nature of changes in local communities. The linkage between these two levels is made both theoretically and empirically by establishing and identifying "mediating institutions" as the actual and specific sites of participation and practice of real individuals and groups. The pattern of interrelations that constitute communities takes form and develops within these mediating institutions, some of which Lamphere identifies as the workplace, school system, housing complexes, and community organizations, to which we add the household, families, and household networks.

These sites are where the changes in the broader institutional arenas, such as, for example, a particular economic sector, are translated into specific outcomes that affect individuals and groups who labor at these "worksites" at the everyday level of social relations and practices. These are the sites where the reality and the relations of race, class, gender, immigrant status, and so on, are constructed and "lived." It is here that these realities and relations are formed as actual practices that establish social location. And this is where these categories and dimensions are realized and concretized as specific mechanisms by which structural inequalities in power and wealth are produced, distributed, maintained, and altered and by which they are incorporated as strategies that define the parameters for the negotiation of social identity. To use an example from Lamphere, large-scale economic changes may decrease the tax base for a community school system, which in turn may lead to hiring and wage policies that result in high teacher turnover, and which, at a particular school, may affect the type and nature of programs offered. And the options for those decisions will surely be considered within the particular configuration of race, class, gender, and immigrant status. This is the site, then, where the changes in macrolevel forces are brought to bear on microlevel relationships.[14]

Within this framework the link between the institutional and the everyday levels is established by tracing the processes of interaction, the patterns of relations, and the strategies and interpretation that form at these specific sites and levels of practice. Using this general approach, we can examine the original issue, that is, what has been involved in the process by which a particular region in Los Angeles has undergone a complete transformation and become a series of Latino communities, how members of these particular communities have lived out and interpreted these changes, and

TABLE 12.1   Latino Concentrations in Southeast Los Angeles

City	Total Population	Latino	% Latino
Maywood	27,850	25,900	93
Huntington Park	56,065	51,579	92
Commerce	12,135	11,042	91
Cudahy	22,817	20,307	89
Bell Gardens	42,355	37,272	88
Bell	34,365	29,554	86
Pico Rivera	59,177	49,117	83
South Gate	86,284	71,616	83

what this means in terms of politics and public policy. I want, then, to use this discussion to suggest what this tells us about how other Latino communities have developed throughout the Los Angeles area.

Using this general framework, the case study focuses on the region of Southeast Los Angeles, once known as the Rust Belt, that includes incorporated cities such as Huntington Park, South Gate, Maywood, Bell, Bell Gardens, Vernon, and Cudahy; unincorporated areas such as Walnut Park; and parts of Los Angeles that have been designated "South Central" by the L.A. City Planning Office. The reason for selecting this region is that it has undergone one of the most rapid processes of change in California. For example, the Latino population in Huntington Park went from 4.5 percent in 1960 to 35.9 percent in 1970 to 85 percent in 1986 and to 92 percent in 1990. And these changes, the transformations, are clearly a function of the general restructuring process, which has affected not only its economic profile but its cultural, demographic, and political makeup as well. And because of the very rapid transformation, it has not been difficult to locate respondents who have lived it.

The degree of concentration of Latinos in this region is reflected in the data for 1990 contained in table 12.1.[15] While the table indicates the high concentration of Latinos in these communities, we need to outline what it was about the restructuring process that propelled the transformation.

Initially, it was part of a more general closing of major manufacturing firms and loss of jobs in California. In the short span of three years, 1980 to 1983, 157,000 manufacturing jobs were lost in the state of California, mostly in the steel, rubber, civilian aircraft, and auto industries. In Southeast Los Angeles, the specifics of the economic restructuring process was a mix of large and small closures and changes. For example, some 8,000 jobs left the city of South Gate in a four-year period early in the 1980s when General Motors, Firestone Tires, Weiser Lock, and Fed Mart closed. During roughly the same period, Chrysler Credit Corporation closed three new car dealerships, Dodge, Jeep Eagle, and Chrysler/Plymouth/Hyundai. While the number of jobs lost, 175, was significant, it was relatively small compared to GM and the other large firms. But another dimension of the effects of restructuring can be seen in this case: the city of South Gate received 20 percent of its sales taxes from these three firms, nearly $5.6 million, and thus its ability to provide services and maintain its operations was considerably undermined.

Other plant closures and job losses included the shutdown in December 1982 of Bethlehem Steel located in the city of Vernon. Over 2,000 men and women were let go that Christmas, and the main union of steelworkers, Local 1845 in nearby Huntington Park, became a food bank to help workers get through that period. In 1989, Dial Corporation discontinued its production of household liquid bleach at its Purex plant in South Gate, and later, in December 1991, it closed all of its operations there. Oscar Mayer was another major Vernon employer that shut down, displacing its entire workforce, most of whom had been with the company for at least ten years. Some of these industrial sites had played a major role in the development of the region over a long period and had established important social ties with the cities; for example, the Dial Corporation had been in the same plant for fifty years and GM had opened its plant in 1936. Despite this, there was virtually no consideration by management of the impact these closures would have on their host cities and communities.

But it was not only job loss that was involved here. The nature of the labor market and labor demand was also transformed. The jobs that were lost were primarily unionized, higher-paying employment with good health, retirement, and other benefits. Yet during the very same period, other sectors were developing which employed low-wage, nonunionized, semiskilled Latino immigrant labor. Thus, although the city of Vernon lost a great number of jobs, its low-wage sector expanded by 8,000 to 10,000 jobs, primarily in the garment industry. It now has more than one hundred garment plants, many with sweatshop conditions and all with a high percentage of immigrant female employees.

The restructuring scenario in Southeast Los Angeles was clearly driven by the dramatic change in economic profile. The closing of major plants and the loss of jobs and revenue that resulted set in motion a process of rapid and complete transformation of the region that included demographic, cultural, political, and household restructuring. While table 12.1 provides an indication of the high concentration of Latinos in the area, what is not apparent is the high percentage of immigrant Latinos. Although it varies by city, the immigrant population is estimated to average close to 50 percent. This is a region that in the 1960s was primarily Anglo. While the restructuring process did not determine the specific processes of community transition and formation, it did, however, create the conditions for them.

Latino immigrants came to this Los Angeles region between 1970 and 1990, driven both by the economic structural changes we described and by some of the consequences of these changes. One of the major reasons for the dramatic increase of Latinos in this specific region of Southeast Los Angeles had to do with the decrease in property values that resulted from the loss of jobs and revenues. The Anglo working class, economically displaced by the forces of restructuring, left the area. Home prices and rents dropped dramatically. And since newly arriving, economically strapped Latino immigrants must of necessity seek out the low-rent areas, they gravitated toward Southeast Los Angeles. Once established as a community, of course, the area attracted more immigrants on the basis of cultural familiarity. Small commercial and retail businesses to service these new communities soon followed. In fact, it was this transition that revitalized the economic base of the region. Thus, for example, in the vital commercial strip along Pacific Boulevard in Huntington Park, nearly 50 percent of the business sites were vacant in the mid-1970s. These were businesses that were oriented both culturally and in class terms to high-wage working-class and middle-class Anglo tastes. When that population left, the businesses collapsed. In their place arose businesses that responded to the needs and tastes of the immigrant Latino, and by the early 1980s, the strip was a thriving commercial zone with nearly no vacancies and an important site not only economically but socially and culturally as well.

LIVES IN TRANSITION

But this is not the whole story. Key to understanding this process of the formation of new Latino communities is tracing the way in which this process of restructuring, with the explosion in immigration, has transformed the lives of those who live in these new communities and how these changes have been lived out and interpreted at the level of everyday practices by both the immigrants and the older generation of Latino residents, whose lives have also been transformed in this process.[16]

It is at this level that we can uncover what the structural changes that have transformed the city mean for those who live in these communities and thereby get a sense of how L.A. is lived and experienced by Latinos. It is through their stories of strategies of adaptation, resistance, accommodation, and transformation that the restructuring process becomes grounded and reveals how one of those "multiple Los Angeleses" has become what it is.[17] To illustrate what some of these experiences and strategies are and how they have functioned in relation to the dimensions of the restructuring process described above, I draw on the ethnographies and life histories of men and women who live or have lived in Southeast Los Angeles. They reveal to us some key insights into the process of creating a new community, the multiple ways in which the restructuring processes have affected Latinos—some benefiting, some losing everything—and about the struggle, full of contradictions, to both engage and resist popular U.S. culture.

This region is heavily Latino, nearly 85 percent Mexican origin, with small pockets of Central Americans, Peruvians, Colombians, and Cubans, some of whom have established small communities of their own and some of whom are spread throughout the area. We carried out our life history interviews with nearly seventy Latino, mostly Mexican, families and households and about twenty households representing other Latino groups. I also spent hundreds of hours with different families and household members, accompanying them as they carried out their daily or weekly routines: sharing meals; attending weddings, baptisms, funerals, dances, parties, and *quin- cenieras;* shopping with them at different markets and commercial sites; eating at many of the small restaurants and food stands in the area; attending meetings of various cultural and rotating credit and burial insurance organizations; attending PTA meetings and meetings of a Spanish-speaking parents organization; and visiting hospitals, doctors offices, and employment and welfare offices.

I present some of the results of this research in two different ways. First, I provide a brief summary of some of the general themes related to the effect of the restructuring on people's lives. While this provides an overview of the range of concerns and perspectives that characterize respondents in these communities, I also present more in-depth analyses of four households that illustrate both the texture of Latino experiences and some of the ways those experiences affect and are affected by broader institutional contexts.

THEMATIC STRUCTURES

We discovered that while the respondents discussed a broad range of topics and issues in their open-ended dialogues, there were certain common themes and concerns that arose out of and in response to their interactions and activities in specific institutional sites, particularly the following: immigration experience, education, language, family cohesion, intra-Latino cultural and class divisions, the work ethic, and discrimination.

However, there are clear differences on these issues along the dimensions of class, gender, country of origin, length of residence, and generation. What quickly became apparent was the extraordinarily heterogeneous nature of these Latino communities. Although it is often assumed that the immigrant experience is the same for most Latinos, we found that this was not the case.

With regard to the immigrant experience, many different stories were told, but there was in all of them the notion of a break, a disjunction and shock that resulted from coming to the United States. Even those who had adopted a very patriotic stance toward the United States recounted having encountered difficulty with the transition at several levels. Even they talked about feeling slighted and discriminated against by non-Latinos simply because they were Latinos. And even those who were critical of immigrants who did not want to assimilate to the new culture still felt a much closer sense of commonality with them and had much more interaction with them than with non-Latinos.

And, of course, we found that some families, both immigrants and longer-term residents, were very nationalistic. The form this nationalism took differed on the basis of immigrant status. For example, the nationalism of second- and third-generation Latinos tends to rest on a selective version and interpretation of what it means to be Mexican, or Cuban, or Puerto Rican that normally coincides with a particular period in the past. So some third-generation Mexicans complained that Mexico had become very different from what they identify as central to being "Mexican."

Still the practices and symbols they continue to engage in as an expression of their Mexican identity are those associated with a previous period. Thus for this generation Mexican music is mariachis and trios, not rock or classical. The same occurs with popular culture, courtship practices, and other areas of cultural identification. Yet there is a basic and common identification as being Mexican.

Within the household and families, the difference in gender roles was a common and major concern and was key in determining the pattern of responsibilities, rights, and privileges. In some households where the gender relations were defined in traditional male-centric patterns, privileging males in terms of power and rights, the women nevertheless were critical of that practice, although they would not express their opinions in front of their male partners. In most instances, however, particularly when women worked outside the home, the assertion of certain claims and expectations about their male partners' responsibilities had clearly been incorporated into the relationship. And they all agreed that the immigrant experience itself—of the women often being alone and having to care for themselves and their children, of being out in the workplace—has changed the gender relations in Latino communities.

The work ethic and education were themes that were often linked and discussed in terms of the requirements for upward mobility. In most of the households of our respondents, the work ethic was simply assumed as a necessity, the identification with this varying according to class differences, but it was a constant for most. Work is seen primarily in instrumental terms. Even the few professionals who talked about this, while they tended to feel more pride in their position, mostly shared this instrumental view. And education was clearly linked to a better job. Most families with children emphasized education for their offspring as the key to a better life. Most of the immigrant households felt that they had to sacrifice to ensure that their children would become educated. And they clearly linked the need for education to the changing economic situation and labor demand.

Last, we found a considerable difference among some divisions according to both class and country of origin. The life histories made it clear that the level of structured and organized interaction between the different Latino groups is very small. And many of our respondents talked about negative images that some of the groups had of each other. These seem to be rooted not only in the fact that the countries they come from have different histories and traditions but also in the way their engagement with the United States is viewed. Thus, for example, among the Mexican households, we found that some clearly saw the other Latino groups as "late-comers" who were now reaping the benefits of their struggles to gain access to jobs and their having established new communities, services, and so on. Some of the Central Americans, in particular, felt that the Mexicans acted as if they were superior and discriminated against their groups in both subtle and obvious ways. Several argued that this was particularly evident in the workplace, where Mexican foremen, floor leaders, and jobbers clearly treated Mexican workers in a preferential way in job assignments, responsiveness to requests and suggestions, and social interaction. They complained that the Mexicans were clannish and treated members of other groups rudely and disrespectfully. Even those Central Americans who did not share this view were very aware of the tension between the two groups.

Some of the families from South America, however, reflected a different view. They seemed much more inclined to view both Mexican and Central American immigrants more in terms of social distance and class standing, or at least self-perception of class standing. Even some who were clearly struggling economically tended to think of these groups as being primarily below them in terms of class. But the interesting thing here is that class was construed not primarily in economic terms but rather reflected a conception based on factors such as social manners, education, and moral values. One can be poor but be superior in "class" to those with higher economic standing. Several of the respondents talked about *una persona educada,* an educated person. The reference here is not to formal education but to a person who knows how to respect others, fulfills his or her obligations, does not intrude or impose on others, and has both the desire and intellect to *superarse,* to better themselves.

TRES HISTORIAS

While these themes provide some of the broad parameters of Latino experiences and perspectives, we can illustrate more clearly the texture of life in these communities by examining the specific experiences of a particular household. The following discussion focuses on four households that have very different characteristics.

La Familia Najera

The Najera household is an extended Mexican immigrant family of seven, including a married couple, Mario (43) and Lucia (36); three daughters, Maria Luisa (15), Isabel (13), and Nancy (3); a son, Daniel (9); and Lucia's aunt, Gloria (38), who has been part of the household for the past four years. They have lived in Huntington Park for ten years; before that, they lived in South Central Los Angeles for six years. Mario and Lucia married in 1974 in Uruapán, in the state of Morelia. At the time of their marriage, Mario was twenty-three and Lucia was sixteen. In 1977, Lucia secured a work permit with the help of a businessman in Los Angeles who had been a boyhood friend of her father. She came to Los Angeles in late 1977 and stayed with the family of a man from her neighborhood who had immigrated to the United States in 1971 and at that time lived in Norwalk. His wife helped find Lucia a job as a domestic, and she later went to work in a garment factory in downtown Los Angeles. Mario crossed the border illegally in 1978 and joined Lucia. He found work in a small neighborhood market in South Central Los Angeles, and they rented their own apartment there later that year.

Since Mario had worked for several years as a butcher in Mexico, the next year he was able to secure a fairly high-paying job in a small but busy meat processing plant in an area close to Huntington Park. Although Lucia stopped working at the factory several times during her pregnancies, she nevertheless continued to work at home, taking in wash and ironing and at one point sewing clothes for neighbors and friends. With their combined incomes, Mario and Lucia were able to save enough to purchase a small home in Huntington Park in 1984.

However, in 1990, a national meat processing plant bought out the firm where Mario worked and restructured the business. Meat was no longer prepared and cut at the facility; instead it served primarily as a retail outlet. The butcher positions were eliminated and of the twenty-six-member work crew, only eight were offered a position with the new firm. The primary work was now packaging meat that was cut and prepared in a central plant in the San Fernando Valley. As a butcher, Mario had made nearly $15 per hour, with plenty of overtime, but his new position paid only $6.40 per hour, with no overtime. His annual income was reduced by nearly two-thirds. Although angry at first, Mario now considers himself fortunate to have been one of the workers who was kept on the job, especially since he has been unable to find a job as a butcher anywhere else.

This experience has had a fundamental impact on the Najera household. Only a few weeks before the firm was sold, the husband of Lucia's aunt, Gloria, was killed, and she was left in Mexico without any means of support. The Najeras invited her to join their household, believing at the time that this would not impose any significant economic hardship. But with the reduction in Mario's income, an additional member in the household placed greater strain on an already difficult situation.

The Najeras have had a difficult time meeting all of their financial obligations and once fell behind in their house payment. As a result, they asked Gloria to find work so that she could contribute to the family income. She worked at several low-wage jobs and is currently a waitress in a restaurant in Boyle Heights. Even Maria Luisa, now fifteen years old, works part-time in a card shop in Huntington Park. The family has discussed the possibility of moving to either San Jose, California, or Las Vegas, Nevada, where friends have indicated that better-paying work is available. But they are reluctant to leave the life they have established over the last fifteen years.

Despite the impact the reduced income has had on the household, the Najeras continue to sustain the network of social and cultural activities they established during their time in Los Angeles. In addition to family friends, both Mario and Lucia have separate networks organized around their activities outside the household. For Mario, this revolves around his membership in a soccer club, which he helped found in 1982. At least twice a week, often more, he attends practices, games, and meetings or just "hangs out" with club members. More recently, particularly on weekends, he has begun to go alone to Mexican dances sponsored by the civic club Morelia in Huntington Park.

Lucia's activities outside the home center on her involvement since 1989 in a Spanish-speaking parents association that was organized to promote greater involvement of Latino parents in educational issues. Lucia attends a general meeting once a month and neighborhood meetings once a week.

The Najeras' story illustrates many of the realities that restructuring promoted, and their pattern of experiences and activities reveals aspects of other sectors of Latino Los Angeles. For example, both of the jobs that Mario held were created by firms servicing the expanding Latino population in the area. The higher-wage job with a larger firm was atypical of the type of positions normally created during the deindustrialization of the area. Eventually, however, that job too succumbed to the same logic of restructuring, albeit in a different sector. One of the explicit goals of the restructuring process was to develop strategies to replace higher-paying, unionized jobs with lower-paying, nonunionized ones. This is exactly what dramatically altered the Najera household. His job as a butcher in a unionized plant provided Mario with a relatively high wage and health and unemployment benefits. However, the new firm circumvented the union and offers no benefits whatsoever. So not only was Mario's direct wage cut by over half, but when the value of the lost benefits is added, Mario's income was in effect reduced by nearly 75 percent.

The Najeras' decision to settle in Huntington Park was also directly related to the process of restructuring that transformed the region. The flight of both large- and small-scale firms and businesses, and the large-scale movement of established households that resulted, brought about a drop in property values that made homes in the region much more affordable than in most other residential areas of Los Angeles. In addition, by the time the Najeras decided to buy a home, the residents of this section of Southeast Los Angeles were predominantly immigrant Latinos, so that they felt that the social environment was a familiar one, offering a full range of services, stores, and commercial outlets staffed by predominantly Spanish-speaking Latinos.

Another dramatic change brought about by the family's altered economic position was apparent in the area of medical care. Before the buyout, Mario's employer contributed $70 a month for a group medical insurance plan with the Kaiser HMO made available through the company. This program covered the entire family, except Gloria, and as a result the Najeras worried little about getting relatively good quality, quick medical care for themselves and, most important, for their children. With the loss of Mario's medical benefits and the significant decrease in family income, family illness now means seeking medical care at Harbor General County Hospital, where charges for medical care are based on income.

In my first visit to the hospital with Lucia and her young daughter, Nancy, I discovered yet another dire reality that thousands of Latinos must confront daily. Nearly three-fourths of the patients in the visibly overcrowded waiting room were Latinos, a large proportion of them children. Discussions I initiated with hospital staff and other patients revealed that waiting periods of six hours are not uncommon, that the staff is understaffed by nearly 30 percent, and that caseloads exceed capacity by nearly 50 percent. In this particular instance, we arrived at 9:30 A.M., but Nancy, obviously in great discomfort from a serious bout with the flu, was not seen by a physician until nearly 1:30 that afternoon. By the time Nancy had some lab work done, was seen once again by the doctor, and had a prescription filled at the hospital pharmacy, it was 3:45 P.M. This is apparently not uncommon. Both Lucia and other patients I spoke with indicated that they expect to spend most of the day at the hospital whenever they seek medical care there.

Another matter that worried both Mario and Lucia was their children's education. Until 1991, both their young daughters, Maria Luisa and Isabel, attended a nearby Catholic school. While the Najeras believed that the girls would receive a much better education there, their real concern was to prevent them from being exposed to gangs, drugs, and violence at the overcrowded public schools in the area. However, Mario and Lucia were forced to transfer their children from the Catholic school because they simply could no longer afford the tuition. This continues to be one of the more painful experiences for the Najera family. Both parents constantly worry about their children while they attend school, and Lucia, in particular, is bitter about this situation.

Accompanying the adult members of the household as they went about their various activities, I learned a great deal about the social and cultural life that the emerging Latino communities in the area have established. Since many of those in the area work Saturdays, Sunday is family day, and on several occasions, I was invited to join the Najeras. They indicated that their routine was fairly typical of other Mexican families in the area. And, indeed, my work with other such households revealed that this seemed to be the case.

After breakfast, the family attends an early Mass at a church where nearly all the other worshipers are Latinos. Then they either visit friends or go shopping. Before the change in their economic fortunes, Lucia said they would have headed for the mile-long commercial shopping strip on Pacific Boulevard to buy clothing or small household items. But these days, they are much more likely to go to the nearby permanent swap meet in Vernon. The latter is extremely crowded with mostly families and resembles the *mercados,* or marketplaces, found in Mexico much more than the traditional swap meet. Stalls are located inside two warehouselike buildings and on the grounds surrounding them. Nearly every conceivable item is available here: plumbing supplies, tools, all sorts of clothing, auto parts, appliances, even car and life insurance. And the smells of homemade Mexican and Central American food from what seem to be dozens of food stands and stalls permeates the entire area. While Mario and the children seem to enjoy this outing, Lucia constantly complains about the noise, the crowds, the disorder, the inferior quality of the merchandise, and not being able to afford to shop either on Pacific Boulevard or at the mall as she used to. And while a few years back they would have had lunch at one of the area's restaurants, they now eat at one of the much less expensive food stalls.

The Rivas

At Mario's workplace, I was introduced to two Salvadoran and one Peruvian co-workers. After several discussions on different occasions, these three volunteered to participate in the research project and I was invited to their homes.

One of these men, Armando Rivas, is from San Salvador and lives with his Salvadoran common-law wife, Teresa, in an apartment in South Central Los Angeles, though both have their main social ties with households in Hollywood and the Pico-Union area. In these communities, different holidays are celebrated; the food is different (for example, the rice is a different color and texture and huge tamales are wrapped in banana leaves instead of corn husks); salutations follow a different ritual; and many words commonly used by the Mexican immigrants have different meanings. The networks for providing information about jobs and housing are based in specific locations established by and frequented by members of these communities. Particular restaurants and meetings of specific social and civic clubs are widely known in these communities as the center of such information. Thus there is always a group of people that congregates in several small retail stores, markets, barber shops, beauty salons, and restaurants along an eight-block stretch of Pico Boulevard, between Union and Normandie just west of downtown Los Angeles. At any given time, there are a whole series of activities taking place there, from card games and dominoes to the dissemination of information on bargain airfares, short- and long-term jobs, housing, news and gossip about specific neighborhoods and even particular families still in El Salvador, and the availability on a barter basis of different services and or goods, such as used furniture and appliances. There is usually a steady stream of patrons having tarot card readings.

The Piñedos

I was introduced to the Peruvian community by Eduardo Piñedo (age 38), who, as mentioned before, works with Mario Najera at the meat processing plant, where he is the accountant and assistant business manager. He lives in a section of South Gate that has larger and more expensive homes. His wife, Magda (age 32), is from Medellín, Colombia, and manages a travel agency in downtown Los Angeles that specializes in booking flights to South America. While the household has a cordial relationship with Mexican and Central American co-workers and acquaintances, their social and cultural linkages are exclusively with other South Americans, primarily Peruvians, Colombians, and Ecuadorians.

The Piñedo household exposed me to yet another segment of Latino Los Angeles, one that reveals the vibrant social, cultural, and night life that is a vital part of these communities. The Piñedos are quite active socially and seem to entertain friends nearly every weekend. These occasions regularly include eight or more people. There is always food, of course, both Colombian and Peruvian. And most drink either the Colombian liqueur, *aguardiente,* or the Peruvian *pisco sour.* And music constantly plays, not as background, but to create a certain atmosphere, so that conversation is always loud and seems to be carried through the music. There seems to be a pattern to the music and the activities. Initially, while conversations are more individual, relatively smooth, popular salsa music is played. After the meal, everyone settles in one area and begins a collective dialogue about a full range of topics, but inevitably, this ends up with the telling of *cuentos,* literally stories, but in reality these are the most current jokes, elaborately told by nearly everyone in rotation. As this breaks up, the tempo of the music picks up and dancing begins. At the end of the session, which can last seven or eight hours, the group once again settles down and listens nostalgically to traditional Peruvian and Colombian music. With some variation, this pattern is repeated in different households the Piñedos visit, and it seems to be an activity organized to both sustain close personal bonds and re-create and recapture some of the cultural practices of their homeland.

This also seems to be one of the objectives of other activities the Piñedos engage in. They regularly attend functions sponsored by both the major Peruvian and Colombian cultural organizations in Los Angeles, always celebrate their respective independence days, and regularly go dancing at several of the salsa clubs throughout Los Angeles and Orange County. Nearly ten years ago, Eduardo established a deejay business that offers exclusively Latin American dance music, such as salsa, merengue, and cumbia, and traditional music from both Peru and Colombia. He often provides the music for some of the social and cultural functions sponsored by various Peruvian and Colombian clubs, as well as weddings, birthdays, and house parties.

The development of the Latino social, music, and club scene that the Piñedos are part of has clearly been a function of the kind of transformation of communities described earlier. While this existed on a very small scale in Los Angeles before the large influx of Latin Americans, it is now a vital part of the local economy. While in the early 1970s only three clubs existed which regularly presented Latin American music, now there are over forty clubs and restaurants in Los Angeles and Orange County that offer a broad range of environments for listening and dancing, from small local restaurants to large, plush, Latin American-style nightclubs. But beyond this development, the changes have promoted a whole new economic sector, including record shops and outlets, radio stations and advertising, as well as several magazines and reviews exclusively devoted to reporting on both local and national Latino nightlife, music, and entertainers. Clearly, this would have been impossible twenty years ago since the constituency simply did not exist.

RESTRUCTURING AND COMMUNITY POLITICS

The processes of restructuring and the pattern of dynamic growth of Latino communities throughout the Los Angeles region that we have described here have not only transformed the region's social and cultural landscapes but have also completely reconfigured the political and policy agenda. Below, I briefly discuss the range of issues that have evolved as a direct result of the type of changes delineated throughout this essay.

The political landscape is now organized around a set of issues rooted in the transformation of the Los Angeles region into one defined by cultural realities and practices that are distinctly non-European in origin. While many of the divisions and conflicts still reflect more traditional economic and political differences, it is really the cultural "foreignness" apparent in the changing faces of Los Angeles that arouses the most passionate hostilities and that manifests itself in some of the issues that define the new political agenda.

Although he was addressing a different issue, Mike Davis outlines in a recent essay what I believe are the central issues at the core of the new politics of Los Angeles.[18] Each of these has evolved from the consequences of the structural changes described above. Even what appear to be more traditional political concerns, such as taxes, crime, and electoral responsiveness, are mediated and framed in terms of these issues. The 1994 California election campaigns have simply served to confirm this.

The first issue, the growth in the number of working poor, arises from the impact of restructuring on lower-income working-class communities. While this has not affected Latinos exclusively, they have been affected disproportionately because of the large percentage who work in the very low wage jobs with no health care benefits created by the restructuring process in the service and manufacturing sectors of the local economy. And the majority of adult Latinos do work: 81.7 percent of Latino males and 56.3 percent of Latina females participate in the labor force. Nevertheless, a majority of the households we interviewed had an annual income of less than $20,000, despite the fact that in 75 percent of them, two or more individuals worked. While not officially poor by the federal government's standards, households that fall in this category are clearly struggling economically.[19]

The political significance of this increase in the numbers of Latino working poor was made clear in the comments of several of our respondents who fell into this category. They indicated that when an entire household works and still has difficulty affording the basics of housing, food, clothing, and health care, they have little reason to believe that they can achieve any economic or social mobility, or feel any loyalty to or stake in the existing system. And the kind of cuts in social, educational, and health services that

have characterized state and local programs for the last few years will exacerbate this perception.

The second issue is the intensification of racial and ethnic hostility and
conflict. If there were any doubts about whether this had any significance
for politics or the policy agenda, the recent campaigns for and against
Proposition 187 surely should dispel them. Despite denials from the proponents of the measure, it is clear that it was perceived by the majority of
Latinos as a racially motivated action. Several of our respondents pointed
out that it was not Canadians, Russians, or Middle Easterners illegally in
this country who were the object of hostility. Rather, they argued that it is
precisely the phenomenon we have examined here, the dramatic growth in
the number of Latinos and their pervasive presence throughout the region,
that prompted support for the measure. Proposition 187 provided the opportunity and mechanism to tap into a level of resentment that must obviously have been building for some time. However, even if measures such as
these are upheld by the courts, they cannot undo the transformation that
has taken place in Los Angeles during the last twenty-five years. Because
of this, the political agenda is more likely to become even more racially
polarized in the foreseeable future.

The last issue, however, is the crux of the matter. It concerns the very
meaning of citizenship and community. While the proponents of anti-immigrant measures present their arguments in terms of economics, jobs, and
the costs of social services, what is really at stake here is what it means to be
a member of a community, which is what citizenship is intended to define.
The literature on citizenship reveals that there are different and competing
conceptions of how to conceptualize it. In the current context of considering the impact of newly arrived immigrants, it is clear that the debate is
framed in terms of a strictly legalistic concept of citizenship. Thus rights
and responsibilities are a function of and are defined by legal criteria. However, an alternative conception of citizenship is grounded in the Hegelian
tradition of defining societal relations in organic terms. This position posits
that citizenship should be a function of an individual's contribution to
the well-being of a community.[20] Thus those who provide the labor and
resources that are the cornerstone of the development of a community
are, through their actions and activity, organic members of a real community.[21]

This is the fundamental issue that needs to be addressed by the political
system. What is clear to me is that dramatic transformations in the demographic, social, and cultural composition of a region are likely to make
ideas and concepts of citizenship and community that evolved from a different reality ineffective ways of confronting and resolving the conflicts and
divisions that are all too apparent in contemporary Los Angeles. It is not
until we reconceptualize what we mean by community, refashion how we

define the criteria for assigning privileges, responsibilities, and rights, that we are likely to begin to find a basis for political and social reconciliation.

NOTES

1. The relationships between changes in the economic configuration of capitalist formation and other areas of social and cultural relations have been the subject of considerable debate. One of the most influential (and controversial) works is David Harvey, *The Condition of Postmodernity* (Cambridge: Basil Blackwell, 1989). For discussions that focus particularly on the cultural changes in the United States, see the collection of essays in Michael Sorkin, ed., *Variations on a Theme Park: The New American City and the End of Public Space* (New York: Noonday Press, 1992).

2. Mike Davis has provided an overview of differing ideological perspectives on social and political change in Los Angeles in his *City of Quartz: Excavating the Future of Los Angeles* (London: Verso, 1990).

3. The distinction here refers to the fact that until the late 1960s, almost all of the Latino population in California was of Mexican origin. The term "Latino" (rather than Hispanic) is used to refer to populations whose origins are from Mexico, Central and South America, and the Spanish-speaking Caribbean. The term is unsatisfactory because of its tendency to treat a group of very different communities as a homogeneous population, but it is nevertheless the term currently used by many Chicano and Latino scholars carrying out research on these communities.

4. This is a multiyear research project designed to study the processes involved in the creation of emerging Latino communities in the Los Angeles region. The initial phase focused on Southeast Los Angeles and included three components: (1) a structural analysis of the changes in the political economy of the region, (2) ethnographic studies of multiple sites of community activity, and (3) life histories of households and families. The ethnographies and life histories were carried out by a team of six researchers based at UCLA. Since 1992, the scope of the project was extended to include other sections of Los Angeles undergoing significant growth in Latino communities.

5. For discussions of some of these factors, see Rodolfo Acuña, *A Community under Siege: A Chronicle of Chicanos East of the Los Angeles River, 1945–1975* (Los Angeles: Chicano Studies Research Center Publications, 1984); and Ricardo Romo, *East Los Angeles: History of a Barrio* (Austin: University of Texas Press, 1983).

6. George J. Sanchez, *Becoming Mexican American: Ethnicity, Culture, and Identity in Chicano Los Angeles, 1900–1945* (New York: Oxford University Press, 1993).

7. The report issued by the Latino Coalition for a New Los Angeles provides a comparative summary of the changing socioeconomic profiles of Anglo, Latino, Asian, and black populations in Los Angeles. See *Latinos and the Future of Los Angeles* (Los Angeles: Latino Futures Research Group, 1993).

8. See, for example, Edward W. Soja, "It All Comes Together in Los Angeles," and "Taking Los Angeles Apart: Towards a Postmodern Geography," both in Edward W. Soja, *Postmodern Geographies: The Reassertion of Space in Critical Social Theory* (London: Verso, 1989).

9. See Michael Peter Smith and Joe R. Feagin, eds., *The Capitalist City: Global*

Restructuring and Community Politics (New York: Basil Blackwell, 1987); and Saskia Sassen, *The Mobility of Labor and Capital: A Study in International Investment and Labor Flow* (New York: Cambridge University Press, 1988).

10. See Soja's essays on Los Angeles as well as Allen J. Scott, *Technopolis: High-Technology Industry and Regional Development in Southern California* (Berkeley, Los Angeles, and London: University of California Press, 1993).

11. Saskia Sassen, "Why Migration?" *Report on the Americas* 26, no. 1 (1992): 14–15.

12. For a discussion of how the restructuring process needs to be conceptualized as more than an economic process, see Robin M. Law and Jennifer R. Wolch, "Social Reproduction in the City: Restructuring in Time and Space," in *The Restless Urban Landscape*, ed. Paul L. Knox, 165–206 (Englewood Cliffs, N.J.: Prentice Hall, 1993).

13. Louise Lamphere, ed., *Structuring Diversity: Ethnographic Perspectives on the New Immigration* (Chicago: University of Chicago Press, 1992).

14. Ibid., 4.

15. These data are from the 1990 census tract tables.

16. For an important study of the process by which immigrants reconstruct identities on a selective basis as a means of maintaining continuity with their past, see Kenya Ganguly, "Migrant Identities: Personal Memory and the Construction of Selfhood," *Cultural Studies* 6, no. 1 (1992): 51–72. Also see Dorinne K. Kondo, *Crafting Selves: Power, Gender, and Discourses* (Chicago: University of Chicago Press, 1990), for an extremely useful analysis of the process of reconstructing identities.

17. For one of the few empirically based studies on the process of social and cultural reproduction in Latino communities, see Douglas E. Foley, *Learning Capitalist Culture* (Philadelphia: University of Pennsylvania Press, 1990).

18. Mike Davis, "Realities of the Rebellion," *Against the Current* (July/August 1992): 16.

19. Based on the data in Latino Coalition for a New Los Angeles, *Latinos and the Future of Los Angeles*.

20. For an insightful discussion of contrasting concepts of citizenship, see Judith N. Shklar, *American Citizenship: The Quest for Inclusion* (Cambridge: Harvard University Press, 1991).

21. John Friedmann's *Empowerment: The Politics of Alternative Development* (Cambridge, Mass.: Blackwell, 1992), provides an alternative model of community empowerment that is consistent with this organic concept of citizenship.

THIRTEEN

From Global to Local

The Rise of Homelessness in
Los Angeles during the 1980s

Jennifer Wolch

Los Angeles became the homeless capital of the United States in the 1980s. In alarming numbers, Angelenos were cast away from traditional anchors of family, job, and community as waves of economic and social polarization resulted in spreading homelessness. In 1990–1991 an estimated 125,600 to 204,000 people were homeless in Los Angeles County at some point during the year, and between 38,420 and 68,670 people were homeless on any given night.[1] Many thousands more were precariously housed, living in fear of eviction or foreclosure, doubled up with family or friends, or constantly on the move as livelihoods and life-sustaining relationships eroded and personal vulnerabilities came to outweigh strengths.

There are many pathways to homelessness in Los Angeles, and as many poignant and disturbing variations on those pathways as there are homeless people. Without detracting from the authority of those homeless voices, it is clear that Angelenos became homeless in record numbers because of powerful systemic forces that shaped their lives in profound ways. These forces, operating at spatial scales ranging from global to local, led to a restructuring of the regional economy, loss of critical welfare state supports, and a shrinking supply of low-cost housing. Combined, they created a swelling population of economically marginalized and precariously housed people. Some of these people became homeless, outcasts from the city's riches and entitlements.

In this chapter, I explore these systemic forces as they were played out in the specific locale of Los Angeles and how, in turn, local governments in the Los Angeles region responded (or failed to respond) to the growing presence of homeless people in their midst. My intent is to show that in Los Angeles, the rise of homelessness during the 1980s was a *process* involving global and local economic trends, macro and micro social forces, and a local politics of rejection and apathy alleviated only rarely by a willingness to assist.

ECONOMIC MARGINALIZATION
AND THE SPREAD OF POVERTY

Economic expansion characterized much of the post–World War II period in Los Angeles, transforming the Southland into the largest manufacturing region in the country, with one of the most important centers of international financial and business services. The Los Angeles "job machine" was not immune from broader structural changes in the economy, however. Periods of economic decline during the 1970s and 1980s, linked to world oil and banking crises and rising global competition, presaged the region's shift from a manufacturing center characterized by a mix of traditional Fordist industries, craft production, and aerospace sectors[2] to a post-Fordist service and manufacturing economy. For many workers, the result was poverty, unemployment, and insecure working conditions. Some of the most severely marginalized became homeless.

Four restructuring trends underlay the transition to a post-Fordist economy: deindustrialization, reindustrialization, public sector contraction, and service sector expansion. During the 1980s, almost half the county's major manufacturing sectors lost employment through deindustrialization and loss of manufacturing to Mexico and offshore locations. Durable goods manufacturing sectors such as autos, rubber, glass, and steel were especially hard hit. Plants closed one after another, and large numbers of jobs were lost as factories scaled back production, canceled expansion plans, and restructured to meet mounting competition. In addition, there was rapid geographic decentralization of jobs to outlying counties of the region. Although Los Angeles County continued to dominate with respect to absolute numbers of jobs, its relative share dipped sharply, especially in manufacturing.

Some manufacturing sectors expanded, simultaneously leading to a reinvigoration and expansion of selected industries in the region.[3] Reindustrializing sectors included high-technology (especially aerospace) and low-technology industries (including apparel, printing and publishing, textile mill products, chemicals and paper). Spurred by Reagan era foreign policy, which highlighted U.S.–Soviet antagonisms, and the associated buildup of the "warfare state," the aerospace sector grew rapidly in Southern California.[4] By 1985, the industry employed over a quarter of a million workers in Southern California, about three-fourths of them in Los Angeles County.[5] Nondurable manufacturing was also reinvigorated during the 1980s. The largest of these sectors was apparel manufacturing; during the 1970s, garment industry employment expanded 60 percent and added (net) 32,000 jobs, for a total of 125,000 jobs (or 12 percent of all manufacturing employment).[6] Growth continued strongly throughout the 1980s,[7] as the burgeoning flow of low-wage (often undocumented) immigrants fleeing political turmoil and economic hardship in Latin America and Asia allowed the region to compete with production centers in developing countries.

During the late 1970s and 1980s, public sector employment contractions were severe. State and local government jobs, accounting for about 13 percent of all Los Angeles County employment in 1976, dropped to under 11 percent by the mid-1980s. The federal share also shrank.[8] Government jobs were lost in all but one year in this period. Federal budget reductions as well as California Propositions 13 and 4 were responsible for the public sector employment decline in the late 1980s. But changes in government service philosophy also were at play. The loss of public sector jobs contributed directly to growth in the private sector, as government agencies embarked on privatization schemes to reduce labor costs and weaken public sector employee unions. Regular employment positions were converted into temporary, part-time, or contract labor in an effort to reduce costs and maintain flexibility in the face of deteriorating budget circumstances.[9]

Employment in services steadily expanded throughout the post-1945 period. Between 1959 and 1980, the Los Angeles region added 750,000 service sector jobs, nearly 40 percent of all job growth (compared to 21 percent for manufacturing).[10] By 1982–1983, the local economy had reached a crucial tipping point; service jobs outnumbered manufacturing jobs for the first time since the 1920s. The service sector's contribution to the economy became even more pronounced as the waves of plant closures hit. Much service sector expansion was paradoxically tied to the region's vibrant manufacturing base, but also to L.A.'s growing role as an international entrepôt.[11] In addition, Los Angeles became a critical node in the emergent global financial services network and began to attract foreign investment in real estate, particularly from Japan, Canada, and, to a lesser extent, South Korea and Hong Kong.[12]

The successive waves of economic restructuring (deindustrialization, reindustrialization, public sector retrenchment, and service sector expansion) left the regional economy in a vulnerable condition. By the early 1990s, California and Los Angeles were in the throes of a severe downturn, more precipitous than that experienced by the rest of the nation. Unemployment rates soared, with record numbers of claims filed for jobless benefits. Some key sectors were hit the hardest. The cold war ended and the national defense budget was downsized, leading to the loss of tens of thousands of defense-related jobs in Southern California.[13] Multiplier effects of this dramatic decline hurt other sectors of the economy. Key nondurable goods sectors that had helped sustain manufacturing growth over the previous decade began to lose employment. Apparel, which had long been the largest job gainer among nondurables, became the largest job loser in 1990 (at least as far as reported employed was concerned).[14] With both business and consumer spending down, other major sectors such as retail and service employment also lagged. And, symbolizing the end of an era in Los Angeles, the local automobile manufacturing industry became extinct when the General Motors plant in Van Nuys closed in the summer of 1992.

Labor Market Polarization and Poverty

Prior to the mid-1970s, Los Angeles's job base was skewed toward high- or medium-skilled labor.[15] But the region experienced steady growth in low-skill jobs and rapid growth in high-skill positions during the 1970s and 1980s, stimulated largely by service sector growth and the spread of sweat-shop-style manufacturing establishments. The new jobs created in the region tended to be concentrated in industries dominated by either low-skill or high-skill employment, producing a somewhat bipolar pattern.[16] There were even more people working in low-wage (compared to low-skill) jobs, as wages failed to keep up with changes in skill requirements. The number of low-wage jobs overall grew at a much faster rate than the total population; between 1969 and 1987, the number of low-wage jobs grew fourfold, while the population of the county grew only 26 percent.[17]

Women, racial and ethnic minorities, and young workers were particularly concentrated in low-skill, low-wage jobs, and their numbers grew rapidly during the decade. Women workers entered the Los Angeles labor force in record numbers during the 1970s and 1980s, many in low-skill jobs. For example, more than three-fourths of all those working as machine operators, assemblers, and inspectors in manufacturing industries were women; more than three-fourths of them were Latinas.[18] The minority workforce was also confined primarily to low-wage jobs. In 1985, minorities made up almost two-thirds of all low-skill workers in Los Angeles,[19] due to long-term patterns of discrimination, lack of resident alien documentation, low formal educational attainment and English-language skills, and the inability of more highly qualified immigrants to obtain U.S. credentials. Last, young people increasingly predominated in the working-age population, but many, especially minority youngsters, were poorly equipped to compete for jobs.

This growing pool of low-skill workers faced increasing competition for jobs, most of which were nonunionized, offered low wages, little job security, and few benefits or opportunities for advancement, and were apt to be part-time and/or temporary. Many formerly well-paid but low-skill union workers were reduced to working for minimum wages in the retail and service sectors. The overall outcome was a pronounced polarization of the wage distribution. The proportion of employees who earned under $11,100 in 1986—the poverty threshold for a family of four—had grown to 17.5 percent of the area's workforce, higher than the national average. The rate of low-wage job growth among male workers also grew faster in Los Angeles than the nation. In 1969, only 7 percent of male workers earned under $10,000; by 1987, the proportion had doubled to 14 percent. At the same time, the high-wage segment of the workforce (11.4 percent) was greater than in the nation as a whole, while those earning between $20,000 and $30,000 fell from 32 percent to 25 percent.[20]

Not surprisingly, poverty spread. In Los Angeles County in 1969, the proportion of full-time, year-round workers in poverty was 8 percent; by 1987, this rate had almost doubled to 14 percent, due to lack of full-time jobs, poorly paying jobs, and lack of employment opportunities appropriate to worker skills and interests. The working-age population in poverty included three main groups: almost one-third were part-time workers (mainly women and Latinos); 14 percent were in low-wage industries (mainly males and Latinos); and more than half had simply dropped out of the labor force (three-fourths of whom were women, and a disproportionate number of whom were African-American).[21] Marginalized by the restructuring of the economy, more and more people looked toward the welfare state to keep them from winding up in the shelters or on sidewalks.

THE RISE OF A REGRESSIVE WELFARE STATE

The surge in poverty linked to economic marginalization was not remedied by the nation's welfare state, despite the rhetoric of a "social safety net" and a "kinder, gentler nation." Rather, mirroring a trend throughout advanced capitalist countries, public resources were shifted from social needs to investment capitalists in the hope of improving the U.S. position in the international economy. Funding reductions and regressive administrative changes were enacted in many welfare programs during the 1980s. This remaking of welfare occurred at federal, state, and local levels. In Los Angeles, a particularly reactionary county government dealt with the swelling ranks of needy people by acting to restrict the level and availability of poor relief and other key social services. More and more people were impoverished, fueling the city's homelessness crisis.

Federal and State Welfare Restructuring

California's tax revolt movement of the late 1970s led to sharp reductions in locally generated funds. Then, in 1981, federal cutbacks in a wide range of social spending and intergovernmental transfer programs further reduced California's fiscal resources and directly affected public assistance recipients. For instance, major changes in the Aid to Families with Dependent Children (AFDC) program in 1981 altered eligibility rules and benefit rates and eliminated work and child care allowances, thus denying benefits to large numbers of recipients who also lost Medicaid and Food Stamp benefits.[22] Federal assistance to state and local governments, mainly in housing, health, job training, human services, community development, and income support, also dropped dramatically throughout the early 1980s. Various federal social service and health programs were converted to block grants and their funding levels slashed, and funding for Food Stamps, child nutrition, and unemployment insurance benefits was cut deeply.

With the recession of 1981–1982, California's fiscal woes deepened. Despite the recovery that followed, overall budget growth was slow, and welfare recipients were favored targets for spending reductions. In the face of rising joblessness and skyrocketing demands on health and welfare services (the state's welfare population grew three times faster than the general population), California's basic response was to slash safety net expenditures. Health services were privatized and scaled back and responsibility for funding shifted to the counties; by the mid-1980s, California's per capita spending on Medi-Cal patients was the lowest among the ten largest states in the nation,[23] and by 1990, the state, once a leader in health services to the poor, was ranked forty-seventh out of the fifty states in terms of per capita spending on indigent patients.[24] Mental health services were deeply cut, and by 1986 California was near the bottom (42d) in terms of its care of the mentally disabled.[25]

The Collapse of Welfare Services in Los Angeles County

Los Angeles County, the most populous in California, was severely hit by the tax revolt, federal social spending cutbacks, and the 1981–1982 recession. Demands on the local welfare system had reached unprecedented levels. But the effects of 1981 federal welfare policies meant that aid grew more restrictive. Thirty-eight thousand welfare recipients were dropped from AFDC rolls, another 48,000 were targeted for benefit reduction, and a further 7,800 were made ineligible for food stamps.[26] Ultimately, about 12,000 AFDC families lost their Medi-Cal benefits after they were cut off from welfare and AFDC caseloads dropped sharply.[27]

However, this was only a brief respite from the explosion of welfare caseloads that was to characterize the late 1980s and early 1990s, when the welfare population grew at an annual average rate of 13 percent.[28] The pressure on county government to respond to increased needs mounted as the decade progressed. The conservative majority on the five-member Board of Supervisors was unwilling to institute new taxes, and favored programs popular with their constituents (such as law enforcement and parks). Such emphases led to drastic reductions in social spending. Three strategies were particularly prominent as the county retrenched: cutbacks, closures, and coercion.

One of the simplest ways that the county managed to cut welfare costs was to defer cost-of-living increases to General Relief (GR) recipients. (GR is a locally funded relief program for those people ineligible for federal or state income support programs.) Between 1981 and 1993, the GR benefit rate rose only $65, to $293. Such penurious policy was justified by the Supervisors' claim that the county's generosity was attracting welfare hustlers. According to Supervisor Deane Dana, California had become a "welfare utopia," and Los Angeles County was the "Santa Claus" for welfare recipients.[29] Welfare "savings" were also achieved through staff reductions. The Department of Public Social Services (DPSS) in 1980–1981 eliminated 20 percent of its total workforce, and hundreds more staff were laid off subsequently. Reductions caused larger caseloads, longer waits for appointments, processing delays, and higher rates of welfare fraud.[30]

In the area of health care, the Los Angeles County Board of Supervisors in 1980 ordered millions in health service cuts, leading to the loss of 1,200 workers, clinic closures, and the reduction of outpatient services to approximately 43,000 clients. Affected services included well-baby clinics, dental services, tuberculosis clinics, and prenatal care.[31] As more state cuts were handed down, the shortfall of funds for the medically indigent increased, prompting further rounds of county health budget reductions and the institution of fees-for-service at county hospitals and clinics.[32]

Mental health services were also slashed. Most state reductions in mental health funding were promptly passed through to local programs, especially community-based clinics and county hospital psychiatric units increasingly burdened by homeless mentally disabled clients. The situation deteriorated to such an extent that in 1987 the chiefs of psychiatry at four county hospitals signed a "Declaration of Conscience," warning that "a desperate level of overcrowding exists night after night in each of our emergency units."[33] Waiting times for an outpatient clinic appointment were anywhere from three to seven weeks. Yet the 1988 county budget included a cut in mental health services of nearly $16 million, making the Department of Mental Health the hardest-hit department in the county.[34]

In 1981, the county closed nine outpatient health clinics in order to save over $11 million. These clinics were primarily located in the low-income, heavily minority communities of the county's traditional south central industrial belt (Norwalk, Compton, El Segundo, Bell Gardens, Wilmington, and Santa Fe Springs). One year later, the county reopened six of the nine clinics, but another thirty-two clinics closed their doors to sick people when they were converted from primary outpatient care units to public health/immunization service centers. South Central communities were most severely affected, along with other neighborhoods in the central districts of the county (fig. 13.1). Only nine basic health centers and four comprehensive health centers remained open for ambulatory patients; and levels of service at the comprehensive centers were reduced. Some hospital-based clinics were also eliminated. These closures were especially painful for South Central residents, since three area hospitals noted for providing care to poor African-Americans had already closed by 1984.[35]

Later in the decade, it was mental health's turn for closures. One-third of the county's outpatient mental health clinics (seven in all) were targeted for closure in the wake of state budget cuts, and six more were forced to scale back services, affecting a total of twenty thousand clients.[36] Later, another clinic in Bell Gardens was added to the list of closures, and five of the twenty that remained open were slated for service reductions.[37] In the final analysis, between 1989 and 1991, eight clinics were actually closed, eight more were "consolidated" (i.e., they added services displaced from closed or contracting clinics), and three reduced their levels of service provision. The closed clinics were located in low-income communities in east and west San Fernando Valley, San Pedro, Wilmington, Arcadia, Carson, and central Los Angeles. The southern portion of the county was again hardest hit by this geography of closures.

In addition to health-related shutdowns, a significant number of the fifty welfare offices of the DPSS were eliminated. Between 1981 and 1983, three AFDC offices and nine GR offices were closed.[38] During the subsequent seven years, two AFDC offices and two GR offices were opened; but four other AFDC offices and five GR offices were closed during this same period.[39] Four food stamp outlets and five Medi-Cal offices were also eliminated (although one new Medi-Cal office commenced operations). In total, fourteen GR offices closed during the decade. Virtually all were located in the county's poorest areas: Long Beach, deeply affected by deindustrialization and rising poverty; South Central, characterized by African-American and Latino populations and declining manufacturing industries; and the inner San Gabriel Valley, a poor, heavily Latino area (fig. 13.2).

As welfare rolls expanded, calls for a more coercive approach to welfare became more insistent. Then-County Supervisor Pete Schabarum proposed forced military conscription of employable GR recipients. Eventually a workfare program for GR recipients was introduced in 1983. But the plan backfired; more recipients than expected applied to participate, overloading the program. Then, opponents attacked the program, claiming that it misused federal dollars and illegally denied benefits to qualified recipients. (These complaints were later substantiated.) In another bureaucratic scheme, many workfare clients were terminated for "lack of cooperation" with the program. Later, the county was ordered by the courts to reinstate these recipients and pay their relief checks.

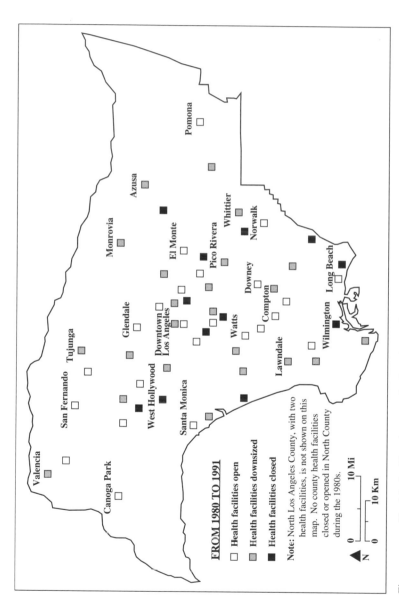

FROM 1980 TO 1991

☐ **Health facilities open**

▨ **Health facilities downsized**

■ **Health facilities closed**

Note: North Los Angeles County, with two health facilities, is not shown on this map. No county health facilities closed or opened in North County during the 1980s.

0   10 Mi

0   10 Km

Valencia

Canoga Park

San Fernando   Tujunga

Glendale

West Hollywood

Santa Monica

Downtown
Los Angeles

Watts

Lawndale

Monrovia

Azusa

El Monte

Pico Rivera

Whittier

Norwalk

Downey

Compton

Wilmington   Long Beach

Pomona

Figure 13.1. Health facility closures during the 1980s.

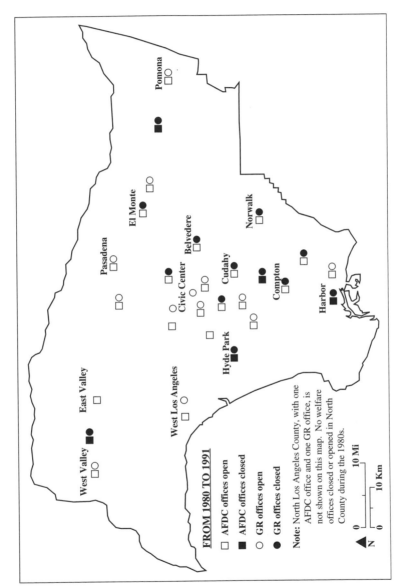

Figure 13.2. Welfare office closures during the 1980s.

The County of Los Angeles also developed a variety of strategies of "bureaucratic disentitlement" to discourage clients from using programs and services to which they were entitled.[40] The most spectacularly inventive examples of bureaucratic disentitlement were found in the GR program.[41] As one local advocate put it, "General Relief is supposed to be a bridge to help people across a crisis, but the county wants to throw the people off the bridge."[42] The GR application process itself was (and is) so convoluted that even trained welfare advocates had trouble with its finer points. The individual forms, separate steps in the application process, and local and state offices that applicants needed to visit for one verification or another were so numerous that many prospective applicants were discouraged. The mentally disabled were especially burdened by the GR process; one such client, plainly eligible for benefits, spent one hundred hours negotiating the system with the aid of a trained advocate, only to be repeatedly denied GR assistance.[43]

Many GR regulations were clearly and deliberately manipulated to achieve caseload containment according to the dictates of county budget contingencies. Once added to the GR rolls, recipients were required to submit a monthly income statement plus a rent receipt showing that they had paid for housing but had not exceeded the housing allowance determined by the GR program. If employable, recipients were also required to submit a number of "job search" forms signed by prospective employers to show that they had been seeking work, and they were required to work for the county nine days each month. Those not employable were required to provide proof of this status by submitting periodic medical and psychiatric examination results. Should any of these requirements not be satisfactorily met, or should a GR client infringe any other DPSS rule (e.g., by appearing late for an appointment with caseworkers), a "60-day penalty" could be imposed, effectively cutting off GR benefits for a two-month period. Approximately 6,000 (10 percent) of the GR program's almost 60,000 clients were slapped with 60-day penalties each month in 1991.[44]

THE COLLAPSE OF AFFORDABLE HOUSING

As the number of economically marginal households grew and welfare supports were diminished, the demand for low-cost housing units expanded dramatically. However, not only did the overall housing stock in Los Angeles grow slowly between 1970 and 1989 (at less than half the national rate during the same period), but the supply of low-cost housing effectively shrank. The private sector was not geared to respond to low-cost housing needs; public housing construction funds had dried up; and the rate of nonprofit affordable housing production was miniscule. Thus the creation of housing to meet new demands rested on traditional forms of new construction, for example, infill apartment and condominium development and far-distant fringe development of single-family homes. But even these modes of housing supply faced growing constraints, especially from slow-growth movements spearheaded by home owner associations. Inevitably, the result of surging demand and constrained supply was a deepening imbalance in the housing market.

As the middle class shrank and fewer households could afford to buy their own homes, home ownership rates fell markedly during the 1980s. This pushed more households into competition for rental units.[45] As a consequence of this tight market, median prices and rents surged. Regional vacancy rates were chronically low. Regional home prices, equal to the nation in 1974, were 55 percent above the national norm by 1985.[46] The upswing in prices continued unabated, almost to the decade's end, with home values (in constant 1980 dollars) rising over 50 percent countywide and over 70 percent in many of the area's smaller municipalities. Rental costs also climbed relentlessly. Between 1980 and 1990, Los Angeles County rents (in constant 1980 dollars) rose over 50 percent.[47] Rent surges were even higher in some smaller communities (up to 64 percent). By 1990, the median rent in Los Angeles County was $570 a month.[48]

As pressure on the housing stock mounted, its physical quality declined and levels of crowding grew, especially in the congested rental sector and especially for the poor. Between 1970 and 1980, there was a 14 percent increase in the number of Los Angeles County units lacking some or all plumbing. This was indicative not only of substandard housing but also of a growing number of illegal conversions.[49] Even more startling was the evidence of crowding. Average household size, which had been declining nationally for the previous thirty years, did an about-face in Los Angeles where between 1980 and 1984 alone, average household size increased by 20 percent.[50] And the proportion of overcrowded units in Los Angeles County grew by almost 90 percent between 1980 and 1990; in some of the county's cities, such as Alhambra, Glendale, South Gate, and West Covina, crowding rates shot up from 150 to over 200 percent, and the proportion of crowded housing reached between 50 and 60 percent in Bell Gardens, Cudahy, Maywood, and Huntington Park. The highest rates of crowding were among recent immigrant households and in central city areas.

The Loss of Low-Cost Rental Housing

There were several key factors fueling the loss of affordable housing in Los Angeles. A principal one was price inflation. Units filtered upward in terms of real costs without cheaper units being added to replace them. Between 1974 and 1985, the number of Los Angeles County housing units renting for $300 or less fell by 42 percent. In contrast, the number of units renting for $750 or more rose by 320 percent.[51] Low-end units constituted 35 percent of the total rental stock in 1974, but by 1985, their share had shrunk to 16 percent. Higher rent units ($500/month and up) grew from 14 percent to 45 percent of the stock.

In addition, the loss of low-cost rental housing was exacerbated by patterns of demolition and new construction of multifamily housing. In almost half the county's largest cities, there was either a net loss of dwelling units or growth rates of under 5 percent over the 1980s.[52] About 4,000 units, mostly rental, were demolished each year in the City of Los Angeles during the decade, and about 1,000 units per year were being converted from residential to commercial uses.[53] After 1987, demolitions of multifamily housing in the City of Los Angeles rose, while new construction permit rates went down. By 1988, the number of demolitions was 75 percent higher than it had been in any previous year during the 1980s. Demolished units were among the most affordable; 80 percent were low-cost rental units, with an average rent of $350 a month. In contrast, rents of newly built units averaged $900.[54] Moreover, the geography of additions and deletions was very uneven. The areas with the highest rates of demolition during 1980–1986 were the west side, San Pedro, and the central city (especially the Central American immigrant district of Westlake). These areas also had high loss ratios (the number of apartments demolished per unit added). The net effect of these combined trends was that there was virtual stagnation in the growth of the rental housing stock throughout the City of Los Angeles, with the exception of the distant northern suburbs of the San Fernando Valley (fig. 13.3).

A variety of local regulations and local political pressures restricted the ability of the housing market to produce additional low-cost units. Building codes routinely rendered "shadow housing" (i.e., units recycled from one housing size/tenure category to another)[55] illegal. For example, building codes allowed the new construction of so-called mingle units (with two master bedrooms) that became popular because of the declining ability of young households to afford home purchase. These units were explicitly designed for two households, but it was illegal to add a kitchen to an existing unit to make it livable for two households.[56] Rent control or stabilization ordinances operative in several cities (including Santa Monica, West Hollywood, and Los Angeles) served to protect existing tenants from the ravages of rent inflation, but for a brief period may have fueled the rate of condominium conversions (until this practice became restricted by law). And local political movements typically led by home owners associations waged campaigns to downzone neighborhoods and block the development of infill and affordable multifamily housing construction.

Last, the flow of federal housing construction funds essentially stopped during the 1980s. Projects already in the pipeline were built, but there was

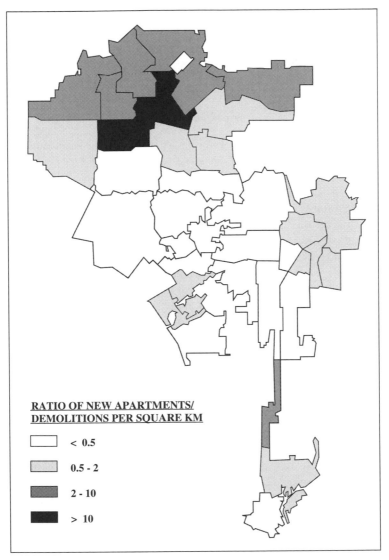

RATIO OF NEW APARTMENTS/
DEMOLITIONS PER SQUARE KM

☐ < 0.5

▨ 0.5 - 2

▨ 2 - 10

■ > 10

Figure 13.3. Net change in multifamily units in the City of Los Angeles, 1980
through 1986.

virtually no net addition to the public housing stock during the decade. In
Los Angeles, only twenty-one projects were completed, with about 8,000
units housing 31,000 people.[57] Federal funds instead came in the form
of rent subsidies (Section 8 certificates and vouchers), which did not normally create new units. A small number of projects (mostly for senior and

handicapped housing) were funded with other public sector sources, but community opposition to these projects was typically intense. With the right to block unwanted projects guaranteed to local communities by the California constitution (Article 34), oppositional forces were usually successful.

The Affordability Nightmare

These housing market dynamics, along with spreading economic marginality, resulted in an affordability crisis of unprecedented severity and magnitude. By 1985, nine out of ten poor households were paying more than 30 percent of their income for housing, and even moderate-income households were facing heavy additional housing cost burdens. Affordability problems hit all racial and ethnic groups, but they were most devastating to the poor and to people of color.

Affordability problems affected both owners and renters, but almost 80 percent of all poor households were renters, and their situation was the worst. Poor renters faced a sheer lack of availability of affordable housing. By 1980, there were already twice as many very low-income renter households as there were units that they could afford. Very important, half of these units were already occupied by nonpoor households.[58] And between 1974 and 1989, poor renter households increased by 43,000 while the number of units they could afford fell by 62,000.[59] During the 1980s, vacancy rates rose to about 4 percent,[60] but available units were predominantly in the upper tiers of the rental market, where rates of construction had been relatively rapid and absorption rates lagged. In areas of affordable housing, vacancy rates were probably below 1 percent. In the subsidized housing sector, the waiting list for Section 8 subsidies was closed in 1986, having grown too long. It was reopened in 1989; interested parties could call an advertised telephone number to request that their name be added to the list. Four days and 180,000 phone calls later, the list was again closed.[61] Among those households lucky enough to obtain a subsidy, only about half were able to find an acceptable unit (i.e., meeting program criteria) within the two months allocated to conclude a rental contract.[62]

Faced with increasing housing market competition as the numbers of home owners dwindled, the proportion of renters paying between 30 and 50 percent of their income for housing grew rapidly. The rates of increase were steepest among the population living below the poverty level. In 1970, 55 percent of households living in poverty were forced to spend more than half their income for housing, but by 1989, three-fourths were spending at this level (more than 20 percentage points higher than for the United States as a whole).[63] Another way to comprehend the housing dilemma facing poor renters is to compare their incomes with the locale-specific "Fair

Market Rents" (FMRs) used by the Department of Housing and Urban Development to approximate typical regional rent levels for standard apartments and determine the level of subsidy provided under the Section 8 program. Fifty-two percent of *all* renter households could not afford the FMR for a one-bedroom unit, and 59 percent could not afford a two-bedroom unit at FMR, using a rent/income ratio of 30 percent as the measure of affordability.[64] Households in poverty simply could not afford FMRs in Los Angeles. The annual income needed to rent FMR units of various sizes was 328 percent of the poverty line for a one-person household, 293 percent of the poverty line for a two-person household, and 226 percent of the poverty line for a four-person household.

Given low vacancy rates and excessive rent burdens, crowding became a sheer necessity as a way to share rent burdens among larger numbers of people. Already in 1970, 37 percent of poor renter households (with incomes at or below poverty level) had been living in crowded conditions; by 1980, this rate was up to 47 percent. Low-income renter households (with incomes up to twice the poverty level) also experienced crowding, the rate climbing from 35 percent to 40 percent from 1970 to 1980. By comparison, other households experienced only a 4 percent increase in crowding (from 12 to 16 percent).[65] Extreme crowding (1.51 or more persons per room) became common. The number of poor renter households living in such conditions rose 48 percent between 1970 and 1980, to 29 percent of the total; the rate for low-income renters rose 41 percent, to 23 percent of the total. Only 9 percent of other households lived in extremely crowded conditions.[66]

Not surprisingly, substandard and unconventional housing units became increasingly common throughout the region. A 1987 *Los Angeles Times* survey estimated that 42,000 garages were illegally occupied in the county, housing approximately 200,000 people. Some of these units were relatively high quality, with full utilities, plumbing, and so on. Many more were substandard in every conceivable way, lacking heat, electricity, and plumbing. The rents for such units were as high as $400 a month; most of the occupants were recent immigrants from Latin America.[67] Other sorts of "dwellings" were pressed into service, although no estimates exist as to their numbers. These included vehicles (cars, trucks, vans, campers, and trailers), tool sheds and chicken coops, and abandoned buildings. Moreover, individual units were illegally partitioned to house more people, and "hotbedding," that is, sleeping in rotation in the same bed, became commonplace. In suburban areas, small motel complexes were taken over by permanent residents, and even large tourist motels were transformed into long-term housing units.[68] Makeshift shelters were routinely constructed under freeway overpasses; the "City of Lost Souls," a twenty-resident encampment built on a freeway embankment, managed to survive for five years.[69] Shacks were constructed along the Los Angeles River's concrete flood-control channel.[70] A market in large cardboard boxes flourished; public storage lockers were pressed into service as shelter. Trees in central Los Angeles were "improved" with platform beds, cushions, and blankets.

FROM HOMED TO HOMELESS

The upheavals in jobs, housing, and welfare state shook loose a new class of homeless Angelenos. The precise number of homeless persons is notoriously difficult to estimate, but there is little doubt that the numbers grew steadily over the decade of the 1980s. Moreover, the geography of the homeless population shifted, consistent with increasingly polycentric and fragmented patterns of urbanization in the region. No longer confined to Skid Row, homeless people became commonplace throughout the urban area, but especially in heavily deindustrialized zones and inner-ring suburbs.

The Numbers Game

During the "S-Night" count by the U.S. Bureau of the Census, designed to include homeless people in the nation's census, enumerators were dispatched to survey in shelters and on the streets. In many places, they were met by hostile and uncooperative people who had been advised not to participate since the count would inevitably underestimate the numbers of homeless and be used as an excuse to cut federal funding for homeless programs. S-Night in downtown Los Angeles turned into a boisterous street party. The 80-degree-plus temperatures of the afternoon had cooled only slightly by nightfall, and few believed that the shelters would be full that night. Despite the heat, many fires were being lit in street-corner cans, and hundreds of people roamed the sidewalks, participating in the free-food gatherings sponsored by the Homeless Outreach Project and other Skid Row agencies. As the count began, one homeless person commented, "Those enumerators don't stand a chance."

Just over a year later, the census figures were published: there were 7,706 homeless people in the City of Los Angeles and 11,790 in the entire county. These counts were promptly discredited. The Los Angeles Shelter Partnership argued that the census had significantly undercounted the shelter population (by at least 30 percent); that in any event, shelters only accommodated about one-third of the total nightly demand; and that street-based counts were notoriously unreliable. Independent researchers noted that enumerators overlooked more than two-thirds of the "decoy" homeless that had been placed on the streets as part of their enumeration evaluation effort.[71]

It seems inevitable that accurate enumeration of the homeless population will continue to be an elusive goal.[72] For most of the 1980s, the most commonly accepted "guesstimate" of the numbers of the homeless in Los Angeles was 35,000. This figure is based largely on the 1984 U.S. Department of Housing and Urban Development survey of homelessness, which reported a "most reliable" range of 31,300 to 33,800 homeless persons at any point in time during the winter of 1983–1984. But other later estimates revealed an enormous fluctuation. A 1984 police count put the number of unsheltered people in the City of Los Angeles at 900.[73] The Los Angeles Shelter Partnership, in contrast, estimated that, based on analyses of AFDC and General Relief homeless caseloads, the city's nightly homeless population was between 19,000 and 31,600; the county's, between 36,800 and 59,100 during the year of the census count. These figures did not include homeless and runaway youth, estimated to number between 3,000 and 5,000.[74]

Local Geographies of the Homeless

In Los Angeles, homeless people historically congregated in the Skid Row district, cheek by jowl with the downtown's glittering "trophy" office towers housing centers of international finance, trade, and business services. Although many of its single room occupancy (SRO) hotels have been demolished in recent decades, the Skid Row district remains relatively intact, compared to other cities in which skid row areas were eradicated through urban renewal. Thus not surprisingly, Skid Row today houses the largest single concentration of homeless people in the Los Angeles region. However, over the 1980s, homeless people became widely distributed across the urban area, as Angelenos living in various parts of the polycentric city found themselves on the streets. Their residence in outlying neighborhoods prior to the onset of homelessness led them to stay within the broad confines of this home "turf" or locale, where they had social ties and more knowledge of community resources. Residence in a neighborhood other than Skid Row was also facilitated by a City of Los Angeles zoning ordinance that permitted by-right homeless shelters of thirty beds or fewer in a variety of commercial, industrial, and high-density residential zones, and by the increasingly restricted opportunities for new shelter and service development in Skid Row itself. Last, the homeless population was no longer composed of older white alcoholic males who historically gravitated toward Skid Row. Rather, the growing diversity of the homeless population, especially the emergence of homeless women and children as a fast-growing component, reinforced spatial decentralization trends.

Systematic surveys of the Los Angeles homeless population have been restricted to Skid Row, while other efforts that threw a wider net, such as the S-night count of the 1990 census, are widely discredited. However, 1991

GR program data on the number of homeless applicants for GR, by regional DPSS GR office, and information on the number of homeless families applying for special homeless assistance funds at DPSS AFDC offices reveal the increasingly decentralized and complex local geographies of Los Angeles County's homeless population. Local wisdom suggests that approximately half the total is located in Skid Row; that is, there are between 10,000 and 15,000 on the streets, in hotels and shelters, or living in other transient circumstances (in cars, on rooftops, etc.). However, it is clear that this is an exaggeration; there are large numbers of homeless people outside of downtown, especially the South Central, South Bay, and west side areas.

Considering homeless families applying for AFDC assistance, the largest proportions of this population applied in offices located in the South Bay, central, and southwestern areas of the county; offices near downtown served lower proportions of these families. However, the sizes of DPSS district office service areas vary widely, as does population density. Thus, on a per capita basis, the highest rates of homeless family applicants were in South Central and southwest of downtown (fig. 13.4). A striking finding is that rates were also very high in the Pomona Valley, the easternmost district service area of the county. Many communities in the San Gabriel Valley to the west of Pomona offer little in the way of shelter and emergency services and refer homeless families to shelters in the Pomona area. Thus the high concentration of such families applying at the Pomona DPSS office may reflect a process in which families in the greater San Gabriel Valley become homeless, are referred to shelters in the Pomona area, and social workers in those shelters refer the families to the local DPSS office for AFDC assistance.

The distribution of homeless single people applying for GR was also decentralized, but there were clear differences from the distribution of applicants for AFDC homeless family assistance. The largest proportion of the county's GR homeless applicant pool was in the greater South Bay area, followed by the west side and downtown. The dominance of the South Bay primarily results from district office closures that greatly enlarged this service area. On a per capita basis, the South Bay receded in importance, while the territory extending from downtown to the west side had the highest homeless GR applicant rates (fig. 13.5; it should be noted that the westernmost portion of district area 10, served by the Rancho Park office, is comprised of Malibu and the Santa Monica Mountains, and so the map overemphasizes its importance). DPSS district offices at the Civic Center, which serves Skid Row; Metro Special, just south of downtown, serving South Central; and Rancho Park, serving West Los Angeles, Santa Monica, Culver City, and Venice, are the primary sites where single homeless people applied for

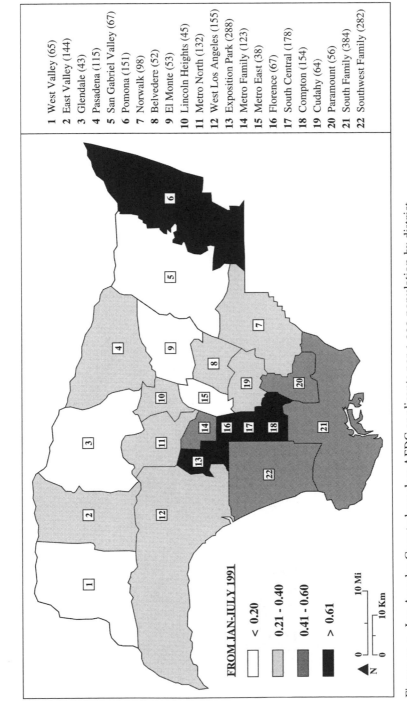

1 West Valley (65)
2 East Valley (144)
3 Glendale (43)
4 Pasadena (115)
5 San Gabriel Valley (67)
6 Pomona (151)
7 Norwalk (98)
8 Belvedere (52)
9 El Monte (53)
10 Lincoln Heights (45)
11 Metro North (132)
12 West Los Angeles (155)
13 Exposition Park (288)
14 Metro Family (123)
15 Metro East (38)
16 Florence (67)
17 South Central (178)
18 Compton (154)
19 Cudahy (64)
20 Paramount (56)
21 South Family (384)
22 Southwest Family (282)

FROM JAN.–JULY 1991

< 0.20

0.21 – 0.40

0.41 – 0.60

> 0.61

0   10 Mi

0   10 Km

N

Figure 13.4. Los Angeles County homeless AFDC applicants per 1,ooo population by district.

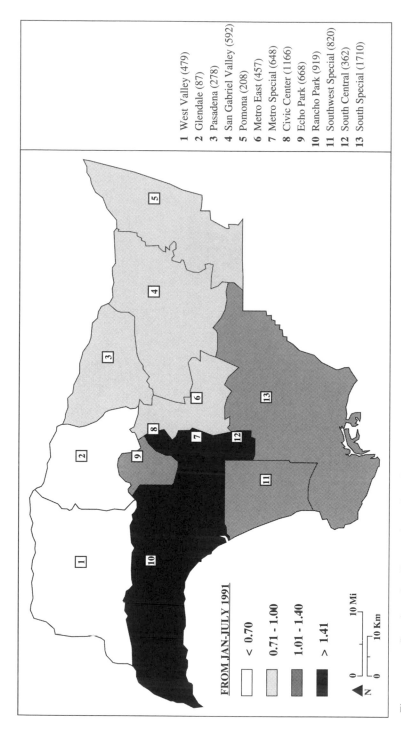

Figure 13.5. Los Angeles County homeless GR applicants per 1,000 population by district.

FROM JAN.-JULY 1991

- ☐ < 0.70
- ▨ 0.71 - 1.00
- ▨ 1.01 - 1.40
- ■ > 1.41

0   10 Mi

0   10 Km

N

1   West Valley (479)
2   Glendale (87)
3   Pasadena (278)
4   San Gabriel Valley (592)
5   Pomona (208)
6   Metro East (457)
7   Metro Special (648)
8   Civic Center (1166)
9   Echo Park (668)
10   Rancho Park (919)
11   Southwest Special (820)
12   South Central (362)
13   South Special (1710)

homeless relief. The Pomona area, so dominant in terms of homeless families, had much lower per capita homeless GR applicant rates.

Homeless people applying for assistance in different parts of Los Angeles County differed from each other in terms of basic demographic and socioeconomic characteristics. A 1987 survey of homeless GR applicants in six major subareas of the county (the Civic Center, which encompasses Skid Row; the inner city; South Central; Long Beach; the west side; and the San Fernando/San Gabriel Valley) suggests these basic variations by place. Although they are in line with the overall regional distribution of homeless GR applicants, the survey's sample sizes are small, thus allowing only a few comparisons. Homeless GR applicants from the Civic Center catchment area, which serves Skid Row, were predominantly single African-American males, over half of which were under thirty-five years old. In contrast, although most homeless applicants in the west side and South Central districts were also males, both districts had higher shares of women. In Long Beach and the west side, homeless respondents were more likely to be white; and in the valley, Latino. The west side had by far the highest proportion under twenty-five years old (75 percent), the valley the lowest. Respondents from the valley were most apt to be married; west side applicants had the highest rate of college attendance, the Civic Center the highest share never graduating from high school, and Long Beach the highest rate of high school graduates. These demographic differences reflect the general populations of the county's subareas and their poor populations, suggesting that homeless people often stay within their traditional geographic zones in the urban region.

THE LOCAL RESPONSE TO HOMELESSNESS

Most cities in Los Angeles County strenuously avoided confronting the homelessness crisis. Most had neither developed a specific policy statement on homelessness nor taken specific actions regarding the issue as they entered the 1990s. And while the largest and most diverse jurisdictions (such as the county and the cities of Los Angeles and Long Beach) had some of the most extensive sets of policies and programs directed toward the homeless, the likelihood of response bore little relation to city size. Several smaller localities had also articulated complex responses to homelessness and had targeted relatively substantial resources to shelter and service provision. But some of the region's larger cities had done nothing to respond to the homelessness crisis, either because they were determined to ignore the problem or because they feared attracting homeless people from other localities. As one local official put it, "Our city would like to do something to help the homeless . . . but frankly we don't want to end up being a magnet for homeless people."[75]

Civic Silences

The vast majority of cities maintained an official silence on the issue of homelessness. They had no policy toward homeless people, homelessness prevention, or homeless programs. Only four jurisdictions in the county had issued a specific policy statement on homelessness: the county and the cities of Los Angeles, Long Beach, and Santa Monica.

The county's 1985 policy called for more lobbying of state and federal governments, greater local coordination and resource creation through public/private partnerships, a variety of specific instructions to county departments to increase access of homeless people to existing resources, and a commission to oversee county efforts on behalf of the homeless.[76] Later, the county established a homeless coordination unit, took on administration of the federally funded Cold/Wet Weather program, and created the Los Angeles Coordinating Council on the Homeless (in 1991). However, the policy did not recommend additional county expenditures.

The City of Los Angeles adopted a formal policy statement with recommendations in 1987.[77] By that time, the city had committed over $1.2 million to homeless-related services, including funding 695 shelter beds and providing food, clothing, and emergency referral services to over 18,000 individuals.[78] Filled with exhortations to "urge," "encourage," or "support" services to be provided by other levels of government, the policy outlined a fifteen-point "Homeless Action Plan." This plan advocated the continuation of ongoing activities, directed consideration of "regional service centers for the homeless," supported the expansion of job training for the homeless, urged federal, state, and county governments to develop "comprehensive" homeless policies, and suggested that the county increase its commitment to improving General Relief. (The city later sued the county in an attempt to compel such an improvement in GR.) Some concrete proposals emerged, including the establishment of a homeless coordinating unit, a homeless services steering committee, an emergency shelter contingency plan, a mobile ombudsman program, and a "move-in" loan program. Many of these actions were taken.

In the following year, Long Beach followed suit and adopted a formal policy statement on homelessness. This statement consisted of a very general resolution by the city council recognizing the extent and origins of the homelessness crisis and adopting "a policy on homelessness that has as its goal adequate housing, food, and medical services for every resident of the City." To demonstrate its commitment, Long Beach called on the county to fulfill its welfare responsibilities to the homeless and indigent, supported state and federal lobbying efforts of the county, and directed city administrators to apply for nonlocal grant funds, establish an advisory committee, and fund a homeless coordinator. The latter two units were in place by 1991.

Santa Monica's policy statement emerged much later, in the context of an emotional debate over the presence of homeless encampments in the city.[79] The policy called for a delicately balanced set of proposals combining greatly enlarged service provision and affordable housing opportunities with rigorous pursuit of public safety measures, for example, prosecution of illegal activities (such as drug dealing), adoption of an anticamping ordinance to prevent people from sleeping in city parks and beaches, and a ban on outdoor meal programs.

Although none of the other cities in the county had a formal policy statement, as required by state law, many made mention of homelessness in the Housing Elements of their General Plans. Typically, these statements were brief and general. For instance, Arcadia's Housing Element claims that "most of the 'homelessness' in Arcadia is generally temporary displacement—job layoffs, eviction or family disputes," the implication being that the city has no real homeless people; their policy is to refer "displaced" persons to agencies located in other nearby cities. In other cities, the Housing Element detailed the support provided to a nonprofit organization to pick up and deliver homeless people to a shelter in a nearby city.

In two cases, though, General Plan statements were more extensive. Pasadena's draft Housing Element, for example, provided an extensive discussion of homelessness, proposed a new zoning ordinance for shelters and SRO hotels, and promoted a range of new and existing city activities to provide shelter and services to the homeless. West Hollywood's General Plan had not only a Housing Element but a Human Services Element as well. As a result, the city created a nonprofit organization to operate a shelter and adopted a strong anticamping ordinance that they began enforcing when city shelter facilities were opened. Much less elaborate but nonetheless surprising were the cases of Huntington Park and La Verne, both small cities with Housing Elements with proactive policies toward the homeless. The new Housing Element in the small, low-income, largely Latino city of Huntington Park provided a detailed discussion of the extent of homelessness there and adopted policies to facilitate transitional housing and SRO hotel development. La Verne, a middle-income Anglo city of 30,000 in the eastern San Gabriel Valley, had been able to find few homeless people but nonetheless had adopted a Housing Element that called for an annual city grant to a nonprofit shelter provider, zoning changes to allow shelters, counseling centers and other services for the homeless to operate in the city with a conditional use permit, and the development of an information/referral brochure for homeless people.

Exclusion through Zoning and Policing

Most cities (about three-fourths) had no specific provisions for shelters, service facilities (such as soup kitchens or drop-in centers), or single room occupancy housing developments. In these instances, such developments were simply prohibited, or else a prospective service provider or developer would have to run the conditional use permit (CUP) gauntlet. Of the jurisdictions with existing or new draft zoning ordinances, ten had SRO ordinances, eight had shelter ordinances, and four had policies directed toward other types of homeless service and housing facilities (including transitional housing). These included the county and its largest cities (Long Beach and Los Angeles) and a scattering of other cities ranging in size and complexity. In most instances, the zoning ordinances were altered to include shelters, SROs, or other service facilities as specifically allowed uses, typically with a CUP; some involved performance standards to be met through the conditional use permitting process, to minimize the impact of public opposition. Interestingly, several cities had recently adopted or were considering transitional housing ordinances, to allow such housing to locate by-right in multifamily residential areas; others, like Huntington Park, were interested in developing SRO units in their downtown centers.

In addition to zoning codes making the siting of homeless facilities difficult, many cities had municipal codes restricting access to public parks during the night, banning loitering and soliciting, and prohibiting trespassing on private property. Laws prohibiting panhandling were also common. But a court decision struck down the state's Penal Code section that had outlawed panhandling, on the grounds that it violated rights to freedom of speech. In any event, these codes predated the homelessness crisis and were rarely used proactively to control local homeless presence or social behavior. Probably the dominant response of cities was complaint-driven enforcement policy. Most cities had no complaints, and so little need for enforcement. On rare occasions, they prosecuted homeless people, usually for loitering, trespassing, or some other minor offense, when their behavior generated a complaint from a resident or local business. More often than not, formal citations were not issued; rather, homeless people would simply be asked to "move along," or would be referred to shelters or services by city police or county sheriffs.

Some cities, however, experienced mounting pressure to actively control the location and behavior of homeless people. To circumvent their inability to prosecute people for panhandling, some cities reported using laws against creating a public nuisance or trespassing to deal with panhandlers. One city, West Hollywood, distributed flyers informing residents that they were entitled to make a citizen's arrest of panhandlers, on a variety of legal grounds; the catch was that the individual making the arrest was responsible for detaining the panhandler until law enforcement officials could arrive and take the panhandler into custody—an unappealing prospect. Concerns about people sleeping in public places or erecting encampments were also voiced by some local jurisdictions, which adopted a variety of responses. California's general vagrancy law was ruled unconstitutional in the early 1980s, leading some cities concerned with the issue to adopt ordinances that prohibited camping or erecting permanent structures in public places, especially parks. By far the most common rationale for such ordinances was that encampments created health, safety, zoning, and fire code infractions. Actual removals were carried out by a variety of public sector jurisdictions. For example, the City of Los Angeles shut down "Justiceville," a 60-person, organized encampment located on a former playground in Skid Row,[80] removed a group of homeless living on the steps of City Hall,[81] and bulldozed a camp of 125 people living behind the Union Rescue Mission.[82]

In addition to such sporadic removals, a small number of cities routinely conducted law enforcement "sweeps" to remove homeless people from public sidewalks and other spaces. For example, the City of Los Angeles in 1987 began routine sweeps of Skid Row streets to eliminate encampments for health and safety reasons. These sweeps were by far the most highly publicized and bitterly contested destructions of homeless encampments in the county. Eventually, the city adjusted its policy of street sweeps, publishing guidelines and posting police and sanitation sweep schedules involving three sweeps per week in Skid Row.[83] Later, these practices were stepped up; all fifty blocks of Skid Row became off-limits to allow for street cleaning Monday through Friday.[84] In addition, the police attempted to confine homeless individuals to those sidewalks in front of the district's six large missions, in the process ousting people from doorways, breaking up sidewalk gatherings, and waking up people sleeping on side streets and taking them to mission area sidewalks.

Less publicized sweeps also occurred in Long Beach, West Hollywood, and Santa Monica. Long Beach adopted an antiencampment policy based on health and safety rationales and conducted sweeps regularly. Like Los Angeles, Long Beach posted sweep days and hours and before each sweep, sent social service personnel to provide verbal notification of sweeps and referrals to shelter and service resources. In West Hollywood and Santa Monica, relatively lenient municipal ordinances and law enforcement practices themselves became targets for community backlash against the homeless and resulted in antiencampment policies and associated sweeps.

Paucity of Funding for Homeless Programs

Los Angeles County received the majority of nonlocal funds for homeless programs and spent the largest number of locally generated dollars as well. A study of funding for homeless programs in the county reported that in 1988, the county received $10 million from the federal government and $14 million from the state of California.[85] Federal funds originated with the McKinney Act; state funds were allocated through a variety of departmental programs, the largest of which was from the Mental Health Department, followed by the Emergency Shelter Program, AFDC Homeless Assistance Program, and smaller programs targeted to homeless youth, the homeless mentally disabled, and victims of domestic violence. In addition, the county administered Community Development and Community Services block grant funds, much of which it distributed to cities to use for various purposes, including homeless programs. Not surprisingly, given its statutory responsibilities for population welfare, the county provided the largest amount of nonlocal funding for shelter and services for homeless people. Hamilton, Rabinovitz and Alschuler, Inc. estimated in 1988 that the county allocated $80.9 million, the largest amounts being channeled through the General Relief Program and other Department of Public and Social Services programs ($65.7 million), followed by health services ($12.2 million). The following year, the county spent an additional $730,000 administering the AFDC Homeless Assistance Program. Apart from these statutory, unavoidable responsibilities, however, the county spent little of its own General Fund revenues on the homeless and fought legal actions attempting to compel them to increase entitlement benefits for GR recipients to reduce their risk of homelessness.

More than half of all municipalities failed to spend any local or nonlocal funds on programs targeted to homeless people. Of those cities that did spend funds to provide shelter or services, about one-third spent local funds, one-third spent state and federal funds, and the remainder combined local and nonlocal funding. Virtually all funds were allocated to service-providing nonprofit organizations. Of the fewer than forty cities reporting some expenditures in the homeless area, only a dozen indicated spending more than $50,000 (table 13.1). Not surprisingly, given its enormous population and widespread homelessness, the largest municipal spender was the City of Los Angeles. By the late 1980s, the City of Los Angeles had been allocating over $1 million in General Fund monies each year to homeless programs. But the city eliminated most of its local funding for the homeless in the early 1990s as additional nonlocal revenues became available and its fiscal problems intensified. By 1991, almost $4 million was being spent on homeless programs, virtually all from nonlocal sources.

However, the city's separately financed Community Redevelopment Agency, mandated by state law to spend 20 percent of revenues on low-income housing, appropriated $1.5 million to purchase 102 mobile homes for transitional occupancy by homeless families in 1987;[86] spent $39 million on homeless-targeted capital and service programs in Skid Row between 1977 and 1986;[87] and in fiscal year 1990–1991, budgeted $8.56 million on Skid Row for shelters, transitional housing, hotel rehabilitation, and service provision.[88]

Overall, expenditure levels were unrelated to city size. To illustrate, West Hollywood, with only about 36,000 residents in 1990, spent about $400,000 on homeless programs, and Santa Monica, with a population of 86,000, spent about $1.3 million, whereas the much larger cities of Long Beach (pop. 429,000) and Pomona (pop. 132,000) spent only $288,000 and $27,000, respectively. Moreover, Torrance, the county's fourth-largest city with a population of 133,000, targeted no funds whatsoever specifically to services for homeless people.

How can we summarize this picture of local response? First, the majority of cities did not respond in any significant way to the homelessness crisis. Not surprisingly, some of these cities were affluent, home-owner enclaves (such as Palos Verdes Estates) that reported having no homeless people living within their jurisdiction and therefore felt little inclination to take action. Other cities minimized the extent of their homeless populations, sometimes claiming that homeless people were just "passing through" on their way to shelters and services in downtown Los Angeles or the South Bay. Homeless people requesting assistance or encountered by law enforcement officers were typically sent to local nonprofit agencies or (more commonly) to services located in nearby jurisdictions. Second, those cities that did respond to the crisis varied dramatically with respect to population size and urban complexity. The cities with the largest-scale homeless coordinating staff and service and shelter grant programs and/or policies (either stand-alone or General Plan Housing Elements) were Los Angeles, Long Beach, Santa Monica, Pasadena, Pomona, and West Hollywood—cities of vastly different scale and scope, ranging from 36,000 residents to over 3 million.

Rather than ecological features, three commonalities appear to have conditioned the extent and nature of the most responsive cities: traditions of progressive politics and service delivery; level of professional and technical staff expertise; and history of public concern about the homeless. Cities such as Santa Monica, West Hollywood, and Pasadena became dominated by progressive forces in the 1980s, emphasizing redistributive service provision. Los Angeles had a long tradition of federal antipoverty programs and nonprofit service delivery (especially in Skid Row) and at least a nominal commitment to serving the poor. Long Beach, much more conservative,

TABLE 13.1 Cities with Specific Spending on Homelessness Programs, 1991

City	From General Fund, CRA ($1,000)	Nonlocal Funds ($1,000)	Total ($1,000)	Calculated as Percent of Total Expenditures	Homelessness Spending Per Capita
Avalon	1		1	0.01	$0.34
Bellflower*	3	3	6	0.04	$0.10
Burbank		50	50	0.02	$0.53
Cerritos	50		50	0.16	$0.94
Covina	14		14	0.06	$0.32
Cudahy		12	12	0.29	$0.53
Downey		15	15	0.03	$0.16
El Monte		30	30	0.08	$0.28
Glendale	240	73	313	0.13	$1.74
Inglewood		40	40	0.04	$0.36
La Verne		4	4	0.02	$0.13
Lancaster	290	50	340	0.85	$3.49
Lawndale		1	1	0.02	$0.04
Long Beach	48	240	288	0.04	$0.67
Los Angeles		3,220	3,220	0.05	$0.92
Manhattan Beach		40	40	0.14	$1.11
Norwalk	55		55	0.15	$0.58
Palmdale	68	99	167	0.53	$2.43
Pasadena	54	85	139	0.04	$1.06
Pico Rivera	12	50	62	0.27	$1.05
Pomona		27	27	0.03	$0.20
Redondo Beach		14	14	0.02	$0.23
San Fernando		24	24	0.16	$1.06
Santa Fe Springs	50		50	0.14	$3.22
Santa Monica**	1,300		1,300	0.75	$14.96
West Covina		12	12	0.03	$0.12
West Hollywood	400		400	1.09	$11.07
Whittier	50		50	0.13	$0.64
Total	2,635	4,089	6,724	0.08%	$1.17

SOURCE: Robin Law and Jennifer Wolch, "Homelessness and the Cities: Local Government Policies and Practices in Southern California," Working Paper no. 44, Los Angeles Homelessness Project, University of Southern California, Los Angeles, 1993.

NOTES:

The figure for Avalon refers to an Emergency Fund for city residents.

The following cities spent an unspecified amount on homeless programs, or an amount which served a wider target population: Artesia, Bellflower, Burbank, Claremont, Gardena, La Mirada, Lakewood, San Dimas, Redondo Beach, Compton, Culver City, Monterey Park, Santa Clarita, La Mirada, Beverly Hills, Torrance.

*Also an unspecified amount on programs serving a wider population in need.

**Also an unspecified amount of nonlocal funds.

nonetheless was a port city and thus home to the typical panoply of rescue missions and soup kitchens. These cities also appear to have had employees with substantive technical expertise in housing, planning, social
services, and community development, familiarity with the range of political issues surrounding homelessness, and knowledge about funding programs and working with nonprofit organizations. Last, in each of these
cities, public controversy served to mobilize local government action. This
prompted local politicians to embark on homeless programming and planning.

Among these proactive places, Santa Monica and West Hollywood stand
out as the most responsive. Simply in terms of per capita spending on homeless programs, these two cities allocated between $13 and $15—eight to
nine times the city of Long Beach, and perhaps as much as four times the
city of Los Angeles.[89] Both cities boasted an ideologically based commitment to generous community service delivery. During the late 1980s, they
found themselves forced to cope with rapidly increasing demands for homeless services. This was partly because of their service policies, but also because of their location (near the beach), social climate (high tolerance for
diversity), and, crucially, the practices of other cities who failed to respond
to the homelessness crisis, except to "dump" their homeless people onto
those jurisdictions offering support facilities and resources. Both Santa
Monica and West Hollywood tried to respond to growing demands, but
despite their reputations as progressive cities, local officials faced a vitriolic
public backlash against the homeless that prompted increasingly stringent
social control measures.

CONCLUSION

During the 1980s, Los Angeles was enmeshed in the powerful dynamic of
economic restructuring driven by complex changes at both global and local
scales. The shift to post-Fordism meant the elimination of thousands of jobs
from traditional manufacturing industries. Additional jobs were lost as the
public sector retrenched, and defense downsizing led to massive loss of
aerospace jobs in the region. Those manufacturing industries that survived
tended to reorganize production (e.g., by using flexible production techniques) in order to enable quick adjustments in workforce and production
processes as market conditions required. A simultaneous reindustrialization
witnessed a spectacular growth in service-related and high-technology industries plus low-technology industries such as garment manufacturing.
The latter were often low-skill and low-waged, the former high-skill and
well-paid. This development contributed to an increasing bimodality in the
region's income distribution.

Economic restructuring left both foreign- and native-born workers (especially African-Americans) facing stiffer competition for the low-skill jobs that remained. Some people were unable to compete and dropped out of the labor force; others were obliged to work in insecure jobs at extremely low wages, often on a part-time basis. Unfavorable labor market conditions led many workers to accept exploitative working conditions and wages, including the absence of job-related benefits such as pensions and health care coverage. The number of working people in poverty grew dramatically.

If poverty, unemployment, and unstable working conditions associated with post-Fordist Los Angeles were crucial preconditions for mounting homelessness, so too were efforts at federal, state, and local levels to remake and partially dismantle the welfare state that had historically protected people from the ravages of the labor market. Over the 1980s, the poor and homeless faced ever-dwindling federal and state health and welfare supports and increasingly hostile and penurious local welfare systems. As a consequence of changes in federal welfare programs that were implemented in the late 1970s, as well as the reforms of 1981, states and localities were faced with a federal government intent on shrinking its financial commitment to the poor and shifting its responsibility for poor relief to lower tiers of government. Some states and local governments worked hard to fill the funding gaps created by federal retrenchment; others simply passed reductions on to clients. Certain jurisdictions, notably Los Angeles County, went beyond federal cutbacks to impose their own even more stringent conditions on local welfare programs. Faced with growing unemployment and poverty and shrinking federal and state resources, the County of Los Angeles sought to deflect mushrooming welfare costs by imposing a harsh regime of relief administration and by curtailing those programs over which they had autonomy (such as General Relief). Inevitably, the situation of welfare-dependent populations deteriorated rapidly.

Given spreading economic marginalization and welfare state dismantling, it is hardly surprising that decent housing was increasingly beyond the reach of more and more households. To make matters worse, the stock of affordable housing diminished over the course of the 1980s. Housing and rental costs surged ahead of the nation at an alarming rate. The rate of housing production could not match the rates of immigration and new household formation in the region. But other important factors conspired to cause a significant deterioration in the position of low-income renters. Demolitions of affordable housing accelerated, the lost units being replaced by upmarket rentals; local regulations and price inflation inhibited the conversion of units through the shadow market. Housing simply became beyond the means of large segments of the urban population. Available affordable units were often overcrowded and of declining quality. Vacancy rates were negligible at the low end of the housing market. The working poor and those on welfare were obliged to compete for the diminishing number of affordable units. People were forced to invent unconventional methods of putting a roof over their heads, including everything from converted garages to cardboard boxes.

With notable exceptions, local government officials remained spectators at the unfolding homelessness crisis. Their (in)actions ranged from suing one another over perceived dereliction of duties to simply transporting homeless people to neighboring cities. Only a small handful of cities tried to tackle the problem, with inadequate resources and amid mounting pressure to back away from their commitments to the homeless. Most cities spent little or nothing on the homeless and did little in the way of adjusting their plans and policies to encourage the delivery of homeless services or to prevent people from becoming homeless in the first place. In a seemingly endless shell game, localities strove to avoid taking responsibility and shifted burdens of providing support for homeless people to other jurisdictions in the region.

Thus have hundreds of thousands of people been impoverished by the complex interaction of global, national, and local economic forces; become marginally housed in crowded, unaffordable dwellings; and found the social welfare safety net swept out from beneath them without much local assistance in sight. They now teeter on the edge of homelessness with little except chance to hold them back. For those that lose this high-stakes game of chance, a new mendicancy awaits on street corners throughout Los Angeles, where homeless people cluster to beg coins from passersby.

NOTES

Materials in this chapter are drawn in part from Jennifer Wolch and Michael Dear, *Malign Neglect: Homelessness in an American City* (San Francisco: Jossey-Bass, 1993). I would like to thank Robin Law, Woobae Lee, and Jong-Gyu Lee for their valuable assistance with portions of the analysis presented here.

1. Shelter Partnership, *The Number of Homeless People in Los Angeles City and County, July 1990 to June 1991* (Los Angeles: Shelter Partnership, May 1992).

2. Edward Soja, Rebecca Morales, and Goetz Wolff, "Urban Restructuring: An Analysis of Social and Spatial Change in Los Angeles," *Economic Geography* 59 (1983): 195–210; Allen Scott and Doreen Mattingly, "The Aircraft and Parts Industry in Southern California: Continuity and Change from the Inter-War Years to the 1990s," *Economic Geography* 65 (1989): 48–71.

3. Edward Soja, "Taking Los Angeles Apart: Some Fragments of a Critical Human Geography," *Environment and Planning: Society and Space* 4 (1986): 255–272.

4. Allen Scott and D. Gauthier, "The U.S. Missile and Space Industry," *Research and Exploration* 7 (1991): 472–489.

5. Edward W. Soja, *Postmodern Geographies: The Reassertion of Space in Critical Social Theory* (London: Verso Press, 1989), 204.

6. Ibid., 207.

7. Los Angeles Economic Roundtable, *Overview of the Los Angeles Economy and Regional Industrial Trends,* Los Angeles Economic Roundtable, Los Angeles, 22 February 1991.

8. Robin Law, "Urban Restructuring and Low Skill Employment: The Changing Location of Work and Home in Los Angeles County" (Ph.D. dissertation, University of Southern California, 1991).

9. Jennifer Wolch, *The Shadow State: Government and Voluntary Sector in Transition* (New York: Foundation Center, 1990).

10. Ivan Light, "Los Angeles," in *The Metropolis Era: Mega-cities,* ed. M. Dogan and J. D. Kasarda (Newbury Park, Calif.: Sage, 1988), 59.

11. Ibid.; and Saskia Sassen-Koob, *The Mobility of Labor and Capital* (Cambridge: Cambridge University Press, 1988).

12. Mike Davis, *City of Quartz: Excavating the Future in Los Angeles* (London: Verso, 1990); and Ivan Light and Edna Bonacich, *Immigrant Entrepreneurs: Koreans in Los Angeles, 1965–1982* (Berkeley, Los Angeles, and London: University of California Press, 1988).

13. Economic Roundtable, *Economic Adjustment Strategy for Defense Reductions,* Economic Roundtable, Los Angeles, 17 March 1992; Robin Law, Jennifer Wolch, and Lois Takahashi, "Defense-less Territory: Workers, Communities, and the Decline of Military Production in Los Angeles," *Environment and Planning C: Government and Policy* (1993).

14. Los Angeles Economic Roundtable, *Trends in Manufacturing,* Los Angeles Economic Roundtable, Los Angeles, 22 February 1991, ii.

15. Law, "Urban Restructuring."

16. Los Angeles Economic Roundtable, *Update on Skill Shifts in Major Sectors (1980–1987),* Los Angeles Economic Roundtable, Los Angeles, 1989.

17. Research Group on the Los Angeles Economy, *The Widening Divide: Income Inequality and Poverty in Los Angeles* (Los Angeles: University of California Graduate School of Architecture and Urban Planning, 1989), 38.

18. Ibid.; and Patricia Fernandez-Kelley, "Economic Restructuring in the United States: The Case of Hispanic Women in the Garment and Electronics Industries in Southern California," paper presented at the annual meeting of the American Sociological Association, 18 August 1987.

19. Law, "Urban Restructuring."

20. Research Group on the Los Angeles Economy, *The Widening Divide,* 35–36.

21. Ibid.

22. Jennifer Wolch and Andrea Akita, "The Federal Response to Homelessness and Its Implications for American Cities," *Urban Geography* 9 (1989): 62–85.

23. "California's Medical Crisis" (editorial), *Los Angeles Times,* 9 February 1987, sec. 2, p. 4.

24. C. Duane Dauner, President of the California Association of Hospitals and Health Systems, as quoted in Joel Sappell, "Hospitals Accuse State of Neglect in Medi-Cal Suit," *Los Angeles Times,* 20 August 1990, sec. A, p. 3.

25. L. May, "State Put Near Bottom in Care of Mentally Ill," *Los Angeles Times,* 19 March 1986, sec. 1, p. 1.

26. Jean Merl, "38,000 in County May Lose U.S. Welfare," *Los Angeles Times,* 14 October 1981, sec. 2, p. 8.

27. Myrna Oliver, "Medi-Cal Drug Cuts Reinstated," *Los Angeles Times,* 4 December 1982, sec. 2, p. 1.

28. Woodbae Lee, "Local Outcomes of Welfare State Restructuring: Los Angeles in the 1980s," Working Paper no. 36, Los Angeles Homelessness Project, University of Southern California, Los Angeles, 1991.

29. Ted Vollmer, "Supervisors Vote Opposition as Dana Breaks Ranks," *Los Angeles Times,* 17 October 1984, sec. 2, p. 1.

30. Richard Simon, "256 Welfare Employees to Be Laid Off," *Los Angeles Times,* 16 August 1983, sec. 2, p. 1.

31. Jean Merl, "Patients, Staff Get Bad News on Squeeze," *Los Angeles Times,* 17 July 1981, sec. 2, p. 1; Jean Merl, "2 State Lawmakers Join in Protest Against Health Care Cuts," *Los Angeles Times,* 22 July 1981; and A. Scott, "County's Poor Seen Delaying Visits to Doctor," *Los Angeles Times,* 19 December 1982, sec. 2, p. 1.

32. H. Nelson, "Fee Emphasis Deters Poor's Health Care, Panel Hears," *Los Angeles Times,* 23 October 1984, sec. 1, p. 3.

33. Claire Spiegel and Victor Merina, "Fund Reductions Imperil Mental Health System, Officials Say," *Los Angeles Times,* 1 August 1988, sec. 2, p. 3.

34. Victor Merina, "County Budget of $9 Billion Leans Heavily on 'Iffy' Funds," *Los Angeles Times,* 15 July 1988, sec. 2, p. 1.

35. Jude Shiver, Jr., "Hospital Closings Called Evidence of Health Care Crisis for Blacks, Poor," *Los Angeles Times,* 20 May 1984, sec. 2, p. 1.

36. Spiegel and Merina, "Fund Reductions."

37. Victor Merina, "Mental Health Clinics' Doors to Remain Open," *Los Angeles Times,* 28 February 1989, sec. 2, p. 1.

38. County of Los Angeles, Department of Public Social Services, *Statistical Report,* 1980–1983; Simon, "256 Welfare Employees to Be Laid Off."

39. County of Los Angeles, Department of Public Social Services, *Statistical Report,* 1980–1990.

40. Michael Lipsky, "Bureaucratic Disentitlement in Social Welfare Programs," *Social Service Review* 58 (1984): 3–27.

41. Gary Blasi, "Litigation Strategies for Addressing Bureaucratic Disentitlement," *New York University Review of Law and Social Change* 16 (1987–1988): 591–603.

42. Gary Blasi, former Legal Aid Foundation attorney, quoted in Ronald B. Taylor, "Supervisors Seek to End Legal Fight over Homeless Care," *Los Angeles Times,* 21 April 1991, sec B, p. 3.

43. Joel Handler, "The Transformation of Aid to Families with Dependent Children: The Family Support Act in Historical Perspective," *New York University Review of Law and Social Change* 16 (1987–1988): 529–533.

44. Penelope McMillan and Richard Simon, "Safety Net Stretched to $341 a Month," *Los Angeles Times,* 21 June 1991, sec. B, p. 3.

45. William C. Baer, "Housing in an Internationalizing Region: Housing Stock Dynamics in Southern California and the Dilemmas of Fairshare," *Environment and Planning D: Society and Space* 4 (1986): 337–350.

46. Ibid.

47. U.S. Bureau of the Census, *Census of Population and Housing* (Washington, D.C.: Government Printing Office, 1980, 1990).

48. Ibid.

49. Baer, "Housing in an Internationalizing Region."

50. Ibid.

51. Research Group on the Los Angeles Economy, *The Widening Divide,* 183.

52. U.S. Bureau of the Census, *Population and Housing.*

53. Los Angeles Blue Ribbon Committee for Affordable Housing, *Housing Los Angeles: Affordable Housing for the Future* (Los Angeles: Office of the Mayor, 1988).

54. Ibid.

55. William C. Baer, "Low Cost Housing as a Resource for the Homeless: Analyzing the Components of Inventory Change for Southern California," Working Paper no. 19, Los Angeles Homelessness Project, University of Southern California, Los Angeles, 1989.

56. Baer, "Housing in an Internationalizing Region."

57. Research Group on the Los Angeles Economy, *The Widening Divide.*

58. Jeffrey Heilman, "Los Angeles' Low-Income Rental Housing: The Demographics and Unit Characteristics of the 1980 Stock," Working Paper no. 20, Los Angeles Homelessness Project, University of Southern California, Los Angeles, 1989.

59. Mark Sheft and Paul Leonard, *A Place to Call Home* (Washington, D.C.: Center on Budget and Policy Priorities, 1992), 8.

60. Jill Stewart, "LA Rentals: A Crisis that is Growing," *Los Angeles Times,* 27 November 1988, I, 1.

61. Jill Stewart, "Housing Seekers Swamp Phone Lines," *Los Angeles Times,* 13 December 1989, A, 3.

62. Steve Renahan, Director of Section 8 Housing, Housing Authority of Los Angeles, personal communication, 1991.

63. Sheft and Leonard, *A Place to Call Home.*

64. Cushing Dolbeare, *Out of Reach: Why Everyday People Can't Find Affordable Housing* (Washington, D.C.: Low Income Housing Information Service, 1990).

65. Research Group on the Los Angeles Economy, *The Widening Divide.*

66. Ibid.

67. Stephanie Chavez and James Quinn, "Garages: Immigrants In, Cars Out," *Los Angeles Times,* 24 May 1987, A, 1.

68. L. Mascaro, "Beyond the Margin," *Los Angeles Times,* 6 July 1991, E, 1.

69. Phil Sneiderman, "Last Rites: City of Lost Souls Can't Escape Judgement Day," *Los Angeles Times,* 9 February 1991, B, 3.

70. Louis Sahagun, "LA River Offers Refuge for Homeless Immigrants," *Los Angeles Times,* 13 August 1990, A, 1.

71. Los Angeles Shelter Partnership, *Homeless Reporter* (Los Angeles: Los Angeles Shelter Partnership, 1991); Michael Cousineau, *An Evaluation of the 1990 Census of the Homeless in Los Angeles* (Los Angeles: Homeless Health Care Project, 1991).

72. U.S. General Accounting Office, *Homeless Mentally Ill: Problems and Options in Estimating Numbers and Trends* (Washington, D.C.: Government Printing Office, 1988).

73. U.S. Department of Housing and Urban Development, *A Report on the 1988 National Survey of Shelters for the Homeless* (Washington, D.C.: Division of Policy Studies, Office of Policy Development and Research, 1989), 18–19.

74. Los Angeles Shelter Partnership, *Homeless Reporter.*

75. Statement made during a survey of local responses to homelessness; for details, see Robin Law and Jennifer Wolch, "Homelessness and the Cities: Local Government Policies and Practices in Southern California," Working Paper no. 44, Los Angeles Homelessness Project, University of Southern California, Los Angeles, 1993.

76. Countywide Task Force on the Homeless, *Homelessness in Los Angeles County,* (Los Angeles: Community and Senior Citizens Services Department, County of Los Angeles, 1985).

77. City of Los Angeles, *Homeless Policy for the City of Los Angeles* (Los Angeles: City of Los Angeles, 1987).

78. City of Los Angeles, *15-Point Homeless Action Plan* (Los Angeles: City of Los Angeles, 1987), 2.

79. Santa Monica Task Force on Homelessness, *A Call to Action* (Santa Monica: City of Santa Monica, 1991).

80. Janet Clayton, "City Studies Condition at Shelter Site for Homeless," *Los Angeles Times,* 5 May 1985, III, 1.

81. Frederick Muir, "Homeless Moved by Chits, Arrest Threat," *Los Angeles Times,* 7 July 1988, II, 1.

82. Louis Sahagun, "Homeless Encampment in Alley Bulldozed," *Los Angeles Times,* 13 September 1991, B, 3.

83. Frederick Muir, "41 Homeless File Claim over Seized Belongings," *Los Angeles Times,* 28 June 1988, II, 1.

84. Frederick Muir, "Police Try to Confine Skid Row Homeless to Areas by Missions," *Los Angeles Times,* 10 February 1989, I, 1.

85. Hamilton, Rabinovitz, Alschuler, Inc., *Confronting Homelessness: What Should Be Done?* (Los Angeles: Greater Los Angeles Partnership for the Homeless, 1988).

86. David Ferrell, "Council Oks $1.5 Million Allocation to Purchase 102 Trailers to House Homeless," *Los Angeles Times,* 29 September 1987, I, 28.

87. City of Los Angeles, *15-Point Homeless Action Plan;* Hamilton, Rabinovitz and Alschuler, Inc., *Confronting Homelessness.*

88. Community Redevelopment Agency Housing Committee, *Central City East, Central Business District Redevelopment Project, Briefing Report* (Los Angeles: Community Redevelopment Agency of the City of Los Angeles, 1991).

89. The per capita estimate spending for Los Angeles includes all city spending, plus Community Redevelopment Agency spending for Skid Row. It does not include any agency spending in other areas, such as Hollywood; however, such expenditures are minor in comparison with downtown spending.

FOURTEEN

Los Angeles, 1965–1992

From Crisis-Generated Restructuring to Restructuring-Generated Crisis

Edward W. Soja

Between 1965 and 1992, the metropolis of Los Angeles experienced a dramatic transformation. Always at the forefront of new urbanization trends ever since its rapid growth in the late nineteenth century, Los Angeles again came to exemplify the dynamics of yet another round of accelerated urban restructuring, in this case one that emerged from the various crises that ended the long postwar economic boom to profoundly reshape the American city in the closing decades of the twentieth century. Many new and different urban geographies took form in the aftermath of the Watts rebellion of 1965; they developed together with impressive synergy over nearly thirty years of rapid economic growth; and at the very point when the restructured Los Angeles was comfortably consolidated as one of the paradigmatic metropolises of the late twentieth century, the "new" Los Angeles exploded in the most violent urban insurrection in American history.

Compressed within the spatiotemporal brackets of this period and place is a remarkable story, one that has implications far beyond the local context. Through its telling can be seen a symptomatic history and geography of the contemporary world, a revealing glimpse of what it has meant to be alive over the past three decades not only in Los Angeles but nearly everywhere on earth. Many places provide similarly revealing viewpoints from which to make theoretical and practical sense of the contemporary world, but few offer such a vivid and variegated panorama of insights as that provided by the Los Angeles experience, from the crisis-generated restructuring that followed the events of 1965 to what I will describe as the restructuring-generated crisis that surfaced in 1992.

LOOKING BACK TO THE FUTURE: LOS ANGELES IN 1965

To outsiders and many of its own inhabitants, the Los Angeles that erupted in the Watts rebellion of 1965 was a virtually unknown city hidden behind the thick sheathing of a hyperactivated American imagination. The academic world of urban studies, still being swayed by the appealing orderliness of Chicago and the indescribable density of power and culture in New York, steered clear of Southern California, leaving all hope of accurate understanding to other observers more in tune with the region's seemingly bizarre exceptionalism. What was more generally known about Los Angeles in both the academic and the popular literatures was characteristically vicarious and impressionistic, built on a collection of heavily mediated images passing, almost by default, for the real thing.

Every city generates such imagery, internally and externally, but Los Angeles was (and is) more specialized in image production and more prone to be understood through its created imagery than any other urban region. On location here since the 1920s are the "dream factories" of what is still called "the industry," mass-producing moving pictures of Los Angeles that insistently substitute reel stories for real histories and geographies. Camera crews "shooting" scenes depicting practically every place on earth (and often off-earth) are a familiar sight on the streets of the city, and a constant local reminder of the confusing interplay between fantasy and reality that pervades everyday urban life, especially in the City of Angels.

By 1965, ten years after its opening, Disneyland had added new layers to this landscape of vicarious unreality. Its imagineered protogeography of America reconfigured the mental maps of the national subconscious to fit the familiar artifice deposited in a tiny corner of Orange County. A cleverly concocted Main Street centered the map and led the all-consuming visitor to separate worlds of fantasy, the future, the frontier, the "happiest places" on earth. With the addition of mass audience television, the blanket of consciousness-shaping imagery was not only thicker than anywhere else, it was more creatively heterogeneous and diverting in Los Angeles, the place where urban imagineering was invented, commodified, mass produced, and projected to a worldwide scale and scope.

Behind these broadcast scenes, however, was another Los Angeles that is only now coming into focus through an almost archaeological process of excavation, a digging process that Mike Davis describes in his *City of Quartz* as "excavating the future."[1] Amid the imagic runes of this extendable past, a clearer picture of the "actually existing" Los Angeles of 1965 is beginning to take shape. What it depicts can be seen as both the darkest side of the American Dream and a crowning moment of twentieth-century urban modernity, a particularly vivid representation of the simultaneously utopian and dystopian urbanization that has been infusing the development of Los Angeles since its origins (see chap. 1, this volume).

More than a century of obsessive Anglofication (posing as Americanization) had increasingly "purified" the population of El Pueblo de Nuestra Señora la Reina de Los Angeles to the point that, in 1960, more than 80 percent of the population were non-Hispanic whites or "Anglos" (to use a term deeply and defiantly rooted in the recolonization of formerly Spanish America). Although the statisticians might quibble, this Anglo population was almost entirely suburban in lifestyle, not unlike the situation comedies of television, constructing places where city and countryside blended together in a new experiential synthesis. This situational synthesis was definitively WASPish, for Los Angeles had for decades contained the highest percentage of native-born Protestants of all the largest U.S. cities. With a substantial dose of irony, Los Angeles in 1965 could be described quite figuratively as "the First American City" (see chap. 2, this volume). An almost crusadelike mentality pervaded this white, often antipapist, and racially proud Christian majority, supremely confident in its successful inhabitation and preservation of an earthly and preternaturally American paradise.

Few areas of Los Angeles contained the conventional densities of urban life, even among the poor and working-class communities of every color, for the city's ghettos and barrios were more suburban than anywhere else in America. "Sixty Suburbs in Search of a City" became the catchall description of life in Los Angeles in the 1960s, and many of those suburbs wore blue collars. Built into this homogeneously unurban sprawl of American Dream-like communities was what two of the best academic treatments of Los Angeles at the time called a "fragmented metropolis" and a "non-place urban realm,"[2] the former reflecting the mass production of suburban municipalities (what a later observer would call "cities by contract"),[3] the latter tapping the rootlessness and artificiality of place-named identities and "proximate" community. Having escaped the claustrophobic tightness of small-town America and the imperfect urbanity of the big cities, well-off Angelenos atomistically constructed far-flung networks of contacts and activities centered around increasingly protected homespaces rather than in well-defined neighborhood communities. The unlisted telephone number and the gated and walled-in residence symbolized this most privatized of urban landscapes. Truly public spaces were few and far between, as what the social theorists call "civil society" seemed to melt into the airwaves and freeways and other circuitries of the sprawling urban scene.

Mass suburbanization and other centrifugal forces had emptied the gridlocked downtown of the 1920s, leaving only a decaying financial and retail center, a few hotels, and the still-imposing Civic Center, which had been recently philanthropically revived by the opening in December 1964 of the Music Center, a product of a fantastically successful effort by the Anglo elite to put their acropolitan culture high up on the map of the city. Still towering over downtown, however, was City Hall, which by 1965 had become a global symbol of the American justice system after being portrayed each week on "Dragnet" and other no-nonsense TV crime shows. "Dragnet"'s sober Sgt. Joe Friday curtly epitomized modernist justice for white America by always insisting on "just the facts, ma'am" in scripts that were checked for verisimilitude by then-Police Chief William H. Parker of the LAPD. No fluffy imagery here, for there was a threatening dark side to life in the brightness of the simulated City of Angels, a tough counterpoint landscape that teemed with stygian dangers, never very far from the glittering surface.

Downtown Los Angeles has been the dystopian Main Street of the world's most visible Noir City at least since the 1920s, a lineage that traces easily from the gritty Bunker Hill of Raymond Chandler to the acid rain-swept streets of Ridley Scott's only slightly futuristic *Blade Runner.* And by 1965, the contrapuntal dark side of the Southern California dreamscape seemed to be particularly rife with what many upholders of the peace were convinced was their greatest threat ever, nothing short of a global alliance of evil forces bent on planetary domination, echoing the many villainous scripts shot on Los Angeles's meaner streets. When Watts exploded in the summer of 1965, the unfolding events immediately appeared to many as the products of a maniacal noir-Disney staging an evil spectacular in Negroland, the darkest and most secretive annex to Noir City. Police Chief Parker, whose name now enshrines the riot-damaged downtown headquarters of the LAPD that was a primary target in the 1992 uprising, not unexpectedly saw everything in black and white, with a little red thrown in for good measure. The revolutionary "monkeys" in the "zoo" of Negroland were running amok, he said, stirred by the "Communists" and their hordes of Hollywood sympathizers. With little accurate knowledge and understanding to distinguish the difference between the two, the real Los Angeles once again seemed to collapse into vivid imagineering. How else could one understand the latest event staged in this dystopic utopia, this place where the unique and the paradoxical are somehow universalized for all to see?

Only well after the rioting, burning, and looting spread to other cities, did a different picture begin to develop of late modern Los Angeles and the deeper—and wider—meaning of the Watts rebellion. Spurred by its increasing role as America's military arsenal for three successive Pacific wars, the Los Angeles region had experienced the most rapid industrial growth of any region in the country after the Great Depression. Federally subsidized suburbanization combined with federally fostered industrial growth to create an exceedingly efficient urban machine for simultaneously stimulating both mass production and mass consumption, one of the crown jewels of the Fordist-Keynesian "social contract" that allowed Big business, Big labor, and Big government to lead the great American postwar boom.

After 1942, when Executive Order 8802 forced war contractors to stop their racist hiring practices, another federally induced ingredient was added to the local mix.[4] One of the largest internal migration streams in American history brought nearly 600,000 African-Americans into Los Angeles County alone between 1942 and 1965. They carried with them the cutting edge of national black politics, enhanced by the growing power of the civil rights movement, the War on Poverty, the dreams of Martin Luther King, Jr., and the raised fist of black nationalism. A second large migration stream, similarly attracted to the hyperactive Los Angeles job machine ever since the Great Depression, added almost equal numbers of relatively poor white Southerners to the cultural mix of the city once called "Iowa's seaport."[5]

Not surprisingly perhaps, both groups concentrated around the huge urban industrial zone (then probably the second largest in the world, after the Ruhr) stretching from downtown to the twin ports of Los Angeles and Long Beach, a zone bounded on its western edge by Alameda Avenue, which in 1965 had become one of the most pronounced racial divides in any American city. On one side of this so-called Cotton Curtain were the factories and jobs and such exemplary white working-class suburbs as South Gate; immediately on the other was a string of equally exemplary African-American suburban communities, many on unincorporated county land and all strikingly bereft of major industrial establishments as well as basic social services: Florence, Watts, Willowbrook, Compton. Despite a tantalizing physical proximity to one of the largest pools of high-wage, unionized, blue-collar jobs in the country, nearly one-third of the African-American workforce was unemployed and almost 60 percent lived on welfare. This south side racial geography provided the immediate backdrop to the urban "civil war" that was part of the events of 1965, once again illustrating how race divides America in ways that often cut across powerful class divisions.

Although concentrated in the Watts district of the City of Los Angeles, the rebellion peaked along the entire corridor just west of Alameda, an area that had become one of the major local, national, and global centers of radical black consciousness in the 1960s. Perhaps nowhere else were conditions more ripe for rebellion. Los Angeles, after a long history of racist administration, zoning, and violence, had become one of the most segregated cities in the country; its mayor, police chief, and dominant newspaper had given sufficient indications that this tradition of recalcitrant racism was still flourishing in the centers of political power; and another obsessive tradition, of McCarthyesque anticommunism, fed by the vicious trials of Hollywood "sympathizers" and the defeat of a vigorous "socialist" public

housing movement in the 1950s, had excitedly centered its attention on up-
pity blacks as the great revolutionary threat to the white American dream.
The mood of the time was captured one month before the August insurrection. In an attempt to stem what seemed to be a rising tide of police
brutality, then LAPD Lt. Tom Bradley formally protested against the widespread posting of John Birch Society literature on LAPD bulletin boards,
literature that labeled Martin Luther King and other black leaders as dangerous Communists and implicitly promoted white and thin-blue-line ter-
rorism against the enemy within (see chap. 11, this volume).

At the national level, urban blacks had assumed, both by default and
by active choice, the leadership of American social movement politics and
were thus the most powerful voice of resistance against the status quo and
racially uneven development of the Fordist/Keynesian economic boom. Although African-Americans in Los Angeles had probably benefited from the
boom more than those of any other major urban region, the segregated
social geography of the larger metropolis all too visibly presented itself as
an extraordinarily polarized mosaic of extreme and conspicuous wealth and
poverty, a consciousness-raising tableau of racially intensified relative dep-
rivation. That the worst civil disturbance of the century would occur where
and when it did was therefore as predictable as the immediate reaction to
it. Thirty-four people were killed (31 by police gunfire), 1,032 were injured,
and 3,952 were arrested (the vast majority African-American). Property
damage topped $40 million and 6,000 buildings were damaged, most heav-
ily along 103d Street, which came to be called Charcoal Alley.

Looked at myopically, the riots, burning, and looting appeared to be a
self-inflicted local wound instigated by the particular frustrations and im-
patience of a long-impoverished and racially isolated population. In retrospect, however, the events were of more global significance. They can be
seen today as a violent announcement that "business as usual" in urban and
industrial America could no longer continue without explosive resistance,
even in the most successful boomtown of the twentieth century. The Watts
rebellion and the series of urban uprisings that followed it in the late 1960s
all over the world (and again in Los Angeles in August 1970, with the Chicano Moratorium, the largest mass protest of Mexican-Americans in U.S.
history) marked one of the beginnings of the end of the postwar economic
boom and the social contract and Fordist/Keynesian state planning that
underpinned its propulsiveness. As occurred a century earlier, the peculiar
articulations of race and class in the United States ruptured the booming space economy at about the time it was reaching its peak performance.
The worldwide recession of the early 1970s, the worst since the Great Depression, helped to confirm the turning-pointedness of the preceding decade, but even more convincing confirmation can be derived from the dramatic restructuring process that has been far-reachingly transforming the

urban landscape and the very nature of urban modernity over the past two decades. As seen from the present, the urban worlds of 1965 have not only been "deconstructed," they have also become increasingly "reconstituted" in many different ways. How this crisis-generated deconstruction and reconstitution took place in Los Angeles provides a particularly revealing story.

URBAN TRANSFORMATIONS

Until the early 1980s, Los Angeles remained as understudied and theoretically incomprehensible as it was in 1965. The little wave of attention that followed the Watts rebellion had passed into the forgetful busyness of a national economy trying to deal with stagflation, industrial decline, and the broadly felt downturn in real income that would later be described as the "Great U-Turn."[6] As another severe recession hit urban America (1979–1982) and Reaganomics began to take hold, Los Angeles was "discovered" by a group of local urban analysts who sought to construct in their studies not only a deeper understanding of what was happening in Los Angeles but also a picture of how these local developments might provide insight into the changes taking place in the regional, national, and global economies. *Urban restructuring* was the central theme of this new literature on the greater Los Angeles region. In the decade from 1982 to 1992, it would generate more significant scholarly writings on Los Angeles than had been produced in the preceding two centuries.

The most influential discovery shaping this new literature came from the realization that the urban region of Los Angeles had developed from the 1920s as one of the world's largest industrial growth poles, that those distracting dream factories of Hollywood stood amid what was becoming the largest manufacturing city in North America. That this industrial expansion was continuing apace during a period of extensive deindustrialization elsewhere intensified the challenge of making practical and theoretical sense of the apparently anomalous Los Angeles experience. Between 1970 and 1980, the entire country experienced a net addition of less than a million manufacturing jobs and New York lost well over 300,000, triggering descriptions of wholesale industrial decline and the rise of "postindustrial" society. In the same decade, however, the far from *post*-industrial Los Angeles region added 225,000 new manufacturing jobs, as well as 1,300,000 people and an even larger number of total jobs in all categories of employment. How could this extraordinary countercurrent be explained? Why had it been so invisible for so long? What impact was it having on the local economy? Was this industrialization in Los Angeles merely a continuation of postwar trends, or was it taking new forms and directions? How could this aggregate picture of a booming regional economy be reconciled with increasing local indications of intensifying poverty, unemployment, and homelessness?

These and other questions initiated an empirical and theoretical exploration of the dynamics of urban restructuring in Los Angeles that was attuned to the particularities of the regional context and, at the same time, connected to more general debates on the changing organization of the national and global political economies. Reflecting the spatial perspective that has informed much of this urban restructuring research, its findings can be summarized around six "geographies," each representing an important dimension of accelerated urban change as well as a particular approach to interpreting the "new" Los Angeles that took shape in the period between 1965 and 1992. As will become evident here and has been demonstrated in different ways in every chapter of *The City: Los Angeles and Urban Theory at the End of the Twentieth Century*, the study of urban restructuring has expanded well beyond the initial focus on industrial change to raise issues of much broader local and global significance.

I. Exopolis: The Restructuring of Urban Form

Los Angeles has been participating in the redefinition of urban form throughout the twentieth century. The classic model of urban form, built primarily around the nineteenth-century industrial capitalist city, presented a monocentric picture of increasing geographic regularity patterned by the dynamics of employment and residential agglomeration. Everything revolved around the singular city center. From its peak densities of population, jobs, and fixed capital investment rippled concentric zonations of residential land use, household composition, and family life. Stretching these concentricities outward were radial sectors that developed particular cross-cutting specializations: zones of industry and commerce, usually one high-income residential area extending from the center to the suburban fringe, and one or more working-class zones, typically associated with tightly segregated communities of racial and ethnic minorities. Cities that had grown large before the nineteenth-century surge in urban industrialization displayed much less regularity, but even in these cases regularities could be found by those who assiduously searched for them.

From its first major urban boom in the late nineteenth century, Los Angeles seemed to have a morphological mind of its own. The classic urban forms were never entirely absent, and glimmerings of them are discoverable even today, but from the beginning the Los Angeles urban fabric took on a very different texture. Although the centrality of downtown Los Angeles has been recognizable for more than two hundred years, the surrounding urban region grew as a fragmented and decentered metropolis, a patchwork quilt of low-density suburban communities stretching over an extraordinarily irregular terrain of mountains, valleys, beaches, and deserts. Both tying the fabric together and giving it its unusual elasticity was first a remarkable network of interurban electric railways and then an even more remarkable freeway system, each visibly focused on the downtown node but spinally tapping a multiplicity of increasingly outlying centers and peripheries (see chap. 5, this volume).

This more flexible and resilient urban ecology seemed to stimulate eccentric specializations and segregations. By 1965, the patchwork of Los Angeles contained a tightly circumscribed African-American ghetto and Mexican-American barrio and, as previously noted, a vast urban industrial zone and a well-defined area of poor whites from the southern states. There were also mini-ghettos and mini-barrios scattered over the landscape, as well as smaller but still significant clusters of industrial production and other specialized land uses, often enshrined in the names of particular municipalities: City of Industry, City of Commerce, Studio City.

By 1965, Los Angeles had become simultaneously eccentric and paradigmatic, a peculiar place yet one that seemed to be symptomatic of the newest trends in American urbanization and modernity. In the 1950s, it was the only one of the fifteen largest cities in the country to grow in population, and even its fiercely ghettoed African-American community was named by the Urban League in 1964 as the best among sixty-eight cities for blacks to live. What has happened since 1965? The answer, as will be true for all the geographies of urban restructuring, involves both significant continuities and pronounced changes in the urbanization process and attendant patternings of urban life and experience. First of all, the population continued to grow at an unusually rapid rate, matched only by other western and L.A.-like cities such as Houston and Phoenix. By 1992, the sprawling regional metropolis had filled in most of a sixty-mile circle drawn around the downtown Civic Center, encompassing the builtup area of five counties and a constellation of more than 160 cities and municipalities. With a population approaching 15 million, Los Angeles today has become one of the world's largest "megacities" (another of the many new terms devised to capture contemporary urbanization trends) and was rapidly catching up to the three other megacities of the so-called First World: Tokyo, New York, and London.

This growth was marked by continued *decentralization* of residential population, industrial establishments, corporate offices, and retail activities into the outer reaches of the sixty-mile circle, following trends established in nearly all North American cities since the end of the nineteenth century. But between 1965 and 1992, this decentralization seemed to break out from its conventional metropolitan boundaries. As before, manufacturing and office development in particular moved outward through the concentric rings and along sectoral zones into satellite cities and suburban green spaces. But increasingly, they burst out even further to fuel what, after the 1980 census, was called (somewhat prematurely, it now seems) the "great non-metropolitan turnaround," when for the first time in U.S. history, small towns and nonmetropolitan counties grew more rapidly than either the central cities or the suburban rings. The suburbs at least were able to rebound in the 1980s (more on this in a moment), but what became clearer was that the scale and scope of decentralization was becoming increasingly *globalized,* that American manufacturing was not only leaving its metropolitan concentrations, it was leaving the country entirely. This meant that the dynamics shaping urban form could no longer be seen as confined within the metropolitan space, even when expanded to include the larger national system of cities. The local was becoming global more than ever before, and this was demanding new ways of understanding the "specificity" of the urban.

The restructuring of Los Angeles exemplified all of these decentralization trends. At the same time as decentralization was occurring, however, there was another major development that was reshaping urban form in Los Angeles and many other metropolitan regions even more dramatically, a *recentralization* process that would place much greater stress on the traditional conceptual frameworks of urban analysis. The primary form of this recentralization can be described most simply as peripheral urbanization or the urbanization of suburbia, but within this slightly oxymoronic phrase is contained what some contemporary observers claim is one of the most radical transformations of urban life and landscape ever seen, a far-reaching deconstruction and reconstitution of urban form. By 1990, the population census would show another historical turn. For the first time, the majority of Americans were living in megacities, sprawling metropolitan regions of more than one million inhabitants.

At the simplest descriptive level, peripheral urbanization refers to the growth of cities in suburbia, the increasing concentration of jobs, factories, offices, shopping centers, entertainment and cultural activities, heterogeneous populations, new immigrants, gangs, crime, and a host of other attributes once thought to be specifically urban in areas that never before had experienced such intensive agglomeration. In recent years, this urbanization of suburbia has triggered a burst of descriptive invention to provide a vocabulary commensurable with the new forms taking shape, with what some have described as "the city turned inside out." Counterurbanization and the growth of Outer Cities are perhaps now the most widely used terms, but the list of alternatives is expanding: postsuburbia, edge cities, urban villages, metroplex, technopoles, technoburbs, technopolis.

Drawing particularly on the Los Angeles experience, I have added another summative term, "Exopolis," literally the "city without" in the double sense of the expanding Outer (vs. the Inner) City as well as the city that no longer is, the ex-city.[7] This double meaning signals an explicit attack on our conventional usage of the terms urban, suburban, exurban, and nonurban to describe divisions within contemporary metropolitan areas. As geographic restructuring works increasingly to blur these distinctions, we must not only revamp our vocabulary but also reconceptualize the very nature of urban studies, to see urban form more as a complex and polycentric regional mosaic of geographically uneven development affecting and affected by local, national, and global forces and influences. Studying Los Angeles (or Tokyo, or São Paulo, or Little Rock) thus becomes a window onto a wider panorama of subject matter than has traditionally been treated in the field of urban studies. This theme and this challenge runs through every chapter of this book.

Four major Outer Cities can be identified in the Los Angeles regional exopolis. None of the four have conventional urban place-names or identities, and they do not appear clearly in official statistical tabulations, but each has been among the fastest-growing "urban" areas in the country over the past thirty years. If identified as distinct cities, each would rank among the fifteen largest in the country. The largest and perhaps most paradigmatic of all outer cities is multiply centered in Orange County, an agglomeration of about fifty incorporated municipalities (none much over 300,000 in size) with a total population of more than 2.5 million. Orange County has been an especially significant focus of restructuring research in all its dimensions and has become a model of sorts for comparative urban studies throughout the world.[8]

Of similar size and even more expansive in recent years is what might be called the "Greater Valley," stretching from Glendale and Burbank through the San Fernando Valley, once the epitomization of American suburbia, to Chatsworth–Canoga Park (administratively part of the City of Los Angeles) and beyond into adjacent Ventura County, with another extension northward into the high desert and canyon country of northern Los Angeles County. In chapter 9, Allen Scott vividly traced the evolution of the high-technology industrial complex that has played a central role in the development of this Outer City, replicating the growth of Orange County that he had described in earlier publications.

A third Outer City has grown along the Pacific shores of Los Angeles County from Malibu to Long Beach, which, with its twin port of San Pedro, has risen to challenge the Randstad and Tokyo-Yokohama as the world's largest port complex. At the center of this Outer City region is Los Angeles International Airport (LAX) and the large agglomeration of office buildings, hotels, and high-technology research and manufacturing establishments that surround it. Sometimes called "Aerospace Alley," this region contains what is probably the country's largest concentration of the American military-industrial complex and has been the seedbed of U.S. weapons and warfare research from the development of the DC-3 to Star Wars.

The fourth Outer City extends from the eastern edge of Los Angeles County to the most developed parts of San Bernardino and Riverside counties. Called the Inland Empire after its wartime industrial expansion in the 1940s and 1950s, this subregion of Exopolis is the least developed of the four in terms of industrial employment and office growth, having suffered significantly from the deindustrialization process over the past thirty years. Its rapid population growth, fed by the sprawling development of relatively cheap housing, has created some of the cruelest repercussions of the restructuring of urban form, especially in terms of what the policy makers call the "jobs-housing balance." Lured by the success stories of other Outer Cities, hundreds of thousands of people have moved to planned new communities in anticipation of soon finding local employment opportunities. All too often, however, the promised jobs do not arrive, leaving huge populations stranded up to sixty miles from their places of employment.

To take perhaps the extreme example, the city of Moreno Valley, located in the far eastern edge of the sixty-mile circle of greater Los Angeles, has reached national attention as an exemplar of the new problems arising in the housing-rich job-poor areas of the Outer City. The 1990 census listed Moreno Valley as the fastest-growing city with a population of over 100,000 in the entire country (of the top 10, 7 were in Southern California). With local employment growth far below what was promised by the community developers, large numbers of residents are forced to rise well before dawn to drive or be taken by vans and buses, often for more than two hours, to the places of employment they held before moving to Moreno Valley. Without a large commercial or industrial tax base, public services are poor, schools are overcrowded, freeways are gridlocked, and family life is deeply stressed as residents contend with the psychological and financial costs of living in a new "edge city" of more than 120,000 inhabitants that is becoming what might be called a new exopolitan slum.

The four Outer Cities of the re-regionalized Exopolis box in a residual Inner City that has been experiencing a dramatic recentralization of its own. Reversing decades of suburban drain (but not the "white flight" that has been an important part of the formation of Outer Cities), downtown Los Angeles and its surrounding Inner City ring has probably doubled in population since 1965 to more than 5 million. This reversal of fortune, like the transformation of suburbia, has been geographically uneven and the highs and lows of development have been changing rapidly over the past thirty years. With seeming irony, while many Inner Cities farther east have experienced continued reductions in population and job densities, that paragon of low-density urbanization has been packing them in. Many sections of the Inner City of Los Angeles now have population densities higher than Chicago or St. Louis, often without significant changes in the built form of housing, creating severe problems of residential overcrowding and homelessness (see chap. 13, this volume). But to gain better insight into the changing exopolitan Inner City, as well as to understand better the shifting regional mosaic of geographically uneven development in the Outer Cities, we must turn to other restructuring processes.

II. Flexcities: The Changing Geography of Production

Accompanying the changing urban morphology of Los Angeles have been substantial shifts in the urban social division of labor and in the corporate organization and technology of industrial production. This important link between industrial restructuring and the restructuring of urban form has been a key focus for much of the new literature on Los Angeles. It has also contributed to a changing emphasis within urban studies more generally and in the practices of urban and regional planning. For most of this century, urban analysis and urban planning have given primary attention to matters of collective consumption: housing, the provision of social services, public welfare policies and anti-poverty programs, the development of mass transit systems, land use regulation, and the emergence of urban social movements around these issues. Today, more and more attention (in money, time, and effort) is being given to the production side of the urban economy and to such questions as how to attract new businesses to stem economic decline and contend with the larger forces of global economic restructuring.

Academic analyses of this powerful relation between industrial and urban restructuring have hinged around a pronounced shift in industrial organization and technology from the Fordist-Keynesian practices of mass production and mass consumption that dominated the postwar economic boom in the United States to what is increasingly described today as a post-Fordist system of flexible production and corporate development that has been at the forefront of urban economic restructuring since at least 1965. Fordist mass production was rooted in dedicated assembly lines and vertically integrated production systems feeding off increasing internal economies of scale that were sustainable only by huge oligopolistic corporations engaged in a relatively stable social contract with the largest trade unions and a federal government dedicated to priming the consumption pump of the national economy through Keynesian practices of demand stimulation and social welfare provision. Under these conditions, it was no great exaggeration to claim that as General Motors or Ford goes, so would go the American economy, for in the automobile industry the entire gamut of Fordist and Keynesian practices were most characteristically manifested.

Fordism continues to be important in the national economy, but the crisis-generated restructuring of the past thirty years has led to the emergence of new leading sectors and new technological and organizational innovations that have coalesced in what some have called a new regime of accumulation, more capable of competing successfully in a restructured national and increasingly global economy. This new regime is characterized by more flexible (vs. hierarchical) production systems located in transactions-intensive clusterings of predominantly small and middle-sized firms intertwined to achieve increasing "external" economies of scope through complex subcontracting arrangements, improved inventory control, the use of numerically controlled (i.e., computerized) machinery, and other techniques that allow for easier responses to market signals, especially in times of economic recession and intensified global competition. With the increasing disintegration of the postwar social contract through union-busting, wage give-backs, corporate restructuring, government withdrawal from most sectors of the economy (with the major exception of the defense industry), and the weakening of the federally sustained welfare safety net (signaling what some have described as a shift from the welfare state to the warfare state), traditional Fordism was no longer sustainable at its former level.

The result of all this was a complex process of unprecedented *deindustrialization* linked to an initially experimental but increasingly focused *reindustrialization* that has had significant repercussions on the regional economic geography of America. Sunrise industries and the growing Sun Belt contrasted with the setting sun of heavy industrial Fordism in the Frost Belt signaled one of the most dramatic regional role reversals in U.S. history, although these metaphors captured only part of the story. What lay behind the shifting regional geography came into clearer focus in Southern California. Still primed by the federal munificence of military Keynesianism and the cold-warfare state that peaked in the Reagan-Bush years, the greater Los Angeles region traced a particularly revealing and apparently economically successful pathway through this profound industrial restructuring. Since 1965, Los Angeles has experienced an almost complete destruction of its Fordist industries, once the largest cluster west of the Mississippi, in a smaller-scale version of what was happening in Detroit, Cleveland, and other centers in the American Manufacturing Belt. At the same time, the resilient regional space economy, built on a few large "systems houses" (as in aerospace and film studios) and many thousands of small and middle-size, often craft-based, industrial firms, flexibly retuned its productive capacity to emerge as one of the world's prototypical post-Fordist industrial metropolises.

Reflecting national trends, the more characteristically Fordist industrial sectors in Los Angeles, including what were once the second-largest concentrations of automobile assembly and tire manufacturing in the country, were wiped out entirely between 1965 and 1992, as was much of the large steel and consumer durables industries. Industrial unions were decimated and tens of thousands of well-paid, often quite senior, and to a significant extent minority and women blue-collar workers, lost their jobs in widespread layoffs and plant closures. Particularly hard hit was the domestic working class (Anglo, Chicano, and black) in the Inner City and in the Outer Cities of the Inland Empire and the eastern San Fernando Valley. Massive white flight from the Inner City, begun in the aftermath of the Watts rebellion, accelerated to near-total abandonment in certain working-class neighborhoods, while large numbers of African-Americans who could afford to do so left the region entirely, triggering in the 1990 census the first decline ever in the black population of Los Angeles County.

The African-American communities left behind in the old riot zone suffered even deeper immiseration than existed at the time of the Watts rebellion, sinking into what came to be described nationally as the formation of a permanent and predominantly black urban underclass—a sad symbol of the degree to which industrial restructuring worked to discipline and punish the main instigators of urban unrest in the late 1960s. More locally, the descriptions were less benign. (See chap. 11, this volume.) Urban restructuring in all its forms was correlated closely with "the Killing of South Central" and "the Making of an American Bantustan," an impounded enclave left to its own subsistence and survival economy of racially defined separate development. Some even equated this abandonment and implosion with a new form of indirect genocide, as mortality rates increased dramatically for almost every African-American age group, especially infants and young male adults. Whatever its deeper causes, deindustrialization and the attendant decline of the welfare state had particularly devastating effects on African-Americans in Los Angeles whose major channels of upward economic mobility had been heavily concentrated in manufacturing and government employment.

Meanwhile, the great Los Angeles job machine continued to churn out new employment opportunities at an almost record pace, oblivious to the decimation of African-American and, to a lesser extent, Mexican-American communities. For most of the period between 1965 and 1992, job generation was even greater than net population growth. The vast majority of these jobs were in nonunionized occupations and most paid much lower wages (with fewer or nonexistent benefits) than those lost through Fordist deindustrialization, creating, among many other effects, a health care crisis of unprecedented proportions as more than a third of the population was left without health insurance. But something else was going on as well, a process of post-Fordist industrial development that was rapidly reconstituting the regional economy in at least three different ways. Receiving the most analytical and popular attention was the development of the "technopoles" of Southern California, the high-technology-based complexes of industrial estates, research and development offices, and supportive business services that propelled the growth of the Outer Cities and clustered around them what is reputed to be the world's largest urban concentration of engineers, physical scientists, mathematicians, computer technicians, and military weapons specialists. It is no surprise that Los Angeles became one of the "textbook" cases for studying the new pathways of post-Fordist industrialization and regional development.

While the technopoles have spun their eddies of industrial growth primarily in the Outer (Flex)Cities, two other forms of flexible specialization have sustained the redevelopment of the Inner City and especially downtown Los Angeles. The first revolves around craft-based production networks and the dense clustering of many small and middle-sized firms highly adaptive to national and global market signals and changes in style and consumer preferences; while the second is built primarily on the provision of specialized financial services and technologically advanced communications and information processing. For each, the Inner City of Los Angeles has been particularly receptive. The garment industry more than matched the aerospace industry (another craft-centered rather than mass-production sector) in the volume of job growth and is now probably the largest in the country, having recently passed New York City. Significantly, the Los Angeles garment industry is highly specialized in sportswear and other clothing that is particularly fad and fashion sensitive and also less susceptible to easy mechanization. Major specializations also exist in furniture, jewelry, printing, industrial design, and the array of services connected to the entertainment industry, where Los Angeles leadership has been established since the 1930s but has grown even more intense since 1965 (see chap. 8, this volume).

Growth in the FIRE (finance, insurance, and real estate) sector has fueled the emergence of Los Angeles as a major challenger to the triumvirate of Tokyo, London, and New York atop the global hierarchy of the "capitals of capital." While extending the region's global reach, this growth has become localized in a dense web of consumer banking, mortgage lending, business accounting, credit checking, information processing, personnel management, building maintenance, and legal services that pulse through the regional economy in ways that probably have greater positive impact than the more cocooned and externally oriented financial districts of New York and London. At the heart of this web is the downtown financial district, but, as might be expected, the FIRE stations are broadly dispersed, with major subcenters in Century City (along the Wilshire Corridor) and Newport Beach, in Orange County.

Helping to sustain these flexibly specialized districts is a teeming underground economy and an immigrant-fed pool of low-wage labor that makes the crackhouse and the sweatshop, the pirate video store and the swap meet, as well as a vast reservoir of underpaid janitors, gardeners, dishwashers, street vendors, homeworking chipboard polishers, and household servants as much a part of the post-Fordist Flexcities of Los Angeles as anything else I have described. Understanding more about this double-sided industrial geography leads us to another key dimension of urban restructuring.

III. Cosmopolis: Globalization and World City Formation

Central to the transformation of Los Angeles has been an expansive internationalization process that accelerated after the major changes in federal immigration policy that took place in that turning point year of 1965. It has compressed within the region the most culturally heterogeneous population of investors, entrepreneurs, workers, and families any city has ever seen. Perhaps as many as 5 million migrants have moved to Los Angeles since 1965, with the vast majority coming from the Latin American and Asian countries of the Pacific Rim. Accompanying this immigration has been an equally global and heterogeneous inflow of capital investment, especially from Japan, Canada, the European Economic Community, the East Asian NICs (newly industrialized countries), and the oil-rich states of the Middle East. Together these flows of labor and capital have probably been more responsible than any other restructuring process for the continued economic growth of the region and the radical changes that have taken place in the regional built environment and the character of everyday urban life. (For the impact on architecture and urban design, see chap. 3, this volume.)

If the industrially restructured Exopolis has turned the city inside out, the new Cosmopolis has turned it outside in again in a far-reaching globalization of the local, a process that has given birth to a new term: "glocalization." After years of relatively unsuccessful local promotion, the development of downtown Los Angeles accelerated dramatically in the 1970s with the influx of foreign capital and the availability of a cheap, unorganized, and seemingly limitless supply of immigrant workers. For the first time, a high-profile central city appeared that was almost commensurable with the size and complexity of the regional economy. Although still far from the heights and densities of Manhattan or Chicago's Loop, downtown development in Los Angeles more directly reflected the effects of economic and cultural glocalization. Its specific geography was split in two, with a half-city of First World skyscrapers and financial power standing starkly above a half-city of Third World cultures and street scenes.

Capping this divisive moiety and holding it together is the governing domestic "Citadel-L.A.,"[9] a band of social control and surveillance that contains, in addition to the so-called cultural acropolis (the Music Center, Museum of Contemporary Art, and the soon to be built Gehry-designed Disney Concert Hall) and the adjacent headquarters of the LAPD, the Times-Mirror Company, and the country's largest Catholic archdiocese, what has become the second-heaviest concentration of local, state, and federal government employment in the country, after Washington, D.C. (the center of the East Coast's most expansive Exopolis). Here, the impact of glocalization on domestic governance and planning is most direct, as local decision making is increasingly affected by global constraints and opportunities. To illustrate, the City of Los Angeles several years ago obtained a loan from the government of Japan to meet part of its budget shortfall, the first time any local government unit in the country ever turned to a foreign source for financial assistance.

Most studies of world city formation have emphasized the concentration of global financial control functions. For the exceedingly heterogeneous world city of Los Angeles, this focus must be expanded to include not only the huge industrial base (eliciting comparisons with Tokyo more than any other major world city) but even more emphatically the extraordinarily global labor force, especially in the corona of diverse ethnic communities that surrounds and sustains the downtown financial, commercial, and government complex. This inner ring is the heartland of the Los Angeles Cosmopolis, a special type of world city where the very nature of urban cosmopolitanism, glocalization, and modern world cityness is currently being redefined.

In this ring of ethni-cities is a dazzling constellation of global cultures that simultaneously reaches out to every corner of the world and draws into Los Angeles an amazing array of "foreign" influences. It also provides an unusually rich testing ground for urban multiculturalism and what can be described as the new cultural politics of identity and difference, far removed from the imagic melting pot of Anglofying Americanization. Reproduced on the streets and in its neighborhoods are microcosms of Hong Kong and Taiwan, Vietnam and the Philippines, Bombay and Beirut, São Paulo and Medellín. There is a Little Tokyo and a vast Koreatown, a huge long-established Mexican barrio and a new barrio filled by a dense mix of Central American migrants representing every faction of the politics of Guatemala, El Salvador, and Nicaragua. An old (from the former Soviet Union) and a new (from Lebanon, Iran, and elsewhere) Armenian community splits its animosities between Turks and Azerbaijanis. Jewish diasporan settlers from Iran, Russia, and New York City debate Middle East politics, while African marketplaces teem with discussions of current events in Cape Town and Addis Ababa and the construction of Afrocentric school curricula.

The list of separate cultural worlds microcosmed in what Charles Jencks has called the "heteropolis" of Los Angeles seems endless, but there is still another dimension to this complex panorama of urban multiculturalism, a growing cultural syncretism that may prove to be the most important new development arising from the contemporary Cosmopolis. Multiculturalism is usually described in two ways, first as the formation of segregated ethnic spaces (ghettos, barrios, Koreatown, Chinatown, etc.) and second as a proliferation of conflictful edges and turfs where different cultural worlds frequently collide in struggles to maintain cultural identity and cohesion. But something else is also happening in the urban borderlands. Multiform "composite" cultures are slowly taking shape and expressing their admixture on the local landscape and daily life: in the creation of new cuisines, designs, clothing, and styles of popular art and music; and in the development of new cultural and political identities. Los Angeles, for example, has been a major center for the assertion of Latino identity (vs. such imposed categories as Hispanic or Spanish-speaking) as a means of uniting the diverse populations whose homelands stretch from Cape Horn to the Rio Grande. Even greater heterogeneity is being synthesized in the growth of Asian-American identity, with Los Angeles again taking a leading role. Many other forms of cross-cultural fusion and coalition building are taking place in the schools and neighborhoods, in community organizations and housing projects, in local government and cultural festivals, in ways that we are only beginning to recognize and understand.

Making sense of the Cosmopolis, the place where the local is being globalized at the same time as the global is being localized, is a challenging task. Contemplating this challenge again, I recall the words of Jorge Luis Borges, whose short story, "The Aleph," I used once before to characterize contemporary Los Angeles.[10]

"The Aleph?" I repeated.

Yes, the only place on earth where all places are—seen from every angle, each standing clear, without any confusion or blending. . . .

How, then, can I translate into words the limitless Aleph, which my floundering mind can scarcely encompass? . . . Really, what I want to do is impossible, for any listing of an endless series is doomed to be infinitesimal. In that single gigantic instant I saw millions of acts both delightful and awful; not one of them amazed me more than the fact that all of them occupied the same point in space, without overlapping or transparency. What my eyes beheld was simultaneous, but what I shall now write down will be successive. . . .

I saw a small iridescent sphere of almost unbearable brilliance. At first I thought it was revolving; then I realized that this movement was an illusion created by the dizzying world it bounded. . . . I saw the teeming sea; I saw daybreak and nightfall; I saw the multitudes of America; I saw a silvery cobweb in the center of a black pyramid; I saw a splintered labyrinth. . . . I saw, close up, unending eyes watching themselves in me as in a mirror.

IV. Splintered Labyrinth: The Repolarized Metropolis

The first three geographies of urban restructuring are tightly interwoven and, taken together, present the most powerful explanatory arguments outlining the causes of the new urbanization processes that have been reshaping Los Angeles and, to varying degrees, other metropolitan regions of the world. The next three geographies can be seen primarily as consequences of or reactions to metropolitan transformation, although they too are marked by the same restructuring dynamic of deconstruction (the breaking down of an older order) and reconstitution (the creation of new or significantly different forms of urban modernity). I begin with the changing social order and, in particular, the increasing and many-sided socioeconomic inequalities that have been so integrally associated with the crisis-generated restructuring of the past thirty years.

Paralleling the spatial structure of the globalized post-Fordist Exopolis is a social and economic structure that has become increasingly fluid, fragmented, decentered, and rearranged in ways that differ significantly from the old class-divided city of the bourgeoisie and proletariat; the neatly apportioned hierarchical city of the wealthy, the middle class, and the poor; and the "two Americas" city of black versus white that was described in the aftermath of the 1960s urban insurrections. This polychotomous segmentation and repolarization has begun to reconstitute the extremes of wealth and poverty and derigidify the social boundaries of class, race, and income grouping, challenging our old ways of understanding the sociology of urbanism.

There are now, for example, more millionaires than ever before in Los Angeles, many constituting a reserve army of the wealthy that includes rock stars and baseball players, computer software specialists and real estate agents, hairdressers and employment headhunters, drug dealers and dentists, as well as thousands of home owners who were lucky enough to buy at the right time in the right place. Never before has the top 10 percent of the income ladder been so heterogeneous, so segmented, and so politically unpredictable. And in many ways, the same can be said for the bottom 20 percent, which now contains representatives from the same occupations and backgrounds as the millionaires and displays much the same political unpredictability.

As is by now clear, urban restructuring in Los Angeles deepened poverty even under conditions of rapid regional economic growth and job generation (see chap. 10, this volume). As many as 80,000 people are now homeless on any given night in the region, and perhaps three times as many are homeless at some point in the average year. But this is only the most visible tip of an iceberg of extreme poverty that broadens into a population of well more than half a million living precariously in housing conditions little better than those of the worst Third World squatter settlements and shantytowns, a situation that has created what is arguably the most severe urban housing crisis in America (see chap. 13, this volume). Many of the more than 1.3 million living below the poverty line in L.A. County in 1989 (the numbers have increased dramatically since then; see chap. 10, this volume) are unemployed and welfare dependent, an unquestionable core of what urban sociologists and policy makers have recently begun to call the "permanent urban underclass." But just as many, perhaps more, are part of the rapidly growing and primarily Latino contingent of the working poor, often laboring for well more than forty hours a week at more than one job for wages that are insufficient to feed and clothe a family.

A perverse symbiosis has developed between the extremes of wealth and poverty in Los Angeles, each feeding the growth of the other. Occasionally, the perversity is exposed in startling ways, as in several clear cases of what can only be called slavery. Immigrants from Indonesia, China, and Central America have been imported (in one case as "entertainers" with cultural visas) and sold to wealthy households as live-in domestic servants. Their passports are kept by their "owners" who provide limited room and board for their services. This new slavery, however, is just one step below what is present in the sweatshops and many other businesses (and households), where undocumented workers are paid subminimal wages at often hazardous worksites and under the constant threat of deportation. The bottom of the poverty iceberg and the new urban social division of labor is indeed broad and deep.

As is clearly shown in many chapters of *The City*, the great Los Angeles job machine has had a "missing middle," bifurcating instead into a small stream of high-paying jobs feeding the new technocracy and a raging torrent of low-wage work (much also involved in feeding the new technocracy) that barely deserves the adjective *subsistence*. This multivalent polarization is no longer easily definable by simple racial, ethnic, occupational, class, or immigrant status categories and binary oppositions. A recent national survey has shown, for example, that Los Angeles contains both the richest and the poorest predominantly African-American communities in urban America, and my guess would be that similar results would be found if such a study were done for Mexican-Americans and Asian-Americans. There are also some indications from unpublished comparative studies of U.S., Canadian, and Australian cities that the polarization and inequality measured among recent immigrant populations extends from the Inner to the Outer Cities, with Los Angeles–Long Beach, Orange County, and San Bernardino–Riverside ranking as the three highest of all metropolitan areas surveyed.

The impact of repolarization also extends deeply into the middle classes, which, as in most of the country, have been increasingly destabilized in their class position over the past thirty years, splitting away from the once robust middle ground of the income ladder in two directions, some upwardly mobile or an least maintaining their comfortable living standards in increasingly multiple job households, while many more, especially women and children, slide downward toward the working poor, the new underclass, and the homeless. The reconstitution of the American middle class has spawned a new vocabulary for urban sociology, with yuppies, guppies (groups of young urban professionals), dinks (double income–no kids couples), woopies (well-off older people), infomerchants and the high technocracy, hyperghettoization and gentrification, glass ceilings and the feminization of poverty. A growing population of "new orphans"—children abandoned by their parents and the elderly abandoned by their children—fill the streets. Workers are "K-Marted" or "Burger Kinged" as their income is cut in half in the shift from manufacturing to the burgeoning services economy.

With the socioeconomic landscape becoming more fluid and kaleidoscopic, there has been an accompanying statistical decline in major indices of racial and ethnic segregation, as Latinos and Asians in particular increase rapidly in numbers and move out from their older staging settlements into new grounds and different lifestyles. The City of Cerritos, for example, near the border of Los Angeles and Orange counties, has recently been named the most racially mixed city in America, with a population in 1990 that was 44 percent Asian, 36 percent Anglo, 13 percent Latino, and 7 percent black. In Gardena, also a city of around 50,000, the four groups are almost equal in size, approaching a racial balancing that may never before have been achieved for any city in history: 32 percent Asian (mainly Japanese), 23 percent for blacks and Latinos, and 21 percent Anglo. Asians have been the fastest-growing segment in nearly all of the wealthiest (and still more than 80% Anglo) areas of L.A. County and have become the largest ethnic group in several cities and the majority in Monterey Park, which has received national attention for its interethnic struggles over language use, with Latinos and Anglos often combining to stop the exclusive use of Chinese and to declare English the "official language."

Equally indicative has been a rapid "recycling" of cities and communities, as one majority is replaced by another. Southeast of downtown, municipalities such as Huntington Park and Maywood have seen their population shift from almost 80 percent Anglo in 1965 to more than 90 percent Latino in a demographic wave that has flowed even farther, into South Central, where Latinos will very soon form the majority of the more than 250,000 inhabitants of this once overwhelmingly African-American section of the City of Los Angeles (see chap. 12, this volume). The broad spread of the Latinos has been so extensive that nearly all the 163 communities listed in a report on the 1990 census, including Beverly Hills, Bel Air, and

Brentwood, had populations that were at least 5 percent Latino. The exceptions were all on the far western flanks of the county, near the border with Ventura County, in some of the stubbornly Anglo beach communities and black elite Ladera Heights, and in the gated communities of the Palos Verdes peninsula.

The number of cities and communities with more than 60 percent black population has shrunk to five: the large (169,000) West Adams–Baldwin Hills–Leimert district within the City of Los Angeles and four small pockets of unincorporated county land (Westmont, West Compton, West Athens, and View Park–Windsor Hills), with a total population of about 55,000. The very names of these areas signal the pronounced westward shift, as well as overall shrinkage, of the core of black Los Angeles. With the growth of Koreatown and Anglo gentrification pushing from the north, and Latinoization obliterating the old Cotton Curtain and spreading through the Watts-Willowbrook-Florence-Compton corridor from the east, black L.A. has not only been compacted, it has become increasingly polarized, with the richest and poorest African-American communities more visibly locked together in their inequalities than ever before. And still farther west, across the San Diego Freeway, a new racial barrier looms in the great Anglo redoubt that runs along the Pacific shores south of Los Angeles International Airport. In this prime stretch of surfurbia, as Reyner Banham once called it, 1,603 African-Americans were counted in the 1990 census in five cities with a total population of nearly 140,000.[11]

V. Unending Eyes: Revamping the Carceral City

The new topography of race, class, gender, age, income, and ethnicity has produced an incendiary urban geography in Los Angeles, a landscape filled with violent edges, colliding turfs, unstable boundaries, peculiarly juxtaposed lifespaces, and enclaves of outrageous wealth and despair. How this immanently conflagratory metropolis was kept from socially exploding until 1992 is wound up in the development of the Carceral City, a geography of warlike fortification and enclosure, of ever-watchful surveillance and creative means of social and spatial control, a place where *police* has become an insistent substitute for *polis*. Provocative descriptions of the Carceral City feature prominently in Mike Davis's *City of Quartz*, probably the best and most widely read of all the books to have been written about contemporary Los Angeles. Merely listing some of the chapter headings and topic outlines of *City of Quartz* provides a telling synopsis of the history and geography of the Carceral City.

Most direct is chapter 4, "Fortress L.A.," a tour de force through the built environment of security-obsessed urbanism. Its headings include "The Destruction of Public Space" (described as a "security offensive" to meet "the middle-class demand for increased spatial and social insulation"); "The Forbidden City" ("taking the form of a brutal architectural edge or glacis that defines the new Downtown as a citadel"); "Sadistic Street Environments" ("hardening the city surface against the poor," with bum-proof bus benches, absent public lavatories, razor-wire protected trash bins, and overhead sprinkler systems that work randomly through the night to discourage sidewalk sleepers); "Frank Gehry as Dirty Harry" (on the fortresslike "stealth houses" of this leading L.A. architect); "The Panopticon Mall" (from the "mall-as-panopticon-prison" to the "housing-project-as-strategic-hamlet"); "From Rentacop to Robocop" (the "frenetic effort" of affluent neighborhoods to "insulate home values and lifestyles" in gated communities, "high-tech castles," "belligerent lawns," and the "voracious consumption of private security services"); "The LAPD as Space Police" (the LAPD's Star Wars-like "metamorphosis into a techno-police"); "The Carceral City" (honing in on the prisons around downtown that contain "the largest incarcerated population in the nation"); and finally, "The Fear of Crowds" (on the increasing attempts to control or prevent all public gatherings and to erase the last vestiges of public space).

Another dimension of the Carceral City is the "sunbelt bolshevism" Davis explores in chapter 3. These "revolutionary" home owner-backed slow-growth insurgencies have created "white walls" of zoning regulations, agile NIMBY protest movements, increasing "suburban separatism," and new "homeowner's soviets" in the attempt to turn back the tide (and the clock) of urban restructuring. In what has been called "the Watts riots of the middle classes," in part to commemorate the victorious tax revolts of the 1970s but also evoking images of the gang power and turf wars of wealthy white adults, there has been what Davis calls "a reassertion of social privilege" by the Anglo middle classes just in the nick of time, given their diminishing numbers and increasingly confusing class identities.

In chapter 5, "The Hammer and the Rock," Davis takes on the police state and the secret and not so secret LAPD-FBI-CIA wars on crime, gangs, drugs, "expendable youth," and the "revolutionary lumpenproletariat." Here one finds one of the most flagrant *continuities* in the history and geography of Los Angeles between 1965 and 1992, a persistent streak of racism, police brutality, right-wing conspiracy theories, secret spy networks, and Blue Knight crusades to save the world from imminent god-forsaken destruction, a streak that spans the chiefly generations from William Parker to Ed Davis to Daryl Gates. Los Angeles remains less densely foot-policed than any other major U.S. city, but it has continued to build on its military defense, space surveillance, and weapons production tradition to produce the most technologically advanced urban armed forces, on the ground and in the air, another vital organ of the mighty militarized technopolis of Southern California.

The policed metropolis is augmented by the quieter presence of what may be the most extensive network of military installations around any major city, a global strike force allegedly prepared to take on any challenge anywhere in the universe. Several military enclosures are scheduled to close down in the 1990s, but their abundance and versatility guarantees a continued impact even if converted to peacetime functions. To illustrate, troops were able to prepare for the Persian Gulf War in the deserts of Southern California, replicating conditions so faithfully that there were special maneuvers around the desert hamlet of Bagdad. At a more intimate scale, lethal weapons are also kept in most households and in many automobiles, creating a heterogeneous, fragmented, and highly mobile militia that also patrols the turfs and edges of the Carceral City, attempting with violence to keep everyone in their place and, increasingly along the freeways, in their proper lane and going at appropriate speeds. In restructured Los Angeles, the potential for violence has been raised to new heights, triggering often-fatal attractions to a disciplinary technology of security and surveillance that patrols the region with endless eyes.

An important and all too easily neglected side effect of these intensified locality struggles has been to focus grassroots political consciousness and energy on what Michel Foucault, who first used the term Carceral City, described as "the little tactics of the habitat," or what contemporary urban scholars call "the politics of place." This recharging of locale and spatial location with active political attachment and identity has spread to the poorest neighborhoods and kindled what have been the most powerful forms of social resistance to the Carceral City and to the other oppressive effects of urban restructuring. Some of these micropolitical struggles have consciously crossed racial, ethnic, class, and gender boundaries to engage in a new multicultural politics of space and place that is significantly different from the polarized politics of binary opposition (black vs. white, labor vs. capital, women vs. men) that formed the basis for most earlier urban social movements. Perhaps never before have the people of Los Angeles, once the quintessential nonplace urban realm, been so politically involved in their immediate neighborhoods and localities, another of the major changes that have occurred between 1965 and 1992 and one that, like the cultural syncretisms of Cosmopolis, must be recognized and built upon by all those who retain some optimism about the future of the region.

VI. Simcities: Restructuring the Urban Imaginary

A sixth restructuring helps to complete the picture of urban transformation. In many ways, it is a deeper behavioral, cultural, and ideological restructuring and is accordingly more difficult to capture in quick descriptions. What it represents is a radical change in the urban imaginary, in the ways we relate our images of the real to empirical reality itself. It is thus at its roots an inherently epistemological restructuring, one that affects our everyday life and how we make practical sense of the contemporary world, what it means to be alive here and now, in a particular place and at a particular time. Rooted in this changing collective and individual consciousness of the contemporary, its new perils and possibilities, the sixth restructuring more directly than any other links the urban transformations of Los Angeles to the broader current debates on modernity and postmodernity.

The simplest way to exemplify this connection is to reassert what I have been saying throughout this concluding chapter, that the restructuring of Los Angeles between 1965 and 1992 provides an unusually clear window onto the contemporary world and that what can be seen through this window is forcefully telling us that traditional ways of looking at and understanding the modern metropolis, following the established epistemologies of urban studies, seem no longer to be as powerful and effective as they once may have been. Taking the argument one step further, I suggest that the Los Angeles experience can be used effectively to illustrate and illuminate the *postmodern transition,* a pronounced shift that has been taking place in the late twentieth century in secular worldviews (what has been called our "discourses" about reality) and in the material conditions and contexts of our lives (i.e., the presumably "real" world itself). In other words, what can be seen through the localized processes of urban restructuring is a more global restructuring of the nature and meaning of modernity, modernism, and modernization as they have been historically comprehended in western industrialized societies (see chap. 4, this volume).

The transition to postmodernity, like the five other urban restructuring processes I have outlined, should not be interpreted as a total break with the past. Just as Fordism remains important in the U.S. and world economies even with the rise of post-Fordist practices and flexible production systems, and the lineaments and lineages of older urban forms continue to be visible in the reconstituted Exopolis, postmodernity has developed through a deep restructuring of a previous "order" of modernity, another process of selective deconstruction and reconstitution that increasingly empowers the new over the old in a context of persistent historical continuities. What defines the postmodern condition, then, is the relative weight given to change versus continuity, to new versus old strategies and structures, in responding to the fundamental question of how we should act on our knowledge of the world we live in.

What's new and what is to be done about what we have newly discovered are the invocative questions that have defined a long succession of changing modernities and modernisms since the European Enlightenment. Over the past several decades, those most comfortable being labeled postmodern in their viewpoints have argued that another new modernity, constituted by significantly different ways of responding to the old questions, has been taking shape from the processes of societal restructuring, from the ongoing deconstruction and reconstitution of the geohistory of the contemporary world. Under these changed conditions, long-established epistemologies and strategies of action and behavior become increasingly problematic and open to question. Their old hegemony is challenged at all scales, from the local to the global, as more immediately adaptive new ways of acting take hold, for better or for worse, in the economy, in politics, in popular culture, and in everyday life. Whether or not one personally adopts an explicitly postmodern stance, one fact seems to be clear: in both positive and negative ways, the contemporary world is becoming increasingly postmodern.

I have elaborated these arguments more fully elsewhere.[12] I will illustrate them here only briefly by examining the impact on Los Angeles of a particularly pervasive and influential postmodernization process: the restructuring of the urban imaginary that arises from what the French theorist of postmodernity, Jean Baudrillard, called "the precession of simulacra," the increasingly widespread diffusion of "hypersimulations" of reality into everyday life and throughout the stretched fabric of the L.A. Exopolis. These hypersimulations or *simulacra* (exact copies of originals that no longer exist—or perhaps never existed in the first place) have always existed in all world religions and in many other forms of cultural symbolism. In the late modern world of Los Angeles, specialized entertainment centers such as Disneyland and Hollywood actively provided consumers with technologically more advanced hypersimulations and fantasy worlds. Over the past thirty years, however, these "real fakes" have escaped from their formerly circumscribed territories and manufactories to infiltrate more deeply than ever before into the intimate everyday life of postmodern urban society, economy, polity, and culture. In these new secular sites and situations, the hypersimulations of urban reality have been blurring, more than ever before, the older distinctions between our images of the real and the reality itself, inserting into the confusion a *hyperreality* that is increasingly affecting where we choose to live and work, what we wear and eat, how we relate to others, who we vote for, how we shape our built environment, how we fill our leisure time—in other words, all the activities that together constitute the social construction of urban life.

The increasing scale and scope of hyperreality is perhaps the most important product of the New Information Society, another of the many alternative ways of describing "what's new" in the restructured contemporary world. The popular media and expanding networks of communications technology have put the "hype" into hyperreality and helped to promote its pervasive diffusion, to create a new electronically enhanced "cyberspace" filled with "spin doctors," "sound bites," "artificial intelligence," and "virtual reality." The degree to which this diffusion of hyperreality has affected national politics, American foreign policy, popular views of the state of the U.S. and world economies and the role of the federal government in our daily lives, opens up a discussion that cannot be completed here. Recognizing these connections is important, however, for it helps to complete the story of urban transformation and brings us closer to understanding why the most violent urban insurrection in U.S. history took place in Los Angeles in 1992.

Los Angeles continues to be the world's most productive and influential center for the manufacturing and marketing of hyperreality. In an increasingly postmodern world, this has not only extended and amplified its global reach and the power of its creative imagineers and spin doctors, it has also had a profound effect on the local urban landscape. At least two new postmodern urban geographies have formed in the dense layers of hyperreality that blanket Southern California, one giving rise to an increasingly comprehensive "theme parking" of urban life and experience, the other creating a spreading "scamscape," a duplicitous spatial terrain in which fraud is practiced with the ultimate in hypersimulated honesty.

To echo the title of a recent book,[13] the New American City can be seen as increasingly recomposed into "variations on a theme park," divertingly organized as a hyperreal world of simulated cultures, lifestyles, and consumer preferences. In the theme-parked city, one chooses to live not only according to old standards of affordability, proximity to work, or access to good public facilities. One also chooses, if such choice is available, a symbolic site that simulates a particular lifestyle theme, that re-creates one's own fantasyland or frontierland or experimental community of tomorrow. The patchwork of specialized residential communities this produces is much more fine-grained in its territoriality than the race- and class-segregated cities of the past, for it contains not only the older segregations but many more new ones as well.

Today in Los Angeles there are specialized Leisure Worlds and Sun Cities for different groupings of the elderly, apartment-blocked marinas for the swinging singles set, gay and lesbian cities such as West Hollywood, an engineers ghetto in the beach cities south of the international airport, and special places and spaces for families committing their children to Olympic competition (Mission Viejo youth won more gold medals in 1984 than all but six or seven countries), or an ecotopian environment, or the California Promise. There are residential developments and urban villages for those who may wish to live in replicas of Cervantes' Spain or a Greek island ("Welcome to Mykonos!" one advertisement proclaims), of Nashville or New Orleans, Little Tokyo or Little Saigon, old-time white suburbia or old New England. These very real and compulsively attractive Simcities, to borrow the name of a popular video game, are available nearly everywhere in Los

Angeles but are particularly dense in the new towns and planned communities of Orange County, home to the original Disneyland but now virtually covered with the most advanced residential complex of hyperreality factories in the world.

In the Inner City, another seedbed of hyperreality can be found. Located here are the creative reproductions and tableaux vivants of all the world's cultures available together for the vicarious experience of millions of itinerant visitors, the "original" models for the most popular (and most postmodern) of all traditional theme parks, Florida's Disney World. Just as one can visit Thailand or Germany in Disney World without having to travel long distances, so too can one taste the food, observe the people, hear the language, and sense the traditions of nearly every nation on earth without leaving Los Angeles County. It takes only a little flight of fancy to imagine the day when visitors to the L.A. Cosmopolis-cum-Carceral City of the future will be able to purchase books of tickets to visit Korealand, Blackworld, Little Tijuana, Olympic Village, Redneck Country, Funky Venice, Off-Earth suburbia, and a technopole or two, tearing off stubs for a restaurant meal, a cultural encounter, or an entertaining night on the town.

In what may be the extreme case of hypersimulation, Disney World's immensely popular re-creation of Hollywood Boulevard is now being authentically copied in Orange County's older Disneyland, with no look back to the long-forgotten and now seedy original, itself being restored along different lines just thirty miles away.[14] But then again, perhaps this is not the extreme case. A recently opened adjunct to the popular movieland tours in the so aptly named Universal City, located up on a hill above the Hollywood Freeway, is CityWalk, described by its imagineers as an "idealized reality, L.A. style," an attempt to "deliver the unkept promise of Los Angeles." A $100 million addition to MCA's "Entertainment City," CityWalk aims to capture the "real" feel of an L.A. street with boutiqued facades borrowed from Melrose Avenue, 3D billboards (with moving parts) copied from the Sunset Strip, and a faux Venice Beach, complete with sand, artificially induced waves, and strolling troubadours. Even history has been prefabricated, with buildings painted "as if they had been occupied before" and candy wrappers embedded into the terrazzo flooring to give "a simulated patina of use." A "new and improved Los Angeles" is needed, so say the project's market researchers, because "reality has become too much of a hassle."[15]

A less entertaining but equally evocative product of this encompassing recomposition of urban reality is the world's most fulsome "scamscape," a highly creative milieu of deception that has taken fraud to new heights of accomplishment. The Los Angeles region, and Orange County in particular, leads the country in practically every kind of legal and illegal fraud: in real estate (always a local specialty), in stock trading (junk bonds were invented in Beverly Hills), in automobile insurance (with carefully scripted and staged "paper accidents" taking place everywhere), in telemarketing (with phone swindlers in "boiler rooms" bilking billions a year), in the defense industry (from faking safety reports on nuclear missile firing devices to charging $1,200 for screwdrivers), in occupational safety and welfare payments (an army of "capper" lawyers is always ready to script fake claims), in politics (with another army of duplicitous "spin doctors" prepared to smear any candidate with whatever "facts" necessary), and in two crowning moments of fraudulent specialization, the first in the savings and loan industry, with Keating's Lincoln Savings headquarters in Orange County leading the way to the largest banking scandal in U.S. history, and the second in the fiscal practices of local government, with the startling bankruptcy of Orange County in 1994.[16] In one of the more than three hundred telemarketing boiler rooms in Los Angeles and Orange counties, a sign at the desk captures the genuine sincerity and public commitment that feeds the hyperreal scamscape. It proudly states: "We Cheat the Other Guy and Pass the Savings on to You!"

How we might explain the growth of this fulsome urban scamscape brings us back to the national scale and to the highly specialized production of hyperreality that was practiced in the Reagan-Bush years. Without resorting to any conspiracy theory or demeaning the patriotic intent of its primary leaders, it can be argued that a neoconservative postmodern politics, already in motion in the late 1960s, accelerated rapidly after the election of a Hollywood actor and ex-California governor as president in 1980. The Republican majority had already been constructed around a "Southern strategy" that thinly veiled an appeal to white racism in the Sun Belt and in the suburbs that bulged with a fearful population fleeing the darker recesses of the inner cities after the urban riots of the late 1960s. In power, the Reagan regime acted boldly to consolidate its support from the "silent majority," one of a dazzling array of hypersimulations used to sell neoconservatism to the American public. It is useful here to remember the difference between simulation and dissimulation. To dissimulate is to pretend that you do not have what you really do have—to lie or to cover up. Watergate was good old dissimulation. In contrast, to simulate is to pretend to have something that you really do not have. When such simulation becomes so intense that you no longer can tell the difference between the simulated and the real, then you have genuinely edged into hypersimulation.

Among the most convincing hypersimulations of the Reagan years was the crusade against "Big Government," a political simulacrum that restructured the national ideology and along with it what I have called the urban imaginary. It was used as an ideological weapon to attack the Keynesian welfare state, to dismantle many antipoverty programs under the continuing guise of a New Federalism, to resimulate the civil rights movement through a cleverly recomposed imagery of "reverse racism" and "political correctness," to explain the origins of recession and the need for a new austerity, and to virtually deconstruct and reconstitute the meaning of liberal democracy and representative government. Family values (during a period when the number of traditional American households of one breadwinner, a wife, and two children declined more rapidly than ever before), Sun Belt and suburban virtues (including the open shop, new industrial growth, and aggressive whiteness), and above all the mythic power of the free market and American entrepreneurial skills combined into the hyperreal substitute for Big Government. Backed by hyperfrauds even larger than the Savings and Loan scandal, such as trickle-down economics, deregulation, and the privatization of the public sector, one of the most undertaxed of all industrial nations rationalized one of the biggest government programs to subsidize the wealthy in recent history. That this could occur during a decade of deepening poverty, devastating deindustrialization, and a gargantuan national debt is testimony to the real power of simulacra.

Behind the simulated retreat from Big Government was increased federal and local intervention into the economy and everyday life, a scam of such proportions that it had to be imagineered by another, more global, hypersimulation. During the Reagan years, a growing tide of factual "disinformation" reconstructed the cold war threat into what would eventually be named a new world order, with the United States as its postmodern Robo-Cop and the mass media as its primary battlefield. This very American hypersimulation, punctuated by events in Granada, Libya, Panama, Nicaragua, and that most postmodern of military spectaculars, Operation Desert Storm, legitimated the domestic reorganization of the welfare state into the more highly specialized warfare state. Military Keynesianism fueled the economy with many billions of dollars for defense, with Southern California continuing to receive the lion's share of all strategic defense initiatives. Continuing to feed off the fears of its majority constituencies, the hypersimulation-addicted neoconservative regime opened an offensive against the inner cities, which were perceived to hold the most serious domestic threats to the new world order. The war on poverty became a war against the urban poor, a promulgation of law and order that militarized the local (and federal) police in a struggle against drugs, gangs, crime, illegal immigrants, and other inner city targets.

As hypersimulations, these powerful images were, and to many still are, genuinely believed to be real and true. Simply stripping away the imagery to expose the supposed reality hidden behind it, however, is no longer a sufficient challenge or an effective critical response. To use a phrase that captures the meaning of both the postmodern condition and the effects of the restructuring processes operating over the past thirty years, reality isn't what it used to be! But while we may not be able to resolve here the political issues emanating from the precession of simulacra and the power of hypersimulations, we can begin to use some of the insights derivable from a postmodern perspective to understand better the urban restructuring of Los Angeles and what happened there in the spring of 1992.

CODA FOR 1992

The preceding descriptions of the Los Angeles experience over the past thirty years have been bracketed between two key turning points. The first is more confidently and hindsightfully defined by the Watts rebellion in 1965, one of the most portentous sparks for the concatenation of crises that marked the end of the postwar economic boom and the beginning of the search for new strategies to restore robust economic growth and avoid even greater social unrest. The six geographies of restructuring can be locally traced back to Watts, and through the window of the Los Angeles experience after 1965 can be seen many comparable crisis-generated restructurings affecting many other areas of the world. This is not to say that Watts in itself was the cause of urban restructuring or that restructuring would not have happened without it. What can be said, however, is that, for Los Angeles, 1965 was a significant turning point and that, for the rest of the world, what happened after 1965 in Southern California provides a particularly interesting and revealing case study in urban restructuring.

The second turning point, 1992, is more tentatively proclaimed, for its sighting is immediate and not subject to the same degree of retrospective understanding. Nevertheless, the events that took place in Los Angeles just before and just after 1 May 1992 seem to be signaling another beginning of the end of an era, a forceful local disruption of (restructured) business as usual that may be a precursor to a more widespread crisis of postmodernity and post-Fordism, just as Watts exemplified the crisis of modernity that marked the end of the Fordist postwar economic boom. This new crisis can be seen emerging from the very practices and strategies that have proved most successful in restoring robust economic growth and effectively controlling social unrest over the past thirty years: in the restructuring of urban form into the stretched fabric of Exopolis; in the flexibly specialized and productive industrial landscapes of post-Fordism; in the formation of a globalized multicultural Cosmopolis; in the widening income gaps and mixed-up class boundaries of the new socioeconomic (dis)order; in the protective fortresses and violent edges of the Carceral City; and in the rise of a neo-conservative urban imaginary of enchanting and duplicitous hypersimulations. What all this portrays, I contend, can be summarized as a movement from crisis-generated restructuring to *restructuring-generated crisis.*

Up to the first years of the 1990s, the bright side of the new Los Angeles increasingly stood out to define one of the great success stories of the late twentieth century. By April 1992, however, the mood had already shifted as all that was so compellingly bright seemed to be self-destructing. *Perestroika* (that potent Russian word for restructuring) and the end of the cold war simultaneously pulled the propulsive rug from underneath the post-Fordist regional economy and removed one of the key ideological pillars that had supported the tightening of social control by local and federal keepers of the peace. As the technopolis went into crisis, so too did its supportive FIRE sector, a coalescence of economic stress that spun into a recessionary spiral that seemed to go deeper in Southern California than in most other regions of the country. Massive job losses hit hard at the upper "bubble" of the bimodal labor market: bankers and brokers, highly paid aerospace workers and the new technocracy, lawyers and real estate agents, yuppies and beamers—those who rode the crest of the most recent boom.

Meanwhile, the Cosmopolis became increasingly unsettled. For every new multicultural achievement in the arts, in business, and in local politics, there appeared new kinds of interethnic violence and conflict as scores of different cultural worlds collided without mixing. More and more poor immigrants were added to the population, but the inflow of foreign capital slowed down and even Japanese-owned hotels, office buildings, and businesses went into bankruptcy. Homelessness dramatically widened its scope and visibility, turning once-sympathetic observers into edgy not-in-my-backyard antagonists. Bulging prisons began releasing thousands of allegedly nonthreatening criminals, and even the most enchanting urban villages seemed to be not far enough away to escape from the growing cosmopolitan violence. In 1992, a record number of violent crimes were committed in Los Angeles County, including 2,589 homicides and more than 800 gang-related killings. There were forewarnings of what might occur, especially in the domestic music of the streets, but the "rap" was incomprehensible to most or was reduced to a mixture of noise and entertainment.

On 29 April, Los Angeles exploded in what appeared to many as a stubborn continuity with the past: police brutality, racism, and social injustice provoking an equally brutal, racially motivated, and Watts-like riot of burning and looting marauders. The more things change, as some would say, the more they seemed to remain the same. Yet there was another dimension to the specific events of 1992 that challenged these appeals to historical continuity left, right, and center. It was difficult to identify and label, but seemed to be coming from another side of postmodernity, from a postmodernism of resistance that had been bred in the new multicultural politics of place, space, and local identity; in a deepened awareness of the surveillant webs controlling the geography of the Carceral City and how to defend against them; in a more sophisticated understanding of the racially and locationally uneven impact of deindustrialization and reindustrialization; in the slowly growing empowerment of a "minority majority" in local politics; and, not least, from the tactical use of media-transported hypersimulations as a means of countering and encountering the neoconservative scamscape. What I am suggesting is that the largest urban insurrection in U.S. history differed significantly from the second largest in being both a consequence and a strategic political expression of the postmodern transition.

Stated differently, whereas Watts marked the first major rebellion against the late modernism of postwar America, the civil disturbances of 1992 may represent the first explosion of resistance to neoconservative American postmodernism and post-Fordism. Both took place in the urban region that was in the developmental vanguard of their respective eras, and each reflected the specific political and economic conditions of its time and place. In 1965, the insurrection was concentrated in the African-American community and emanated directly from the modernist politics of the civil rights movement and black nationalism. In 1992, although initially concentrated in nearly the same areas and led again by young black men, the insurrection was decidedly more global and cosmopolitan, and was fought more like Operation Desert Storm than like the Vietnam War. As the word of the Rodney King verdict spread from the courthouse in Simi Valley (the primarily Anglo working-class edge city in Ventura County that had become a favorite place for policemen and white families escaping the now-foreign Inner City) to the symbolic corner of Florence (the name of one of the major communities affected by the burning and looting of 1965, now primarily Latino) and Normandie (a street running north into the heart of the new Koreatown), two series of events conjoined, one local and immediate, the other global and hypersimulated, with news networks broadcasting to the world more and lengthier images of Los Angeles than had ever been seen before.

The most memorable pictures, involving the beating of Reginald Denny, were characteristically ambiguous. To most, they conveyed clear visual evidence of violent frustration and anarchy, the absence of order and the lack of concern for human life. To others, there was another reality here, one arising from the consciously televisual enactment of resistance and rage to a long history of unpunished police brutality brought to a head when the "truth" conveyed by the all-seeing video camera had been denied in a Simi Valley courthouse. As if to reassert the power of one visual hypersimulation against another, Police Chief Gates donned the war apparel of his SWAT teams to arrest the presumed gang-bangers so visible on everyone's TV screens. This gave rise to a disturbing question, one that the beaters of Reginald Denny may have intentionally wanted to raise: If the videotape of many white men kicking and beating up a lone black man could be dismissed as a misleading picture of reality, would it be possible for the same result to occur with a videotape of many black men kicking and beating up a lone white man? For many, this was an irrelevant question. For some, it was and is crucial.

The local events and images spread well beyond South Central Los Angeles. With less well reported details, Long Beach, the region's second-largest city, exploded as violently as anywhere else. The Salvadoran barrio in Pico-Union was also particularly active, drawing in a small army of immigration officials who, against established local policies, quickly deported hundreds of allegedly undocumented workers. More than 50 percent of those arrested at the peak of the riots were Latino, versus 36 percent black, and it was not only blacks and Latinos that participated in the looting. Anglo yuppies with car phones raided computer stores and camera shops, while others gathered into vigilante groups to defend their neighborhoods against all intruders. In another symbolic act, an especially ecumenical group immediately struck deep into the Citadel-L.A., attacking the Parker Center headquarters of the LAPD as well as City Hall and other institutional centers of power and surveillance. The flames fanned outward into the San Fernando Valley, Pomona, Long Beach, the South Bay, and other parts of the Outer City and leapfrogged to the region's outermost satellite, Las Vegas. Sympathetic rebellions were sparked in the Bay Area, Atlanta, Omaha, Minneapolis, Toronto. Moment by moment, the local events became regional, national, and global at the same time and at an unheard of speed and intensity.

Again, there is much more to tell as Los Angeles rebuilds, or, perhaps more accurately and hopefully, begins another round of crisis-induced restructuring, for if there is one general conclusion to be derived from the events of 1992, it is that the restructuring processes of the past thirty years, especially where they appear to have been most advanced and successful as in Los Angeles, produce new conditions for economic decline, racial and ethnic oppression, and social upheaval. This dialectic of extremes, of utopian dreams and dystopian nightmares, of paradigmatic successes and exemplary failures, has always characterized the history and geography of Los Angeles, giving pause to any categorical predictions about its future. All that can be said in closing is that Los Angeles, as always, is worth watching.

NOTES

1. Mike Davis, *City of Quartz: Excavating the Future in Los Angeles* (London: Verso, 1990).

2. Robert M. Fogelson, *The Fragmented Metropolis: Los Angeles, 1850–1930* (Cambridge: Harvard University Press, 1967); reissued with a foreword by Robert Fishman, by the University of California Press (1993). The vision of Los Angeles

as a "nonplace urban realm" can be found in Melvin Webber, "Culture, Territoriality, and the Elastic Mile," *Papers of the Regional Science Association* 11 (1964): 59–69.

3. Gary Miller, *Cities by Contract: The Politics of Municipal Incorporation* (Cambridge: MIT Press, 1981).

4. The year 1942 was an especially interesting one for Los Angeles. The first concentration camps were created to remove Japanese-Americans from their property and businesses in the city, a Japanese submarine shelled an oil field near Santa Barbara, and a purely imaginary air raid led to a crazed scenario in which a "hostile aircraft" was reported to have been shot down on Vermont Avenue. Five citizens died in this imaginary invasion, three from car crashes and two from heart attacks. In the same year, Camp Pendleton Marine Corps base was founded and the "Sleepy Lagoon" murder triggered another racist-enhanced frenzy in which as many as 150 Mexican-American "boy gang" members (as they were then called) were arrested for the death of one youth at a party in East Los Angeles.

5. Significant changes in U.S. immigration laws were made in 1965, following the end of the bracero program in the previous year. The continuing hunger for cheap foreign labor to feed industrial growth and assist in disciplining the burgeoning domestic workforce would stimulate the extraordinary immigration from Mexico, Central America, and Asia in the succeeding decades.

6. Bennett Harrison and Barry Bluestone, *The Great U-Turn: Corporate Restructuring and the Polarizing of America* (New York: Basic Books, 1988).

7. Edward W. Soja, "Inside Exopolis: Scenes from Orange County," in *Variations on a Theme Park: The New American City and the End of Public Space,* ed. Michael Sorkin, 94–122. (New York: Noonday Press, 1992).

8. Ibid.; Allen J. Scott, *Metropolis: From the Division of Labor to Urban Form* (Berkeley, Los Angeles, and London: University of California Press, 1988); and R. Kling, S. Olin, and M. Poster, eds., *Postsuburban California: The Transformation of Orange County since World War II* (Berkeley, Los Angeles, and London: University of California Press, 1991).

9. Edward W. Soja, "Heterotopologies: A Remembrance of Other Spaces in the Citadel-L.A.," *Strategies* 3 (1990): 6–39.

10. Edward W. Soja, "Taking Los Angeles Apart: Towards a Postmodern Geography," chapter 9 in *Postmodern Geographies: The Reassertion of Space in Critical Social Theory* (London: Verso, 1989), 222–248.

11. The number of census tracts in Los Angeles County with no African-American residents has dropped, however, from nearly 400 in 1960 to as few as 4 in 1990, a mark of the success of antiracist legal struggles in the Los Angeles housing market.

12. Soja, *Postmodern Geographies,* "Heterotopologies," "Inside Exopolis," and "Postmodern Geographies and the Critique of Historicism," in *Postmodern Contentions: Epochs, Politics, Space,* ed. J. P. Jones, W. Natter, and T. Schatzki, 113–136 (London: Guildford Press, 1993).

13. Sorkin, *Variations on a Theme Park.*

14. The "real" Hollywood Boulevard still retains a powerful hold on at least one segment of the American urban imaginary. It is the main axis for the country's largest community of runaway and homeless youth. For an analysis of the struggles

between runaway youth, their institutional providers of services, and the redevelopment planners (both public and private), see Susan M. Ruddick, "Redrawing the Maps of Meaning: The Social Construction of Homeless Youth in Hollywood" (Ph.D. dissertation, Urban Planning, UCLA, 1992).

15. *Los Angeles Times,* 29 February 1992.

16. The Orange County bankruptcy occurred after this chapter was written. For an interpretation of its causes and consequences as well as a more detailed discussion of the six geographies of urban restructuring in Los Angeles, see Edward W. Soja, *Thirdspace: Journeys to Los Angeles and Other Real-and-Imagined Places* (Oxford and Cambridge: Blackwell Publishers, 1996) and its companion volume, *Postmetropolis,* forthcoming from Blackwell in 1997.

ILLUSTRATION CREDITS

Figure 1.2: From *An Atlas of Population Patterns in Metropolitan Los Angeles and Orange Counties, 1990,* by Eugene Turner and James P. Allen (Northridge: California State University, 1991).

Figure 5.1: From *Los Angeles: An Illustrated History,* by Bruce Hensell (New York: Alfred A. Knopf, 1980). Used by permission.

Figure 5.2: "The S-Curve of the Third Avenue El," from *32 Picture Postcards of Old New York,* by Hayward Cirker (New York: Dover Publications, 1976). From the collection of E. B. Watson. Used by permission.

Figure 5.4: Courtesy Los Angeles Public Library, Security-Pacific Photographic Collections.

Figure 5.5: Courtesy of the California Historical Society, Los Angeles History Center Title Trust and Insurance Collection.

Figure 5.6: From *The Fragmented Metropolis: Los Angeles 1850–1930,* by Robert M. Fogelson (Cambridge: Harvard University Press, 1967). Used by permission.

Figure 8.1: From *An Introduction to Design and Culture in the Twentieth Century,* by Penny Spark (New York: Harper & Row, 1986).

Figure 8.3: From *High Styles: Twentieth-Century American Design,* by Lisa Phillips et al. (New York: Summit Books, 1985).

Figure 8.6: Photo by Salvatore for Athena.

Figure 8.7: From *Design Now: Industry or Art?* by Volker Fischer (Munich: Prestel-Verlag, 1989).

Figure 8.8: From *Contemporary Classics: Furniture of the Masters,* by Charles D. Gandy and Susan Zimmermann-Stidham (New York: McGraw-Hill, 1981).

Figure 8.9: Photo by Roger Rosenblatt.

Figure 8.10: Courtesy Mimi London, Inc.

Figure 8.11: Courtesy California Pacific.

Figure 9.3: From *Census of Population, 1950* (Washington, D.C.: U.S. Bureau of the Census, 1950).

Figure 9.4: From *California Manufacturers Annual Register,* California Manufacturers Association (Los Angeles: Times-Mirror Press, 1995).

Figure 9.5: From *Census of Population, 1950* (Washington, D.C.: U.S. Bureau of the Census, 1950).

Figure 9.6: From *1970 Census of Population and Housing* (Washington, D.C.: U.S. Department of Commerce, Bureau of the Census, 1970).

Figure 9.7: From *California Manufacturers Annual Register,* California Manufacturers Association (Los Angeles: Times-Mirror Press, 1973).

Figure 9.8: From *1990 Census of Population and Housing* (Washington, D.C.: U.S. Department of Commerce, Bureau of the Census, 1990).

Figure 9.9: From *1990 Census of Population and Housing* (Washington, D.C.: U.S. Department of Commerce, Bureau of the Census, 1990).

Figure 9.10: From *1990 Census of Population and Housing* (Washington, D.C.: U.S. Department of Commerce, Bureau of the Census, 1990).

Figure 9.11: From *California Manufacturers Annual Register,* California Manufacturers Association (Newport Beach: Database Publishing, 1991).

Figure 9.12: From *Annual Planning Information, Oxnard-Ventura Metropolitan Statistical Area* and *Annual Planning Information, Los Angeles-Long Beach Metropolitan Statistical Area* (Sacramento: State of California Health and Welfare Agency, Employment Development Department, 1992).

Figure 9.13: From *County Business Patterns* (Washington, D.C.: U.S. Department of Commerce, Bureau of the Census, various years).

Figure 9.14: From *County Business Patterns* (Washington, D.C.: U.S. Department of Commerce, Bureau of the Census, various years).

Figure 9.16: Data courtesy Rocketdyne Division, Rockwell International Corporation.

Figure 13.1: From "Restructuring the Local Welfare State: A Case Study of Los Angeles," by Woobae Lee, Ph.D. dissertation, University of California, 1994.

Figure 13.2: From "Restructuring the Local Welfare State: A Case Study of Los Angeles," by Woobae Lee, Ph.D. dissertation, University of California, 1994.

Figure 13.3: From "Dynamics of Rental Housing in Los Angeles 1980–1986: Changes in Affordability and Supply," by Jeffrey Heilman, Working Paper 21, Los Angeles Homelessness Project, University of Southern California, Los Angeles, 1989.

INDEX

Aalto, Alvar, 56
Actualidad, 369–370
Acuña, Rodolfo, 367
Adler, Sy, 132
"Aerospace Alley," 436
Aerospace/defense industry: decline since late 1980s, 278, 297, 306; growth after World War II, 9, 277, 436; growth from 1920–1940, 7; growth in 1980s, 317–318, 391; origins in amateur aviation, 241
Aerospace Museum, 58
AFDC Homeless Assistance Program, 416
African-Americans: burden of civil rights movement failure, 351–352; development of underclass after 1965, 440; early civil rights and political organizations, 341; economic strength of early community, 340–342; exclusion from local politics, 339–340; faith in urban ideal, 337–338; future prospects of, 359–361; gangsta culture, 360; income inequality among, 446; as LAPD officers, 352, 353; loss of unity after 1992 riots, 357; majority population areas in 1990, 448; migration from central and south central city, 345–346; political leadership, 336–337, 348, 350–351; population change in 1990s, 440, 448; population growth before 1990, 10, 324, 334*n*31, 340, 342–343, 430;

residential segregation, 10, 342–346, 430, 461*n*11; "spatial ghettos," 343; unemployment in 1965, 430
Ain, Gregory, 183*n*31
Air quality management: Air Pollution Control District (APCD), 191; Air Resources Board, 224*n*50; "Black Monday" smog attack, 166, 190; bubble concept of regulation, 205, 214; California emission standards, 223*n*49; end-of-pipe regulation, 214; EPA national standards for air pollutant concentrations, 214; firm-by-firm regulation, 213; mobile source regulation, 191; Motor Vehicle Pollution Control Board, 191; regulation of industrial air emissions, 213–214; State Air Resources Board, 191; stationary source regulation, 191; use of markets for regulation, 212–216. *See also* South Coast Air Quality Management District (SCAQMD)
Alameda Avenue (Cotton Curtain), 430
Aldrich, Lloyd, 126–127
Alexander, Robert, 168–169
Alhambra, 401
American culture: contradiction between values of nature and material progress, 25–26; and individual fulfillment, 26–29; origins and sources of, 23–24; racism and violence in, 24–25; suburbs, 25, 26
American Seating, 256

Compositor: J. Jarrett Engineering, Inc.
Text: Baskerville
Display: Baskerville
Printer: Edwards Brothers, Inc.
Binder: Edwards Brothers, Inc.